COLLEGE OF ALAMEDA LIBRARY
008185
WITHE

D0960813

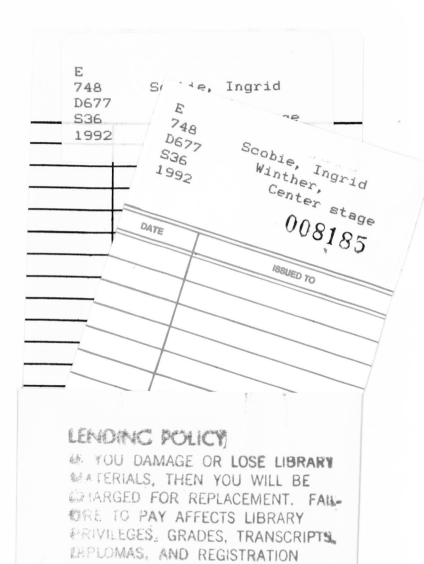

E
748
D677
S36
1992

Scobie, Ingrid

E
748
D677
S36
1992

Scobie, Ingrid
Winther,
Center stage

008185

DATE	ISSUED TO

LENDING POLICY

IF YOU DAMAGE OR LOSE LIBRARY
MATERIALS, THEN YOU WILL BE
CHARGED FOR REPLACEMENT. FAIL-
URE TO PAY AFFECTS LIBRARY
PRIVILEGES, GRADES, TRANSCRIPTS,
DIPLOMAS, AND REGISTRATION
PRIVILEGES OR ANY COMBINATION
THEREOF.

AUG 21 1996

WITHDRAWN

CENTER STAGE

Helen Gahagan poses as a crook who goes straight, in the 1923 revival of the famed melodrama *Leah Kleschna. Courtesy of the Carl Albert Congressional Research and Studies Center, University of Oklahoma*

Ingrid Winther Scobie

CENTER STAGE

Helen Gahagan Douglas
A Life

New York   Oxford
OXFORD UNIVERSITY PRESS
1992

Oxford University Press

Oxford   New York   Toronto
Delhi   Bombay   Calcutta   Madras   Karachi
Petaling Jaya   Singapore   Hong Kong   Tokyo
Nairobi   Dar es Salaam   Cape Town
Melbourne   Auckland

and associated companies in
Berlin   Ibadan

Copyright © 1992 by Ingrid Winther Scobie.

Published by Oxford University Press, Inc.,
200 Madison Avenue, New York, New York 10016

Oxford is a registered trademark of Oxford University Press

All rights reserved. No part of this publication may be reproduced,
stored in a retrieval system, or transmitted, in any form or by any means,
electronic, mechanical, photocopying, recording, or otherwise,
without the prior permission of Oxford University Press.

Library of Congress Cataloging-in-Publication Data
Scobie, Ingrid Winther, 1943–
Center stage : Helen Gahagan Douglas, a life /
Ingrid Winther Scobie.
p.   cm.   Includes bibliographical references and index.
ISBN 0-19-506896-3 1. Douglas, Helen Gahagan, 1900–   .
2. Legislators—United States—Biography.
3. United States. Congress. House—Biography.
4. Actresses—United States—Biography.   I. Title.
E748.D677S36   1992   328.73'092—dc20
[B]   91-17186

2 4 6 8 9 7 5 3 1

Printed in the United States of America
on acid-free paper

For Jim
And the memories of the intertwining
of our minds and hearts,
and of our shared dreams

Contents

Introduction

IN THE 1940s, Helen Gahagan Douglas, the first actor and Hollywood figure ever to move successfully into national electoral politics, became a widely respected liberal member of Congress. By 1948, when she ran for her third term, she ranked at the top of blacks' and labor's list of critically valuable politicians on Capitol Hill, played an active role in refining postwar foreign policy as a member of the House Foreign Affairs Committee, and bravely stood out as one of few members of Congress willing to oppose legislation curtailing civil liberties as the Cold War developed. A tall, stunning woman who presented herself in a dignified and fashionable style, Douglas had a vivacious, warm, magnetic, self-confident manner that motivated people to political action and created loyal staff members and friends.

Douglas had a most unusual background for a member of Congress. She was born in 1900, the middle child in Lillian and Walter Gahagan's family of five. Walter had a very successful engineering firm in Brooklyn, and he raised his children in the city's posh Park Slope neighborhood adjacent to Grand Army Plaza and the beautiful adjoining Prospect Park. From a young age, Helen showed intense interest in theater and a dislike for academics. But she eventually gained the necessary credentials to enter Barnard College in 1920. Two years later, despite parental opposition, she accepted a contract for starring roles on Broadway. In 1928, she began intensive voice lessons to add operatic roles to her repertoire. In the famed producer David Belasco's last play, *Tonight or Never*, she fell in love with Melvyn Douglas, her leading man. The two married and moved to Los Angeles, where Melvyn enjoyed a successful movie career. Helen's performing opportunities dwindled, and eventually she became involved in political concerns, at first the state's migrant problem. Two children born in the 1930s added parenting responsibilities. A friendship with Eleanor Roosevelt drew Helen quickly into Democratic Party politics in the early 1940s, providing preparation for her foray into electoral politics.

In this book I place Douglas's life in the context of early twentieth-century upper-class Brooklyn society, commercial Broadway theater in the 1920s, the Hollywood social and political milieu of the 1930s, female voluntarism in politics during World War II, and postwar liberalism. I look at how a female member of Congress with unusual credentials and wealth became powerful as a member of the second generation of post-suffrage women. I redefine congressional power, taking gender differences into account, and argue that the skills of a mature and talented actor can serve as excellent preparation for American-style politics. I also address questions arising from Douglas's determination to carve out her own professional directions while coping with her complicated home life as a wife and mother. This personal and public conflict shaped her professional style and choices.[1]

My investigation into the life of Helen Gahagan Douglas began in 1968 when I was a twenty-five-year-old history graduate student at the University of Wisconsin, Madison, specializing in social and political history. I was working on my dissertation, which dealt with anti-Communist legislation in California in the 1940s. At the insistence of my thesis advisor, I gathered materials about the 1950 United States Senate race in California between Douglas and Richard M. Nixon. As little related to my thesis topic, I stored the materials away. I do remember how strange it was to be working on a California figure at the University of Oklahoma. Apparently a university archivist, in Washington to collect papers from defeated Oklahoma members of the House of Representatives, passed by Douglas's office door to offer his condolences about her Senate defeat by Nixon. In the course of the conversation, he learned she had no plans for depositing her papers in an archive and asked if she would be interested in considering Oklahoma. Flattered by the interest, she agreed immediately.

At this stage of my life, I was also a bride of a noted Latin American historian, James R. Scobie, and the new stepmother of his two preschoolers. The story of writing my Douglas biography follows the contours of my changing life—to professional historian and mother of four, to widowhood in 1981, and finally into my first tenure-track job with the challenge of single-parenting four children. The adventure also follows my evolution from a traditionally trained historian to a self-taught women's historian. While it seems a long time to have had a book brewing, this span of years of living with this project has profoundly affected both my life and my view of Douglas.

From 1970 to 1973, I served as the assistant executive secretary to the Organization of American Historians. During these three years, I concentrated on my marriage, raising my two young stepchildren and our new baby, my challenging job, and some research and writing. Only later did I look back and realize my naïveté about gender issues in academe, including my own professional life; my insensitivity to other women's struggles; and my lack of awareness of what a "balanced marriage" for a professional couple really meant. My first positive response to women's history came in 1973 when I received a letter asking me if I could present a paper for the Western History Association annual meeting on a western woman (anyone, it did not matter) for a session on women (no specific topic). I jumped at the chance; I was still at the stage where I received few invitations to give papers. I had those materials on the 1950 Nixon–Douglas campaign. As I prepared my paper, I found my study fascinating. By chance, I received considerable press attention at the meetings because President Richard Nixon's vice-president, Spiro Agnew, had resigned that morning. I happened to be four months pregnant and found myself mystified when the photographer for the *Fort Worth Star-Telegram* took a close-up shot. When I asked him why, he indicated that the paper would not publish photographs of pregnant professional women. I was really taken aback, and a bit angry. I associate the beginning of my interest in women's history and equal treatment of women with this paper and the convention.

After the meetings I returned to the University of Oklahoma to work in the Douglas papers to prepare my piece for publication.[2] As I rummaged through Douglas's theater scrapbooks, opera programs, and political speeches, I got hooked. Though I admit to the allure of writing about a glamorous public woman married to a celebrated movie star, what most intrigued me was the question of how a wealthy actress–opera singer from Hollywood managed to get elected to three congressional terms from an inner-city Los Angeles district in which she had never set foot prior to campaigning, and then nominated as the Democratic candidate for the United States Senate in 1950. The fact that in 1973 Helen and Melvyn, both in their early seventies, were alive was also important. When I discovered a group of over three hundred unidentified photographs in her papers, I got permission to take the photos to New York to work with Douglas on the identification process. Thus, in December of 1973, we spent two days, occasionally with Melvyn, poring over the photographs. Helen frequently asked Melvyn his opinion of who an individual might be in a photograph, but she generally argued with his reaction and rarely agreed with him. I gained my first insights into their relationship by listening to them interact.

I had a horrible experience on my way to Douglas's apartment, located at 50 Riverside Drive on the corner of Seventy-seventh Street, two blocks west of Broadway. I was by then six months pregnant. I had donned a pantsuit for the cold and rainy day. I felt self-confident and excited. My arms were loaded—a heavy suitcase with the photographs in one arm, a briefcase with books, tape recorder, and various supplies in the other, and an umbrella wedged in somehow. It did not occur to me to take a cab; I always used the subway, particularly for long distances. After battling crowds, I emerged at the Seventy-ninth Street and Broadway exit with a sigh of relief—only four more blocks. But I soon realized my new maternity pantyhose were gradually slipping down over my enlarged belly, carrying my slacks with them. With no restaurant in sight, I finally stopped in the secluded entrance of what turned out to be a synagogue. As I began pulling myself together, an elderly man approached the door. He only wanted to enter the building, but I became terrified and left immediately, still disheveled. When I arrived at the Douglas apartment, I was completely undone. I barely greeted the famous woman I had come to see, asking only for the bathroom. It was Douglas, not me, who played the role of putting the other at ease. After a cup of hot tea and a quick rundown about my husband and children, I finally calmed down.

No matter the number of times I tell my students how *not* to arrive for a first interview, I am convinced that the humiliating incident affected my visit, and in turn, our relationship, in positive ways. The situation could of course have had quite opposite consequences. Unexpectedly we met as private, not public, women. While we changed roles back to public women as we began to talk about the photographs and many other subjects, a bond had formed. When I left, I sensed that Douglas liked me personally and intellectually, that she was pleased to have a professional historian, not a journalist, take an interest in her life, and that she trusted me not to misuse information she had given me. I parted with the comment that some day, when I emerged from child-rearing, I planned to write her biography. She smiled but said nothing.

The Douglas project sat for four years, until 1977. But I began to grow as a novice historian of women. I taught women's history for the first time in Buenos Aires as a Fulbright professor. I also became acutely aware that my husband and I did not share parenting and household chores in as well-balanced a fashion as I had thought. In 1977, we moved from Indiana University to the University of California, San Diego. Thus began another segment of four years, from 1977 to 1981, during which I became active professionally despite being knee-deep in children, ages three to fifteen. I taught part-time, but more important, I had the opportunity to explore Douglas's life once again. The Regional Oral History Office housed in the Bancroft Library at the University of California, Berkeley, was working on a major project with Douglas and various friends and colleagues. I was asked to help edit and conduct interviews. My growing perspective on women's lives influenced the structure of my questions. In the fall of 1979, as my teaching responsibilities ended, I began serious work on the Douglas book. I traveled first to Fairlee, Vermont, where the Douglas family summered.[3] Douglas had agreed to see me briefly in September. My goal was to gain access to her private papers, which covered primarily her activities after the 1950 campaign. I was nervous. She did not feel well; breast cancer that had developed in 1972 had recurred in 1976, spreading to her bones. She had scheduled hip-replacement surgery for October. But as we began talking, she became increasingly open and friendly. After lunch she suddenly suggested that since I was going to be reading all her personal letters, I might as well start with her summer correspondence while she napped. I covered her frail body on the dayroom couch, closed the door, and began to read. Before I left late that afternoon, she had invited me to stay with her in New York in December to go through her papers, on the understanding that I would not interview her. She was working diligently to complete her autobiography and had limited energy.

The New York visit provided essential research materials for the post-campaign years, offered insights into Douglas's private life, and proved emotionally exhausting. I arrived in early December at suppertime and set my bags in Melvyn's bedroom, which I was to use while he was on location in San Francisco filming *Tell Me a Riddle*. It took me about twenty-four hours to get over the excitement of sleeping in a movie star's bed with an Oscar and other awards two feet away. Mary Helen, the Douglases' daughter, was living at the apartment to help care for her mother. Douglas's days, unlike the hectic pace of years past, followed a simple routine. She rose about 9:30, ate breakfast in bed, consulted with the elderly maid who had worked for the family for years, and then turned to her writing. Three unemployed actors helped out—one typed the handwritten pages of Helen's manuscript and two others alternated cooking dinner. Helen generally rested in the afternoon, worked a bit more on her book, and often concluded the day dictating correspondence to Nan Stevens, her long-time secretary. If Helen had not invited company for dinner, she, I, and sometimes Mary Helen dined and then watched television, played cards, or chatted. Helen and Melvyn telephoned each other frequently to check on each other's health and to share the day's events. Occasionally a friend dropped by the apartment; several times one or a few guests were invited to dinner— extended family or close friends. Helen left the apartment only for brief walks. She included me in the conversation with visitors and dinner guests, and I often accompanied her on walks—occasions I found delightful.

Other than these few diversions, my daytime work pattern was varied only by occasional errands I did for Douglas, episodes that offered clues to her temperament. Despite my careful adherence to a detailed grocery list when I shopped, for example, Douglas never failed to chastise me for spending too much money, a reflection of her years of concern, often unwarranted, about lack of sufficient funds. The execution of one errand helped explain the remarkable devotion of certain female friends and staff that I had never understood. In this instance, I offered to track down some bedroom slippers that Douglas needed. I proceeded down Fifth Avenue, which was overflowing with shoppers and slick with falling snow. I stopped in every major department store, starting at Sixty-fifth Street, each time without success. The temperature dropped as the sun gradually went down. I suddenly wondered, why am I doing this? Something kept me going, a need to please her beyond any reasonable expectations. I knew that Douglas could make people want to please her to the point of creating a dependent relationship; I had fallen into that trap. I finally found the right slippers, and I hurried back to Riverside Drive. I felt frightened; I realized that I had become too involved. I knew I had to back off, to distance myself to maintain detachment and scholarly integrity. A similar situation occurred again in the spring when she asked me to help her complete her autobiography. While I did a few simple research tasks that seemed overwhelming to her, I turned down the opportunity to become substantively involved. I had learned my lesson.

My opportunity to spend substantial time with Douglas offered me, as a biographer, a most unusual opportunity. While I could only imagine what she was like in her younger years, the experience provided something concrete for my imagination. But while personal contact enriches interpretation, it decreases objectivity. I was constantly aware of a fine line I could not cross. When I inadvertently crossed the line (as in the case of the slippers), I pulled back immediately. Helen, too, had her own line, but it was less defined. Sometimes she would open up about her feelings concerning Melvyn or the children. I realized I was learning far more than I would eventually include in my book. The timing of this visit was indeed fortunate; she died six months later, in June 1980.

In the spring of 1981, I received a substantial grant from the Research Division at the National Endowment for the Humanities. I had been earlier encouraged by smaller grants from the Eleanor Roosevelt Institute and the American Philosophical Society. I knew the NEH money would really get the project underway. But as I was putting the finishing touches on a paper about Douglas and Eleanor Roosevelt for the 1981 Berkshire Conference on Women's History, my world fell apart.[4] With no warning, my husband collapsed; he died immediately. The eventual explanation: "probable cardiac arrhythmia." I knew I had to move away to progress in my career. I accepted a tenure-track position in women's history at Texas Woman's University in Denton, Texas, near Dallas. Living in Texas, teaching full-time, and raising four children (now ages eight to nineteen) away from anything or anyone familiar proved challenging and exciting, as well as sad and lonely. But my life had silver linings. I now lived in a state intimately linked to Douglas's closest congressional friend, Lyndon B. Johnson. Texas also had a network of politically savvy women of which I became a small part. These women, including Sarah Weddington, Ann Richards, and Liz Carpenter, brought some reality to my analytical perception of political women. Liz Carpenter also provided insights into Douglas (she was a young Texas journalist on the Hill during the 1940s) and widowhood. I also became involved in community theater in Denton, rekindling an old interest.

Although my family commitments would not permit the time required for acting, I combined my past theater experience with artistic training as a child and in college and began working with costumes, eventually designing for numerous productions and even winning awards. These new realities in my life increased my understanding of Douglas.

During this transition period, I substantially revised my interpretive framework. My first breakthrough was a realization that Douglas's professional life could not be analyzed as three separate careers—acting, singing, and politics— it was an integrated whole. Douglas was an actress accustomed to success and attention throughout her lifetime. As she moved to different arenas for acting, only her stage and audience changed. Not all actors can move from the theatrical to the political stage, but Douglas could. The growing literature of the post-suffrage generation of women reformers and the question of dual-career marriages also helped me understand Douglas. Historians began, for example, to re-create the female world that shaped Eleanor Roosevelt, who in turn helped define a new political milieu for women. Although Douglas's background did not parallel any pattern of political female participation, she did excel within the pre-existing female-defined structure in her Women's Division work. She also came of age during a time when discussion abounded about the possibility of continuing a career and marrying. Her relationship with Melvyn and her children reveals her struggle to pursue her career and to take responsibility for the domestic health of their private life. The story of their relationship suggests the difficulty of maintaining a healthy dual-career marriage.

Another breakthrough occurred as I read in the political science literature on congressional power. While this literature dealt exclusively with men, I found I could apply certain assumptions and models to Douglas. When she entered Congress, she discovered quickly that to have any sort of impact, she would have to play an untraditional role. The first basic rule of legislative success—to specialize—did not interest Douglas. She considered herself a generalist fighting for an overarching plan for postwar America. Douglas saw political issues in terms of right and wrong. She had faith that government, run for and by the American people, should be improved through the power of the voter. She had little inclination to learn the intricacies of legislation. In her campaign manager Ed Lybeck's words, "Helen could not have gotten a bill passed making December 25th a holiday" even if she tried. He added, however, that "she was a light in the window for liberals at a time when things were very dark." She had no intention of ingratiating herself with her colleagues. She got along with those who thought about issues as she did; she viewed the rest as her enemies or simply incompetent. The role that did work for Douglas was that of a self-appointed whip. She had a distinctive flair that set her apart from her colleagues, yet her style was not unknown to the House or Senate. Political scientists have variously typed these legislators as outsiders, mavericks, crusaders, and agitators. Generally, the fewer rules that such legislators followed, the faster they became cast in this nonconformist role. Political scientists Ralph K. Huitt and Robert L. Peabody wrote that outsiders feel "impelled to stand for principle absolutely, preferring defeat on those items to half-a-loaf." They like "to tell people what they should and frequently do not want to hear." These types take themselves very seriously, often lacking a sense of humor. While I had to add a gender component, these conceptual models fit Douglas well.[5]

Materials on her private life made it clear that Helen's relationship with her family in the 1920s and, after 1931, with Melvyn and their two children played a significant role in defining her professional choices. On the one hand, Douglas could take risks that were not possible for most women. As a young actress she could be choosy about acting roles because she did not have to make her living from her salary; her wealthy father supported her. With Melvyn's income as a prominent Hollywood leading man, she could continue to make choices about acting and singing opportunities. As Democratic national committeewoman and head of the Democratic Party's Women's Division in California, both appointed volunteer positions, she had the resources, unlike most others in a similar post, to set up an office, hire a staff, and fly all over the country to speak. She worked and socialized easily with Washington politicians. With her children in boarding schools and a secretary, maid, gardener, and cook, her time became increasingly her own once Melvyn joined the Army in 1942.

Douglas's personal life complicated her public life. Her decision to move to Los Angeles in 1931 when Melvyn had a movie offer decreased her acting and singing opportunities. She did not want to leave Los Angeles for long periods of time to perform in New York and Europe. For various reasons Helen Douglas did not have a film career. Eventually politics offered her a new stage; but after her Senate defeat she lost her political base when she agreed to move back to New York so that Melvyn could pursue a stage career. She also promised that she would shoulder full responsibility for their teenaged children, although this did not prevent very active involvement as a lecturer, performer, and political model for women. Over the course of her full and rich life, her attempt to balance her professional interests with her marriage and children demonstrates the challenges faced by many twentieth-century public figures.[6]

I gathered primary materials for this book both from libraries and from individuals. I particularly appreciate Jack Haley and John Caldwell at the Carl Albert Congressional Research and Studies Center and Western History Collection, University of Oklahoma; Willa Baum, Malca Chall, and particularly Amelia Fry-Davis of the Regional Oral History Office at the Bancroft Library, University of California at Berkeley, from whom I learned professional interviewing techniques and much about Douglas; and Richard D. Kirkendall and John

Bodnar, former and present directors of the Oral History Research Center at Indiana University, Bloomington, who agreed to transcribe my interviews. I appreciate the courteous and helpful staffs of the following libraries and archives: Manuscripts Division, Bancroft Library; Special Collections, Theater Collection, and Department of Public Administration, University of California at Los Angeles; Special Collections, Honnold Library, Claremont Colleges; University Archives, Occidental College Library; Huntington Library, San Marino, California; Margaret Herrick Library, Academy of Motion Pictures Arts and Sciences, Los Angeles; RKO Pictures Archives, Los Angeles; Los Angeles Public Library; Special Collections and Eagleton Institute of Politics, Rutgers University; Museum of the City of New York; Long Island Historical Society; Brooklyn Public Library; Shubert Theatre Archives, New York City; New York Public Library, particularly the Theatre Collection at Lincoln Center; Manuscripts Division, University of Washington; Manuscripts Division and Film Archives, State Historical Society of Wisconsin; Archives of Labor History and Urban Affairs, Wayne State University; Historical Society of Troy, Ohio; Lyndon Baines Johnson Library; Franklin D. Roosevelt Library; Harry S Truman Library; Registrar's Office, Barnard College; Manuscript Library and University Archives, Columbia University; Theatre Archives and Manuscript Division, Princeton University; and the Manuscript Division of the Library of Congress. Other libraries sent me useful materials, including the Berkeley-Carroll Street School in Brooklyn; the Stone Leigh-Burnham School in Massachusetts, which houses the records of the Capen School; Forbes Library in Northampton, Massachusetts; and the University Archives at Dartmouth College.

Numerous Douglas friends and colleagues provided insights into Douglas's professional activities, personality, and private life and first-hand impressions of the atmosphere and intellectual milieu of Hollywood and Washington in the 1930s and 1940s. These interviews complemented other interviews with Douglas or about her life, including the Douglas project and other major projects at the Bancroft Library's Regional Oral History Office; UCLA Oral History Program; interviews conducted by Elizabeth Evans, Douglas's cousin; the Melvyn Douglas project housed at the Oral History Research Center at Indiana University; and interviews at the Johnson, Roosevelt, and Truman presidential libraries. Many of these people also shared personal correspondence and memorabilia. I wish to thank each of these individuals: Tom Arthur, George Abbott, Martha Allen, Leisa Bronson, George Byron, Liz Carpenter, George Cehanovska, Marguerite Clark, Susie Clifton, Wilbur J. Cohen, Eloise Cohen, Virginia Foster Durr, Philip Dunne, India Edwards, Creekmore Fath, Roy Greenaway, Sharon Lybeck Hartmann, William Malone, Dorothy McAllister, Carey McWilliams, Paul Meyer, H. L. Mitchell, John C. Packard, Jr., Claude Pepper, Esther Peterson, Allen Rivkin, Easton Rothwell, Anne Seymour, Elizabeth Snyder, Paul S. Taylor, Esther Van Wagoner Tufty, John A. Vieg, Jerry

Voorhis, Terrell Webb, Claire McAllister White, Wilson W. Wyatt, Sr., Jacob Zeitlin, Mickey Ziffren, and Paul Ziffren.

Helen Douglas's family also provided important assistance. Melvyn let me read the hundreds of letters he received after Helen died; and Walter and Gay Gahagan, Helen's brother and sister-in-law, talked with me at length and shared family materials. I am particularly indebted to Mary Helen Douglas and Peter Douglas, Helen and Melvyn's children, who gave willingly of their time, memories, photographs, and other personal items. Perhaps most important, I appreciate their faith in my work.

I must single out Alis De Sola, Helen's lifelong friend from Barnard days, and Nan Stevens, the Douglases' personal secretary and close friend after 1950. I spent hours talking with Alis; her sharp memory plus her ability to see Helen's shortcomings as well as her strengths provided critically important perspectives. Except for the one time I stayed with Helen, I lived in Nan's apartment over the ten-year period when I came to do research in New York. She shared materials with me such as her correspondence with the Douglases and her daily calendars that reflected the activities of Melvyn and Helen. We cooked together, walked her dogs, played Boggle endlessly, and ate Chinese food at her favorite spot around the corner from her apartment at Broadway and Ninetieth. She punctuated our time together with her marvelous sharp wit, generosity, and the warmth of friendship. Her sharing of her memories of years of being part of the Douglas family provided me an insider's view few biographers enjoy.

I could not have written this book without generous funding. The Eleanor Roosevelt Institute at the Roosevelt Library and the American Philosophical Society awarded me grants in the early stages of research. Critical to continuing and completing the project was a major grant and subsequent supplement from the Research Division at the National Endowment for the Humanities. I am also most appreciative of the flexibility the Endowment permitted when events in my personal life required a considerable postponement of the project. The Carl Albert Congressional Research and Studies Center at the University of Oklahoma awarded me a Visiting Scholar's Travel Grant which I very much appreciate. Two universities deserve mention. When I received the NEH grant, the Department of History at the University of California, San Diego, appointed me a research associate and provided an office, phone, and faculty research privileges. At Texas Woman's University, Elizabeth Snapp, director of libraries, facilitated my research in many ways. The university also granted me leaves of absence to complete the book. My department chairs and colleagues patiently worked around my periodic absences from my teaching and university responsibilities, and I received a departmental travel grant in 1991.

Friends read all or parts of the manuscript and offered important insights. James T. Patterson and Susan Ware, both accomplished biographers, slugged through two drafts and parts of a third in the manuscript's late stages, offering invaluable comments and encouragement. John Alexander Williams read early drafts and helped me shape my focus. Others also read the manuscript and offered important conceptual, factual, and editorial comments: historians Robert E. Burke, Roger Daniels, Thomas Dublin, and George M. Juergens; psychologist Robert Gatchell; social worker Laura Neal-McCullom; and literary writer Barbara Winther. The following read selected chapters or related writings: Arnold P. Gass, Joyce Bernard, David Burner, Bruce Dierenfield, D'Ann Campbell, Jean A. Creek, Peter Fiske, Tim Hoye, Laura Kahlman, Steve Kovacs, Charles Morrissey, William Scobie, Jill Scobie, Joan Wall, and John Wickman. Michael Gottlieb read chapters and listened, questioned, and encouraged me daily in the last crucial months of this book. Over the years, students at various universities assisted me with xeroxing and the periodic reorganization of materials: Carol Ann Allen, Tom Cromwell, Bill Fredericks, Diane Lanier, William Scobie, Jared Williams, and Diane Williamson. Brian Hart was particularly helpful and meticulously careful in the final stages. My mother, Mary Galey Winther, transcribed early interviews and secured translators at Indiana University for the opera reviews in Hungarian, Dutch, German, and Czech. Susie Clifton spent considerable time locating census tract data on the Fourteenth Congressional District and other helpful materials. Elizabeth A. McNamara, Victoria Sanders, and David Washburn provided valuable advice. I also wish to thank Sheldon Meyer at Oxford, whom I have respected for many years, for his confidence in my manuscript; and Gail Cooper, my talented and precise editor, for her comments and guidance.

Many friends continued to have faith in me as an historian over the past fifteen years during the long period of childrearing complicated by my husband's death. Several made a critical difference: Joan and Sam Baily, G. Cullom Davis, Thomas Dublin, Paul W. Glad, G. Wesley Johnson, George Juergens, David Kyvig, Gerda Lerner, John V. Lombardi, Steve Kovacs and the late Katherine Kovacs, James Kirby Martin, James T. Patterson, Elizabeth Israels Perry, Janet and Alex Rabinowitch, David Ringrose, the late Nancy A. Roeske, Harry N. Scheiber, Susan Ware, Nancy Weiss Malkiel, and John Alexander Williams.

I must mention the importance of my family. I shared a significant personal and professional partnership for fifteen years with Jim Scobie to whom I have dedicated this book. He helped me shape this project intellectually in the early years, shared household responsibilities and took care of the home front while I conducted extended research trips, and, most important, believed in me and loved me. When I took the whole family with me to Oklahoma, however, he did protest that Norman (especially the record hot summer of 1980) could not compete with Buenos Aires, his base of research. I only wish he could read the finished product. Our four children, Bill, Clare, Kirsten, and Bruce, also influenced the book. Without them I might have completed this project long ago, but I would not have gained first-hand experience in combining a career, marriage, and parenting, an important theme in the book. They also believed in the importance of my work, which means more than they know. Kirsten and Bruce, now in their late teens, have never known life without the constant pressures I felt from "the book." They have been very loving and unusually patient and interested. I also owe much to my late parents—my mother, Mary Winther, who made me believe that women can somehow do it all, and my father, Oscar Osburn Winther, who introduced me to the historical profession.

Denton, Texas   INGRID WINTHER SCOBIE
Summer 1991

CENTER STAGE

1

Growing Up in Brooklyn

IN 1897, thirty-three-year-old Walter Hamer Gahagan II brought his bride, Lillian Mussen Gahagan, aged thirty-one, to Brooklyn. Both had small-town Midwestern roots. Walter, a contracting engineer and a large handsome man of tall, erect stature, had grown up in Troy, Ohio. The diminutive, attractive Lillian, a former schoolteacher and millinery store manager, had been assisting her father in managing a hotel in Lodi, Wisconsin. The two moved to the New York area because the St. Louis firm Walter worked for had sent the talented, ambitious engineer to supervise the construction of the Manhattan pier of the Williamsburg Bridge linking Manhattan to Brooklyn. He had just completed a job supervising the construction of a series of bridges across the Snake and Red rivers in Arkansas and several railroad lines, including one in Wisconsin. He had met Lillian while on the job in Lodi.[1]

Several generations of Gahagans had established reputations as civic-minded, prosperous farmers in Troy. In 1796, Walter's great-grandfather, William Gahagan, Pennsylvania-born and of Irish descent, joined a group of Cincinnati settlers who moved fifty miles north and founded Dayton, Ohio. Gahagan eventually bought land in Troy, slightly to the north. Canal building in Ohio in the 1820s boosted the economy of Troy and the Miami River area. Spacious brick and frame houses (many have been carefully restored by today's local residents) lined the streets. In 1863, during the Civil War, William Gahagan's grandson, William Henry Harrison Gahagan, married Hannah M. Smith, a schoolteacher from a neighboring town. Their three children included Walter Hamer, born in 1866, and two younger daughters, Bessie and Mary. In the early 1870s, the family moved into the large, comfortable home built by William's father in downtown Troy. The handsome two-story white brick colonial house, with large windows and surrounded with fruit trees, is still a distinguished landmark in Troy. Shortly after moving into the house, William died of a wound he received while serving in the Ohio Volunteer Infantry during the war. Despite the emotional, physical, and financial hardships, Hannah continued to farm until she had raised her children, and she succeeded in providing a stable home.[2]

Hannah, a handsome woman, dressed impeccably and carried herself with a dignified air. She wore a wig to hide the loss of hair from an early bout with typhoid. A warm but reserved, even austere person, she reared her family with a strict hand. Hannah's strong commitment to education, a reflection of her two years at Ohio's Antioch College, resulted in her emphasizing to her children the importance of reading and high academic performance. Deeply religious and an active member of the Presbyterian church, she expected regular church attendance from her children. She also kept a close eye on their social behavior. Although she did not have the resources to send all three children to college, she mortgaged the farm so that Walter, who wanted to be an engineer rather than a farmer, could go first to Ohio State Technical School and then to the Massachusetts Institute of Technology, from which he graduated in 1887. Once the children were grown, Hannah moved closer to town. Her activities reflected those of typical late nineteenth-century middle-class women who viewed involvement in social reform as an extension of their household duties. Hannah involved herself as a leader in the church, the Daughters of the American Revolution, the Women's Christian Temperance Union (WCTU), and the Altrurian Club, a local women's literary and social reform group. In 1896, two years after Ohio passed a law permitting women to vote for and serve on local school boards, Hannah successfully ran for a position on the board.[3]

Unlike her husband, Walter, Lillian Gahagan had an insecure and unhappy childhood. Her father, James Mussen, was born in 1830 in Vermont and moved to New York as a teenager. When he was seventeen, he left home to farm on his own, first settling in Illinois and then joining the surge of population moving into Wisconsin. In 1850, he married a Welsh girl, Tamer Griffith. Eventually the family moved to Dane County, settling in Roxbury near Madison. Lillian, born in 1866 and one of seven children, barely knew her mother, who died of pneumonia in 1873. Although only a child when her mother died, she never forgot that her mother had a beautiful singing voice; music had also been important in Tamer's childhood. One year later, James remarried, but his new wife, Rebecca Holcomb, deeply resented Lillian. The child disliked her stepmother, and as a young teenager she moved in with a minister and his wife, who provided the first happy home she had known. She attended high school in nearby Lodi, secured teaching credentials, and began teaching in a small schoolhouse in Rice Lake, several hundred miles north. Later she opened a millinery shop.[4]

In 1891, James married again and moved back to Lodi. Lillian loved her second stepmother, Ida Waterbury, and in 1894, Lillian moved home to help her father run a newly acquired hotel, the Briggs House. Although she had little time for outside activities, she sang in the church choir, delighting the local residents with her lovely voice, which she had inherited from her mother. The hotel proved a successful venture for Lillian's father. During the 1890s, the massive railroad expansion that Wisconsin had experienced since the Civil War had finally reached Lodi, and the Briggs House provided comfortable quarters for many working on the railroad line—including, in 1896, Walter Gahagan. He admired Lillian's beauty, her determined and self-reliant character and her management skills, traits he saw also in his mother. He also found himself enchanted with Lillian's voice.[5]

One can only speculate what attracted Lillian to this well-educated, successful engineer who suddenly appeared on the Wisconsin frontier. She was undoubtedly flattered by the attention Walter paid her, and she enjoyed his company. She realized he would provide a financially and emotionally stable family life at a level of society Lillian was not accustomed to but perhaps aspired to reach. Most likely, however, Walter was not the first to seek Lillian's hand in marriage. She valued her freedom to make choices. For fifteen years, since her early teens, she had made her own decisions about where she lived and how she supported herself. She loved her bicycle, a symbol of independence and the new interest women had in physical fitness. With a bike in Lodi, she did not have to depend on others to get her around town. When Walter finally proposed marriage, after a year of formal courting, Lillian may very well have seen her options as marrying Walter, who would expose her to a world of culture, education, and wealth in which she could continue exploring her own personal development; marrying someone with a similar economic background and becoming immersed in a more traditional life of burdensome domestic responsibilities; or remaining single and maintaining her autonomy. Although she finally agreed to marry Walter, she did not like the early signs of his determination to control their relationship, which would necessitate her abandoning her independent ways. Lillian agreed reluctantly to a trip to Troy when Walter insisted that his mother must approve of his choice of a bride. Fortunately, she did receive Hannah's blessing. Walter also insisted that Lillian sell her beloved bicycle that had provided her so much freedom. The couple married in Lodi and left shortly after for New York City.[6]

Soon after the Gahagans had arrived in Brooklyn, Walter realized that the New Jersey–New York metropolitan area offered excellent professional opportunities. Brooklyn, a city of nearly one million people, had only a handful of contracting engineers.[7] He realized that with ample work nearby, he would not have to travel extensively as he had during the previous ten years. Walter left the St. Louis firm in 1899 and formed his own company, the Gahagan Construction Company, which became very successful. He secured an office at 189 Montague Street, the main commercial and residential street in the heart of Brooklyn Heights, the city's center, two doors from the Manufacturers' Trust Bank. He also bought a small home at 118 Berkeley Place in the fashionable Park Slope residential area, about two miles from his office. Lillian had given birth to twin boys, Frederick and William, in 1898. Two girls followed in quick succession, Mary Helen in 1900 and Lillian in 1902. The arrival of Walter Jr. in 1910 when Lillian was forty-four added more bustle to the household. The entire family was handsome, fair-skinned with brown hair. Mary Helen, or Helen, as she was called, was born in New Jersey rather than Brooklyn. In the summer of 1900, the Gahagans had rented a home in Boonton, where Walter's firm was constructing a large reservoir. Although Lillian had planned to deliver her baby in Brooklyn, she went into labor so late in the evening of November 25, 1900, that she had no time to return to Brooklyn. Thus Helen was born in Boonton, an event that local residents liked to call to the attention of visitors when their native daughter became a well-known theatrical and political figure.

Although Walter would have preferred to raise his children in a small town, he found Brooklyn an acceptable urban environment for his family. Many professionals chose to live in Brooklyn, which had developed a reputation as Manhattan's bedroom community, the "city of homes and churches."[8] Newcomers liked the identification with friendly neighborhoods, reminiscent of small towns and villages where many of the residents, like Lillian and Walter, had grown up. By the turn of the century, Brooklyn had also developed into a significant industrial, commercial, and cultural center, the country's fourth-largest city. Immigrants, particularly Irish, East European Jews, Poles, Italians, and Scandinavians, made up over half the population. Only a few blacks lived in the area. Brooklyn, like its larger neighbor Manhattan, developed its port into a major shipping center and encouraged the growth of related manufacturing, trading, and banking concerns. By 1900, transportation links and political changes brought the two cities together, enhancing economic ties. In 1883, the Brooklyn Bridge, the world's largest suspension bridge, had linked Brooklyn with the southern tip of Manhattan, and horse-drawn trolleys permitted easy transportation back and forth. It was also only a short walk across the bridge to Wall Street. By 1900, railroad lines extended across the bridge, adding to the ease of communication. Political consolidation of the five New York boroughs in 1898 further unified the two cities. Nevertheless, despite Brooklyn's complex economic interrelationship with Manhattan and the similar social fabric of the two cities, Brooklyn retained its own individuality.[9]

*

Helen grew up in a household with two strong-willed parents whose values reflected their childhood experiences. Although he was only ten when his father died, Walter valued the time his father had spent with his children, and he took a deep interest in his brood of five. He remembered his mother's struggle to keep his family together, and he believed in the strength of a strongly knit family. Like his mother, he viewed hard work, constant reading, and formal education as the essentials for success. He did not like to attend church, despite his upbringing, but he closely monitored the moral and social values of his children. Lillian also brought to the marriage a commitment to education and strong ties to the Episcopal church, which had reassured her mother-in-law. Lillian's unhappy childhood had taught her that idleness had no place in women's lives. She believed that single women must be prepared for a job and that married women, if they chose, could also have a career. Walter quickly dashed her hopes for a dual-career marriage when she had an opportunity, shortly after moving to New York, to take singing lessons with the idea of eventually training as an opera singer. As Helen recalled, her father said, " 'Now, Lillian, either you give up this notion of opera or you go back to Wisconsin.' Mother gave up the notion of opera. But she did not give up singing." She simply did not perform professionally. But " 'it was a bitter pill to swallow.' " Walter believed in a traditional division of work and home for husband and wife, despite the fact that his mother had managed the family farm. But he respected his mother's active community work and encouraged his wife to follow Hannah's example.[10]

In 1905, the year Helen turned five, the family moved to a much larger and quite imposing house in Park Slope. This relatively new, posh neighborhood of stylish, imposing brownstone homes—both rowhouses and freestanding mansions—and elegant churches had become one of the most fashionable neighborhoods in Brooklyn. Park Slope developed after the Civil War when the original area of upper-class housing in Brooklyn Heights, still the main business center, grew crowded. The state legislature had contracted with Frederick Law Olmsted and Calvert Vaux, the noted landscape architects who had designed Central Park, to draw up plans for an equally magnificent area in Brooklyn. After drawing plans for a park modeled on the Romantic naturalism of English gardens, the men also structured the outlines of an adjacent residential area, one of the first suburbs, with the goal of creating for the upper class a "tranquil environment" with cultural and recreational opportunities nearby. A huge plaza, eventually called Grand Army Plaza, was built adjacent to the park. With a central fountain and an enormous, ornately carved memorial arch in the center, the plaza, reminiscent of Latin American plazas, became the site for the Brooklyn Public Library, the classy social Montauk Club, and other important public buildings. Beginning in the 1870s, but increasingly in the next two decades, developers built homes in a range of architectural styles in an area five blocks deep that wrapped around the park and plaza for about twenty blocks. Upper-class and upper-middle-class professionals, primarily native-born, quickly took advantage of the opportunity to move out of Brooklyn Heights.

The new Gahagan home, a very large, fenced-in brownstone house at 231 Lincoln Place between Seventh and Eighth avenues, was only one block from the plaza and close to the park. The three-story, ivy-covered Berkeley Institute, a first-rate private school for girls, was down the street a block. The school, founded in 1886, met the needs of the growing number of Park Slope families who wanted a good college preparatory school for their daughters. The boys also attended school nearby. Most of the homes on neighboring streets—Seventh and Eighth avenues, St. John, and Berkeley—were large row houses with garden areas in the rear of the lots. But the homes on the odd-numbered side of the 200-block of Lincoln Place were freestanding with ample garden areas on both sides and in back. They also were considerably larger than other homes in the Park Slope neighborhood. While twenty- by forty-foot houses were not uncommon, the Gahagan home measured about ninety-five feet by eighty feet. The Gahagans bought an empty lot between 231 Lincoln Place and the corner of Eighth Avenue, which further enhanced the attractiveness of their home. "It was one of those quiet areas with enormous houses" enjoying constant police protection, Helen remembered, "really the Park Avenue area of Brooklyn." The horse-drawn carriages and vendors' cries provided the major outdoor sounds, often less raucous than the inside voices of vivacious children. As the ground was higher than in other sections of town, residents enjoyed cooler air during the hot summers.[11]

The Gahagan home was actually a duplex. The two entrances, each with a high stoop leading to the door, led into identical homes. Interior doors connected the second and third floors of the duplexes to each other. A roomy basement, the site of the original kitchen, offered extra storage space and servants' quarters. Steep, narrow staircases that led up to the two upper floors had banisters. Much to Walter's dismay, the spirited Lillian taught the children how to slide down the banisters. On the first floor each side had its own kitchen, dining, and living room. The Gahagans used the long and narrow rooms on the second and third floors for bedrooms. The front second-floor bedrooms, one of which was Walter's, had a small balcony. Lillian also had her room on the second floor, as did Lilli and Helen, who shared a room. The house was high enough so that Helen could look out at the lovely park as she lay on her bed. The boys took over the third floor on both sides of the house.

Walter and Lillian created an ambience in their home reminiscent of the Gahagan house in Troy. They decorated the spacious, high-ceilinged rooms with fine-quality but not ostentatious furnishings. Walter added large windows. "There never seemed to be enough," Helen recalled, who developed her passion for huge windows at an early age. The light streaming in through the windows, the books lining the walls, and fine paneling throughout the house gave the rooms an inviting, comfortable feeling, a mood Helen sought to emulate in every house she lived in after she married. The books reflected the avid reading habits of the entire family, particularly Walter and Helen, "inveterate readers" like Walter's mother Hannah. Lillian bought fresh flowers regularly for the house. At night, gaslight gave a glow to the rooms, and in the winter, fires in the marble fireplaces throughout the house added to the coziness of the environment.[12]

Shortly after moving to Lincoln Place, Walter realized he needed more help in his growing business. Convinced that family should "stick together," Walter tried to persuade both his brothers-in-law who lived in Troy to join the firm. Bess's husband, Ben Schaible, did not want to leave his father's jewelry business. But George Clyde, Mary's husband, agreed to join the firm, and they moved into the empty side of the Gahagan house. Their only child, Walter, several years older than the Gahagan twins, joined the boys on the third floor. Helen became infatuated with her cousin and trailed him around as much as he would tolerate. He died suddenly of pneumonia when Helen was a teenager; the loss deeply saddened young Helen.[13]

Lillian ran a smooth household. She hired servants, a luxury neither she nor Walter had experienced as children. She generally employed Swedish or German immigrants who required considerable training, but they did free Lillian from the drudgery of household work. She closely supervised the children's myriad activities. She was "gentle, quiet, but went her own way and ran everything," yet to the children, it seemed as if the house just "ran itself." Crises rarely distressed her; somehow she believed that "everything would work out," a philosophy that undoubtedly had emerged from her childhood years. She once told Helen, "Don't argue. If it's right . . . for you, it will happen. . . . Everything would come out right—It couldn't be wrong." Helen developed this Pollyanna attitude towards life. Lillian received a household allowance from Walter that was frequently insufficient. She worked around her dominating husband by periodically overdrawing the bank account, somewhat to Walter's embarrassment, since he was on the bank's board of directors.[14]

Lillian also took over the job of developing well-rounded children. This meant, first of all, a sound religious education. She had less interest in her children's living up to the "literal word" of the Bible, however, than in the development of their character. Helen hated going to Sunday school at the local St. John's Episcopal Church each week. "I never could understand how God could be three-in-one." Lillian also insisted on constant exposure to music and art. Though it was traditionally part of a woman's finishing education, Lillian required piano lessons for both the boys and the girls, although she insisted the girls continue with additional tutors in the summer. At one point, she required Helen to take ballet lessons so she could "dance like Anna Pavlova," but these proved to be a "disaster." She often invited musicians into their home to perform, and she took the children on Saturdays to the nearby Brooklyn Art Museum. From the time Helen was ten, Lillian took her reluctant daughter every week to the Metropolitan Opera. Recalled Helen, "I would be so unhappy sitting through long operas and I'd complain, 'They're all so *fat*, Mother.' " Lillian would simply tell her to stop looking and just listen. When Helen commented that she wanted to be an actress, her mother responded: " 'Why do you want to be an actress? Why don't you want to be something really worthwhile—a *singer?*' "[15]

The broad-shouldered Walter dominated the family's interactions when he was at home. He ingrained in his children a series of rules that stemmed from his business principles. "Your word is your bond," he always told the children. "If your word isn't good, you're not worth anything"; no job was ever too small, rather the question was whether one was "big enough to do the job"; no person was "too humble" for a friend; one should always try to "make everybody's life and every place you've been better because you've been there." In addition to these rules, Lillian admonished her family never to say "ugly things about people" and never to waste time. Despite the family's high social status, Walter recalled as an adult, the children were not conscious of who belonged or who did not belong to a particular group or club. Helen also made no reference to her parents' becoming involved in a high-society social life. Neither Helen nor her sister Lilli experienced the life of debutantes; neither had a coming-out in New York society. The parents expected all their children to excell to their capacity.[16]

Walter included his family as much as he could in his work. The children heard much talk about the engineering business, from construction problems to the art of bidding for jobs. Like her twin brothers, who eventually took over the business, Helen found it fascinating to observe a particular job in progress. She vividly remembers taking off on her own on one such visit—in a manner more typical of an adventurous young boy than a "proper" young lady—and scrambling down the excavation to the work site for the New Jersey–New York tunnel under the Hudson River. Her father, who had recently lost a worker when the opening to the excavation collapsed, was horrified to discover Helen at the entrance to the tunnel. Walter also exposed his children to his work in another way by inviting his colleagues, Brooklyn's conservative Republican business and community élite, into the house. His community contacts branched out widely. In addition to his own business, he was a director of the Manufacturers Trust Company and the Northside Holding Company, a member of the élite Montauk and Brooklyn clubs, the Masons, and several professional organizations. Lillian, too, brought in women she met in her church and other civic groups, including the Chicago Club, and, in the 1920s, the Theater Club.[17]

In general, Walter and Lillian tried to let their children develop their own interests without too much interference. It was a "noisy, gregarious, affectionate family." Both Helen and Walter Jr. remembered that "everybody was doing their own thing." He likened the family lifestyle to the play *You Can't Take It with You*; Helen's analogy was to *Life with Father*. Both recollections suggest a behavior structure imposed by both parents that the children continually challenged. Lillian eventually backed up whatever the children wanted to do. The twins Fritz and Bill, tall like their father, had very different personalities. Bill, the "prince" of the family (in Walter's words), was much more assertive and self-assured than the quiet Fritz. Both excelled in school, played football, and attended Williams College. Helen, the middle child, tall and statuesque as she grew older, was rebellious, loving, mischievous, and playful. She loved to act and found that it drew people's attention. Lilli, the prettier and more sociable of the two girls and physically more like her mother, sometimes envied the attention that Helen received. Walter, the "baby," was the center of much attention until the older children left home. Then he felt very lonely, without adequate parental support.[18]

Although everyone in the family had busy schedules, both Walter and Lillian insisted on the family's gathering together for dinner. Walter could not always be home for dinner because of work responsibilities, but when home, he clearly dominated the conversation. A spirited and competitive atmosphere typified the dinner hour; the children learned quickly that they had to be assertive if they wanted to be heard. Family councils often followed the evening meal. While Walter listened to his children, his opinions generally prevailed. On Sundays, Walter often took the family to dine at the Montauk Club, located a block down the street. The club, according to a contemporary observer, "took high rank among the social organizations of Brooklyn" and kept up with the "constantly increasing needs of a fashionable and exclusive section of the City." The club offered luxurious dining. Copied after the famous clubs in Manhattan, Philadelphia, and Boston, the ornate, four-story building, built of brownstone, brick, terra cotta, and copper, is still standing as an imposing structure on Grand Army Plaza. Inside, the carved mahogany paneling and heavy dark wooden banisters gave a rich feel to the halls and rooms, which included a reading room, a billiards room, a private salon for ladies, and a formal dining hall. From the top floor, one could see across to the New York harbor, Staten Island, and the New Jersey shore.[19]

In the summer Walter insisted that at least Lillian and the girls get out of Brooklyn; the twins had to work for the firm once they were old enough. They and their father would join the rest of the family for a brief vacation. Until Helen's early teen years, she and Lilli also visited their grandmother in Troy and occasionally family in Wisconsin. Walter undoubtedly felt that his young daughters would profit by spending time with his mother, who was strict and austere but also cared deeply for her grandchildren. A cousin of the Gahagan girls commented: "Grandmother wasn't too broad-minded. She believed in God, the American flag, the DAR, and the Presbyterian Church," and "no and's-if's-or-but's about it." The grandchild also observed that her cousin Helen inherited her strong-willed nature from her grandmother, although clearly Helen's father had the same character. When Helen was in Ohio, she enjoyed visiting not only her grandmother but also her cousin Martha Schaible, who was about Helen's age. The two had more in common with each other than with Helen's sister Lilli during these years. Martha recalled that Lilli "always had beaux on her mind. Helen and I weren't interested in boys; we were interested in books and other things that Lilli couldn't have given a hoot about." Helen and Martha read poetry together, and Helen loved to be dramatic. "I can remember being up in grandmother's front bedroom where Helen stayed, and she would act parts of a poem or of a play," hoping to make Martha cry. "If she could make me cry, she was very successful."[20]

In 1912, when Helen was twelve, Lillian took the children on their first visit to Europe, a trip that made a deep impression on Helen. While the boys took a bicycle trip down the Rhine, the girls stayed with their mother in Baden-Baden in the Black Forest, visiting museums, attending concerts, and shopping. Two years later, however, Walter decided that he was tired of the family's constant traveling. He thought a country home for summer retreats would be better for his four adolescent children. The family bought Cliff Mull, a lovely Victorian house built in 1889 on small, crystal-clear Lake Morey near Fairlee, Vermont, about thirty miles north of Hanover, New Hampshire. The house, which Helen thought "looked like a birthday cake," had a wide porch that wrapped almost entirely around it. The house sat atop a wooded hill thick with maples and white birch, with the lake barely visible through the trees during the summertime. Walter added windows, built sleeping porches for the children off the upstairs rooms, enlarged the living room, and put in a tennis court. The Clydes bought a separate cottage nearby. Two years later, Walter's sister Bess Schaible, Martha's mother, died suddenly. Each summer after that, Martha and Grandmother Hannah joined the Gahagan compound.

Helen loved Vermont from the very start. Remembered images of Cliff Mull helped her get through the long and often dreary New York winters. The summers had a similar routine. Lillian structured the children's mornings, including Martha's, with tutoring and the chores. Instruction included piano, diction, and classes in how to read poetry "properly." One tutor, whom they despised, made the girls do vigorous exercises in the heat of the day. They also had to take riding lessons. Helen liked riding but hated the classes in the disciplined art of horsemanship. But by afternoon they were free, and the girls often joined their brothers or other teenagers from surrounding houses in outdoor activities. They almost always swam in or canoed on the lake. Often they rode horses, played tennis, or walked in the woods. They took picnics with them and occasionally enough supplies to camp out overnight. Sometimes a group would walk the four miles into town to the local drugstore for homemade ice cream topped with marshmallow and chocolate sauces, "as if we had never had ice cream before in our lives." Helen also enjoyed reading, perched on a smooth rock away from all the activity. As in Ohio, Martha and Helen tended to pair off together. As they grew older, boys came by to visit the attractive teenage girls, but neither Helen nor Martha had Lilli's interest in dating. Helen never ceased practicing acting skills. She did eye exercises in front of a mirror, for example, trying out changes of emotion. One day she practiced flirting, using the twins and their friends as "subjects." When they had had enough, they "picked me up bodily, carried me out of the house and down three flights of stairs, and threw me into Lake Morey."[21]

As Helen was growing up, she developed particularly close feelings for her father. In her autobiography, Helen frequently points out the ways she and her father were alike. She sought in many ways to please him. She acquiesced to his determination to supervise her social life; even when she was an adult, he continued to exercise considerable control. She learned to get around the domineering side of his personality so that she could develop a friendship with him. She discovered, for example, that late in the evening he became gentle and mellow. She would persuade him to come downstairs for midnight snacks of fruit, cheese and crackers, and her favorite, onion sandwiches, long after her mother had gone to bed. Unlike other times when he tended to lecture the kids, he relaxed, chatting about problems in his work and listening to her stories of friends and school.[22]

Helen also, perhaps unconsciously, sought her father's approval by demanding she be permitted to do everything her twin brothers could do, particularly when it came to sports. She participated in activities from golf and skiing to boxing, although she often ended up getting hurt and dropping the interest. She did excell in horsemanship. In Europe, she felt jealous that the twins had bikes. One day she insisted that she ride up a mountainside. She finally got her way, and on the way down she slipped in the mud and badly sprained her ankle, much to her mother's disgust. For several years in Vermont, Helen resented the fact that she could not drive the Ford because she was not old enough to have a license. Determined not to be denied a privilege that her brothers enjoyed, she begged her brothers to teach her, but they refused. In typical style, she decided to try it herself. One morning, while everyone was still asleep, she cranked up the auto, enjoyed a pleasant ride through nearby towns, and returning to Cliff Mull without a mishap. But just as she was approaching the house, family members raced towards her. Startled, she put the car in reverse and rammed the car into a tree.[23] At the same time that Helen tried to identify with her brothers, she set herself apart from her sister. Lilli always felt overshadowed by her older sister. She felt that Helen was her father's favorite, although Lilli took some solace in believing that her mother favored her.

While on the one hand Helen sought her father's approval, she struggled with him on certain major issues that created serious tensions in the relationship. Unlike her brothers, she had no interest in performing well academically. Her father did not want "a home cluttered up with dumb females who couldn't take part in anything," Helen recalled; "he had no patience with stupid women." In fact, she believed that initially he had not wanted girls, only boys. Also from a very young age she insisted, against her father's will, on becoming an actress. Her father opposed an acting career because he felt it improper for a woman to go into the theater; he believed "all actresses were tarnished." Yet Helen could never understand "why a talented actress should be less honorable than a talented engineer." Her mother also opposed her daughter's desire to act, but not because she had believed it "inappropriate" for ladies. She wanted Helen to become an opera singer, a goal Lillian herself had never achieved. She was also upset with Helen's unwillingness to take her schoolwork seriously.[24]

Helen's perpetual dislike of school began in kindergarten, when Berkeley dropped her behind a grade because she could not spell, a problem that continued to plague her as an adult. The goals of the school, however, certainly met her parents' expectations of a superior educational institution for refined, upper-class young women. Aimed at providing a "complete education," particularly for the college-bound young lady, the school offered a broad curriculum and a disciplined structure. Beginning in first grade, classes included English, mathematics, geography, nature study, and art, with foreign languages added in the third grade. The goal was to "awaken such natural interest in study" and to "establish right habits of control and self-reliance." The school also expected good manners. A list from the headmistress of proper behavior for walking to and from school, entering the building, the classroom, and attending school parties—including speaking in "agreeable, cultivated tones," acquiring a "bearing well-poised and gracious," and avoiding loud laughter or "petty rudeness"—reminded the girls of "customs as old as courtesy itself, observed by gentlewomen everywhere."[25]

But studying such things as plants and insects, the earth's motion, stories of New York history, and mathematical concepts never awakened Helen's curiosity. Even in the primary grades, with 69 a failing grade, her school marks hovered in the 70s and low 80s. Although the honor roll recognized students for excellence ranging from scholarship to attendance, deportment, and voice, Helen never made a single list. Her grades improved in the fifth grade, but then dropped continuously until the eighth grade, at which point she failed German and algebra, dropped history, and was absent thirty-eight days and late another fifty-nine times during the school year. Despite her dislike of school, the fact that she attended a single-sex institution where women could excell without competing with men contributed to her determination to overcome gender barriers. Even at this stage, Helen knew that she much preferred to spend her time making up stories and acting them out rather than studying. But her teachers had little patience with Helen's natural talents and interests. They had no place in the Berkeley Institute. She remembers one morning before going to school she decided to portray a "pale heroine." The unamused teacher inquired sarcastically whether Helen had fallen into a flour barrel, much to her chagrin. But at home at least she was not stopped from her daydreams and play-acting. She saved her allowance for Saturday theater matinees. She even used her father's billiard table until he realized what she was doing and banned the use of that stage.[26]

Helen's dispirited academic attitude did not affect her enthusiasm for the school and her friends. Her classmates liked her and in fact elected her more than once to be class president. Finally, in the spring of her freshman year, Helen suddenly found an avenue at school in which she wanted to excell. A new elocution teacher and noted drama coach, Elizabeth Grimball, added Dramatics to the English curriculum. She realized quickly that this academically rebellious teenager had exceptional talent and carefully cultivated and encouraged her new pupil. And Helen needed a mentor who could encourage her, as well as provide direction and opportunities. Before long, Helen began starring in plays and participating on the debating team. One school yearbook noted that Helen's performance as Queen Elizabeth in an original play by Grimball was "remarkable." In debating, Helen found that "everyone wanted me on their side." She never cared which point of view she argued unless the topic concerned Irish independence. She had an intense interest in anything Irish, for she always considered her Irish blood dominant, despite the fact that the Irish in her family was more than five generations back. Helen received 90s in Grimball's class, but this enthusiasm did not rub off on her other courses. She failed geometry and received 70s in the rest of her classes. Grimball's encouragement got little support from the Gahagan household. "Father tolerated my obsession with Elizabeth Grimball's department" until he found out that his daughter cut classes one day to sell war bonds with Broadway stars, including Al Jolson, on the steps of the New York Public Library. "He was furious," she recalled.[27]

As Helen's enthusiasm for Grimball's class grew, her performance in her other subjects continued to decline. At the end of her sophomore year she failed every subject—algebra, chemistry, English, German, and Latin—except elocution and gym. Her father waited until the family reached their summer home in Vermont before he talked to her about her grades. The intervening days were torture. Helen recalled that the lecture, reminiscent of the behaviorist's belief in rational control of emotions, lasted all day. " 'You know, you're ignorant,' " her father told her. " 'One can support women [only] if they're educated' "; did she just want to be a " 'breeding machine?' " he asked. " 'Just because you can talk a lot, and read a lot, you think you are educated, but you're not.' " If it took until she turned forty, she was to go to college and " 'forget about acting.' " She needed to learn to think about what she read, her father argued, in order to control her emotions so that she was "less likely to be manipulated." Helen spent all the next day climbing the rocky hills, thinking about how unfair it was that her parents had never encouraged her theatrical talent. But she finally decided that if she obeyed her parents, their attitude towards acting might change. She suggested to her mother that she enroll in a summer tutoring program at nearby Dartmouth College.[28]

In the process of looking into Dartmouth, she learned of the Capen School, a girls' college preparatory school in Northampton, Massachusetts, with close connections to Smith College. Much like the Berkeley Institute, the Capen School aimed to prepare women for a "higher course in education and a larger life of refinement and usefulness to society." She requested admission for fall. Despite her poor grades, she was accepted. She stayed two years and for the first time tried to apply herself to her schoolwork. Although she did not find herself any more stimulated by her courses at Capen than at Berkeley, she learned she could pass by memorizing the material. She could not resist organizing a dramatic group on the sly, much to her parents' dismay. The girls produced George Bernard Shaw's *St. Joan*. "Of course," she said, "I played Joan." She also played Queen Elizabeth in another production.[29]

Most of the college-bound Capen girls entered nearby Smith, but as long as Helen's parents expected her to attend college, Helen preferred the more cosmopolitan Barnard College in New York City, a choice with which her parents concurred. They no doubt liked the idea of her being close to home; Helen wanted to be near the New York theater district, not at some country school. Helen was particularly delighted that Elizabeth Grimball had left the Berkeley Institute to run an Off-Broadway production company, Inter-Theatre-Arts, Inc., a school for actors that also provided production opportunities for little-known playwrights. She had continued to be an important supporter and friend of Helen's. In the summer of 1920, before Helen took Barnard's entrance exams, she went back to Dartmouth for tutoring in Latin from the noted Harry Edwin Burton, Daniel Webster Professor of Latin. He told Helen that she could not possibly make up for what she had lost by not doing well in her previous Latin classes. He did, however, provide hints for guessing words from the Latin stems. Fortunately, she passed the required examinations.[30]

A coordinate college with Columbia, Barnard provided women with an alternative to both strictly women's colleges and coeducational schools. The school had originally been created as a day school to provide New York girls an opportunity to share in the education that men received at Columbia. Eventually

Barnard hired its own faculty and built dormitories to create a campus life of its own, but the two schools remained closely linked. Barnard, like Smith, was one of the seven élite women's colleges in New England, founded in the last two decades of the nineteenth century. This group also included Wellesley, Mount Holyoke, Vassar, Bryn Mawr, and Radcliffe. In these prestigious schools, as Helen Lefkowitz Horowitz has pointed out in *Alma Mater*, women broke away from the "common notions of femininity of their era. Through college organizations, athletics, and dramatics, they learned the masculine routes of power: how to cooperate, how to compete openly, how to lead." [31]

The student body at Barnard in 1920, numbering around 850, included a wide range of academically talented girls, still primarily from New York City. "From the very first, the Committee on Admissions was not looking for grinds but for capable young women," one historian of Barnard College commented. During the four years, the faculty aimed to put a "fine edge" on the "vigorous common-sense abilities" the girls already possessed. Those whose families had more limited resources came as day students and "kept campus life from being too cloyingly girlish and secluded." Others chose Barnard so they could be in New York during the debutante season, although they still had to meet the college's stiff academic standards. Barnard also had a sizable number of Jewish students, unlike her sister schools, which broadened the intellectual atmosphere. In the 1920s, this created a "Jewish problem" in the mind of the dean, Virginia Gildersleeve. While she did not object to Jewish students, she felt that the increasing numbers of immigrants from Eastern and Central Europe and Russia represented a " 'particularly crude and uneducated variety of Jew.' " These three groups, added to the typical upper-class young woman, provided a different mix than that found at the rest of the Seven Sisters. [32]

The students who lived on campus—the wealthier; those who lived outside of an easy commute, such as Staten Island, Flushing, Brooklyn, or New Jersey; or the few from more distant states—stayed in the one dormitory, Brooks Hall, or in the adjacent apartments purchased for overflow housing needs. Although many girls came to college and married immediately after graduation, Barnard had an impressive number of students who chose either to attend graduate school or to work after their college years. Alumnae found both traditional women's jobs as tutors, secretaries, clerks, and social workers, but also positions as lab assistants, chemists, researchers, editors, and statisticians. Helen entered with the idea of becoming an actress; marriage was not a concern to her or her parents. In fact, they would have been distraught had Helen indicated an interest in marriage at this point in her life. [33]

Although World War I did not dramatically change the type of student attending Barnard, it did affect student concerns. The bobbed-haired, smoking, painted flapper emerged at Barnard as the symbol of women's sexual liberation, as she did all over the country. While "flapperdom did not particularly bother the college," the faculty did discover "beneath the mask of dead white powder and staring rouge" a "new creature" who was "desperately in earnest about the world and her part in it." Barnard responded with curriculum changes that students as well as faculty and administration helped initiate. In 1921, the college started a Department of Government. Two years later, Raymond Moley took over as head of the department, only one of many eminent scholars Gildersleeve attracted to the faculty. The college added new courses that reflected a perceived expansion of career opportunities for women as a result of the war and expanded efforts to develop courses that made use of the resources of New York City. In addition to curriculum changes, Barnard women had ample opportunities from compulsory assembly and public lectures to learn about the "outside world" from distinguished speakers, such as John Erskine, who lectured on poetry, or Arthur Hopkins, who spoke on the need for theater to "give us a better understanding of our fellow men." Students could also take trips into the city to observe, for example, a tenement house while taking a sociology course. In addition, the college had a tradition of student "stump speaking" in "The Jungle," a beautiful wooded area between Barnard's buildings, designed by Olmstead, the same famed architect who laid out Brooklyn's Park Slope.[34]

Thus Helen entered a college that offered her a wide range of intellectual challenges for a woman of her era. But she avoided most of the ferment around her. She lacked the scholarly incentives Gildersleeve valued in her students. Helen was certainly intelligent and vivacious, but she had no interest in learning just to learn. She had to be interested in a subject in order to apply herself. She continued to ignore current events; in her autobiography, for example, she makes no mention of the impact of World War I. Yet eventually, as one college friend said, Helen "became a good imitation of an intellectual." It also seems likely that the "refined and energetic" dean and the politically and socially active students served as feminist models for Helen, even though at this point this academically undisciplined student had one goal in mind, to become an actress. Simply put, she was "obsessed by the theater."[35] One can only speculate why Helen still wanted to become an actress. It gave her a creative outlet for her restless energies and also satisfied her need for attention. Acting provided one way of perceiving the world, of understanding different personalities, of comprehending human problems, and at times of avoiding introspection. Helen also realized that on stage, men and women were both important, and she did not have to compete as hard as in other professions to be treated equally.

It took Helen a while to find her niche at school. Her major concern initially was getting through her freshman courses. Her day began with Freshman English. Her professor, Ethel Sturtevant, also taught theater classes. One student in the class, Alis De Sola, particularly disliked Helen. Alis, a sophisticated, petite young lady, impeccably dressed and quiet, sat in the back of the room.

An academically talented girl well prepared for college, she had lived most of her childhood abroad. She was, in her own words, "snooty as hell" and somewhat of a "rebel." She certainly felt she did not need beginning English, given her previous education, and thus felt "brash and contemptuous of Sturtevant." Every day, Alis would observe with disdain Helen rushing into class at the last moment as if she had just gotten out of bed, her "hair all mussy, her stockings torn." Helen sat in the front row, raised her hand constantly whether she knew the answer or not, and "always yelled." Helen, Alis observed early on, definitely needed the course, for she had no idea how to organize material. Helen, in turn, found Alis equally uncongenial. Alis mumbled when she talked. She also came across as a snob, a trait Gahagans found distasteful. Helen did admire Alis's beautiful long hair, carefully wrapped around her head. But when Alis cut it, Helen lost whatever positive feelings she had for her fellow student.[36]

Much to the dismay of both girls, Helen recalled, Sturtevant decided that the girls were both interesting women and "kindred spirits." She put them together on a team to debate the question of Irish independence. Both believed in the independence movement, but for entirely different reasons. Alis loved Irish Renaissance writers, while Helen still believed she was Irish. Alis, in charge of the pro-independence team, decided that Helen could not handle the intellectual arguments but she could present the emotional side of the case. One evening, when Alis came by Helen's apartment to work on the debate, Helen suddenly "flung her arms" around the startled Alis, saying, "I love you!" And that, Alis later recalled, was Helen—a "free spirit" and "utterly uncontrolled." From that point a deep and close friendship began to develop that lasted throughout the lifetimes of the two women. The two began spending as much time as they could together. Despite the fact that their academic lives took very different paths, they often had courses together, and they enjoyed each other's company.[37]

Fortunately for Helen, Barnard had a strong tradition of dramatic activity, typical of the élite women's colleges but less so of coeducational schools. In 1913 the college organized a club, Wigs and Cues, to manage most student productions. In addition, individual instructors frequently had their classes put on original student plays. One of Helen's professors, Minor Latham, the personable English Department chair, had her students write and produce miracle plays, a centuries-old form based on religious themes. "She taught her students how to bring their ideas to life upon a stage." Latham also took advantage of the nearby professional stage. Her classes attended Broadway productions, and she and other faculty members often recruited professionals to assist with student performances. Occasionally Columbia and Barnard collaborated on productions, which provided increased production resources, male cast members, and a relaxed coeducational experience. In addition to a strong theater program, the college also had a long-standing tradition of Greek Games "drama-tizing women's new access to liberal learning." The games, played in April, first developed in 1903 as an athletic contest between freshmen and sopho-mores in an era when a "Greek flavor permeated the whole undergraduate life." Gradually, the competition developed into a much more intellectual and esthetic event. Each year, the students dedicated their games to a particular god or goddess. In preparation, they studied clothing, lyrics, music, poetry, and myths surrounding their god and the Olympic tradition. As Gildersleeve later wrote, the games were "a striking example of the modern use of play and pageant in education. They lead some four hundred girls back into what seems like that bright and beautiful world of ancient Hellas . . . when the atmos-phere was clear and untroubled, and the spirit of the world fresh and strong." Helen soon discovered a place for herself in both the Greek Games and Wigs and Cues. During her freshman year, her class selected her as the lead in the games, the "daring Atys," a part Helen played well. In her sophomore year, she was in charge of the Games Advisory Committee, which required hours of planning. This leadership position in one of the most important Barnard activ-ities provided important training in organizing educated women.[38]

Helen's most creative efforts, however, came through her activities with Wigs and Cues, especially during 1921–22, her sophomore year, when she headed the organization. In the fall of 1921, a number of the students persuaded the faculty to let them produce for their December play something more challeng-ing than second-rate Broadway shows. They chose the American debut of *And Pippa Dances* by Gerhart Hauptmann, a leading German writer and Nobel Prize winner for literature. Helen directed the play rather than acting. The story revolved around the reactions of men of different philosophical leanings to a beautiful little Italian girl, Pippa. Stage direction demanded an under-standing of the abstract nature of Hauptmann's thought, and many felt the selection "much too difficult to be presented by a college dramatic society." Fortunately, Helen profited from the keen interest that several New York pro-fessionals, including the well-known Broadway producer of Hauptmann plays, Emmanuel Reicher, took in her production. When the play opened in mid-December it received wide acclaim. Reviewers were enthusiastic about Helen's directing. One commented that Gahagan and the cast "attacked the play with such reverence. Never once did they forget the lyrical quality, the consciously artistic tone, and the involved symbolism." That December proved a high mark for Helen and other Wigs and Cues members in other respects as well. They sponsored an Assembly speaker Kenneth MacGowan, a director of the Theatre Guild and an editor of *Theatre Arts Magazine*. In addition, two Broadway stars came as the group's guests at their December Tea—the young, talented Katharine Cornell, playing in *A Bill of Divorcement*, and actor-director Louis Calvert. A week later Helen appeared as the Snow Queen in a play produced by Elizabeth

Grimball at Inter-Theatre-Arts. On top of everything else, Helen directed one of four miracle plays that her class with Latham produced early in January.[39]

As might well be expected, Helen concentrated almost entirely on her theater opportunities. She knew she wanted to study only enough to get by. She managed to maintain about a B— average her freshman year, although she took an "incomplete" in English her first semester. Her grades the next year, when she took English classes primarily, were less impressive. She failed both history and physical education. Fortunately, she had friends who helped her through her other courses. Helen was always "candid with her friends, and also had a way about her that engendered almost a worshipful quality in some of her friends' feelings towards her." She was a "goddess," said Alis, "a nice goddess you know, and in many ways she was lots of fun as a person." And they enjoyed doing things for her.[40]

Helen's most exciting theatrical adventure at Barnard had its inception in Professor Sturtevant's class, "Epic and Romance," in the spring of 1922, a class she took with Alis. They both found the Irish epics fascinating, given the "obsession" they both had with "all things Irish." Sturtevant suggested that for their term paper they dramatize an episode from an epic story that particularly appealed to them, entitled *Tain Bó Cuailnge*. The story revolved around Cú Chulainn, who was under the spell of a fairy queen for a hundred years. He begged to return to Ireland, but the queen would not let him, and he eventually killed himself. Alis did most of the writing, while Helen helped structure and organize. The girls found themselves so excited about their one-act play, which they called *Shadow of the Moon*, that they showed it to Grimball. She found the play charming and arranged to produce it with Helen playing the role of Fand, the fairy queen. An enthusiastic alumna, writing in the *Barnard Bulletin*, noted that the play "reminded us of the best that there is in O'Neill." And as for Helen Gahagan, "she can act!"[41]

The professional production of the play, exciting enough for a sophomore in college, ultimately proved to be her ticket out of college and onto the Broadway stage. Among those whom Grimball had invited to see *Shadow of the Moon* was her close colleague, Harry Wagstaff Gribble, a playwright who had attracted considerable attention with a recent Broadway play, *March Hares*. Impressed with Helen, he asked her to play the lead role in his new play, *Shoot*, which he and Grimball planned to have Inter-Theatre-Arts produce. Helen accepted, unconcerned that rehearsals came during exams. Alis and some of her friends, knowing that she would never pass her philosophy course without pressure, locked her in a room, threw the key out the window, and forced her to study. "I swear to God," said Alis, "she never opened the book and she skipped most of the lectures." She managed to pass the course with a C. During the production of these two plays, Helen had to cope with a displeased father. Walter had accepted Helen's involvement in Barnard theater, as long as she confined herself to academic courses and college activities. But when he learned that Grimball planned to produce *Shadow of the Moon*, he blamed Sturtevant, in whose class Helen and Alis had written the play. Although generally a cordial gentleman, Walter had little control over his temper when really angry. In a rage, he went to see the professor. "He was a brute, acting like a mad man," Sturtevant told Alis afterwards. "I could not believe he was her father." Walter then implored Alis, whom he liked because he saw her as a serious student, to persuade Helen to finish college. "Helen should graduate," he argued; "then she can do what she wants." Alis countered, "Look, she doesn't give a damn about it. And it really has nothing to do with what she is going to do later."[42]

Walter's protests were in vain. The stakes were too high for Helen; she could not resist the opportunities that began coming her way. Thus, when producer John Cromwell, who saw her in *Shoot*, tapped her for the part of Sybil Harrington in *Manhattan*, an Off-Broadway play he planned to produce at the MacDowell Theatre in August, she accepted. Cromwell found Helen so talented that he persuaded his friend Grace George, actress and wife of a crusty, tough, established Broadway producer, William A. Brady, Jr., to see a performance. Grace George had a reputation for finding young actors and actresses, among them Douglas Fairbanks. She reported back to her husband that he had to take a look at Helen. When Brady watched her, he asked if he could pull her out of *Manhattan* and cast her as Anne Baldwin, the lead in a new Owen Davis play, *Dreams for Sale*, about to go into rehearsal for September production on Broadway. Although Helen found the ingenue role "silly," she told Brady " 'I can play it on my eyebrows' " and agreed to take the part. This was her big chance.[43]

2

Broadway Stardom Overnight

GAHAGAN'S PRODUCER, the aging William A. Brady, Jr., a "blustering, rough-tongued Irishman," had little in common with the young actors with whom he contracted. A boxing manager as a young man, Brady eventually turned to acting and theater management. He produced melodramas in the West before moving to New York. After a period of staging spectacular events, including a boxing match in the Metropolitan Opera House, which created a considerable sensation, he turned to legitimate theater. He first acquired the Manhattan Theatre for his productions and then built the Playhouse in 1911. He worked closely with his actress-manager wife, Grace George, an aloof, exquisitely groomed and cultured individual, and one of the few women to penetrate theater management ranks. Brady had an impressive list of stars under contract to him during this period, including Humphrey Bogart and Katharine Cornell. Although Brady produced the works of a wide variety of playwrights, he had collaborated closely for years with Owen Davis, the author of the play in which Brady cast Gahagan, *Dreams for Sale*. Davis had written successful melodramas for over twenty years before he turned to more serious writing for Brady. Many of Davis's plays became vehicles for Brady's actress daughter, Alice Brady. In the 1921 season, Davis received critical acclaim for his work, *Detour*. A year later, *Icebound* earned him a Pulitzer prize. Producer George Tyler described Davis as "at present the most successful and capable playwright in America."[1]

Although Gahagan accepted Brady's offer, she knew that the consequences of such a decision would have dire repercussions at home. Walter Gahagan's attitude was commonplace among men of his generation. Actors' lives had always been outside of the norm—constant travel with poor conditions, strange working hours, and physical proximity with the opposite sex—which suggested illicit sexual behavior. The actress was "seen as a pariah in Victorian eyes because her mobility and professional equality did not enable her to fit into a world where a woman's sphere was solely the home and the family."[2] Tension at the Gahagans climaxed the night before *Dreams for Sale* opened. Brady threatened that he would not open the play unless Helen signed the contract. She told Brady she would talk to her father and let him know the following day. Her friend, producer Harry Gribble, with whom she had done *Shoot*, had come to the final dress rehearsal. He realized the pressure and panic that Helen felt. He accompanied her home to talk to her father and stayed well into the night. Her mother stayed out of the way. As the exhausted actress was drifting to sleep, she could hear through the open windows her angry father shouting that "his daughter, by God, was not going to be an *actress*"; that she was going back to Barnard.

The following day, according to Helen's recollections, she went to the theater with considerable apprehension. Brady stormed into her dressing room. As was frequently the case, he had been drinking heavily. He spoke harshly to his newest discovery. He stuck in front of her a three-year contract with an option to renew for two more years. Helen remembered the almost unbearable tension she felt. Yet this seemed the moment to stand up to her father, and she signed. Brady was so pleased that she "felt like one of his prizefighters . . . about to climb into the ring." After the performance, dozens of friends, and more important, her entire family made their way backstage. Her father, "sad and withdrawn," made only one comment to the exuberant Brady: "Keep her clean." Helen expected this reaction from her father. But her mother startled her by saying that she would only be proud of Helen when she *sang* in the theater. Despite her parents' attitude, she did not regret her decision.[3]

Although the audience had responded enthusiastically, no one expected the overwhelmingly positive response of the reviewers. Even the self-confident Helen found herself somewhat taken aback. While the critics found little literary merit in *Dreams for Sale*, this did not deter them from noticing this twenty-two-year-old "new girl on the block." The *Brooklyn Daily Eagle* crowed over the success of a local girl making good—"A Brooklyn girl has conquered the world of Manhattan overnight." The exuberant Gilbert Seldes, a critic for the *Dial* and noted for his sound reviews, wrote that Gahagan as a newcomer "has made the most jaded first-nighters sit up." Not since Helen Hayes had "any unknown scored so superlatively, and with such generally conceded prospects for a brilliant future." Heywood Broun called hers the "most sensational debut of the season" and "ten of the twelve most beautiful women in the world." He added that the "most exciting thing which can happen to a critic in the theatre is to discover, or think he has discovered, a new star," and Gahagan strongly reminded theatergoers of Ethel Barrymore. Colgate Baker, writing for the *New York Review*, commented that "the day of miracles is not past for William A. Brady." He still had his gift of "doing the amazing and extraordinary," for he had found a "real acting genius. . . . This is a real event, folks." Helen even made the cover of the noted *Theatre Magazine* for October. Not all critics, however, offered such generous praise. Alan Dale of the *American* said that Gahagan reminded him "of an amateur playing at being a star. The only thing lacking was stellar quality." She seemed to have been taught, he continued, that unless she is "in the center of the stage she needn't consider herself on the stage at all." Burns Mantle agreed with H. Z. Torres that she lacked the skill to play the character.[4]

Despite mixed reactions, the *New York Mail* speculated that Gahagan was probably the "happiest actress in New York" when she woke up to "find herself heralded as the most promising young leading woman" at the beginning of the season. She certainly seemed excited, a bit silly, and naïve when eager journalists badgered her for a personal interview. "I don't see how I can be interviewed yet because I haven't been on the professional stage long enough to have very decided opinions or to give advice to girls," she said to the *Brooklyn Daily Eagle* reporter, which suggests that she felt she suddenly had become a role model. She commented to another journalist, reflecting her somewhat sheltered life and prudish outlook, that she wished she did not have to kiss on the stage. "I don't like it at all," she complained, but she supposed that she would eventually get used to it. "After all, promiscuous lovemaking a few feet behind the footlights is a necessary cog in the machinery of the play."[5] Gahagan also revealed a glimpse of her ambitious thoughts for the future, ideas shaped both by her two years of classroom and stage experience at Barnard and by her inordinate self-confidence. Her greatest desire was to appear in Henrik Ibsen's plays. She also wanted her own theater, where she could "produce and manage the plays that I hope to write." Alis De Sola remembered clearly one evening after a rehearsal for *Dreams for Sale*. Helen was "full of, well, hope is too weak a word really; there was a certainty about her future career." She commented to her friend, in a manner reflecting the self-confidence her parents had instilled in her, " 'You know, I know anything I really want, anything, I can get. I just have to want it enough.' "[6]

Helen Gahagan entered the New York professional stage in 1922, early in one of the most exciting and vibrant decades in the history of American drama, a time of unprecedented artistic expression and commercial success. The best of the New York producer-managers, often actors or playwrights themselves, generally based themselves at one theater and worked to develop a reputation for popular productions. They constantly looked for new talent to attract playgoers. Gahagan worked under three of the major producers of the 1920s: Brady, George

Tyler, and David Belasco. Only a handful of others shared the domination of production in the 1920s—the Shubert brothers, Daniel Frohman, George M. Cohan, John Golden, and A. H. Woods.

Gahagan's role models dated back to the early 1800s. The theater became, as early as the mid–nineteenth century, one of the few professions where women could experience both financial independence and professional equality. In the mid–nineteenth century, actress Olive Logan gained the attention of feminists such as Elizabeth Cady Stanton and Susan B. Anthony with her lectures and writings on female equality. In 1868, Logan published what she claimed was "the first explicit American assertion" that the theater was a place for women to achieve equality and independence. As she viewed it, there were "two branches of industry in this world where men and women stand on an absolutely equal plane in the matter of cash reward. These are literature and drama." Pre–Civil War audiences also enjoyed such actresses as Charlotte Cushman and Anna Cora Mowatt, but the young English child actress Louisa Lane, who came to the United States in 1827, quickly became the leading actress and female theater manager. She and her Irish actor husband, John Drew, had three children who became leading actors, Georgiana, Louisa, and John, Jr. Georgiana married actor Maurice Barrymore, and they and their three children, Ethel, John, and Lionel, became the most outstanding family of actors in the twentieth century. Gahagan acted with John Drew, Jr., and all three Barrymore children performed on the New York stage in the 1920s. In addition to Ethel Barrymore, actresses whose style and talent influenced the decade Gahagan acted in included Rose Coghlan, Lillian Russell, Julia Marlowe, Maude Adams, Margaret Anglin, Laurette Taylor, Lenore Ulric, and Pauline Lord. Gahagan also looked for inspiration to several leading European actresses, particularly the great Italian, Eleanora Duse, and Sarah Bernhardt from France.[7]

Despite the superior pool of talented actors and creative theater entrepreneurship, the general quality of plays produced in the United States prior to the 1920s was poor. Producers had little interest in new European dramatists such as August Strindberg, Henrik Ibsen, and George Bernard Shaw, or the new techniques emerging in companies like the Moscow Arts Theatre. Furthermore, American playwrights produced little of literary merit. American popular taste seemed increasingly to favor vaudeville, minstrel shows, and circuses, which further discouraged production of better plays. The situation began to improve, however, during the decade just prior to the 1920s, the years when Gahagan's interest in the theater was maturing. A burst of criticism, led by universities, attacked the poor quality of commercial theater. One of the chief critics, Harvard English professor George Pierce Baker, pioneered the introduction of drama courses in the university curriculum. Graduates of his famous Workshop 47, including producers, directors, actors, set designers, and dramatic critics, made their mark on Broadway during the 1920s. Elizabeth

Grimball's theater instruction at Berkeley was unusual for a secondary school at that time, and Barnard had developed one of the most extensive theater programs in the country by the time Gahagan entered in 1920. Helen Gahagan was one of the first actresses in the 1920s to receive training in an academic setting rather than in the customary venues of stock companies or drama schools.[8]

The "little theater" movement, dedicated to artistry and creativity, also influenced the quality of commercial theater by creating competition. The good New York groups, including Elizabeth Grimball's Inter-Theatre-Arts group, enlarged the offerings to New York theatergoers. The Washington Square Players, organized in 1915, lasted only three years but produced dozens of plays, many of them by new playwrights. It also offered a launching pad for talented actors such as Katharine Cornell and Rollo Peters. A small group of Washington Square Players founded the Theatre Guild, which became a full-fledged art theater. Eventually it became competitive with Broadway productions. Another important group, the Provincetown Players, provided a stage for the leading American playwright of the 1920s, Eugene O'Neill, which led the way to his eventual commercial success. Actors and publications also challenged the commercial theater. In 1913, a group formed the Actors' Equity Association to fight producers. In 1919, actors called a strike to end financial and workload exploitation. In addition, two publications dedicated to drama as a serious art form came into being in the decade before the 1920s, *The Drama* and *Theatre Arts Magazine*. Articles on all phases of the theater brought new attention to quality productions.[9]

These changes helped make possible the rise of a creative group of American playwrights and a serious school of dramatic criticism. Many young and talented writers saw their plays produced in the 1920s, not only off-Broadway in the little theaters but in the commercial theaters as well. These new voices included not only O'Neill and Owen Davis, but also Maxwell Anderson, Sidney Howard, S. N. Behrman, Elmer Rice, and George Kelly. Rachel Crothers was one of the few women in this select group. With better plays came an improved group of theater critics. Four trained at Harvard with Baker, including Brooks Atkinson, Robert Benchley, and John Mason Brown. To this group must be added the scholarly Joseph Wood Krutch, Kenneth MacGowan, Burns Mantle, Percy Hammond, Gilbert Seldes, Stark Young, George Jean Nathan, and Alexander Woollcott. These men had a positive impact on the American theater by elevating theatrical criticism, but they also developed tremendous power over the commercial success of the plays and the reputation of the actors. Playwrights, actors, directors, and producers alike both respected and feared these critics. Opening-night reviews often determined the commercial success or failure of a play.[10]

The 1920s, therefore, could not have been a better time for actors in terms of the new energy and improved quality of Broadway productions. Gahagan, though talented, energetic, self-confident, and attractive, entered a competitive market. When William Brady offered her a lead role in a Broadway production and a contract guaranteeing starring roles for five years, he was offering her an opportunity that came to only a handful of the country's best actresses in a highly competitive market. Few, no matter how talented, stepped from any preparatory environment—stock company, drama school, or college theater—to a starring role on Broadway with a leading producer without a long and often discouraging apprenticeship. And to have this chance at the pinnacle of American theater was the chance of a lifetime. One critic commented that by the 1920s the stage had reached the "Golden Age, so far as young actresses are concerned, and that if the young dramatists, the young actors, and the young audiences were half as shining, darkness would be dispelled from the theatre."[11]

Despite the praise for Gahagan's first performance, *Dreams for Sale* failed miserably at the box office, closing after thirteen performances. As Brady looked for another play, it did not take him long to discover that he had signed on a most independent young lady, one unwilling to take any part just to gain more stage experience. She rejected numerous scripts. Finally, in desperation, he lent her to a new producer in town, Maurice S. Revnes, for *Fashions for Men* by the Hungarian Ferenc Molnar, a prominent European dramatist. Molnar, "the most popular and brilliant of the Hungarians," was best known for his play *Liliom*. He had five plays scheduled for the 1922–23 season. *Fashions for Men* was not one of his more distinguished works, but Gahagan was fascinated by the idea of acting in one of his plays. The story revolved around Peter, a Budapest haberdasher, played by the acclaimed O. P. Heggie. Everyone except his gentle, simple bookkeeper Paula, played by Gahagan, took advantage of Peter. The play opened at the National in early December of 1922. Although Heggie received the most critical attention, Woollcott and Hammond agreed that Gahagan's performance had not disappointed them. Lewissohn praised both performers in *The Nation* but called the play brittle and factious. Torres wrote that Helen played Paula with "rare intelligence," although Mantle found her merely pleasant and competent. After a respectable ninety performances, the play moved to Chicago for a short but well-received run. The producer renamed the play *Peter and Paula* to avoid the confusion encountered in New York, where some thought the title *Fashions for Men* suggested a style show.[12]

In anticipation of the closing of the play, Brady loaned both Gahagan and Heggie to the new production team of Lester Bryant and John Tuerk to do *Chains* by a young playwright, Jules Eckert Goodman. Brady felt that the play, which challenged traditional ideas about women, could "restore Chicago's importance as a city where plays are seen for the first time." *Chains* fell into the genre of dramatic works that confronted conventional ideas about women's psychological and economic independence. From Ibsen's *A Doll's House*, which dramatized the trapped housewife, to J. M. Barrie's *The Twelve Pound Look*, about the importance of women's economic freedom, plays and the actresses portraying these roles influenced thousands of women. Brady came to Chicago to help supervise the rehearsals that occurred simultaneously with the final performances of the Molnar play. Helen recalled: "Brady stood at the back of the theater, a cigar clenched in his teeth, and bellowed orders at us. The tension he produced was exhausting." But the nature of the play and the opportunity to work again with Heggie made it bearable for Helen. She played the lead role of Jean Trowbridge, a young, single girl who gave birth to a baby. Despite pressure from the parents of the baby's father, Jean refused to marry her boyfriend. Helen liked the part of Jean. "When I plead the case of Jean Trowbridge," she contended, "I plead the case of a modern girl and the trends of modern thought. . . . Why should any girl marry a man she no longer loves just for the sake of respectability?" The *Chicago Tribune* reviewer wrote that Gahagan "gloriously" brought the character to life; other reviews were, for the most part, excellent. Audiences and critics in Chicago craved good theater much more than in the over-saturated New York market.[13]

That fall, just one year after Gahagan had made her debut in *Dreams for Sale*, Brady brought the successful *Chains* back to his own Playhouse Theatre in New York. It ran for over four months, closing finally in Philadelphia. Gahagan's reviews were, once again, good. Colgate Baker said that Miss Gahagan has the "mystic stuff of which great actresses are made," and, just as important, she knew how to use it. Some critics complained about her exaggerated facial expressions and her habit of dropping lines. Augustus Thomas, however, a prolific playwright and executive chairman of the prestigious Producing Managers' Association, wrote her that when he saw her in *Chains*, "I thought you the most promising and vibrant thing that I have seen in the American theatre in a generation." Heywood Broun's comments summed up her current status as an actress. She "gives promise," he said, "of being one of our great actresses some of these days. High talent is all that should be said now. Luck and ever so many other things must break right for the highest fulfillment of an undoubted gift."[14]

Gahagan found that rehearsals for her next play, again with Brady, had an air of excitement about them. She had the lead in C. M. S. McClellan's *Leah Kleschna*. Often called the first and best "crook play," it had been originally written for the prominent post–Civil War actress, Minnie Maddern Fiske. Brady gathered an outstanding cast for this revival. Once again Gahagan had an opportunity to work with some of Broadway's best, including William Faversham. Brady invited Detroit's Jesse Bonstelle, one of the few noted female directors, to direct this performance. Even more meaningful to Gahagan, however, was Fiske's presence at rehearsals, despite the constant comparison between her performance and Fiske's. To the younger actress, the great Fiske, her favorite actress, was the "mother of the school of modern histrionic art" where acting talent, not personality, dominated. Gahagan also felt considerable pressure because *Chains* was still in production in Philadelphia. She worried constantly that her train would be late and the cast, several of whom she found temperamental, would be kept waiting. As she expressed dramatically and immodestly to a reporter: "Imagine! William Faversham, Lowell Sherman, Arnold Daly . . . and all those other notables of the stage waiting because the train I was on was late! It was a thought that might chill the blood of a more hardened campaigner than myself." She undoubtedly loved the attention and sense of importance.[15]

Gahagan's close attention to the direction of Bonstelle and Fiske paid off. She thrilled to an opening-night telegram on April 21, 1924, from Fiske: "Your sincere and beautiful acting of Leah will go to the hearts of the people just as it went to mine." Critics of pre-Broadway openings raved. The play "electrified" New Haven audiences. The *Philadelphia Ledger* called Gahagan the "most-discussed actress on the American stage," although in Boston, the *Herald* regretted that her diction was "faulty and sometimes unintelligible." New York reviewers, for the first time, spoke less of promise and more of her developing talent. She even made the gossip column, a somewhat undistinguished measure of her growing stature. Someone, the *Herald Tribune* reported, had seen Helen Gahagan "tripping northward past the Astor wearing something in sleek, black silk." The play ran for a month in New York and then moved on to Boston and Chicago. By the time the production reached Chicago, Helen felt exhausted. She threatened to leave the cast unless the producers agreed to cancel the profitable Sunday evening performances. Thus she "accomplished single-handed what all the Equity's forces and all the reformers' men couldn't bring to pass," a journalist wrote.[16]

Helen's press interviews reveal an increasingly self-confident and beguiling young woman. In a discussion with a Philadelphia reporter, she traced, as she phrased it, her "meteoric rise to stardom," recounting how she had used her father's billiard table until banned from it, had given skits for friends, often amusing impersonations of their parents "which afforded many mirthful scenes," and her "stirring speeches" for the Liberty Loan committee. And now "to think after two short years my name is up in electric lights . . . where all those that pass by can see." She also began accepting invitations to speak to large groups, including an audience of four hundred at her mother's Theatre Club meeting at the Astor Hotel. In one speech she emphasized the importance of reading plays and taking children to the theater, praised hard-working actors who gave their entire life to their work, and clarified how drama, to her, encompassed all other arts.[17]

Despite feeling triumphant about her successes, Helen was exhausted from the intense spring. To get away from the pressure, she went to Europe for the summer with her mother and teenage brother, Walter. Gahagan expected that the highlight of her trip would be the opportunity to meet Molnar in Hungary. In an interview, she indicated that Molnar was "friendly, somewhat bald," and "he loves to eat and his figure shows it. . . . He was wonderfully nice to me. I enjoyed talking with him though we had to speak in German." Her later account of the incident, however, proved far less positive. As she recounted in her autobiography, she bumped into the playwright unexpectedly one evening in a café, and he merely "extended his hand but didn't rise or speak. The cold silence stretched interminably." Embarrassed, she left immediately. Whatever the truth about this encounter might be, she did enjoy local Hungarian public-ity as a new American actress who had performed in a Molnar play when she made the cover of the popular magazine *Ma Este*. She also visited museums, shopped, attended plays, and met Hungarian colleagues. Fascinated with the new European experimental theater, she returned rejuvenated and anxious to get involved in the avant-garde plays produced off-Broadway. [18]

When Gahagan returned to New York and realized that Brady had nothing of interest to offer her, she took the opportunity to try out for an Off-Broadway production. Much to Brady's disgust, she accepted a part in the drama *Beyond* by the German expressionist playwright Walter Hasenclever, which the Prov-incetown Playhouse was producing. The play consisted of twenty-two scenes and dealt with the affair of a recently widowed young woman and her hus-band's best friend. The play opened in January for a two-week run. Gahagan found the challenging part a welcome change from commercial Broadway. Students of the new trends in theater found it a "laboratory experiment of tremendous interest" and the "most advanced piece of expressionism ever pre-sented" in the United States, but the regular critics disliked it. George Jean Nathan called the play "just about as dull a few hours in the theatre as the human brain can picture." The *New York Evening Post* reviewer declared that "the easiest way out for a reviewer of this play is to tag it a dramatic curiosity, ultra modern in design and experimental in its execution," but concluded that it was "a racking, terrible experience." The *New York Evening World* thought the title *Beyond* quite apt since the audience never grasped the meaning of this "most unintelligible of all the expressionist plays. If you get fun out of embod-iment of soul-states, then *Beyond* will give you a rousing evening." Hammond of the *New York Herald Tribune* arrived late. He listened a bit in the foyer and then gave his tickets to the doorman. He returned home to sit by a fire and read a good book. The next day, when he learned that Woollcott had panned the play as "an intolerably aching void" despite its two gifted young players, Hammond declared himself the most fortunate of critics. One reviewer, how-ever, actually enjoyed the play. He said about Gahagan: "Such a combination . . . of beauty, grace, sure technique, and intelligent comprehension of a role is seldom found in the theatre. This young lady with the timbered, quavering

voice, the tragic eyes, and the bitter lips of Ethel Barrymore" gave a performance that rose "to the heights of greatness. . . . The spectator sat petrified
with heart pounding and hands feverishly hot. . . . Miss Gahagan is a mystic."[19]

After the first-night reviews, the rough-hewn Brady scribbled a pencilled note
to Helen in his almost illegible handwriting on rough brown paper, which read:
"Dear Helen Gahagan. I see by the papers that the play did not go over and I
am writing this to tell you to call on me for assistance and advice at any time
and place while I am capable. When I am not at the office I am home and
you are always welcome as long as I live. Don't be discouraged. You have had
a lot of luck and a little bad luck. . . . Remember it's always well that one
has a friend when the going is hard. Next time you play don't play unless I tell
you you are right." Although no answer from Gahagan has been found, she
surely was touched by this rare show of tender feelings, yet not regretful she
had chosen to do the play.[20]

During these initial years in the theater, Helen's parents tolerated her acting.
She did not quarrel with her father's determination to keep a close watch on
her; her rebelliousness had simmered down. But when Walter discovered she
was sharing a water cup with the other cast members, he insisted she use her
own cup, a silver one. She continued to live at home. Either he or the twins,
graduate students in engineering at Columbia, delivered her to the theater door
and picked her up immediately following the performance, unless she and Alis
De Sola, who lived in New York writing plays, had after-performance plans.
Walter saw Alis as an acceptable chaperone. Helen's mother often accompanied her when on tour, as did Minnie Mae Fleming, a Barnard classmate. De
Sola recalled that Minnie Mae "adored" Helen and fussed over her like a "mother
hen," picked up her clothes that were strewn around the room, and generally
treated Helen as if she "owned" her, attention Helen relished.[21]

Gahagan's relationship with her father changed in the spring of 1925 when
Gahagan was twenty-four. Up to that point, Helen felt that though her parents
attended her plays regularly, her father continued to be disappointed in her
choice to be an actress. But one evening, after the play, Gahagan noticed a
"stillness and sadness" about her father that "caught my heart," a look that
almost frightened her. It suggested a loneliness, even a feeling of abandonment. The next morning, her father commented casually: " 'I build bridges,
Helen. You build character. I see very little difference.' There were no more
lectures about finishing my education, or about the ignominy of acting. The
long struggle between us was ended." While Helen's memory seems somewhat
pat, what is important is that she considered this period a time of change. Her
sense of a breakthrough with her father had an important effect on her. Theater
no longer represented the "forbidden fruit." Any decision to continue as an
actress or to develop new directions was finally independent of the desire to

rebel against her father. Yet despite Gahagan's increasing independence from her family's apronstrings, she remained in close touch with her family. Walter's eighty-two-year-old mother, Hannah, still leading an active life in Troy's social circles, fell off a ladder and broke her leg. She came to Brooklyn at her son's insistence. She regretted leaving Troy but became involved in Brooklyn's activities by teaching Sunday school, frequenting the Brooklyn Academy of Music and the Art Institute, and working on the family genealogy. She tried to impose her values on the family, and she insisted on having the American flag behind her dining room chair at all meals. Much to Helen's surprise and delight, her grandmother supported Helen's decision to enter the theater. "I remember she looked at me and, almost whispering, said, 'Well, you can teach in the theater too.' "[22]

Helen was greatly saddened by her sister Lilli's decision to get married in the fall of 1923, and their parents were deeply distressed. Like Helen, Lilli had completed only two years at Barnard and had also rebelled against her parents' strict discipline and high academic expectations. She was also angry at her sister's theatrical success. A family member commented that Lilli's marriage was as if she finally "beat Helen at something." Lilli had always walked in Helen's shadow, despite vast differences in temperament and talent. At the Berkeley Institute, at Capen School, and again at Barnard, she, too, became involved with the theater, only to find herself compared to her more driven and talented sister. This constant comparison to Helen "twisted Lillian's life." She was like a "miniature version of Helen" without Helen's personality. Walter bought a house nearby for Lilli and her husband, Robert Walker, and another for Fritz, the first twin to marry, to keep the family close by and undoubtedly to continue to have the opportunity to influence his children to the best of his ability. But he could not stop Lilli from further complicating her life by beginning a family immediately. When Lilli left home, Helen missed her tremendously. Although they had not developed a close friendship, they cared deeply about each other.[23]

Helen developed a lifestyle as an actress that reflected both the rigorous demands of acting and her own peculiarities of personality. She generally slept in until at least ten o'clock. After a relaxing bath, she returned to bed to have a breakfast of toast and coffee and to read. Even as a young woman, Gahagan realized that leisurely mornings were critical to conserving her energy. An avid book-buyer, she enjoyed biography and books on science. She revealed to a newspaper reporter that she never read either novels or newspapers. If a journalist wished to interview her, she scheduled the reporter for the late-morning period when she was back in bed. She wore elegant robes and wrapped a turban around her head. This informal setting generally startled the first-time interviewer, unaccustomed to talking to a star still in bed, which probably added a seductive illusion to the scene. In the early afternoon, Gahagan went from her home in Brooklyn into Manhattan for various lessons. She scheduled twelve lessons weekly, including music, dance, diction, and language classes in French and Italian. On matinee days, she had to go directly to the theater. Otherwise she shopped, went for walks, or occasionally gave talks on the theater to business clubs or university drama classes. In order to regain her energy on days she had two performances, she either took a long walk after the matinee or relaxed on a cot she brought into her dressing room. When resting, as she told one reporter, she would "slip into a pink crepe peignoir" and lie on her back, her hands beside her, in an "absolute state of relaxation. . . . I forget everything. Those two hours are like a rebirth." She generally had a light dinner of fruits and vegetables before dressing for the evening performance.[24]

After Walter Gahagan became more permissive about his daughter's social life, Helen often met friends in the old cafés on Second Avenue, such as the Café Royale. Frequently she and De Sola would meet a small group of theater people, although generally not from Gahagan's current cast. Helen also did things with her cousin Martha Schaible. After graduating from Smith, Martha entered graduate school at Columbia and moved into the Clyde side of the Park Slope duplex with her grandmother Hannah. "Helen was lots of fun when she was young, and not so desperately and intensely concentrated as she was later on," De Sola recalled. Friends tended to put her on a pedestal, attention Gahagan enjoyed. They liked being around her because she was warm, honest, and effervescent, and a certain charm exuded from her disorganization and utter lack of self-consciousness. But she was also a very self-centered person during these years. "Helen was Helen's greatest interest," De Sola recalled. She showed no curiosity in the world outside her small, confined life of the theater and her family, an attitude reflected by her refusal to read a newspaper and her irritation with her mother when reminded to vote in the 1924 presidential election, her first opportunity to cast a ballot. Despite social friendships, Helen, like the rest of her family, never shared inner feelings with others. She "withheld her deepest feelings from herself as well as from others"; she never wanted to "look inside."[25]

Gahagan's relationships with men during this period were both refreshing and shallow, like her relationships with people in general. Throughout her twenties, she never developed lasting entanglements, nor did she think seriously about marriage, although she claimed that she was frequently engaged. The popularization of Freudian theory made her and her friends aware of their sexuality from an early age. But she had an attitude of superiority towards men, Alis De Sola recalled. Helen was more "enchanted by the *idea* of being in love, rather than being in love. [She] had a very drastic effect on men. She looked lush and sultry, but she *wasn't* lush. She was really a puritan," like her parents. Men found her so beautiful and "so damned innocent" that the combination "floored" them. Even if she might finally decide to "go to bed with a man," Helen confided to Alis, *"he* couldn't function!"[26] Her aversion to serious associations with men may well have reflected a fear of intimacy with men, a concern that marriage would adversely affect her acting career, and a way to gain her father's approval by shunning sexual encounters. A potential relationship with Leopold Stokowski, conductor for the Philadelphia Orchestra, illustrates her father's strong protests to any involvements. Stokowski pursued her in the spring of 1924 when she was doing *Chains* in Philadelphia after he saw her in a performance. He first sent her tickets to one of his orchestra performances and then invited her to lunch. The following day, she received a phone call from a "Philadelphia matron" who told her to stay away from Stokowski if she valued her reputation. "Father's long arm had reached me in Philadelphia." Although Gahagan tells the story to indicate her father's control, the incident also suggests Gahagan's desire to portray herself as both a picture of innocence and yet attractive to desirable single men. It also reflects manipulative behavior, teasing men and then shutting them out.[27]

Helen portrayed an image of demure sensuality, mystery, and strength, both in person and in formal studio photographs, but the combination varied depending on her mood. She had had plenty of practice as a youngster posing in front of a mirror and for friends. As cultural historian Martha Banta commented, during the first two decades of the twentieth century, as Helen was growing up, posters of all sorts abounded, including patriotic posters, advertising posters, theater posters, and movie stills. "Under such conditions, a young thing could not start too early to rehearse for the poses that constituted one's existence within a 'universe of signs.' " With different poses, a woman could "act out her dreams," "order her inner life," or "make a political statement."[28]

Helen's striking, fair-skinned, oval face, with an elongated nose and soft but penetrating eyes, complemented her well-proportioned body. While she was not slim, she was often referred to as slender, statuesque, and graceful, with a "Grecian loveliness of face." Her long arms and fingers added grace to her tall physique. She revealed various images in her photographs and occasional portrait paintings in the 1920s, images that changed in the 1930s after she married, and again in the 1940s when she entered politics. Helen's first publicity shots revealed a smiling, young, dignified girl, looking directly into the camera, with short brown wavy hair. This look soon changed to other images—sometimes demure, at other times more sultry, or even exotic with a turban. She grew to prefer showing a right profile, casting her eyes downward to the side, perhaps to avoid any invitation to men. Although she kept her hair fairly short, she varied the part in her hair, from the center to the left side, as well as the size and shape of her eyebrows. Sometimes she sought a heavy, fairly curved look; at other times a thinner, straighter brow suited her. In stark contrast to this soft impression that Helen sought, artist Hans Stengel portrayed her during

Beyond as an angular, haughty woman—really a "wicked witch" look—reflecting another side to her public personality and, most likely, his view of her role in the play. The sketch was entitled "Hans Stengel's Impressionism of Helen Gahagan's Expressionism." On the other hand, one columnist wrote that no photograph could do justice to her beauty.[29]

Helen increasingly selected sensual clothing for her photographs. Initially she wore soft, high necklines, but after several years she often chose low-cut gowns. For a full-length painting that appeared on the cover of *Theatre Magazine* in 1925, she posed in a stunning, sleek, strapless, dark-green satin gown. The neckline of the dress rose to a point, eliminating any indication of cleavage. She added a beautiful ornamental metal belt that lay gracefully around her waist and then fell into a V down her abdomen. She draped a wide, sheer, cranberry-tone scarf over her left arm and added a delicate antique chain around her long neck, with an elegant pendant that rested on her dress. She stood full-face with a quiet yet vital composure, with her left side to the painter. This painting represents a good composite of her 1920s images—sensual but not erotic, gentle yet mysterious, big-boned but stunning.

During the spring and summer of 1925, Gahagan did two more plays on loan from Brady, *The Sapphire Ring*, by the Hungarian Laszlo Lakatos, and Kane Campbell's *Enchanted April*. Both had short runs. During these months, Helen seemed to feel increasingly frustrated and restless. After only three years on stage, she had scored a series of successes. But she felt trapped in the system, impatient with the lack of good roles offered her. She could turn down a role, but Brady would not let her select plays. She could have attempted to get more involved with one of the little-theater groups, as she did when she played in *Beyond*. But she would have had to forego the luxury of a substantial guaranteed income. While Gahagan did not need the money, as her father had the means to support her, she liked the idea of earning a good salary. Brady had started her at $175 per week and gave her periodic increases. She also would have been out of the limelight, the lights of Broadway, which she enjoyed.

In the fall, despite a summer respite in Europe with her mother, her frustrations that had begun to build earlier in the year continued to grow. She knew that her problem was a lack of challenge, but she found it difficult to know how to redirect herself. She had the urge to move on in new professional avenues, but she did not have a clear idea of what direction her work could go. Part of her trouble was her refusal to be introspective, to analyze what she wanted. Also, opportunities to explore different options did not present themselves. She continued to contemplate writing plays. As she glibly commented to one reporter, "The stage has always interested and fascinated me, but it was as a playwright that I had really intended to make my start, and not as an actress." She had hoped that *Shadow of the Moon*, the play she and Alis wrote at Barnard, would open at a Broadway theater "with all the first night critics and first night audiences to pass judgment on my brainchild. However, my play gave me my histrionic beginning and I suppose I ought to be content, for the theatre has been very nice to me. Yet I still believe my forte is playwriting. I want to create rather than interpret. . . . Just when I will find the time to write my next play, is, of course, problematical."[30] Despite this assertion of talent as a writer, however, Gahagan had never shown strength in that area. In fact, De Sola had written *Shadow of the Moon*, while Helen helped structure the concept of the play. While Gahagan never did explore either writing, producing, or working much with Off-Broadway repertory groups, she made one major change. When her contract with Brady expired in the fall of 1925, she moved to another manager, the sixty-year-old George Tyler, rather than take the two-year option with Brady. Tyler promised her more interesting parts, which reflected a difference in the sorts of productions that Tyler produced and Gahagan's changed status as an actress.[31]

A veteran of Broadway, with over three hundred productions to his credit, Tyler had a reputation as one of the most daring producers in the business. His willingness to take risks, argued one observer, was matched only by Oscar Hammerstein and Morris Gest. Like Brady, he managed dozens of well-known stars, including Minnie Maddern Fiske, Tyrone Power, William Faversham, Margaret Anglin, Helen Hayes, Lynn Fontanne, and John Barrymore. Credited for initiating the New York interest in George Bernard Shaw with his 1905 production of *You Never Can Tell*, Tyler remained in the mid-1920s "a power of the American Stage and the . . . only really independent operator on a large scale who has survived." He traveled abroad every summer to remain in close touch with European producers, directors, and playwrights.[32]

Tyler's new star had matured since her early days with Brady. By 1925, critics no longer considered her a newcomer with potential. She had developed into a first-rate actress. The continued comparison to Ethel Barrymore suggested Gahagan's style of acting and her physical description. Although Helen's weight had gone up and down as a child, she kept herself slender in her early years on Broadway. Despite her youth, she had a dignified bearing, accentuated by her height (5' 7") and long limbs. She had a supple body that she used to her advantage as well, sometimes even to the point of overacting. Gahagan was an emotional actress who felt most comfortable with parts she could identify with. Although she liked being the center of attention, she eventually became a good ensemble player. Percy Hammond, after talking to fellow critics and producers, listed fifteen actresses he predicted would take the place of the greats such as Lenore Ulric, Frances Starr, Ina Claire, Anglin, and Fiske. His list included Gahagan, Helen Hayes, Cornell, Fontanne, and Eva Le Gallienne. He commented that Gahagan was "one of the best in reproducing the patrician style, dignified, elegant, and decorative." Furthermore, Hammond continued, "Mr. Broun's description of her as 'The Twelve Most Beautiful Women in the World' is generally accepted as authentic." Theater veteran George Abbott called her a "strange classic beauty."[33]

Tyler offered Gahagan the lead in *Young Woodley*, a play that provided her first opportunity to perform in a first-rate dramatic work. Tyler, who maintained close contact with colleagues in the English theater, had learned of the availability of the play from his friend, producer Basil Dean. The author John Van Druten, a British schoolteacher and writer in his early twenties, had written plays before, but *Young Woodley* was his first critical success. The story took place in an English boarding school and centered on an affair between Woodley—one of the students, a daydreamer in need of support and love; and Laura—the young, unhappy, and unloved wife of the insensitive headmaster. A London West End theater had production rights to the play, and it was in rehearsal when the national censor banned the play from production on the grounds that it criticized the British school system. While Van Druten vehemently denied the charge, seeing his play as a study of adolescence, Tyler took advantage of the situation and secured the American production rights and persuaded Dean to come to New York to direct the play. Tyler cast Gahagan as Laura and the very popular, dark and handsome Glenn Hunter as Woodley. Hunter had acquired quite a following from the hit film *Merton of the Movies*. Gahagan was delighted with the script. As in *Chains*, she played the part of a woman willing to go against society's rules in order to achieve some measure of happiness and independence, the kind of rebellious role she apparently enjoyed playing. These sorts of characters allowed her to act out repressed feelings of sexuality and defiance. Helen became so involved with the part that in the second act, when her husband discovers her kissing Woodley, "I break into a cold perspiration." She quipped, "It is a wonder I don't get pneumonia."[34]

The play opened first in Boston at the Hollis Street Theatre at the end of September in 1925, and then moved to Philadelphia where it received generally good reviews, although playgoers wrote numerous complaints to Taylor that they had trouble hearing Gahagan—a problem that had consistently plagued her. Tyler wrote the actress a curt note, reflecting his constant obsession with money: "We have had so many complaints of indistinctness that I feel I simply *must* write you this line requesting you to try and rectify the fault. . . . On three different occasions we have been compelled to refund money to those who complained. If the condition is allowed to continue it will undoubtedly shorten the run of the play which would be most deplorable. Won't you *please* speak up at *all* performances." She evidently took Tyler seriously. Helen assured her manager several days later that her diction problems were over. "You ask if people can hear me," she wrote. "I want to tell you that if I stood on a high building and wished to send you a message . . . in your office . . . you probably could hear. Thus—I am being heard and despite everything I shall continue to be heard."[35]

When the play moved to the Belmont in New York at the end of November, it attracted unusual attention. One critic praised Van Druten for his "positive genius for knowing what everyday people do and feel." Parents brought their children. High school teachers used the play as a subject for school and club lectures, and the Columbia University drama faculty found it "fraught with valuable significance." Burns Mantle included it as one of the best ten plays of the season in his annual review. Critics also praised the acting, although they generally gave Hunter the better reviews. The play did so well in New York that Tyler wanted to take it on tour after the summer break, despite the expense involved and Gahagan's reluctance to tour. After playing *Young Woodley* for nine months, three times longer than any run she had experienced, she wanted to move on to other things. Still thinking about writing, she began talking about revising *Shadow of the Moon*. Nevertheless, she finally agreed to tour when Tyler promised that he would pull her out of the play after three months to play the title role of Rose Trelawney in a revival of *Trelawney of the Wells* by the English playwright Arthur Pinero. Gahagan also got a much-needed break by taking a trip with her mother to Italy.[36]

The tour played to packed houses, much to Tyler's delight, but Helen found the constant repetition monotonous. Her mother came along. This helped relieve the boredom. Gahagan also took dozens of books, which fascinated reporters. A Cincinnati reporter wrote that "Miss Gahagan confines her apparel to one suitcase and a band box. . . . The large travelling case which goes to her hotel room is crammed with books. . . . no best sellers . . . but standard and erudite works" in philosophy, art, music, biography, and literature. She also brought French, German, and Italian grammar books to study. Gahagan decided that another way to break the tedium was to regard each stop as a new challenge. "I study each new city," she said, sounding a bit like a politician. To be "successful on the road you must constantly have your hand on the pulse of the country and cities you are travelling through." In fact, "cities are people, I believe, and if you don't take the trouble to become acquainted, they will have none of you." Reporters regarded her as serious and intellectual; one certainly did not discuss "frivolous topics" with her, commented a Cincinnati writer.[37]

Gahagan also developed several romantic liaisons on tour, which also helped provide distraction. She saw a good deal of Van Druten, who had come along on the trip to make advance lectures to universities and clubs. Unlike many other temporary acquaintances she made in her plays, this friendship continued for over a decade. Gahagan later credited Van Druten with forcing her to respond to fan mail. He constantly pestered her because she did not answer her fan letters, often from men who claimed to have fallen in love with her. She told Van Druten that she could not be bothered, which is typical of a person who lacks a certain sensitivity and feels threatened by such direct expression of sexual adoration. It took too much time, she argued, and she had never learned to type. Eventually she gave in and hired a secretary. Another member of the company, Beauvais Fox, the play's business manager, also became enamored of the leading lady. When she left the tour, he wrote her an emotional letter. "Helen dear, I am devastated missing you"; signing it "your elegiac friend." He also added a bit of gossip. Van Druten, he wrote, had developed trench mouth "and by what blonde or brunette, not of my scheduling." Gahagan and Hunter, however, kept their love on stage; they apparently had little in common. Reporters found the two fascinating opposites. Hunter, moody and temperamental, flaunted his income, one reviewer noted. The actor drove a Peugeot with Max, his schnauzer, in the back seat. A chauffeur, his secretary, and all his luggage followed in a Lincoln. He complained constantly and tended to worry excessively about his health.[38]

The most important relationship that Helen nurtured on tour was with Tyler. During the tour, the two corresponded frequently. The relationship had lost its initial formality before the *Young Woodley* tour. Gradually she began to see her new manager as one who understood her and cared for her. Tyler at first played a paternalistic role. In time, however, he fell in love with her. Gahagan loved him too, although one can only speculate about the exact nature of her feelings. She apparently did not share the romantic and sexual attraction that Tyler felt for her. Rather, he represented more of a father figure to whom she could pour out her feelings and who could help her achieve her loosely defined goals. Their correspondence, which began during the *Young Woodley* tour and continued over the next three years, expressed Helen's ambitions, a confused sense of direction, bewilderment about how to achieve happiness; all overlaid with her whimsical, free spirit. In addition, the letters reinforced the perception of others that Helen cared about little else besides her career, family, and those who might help her achieve her goals.

As Helen's time to leave the tour neared, she began to think about new directions, revealing, characteristically, tremendous energy without much sense of exactly how to direct it. In one note she told Tyler that she had been "planning how my theatre was going to be built last night. Won't it be wonderful someday." In another letter, she poured out her feelings. "My energy is growing apace. Sometimes I feel I must burst with it. And I have had a vision [that] within five years I shall have made Europe and America love me. If you doubt me, keep this letter as proof." She asked Tyler to get her the rights to George Bernard Shaw's *Saint Joan*. He knew, she wrote, how she felt about *Saint Joan*. "I was born to play the part and I know it will be successful again in New York. It's a real play, modern and a plot people will be thrilled with forever." She also wanted him to think about her doing an Ibsen play and possibly a play written from a new book on Leonardo da Vinci that she had found fascinating. Tyler wrote back that he would investigate all these possibilities, although *St. Joan* was out because Julia Arthur had toured with it throughout the country. He then addressed her ambition, showing shrewd insight. "I quite understand how you feel. In fact I have sometimes wondered why you waited so long to pour it all out. Just the same you *must* curb yourself. There is hardly a doubt but that you will accomplish a great deal—will go very far—but you can't do everything, and if you allow yourself to grow excited every time you read anything worth while you will let yourself in for a constant state of exhaustion—if not yourself, then your manager."[39]

Helen answered that she was looking forward to coming back to New York to star in *Trelawney*, playing the role of Rose. "I feel as though a new phase of life were to open up for me—that my first apprentice work is finished and that my study from now on has at least a good solid foundation. . . . I feel as though I had great wings on my back and that I were going to fly to New York instead of taking the train. I may do it yet, and then you will have to throw great ropes up in the air or I shall be lost somewhere and at the same time rehearsals will begin I shall be seen on some great cloud dangling my feet." She added, "I promise not to wear you or myself out with my enthusiasm. I wept when I read your letter—was that too silly? Goodbye and love, Helen."[40]

Tyler began rehearsals for *Trelawney* in January. The play, still considered the best of Pinero's plays, was originally produced in London in 1898. It had been revived various times, including in 1911 with Ethel Barrymore and as recently as 1925 with Laurette Taylor. Tyler intended this production to tour, with only a relatively short run in New York. He had gained a reputation for successful revivals of old favorites in the 1920s, such as Newton Booth Tarkington's *The Man from Home*, and two eighteenth-century favorites, *The Rivals* and *The School for Scandal*, both by Richard Brinsley Sheridan. But his principal financial successes turned out to be two in which he used Gahagan in the lead roles—*Trelawney*, and Victorien Sardou's *Diplomacy* the following year. *Trelawney* revolved around Rose, a Sadler's Wells actress who feels she cannot go on acting in plays that have no meaning, which struck a resonant cord with Helen. The play was like a "delightful old book . . . with a soft and romantic loveliness that . . . has almost passed out of our lives." Tyler assembled sixteen stars. Critics hailed the cast as "one of the most sensational . . . ever put on the American stage." The distinguished cast included the spry, eighty-two-year-old Mrs. Thomas (Blanche) Whiffen, O. P. Heggie, Rollo Peters, Robert Lansing, Lawrence d'Orsay, and Pauline Lord (replaced by Peggy Wood on the tour). Whiffen had played in the original cast as well as the 1911 revival; others had also had parts in previous revivals. The most important star among this group was John Drew, aged seventy-three, son of Louisa and John

Drew and uncle of the Barrymores. Clearly he was the biggest drawing card and the tacitly accepted leader among the actors.[41]

Gahagan could not have played with a more distinguished gathering of actors. Opening night in New York provided a "claqueman's holiday, and the applause for Drew lasted several minutes." The tour proved even more successful than *Young Woodley's*. Newspapers wrote full-page stories detailing the history of the play, the cast, and the Drew-Barrymore family. In Cincinnati, reviewers regarded Gahagan as a native daughter, playing up all her homey comments about Troy. Many of the tour cities, such as St. Paul, St. Louis, Indianapolis, Detroit, and Spokane, not to mention smaller towns like Madison and Yakima, feasted for the first time on such a large group of outstanding actors. In Washington, D.C., dour President Calvin Coolidge, who was normally unresponsive at most plays, surprised the cast when he both laughed and applauded. Helen wired Tyler that he should bring the play to Europe, England, France, Berlin, Vienna, even Budapest, but he did not follow up on that suggestion. In every city, the play shattered box-office records by generally grossing between $30,000 and $50,000.[42]

Gahagan told Tyler that the tour had been delightful, in large measure because of the unusual compatibility of the group. She wrote him on stationery from the Portland Hotel. "Some people collect towels, spoons, bits of furniture which they bite off." But "my weakness, I must confess, is paper. I cannot bear to leave it behind me. I always live in the expectant hope of an outbursting river of words and paper is my one fortification." Various family members of the actors toured with the cast, including Helen's mother. Peggy Wood commented that the "real team work and unostentation of this greatest aggregation of stars ever assembled" astonished her. The group grew even closer when Drew became ill and had to leave the cast. He died six weeks later in San Francisco.[43]

Helen enjoyed the new opportunities she had with Tyler. He provided her with higher quality productions and roles than those offered by Brady. She worked with unusually excellent casts that included greats of the early decades of the twentieth century. While she kept hoping for chances to perform in the classics, she resisted leaving Broadway to work in Off-Broadway, avant-garde, or regional repertory theater where she might have broadened her experience. She was a talented actress, but she lacked the long years of craft training of her colleagues, and that eliminated her from competition for the best of Broadway's productions. Even so, many an aspiring actress would gladly have traded places with her. Despite her periodic disillusionment with her career, she did not see acting as a temporary endeavor. Yet she often fantasized about taking on new challenges in the theater, including directing, playwriting, and even theater management.

To what degree did Helen Gahagan fit the profile of the woman of the 1920s? Dorothy Bromley offered one description of the "Feminist—New Style." She argued in part that the professional, public women of the postwar decade differed in many ways from those in the decades preceding the war. The modern woman, she argued, believed she had a good mind and sought a challenging job, but did not discard the notions of relationships with men, marriage, or a family. Furthermore, the new woman believed in the efforts of individual women rather than groups, although she also offered support to women coming along behind her. Helen certainly prided herself on the quality of her mind and demanded challenge as an actress. She had no fear of failure or insecurity. She sought support from individual men and women, not groups of reformers. She also enjoyed men; in Bromley's words, she talked to a man "because he has ideas that interest her or because she finds it amusing to flirt with him." But she did not assume that marriage and children were necessarily part of her future. Although she never categorically eliminated the possibility, she gave the matter little thought. She most likely figured that if she really fell in love, she would deal with it at that point, and everything would work out. Up to this point, she had demonstrated little in the way of a systematic plan for reaching her long-range goals. She simply moved from day to day. Helen was also self-centered. She apparently did nothing to help other actresses progress, although she did argue for women's rights through the roles she played. Yet she had an utter lack of interest in the world around her—the wider international scene, national events, or the social and economic problems that existed within blocks of her home and Broadway's select theaters.

Despite these differences, however, Bromley's summary of the feminist construct of the 1920s describes Gahagan well. Women of this era, Bromley wrote, took "a keen pleasure in using [their] mind[s] . . . and in learning to think clearly." They knew it was their "twentieth-century birthright to emerge from a creature of instinct into a full-fledged individual who is capable of molding her own life." And, historian Susan Ware added, "the key to understanding this new woman . . . is to recognize her highly individualistic approach to both personal and professional life."[44]

3

Trying a New Stage:
Grand Opera

IN THE LATE SPRING of 1927, as soon as the *Trelawney* tour ended, Gahagan hastened home. She felt exuberant about her secret summer plans to devote herself full-time to voice lessons. She had kept these plans to herself except for sharing them with Tyler. As she wrote him in anticipation, "this spring finds me oh so happy, so happy."[1] Gahagan thought of her new singing direction as an answer to her unsettled feeling, although she did not contemplate leaving the theater at this point. While she could presumably count on Tyler's providing her with more interesting roles, no evidence suggests that she had any particular interest in refining her acting skills. Gahagan had thought about learning to sing since childhood even though she had not taken any action in this direction. But her mother had more in mind than just exposing her daughter to opera when she took her to the Metropolitan Opera as a youngster. Lillian clearly hoped that Helen would decide to become a singer. Unconsciously, if not consciously, she wanted her daughter to accomplish what she herself had been denied. Lillian was disappointed that Helen preferred the theatrical stage and never missed a chance to let her daughter know that she felt let down by her daughter's choice. Helen was sensitive to the pressure.

One day, Giuseppe Bamboschek, the orchestra conductor at the Met and a family friend, visited the Gahagan home. He listened to Helen sing and concluded, " 'Well! We must find you a *teacher*, a good one.' " Helen was willing to see who Bamboschek could discover. In the spring of 1926, during the New York run of *Young Woodley*, Bamboschek called to say that he had found the ideal coach for Helen, Madame Sophia Cehanovska, a Russian voice instructor who had come to the United States in 1922. Helen immediately liked the eccentric Cehanovska, whom she called "Madame." Lillian was obviously very pleased that Helen had finally decided to develop her voice. Cehanovska, a former voice instructor with the Imperial Conservatory of Petersburg, had first-rate credentials. She and her husband Vincent, director of the Imperial Bank of St. Petersburg, had lost much of their savings during the Russian Revolution. When Vincent died in 1921, Sophia escaped from Russia to Turkey to join her daughter Vera and son-in-law Sasha, both singers. She persuaded one of her prize students, who had become almost like a son, to join her. Later Vera and Sasha chose to go to Germany, and Sophia and her new "son" George, who took Cehanovsky as his last name, decided to go to New York. The two barely eked out a living. George sang in Russian restaurants, and Sophia taught voice lessons. In a short time, however, George joined the San Carlos Opera Company, and in 1926 he secured a full-time contract as a baritone with the Metropolitan Opera. He remained there for the rest of his career.[2]

Initially Gahagan could only take lessons intermittently because she toured much of the year, first with *Young Woodley* and then with *Trelawney*. The part of Rose Trelawney required some singing, which created a stir with the reviewers, who discovered a "rich and delightful singing voice."[3] While on tour with *Trelawney* she decided she wanted to spend the summer working on her singing. Madame agreed to take her on full-time as long as Gahagan traveled with her to Germany for her lessons. Cehanovska had planned to spend the summer with Vera and Sasha who had settled in Bad Reichenhall, a popular health spa. Therefore, in June, Gahagan, her mother, her brother Walter, George, and Madame set sail for Europe. Madame's method of instructing Helen that summer included lengthy daily exercises and one operatic role, Santuzza, from the Italian opera *Cavalleria Rusticana*. The opera, by Pietro Mascagni, won a prize after its premiere in 1890, and it became a sensational hit throughout the music world. The simple story, set in a Sicilian village, tells of the tragic results of an affair that Santuzza's boyfriend has with a married woman. The music is emotional, full of melodic solos, a good piece to learn on, and one appealing to Gahagan's dramatic proclivities.

Gahagan threw herself into her lessons with an intensity that worried even her mother. In desperation, Lillian bought Helen some Agatha Christie novels and insisted she read them at night to break her work cycle. Gahagan also allowed herself the "luxury" of walking around the beautifully manicured grounds of the spa. She wrote Tyler that Bad Reichenhall was a "famous cure place and the people look as though they ought to be cured. None of the men have any hair (it's most extraordinary, they look like caricatures of daschhounds) and the women like the four fates multiplied."[4] By the end of the summer Gahagan had mastered her first role. She became so absorbed, in fact, that she abruptly decided to leave the theater and continue singing full time. Helen's cousin Martha Allen commented that Helen "got sort of bored with the theater, and it was a new challenge." Although Helen was twenty-six, she seemed unconcerned that she was quite old to begin serious voice training. Her mother had been told at age thirty-one that she could develop into a professional singer. But she had been singing regularly in church for years and may well have had a better voice. While Madame initially expressed hesitation about Helen's abandoning a successful stage career for uncharted territory, she also wanted to teach Helen. Martha recalled, "I think Madame had great faith in her [and] it was quite a financial plum." She did not, to Martha's knowledge, need any other students to support herself financially as long as she was Helen's instructor.[5]

The day after Gahagan returned to New York in mid-September of 1927, she dramatically made an announcement to the press that she had canceled all theater engagements. She planned to "devote herself to grand opera exclusively." She had thought carefully about this decision. "This may sound surprising, but few of my friends will be astonished. You see, they think I'm crazy anyway, and are prepared for almost anything I do. Of course, the Metropolitan Opera Company is my aim, but I have only a hope and no assurance that I will attain it. If I fail—well, you'll see me back on the stage fast enough." Tyler was distraught. Gahagan had a five-year contract with him and he had her next play in rehearsal. He also knew he would see much less of her. Gahagan felt guilty, but not guilty enough to notify Tyler of her decision before she left Europe. Gahagan did make one concession, which she considered magnanimous. If, she told him, he ever desperately needed her at a later date, she would act for him at no salary.[6]

Gahagan's decision revealed an egotistical and selfish side. Despite her father's dictum that people never went back on their spoken word, she had broken a written contract on the eve of the fall theater season. Once again she had acted impetuously. When she quit Barnard, she left behind activities that had lost their novelty, a life from which she felt she had extracted all the personal gain and satisfaction she could. She did not appear to have any interest in the long-term payoff of a college education if the short term did not offer what she thought she wanted. She also freed herself of resentment against her father when she left school. But this time the decision was unprofessional and thoughtless, considerably inconveniencing Tyler. He had treated her well and had elevated her to a status among established actors that perhaps she did not yet deserve.

The opportunity to explore and develop a new career direction without having a job once again made her professional life dramatically different from that of her theater colleagues. Most actors, even stars who counted on fairly steady work, simply could not afford to stop work for an undefined amount of time. Helen had accumulated some personal savings, but she counted on her father's financial backing to hire a full-time teacher and to live independently. Although she did not indicate in her memoirs her father's attitude towards the change, he supported her financially. Possibly he felt more comfortable with Helen under Madame's protective care. The new professional direction obviously pleased her mother. Her theater mentors, particularly Elizabeth Grimball and Harry Gribble, thought she had made a terrible mistake. The most necessary support at this point, however, came from Madame. Once she realized that Helen was serious about her study, she lavished time, energy, and affection on her new student. Just as Grimball had guided her in her initiation into theater, so did Cehanovska in opera.

This strenuous period of study, which began in the summer of 1927 when Helen was twenty-six, continued for the next two years. Gahagan moved into a tiny apartment on West Eighty-ninth Street in the same building as Madame and George to avoid the long commute from Brooklyn. Her cloistered routine represented a drastic shift from the daily activity she had become accustomed to, but she seemed to relish the change. She wanted to learn quickly so she could begin performing. Her day began at seven with several hours of practice. She had a two-hour lesson in the late morning, followed by more practice until late at night. She resisted having a telephone. At the insistence of her parents, she agreed, but only on the condition that she, not her family, would initiate calls. She ate erratically, causing Madame much concern, and began gaining weight.[7]

In the spring of 1928, Tyler came to Gahagan to make good on her commitment to do a play if he needed her. He had had a terrible season financially. He produced nine plays, each with excellent casts. All had failed. He was disgusted. "Nobody comes. . . . They're afraid they will look upon an intelligent performance," he wrote a friend in England. He commented to Jesse Bonstelle that the chance of a success for a new play was about five percent. "I can make more money shaking dice than continuing that sort of a game. In the future, I propose to do the type of play which will allow me to create my own audience, *viz.* classics and important revivals. And that's that." Thus he hoped that another revival, the spy melodrama *Diplomacy*, and one of the "greatest of yesterday's living room dramas" written by the famed French playwright, Victorien Sardou, would break his losing streak.[8] In his inveterate style, Tyler pulled together an unusually fine cast. Two of the three principal parts he gave to Frances Starr and William Faversham, but the cast also included Rollo Peters, Jacob Ben-Ami, Charles Coburn, Georgette Cohan, Tyrone Power and Margaret Anglin, in a small role but as a principal draw (she had appeared in the 1901 revival). Tyler had counted on using a British actress as the principal lead, the part of Countess Zicka. But when she became ill, he turned to Gahagan to play the part. He also asked if he could borrow money. She agreed without hesitation to take the role and also lent him $5,000 from her personal savings.

Tyler took the show on an extensive tour and then back to New York for several weeks of performance. The entire cast and production drew rave reviews, and the play proved a financial winner. Reviewers generally singled out several actors for special comment, including Gahagan. The *Pittsburgh Post Gazette* called the cast "as nearly perfect as any cast could be." Gahagan's "work was a supreme triumph of the actor's art. You see her thinking." In St. Louis, the *Globe* review called Gahagan "colorful and genuinely emotional, with especially effective moments in the conflict between jealousy and love, and in the final crumbling of her spirit." The *St. Paul Pioneer Press* pointed out Gahagan's "fine performance," calling her a "rich and radiant creature [who is] always brilliant and engrossing." While on tour, Gahagan used free moments to pore over opera scores and vocalize whenever she could find a piano. In Des Moines, as she recalled, she went into a music store, closeted herself in a practice room, and forgot the time. Five hours later she found herself locked into the shop and barely able to return in time to appear on stage.[9]

When the play opened in New York, reviewers also gave the production good reviews; the *New York Times* called it a "ten-star constellation" providing an "exceptionally agreeable and interesting" evening. Gahagan created a considerable stir among the critics, who chided her about her considerable weight gain. One headline read: "When Helen Gains Art Gains and Vice Versa." The article went on: "When Helen Gahagan swept onto the stage of the Erlanger Theatre Monday night as Countess Zicka in the opening performance of *Diplomacy* you couldn't hear her [opening line] for the gasp that went up all over the house. For lovely Helen had grown so . . . plump." Her face and voice were as glamorous and enticing as ever. But "something had happened to her figure that made it impossible for the sun to shine on her toes." It seemed that all she had done since leaving the Broadway scene was "to accumulate pounds of very unnecessary avoirdupois." But in reality she had been studying singing "with an eye on the Metropolitan footlights. And have you ever seen a prima donna? That's the answer, boys and girls, to Helen's change of form."[10]

Gahagan had always watched her weight. In college, she trimmed her slight plumpness, and she kept the weight off during her acting years. But once she began singing, she felt little compunction to be careful. The total lack of exercise and an unvaried routine also made her weight difficult to maintain. As she gained weight she tried to convince herself that she needed the extra pounds. An article she saved entitled "Must Opera Singers Be Fat?" pointed out that strenuous exercise adversely affected the larynx and vocal cords, and fat in the tissues allowed singers to relax their throat muscles more. The "stout singer" generally had a more resonant voice, the author asserted. Gahagan also clipped a review of an art exhibit opening that read "flappers as plump as cherubs are forecast as the coming ideal of feminine beauty in America, judging by the total lack of thin nudes in the paintings." Gahagan snapped at the press: "Just now I weigh but 150 pounds, stripped, and that is twenty pounds more than I weighed last year. But day after day since then, I've sat at a piano and sung for ten hours at a time." She did not smoke, drink, or stay up late, all things that might have helped her keep her weight down. "Furthermore," she protested, "it's of no importance what I weigh." Nevertheless, she agreed to take off ten pounds in a hurry to help appease the audience response, as well as permit a costume change to a more tightly fitted gown. Her loose-fitting dress accentuated her larger size and "made her look like a middle-aged Viking in modern garb."[11]

In her press interviews, Gahagan made it clear that while she had returned to acting temporarily, she had not left the stage. She simply had moved from the dramatic to the operatic stage. She said again with assurance that she hoped to become "one of the great operatic figures of the world" because she knew she had a good voice. "I'm going to sing because I must sing." She claimed that a singing career had been her ambition for years. "It's nothing for me to boast . . . that I have a singing voice. It's all inheritance, not an acquisition." Although her friends thought her courageous, she said, "I do not claim courage because I've never felt fear." But whether she could achieve as a singer was simply up to the Fates, she declared.[12]

Despite Gahagan's eagerness to return to singing, *Diplomacy* turned out to be a thoroughly enjoyable break from her long hours of voice training. Gahagan and Tyrone Power enjoyed a romantic fling during this play. When the play ended, he sent her flowers and a sweet note. "Dear Helen. You are covered with flowers—covered with all of beauty. . . . Alas, the days are ending 'Diplomacy' but I shall never forget the happiness that has been [mine]." Gahagan wrote Tyler in Europe that "it has been a very happy company and if it weren't that I have to get back to my lessons I would be more than sorry that it is over." She hoped he understood that she had to reach a certain level in voice training so that she could find out if she would be happy as an opera singer. "You can't know what a great struggle for me it is to stop [acting] even for a short time, but some instinct makes me proceed as I am. Being Irish, I cannot help but feel that is the only course to take."[13]

Gahagan resumed her voice lessons in the summer of 1928 near Ravinia, the opera center outside of Chicago where George Cehanovsky was performing. By the time Helen returned to New York, Madame had her working hard on Giacomo Puccini's *Tosca.* During the winter, she gradually began adding other classical roles, including Aïda. She occasionally broke her pace with lectures to drama students at Clark University but generally worked intensively. Although Madame felt that her student had progressed rapidly, no definite plans for performances emerged until Gahagan met one of George's friends, Czech baritone Pavel Ludikar, after a Met performance. He and Helen became friendly, and when Ludikar heard her sing, he suggested that they might do *Tosca* together in Czechoslovakia for her European debut. By the spring of 1929, these plans materialized. Ludikar had arranged for performances in the opera house in the mining town of Ostrava. In June, Gahagan and Madame made preparations to sail, although they had made no other performance plans. Madame assumed that these could be worked out more easily once they reached the Continent, particularly during off-season.

On the boat, Gahagan learned that Otto Kahn, director of the Metropolitan Opera, was, fortuitously, also a passenger. She wasted no time in gaining his attention. She persuaded him to listen to her sing, and, as she wrote Tyler, Kahn appeared "enthusiastic" about her voice. Apparently he also found her personally attractive, and Gahagan, whether she found Kahn appealing or not, did not discourage his interest in a rendezvous in Vienna. She wrote Kahn afterwards from Paris where she was staying while her *Tosca* costumes were being made. "Don't be surprised to hear your name called very loudly from the mountain some morning. . . . At just this time last week I was having a beautiful ride with you through Vienna. . . . I write you on Sunday so that you will have to think of me . . . and in this hour I put a spell upon you, that hereafter forevermore Sunday is my day—and on this one day . . . you must think of me." Kahn responded, wishing her good luck for her debut in Ostrava. He added, with a note of sarcasm, "For all I know, [Ostrava] may be in China, or darkest Russia, though I presume it is in Czecho-Slovakia. I have the pleasantest recollection of the Sunday near Vienna, of the meadows. [I do] not need your Irish spell to direct my thoughts on Sundays and to wish you well, both personally and professionally. I hope to have the pleasure of meeting you in Paris, where I expect to arrive on June 3." [14]

Despite the encouragement Gahagan felt from Ludikar and Kahn, Helen's debut proved to be less than ideal. Much to her horror, she learned upon her arrival in Ostrava (not noted as a culture center) that the company had planned only one rehearsal. Ludikar had inadequately briefed her on stage blocking, and she found herself left to improvise. Fortunately the second performance went much better than the first. She wired Tyler immediately that the opera had gone well, following up with more details in a letter. "The notices were wonderful. Everybody thinks I have been . . . a concert singer for years. They would die if they thought I had learned everything in two years." Ludikar "is a great actor and the best Scarpia I have ever seen." She also sent a release to the *New York Times* that raved: "Helen Gahagan . . . has emerged as one of the outstanding American successes of the present continental opera season." [15]

Helen's enthusiasm and a language barrier resulted in her distorting her assessment of her reviews. Although they certainly were not bad, particularly since this was her first opera performance, the star was the Czechs' own Ludikar. One review said: "What makes this production so interesting, of course, is the guest appearance of our great Pavel Ludikar, whose name ranks among the most popular and most glorious artists of the world." A second review in the same paper praised Ludikar extensively and then politely turned to Gahagan. "Also appearing with Ludikar was an American singer Helen Gahagan. . . . Only after further theatrical experience will [she] be able to express every necessary emotion so that Puccini's heroine can be the emotionally rich and hotly passionate woman she is supposed to be." Furthermore, Gahagan's voice did not yet have the "proper fullness for Tosca, especially in the lower register. This, however, can be overcome with further development. A good indication that this may come to be, are her nice highs and the consistent, basic sound of her voice." [16]

Soon after the *Tosca* performances, Gahagan received a letter from Tyler. Hurt that she had been too absorbed in her new adventure to write him before her opening performance, he wrote: "Why all the silence? I have hoped and prayed to hear something of you and your progress, but not a line. . . . Why this Glenn Hunter indifference to your manager? Have you found a husband or any terrible thing of that sort?" Gahagan assured him that she could never forget him. "How can you ever be for me anyone but my dearest one and only manager?" Already discouraged, she confessed that she was not really sure that she wanted to do her singing in Europe, for "I shall die of loneliness and cold." She had been "working desperately hard all the time learning new things—especially for concerts. . . . Sometimes I am so tired I think I can not live through it—that I will drown before I can swim to the shore of this new career but somehow at the 11th hour things seem to go and things look easier." Once she finished singing in Europe, she told him, she wanted to sing *Tosca* and *Cavalleria* with Ludikar and the Philadelphia Opera Company and audition at the Met. Next she wanted to sing in cities like Washington and Baltimore. "I think we will make a lot of money—I say we because I want so much for you to do my concerts. We can start with one if it goes, another, etc. I think they will be very successful." With a weak attempt at humor, she joked that "people will come if only to hear how I can't sing." [17]

She closed her letter with a stream of disjointed feelings, closer to any expression of romantic feeling toward Tyler than she had previously revealed. But her effusion of emotion most likely resulted from loneliness and affection rather than romantic feelings. "How many times I have longed for you and spoken of you. Especially whenever I get very tired I feel you very near me—that first night I sang Tosca you were with me all the time." She described her exhaustion. "After the performance I was so tired I could scarcely move my body. And between the first and second performances I cried continuously and I tried to remember I had to sing and that one can't cry and sing. But it was no use. But anyway the voice was as fresh as though I had been sitting in an arm chair all my life. Five complete performances, counting rehearsals, of Tosca in one week. . . . The worst mountain is climbed and all the rest is easier no matter what heartache comes." In her closing sentences she made it clear that she was not seriously in love with Tyler. "I hope you realize by this time I am not the marrying type. You and my mother, I think, are the only people who think I am. It never ever occurs to me to think about marrying. It won't be very long now and I shall see you. But I shall send you word in the meantime." Tyler was excited to hear from her. Her "blessed note" had arrived and he had arranged for a story to be sent out covering all the details she had written. "Your successes are such a joy to me; and the fact that you are taking the bull by the horns and coming to Philadelphia to sing . . . delights me." He was certain that after a few more performances, she would be able "to give a fine demonstration. Furthermore, your voice is so fresh and new that you will have a much better chance . . . than if you wait until later." [18]

A letter to her mother, written at the end of July while preparing for her Bad Reichenhall performance, revealed her general emotional state after this first group of concerts. Elated but also very nervous and tired, she reported that she was staying alone in Bad Reichenhall because Madame and Vera had moved to a villa to "have better air." She decided to remain in her hotel because the thought of moving was just too much. She loved the food and the service, even though the room was so small "you can just turn around." She was working hard, learning about thirty songs which was about seven or eight times more than she would need. She felt encouraged to see her pictures and name "literally plastered all over" Bad Reichenhall. But she had no confidence that people would come, especially since her concert followed that of Sigrid Onegin, "one of the biggest concert singers in the world—a beautiful voice and fat, like a cow." So just in case no one bought tickets, she had bought a hundred tickets to pass out to people. "But the darned place holds 1,000." Although things were going better than she had hoped, "there is such a strain connected with it." In addition, she was out of money. "It seems extravagant but in my life I have never been less extravagant." At least she did not have to pay to sing, but her expenses seemed to mount up: her costumes, lessons, the agent, and living expenses. "Getting to be a Prima Donna is not easy from many angles." But maybe it would all be worth it because Tyler hoped to get her a contract for a singing role in a movie. [19]

Although Gahagan was ready to go home, she had to concentrate on the engagements that materialized through an agent Madame had Helen hire. She sang several concerts, including one in Bad Reichenhall that included arias from *Tosca*, *La Gioconda*, *Thaïs*, and *Manon Lescaut*, as well as some German lieder. She became particularly excited over singing with an orchestra, which she had never done before. She also added *Aida* to her repertoire, singing the complete *Tosca* and *Aida* in Augsburg, *Cavalleria Rusticana* in Pressburg, *Tosca* and *Aida* back in Ostrava with Ludikar, and winding up with *Tosca* at the Salzburg Festival in October.

Later reviews were better than her first; several took note of her acting ability. One critic said that Gahagan had "a big voice, especially rich in the high register, of beautiful sound. In her entire performance she displayed her talent for the stage. Whether her program should have been so multilingual, can be disputed. It is understandable that the American singer struggled a bit with the German language." When Gahagan was back in Ostrava in September, singing again with Ludikar in *Aida*, the critics treated her more kindly. One commented: "Turning to the performance of the actress . . . it is necessary to speak with no little respect." Just to "command" vocally the part of Aïda required considerable talent, he said. She had appropriate characterization, although she lacked a "fervor of expression." Nevertheless, her voice "resounds with proper brilliance in the upper register of a dramatic soprano. . . . It's been a long time since so powerful and constant applause has been heard in an Ostrava theater." A reviewer representing a sophisticated Prague journal ventured to Ostrava, most likely to hear Ludikar, and wrote a fairly complimentary review about Helen. He was particularly impressed with her ability to play opposite the Czech virtuoso; she delivered an "excellent, well-studied performance" although he noticed some vocal problems. She finished her tour in Salzburg in October where her Tosca was quite well received. One reviewer commented that "her soprano voice, secure in all registers, is full of sweetness and warmth. . . . Even if her strength was in the area of lyricism, she also knew how to project the dramatic highlights . . . thanks to her natural acting, noble gestures, and convincing mimic art." [20]

Ostrava's more positive reception buoyed the novice singer. She wrote a breathless letter to Tyler, telling him that the theater had been sold out for each performance; tickets sold at double price; "the people seemed to love me, even if I am a miserable foreigner." At that point, she believed that she would become a "very fine singer and it makes me happy. When the orchestra plays I have the sensation of flying." She felt it had been worth the hard work. "I feel like a fish in water . . . and it is such a luxurious feeling. Please dear Mr. Tyler don't print what I write you." Yet she felt relieved to be coming home; she missed the people she loved. She instructed Tyler to send her picture to either *Vanity Fair* or *Vogue*. The partner of Condé Nast, publisher of these magazines, had promised to do all he could to help her. [21] It is interesting that Helen's self-esteem rose so dramatically from her reception by what must have been a culture-starved audience, not a sophisticated one. Surely she must have been aware that success in Ostrava did not necessarily lead to success on the major opera stages. But while she does not directly mention Ludikar's support, his plan at that point to sing again with her the following spring and in proposed concerts in larger cities apparently justified her hopes for continued success.

Gahagan finally left for New York in October 1929 on the *Mauretania*, full of plans to make money and a singing name for herself during the winter opera season in the East, and to sing with the Metropolitan Opera—all this despite the stock market crash and its unpredictable impact on the performing arts. But little happened. Tyler had no luck with his own dramatic performances, let alone finding singing work for Helen. One newspaper published an article that suggested that Gahagan had joined the Philadelphia Opera Company with Ludikar's help. But the news had no basis. In fact, during the entire winter she sang only once, at a January benefit for the Berkeley School at the Brooklyn Academy of Music. Her father paid the expenses. Even that performance proved difficult, for she had a severe case of influenza for three weeks prior to the concert. She did at least manage to have a Met audition that Kahn arranged, but to no avail. "Maestro Papi later told George [Cehanovsky] that I sang well but he'd heard me breathe," recalled Helen in her autobiography. But it is doubtful that, no matter how talented she was, the Met had any interest in hiring an unknown singer while facing the possibility of a shortened season and having to fire some of its regular singers. It became painfully clear that if she wanted to sing, she had to return to Europe.[22]

With a heavy heart, therefore, Gahagan set sail with Madame in the spring, with the plan of staying two years. She had no definite bookings; she was counting on her agent, Walter Hofstötter, for adequate arrangements. This time Madame planned to stay with her daughter, Vera. Although Cehanovska intermittently coached her pupil, Gahagan was essentially on her own. Rather than exhilarated, she found herself lonely and sad. She missed her family tremendously, particularly because she sensed that her father's health was failing. Without telling Madame, Gahagan began making secret plans almost immediately that would take her back to the United States by fall. The opportunity to return arose from quite unexpected quarters. Producer David Belasco, often referred to as the "dean of Broadway producers" and noted for his meticulous casting, was determined to get her for the lead in a new play, *Tonight or Never*, by the Hungarian playwright Lili Hatvany. Once he had made up his mind to get a particular actor for a part, Belasco persisted relentlessly, and his determination to get Helen proved no exception.

Belasco, the son of Portuguese Jews, grew up in California. His father, a harlequin, and his Gypsy mother sent David to a Catholic school. He deeply admired one of his priest teachers, which accounted for the priest's collar he wore in later years. He eventually ran away from school and roamed the West Coast, playing some two hundred roles as an itinerant actor and gaining experience as a playwright and stage manager. Eventually, opportunity led him to

New York, where he launched a creative and successful career as a producer. In 1910 he built his own theater, the Belasco, where his conglomeration of priceless artwork, religious artifacts, and theatrical props became legendary. Unlike Brady and Tyler, the two producers Gahagan had worked with up to this point, Belasco became much more involved with the minute details of the staging of plays. He spared no expense in creating realistic staging, which resulted in elaborate scenery, mechanical devices for dramatic effects on stage (he was the first to produce rain on stage), and, in particular, superb lighting. He worked closely with only a few stars, looking for the right play for their particular talents. Once he cast an actor in a part, he expected the actor to "play to the full, every shade of meaning developed, every opportunity seized for the rounding out of the picture." It was not surprising, then, that those whom Belasco developed attributed much of their success to his meticulous training. He used the same care in selecting his supporting cast that he did with his stars. As one critic said, his plays had "the most uniform and best ensemble work in America."[23]

Belasco generally took on new actors in the early stages of their careers. But in casting *Tonight or Never* he felt that no one but Gahagan met his standards for the lead role of Nella, a frustrated prima donna. In the story, Nella's voice coach was convinced that in order for the singer's voice to improve she must have an affair. Eventually she falls for an "unknown gentleman," and her singing improves dramatically, just as her coach predicted. Nella then learns that her lover is really a talent scout for the Metropolitan Opera in disguise. He offers her a contract and asks for her hand in marriage. Gahagan found Belasco's offer appealing because it provided a way to get back to the United States by fall. She did not have any particular interest in working with Belasco or in returning permanently to the stage. She really had not thought beyond getting out of her European trip. Her contract guaranteed a salary of $1,000 a week for the first season, a top salary for a Broadway star, with an option at $1,200 per week for the second year. This offer was particularly good in light of the generally bleak financial picture of legitimate theater. New York had lost audiences to the movie industry, and many top-flight actors had moved to Hollywood. The stock market crash intensified the situation. In the 1929 season, fewer than ten percent of the productions showed a profit; every New York producer lost money. As one producer summed up, "The theatre in America has simply gone to hell and there is very little chance of improvement." By the summer of 1930, everything was in chaos, and "nobody seems to have any money." Only a producer with Belasco's resources could mount a successful show.[24]

Tyler knew of the dealings between Gahagan and Belasco, and she mentioned to Tyler the contract terms she hoped for, suggesting he might become involved. But evidently Tyler stayed out of the negotiations, and she ended up bargaining through a new agent. In desperation, Tyler suggested that he could commission a play to be written for her with a singing role or anything else that would make her happy, but to no avail. She had made up her mind. She justified the decision with the comment that the play was, "in a way, written for me and will be like a continuous audition." Once Helen knew that she would go home in October, she turned her attention with a clearer mind to the engagements that Hofstötter had lined up. She finally had a chance to do the first role she had learned, Santuzza in *Cavalleria Rusticana*, which she performed in Salzburg in June. She repeated *Tosca* in Salzburg and Vienna during July. Although she once again received mixed reviews, critics generally felt she showed a marked improvement over the past year, even suggesting that she might have a singing career ahead of her in Europe, if not in the United States. She belonged to the group of "the most celebrated actresses" who had switched to opera. One Salzburg critic commented that while the "excellent" singer Helen Gahagan did not have a romantic voice, it was "sensitive," and she displayed "sonorous projection" and "brilliance." In Vienna she sang outdoors in a crowded garden during a blustery windstorm, which detracted considerably from her performance. Even so, one critic commented on her "striking appearance, convincing acting, and marvelous well-trained, dramatic voice."[25]

Gahagan still did not write Tyler, which upset him considerably. Tyler was hurt and distressed about the Belasco contract and also worried about her. He wrote a friend, asking if he had heard from her. "She is the most adorable thing and never does anything wrong to anybody." Her voice was too good for her to have failed, so why had she not written? He wrote Gahagan at the end of July, hiding his personal feelings with a businesslike letter. "Why the silence? I can't help but feel that there has been a little double-crossing somewhere. . . . I need your assurance that you don't feel that I in any way have neglected your affairs." She sent him a cryptic cable August 14: "Accepted play because in need of money. Thought you knew. Letter follows. Devotedly as always. Helen." Two weeks later she finally managed a letter. Gahagan wrote that she had been too busy to communicate because she had made five trips for various singing engagements. Each time she returned, she had to study new music and regain her strength from the trip. "The thought of writing made me sick." She had not even written her own family for two months. But when she received his letter, she realized he did not know she had agreed to perform in the Belasco play, and that he was obviously "annoyed." Begging him not to be upset, she indicated that had she thought he really opposed her doing the Belasco play, she would not have agreed to do it.[26]

She explained why she accepted the offer.

I am in great need of money, and I cannot live on the money people tell me I can live on in Europe. To make these trips costs a small fortune. . . . I am afraid when I got over here I got a little "panicky." And I feel rightly so. I lost practically all the money I had saved in the market and it is an awful feeling not to have any money in back of you. Of course there is always Father but he has had a trying year and many responsibilities and anyway neither he nor you would believe how much money I need. I can go without jewels and an abundance of clothes but I hate cheap things and if I have to steal, my costumes have to be right. I can't ride second class in trains because the people smell, and I can't go to dirty, cheap hotels because I get sick. And I have to be able to send as many cables and telegrams as I feel necessary and when I want to hear music I go, and for the theatre the same. I can't take buses, subways, and streetcars. I can't and never could. Partly it's a matter of strength. If I were to insist and make myself do all these horrible things, I would have no energy or strength to work.

She had no interest in the sort of social life her contemporaries led. "But for a deeper reason, I know I shouldn't last more than about two or three years. I have a funny set of nerves. I can't bear to be pushed or crowded and I grow frantic with noise and confusion. I don't allow myself to be hysterical but I am an essentially hysterical person."[27]

In addition, she told Tyler, she felt that she had exhausted her current possibilities for European performing. She thought the Italian theater was "corrupt," and although she had opportunities in the German-speaking countries, she had to begin to learn German roles, which she figured would take another year. She really did not want to stay in Europe for another year, because to "remain another year outside the theatre is morally bad." She felt she should earn money acting and then return to singing. Although she was not particularly happy at the idea of working with Belasco, he had offered a play with music. "I hate change and I really love you and feel you are part of my family. And to be in the hands of a complete stranger—it is unpleasant. But it seemed the only thing to do. . . . Perhaps I worked everything out in my brain all wrong." She certainly could not "bear it" if he remained cross with her or if he thought she had left him for good.[28]

She closed her letter with details of August and September. She had canceled some concerts for Vienna in August because she did not like the idea of singing outdoors again, but she had agreed to other appearances. She planned to begin rehearsals with Belasco immediately upon her return. She urged Tyler to cable her so that "I know you understand and believe that my affection for you is the same and will always remain the same. Perhaps I have made a mistake. If so, I know you will forgive me and continue to love me as I love you. Helen." Tyler answered immediately. He assured her that he was not annoyed nor did he wish a financial interest in her Belasco contract. He simply wanted to help her. "I only wish I had a success or two in order that I might send you a peck of gold."[29]

Gahagan's letter to Tyler suggested that she had confronted some new realities. She had lost money, her father had experienced a slowdown in his business and was physically feeling very poorly, and she was earning little money. She could not even consider living below her accustomed standard, as she felt certain that would mean dirty hotels and smelly crowds. In order to stabilize her economic situation, she had to return to acting and accumulate some savings once again so that she could continue her singing. But she did not know definitely if she wanted to continue, because it meant learning German roles, a challenge that did not appeal to her. Although she had felt frustrations in her acting career, performance on that stage had come easily for her, unlike her singing. She was an excellent actress—an average singer. Cehanovska, like Elizabeth Grimball, had provided her the tools of a trade. But while Grimball's connections resulted in Gahagan's securing a contract with a leading producer, Cehanovska essentially left her to take her new skills and succeed on her own. This meant working her way up slowly, something Gahagan had never done before and showed no inclination to try. She was an indulged young woman, a prima donna. She certainly deluded herself to think the Metropolitan Opera or any other top opera company would hire her.

Although Helen had planned to return in October, she received a wire informing her that doctors had diagnosed cancer in her father and asking her to return home immediately. Reluctantly, her European agent Hofstötter canceled all her remaining obligations, and she sailed on the first available ship. Gahagan wrote in her autobiography that she returned to New York solely because of her father's illness and then accepted the Belasco offer once home. She did not hint at the other reason, that she did not want to stay in Europe. This significant discrepancy, like other distortions in her memoirs, suggests that she either grew to believe that this story was accurate or she consciously distorted the facts. In either case, she did not want to present herself publicly as lacking direction or dedication.

Once Gahagan reached New York, Belasco prepared to cast the "unknown gentleman." He had waited until he could see Gahagan with potential actors. "I make it a rule to bring together my future hero and heroine before I make my selection," he told Henry Albert Phillips of the New York Herald Tribune during the run of Tonight or Never. "I listen to their voices. I see how they take to each other. I can't explain it, but I can sense how they will play together, in each other's arms, or kiss each other. For they must not be afraid to kiss. If there is love at length, it must be decent. They have got to play straight with me and each other. I have always found this of great importance in casting." He carefully observed Helen's unenthusiastic response to various possible leads. Then he showed her a picture of twenty-nine-year-old actor Melvyn Douglas, new to the Broadway scene but not new to acting. She was not impressed. "She had an aversion to blond men whom she considered 'shallow,' "

Melvyn remembered. Belasco begged her just to meet Douglas once; she reluctantly agreed.[30]

The recollections of this meeting that Helen and Melvyn wrote in their autobiographies provide an interesting public statement about each other. Melvyn recalled that when he came into the casting room, he realized he had met this theater star before in Detroit. Jesse Bonstelle had entertained the touring cast of *Diplomacy* in 1928. Melvyn attended the party and he remembered being disappointed that Helen paid no attention to him when he met her, and she stayed only briefly at the party. When he saw her in Belasco's office, "Helen was standing in front of the desk with her back to the door, one hand poised on her hip as if she was about to push past me out the door. I heard the rat-a-tat-tat of her nails drumming impatiently on the desk top." When Belasco introduced the two, Melvyn continued, "Helen half turned and peered over the top of her white fur collar. The light from the lamp caught a gold earring and lit her eyes. She stopped, stared openly at me and abruptly, her hand slid from her waist to her side. . . . After a few minutes of forced conversation I was dismissed—and ran down the stairs for dear life." Helen wrote that she had little hope for the play's flimsy story unless the leading man turned out to be extremely attractive; she had no confidence that such a man would materialize. But when she saw Melvyn, he "didn't resemble the callow picture" that Belasco had shown her. "Here was a mature man . . . tall, broad-shouldered, slender, and exceedingly handsome. His speech was cultivated, his bearing aristocratic, and his personality magnetic. Not since my cousin Walter had any man affected me as he did at first sight." After a short conversation, Melvyn left, and Helen responded to Belasco's inquiry as to her reaction with a brief, "He will do."[31]

4

Early Years of Marriage

ALTHOUGH ATTRACTED to each other, Helen and Melvyn did not begin to see each other socially until Helen invited him over one night to practice some scenes. As she later reminisced, she had felt concerned that Belasco kept avoiding rehearsing a scene in the second act when the two made love on stage. When she realized that Belasco felt uneasy asking for a realistic portrayal, she assured him that she had played a similar scene in *Tosca* many times. She then invited Melvyn to her apartment on Central Park South with the pretext of rehearsing several scenes. She had been "obsessed with thoughts of him. My longing to be alone with him became a consuming desire." She did not tell him until he arrived that she wanted to work on the love-making scene. The home rehearsals apparently went well. After that evening, they saw each other off the set almost daily and fell deeply in love. Belasco commented, "I've seen many romances in the theater, but none so fine, so old-fashioned and honest" as this one. His definition of "old-fashioned" most likely had a modern twist. Helen found that unlike in her other relationships, she shared with Melvyn deep interests in the theater, music, and reading. They had mutual respect for and interest in each other's individuality and an obvious sexual attraction for each other. Once their relationship became public and reporters quizzed her, she explained it all with her serendipitous attitude. "I don't know what happened to me. Call it intuition. Call it love at first sight. I'm Irish, so I'll call it fate."[1]

Although the initial attraction between Helen and Melvyn was understandable, particularly given the romantic setting in which the affair was taking place, the two had little in common in background and temperament.[2] Melvyn's Jewish father, Edouard Hesselberg, a professional pianist, grew up in Riga, in the Baltic area of the Russian empire. His mother, convinced that Edouard had musical talent, worked with him daily on the piano from the time he was three. At the age of seven, he impressed his audience with a Beethoven sonata. He enjoyed continuous success in his performances, and in his late teens, his family smuggled him out of the country so that he could avoid military service. Many worried that under the Czarist regime young men might be forced to abandon their careers. Edouard eventually made it to the United States, found a teaching position in piano in Denver, and fell in love with Lena Shackleford, a Kentucky girl of Scottish and English background. Lena, a divorcée with one child, had grown up in the South and had moved to Denver where she taught kindergarten. Lena's parents, both overtly anti-Semitic, showed little enthusiasm for the couple's relationship and decision to marry. Although they did not prohibit the marriage, they made continual critical comments about Jews.

The young Hesselbergs moved from one teaching position to another. They went first to Wesleyan College in Macon, Georgia, where, on April 5, 1901, Melvyn was born. A second child, George, was born two years later. Lena's child by her first marriage, Melvyn's step-brother, spent little time with his mother's new family. After Macon, the Hesselbergs moved to the Belmont College for young Women in Nashville, Tennessee, for some years, with a year out in Germany for Lena's health. As Melvyn approached his teenage years, the family moved to Toronto, where Edouard headed the piano department at the Toronto Conservatory of Music. After five years he moved to take a similar position at the University of Nebraska and eventually moved once again to Chicago to teach privately.

Melvyn never felt particularly close to his parents, and he did not enjoy all the moving. His father, a quiet but "terribly emotional" man, had little interest in guiding his children in any way except through "haphazard" discipline. Melvyn recalled: "He had a tremendous temper and utterly lost control of himself during these tempers. He used to beat us, [until well into our teens]. I can remember [our] being taken down into the cellar and really beaten because of very minor discrepancies in our behavior." When George was about six, for example, his father tried to teach him the sequence of meals. Because the child could not master this concept, he was "thrashed until he was able to say breakfast, lunch, and dinner." Melvyn's principal recollection of his mother's concern with teaching values to her children emerged from her enthusiastic involvement with a strange mixture of religions and religious ideas. She joined several evangelical cults, believed strongly in puritanical values about sex, and eventually became a Christian Scientist. She read Bible stories to the boys all through their childhood. Perhaps because of the strong anti-Semitic feelings of Lena's parents, neither Hesselberg ever mentioned Edouard's Jewish background to Melvyn and George. Lena always called her husband a "foreigner."

The few religious customs he practiced, such as burning a candle to commemorate the anniversary of his parents' death, were dismissed as "foreign customs."

During his late teens, Melvyn grew to know and love two aunts on his father's side: Cora, a noted pathologist, and Rhetice, a talented violinist. Because their intellectual interests paralleled Melvyn's, he became much closer to these aunts than to his relatives on his mother's side. Melvyn felt particularly close to Cora, who became almost a mother to him. He could open up to her emotionally in a way never possible with his mother. Cora, he said later, "was absolutely dumbfounded to discover that I knew nothing about the Jewish side of my family." He gained from her a sense of his father's background. He learned, for example, that many of his relatives had admired Tolstoy and had sympathized with Russian radicals. His grandparents had survived two Russian pogroms. These stories reinforced his later memory of his father's tales of anarchists and assassinations of royalty and the upper class. Conversation about hopes that the Russian Revolution would provide a better life made these rebels take on a "kind of heroic aspect." Cora encouraged her nephew to read the Russian writers, such as Tolstoy and Dostoevsky, which only further encouraged his "empathy with the oppressed." Melvyn said later that his aunts stimulated in him an "interest in the necessity to try to set things right, not only in the nation but in the world so far as people and people's lives were concerned."

Melvyn wanted to leave home from his early teenage years. In Toronto, when he was only fourteen, he ran away and joined the Army, but his parents found him and pulled him out. He hated his schools, as they catered to upper-class English families, and he did not enjoy his own family life. He developed a keen identity with the children on the "wrong side of the track, with the have-nots rather than the haves." His family tended to associate with people wealthier than they, which made Melvyn more acutely aware of class differences. When the family moved to Nebraska, he tried once again, in 1917, to join the Army after he was kicked out of high school with a large group of rowdy fraternity brothers. Though only sixteen, he managed to get by the induction officials, but much to his disappointment, he did not get overseas because the war ended. During this year, he remembered, he changed dramatically from a "naïve and innocent youngster" to a more sophisticated, thoughtful young adult. For the first time, he began to think seriously about his relationship with his family. He strongly questioned his mother's religious ideas. He also became increasingly uneasy that he did not really know his father or how to deal with this "strange relationship, strange lack of knowledge" about where he stood with his parents. This self-questioning stimulated "voracious reading" in a broad range of literary, political, and philosophical works, which in turn led to a "lust" for a new kind of life.

Once out of the Army, Melvyn returned home, but "home" had moved from Nebraska to Chicago. His father's income had decreased considerably.

Melvyn could not attend college; in fact, he had to begin supporting his parents financially. He first sold hats in Marshall Field's and made some friends in the various artistic, literary, and theater communities. One of his new friends was William Owen, a theater director. Melvyn immediately jumped at the opportunity to share an apartment with him because he could no longer tolerate the tense atmosphere at home generated by his parents' increasingly unhappy marriage. This new friendship rekindled an interest in the theater that a teacher had initially sparked during Melvyn's sophomore year in high school. He performed with a group Owen organized. When Owen joined the drama department at the Cosmopolitan School of Music, he hired Melvyn as his assistant. A group from the school toured the Midwest. Melvyn found himself acting continuously, learning by the apprenticeship method, playing primarily Shakespearean roles. He later toured with another Shakespearean company. When this group became stranded in Toronto, he rather presumptuously set himself up as an acting instructor; but after six months, he had no money for himself, let alone for his parents.

At the same time that Melvyn branched out into acting, he continued to immerse himself in the "yeasty" ferment of intellectual Chicago. He particularly admired the ideas of socialist labor leader Eugene V. Debs and the famous defense lawyer Clarence S. Darrow. Melvyn even participated in activities at Chicago's famed settlement house, Hull House, and spent hours at the Dill Pickle Club, a hangout for a "wonderful mishmash" of people, primarily leftists. He felt part of the generation of the 'twenties, a period of "breakthrough, of experimentation . . . of rebellion and knocking down the old barriers." Yet none of this talk led to participating in the political process. Conservative national politics held no excitement for restless youths anxious for action. "It was all a kind of dinner-table business, sitting around with beer and hot dogs." After a couple of years with Owen, Melvyn briefly joined a Chautauqua group, and then had an opportunity as a leading man with a stock company based in Sioux City, Iowa, his first real commercial job. His salary of $50 per week did not stretch very far, as his financial responsibilities for his parents were growing and he had to buy his own costumes. When the group reached Madison, Wisconsin, he took advantage of an opportunity to form his own company. Living in Madison made him more acutely aware of his desire for more education, but he knew that he could not afford classes. But nothing could stop him from seeking out intellectually stimulating people. His acquaintances soon ranged from the economist John R. Commons to the architect Frank Lloyd Wright. He also married during this period. He and his wife had one child, Gregory. The couple had little in common, and the relationship lasted only a year. When the two divorced, Melvyn gave his parents his meager savings, left his wife and baby, and escaped his responsibilities by taking off for Europe.

Melvyn spent most of his time in France, avoiding Americans so he could learn French. He enjoyed the challenge of living cheaply. He took a long bike trip around southern France, read French writers, and attended lots of theater. As he recalled, he eventually confronted the fact that he was not as good an actor as he had thought. If he really planned a career in the theater, he would have to "buckle down." Thus, when he returned to New York in 1925, he "pounded the pavement," as did so many hopeful actors at the time, using his free time to go to as many plays as he could afford at the cheap balcony rate offered to unemployed actors. But he had no luck until director Jesse Bonstelle visited from Detroit, looking for actors for her company. Melvyn managed to persuade Bonstelle to hire him. He stayed two years with Bonstelle, a period in which he recalled maturing tremendously, particularly in the second year when he got promoted to the position of leading man. With Owen, he had never advanced beyond a superficial playing of a character. Owen believed actors learned by mimicking other actors. With Bonstelle he learned to analyze his part and to realize that character interpretation could vary enormously with the actor's understanding of the character's motivations. While in Detroit, he once again sought out stimulating company, and his reading turned to writers such as Walter Lippmann and H. L. Mencken's *American Mercury*. Although Detroit did not have the "rowdy, Bohemian . . . radical atmosphere" of Chicago, he met some musicians, journalists, and theater critics, and, through the Bonstelle company, outstanding actors. Bonstelle "seemed to have had an extraordinary knack for latching onto people who were just about to make it as big shots in the theater." During Melvyn's stint with her, for example, he met Katharine Cornell and her husband, Guthrie McClintic, and Ann Harding. Bonstelle also gave him a chance to learn about the business side of her company.

In 1927, Melvyn decided to try New York again. Armed with a letter from Bonstelle for her producer friend William Brady, Helen's first producer, he managed to get a three-year contract. Brady first made him change his name, ostensibly because "Hesselberg" would not fit on a marquee. More likely, he did not like the Jewish-sounding name. Melvyn chose "Douglas," his grandmother's maiden name. For two years, Brady only gave Melvyn parts in shows appearing outside of New York. Eventually, however, Melvyn worked up to leading roles in fairly interesting plays. He also felt relieved that he had a guaranteed salary of $125 per week. He made his Broadway debut in A *Free Soul*; the turning point for Melvyn proved to be a play called *Reception*. Some Belasco scouts attended a production and recommended him to Belasco for the part of the "unknown gentleman" in *Tonight or Never*.

Gahagan found the several weeks of rehearsal stimulating romantically and intellectually and, much to her surprise, an energizing acting experience. She discovered that working with Belasco was very rewarding. She had never before experienced a director who meticulously guided every movement of his actors. He went to any lengths to produce a desired effect. For example, he once stuck Frances Starr with a pin to show her how to scream realistically. Belasco always had a completed set at the first rehearsal, not just the customary last three or four before opening night. In *Tonight or Never* Belasco insisted that Helen use her own china when she drank tea, her own books, and personal items as table ornaments in order to feel at home in the setting. He asked her to rehearse in a long gown to become accustomed to wearing one in the play. He provided fresh gardenias daily for the set. Helen became close to Belasco, frequently lunching with the white-haired gentleman, always dressed in his priest's black shirt and reversed collar. They ate upstairs in his eclectic study crammed with the props and artwork he had gathered for sixty years. Photographs of Belasco filled the few remaining vacant spots on the walls.

The play opened in New York on November 18, 1930, just before Helen's thirtieth birthday, on a sad note for the cast. Belasco had developed a severe case of pneumonia during the out-of-town performances. For the first time in his career, he could not attend opening night. He telegrammed Helen. "Not being at the dress rehearsal was hard enough for me to bear but missing your beautiful first night breaks my heart. I wanted to see your triumph. You are a dear wonderful girl and a superb artist. And all my heart is with you for your great success."[3]

Critics liked the play, and so did the audiences. It ran for 267 performances, impressive in normal times, even more so given the economically depressed state of the country. Belasco had developed such a reputation that audiences always looked forward to exquisitely directed productions and whatever new "marvel of gears and voltages will be disclosed." No matter what the play or who the actors, many came solely because of the quality of the production and his "shrewd sense of the theater." In the case of *Tonight or Never*, Belasco had taken a weak, unoriginal play and with "the magic of his genius at casting, by the skillful creation of a seductive atmosphere through lights and settings, by deft direction, transformed what might well have been commonplace into a delightful evening." Or, as the *New York World* said, the play provided an antidote to the Depression by taking the audience out of their "dull lives."[4]

The play proved a triumph for Helen. She was the "wonder of the season," the only actress who could act and sing this role. She sang *Tosca* in the play "as it has never been sung before." She had slimmed down again to her pre-opera weight and looked trim and lovely. She was like a "du Maurier drawing, length, poise, grace, all merging into charm. Helen Gahagan has everything." Another critic said that he had seen each of Gahagan's plays, "but not until last night would I vote for her admission into the halls where are niched the greats of our contemporary theatre. It took a Belasco to do this." Two critics included her in their list of top five actresses of the season. Melvyn also scored well as Nella's lover, and critics could not resist comments about the love scene. The *New York Evening Post* commented that Douglas "carries off his part with ease, and, when he is called upon to bite the lady's neck [he] bites it with an urbane and gentlemanly manner marvelous to behold." But no one questioned who was the star.[5]

In later years, both Melvyn and Alis De Sola indicated they thought Melvyn, not Helen, the better actor. Melvyn knew that while Helen "had reached a more prominent place in the theater at that time than I had . . . she hadn't begun to have as varied and wide a background in the theater as I had." Alis was a bit more blunt. Melvyn had "enormous technique," whereas Helen fit the "distinctive actress" category, who "radiated a glow," Alis recalled. When Alis attended opening night of *Tonight or Never*, she was "furious" because she felt "Melvyn acted rings around Helen. . . . He made her look amateurish." She also did not like her first impression of his personality; she found him "aloof" and "chilly." She eventually changed her opinion and realized later that Melvyn appeared distant because of his "extreme introspection." He also told Alis that he initially assumed most of Helen's friends were "just an adoring society . . . here's the queen and here we are."[6]

Regardless of who was the better actor, Helen drew the attention from the press. They quizzed her about her apparent return to the theater. She evaded the questions with typically flip answers that covered up her indecision. She informed one reporter that she had been preparing eight operatic roles that "would have established me on the Continent," and she intended to return to finish what she had started. On the other hand, she commented, " 'Maybe I'll go on to Hollywood and make money enough in the sound films to put on my own opera.' " The reporter continued: "So she rambles, archly 'play-acting.' . . . A born prima-donna. Except that she gets her way with a smile—not a tantrum." Reporters also continued to be drawn to her beauty. Sometimes Gahagan dismissed this fascination; at other times she chatted amiably about her "beauty secrets." In one interview during the run of *Tonight or Never*, she indicated that she did not take milk or champagne baths, although she did luxuriate in three to four baths each day. She felt convinced that fresh country air best enhanced her skin. As for creams, she used commercial cold cream rather than her mother's homemade variety which, she contended, smelled awful. She wore no makeup, only faint, flowery, pure perfumes which she thought added "grace and charm."[7]

While Helen was relishing her greatest stage triumph and the emotional high of her love affair, she also had to cope with the trauma of the death of her father, who died of throat cancer in mid-December on the first day that he could muster the energy to attend a performance of *Tonight or Never*. Walter had never met Melvyn. In fact, she may never have told him that she was involved in an intimate relationship for fear he would disapprove. But her father got a first-hand impression of how they felt about each other by watching them act that afternoon. He also heard his daughter sing on stage for the first time. Walter gave his daughter a hug and commented, " 'It was beautiful, Helen. Now I know what you wanted.' " That evening, just before the beginning of the performance, Helen received a call from her family. Her father had died quietly while eating dinner alone in his bedroom. Her professional discipline carried her through the performance, but she did not find it easy. When she returned home, she found the family clustered around her mother. But no one cried. The children had been taught to bottle their deep emotions inside. Lillian considered an outward display of emotion as a lack of tough character. Brooklyn residents turned out in force to pay their last respects; Walter's bier sat in a small room filled to the ceiling with flowers. Visitors included nuns from a nearby convent, who appreciated Walter's thoughtful gestures over the years, and the neighborhood newsstand boy, to whom Walter had always spoken kindly. Over three hundred, including the *Tonight or Never* cast, attended the service, held in the family living room. The family buried Walter in the family cemetery in Troy, but Helen could not participate in this final goodbye because of her obligations to the play. Helen's father's death added new dimensions to her relationship with Melvyn. Losing her father meant a loss of both financial and emotional support, which Melvyn could supply. This loss may also, however, have had a liberating effect.[8]

Tonight or Never continued to play to capacity audiences. In March, Belasco had recovered sufficiently to attend a performance. This occasion proved to be a happy though teary occasion for the cast, crew, and audience. Belasco had always engendered fierce loyalty in his actors, but a poignancy had enveloped this production as if people knew that it would be his last. Gahagan led him on stage, and a wave of thunderous applause shook the stage sets, echoing for nearly ten minutes, while the pair, the elderly producer of four hundred plays, and the thirty-year-old star, bowed hand in hand.[9]

Despite her feeling that she ought to be offering emotional support to her mother, Helen continued to spend most of her free time with Melvyn. In the spring, they decided to get married. When Helen presented two choices to her mother, marriage or living together, her mother did not react positively to either choice. She remembered what had happened to her own career ambitions when she married, and she worried about Helen's singing career. She finally consented to a wedding, however, and planning the event turned out to be therapeutic for the whole family. The couple chose Melvyn's thirtieth birthday, April 5, as their wedding date. Helen asked Helene Pons, her *Tonight or Never* costume designer, to create a simple but elegant gown. Helen and Melvyn planned a simple ceremony. They wanted it in Helen's home, a larger Park Slope house where her parents had moved several years before. On the day of the wedding, dozens of telegrams came from out-of-town friends, including a touching one from the couple's mutual friend Jesse Bonstelle. Their relationship, she felt, seemed the "finest and most congenial companionship I have seen in a long time. I love you both and hope that your ship will sail serenely and successful in pleasant waters with just enough rough weather to weld you closer together." [10]

Helen descended the staircase, radiant, slim, and beautiful in her satin and Valenciennes lace gown with a long train trailing elegantly behind her. William, the first-born of the twins, gave her away. She wore a small lace hat with no veil, and, not surprisingly, carried gardenias mixed with lilies of the valley. A family friend, the Reverend Parkes Cadman of the Central Congregational Church, rather than the priest from St. John's Episcopal Church, officiated. Melvyn's father and George Cehanovsky performed a "magnificent concert" for the guests, who included the entire cast of Tonight or Never. That night many of the happy crowd trooped downtown to see the evening performance. "To our intense embarrassment," remembered Helen, "they howled with approval during our love scenes." Melvyn, too, recalled the "raucous audience." They particularly liked the scene when Melvyn, seated by Helen, reached around her with one arm and placed his hand on Helen's breast, a gesture that was "exceedingly daring" at the time, Melvyn commented. [11]

The wedding made marvelous newspaper copy. Not only was it a society wedding, it was the marriage of a famous Brooklyn actress and a lesser known but first-rate actor. Helen fielded questions about her honeymoon with one of her typically abstract imaginary comments. They would, of course, defer the honeymoon until the play closed for the summer. And then "we won't just go to some hotel and sit around all dressed up. We will go to China or Africa or Egypt or maybe take a walking tour through Ireland." And as for her role as a wife, she smiled: "Am I going to cook and sew for my husband? I am not! Anybody can roast chicken . . . fry eggs, darn a husband's socks and bake apple pie. Of course, I could learn if I had to. But I won't be that kind of wife. No, I'll never leave the theatre, until I'm 95. I'm going to be the most devoted, loving wife in the world. But never a housewife!" She offered no hint of her self-perception as a mother, except to comment about Melvyn's son Gregory, "a fine little chap" who would probably stay with Melvyn's parents. Questions regarding her professional future required even more vagueness. One persistent reporter wondered if Helen would follow her husband even if it meant that she could not "remain a star in her own right." Helen answered, "Being Irish, I just leave that to the fates. I started acting when I was five years old, and I love the stage. Something called me to grand opera later. But I am always mad about what I am doing at the moment, and I am fascinated" with Tonight or Never. "The only really strange thing about my career thus far is my falling in love. I don't think it was charted. It just happened. I always said I would never marry." The publicity certainly did not hurt the play's box office receipts. The week before the ceremony the play grossed $14,000; the week following, $17,500; and the grosses stayed high. "That's what romance can do for the box office," quipped a reporter for the *New York Sun*.[12]

Although many close friends attended the wedding, two special ones could not come, Tyler and Belasco. For Tyler, the wedding symbolized the end of a romantic fantasy, an unreciprocated love. Helen had perhaps misled Tyler with her uninhibited letters and warm expressions of affection. But for her, Tyler had never been more than an important support for her theatrical ambitions. At this point, she was unclear about her professional directions and did not need him. Tyler sent Helen a thinly veiled excuse. "My dentist has today pulled so many of my teeth and made such a sight of my mouth that I must abandon the thought of seeing you married. I suppose I should say 'pleasure,' but I hardly feel it to be just the word. You are really going out of my life, and it hurts like the dickens to realize it, so I suppose I should keep away even if I had a full set of teeth and a decent suit of clothes." But he wanted her to know that her happiness was very important to him. "There is no one in this world more entitled to all the capital prizes of life than you are—and I speak with surety. Honestly—I think that of all the glorious people I have known your character is the finest. God bless you." Belasco felt too weak to travel to Brooklyn. Helen sent him a basket of roses, a gesture that touched him deeply.[13] He died nine days later. The publicity following Belasco's death documented his reputation in the world of theater and the city of New York. His pallbearers included Al Jolson, George M. Cohan, Daniel Frohman, Mitchel L. Erlanger, and New York mayor Frank Walker. The praise also bespoke the professional stature Helen had attained as an actress.

A flurry of activity and change followed in the months after the wedding. An impending move to Hollywood dominated the young couple's plans. During the run of *Tonight or Never* Melvyn had signed a contract to do the play's movie version with producer Samuel Goldwyn. Goldwyn and actress Gloria Swanson, both affiliated with United Artists, had attended a performance of *Tonight or Never*. Swanson, one of the biggest draws of silent films in the 1920s, persuaded Goldwyn to buy the movie rights. She saw *Tonight or Never* as a good vehicle for a comeback from severe financial problems and a sagging career, plus an opportunity to sing in a film. The producer hired the entire Broadway cast, with the exception of Helen, and offered Melvyn a seven-year contract. Melvyn accepted without hesitation. Although he realized that he had reached a new level of desirability on Broadway, he had financial obligations to his parents and his son Gregory. In addition, he hoped he might become involved in some interesting film work.[14]

Goldwyn made his offer before Helen and Melvyn had announced their engagement. Initially it made Helen hesitant about marriage. She worried, as did her mother, about whether she would be able to continue her own career. She would have to leave the secure world of her family and friends. She worried about being away from the family. The twins had taken over the business, but Bill, shortly after his father's death, had suffered a nervous breakdown and eventually moved away from New York. Lilli had divorced her husband and was looking for a job, determined to support herself and her three children. While Melvyn had moved continually throughout childhood and had wanted to leave home since his early teens, Helen had never ventured far from New York except when she sang in Europe, an experience she did not particularly like. When she toured in the United States, her mother and, sometimes, her sister or friends had generally accompanied her. After several days of indecision, she decided to go ahead with wedding plans. "Helplessly in love," she quipped. She deeply loved Melvyn; the religious, financial, social, and family life differences did not deter her. Her Pollyanna attitude convinced her that somehow everything would all work out. Once she had made up her mind, Helen pushed her doubts and insecurities aside. RKO did invite her to make several screen tests that spring, and she received a verbal offer that made her feel a bit better about her options. But as Melvyn recalled, "I think that Helen was always, from the beginning, rather sad" about the move. As if to indicate she had no intention of slacking off in her career, she kept her maiden name, a practice that was going out of style with the New Woman of the 1920s.[15]

When the play closed, the newlyweds took a two-week honeymoon in Europe. Helen also had to prepare for her American debut at the Cleveland Grand Opera Company's 1931 summer fund-raising festival. The occasion attracted a wealth of talent. Over thirty soloists from the Met participated, as did several opera companies, including the Chicago Civic Opera at Ravinia and the Philadelphia Opera. Featured singers included Met stars Anne Roselle and Elda Vettori, Russian singer Alida Vane, and Gahagan, billed as "a European opera and American stage star." Gahagan performed respectably "despite evident nervousness" before a sell-out audience and difficult singing conditions. The singers performed on a 125-by-75-foot stage without a back, set in a 100,000-seat baseball stadium. The audience, seated in a roped-off section of 20,000 seats, were so far from the stage that they could see very little. Hearing was also a problem, further complicated by the stadium's proximity to the boat docks and railroad yards. Helen invited Madame to come to Cleveland. Their meeting was bittersweet as neither woman knew what lay ahead. But Madame, who had never met Melvyn, "got along famously" with the bridegroom and at least felt reassured about the marriage. Gahagan's agent, Murray Williams, had made certain that Met manager Otto Kahn had someone in Cleveland to hear Gahagan and report back to him. But no invitations came out of the Cleveland performance.[16]

After the festival, the Douglases took off for California by train. Steaming hot weather made the trip miserable. Los Angeles provided some relief from the heat, although little else about the city seemed appealing. Melvyn wrote his mother that Los Angeles and Hollywood had at first a "most depressing effect upon us. Everything seemed to be the emanation of a delirious vaudeville actor's nightmare." While looking for a place to live, they stayed in a "garish hotel that made things even worse. . . . All together we felt like two lonely souls lost in one of those little Nemo's dream places which used to appear in the funny papers." The "natives" seemed friendly, he reported, but he and Helen found Hollywood people and attitudes very strange.[17] The Douglases' first impressions quite accurately described Hollywood, once called the "dream suburb of Los Angeles." The uncommon atmosphere of the film colony in 1930 had developed over the years, particularly during the previous fifteen years, as the film industry became increasingly successful. As the top weekly salaries for movie stars ranged from $2,000 to $10,000, compared to $1,000 on the New York stage, many Broadway actors made their way to Hollywood in the 1920s, an influx that increased after the development of sound movies in 1929. New York directors, writers, and producers, and enterprising businessmen from all over the country also found irresistible the attraction of money, Hollywood's egocentric environment, the appeal of a new art form, and the sunny climate.

The community of Hollywood these film people belonged to was defined, not by geographical boundaries, but by "the industry." Members lived all over Los Angeles, yet as long as they drew a salary from the producers, they belonged to the "rigidly stratified community," where income alone defined an individual's social status. If one's salary slid, status declined accordingly. If people left the film industry, regardless of accumulated wealth, they no longer belonged. Members of this new Hollywood rarely enjoyed inherited wealth. The élite often flaunted their high incomes with pretentious houses, expensive clothes, and an ostentatious style of living. The film industry flourished during this period because movies quickly replaced theater outside of New York as the social outlet of middle America. By the mid-1920s, over fifty million crowded more than 20,000 movie houses each week. Americans liked the admission cost, only about 20 percent of theater ticket prices. They also became avid fans of movie stars, thus encouraging the star system. Early stars included Mary Pickford, Charlie Chaplin, Gloria Swanson, and Douglas Fairbanks.[18]

Anxious to escape the Hollywood environment, the Douglases began immediately to search for suitable housing. One of Helen's friends who had moved from New York to Hollywood suggested Beverly Hills or Malibu. After visiting them, the Douglases decided those were two communities where they would never live. The expensive houses in these so-called "desirable" neighborhoods, Melvyn wrote his mother, looked like "fantastic nightmares" with "cheap bizarre decoration." The Douglases finally located a home they found very attractive and more reasonably priced on Greenleaf Street in Van Nuys, a community in the San Fernando Valley northwest of Hollywood. It only took twenty minutes to drive from there to Melvyn's studio. The large and airy house had a garden full of roses, which Helen loved, a tennis court in need of repair, a swimming pool, although not a "glamorous" one, and plenty of space for their two new Pekingese to romp. No houses existed within several blocks, nor were many streets paved. "We thought we were living way out in the country on a prairie."[19] Once Helen hired help, the two settled into a routine organized around Melvyn's rehearsal schedule for *Tonight or Never*. Although Helen worked her voice practice into this routine, she did not find the shift from New York easy. It did not take long for reporters to discover that the Douglases made interesting copy as they did not fit the Hollywood mold. One writer dubbed Helen the "Mystery Woman of Hollywood" because she had no interest in parties, nor did she "give a hoot" about the community's élite. Neither she nor her actor husband seemed to need Hollywood, choosing instead to escape to Van Nuys. Their early friends tended to be those in the *Tonight or Never* cast.[20]

Melvyn had mixed feelings about his first experience on a movie set. He quickly realized that the "well-defined social strata" defined the movie colony at work. "There is a decided flavor of caste" among the movie folks, he wrote his parents, "which we find obnoxious." It resulted in a "pretentious arrogance on the part of the higher-ups and a rather nauseating servility on the part of the others." As for working with Gloria Swanson, she seemed "pleasant enough," although it was impossible to compare her with Helen. Goldwyn had finally decided to eliminate most of Swanson's singing, which Melvyn thought a good idea. "Her voice would dispel any illusion as to her being an opera singer, even a third-rate one." He also thought it amusing that Swanson was pregnant, necessitating the remaking of her entire wardrobe. Although Melvyn was not particularly pleased with the final result, reviewers liked his first movie. The *New York Times* wrote that Melvyn's "bright interpretation rather puts Miss Swanson in the shade." Her performance certainly "falls short of Helen Gahagan's" in the stage production. Goldwyn felt pleased that he had discovered in Melvyn a "strictly American leading man" with his "clean cut blond good looks" in contrast to the more Latin type such as Rudolph Valentino. He anticipated that Melvyn would do well in upcoming films.[21]

While the filming occupied most of Melvyn's time in September and October, Helen enjoyed a much-needed rest. She generally drove Melvyn to work and then returned home to practice. She occasionally indulged with a trip to a masseuse. She avoided going into the city as much as she could. Melvyn bought her a Pierce Arrow limousine to remind her of trips to the New York theater in her father's Pierce Arrow. When one of their servants drove her into town, she drew the blinds so she could forget that she was in California. Before long, however, an opportunity came her way. David Belasco's brother Edward, and his partner Homer Curran, who ran the West Coast Belasco operations, contracted with Helen to do the stage production of *Tonight or Never* in November and December. This opportunity not only gave her something to do, but more important, offered immediate West Coast visibility. Melvyn even hoped it would result in a picture offer for her. She did not particularly enjoy the production, however, because it took her away from Melvyn for several weeks, and her performance was so associated with her romance with Melvyn. Although the original cast was able to join her once the Goldwyn filming had ended, Melvyn could not play his Broadway role; he had to move immediately into rehearsals for another movie. Professionally, however, she was a hit, particularly in Los Angeles, where film celebrities packed the theater on opening night.

After *Tonight or Never* closed, Helen had no idea what would follow. Aside from a Christmastime performance singing with the San Francisco Symphony, she had no other engagements. When inquisitive reporters tried to find out what plans she had, she threw out numerous possibilities. Maybe the play would travel to London, she commented, or tour in the United States. She might appear with the Cleveland Opera or maybe the movies. But "it isn't my way to guide the trend of my life or its work," she declared. She did know that as long as Melvyn had a contract in Hollywood, she did not want to consider anything but brief commitments away from Los Angeles. But Gahagan tried to maintain a cheerful front. She wrote Tyler that "building up an audience out here in the face of the movie people is fun." She knew, however, that the possibility of doing good plays in Los Angeles was slim. Although the city had some respectable stage productions, it was, without question, a movie city. As one reporter pointed out, most of the innumerable stage productions played by "young hopefuls waiting for screen chances" lost money. The city was "too picture-conscious"; it took "its celluloid personalities and studio activities more seriously than Broadway takes its show world." Although she would have welcomed appealing opportunities in film, nothing turned up during the Douglases' first fall in Los Angeles. She continued to negotiate with RKO but neither side could agree on contract details. Nor did any offers come from other studios, although she occasionally read scripts. Actually, despite her claims to the contrary, she did not fit the image of the 1930s movie star, and perhaps Gahagan knew this intuitively. Her beauty, height, big frame, and large-gesture style of acting, so appropriate for the stage, precluded her portraying the typical diminutive glamor girl of the 1930s. In addition, she was not interested in any of the scripts that did eventually come her way.[22]

Two performing opportunities finally materialized for early 1932—a talent show and a vaudeville appearance, both in New York City—which she must have accepted in almost total desperation. In the talent show, Gahagan joined a group of singers, orchestras, and concert bands in a pageant to celebrate the history and development of the State of New York. The highlights of the extensive assemblage of talent included Gahagan singing various songs with Rudy Vallee and his dance band, composer Jerome Kern conducting a review of his songs he entitled "Kerniana," and an appearance by Lily Pons, a newcomer to the Metropolitan Opera who had won wide acclaim. Gahagan's participation in the talent show was surprising enough, but her appearance in vaudeville suggests a real ambivalence about her performing. She obviously did not want long periods away from home, but she was willing to take almost anything just to stay on stage. Gahagan appeared at the Palace, a leading vaudeville theater. She shared top billing with Buck and Bubbles, "undoubtedly the best of the colored commercial dancing teams." Although her voice clearly was "much better than vaudeville usually produces," she suffered from severe stage fright, according to one reviewer, a common problem with first-time performers at the Palace. She sang a concert of classical and semiclassical songs. One critic summed it all up well. Gahagan's "appearance in vaudeville is somewhat of an experiment and it does not seem to be her metier." She had too good a voice for this type of program. "The whole scheme is too incongruous; Miss Gahagan and Buck and Bubbles. They just don't run together." Neither performance proved particularly satisfying, but at least she was well paid.[23]

Despite Gahagan's reluctance to look for plays in New York after moving to Los Angeles, she could not bring herself to cut off her Broadway ties completely. She renewed her contact with Tyler, begging him to find her a good play. It was not an easy task, because the Depression had magnified the drain the movie industry had already made on legitimate theater. As did many producers of the old school who had not established ties to Hollywood, Tyler found his fortunes waning in the early 1930s. But the most annoying hindrance Tyler encountered in working with Gahagan was her indecision. Every time he thought he had a good possibility, she would back down. Yet he continued to help her because he cared about her. Gahagan took advantage of that devotion. She also cabled her friend Van Druten, the author of *Young Woodley*, inquiring if she could do his play *Behold We Live*. He indicated that he did not want to produce it in the United States at the present time, but he left open the possibility of her acting in one of his plays in the future.[24]

Despite her inconsistent efforts to get a contract in New York, Gahagan knew that only movie work would allow her to base herself in Los Angeles. A year later, the Depression had begun to take its toll on the studios. Nevertheless, early in 1932, RKO still seemed interested in negotiating with Gahagan. Thus, while in New York in January for her talent show and vaudeville concerts, Gahagan met with studio representatives for publicity interviews, contract negotiations, and discussion of her first film. In February, however, the studio underwent a shift in management, filed for bankruptcy, and backed off from signing a contract.[25] Helen became agitated with this turn of events. She wrote Tyler that she had been having a "hectic time fighting with the movie people over plots and contracts. I who never fight with anyone—it makes me feel like a shrew. It seems I am in a very precarious position at present but I am sure everything will straighten itself out." In early March she appealed her case to the Academy of Motion Pictures. She claimed that she had refused numerous lucrative theater and opera offers and had declined to discuss possible film contracts with Universal and Fox Studios. RKO, in its defense, countered that although the studio had held various meetings with Gahagan to draw up a contract, neither side could agree on terms and therefore nothing existed in writing. Furthermore, the studio had not announced any agreement to the trade papers, nor did it know of any competing offers to Gahagan either on the stage or from any other movie studio. The Academy held a hearing and decided in RKO's favor because no written contract existed. But it reprimanded the studio for unprofessional behavior by misleading Gahagan and extending negotiations over an unnecessarily long time.[26]

As the spring of 1932 turned into summer, after a year in Hollywood, nothing really appealing had yet presented itself. Gahagan floundered. "Honestly, I don't know what I want most to do—stage, opera, or screen," she admitted. She even tried writing a play in 1932, which Edward Belasco had promised to produce. This writing endeavor fizzled. But when she received an invitation in the summer of 1932 to do a benefit performance of *Aida* at the Polo Grounds in New York, her spirits rose quickly. "Don't think I'm not the happiest girl alive" to be singing this opera engagement, she told a New York reporter. Unfortunately the experience did not come up to her expectations. The stage turned out to be nothing more than a jerry-built affair "which lay squatly across the home plate." She could not hear the orchestra, and her projection suffered from the lack of acoustical props. But at least the "tumultuous applause of some 5,000 in the grandstand" suggested an appreciative audience.[27]

Following *Aida*, Gahagan accepted an offer from Belasco and Curran for the lead in the Jerome Kern operetta *The Cat and the Fiddle*, a current hit in New York and London. They scheduled a ten-week run in Los Angeles and San Francisco. Although she had to be away from Melvyn for several weeks, she accepted and enjoyed the production. As with *Tonight or Never*, both the critics and the audiences loved her. The *San Francisco Chronicle* said that Gahagan "was never more irresistibly alluring than in this role. She carried herself with a dignity that lifted the entire tone of the vehicle and her superb voice gave the Kern melodies . . . a warmth that never ceased to be patrician." Actress Connie Palms, a good friend of the Douglases, recalled Helen's performance as "utterly enchanting, very real. Beguiling. The audience was in the palm of her hand." Palms was struck with how "beautifully" Gahagan moved;

"it's surprising because she's such a tall person." The other leads also had excellent voices, leading reviewers to call this performance superior to the Broadway run. The operetta proved such a success that it ran several extra weeks in San Francisco and returned for the Christmas holidays after the Los Angeles productions.[28]

While Helen tried during the year following her marriage to settle into a satisfying professional routine, Melvyn chafed under his contract with Goldwyn. After *Tonight or Never*, he made seven films on loan to other studios, but he summed them all up as "junky stuff." He enjoyed a couple of the roles, however, and had the opportunity to work in a lead role with some of Hollywood's top stars. Despite poor-quality material, he generally received favorable reviews. His movies ranged from *As You Desire Me*, an MGM movie adapted from the Luigi Pirandello play in which he played opposite Greta Garbo, to a "godawful" film for RKO entitled *Prestige* with Ann Harding, which took place in an African jungle. At Paramount he did a gangster movie, *The Wiser Sex*, with Claudette Colbert. He had a role in Universal's film version of the J. B. Priestley horror story *The Old Dark House*, playing with Charles Laughton and Boris Karloff, and he appeared in another jungle story, *Nagana*, about a scientist in South Africa who tried to cure sleeping sickness. He actually liked his role as a mad scientist who experimented with bats in *The Vampire Bat* for Majestic. He poured out his frustrations in a letter to Helen after only six months of filming. She was in San Francisco performing in *The Cat and the Fiddle*. He felt sick of "this whole damned movie racket," torn between the desire to "chuck" everything and the reality that only by sticking with his commitment could he become independent. Maybe if she could land a contract it would help, but he hated to think of her doing anything she did not really want to do. Helen had such "a tremendously vital and exciting" opportunity ahead of her on the stage and in movies, and "nothing should be allowed to stand in its way."[29]

Melvyn's unhappiness stemmed from various causes. Although fascinated by the technical advances of the movie industry, he realized that most of his early films had little artistic merit. Even if studios had assigned him more challenging roles, screen acting did not offer him the same sense of power as on the stage. Movies were made in segments, so that he missed the "thrill of creation" he experienced on the stage. He also hated the lack of control over the films he made. He felt like a "mere chattel" in the hands of Goldwyn compared to the way Brady treated him. Financially, however, Melvyn did well. Though the studios had considerable financial trouble during the early 1930s, Melvyn had a guaranteed salary ample enough to live very comfortably and still save two-thirds of what came in. He could support his parents and Greg. He re-

called in later years that he felt guilty that he and Helen were "relatively un-
touched" by the Depression. He also realized that the publicity from his films
helped his position in the theater.

Melvyn's distress continued to grow. In August 1932, he approached Goldwyn and pleaded to be released from his contract. Melvyn had no specific plans
other than to get out of his present situation. Much to Melvyn's surprise, Goldwyn agreed, but he made Melvyn promise that if he decided to return to films
within the year, he would give the producer first option. Melvyn's new freedom
meant that he and Helen could reevaluate how to manage their two careers
more effectively so they could have more professional satisfaction and less time
apart. They often had only Sundays to themselves when both were in Los
Angeles. They led a quiet life, played tennis and bridge, attended concerts,
and occasionally invited a few friends, mainly members from the *Tonight or
Never* cast or an occasional person Melvyn met during a filming, for an informal meal. The couple both disliked it when one of them had to be out of
town. They phoned constantly and sent frequent telegrams and letters. Melvyn
wrote in one letter: "I adore you, darling. When you were so unhappy over the
phone the other night, I was in a frenzy; I felt so damned impotent at not
being able to take you in my arms. . . . You are everything I have ever dreamed
of, and that's a lot because I have ambitious dreams. I don't show things the
way you do, darling, but I feel them." Telegrams sometimes conveyed news
but more often just their love for each other. From Melvyn: "Good morning
darling. I love you. Your wire received. It was sweet." [30]

The Douglases immediately began to think up ways to be together. Helen
planned to tour the West with *The Cat and the Fiddle* beginning in January
1933. The two hoped to figure out a way for Melvyn to travel with the company. Belasco was "crazy" to put them together in a play, so that was another
possibility. In addition, they began negotiating with close friend and upcoming
playwright Dan Totheroh to write a play for them to do together. They hoped
that a commissioned work would ensure quality as well as balanced roles. Although several papers announced that Helen and Melvyn would do a film
together, *Brief Moments*, this news proved to be rumor only. One reporter bet
that Melvyn and Helen "will one day soon become as popular a team as Alfred
Lunt and Lynn Fontanne. . . . They belong together the way marshmallows
and mayonnaise don't." But all these plans evaporated when Melvyn impulsively proposed that they take off and go around the world. The idea came to
him while visiting Helen near the end of the second San Francisco run of *The
Cat and the Fiddle*. The cast had just learned that tour plans had fallen through.
One evening, while they lay in bed listening to the boat whistles from the bay,
he suggested that they get out of Hollywood and take a trip around the world.
Helen agreed instantly, and Melvyn bought tickets the next day. Although he

no longer had financial problems, he continued to worry about money. He felt relieved that the ticket prices, $750 apiece, were cheaper than living in Los Angeles.[31]

Within two weeks, the carefree and happy couple, traveling as "Helen and Melvyn Hesselberg," boarded a small French cargo boat heading down the western coast to Mexico. "We weren't what you'd call model tourists," Helen recalled. They did not use guidebooks or maps, nor did they plan an itinerary. They avoided tourist spots. "We just went where fancy led us." They made a real effort to see as much local theater, dancing, and puppetry as possible, often meeting local actors and visiting their homes. After going through the Panama Canal, the Douglases sailed to Le Havre and spent two weeks in Paris ("religiously avoiding Notre Dame and the Louvre"). They had a reunion with Melvyn's parents and Gregory. Melvyn had arranged for them to live in Europe for a few years after the wedding in 1931. The Hesselbergs had agreed to care for Gregory, so Melvyn and Helen had not seen the three since moving to California.[32] Melvyn and Helen also had some surprising news in Rome. Since leaving Los Angeles, Helen had suffered periodic spells of nausea. She finally agreed to see a doctor, who diagnosed her discomfort—pregnancy. At first Melvyn thought they should return immediately, but Helen thought the idea ridiculous. Helen recalled that when Melvyn discovered that it would cost them more to return than to continue on their trip, he acquiesced in Helen's urging that they go on, indicating a conflict between the financial insecurity he had lived with all his life and his concern and worry about Helen. One can only speculate on how the two felt about having children. A close friend recalled that Melvyn, not Helen, was interested in having children. His sense of responsibility for Gregory, however, seemed confined to financial support. Helen's response to the news that she was pregnant indicated little concern about any sort of medical complications and no apparent desire to have an abortion.

After the family-oriented time in Rome, the two traveled to Marseilles and then sailed to Port Said, Egypt. At that juncture, they decided to take a side trip to Palestine. The unexpected detour proved to be a moving experience. They both found the development of the land and the early kibbutzim innovative and exciting. Melvyn found himself overcome with emotions when they visited the Wailing Wall. Never before had he experienced a sense of belonging to the Jews. He also felt attracted to their combination of socialism and capitalism in their political ideas. He had found his people, "an umbilical cord." After Egypt, they went down through the Red Sea to Singapore and across to Indonesia and Bali, where they stayed almost a month. They enjoyed the native dances and ceremonies, and Helen impulsively decided to participate in a ritual that a local witch doctor performed on pregnant women. After much negotiation, as Melvyn recalled, the two garnered an invitation to the witch doctor's hut. "The ceremony consisted chiefly of incantations, a kind of melodious, sing-song business of mumbo-jumbo which was very impressive." Then the man rose, pressed his lips "fervently" to Helen's forehead as if "conversing with her brain," and predicted a boy. A second, rival witch doctor immediately invited them to his ceremony, replete with lotus blossoms and tiny bells. He also predicted a boy.[33]

The next stop was China, where Melvyn developed malaria. He ran an extremely high fever and lost considerable weight, but once he had recuperated enough to begin exploring again, they spent considerable time attending theater productions and visiting universities. One theater custom that amused Helen was the practice of throwing hot towels. One evening, with the temperature about 110 degrees, "white objects began to hurtle through the air." These "objects" turned out to be steaming hot towels that the audience used to cool themselves off. The honeymoon ended in Japan. Helen became absorbed in studying Japanese theater as reflected in the kabuki theater and the Tokyo puppet shows, which used life-size puppets. At least technically, she felt, the Japanese began where American theater left off by utilizing, for example, a wide variety of equipment for staging and lighting, including a revolving stage. Melvyn noted a marked difference between the relaxed, charming Chinese and the Japanese, in whom he noted both aggressive behavior and a strong identification with their military traditions. He had a definite feeling that Japan was preparing for war.[34]

This relaxed, happy, and interesting trip, which lasted almost nine months, cemented the Douglases' relationship. It might well have lasted longer had not the baby's October 1933 due date dictated a return to California. As October grew closer, the Douglases became increasingly excited about their impending parenthood. But both plunged immediately upon return into re-establishing their professional careers. They had decided to move back to New York and return to the stage. Melvyn did one quick movie just to build financial resources back up. Helen began preparations for them to jointly produce a play that Dan Totheroh had written for them during their absence. Both felt content about their new direction. During these years, they enjoyed a very happy, special marriage. They were deeply in love. Helen helped open Melvyn so that he was more relaxed and outgoing with other people, although he always remained introspective and self-analytical. He also learned from her to trust people. Melvyn sensitized Helen to worldly issues, took her outside of her narrowly defined world and encouraged her in a gentle, persuasive way to care about how people lived in other cultural, political, and economic circumstances, and to gain "intellectual clarity." He also helped diminish to a small degree her "fairy tale" view of life.

5

A Lack of Direction

THE DOUGLASES WERE PLEASED to be working with Dan Totheroh. A native of San Francisco, Totheroh began writing plays when he was thirteen. He received considerable attention in New York during the 1920s with his play *Distant Drums*. Although another script, *Wild Birds*, produced by Cornell's husband Guthrie McClintic, did not succeed financially, it gained critical acclaim. One critic commented that while not all of Totheroh's plays were successful, each had "force, tremendous honesty, and a curiously haunting style of writing." The Douglases were ready to move to New York. This opportunity seemed to be what they were looking for.

The couple planned to go into rehearsal about six weeks after the birth of their baby and open on Christmas Day in San Francisco. They then hoped to take the play to New York. But first they had to secure financial backing. Helen turned to Tyler for help. In early October she wrote him a spirited, self-confident letter. Melvyn and she were both "so happy about each other, the baby, and the new play . . . that we keep pinching ourselves to make sure it's true." But they needed money to produce *Mother Lode*, and she thought this would be a good investment for Tyler. As she exuberantly pointed out, she and Melvyn thought the play a "magnificent" work, and "all" of San Francisco was looking forward to the play after seven months of extensive publicity. The characters were glamorous, well-known San Francisco historical figures, the locals liked Totheroh's work, and with her and Melvyn acting, how could the play fail? She reminded Tyler of her West Coast popularity. "I had the biggest success in San Francisco with *The Cat and the Fiddle* of anyone in years." She begged him to respond right away, since she was about to have her baby. Tyler, however, had learned long before that Helen's enthusiasm could be misleading, and he refused to get involved. So the Douglases temporarily shelved the play.[1]

On October 9, 1933, Helen gave birth to a healthy baby boy. The Douglases could not decide on a first name, so they temporarily named him Gahagan Douglas. Melvyn left for New York shortly after the baby was born to look for work, as they were out of money. Helen planned to join him with "Baby" once she regained her strength. Melvyn got a part almost immediately in a comedy by Jesse Lynch Williams, *No More Ladies*, directed by Helen's friend from college days, Harry Gribble. Six weeks later, Helen was ready to go. She wrote Tyler: "Little Gahagan Douglas whose first name we think will be Michael, sends you much love." *Mother Lode* was still on hold, and she was about to join Melvyn in New York in a permanent move. "Oh dear me, but we are glad we are coming back to New York. I could scream for a job. If it only weren't so cold. We have both been in such a hot climate especially this last year. And I can't wait to work. For the next ten years I would like to work without interruption."[2]

Just before Helen left Los Angeles, she unexpectedly received another play from Totheroh. This one, entitled *Moor Born*, centered on the Brontë sisters. She got so excited when she read the play that she called up Totheroh in the middle of the night to say she simply had to play the part of Emily. Despite his reminder that no one had shown interest in producing it when he made the rounds three years before, Helen was determined to do the play. She began looking for money as soon as she reached New York. She eventually persuaded John Tuerk, the Brady protegé who had directed her in the Chicago production of *Chains* ten years before, to produce it with the understanding that Melvyn would direct it. The Douglases gathered an excellent cast, including Frances Starr, Edith Barrett, and Glenn Anders. Since finances were tight, Melvyn directed for no pay, and all the leads accepted minimum Equity scale. Although Melvyn found this first opportunity to direct both challenging and important for his career, it imposed enormous pressures, since he was still playing in *No More Ladies*. He had little time to spend at home with Helen and his six-month-old son.

Moor Born opened in early April and received mixed reviews, which meant that it had only a short run and lost money. Yet even if the play had run longer, the likelihood of its making money remained slim. In the 1930s, in contrast to previous years, a play generally had to be sold to Hollywood for film rights to turn a profit. The acting and directing, however, received excellent critical comments. The short run and the reviews of the play's quality did not matter to Helen. She found herself satisfied professionally. Her performance proved to be the most sensitive of her career; the role had depth and the director knew her strengths well. Rehearsals became a continual intellectual discussion about the Brontës. Brontë enthusiasts who jammed the dressing rooms after the play more than compensated for the general lack of popularity of the play. Although the acting proved strenuous, particularly for a recent mother, Helen reveled in the role of Emily. "I would rather have had my six weeks as Emily Brontë than star for a year in a hit," she remarked. One reporter, interviewing her before a performance, found her so eager to talk about the part that she had to be reminded to continue applying her makeup. She identified with Emily. She, like Emily, liked the countryside, enjoyed being alone, and preferred to reason things out on her own. Helen felt about Vermont much as Emily did about the moors, where she found in the solitude many delights, and "not the least and best loved was liberty."[3]

Just as important to Helen as a satisfying role was the fact that she and Melvyn were once again working together. They constantly discussed the play. "I know that many husbands and wives find it difficult to work together, but Melvyn and I have been very successful," she said, even though he demanded a great deal more from her than from the rest of the cast. She felt the relationship worked because during their discussions "I cease to be Mrs. Melvyn Douglas. I'm Helen Gahagan, an actress whom my director is trying to improve." They never allowed arguments about the play to intrude into their personal lives. Helen assured reporters that she and Melvyn had a "sublimely happy" marriage. In five years they had never quarreled, although they argued "like the devil—so much so that anyone who happens to be around thinks we're about to tear each other to pieces. But those arguments always are about abstract things. And we enjoy them because they sharpen our wits." In addition to regaining a positive feeling about her professional work, Helen also enjoyed the baby. She was pleased to secure Frau Gaehler as a maid, a woman who had worked for her family for many years. She had encountered, however, considerable adverse reaction to her pregnancy, criticism that she thought "obscene." She found people acted "as if it were extraordinary for an actress to have a baby." She mounted baby pictures all around her dressing table and talked about him without hesitation to whoever would listen. During one interview, she had the baby on her lap. She assured the reporter that he would not interfere, for he was "terribly well mannered" at age six months. Yet "Turnover" (Gahagan's current nickname) "came near to stealing the interview." When asked if the baby had changed her way of life, Helen responded that her life had not changed a bit. "That worries me, the way people think having a baby is going to change everything. Isn't having a baby the most natural thing in the world?"[4]

During *Moor Born* and for a few weeks after it closed, it seemed that the Douglases' life had actually settled down. But not for long. In the summer, Belasco and Curran asked Helen to take the lead in the road production of Maxwell Anderson's *Mary of Scotland*. The play had enjoyed considerable success on Broadway with Helen Hayes in the title role. Gahagan could not resist the offer, despite the fact that it would take her away from Melvyn and their nine-month-old baby for over two months. She entrusted the baby to Frau Gaehler, who took him to Vermont while Melvyn continued in *No More Ladies*. He made one trip to Vermont while Helen was gone and reassured her that all was well with the child. Helen enjoyed the challenging role almost as much as that of Emily in *Moor Born*. She found her co-stars, Violet Kemble-Cooper as Elizabeth and Ian Keith as the Earl of Bothwell, superb colleagues. The lavish set and costumes added to the glamor. The cast played to full houses, and once again Helen received rave reviews. In Los Angeles Gahagan "achieved glowing recognition before an ermined crowd," one critic wrote. The public response proved so overwhelming it even caused a run on books about Mary of Scotland at the public library.[5]

The press asked questions about her acting as well as her wardrobe and the baby. Although Helen found the subject of fashion boring, she agreed to talk about it. She dressed, wrote one fashion editor, "like any sophisticated modish woman of fashion, in flawless, simple, carefully planned clothing . . . never showy or exaggerated." Gahagan revealed she shopped for clothes in much the same way as she handled most other household or child-rearing tasks—by finding a competent person to do it for her. When she needed clothing, she simply called her favorite shop and had them send someone out to see her. If they did not have what she wanted, they made it for her, a habit reminiscent of her childhood when her mother had a full-time seamstress. If she really liked a hat or dress, she had it copied in various colors. She had no interest in fashions for the baby since he wore diapers and shirts in the winter and "wickies" in the summer. She had given his dresses away because she thought he looked absurd in them. He still had no name. She and Melvyn called him "Baby" or "Sweet" or "anything else that comes to our lips [since] Gahagan really does not lend itself to the caressing conversation between a parent and a baby." Helen loved singing lullabies to him as he seemed to enjoy it. "He puts his head back, dog-fashion, and howls." Babies were wonderful, she mused. "I'd have twenty of them—they're so nice—if I only had the time."[6] This comment suggests that while Helen and Melvyn clearly loved the baby, they had not yet developed any deep sense of maternal or paternal attachment. The failure to name the child after nine months seems to underline the Douglases' inability to deal with the child as an individual. Helen did take note of gender distinctions by getting rid of his dresses, but her apparent tendency to dress him in the same basic clothing day after day makes one wonder how often the child was dressed up and taken on family outings. While he was cared for in a loving way, it seems logical to speculate that Gaehler took care of the daily tasks such as diaper-changing, bathing, feeding, and night wakings, while Helen played with him when she had time. Evidence does not suggest that Melvyn spent much time with the infant.

When the tour ended, Helen hurried to Vermont to pick up the baby before returning to New York. *No More Ladies* had closed, and Melvyn had turned his attention to trying to mount a production of Totheroh's *Mother Lode.* Totheroh and his colleague George O'Neill had strengthened the script with a re-writing. He and Helen organized the Mother Lode Players, Inc., in November 1934, and eventually Melvyn put $25,000, most of his savings, into the production. He and Helen planned to play the leads and Melvyn would direct, all for no salary. The Douglases felt very fortunate to get Beulah Bondi to take the third major role. Everything seemed right for a success. But critics tore this production apart. Brooks Atkinson of the *New York Times* pointed out that he and his colleagues had looked forward to the play, since Totheroh and O'Neill were "two of the most poetic spirits that have been hovering about our theatre." Unfortunately, *Mother Lode* was not of the quality they expected. Other critics called the play "vague and confusing," "dramatically inadequate," and "philo-sophically pretentious," and the respectable acting did not save the play. Need-less to say, the cast and the playwrights found the criticism demoralizing. Even worse, the Douglases had lost Melvyn's savings, and Helen apparently had no resources at that point.[7]

The tight financial situation and lack of any offers for New York productions encouraged her to accept a most unexpected approach from RKO. The studio, which had recovered from its financial distress and reorganization of the early 'thirties, asked her to play the title role in the film version of H. Ryder Hag-gard's late–nineteenth-century science fiction fantasy, *She.* RKO calculated the time was right for the movie because of the box office success of two other films of the same genre, *King Kong* and *Tarzan of the Apes.* The studio allo-cated $500,000 for the film, a fairly high figure at the time, and offered Ga-hagan a weekly salary of $2,250. The well-known Merian C. Cooper was hired as director and Randolph Scott as the male lead. Perhaps because Gahagan felt financial pressure, she accepted without seeing the script. She did spell out other conditions, however, including first-class train accommodations for her-self, the baby, and Gaehler, the maid. Her contract also included options for five additional films and the proviso that the studio arrange her annual layoff period of twelve weeks to occur at a time that would permit her to do a Broad-way show. She made it clear that her acceptance of the contract did not mean that she would be less discriminating about future parts. "If I decide to do more, I would like . . . to choose my material. . . . I should hate to feel I was contracted to stay anywhere for a year."[8] Despite her and Melvyn's deci-sion to live in New York so they could act on stage, Helen apparently was willing to consider more than one film. The two were clearly experimenting with ways to be satisfied personally, maintain their intense and happy marriage, and try to integrate a baby into their lives.

RKO felt fortunate to get Helen and overlooked their past bitterness. Unlike the typical female role of the 1930s, the part of "She" called for a woman of Gahagan's large build, stately, dignified manner, and style of acting. Cooper so respected her acting talent that he tried unsuccessfully to purchase half of the film options from RKO. Helen told Melvyn that Cooper wanted as much as she did for her to be a successful movie star. "I am believing him and hoping for the best." These comments suggest that part of her could not let go of a dream to act in movies. Perhaps the *Mother Lode* experience had dampened her enthusiasm of the previous year to live in New York so she and Melvyn could act on stage.[9]

Helen left Melvyn in New York in mid-February of 1935. She persuaded Alis De Sola to come with her to Los Angeles for the filming. She and Alis had not seen much of each other since the mid-1920s. After graduating with high honors from Barnard, Alis began writing plays and short stories. She also entered into what turned out to be a disastrous marriage; the two divorced in the early 1930s. She and Helen had never lost their deep love for each other, and going to Hollywood proved to be a delightful break for Alis. Once in Los Angeles, Helen and her entourage settled themselves in a hotel apartment. When Helen's mother joined them, however, and Helen hired a cook, the hotel quarters became cramped. Helen finally rented a small but attractive house at 434 Rossmore Street in Hollywood, not far from the studio. Helen particularly liked the garden. It gave her sixteen-month-old baby, who had finally been named Peter, a chance to play outside. As soon as Gahagan felt settled, she and De Sola turned their attention to the script. The story took place in the strange icy region of "She" in the Kingdom of Kor where the 500-year-old cruel Goddess of Kor preserved her life by bathing in an eternal flame. Gahagan and De Sola thought the script was "ghastly," and even more dismaying, Helen found her role "superficial." The two began rewriting her part so that her lines were at least "sayable," and eventually a good studio writer worked over the rest of the script.[10]

Before filming began, Helen had to go through several tiring weeks of practice shots and long periods with makeup and costume people. "I guess I get too nervous," she wrote Melvyn, "but everyone gets me so excited." She enjoyed visiting with Totheroh and O'Neill who had come to Los Angeles to see if they could turn their bad luck around by trying their hand at movie scripts. She also spent time with Melvyn's parents, who had returned from Europe. Edouard was in poor health. Melvyn had secured a small house for them in Los Angeles. Gahagan found the actual process of filming intimidating and frustrating. The lack of sequence in shooting scenes proved difficult for her to handle, and the cameras, cranes, and lamps—she described them as looking like "man-eating machines"—gave her stage fright when they moved close to her face. She hated having to get up early and remain beautiful from nine in the morning until six at night with dozens of experts fussing over her hair, her makeup, and her costumes. She developed an overwhelming impulse to "go out to the nearest mudhole and get in it." She did find the practice of watching a film come to life fascinating. De Sola recalled how absorbed Gahagan became in the daily viewing of the "rushes," scenes shot during the day. One afternoon, as she watched her face grow larger and larger until it filled the screen, she leaned forward and exclaimed, " 'God, that's beautiful!' "[11]

Midway through the filming, Cooper shifted his conception of the image he wanted Gahagan to project. This resulted in considerable reshooting. Initially, he wanted her "regal, stately, and cold." But then he decided he preferred her to appear sexy, entailing a complete remake of the costumes. This shift drove the costumer to the "hysterical stage," Helen wrote Melvyn. She believed that Cooper changed his emphasis because he felt that she was "too mental. . . . Any woman who can talk becomes mental in [the studio's] eyes. Anyway, 'make her sexy' is the Gahagan slogan." One of Helen's costumes, a chiffon outfit, caused considerable comment around the studio, and brought a reaction from Melvyn as well. "To think of you running around the set with nothing but a chiffon robe," he wrote. "Well, well, well. You certainly got into the high-powered sex-appeal class quickly. I hope, Miss Gahagan, it doesn't give you any bacchanalian ideas, at least not until I arrive. . . . Anyway, I'm glad its a chiffon robe and not a leopard skin. I don't think I could stand a leopard skin."[12]

De Sola's favorite chiffon robe story recalled the shooting of a scene when Gahagan descended a long flight of stairs. Cooper told her to remove various layers of chiffon until she ended up with only a single layer and no underwear. In the finished picture, because of the lighting, "she didn't look naked," but on the set "you could see everything," almost her pores, and "everybody just gaped." Helen, unaware of this, remained "serene" and "totally oblivious." She drew the line, however, when she was asked to pose for shots with only a bra and short panties. The publicity people thought they could "make great posters with me standing naked in a flame" she told Melvyn. Gahagan handled the constant attention from fan magazines much as she had in New York. She acquiesced to interviews only if the writers visited her when she was resting in bed in the mornings. Completely uninhibited, it did not bother her in the least to receive callers, mainly men, with her hair in rollers and cold cream on her face. The men had never seen a star "in such a condition," De Sola commented, but after the initial shock, they relaxed.[13]

The shooting finally ended in April. On balance, Gahagan had not enjoyed the experience. Although RKO held an option for further films, she had little interest making others. *She*, released in July, received mixed reviews. Some found it dull, slow, and somewhat silly. Others thought it top entertainment "if you like the real and unreal and furious action." The *Miami Herald* said Gahagan was marvelous and seemed to have the "wisdom of the centuries."

The *St. Paul Dispatch* commented that "even for movie fans who have un-wavering faith in Hollywood's banshees, white zombies and lugosi vampires," *She* offered more than the usual Hollywood fantasies and was "crammed with the best nightmare material . . . in years." Some thought RKO wasted Helen's talents, but others thought her ideal for the part because her weight, at 135 pounds, did not present a problem 2,000 years ago when "loveliness in women had nothing to do with a weight chart which never rises above a hundred and four and a thirty-inch hip measure."[14]

While Helen was filming *She*, Melvyn went through a frustrating and un-happy period in New York. When he and Helen had moved to New York in November 1933, they intended to stay permanently. Melvyn had no interest in returning to the movies or even in combining the stage with filmmaking. After Helen left in February 1935 to film *She*, Melvyn had another successful di-recting opportunity, Sean O'Casey's *Within the Gates*, an "extraordinarily po-etic work" that he enjoyed "enormously." A role in Louis Bromfield's *Deluxe* followed, but the play did not do well and closed in March. Melvyn became worried about staying in New York because no opportunities came along, and the fall season looked unpromising. Yet he feared that returning to film would result in the disappointing experience he had had in the early 'thirties when the scripts did not challenge him. He finally decided to contact an agent about a movie contract that would allow him regular time off to get back to New York. Nothing materialized except an MGM contract, which Melvyn turned down because it paid only $1,000 a week. Although he became increasingly impatient, he did not think it wise to leave New York until he had a contract in hand, in part because of the rumor that the film industry might move to Florida. Helen, however, with her impulsive outlook, urged Melvyn to come to Los Angeles and not worry about a contract.[15]

By April, Melvyn felt even more depressed, a mood compounded by extreme loneliness. At the beginning of his separation from Helen, his plays and some social life with Helen's siblings, Walter and Lilli, and other friends had kept him busy. Once *Deluxe* closed, however, Melvyn seemed engulfed with sad-ness. One night he woke up startled, certain that Helen and Peter were in the bedroom. During the run of *Deluxe*, Helen had arranged for a flower to be sent to Melvyn each night. "Each evening when the flower arrives . . . I am suffused with a warm weakness and a few tears. So write me often and keep me warm." Helen's loneliness came over her in "great waves," she wrote, al-though the family and filming kept her busy. She hoped her hairstyles, hair pieces, makeup, and costumes in the movie would please him. She urged Melvyn to write more, even though he wrote at least twice a week to her weekly letters. Once when she had not received a letter from him in a while, she became cross on the phone. Melvyn wrote, "You were so harsh over the phone about not having had my letter that I was upset for hours. Sweet, it wasn't my fault you didn't get it." Each of Melvyn's letters, though full of news, included a tender portion and an indication that he was becoming more emotionally attached to Peter. "Darling, I am with you constantly. I am afraid you are ingrained into my system. Do write as often as you can and tell me all of Peter's accomplishments." Helen wrote in one letter, "Peter is so sweet." He "kisses his hands all the time and kisses all his toys, flowers, etc." One night he sang himself to sleep. He was growing fast, and he probably would be as tall as his six-foot-six Uncle Walter. The warm weather had turned his cheeks pink, and he ate constantly. If Melvyn did not come soon, she warned, he would "miss the best part" of Peter. He had just begun to play, and "it's too cute." Melvyn asked Helen not to go to the beach with the baby for that was "one of the things we must do together. God, how I miss you two. Everything else is pointless."[16]

By mid-April, Melvyn decided to take his chances and left New York. Much to his surprise, once he got to Los Angeles, Columbia, Paramount, and RKO all wanted him. His first film, *She Married Her Boss* with Claudette Colbert, turned out to be an enormous box office success, and the next two—one was *Annie Oakley* with Barbara Stanwyck—also did well. By winter he had two favorable contracts, with Columbia and MGM. Although he could not arrange his schedule to return occasionally to New York, his concern about financial security subsided. This success was dampened, however, by his father's death, an event he found it very difficult to adjust to. He had grown closer to his father, who had mellowed considerably in his later years. Melvyn's reckoning with his Jewish background also intensified his affection. But his mother seemed relieved. She developed into a much happier woman after her husband died; she continued to live in Los Angeles, joining various organizations of film-star mothers and enjoying a pleasant social life. Melvyn later realized that much of his intense drive to find satisfaction in his work resulted from his feeling that his father had been "lazy about his music. . . . He lacked this sense of urgency . . . this compelling need to fulfill his capabilities."[17]

Melvyn's career in film took off rapidly. With a double contract he finally had some script control, which meant an improvement in the quality of the movies he selected. He began to make films on loan to Paramount and RKO. He had reached a stage in his career when he almost always played the leading man opposite Hollywood's top stars, and his salary went up accordingly. By 1937 his credits in a variety of gangster, thief, and comedy films included *The Gorgeous Hussy* with Joan Crawford; *Theodora Goes Wild* with Irene Dunne; *Angel*, starring Marlene Dietrich and directed by Paramount's prize, the distinguished German immigrant, Ernst Lubitsch; *I'll Take Romance* opposite Grace Moore; and *There's Always a Woman* with Joan Blondell. Although he was not particularly happy back in Hollywood, he certainly found it more stimulating than his initial stint in 1931–1932. As a *New York Times* reviewer noted in 1936, Douglas demonstrated on screen the "self-assurance of a man whose position in the cinematic scheme of things is unquestioned."[18]

The Douglases moved into a large, seventeen-room, elegant Spanish-style home in the 300-block on South Hudson, just off Beverly Boulevard and near the Wilshire Country Club, an affluent area. The tile-roofed house enclosed a lovely patio surrounded by palm trees and numerous plants and shrubs. Large archways separated the patio from the inside of the house, and a wide, second-floor balcony overlooked the patio. They gave a housewarming party in April of 1936, also celebrating their fifth wedding anniversary, Melvyn's thirty-fifth birthday, and Dan Totheroh's impending vacation escape to Bali. The guests, who dined on enchiladas from Helen's favorite Mexican restaurant, were primarily old friends, among them William Brady and Grace George, who were vacationing in Hollywood; Beulah Bondi, who had played in *Mother Lode*; Owen Davis, the author of Helen's first Broadway play, *Dreams for Sale*; and George O'Neill, Dan Totheroh's good friend and colleague. Other friends whom they spent considerable time with, such as actor Ralph Bellamy, were unable to come to the party. Their circle of friends still came from the theater, not the film world. As Melvyn said, in movie-making, people met on the set, rehearsal time was short, and generally the cast spent little time together. In contrast, strong relationships developed during the intense rehearsal time for a stage production, and one generally became closer to the cast.[19]

During these months, Helen and Melvyn also became increasingly concerned that Peter have more stimulating activity. He was spending most of his time with the maid. When he turned two in October 1935, the Douglases enrolled him at a reputable private school, the Buckley School, where his day included games, clay modeling, woodcraft, reading, dancing, singing, and French. The *Los Angeles Times* commented that "Peter is believed to be one of the nation's youngest schoolboys." Helen and Melvyn enjoyed him as often as time permitted. Helen, in one of her expansive moods, told a *New York World Telegram* reporter that she had been happy growing up in a large family and she just loved children. She hoped that eventually they would have six.[20]

Despite Helen's aversion to the Hollywood lifestyle, she occasionally played the part of society wife, particularly if she could earn some money at it. She even wrote a series of articles for the *Los Angeles Examiner* describing her favorite outfits, which revealed something of how she and Melvyn spent their leisure time. She selected her white wool cape that she used for sailing; a navy sailor-style coat made of the Latin American fur vicuña, which she wore to the Santa Anita race track; and an imported gray and red tweed suit complemented with a red, broad-brimmed hat for various business purposes. Although she saw herself as "one of the strictest advocates of the tailored mode for streetwear," she designed herself a feminine blue-and-white organza party dress for garden parties and wore a light blue sharkskin pajama suit for lounging at home. She had an aversion to slacks. She even wore dresses to rehearsals, she explained, because she found them more comfortable, and she believed women should dress in feminine clothes. Although she did not mention this, dresses also flattered women with a big build.[21]

With Melvyn back in Los Angeles and the New York move aborted, Helen's professional prospects seemed dismal. She had finally had a break in film, and she did not like it. Perhaps if interesting scripts had come her way, she might have done another movie. But this did not happen. Although she had rewarding experiences with Totheroh's plays in 1934, the Douglases had taken the responsibility for mounting these productions. No other offers had come along. Tyler died shortly after Melvyn moved back to Hollywood. Although Tyler had not secured a play for Helen since the 1920s, she had few other inside connections. She generally remained choosy about what she would do. While she was a talented stage actress, she had succeeded without investing the years of concentrated energy that result in continued improvement as had her contemporaries, such as Katharine Cornell or Helen Hayes. Her one experience in the movies had not altered the producers' opinion that she had limited possibilities in film. And the fact that Melvyn's film career was becoming successful so quickly might well have made her want to avoid being compared unfavorably to Melvyn.

Helen decided to turn to her remaining option, her music. As she explained to a reporter, "Life is too short. I have other interests and I'm not going to let myself get tied up in a bow knot like so many of my theater friends who work themselves into a nervous breakdown over their difficulties with the studio."[22] Although she had not sung much professionally since moving to California in 1931, she had practiced regularly. But she was thirty-four, five years older than when she did her 1930 European tour. In the summer of 1935 she became more assertive in her planning. She decided to prepare for recitals and to accept attractive opera invitations. She secured an agent and asked De Sola to develop a publicity brochure. Gahagan also persuaded Madame Cehanovska to move to Hollywood along with George so that Helen could start regular lessons. As an inducement she suggested that George might find movie work. Madame agreed to come, at least for a brief time.

Gahagan felt encouraged when she received three opera invitations, the first she had received since she sang *Aida* at the New York Polo grounds in 1932. She accepted two of the invitations, one from the San Francisco Opera for the lead in Giacomo Puccini's one-act *Suor Angelica*, and the second from the Los Angeles Civic Light Opera for a two-week run in the title role of Franz Lehar's operetta, *The Merry Widow*. But she turned down an opportunity to sing Amilcare Ponchielli's *La Gioconda* with the St. Louis Opera on the grounds that she did not like the opera—a finicky attitude for someone trying to break back into the opera world. Gahagan received good reviews for both West Coast performances. She particularly enjoyed playing the part of the glamorous Sonia in *The Merry Widow*, set in turn-of-the-century Vienna. Melvyn often dropped by rehearsals, tactfully offering directing advice. On opening night, early in May 1936, she impressed both the critics and the fashionably gowned, responsive audience, which included many movie celebrities "who came to pay tribute to Helen Gahagan." Well-dressed and handsome Peter, not quite three, sat in the audience, his first opportunity to see his mother perform. At her first entrance, he said quietly, "Hello, Mommy." But later, when she had to struggle with another performer, Peter said loudly, "You let my Mommy go, *you nasty man!*" [23]

In the summer of 1936, Helen pushed ahead with her plans for a concert series and secured two engagements. She asked De Sola to write some advance stories for the cities where she had contracts. Stark Young, the long-time theater critic for the *New Republic* who had become a personal friend, helped De Sola, as did Walter Pick, Helen's cousin, who worked with the agent on the recital planning. But Helen was caught off-guard by an invitation from the prestigious New York Theatre Guild to co-star with Clifton Webb in the Guild's opening play of the 1936–1937 season, *And Stars Remain*, by Julius and Philip Epstein. Gahagan dropped everything and left for New York. She could not pass up an opportunity in which she knew she could excel, rather than gamble on singing, which had an uncertain outcome. Furthermore, despite her stated determination to stay near Melvyn and Peter, parenting priorities became secondary when the right performing opportunity came along. The Epstein brothers, both young radicals, wrote *And Stars Remain* as a satire on contemporary political attitudes. Helen was initially flattered by the opportunity to perform for the established Guild, but she quickly lost her enthusiasm for the play. She did like working with Webb, however. "Clifton is awfully good, if his fairy qualities wouldn't show so terribly," she wrote Melvyn. But as the rehearsals progressed, she and the other cast members became frustrated with Guild members who continually insisted on rewriting the second and third acts. [24]

After three weeks of rehearsals, she told Melvyn that the cast had gone through three versions of the last act and at the moment had no version, "unless the Epstein boys have evolved a new one overnight." She was also finding her own role "dull and vacillating." Although Helen increasingly disliked the play, it pleased her when on opening night Noël Coward and Maxwell Anderson, among others, "said the nicest things." "They all think it's a horrible part," she wrote Melvyn, but at least "I am simple, believable, and have great charm and real warmth." Reviewers wrote off the play as "thin" and "silly" and generally agreed that the Guild had wasted Gahagan's talents on a "largely unrealized role." Yet despite the fact that she called the play an "ordeal," she knew that when it closed she would be sorry. "It's so wonderful to be back in the theatre," she wrote Melvyn. Helen mentioned future possibilities in almost every letter; she even spoke of a play in England.[25]

Helen kept herself busy in her free time with a social life that revolved around the theater and the large Gahagan family. She attended plays, generally with a member of her family, Alis, or actress Laurette Taylor, one of her few theater friends. Gahagan continued her singing every day. She could do some "cheap concerts" around New York, she wrote Melvyn. She went to various parties and occasionally entertained. But she disliked formal teas, even those in her honor, such as a "stupid" one a drama club gave for her. Her co-star Webb hosted an interesting party where the guests included Lynn Fontanne, Alfred Lunt, Guthrie MacClintic, Cole Porter, and writer Donald Ogden Stewart. Helen did not leave until after five o'clock in the morning. She wrote Melvyn the next day that her brother Walter gave her some medicine to prevent a hangover since she had drunk quite a bit of champagne. "So don't worry," she assured Melvyn. Despite an active social life and the security of her family around her, Helen seemed very lonely. She wrote Melvyn that his letters were like "candies"; she always saved them to open last. When they were back together, she wrote, "you will have to continue writing me anyway. It gives me such palpitations of the heart when I see your handwriting . . . you are around me so strongly I feel your love all the time. . . . please know that I am kissing you" in every moment. "Darling, I ache for you. Everything is so hollow, so dull. I don't know how I get along at all. . . . It does not matter what else happens to me in the world for you have loved me and that is enough. . . . How in the world did I find you, dearest?"[26]

Melvyn's letters reveal the toll that nonstop film production for a year and a half had had on him. He was envious of Helen's opportunity to return to the stage. He felt desperate to "get out of this God-damned place. . . . You seem like you are in another world . . . like some bright place" one dreams of getting to eventually. He felt the MGM contract around his neck, and he longed for a simpler life. He disliked movie actors more than ever because he felt they were "groups of exhibitionists all floating in a soup of adulation. But maybe they aren't any worse than lots of other people." Too many people had no feeling of connection to the world around them. Helen and Peter gave him his sense of identity. One day, he recounted, he woke up so tired that he decided to call in sick. Suddenly the studio doctor showed up, and he had to "put on an act. Fortunately he was stupid and my hands and feet were cold [so] I just had to convince him that my stomach was upset. It was very funny and now I feel like a naughty child." He detailed an encounter with the notorious Hollywood gossip columnist Louella Parsons, who wanted him and Irene Dunne to do a broadcast for her program. Because Parsons had recently come out with some nasty gossip about Melvyn, she had "crawled on her belly" when she called, and he let her crawl. She was like "melted butter, a little rancid."

He asked Helen, "Do you think I should have told her to go to Hell?" After some thought, Melvyn decided not to make a fuss.[27]

When Helen left for New York in September 1936, Melvyn moved out of the Hudson Street house, which had had its housewarming only five months before, into an apartment. He kept Peter, now three, for the first two months. At the end of October, Melvyn sent Peter to New York at Helen's suggestion; she wanted the toddler to become acquainted with his Gahagan relatives. Both Lilli and her brother Bill had children near his age. Instead of putting him into school, Helen kept him at her apartment. As she had many of her days free, she or Gaehler took him to the park often and visited friends and family. Helen enjoyed his curiosity and observed his rapidly growing vocabulary. Peter loved to sit at the piano and turn the pages of her music. He would inquire, pointing to the music, "What is this all about, Mommie?" He also "read" books, commenting one day that " 'books were man's best friend.' " He explained to his startled mother that he had learned this expression from his grandmother Lillian. Peter often "wrote" letters to his father, messages dictated to Helen. His favorite line was: "Dear Daddie, have a good time in the studio." Melvyn found that "ironic, to say the least." Helen assured Melvyn that Peter had become his father's boy and was no longer her baby. "He puts your picture under his pillow every night and kisses it." Melvyn worried about Peter's not attending a nursery school. He realized that it was good for him to play in the park all day, but he felt that the games and activities that he had learned in the Los Angeles school were important for his creative development. More to the point, he suggested that Helen was indulging him too much. Yet he supposed Peter should have fun while he could. Helen responded that she thought school could wait until the weather turned bad.[28]

Helen also took Peter to the openings of Melvyn's films, special events for all the Gahagans and their friends. Peter found it difficult to understand where his father went when he left the screen, she wrote Melvyn, and Peter cried because he could not see him in person. Helen clipped all the New York notices for Melvyn and passed along everyone's comments, particularly her own. While she was pleased with *Gorgeous Hussy*, for example, she felt that the filming and lighting did not do justice to Melvyn's acting in *Theodora Goes Wild*. The studio "gave all the breaks to [Irene] Dunne. I suppose they had to because she is so god-awful looking in life." But there were no flattering shots of Melvyn. Melvyn gently responded that "naturally she got the breaks as she was the star." Helen also could not resist telling Melvyn that he had put on an unnecessary ten pounds. "You get away with it in this picture but dearest you must diet." She admitted that she also had put on weight and also needed to cut back. Melvyn joined Helen in December after he negotiated a leave of absence from MGM with the hopes of having several months' respite from making films. But he had a chance to do only one play before the studios called him back. Helen remained in New York through Christmas, still hoping acting or singing opportunities would come up. But none of the vague ideas that people bandied about ever materialized. She even thought a singing part in an MGM movie might come through. "Everything is so nebulous and illusive," she wrote Melvyn; "I feel exactly like a balloon floating in space." She admonished him in the same letter to cut back on his smoking and go to bed at a reasonable hour. Maybe trying to control Melvyn's behavior, particularly from long distance, soothed her frustrations.[29]

This period of gloomy separation ended abruptly in February 1937 when Helen received two invitations for recitals. Her spirits revived; she returned immediately to Los Angeles; and the two moved back into the Hudson Street home. Suddenly their life resumed some semblance of normalcy. The first item on her agenda was an appointment for publicity shots. Helen had hired Walter Pick, her cousin, to organize all the details of her tour. Ten years younger than his cousin Helen, the handsome Pick had come to Los Angeles with the promise of a movie contract, which did not materialize. He gradually worked into a regular job with the Douglases, handling correspondence, cueing Melvyn on his lines, planning Helen's recital tour details, and generally helping out with other professionally related tasks. Pick wrote De Sola about the day the photographer took the publicity pictures. Helen wore the "most stunning clothes you ever saw. . . . I almost died laughing at Helen for they took the first pictures at a cemetery right on Hollywood Boulevard! The next group were taken with a barn as a background and right next to a trash pile. Anyone but Helen would have gone mad as there was a designer, a hatter, a newspaper woman to interview Helen, a girl from the hairdresser's and a maid to press her clothes—all dashing about with us. In addition there was the photographer and his wife and myself. It is too bad you are not here for all these rare moments."[30]

Gahagan left for her first concert, scheduled in Dallas, in early March. Minnie Mae Fleming, one of her Barnard friends, had arranged this appearance as a society fund-raiser for Barnard College. Gahagan's program included four Franz Schubert songs, five from the Dichterliebe Cycle by Robert Schumann; an aria from *Cavalleria Rusticana*; lieder from Strauss, Wolf, and Brahms; and some Russian songs of Tchaikovsky, Gorodine, and Gretchanioff. Her accompanist during this period, Sanford Schlüssel, had an excellent reputation. Her reviews in Dallas were quite complimentary. The program for the concert in San Francisco differed only slightly from that in Dallas, but the critics were not as kind as in Texas. One commented that she made too much noise while breathing, although he acknowledged that her high tones were "exquisitely flutelike." In sum, said the *San Francisco News*, perhaps she would never reach the point where she could "vie with the great in passing the acid test of the recital stage," but she still was good. A third concert at the Met, which Helen thought definite, fell through.[31]

But a most exciting opportunity to sing once again in Europe materialized in the late spring—a six-week summer tour planned by Walter Hofstötter, the manager who had organized her tour in 1929–1930. He arranged a series of concerts in Paris, Prague, Budapest, and Munich in June and July of 1937, culminating at the Salzburg Festival. Gahagan worked diligently to expand her repertoire. She had finally mastered German. In addition to popular material like the complete Schumann Dichterliebe Cycle of sixteen songs and those of various German lieder composers, she had added more selections from Schubert and Richard Trunk, songs of several Austrian composers including those by the aging but still popular Joseph Marx, avant-garde music of Serbian Rodolphe Reti, and music of two additional Russian composers.

Although Gahagan looked forward to her European trip, she and Melvyn worried about the political situation. The first warning signal came before they left for Europe, when Hofstötter refused to let Gahagan bring her accompanist Schlüssel. He reasoned that she should have a European, not an American, accompany her, but Helen assumed that he objected because Schlüssel was Jewish. Hofstötter secured an Austrian pianist, Fritz Kuba. Gahagan's uneasiness increased once she reached Europe. Hofstötter had scheduled her in Munich and Bad Reichenhall despite her instructions to bypass Germany. Since Kuba could not enter Czechoslovakia, she had to hire another substitute. Furthermore, Hofstötter said if she sang German lieder in Prague, a riot would take place. This time she balked. If she could not sing German songs she would not sing, for "music lovers would not hold Brahms, Schumann and Marx responsible for the Nazi movement." Despite Gahagan's anxiety, the trip went smoothly. She stayed first in Paris, working hard on her Marx songs. She wrote Melvyn, "I literally saw nothing but the hotel. . . . But I did finally learn the damn Marx songs." She sang them over Paris radio and was taken by surprise when Marx heard the program and found her interpretation of his music "enchanting." He asked if he might go along on the tour, accompanying Helen when she sang his songs; not surprisingly, she welcomed his interest and support.[32]

After her Paris concerts she traveled to Prague, where she sang in the Municipal Library. Hofstötter's fear of her singing German songs was unfounded, although she did not like Prague. She found the city dirty and dreary, and "the people all looked like peasants," observations reminiscent of her disdainful attitude towards European cities and ordinary people in the summer of 1930. She received mixed reviews. One critic noted that she was not of the quality necessary for opera, but "she is fitting beautifully into the more intimate atmosphere of the 'lied.' " After her second concert a few days later, one reviewer complained that the concert season had already dragged on long enough, and "now this singer from somewhere over the ocean has arrived to take the podium and have the last word." Nevertheless, despite his skepticism about female American actors and singers, he remarked that Gahagan's voice was first-rate, with great range, a powerful sound, and a clear but somewhat sharp higher register. Gahagan's next stop, Budapest, was "like coming to heaven. The whole city here is so clean and light and airy." Excitement hovered over her arrival because the popular Marx planned to accompany her. She sang in the small concert hall of the Musical Arts Academy. In spite of much anticipation, however, reviews once again proved less than enthusiastic. One reporter noted that she did not seem to know much about Hungary, but when he suggested that she pay more attention to the Hungarian composers such as Béla Bartók, Zoltán Kodály, and Ernst von Dohnányi, she took out a little red pencil from her purse and wrote down every name in a gold-margined notebook. One reviewer asked her why she had come in the summer as opposed to the regular opera season; she explained she had a radio contract with NBC and was only free in the summer.[33]

She then traveled to Germany for concerts in Bad Reichenhall, then to Innsbruck in Austria, Scheveningen, the Netherlands, and back to Munich. She confined these programs to German songs. Marx accompanied his own compositions, and Kuba played for the remainder of the program. In Innsbruck, the reviewer said that she had a bad habit of singing with her hands, which Germans could not understand because they believed it "restricted projection." The Dutch critics thought her German pronunciation abominable and her performance superficial. According to one devastating review, "her voice came up short measured against the standard which people apply here since it is one-dimensional and is often lifeless. . . . The sound, which carries well, therefore takes on a metallic quality." Gahagan, critics suggested, should limit herself to stage or film. "The art of song does not become her. . . . How could anyone have *so* little understanding of Schumann's Dicterliebe. . . . The audience was small and applauded out of politeness." Her final concert was in Salzburg. Gahagan appeared with Hans Duhan, a noted Austrian baritone with the Vienna State Opera. With the exception of two Rinaldini songs, she planned an entire evening of Marx while Duhan sang a variety of lieder. The *Donnerstag* gave them good reviews. Duhan's singing was "especially sonorous" and Gahagan had "a sparkling, theatrical type soprano which is also obvious in her rendition of 'lieder.' " Unlike previous critics, this reviewer thought she handled German "with absolute security."[34]

Helen felt exuberant about her concerts, despite the mixed critical response. She judged her success by the audience response and comments she heard. "I was scoring a hit everywhere," she wrote home, particularly in Prague, Munich, and Budapest. "They went wild" in Prague, she wrote Melvyn. "They said they had *never* heard a foreigner sing German as I did." She asked Melvyn to tell the people at the Hollywood Bowl, where she was scheduled to make her debut immediately after returning, that in Innsbruck the audience demanded "encore after encore until my voice felt like a husk and I was crying from sheer tiredness. But, oh, it was grand!" The material she sent for the Hollywood Bowl's concert program exaggerated her European reception. Helen Gahagan had had a "terrifically successful concert at Salzburg," said the blurb, "where she was accompanied by Joseph Marx, accredited as the greatest living European composer after Strauss." She wrote Melvyn that "it seemed almost impudent that a young singer like myself," with only a few years' experience, "should brave the critical ears of those musically wise people." [35]

Gahagan actually believed she had scored a real success, and perhaps she had with many of those who came to hear her sing. She apparently discounted the critical reviews or in some cases never read them. She left Prague before the reviews came out and wrote Melvyn, "I hope they were good, I don't see how they can be anything else but you never can tell." It is logical that she and her publicity people would select the best quotes for advertising brochures, and possibly that was all Helen read. Yet Helen typically felt enthusiastic about her performances. Her tendency to have a rosy outlook meant that she did not dwell on the negative, and she could scarcely be characterized as modest. The trip was marred, however, by the tense political situation in Europe, and Helen was relieved when her sister Lilli joined her in Germany. Both were conscious of daily military maneuvers. Their most alarming incident occurred shortly after the Salzburg Festival. Helen had just received an invitation to sing *Tosca* at the Vienna Opera that fall, and she had scheduled an appointment to discuss plans at a local coffeehouse with a friend of Marx's, an English music critic whom she knew only slightly. The man launched into vicious anti-Semitic talk and asked Helen if she would be willing to report to him any anti-Nazi activity in the United States. Helen became anxious and upset and ended the meeting abruptly. The following day, when Hofstötter put Helen and Lilli on the train for their return trip home, she heard the conductor say to her manager, " 'Steh auf!' Hofstötter jumped to his feet at once and stood at attention." Helen did not know if this meant Hofstötter was a Nazi, but his military response petrified her; she felt as if she had been "hit in the solar plexus." She was impatient to get home, although she still planned to return in the fall to sing at opera houses in Vienna, Prague, and Budapest. [36]

Helen found the boat trip dreadfully slow. She missed Melvyn, and Hofstötter had booked them in inside staterooms that were unbearably hot. The only place she and Lilli could escape the heat was on the deck, and Helen caught a terrible cold. "If Hofstötter had been there," she wrote Kuba, "I would have beaten him." Pick wrote De Sola that Melvyn was "goddamn bored" with the Grace Moore picture he was working on at present, and it was even worse with

Helen being away. "He goes around like a chicken with its head cut off." Gahagan reached home shortly before her Hollywood Bowl performance. Despite laryngitis, she still planned to perform. But after the rehearsal the afternoon of the concert, she decided she could not sing that evening, despite her doctor's opinion to the contrary. An amused reporter for the *Los Angeles Evening News* commented that "deuces were wild last night at [the] Hollywood Bowl, with a complete new deal all around. The fun of guessing what would turn up next on the program kept the audience sitting in for another hand through an entire concert that was definitely not the scheduled one." Conductor Fritz Reiner and the Bowl orchestra opened with the Berlioz "Roman Carnival" overture, with a "gallant 'show must go on' fervor," while "frantic phone calls and a careening taxicab brought George Cehanovsky to pinch hit for Miss Gahagan." At the insistence of the program's organizer, the voiceless Helen, feeling quite ridiculous "decked out" in her formal gown, appeared briefly "with low and silent bows to the audience" and accepted a huge bouquet of flowers. Bowl talent scouts, meanwhile, "sleuthing among the audience," spotted Met tenor Mario Chamlee enjoying the concert. They gave Chamlee a pep talk, and he dashed home and grabbed some music. The small but enthusiastic audience took the changes in stride and, according to one reviewer, found the concert much more fun than the originally scheduled program. Gahagan found the whole experience humiliating. She decided later that her problem was less the laryngitis than an emotional block about singing German songs after her experience in Salzburg.[37]

Shortly after returning home, she and Melvyn began building a home despite Melvyn's uneasiness about what he called his "gypsy" pattern of moving back and forth to New York. Although Helen had moved just as much, she had tired of renting and moving about. The idea of building a dream home offered tremendous satisfaction. She wanted a home that fully satisfied her need for a sense of permanency and to be surrounded by a home full of light. They bought a beautiful three-acre lot in the hills above the Hollywood Bowl, a residential area called the Outpost Estates. Although it was a wealthy neighborhood, its large custom homes bore no resemblance to the pretentious mansions of nearby communities like Beverly Hills.

The Douglases asked their architect, Roland Coates, to design a one-story home to nestle in the hilly terrain and satisfy Helen's passion for spacious rooms and ample light. A long S-shaped driveway wound up the steep hill off Senalda Drive to a large entry next to a three-car garage. Except for the door, painted a soft, warm red, the rest of the wood-paneled exterior was light gray complemented with white shutters. A balcony ran across the entire front of the house, providing an excellent view of the city and, when the fog had burned off, of the ocean. Each of the rooms had high ceilings and huge windows, and most had access to the outside. The living room and Helen's bedroom had fireplaces and lots of bookshelf space. The cozy kitchen included two adjacent servants' rooms. Melvyn and Helen had a two-bedroom suite off a wide hall, and two other bedrooms came off a second hall. In back, a large patio surrounded a small swimming pool. A steep bank, filled with eucalyptus trees that filtered the sunlight, rose high above the back property line and provided privacy. Although the Douglases had a sizable income, principally from Melvyn's film work, the cost of the house, $55,000, seemed "prohibitive" to them.[38]

Little art adorned the house, but hundreds of books from Melvyn and Helen's collections lined the walls. Handsome furniture, much of it designed by Coates and covered with bright, expensive fabrics, provided dramatic focal pieces. The Douglases eventually hung a number of somber Käthe Kollwitz drawings of Nazis. In general, however, the house had a warm and inviting atmosphere. Pick recalled that "it was smart, but very comfortable, and not at all ostentatious"; very French Provincial. Even Melvyn, who had a difficult time adjusting to the enormous rooms he said could house a "camp of gypsies," grew to love their home. The house fit the Douglases' informal lifestyle. In their early years in California, they had done relatively little entertaining. Since their base shifted back and forth between Hollywood and New York, they had little time or energy to cultivate friends.[39]

Once they finally made up their minds in 1935 that California was their home, however, they branched out and began to develop new acquaintances. They entertained casually and frequently. Among the Hollywood set, they gravitated primarily to writers. Neither management types nor fellow actors, with a few exceptions, appealed to them. Both also used the house for business meetings and media interviews. As a couple they abhorred the social climbing and "brutal petty snobbery" typical of the upper echelons of the movie industry. Although they dressed handsomely (Helen enjoyed her furs) and owned two Cadillacs, they enjoyed these luxuries for their own sakes rather than as a means of identifying with their wealthy Hollywood co-workers. They found the elaborate parties that were so much a part of Hollywood society repulsive and disliked the flashy clothes and the fast-paced life that provided grist for Hollywood gossip columnists like Hedda Hopper and Louella Parsons. On rare occasions Helen would lend a hand to society fund-raisers, but she felt no need to spend time or energy mixing with the Hollywood élite. Melvyn recalled one of many experiences he found utterly distasteful. He picked up Peter from a birthday party; each of the hundreds of children received costly gifts and a circus had been hired for entertainment.[40]

The Douglases' busy schedules demanded considerable household help, and the number of servants varied with availability and changing needs. In the late 1930s their servants included a Russian cook, a live-in German couple who served as butler and maid, a gardener, and a nurse. On the cook's day off,

Melvyn often did the cooking. Helen shopped occasionally, particularly at the Farmers' Market, where she picked out whatever looked delicious. Walter Pick's responsibilities had increased so that he handled all correspondence and publicity and helped with entertaining. "It was almost a religion working with Helen and Mel," he recalled; "they changed my entire life."[41]

Although supervising the building of the new house occupied much of Helen's time in the fall and winter of 1937–1938, she also had a busy fall professionally. She prepared a series of radio programs for 1938 release, did a fall concert tour in Ohio, and prepared for her trip to Europe in January and February and two spring concerts in Los Angeles and Toronto. The time-consuming radio series proved to be a disaster. She recorded twenty-six programs in a soap-opera series for MGM called "Love for a Day," which was intended as a vehicle for Helen to sing. Although the pay was high, her principal motive for signing the contract was the opportunity to perform in a new medium. Unfortunately the series failed, in large measure because of poorly written scripts. The Ohio tour proved more satisfying than the radio venture. She excluded all German literature from her programs except the Marx songs. She sang in three Ohio cities—Dayton, Springfield, and Cleveland—where the audiences and critics received her enthusiastically. The local musical groups that sponsored her tour went out of their way to treat her as a native daughter returning home.[42]

When she returned to California, however, she had a difficult winter. She had her tonsils removed in December. "The poor girl suffered terribly," Pick wrote De Sola. Worried about her concert commitments, Gahagan flew to New York for some lessons with Cehanovska, who had moved back East. Helen returned full of her mentor's advice for protecting her voice. "Don't forget to do your mouth and lower jaw exercises a little each day," her instructions read. "Make grimaces with your face, to the left and right, yawn, and stick your tongue out like a poorly reared little girl."[43] Helen's European plans fell through, despite considerable correspondence with Kuba about details. In her autobiography, she commented that after her Salzburg experience she had no intention of returning to Europe. But her letters to Kuba suggest that until January 1938, even after her operation, she worked hard to arrange a schedule. The trip did not materialize, for reasons more complex than she remembered. The European situation had worsened since summer. In addition, her surgery postponed any singing until spring. She also became pregnant in November. But she did perform in Los Angeles and Toronto in the spring of 1938. By the time of the Canadian concert in April, she was five months pregnant and found singing very uncomfortable.

Except for her decision not to sing in Europe, Helen showed no outward signs of losing interest in her professional work as an actress and opera singer. Nevertheless, her performing career had drifted for some time, and she must have realized that. Pick felt the decline began when she canceled the Hollywood Bowl concert, which was intended as the "springboard" to United States engagements. After the Bowl incident, she no longer had the "same great drive."[44] Chances to sing in the United States had been limited all along and showed no signs of improving. She had never given up on the Metropolitan Opera, occasionally using her connections to audition. But she got nowhere. Despite great hopes for a major concert tour, her American bookings during the fall of 1937 and spring of 1938 were second- and third-rate. Hitler's takeover of Austria in 1938 and Czechoslovakia in mid-1938 and 1939 shut out European possibilities. Broadway performances became too complicated, and theater opportunities on the West Coast continued to decline. Film seemed a dead end, and her one radio venture failed. And she was expecting another child.

Up to this point, however, in spite of the bicoastal nature of the Douglases' careers, the couple had a very strong and romantic marriage and a loving household. In 1936, when quizzed by a reporter who seemed convinced that actor–actress marriages could never work, Melvyn retorted, "One of the secrets of successful marriage lies in . . . the community of interest our work in the films and on the stage has given us." Helen, not Melvyn, however, took full charge of household and parenting management. Dual-career marriages were becoming more acceptable in the 1930s, but the home still remained the province of the wife. When Helen acted in New York, she either took Peter with her or made certain that proper nursing care was provided. Unlike the vast majority of married working women, Helen had the financial resources to hire as much household help as necessary. Yet Helen spent considerable time with Peter, as did a new babysitter, Evelyn Chavoor, a student at the University of California, Los Angeles. "Evie," as she was called, who began helping out the Douglases in the fall of 1936, came from an immigrant Syrian family. Her father sold the Douglas family fresh fruits and vegetables from his truck. Peter was enrolled in school at three, perhaps partly to get him out from underfoot but also because Melvyn, more than Helen, continued to feel he needed to be in a structured and disciplined learning environment. While preschool enrollment is common practice today, that was not the case in the 1930s. Despite preschool, Peter remained an indulged child, Pick recalled; "difficult" even at an early age. When he misbehaved, neither parent could spank him. "I spanked him a couple of times." Then Melvyn and Helen would "break down, they'd just weep." Both found the process of trying to parent successfully very frustrating.[45]

6

The Move to Politics

WHILE HELEN'S PERFORMING FUTURE looked increasingly bleak, Melvyn, in stark contrast, continued to climb in prestige. He became one of Hollywood's highest-paid leading men, known for his fine comic timing, his handsome looks, and his ability to play well opposite Hollywood's female stars. Although Helen claimed later that she never felt jealous of Melvyn, a statement underscored by Walter Pick, she had always felt that they should both be equally successful and happy in their careers. His star was rising and with it his income. Helen's star was on the decline; she was vulnerable in 1938 to being pulled off in another direction. [1]

In the fall of 1937, Helen and Melvyn became drawn into the swirling political ferment in Hollywood. Helen's political awakening had occurred in Salzburg, a sudden, dramatic awareness of a world outside her own personal concerns. Melvyn encountered pro-Hitler sentiment in Americans on his boat trip back to the United States after accompanying Helen over in June. He found himself seated at the captain's table one evening with several Midwestern businessmen who were "viciously anti-Roosevelt—'that crippled bastard in the White House'—and completely admiring of Hitler and what he was doing in Germany." After hearing this viewpoint repeated throughout the trip, he recalled, "I was congealed with a kind of horror. It occurred to me that this probably represented a large, large body of opinion in our country, in which there was . . . very little understanding of the implications of what was going on in Germany." [2]

The Douglases' heightened awareness coincided with a dramatic change in the political climate in Hollywood. In the early 1930s, Hollywood had been a "never-never land of sunny skies, sleeping Beauties, and ivory towers," a center of political indifference. The politicization of the movie capital began with the formation of the Screen Writers Guild in 1933 and heightened during the End Poverty in California (EPIC) campaign in 1934 when socialist Upton Sinclair ran unsuccessfully for governor on the Democratic ticket against the conservative Republican, Frank F. Merriam. Artistic Jewish immigrants escaping from Nazism, like director Otto Preminger and composer Max Steiner, moved into Hollywood after 1933 and provided further impetus for a liberal, anti-fascist political consciousness.[3]

During these years, the conservative producers constantly conflicted with the liberal sentiment of the artistic community—initially the writers, a conflict that played itself out in disputes between labor and management. Louis B. Mayer even considered moving his giant studio to North Carolina. Soon thousands of other members of the artistic community of all ethnic and economic backgrounds joined hands with the screenwriters. By 1937, the community had become a hotbed of radical and liberal activity as political refugees continued to pour in, with fresh stories of fascism and Nazism. Hollywood celebrities like the Douglases, Lillian Hellman, and others who had recently traveled abroad verified the stories; still others, such as lawyer and writer Carey McWilliams, wrote compellingly about Hollywood's reaction to the fascist menace. As a result, Hollywood experienced "the most successful, most internationally oriented left-wing mobilization ever to occur in the United States." A writer in the *Screen Guild Magazine* wrote in February 1937: "We're up to our necks in politics and morality right now. Nobody goes to anybody's house any more to sit and talk and have fun. There's a master of ceremonies and a collection basket, because there are no gatherings except for Good Causes."[4]

Larry Ceplair and Stephen Englund, in their meticulous study *The Inquisition in Hollywood*, noted the deep radical sentiment of the early writers and "the presence of radicalizing historical factors like the Depression and . . . the New Deal, an awakening labor movement, and a revitalized Communist party." Atypical of radicalism in other areas of the United States, this atmosphere "provided a foundation for the reconstruction of a left-wing movement and culture" that had not been present in the country since the post–World War I Red scare. While the public found it difficult to accept the politicization of the movie world, as many regarded actors as unreal people with emotions and no ability to think, filmmakers became aware of the power of their names and potential political influence. Actors, directors, producers, and writers signed petitions and began making speeches in the typically emotional style of the movie community. Yet despite outside criticism and skepticism about the film industry's venture into political causes, many in Hollywood were thoughtful, serious, and effective speakers against fascism.[5]

This political mobilization was reflected within the Democratic Party throughout southern California, but most particularly in Los Angeles County. Hundreds joined either the Motion Picture Democratic Committee or the Studio Committee for Democratic Political Action to work for the gubernatorial challenge of Democratic candidate Culbert L. Olson against Merriam, a successful effort. Others also joined various organizations within a loose coalition of groups dedicated to causes including Communism, the New Deal, and anti-fascism, informally termed the Popular Front. Although these groups each focused on a specific cause, they all agreed that Roosevelt should take a stand against fascism both abroad and at home and should aid victims of fascist regimes, feelings greatly intensified by the fascist takeover in Spain by Generalissimo Francisco Franco. They also wanted to help protect the trade union movement against big business and supported New Deal domestic reform legislation. Hollywood's enthusiastic endorsement of causes provoked an almost manic response from the right, as manifested at the private level with corporate pressure and in both California and United States governmental organizations. The United States House Un-American Activities Committee (HUAC), initially called the Dies Committee after its chairman, Martin Dies, and later the California Un-American Activities Committee headed by the formerly liberal musician Jack B. Tenney, held numerous hearings in Hollywood. These investigative bodies were convinced that the Communist Party had organized all Popular Front organizations and members were either party members or at a very minimum, "fellow-travelers."

The most influential front organizations originating in Hollywood in 1937 included the Hollywood Anti-Nazi League, the Motion Picture Artists Committee to Aid Republican Spain, and the Motion Picture Democratic Committee. Other nationally well-known organizations with active Hollywood chapters, whose membership came into question almost immediately and again after World War II and during the McCarthy period, included the American Youth Congress, the Joint Anti-Fascist Refugee Committee, the Abraham Lincoln Battalion, Labor's Non-Partisan League, the Writers' and Artists' Committee for Medical Aid to Spain, and the National Lawyers Guild. The Hollywood Anti-Nazi League, spearheaded by screenwriter Donald Ogden Stewart, actor Fredric March, director Fritz Lang, and composer Oscar Hammerstein, became the most successful in the country. The League "served as a prototype" for Popular Front organizations; "a small nucleus of activist-celebrities" started the groups, which were run behind the scenes by a few salaried staff members and hundreds of volunteers. The group's most visible members included leading screen actors and writers of various political persuasions, from liberals to Communist Party members, but studio people of all crafts and even some non-Hollywood people joined in great numbers. The League became officially organized in the summer of 1936, when over 10,000 people gathered for a meeting where speakers such as Eddie Cantor, Hammerstein, Dorothy Parker, Gale

Sondergaard, Mayor Frank Shaw, and John Lechner of the American Legion spoke out strongly against fascism. At its height, the membership totaled between 4,000 and 5,000. As did most front organizations, the group represented a wide range of political views. Members of the American Communist Party consistently helped organize the Anti-Nazi League and all other front groups, despite their small numbers. Yet it was almost impossible to identify party members because of the common outlook they shared with liberals on fascism and social reform. Paul Jerrico, an active Communist Party member in the 1930s, said he thought Hollywood had no more than about 300 party members in the late 1930s. Noted screenwriter Philip Dunne, a politically active liberal Democrat and close friend of the Douglases, estimated about 250. These independent judgements from two different political vantage points underscore the awareness of the small numbers of actual Communists.[6]

During the early years of Hollywood's entrance into politics, the Douglases showed no interest in political participation. Melvyn had felt keenly about political and social issues as a teenager and in his early twenties, but he had never become active in organizations. He and Helen occasionally discussed politics in the early years of their marriage, but their professional and family concerns dominated their lives. In her extensive correspondence with Melvyn from 1931 to mid-1937, the only comment she made about events outside her own world concerned the 1936 election. "Wasn't the Roosevelt landslide wonderful. That shows a very hopeful sign for America, doesn't it? And certainly should curb Hearst's power." But she was singlemindedly oriented to her career and family. By the end of 1936, however, Melvyn showed signs of changing. In a letter to Helen in December 1936, he wrote that many people, particularly actors, had no identification with the world around them. When people lost that sense of identification they "are adrift, and begin to clutch at straws like the proverbial drowning man." These feelings were probably intensified by the fact that he was not entirely satisfied with screen acting. Helen listened to Melvyn's concerns, and after her experience in Europe both were ready to join the anti-fascist protest. They became members of the Hollywood Anti-Nazi League and also supported a group of fifty-six other prominent Hollywood people in signing a "Declaration of Independence" declaring a boycott of Nazi goods.

Initially Melvyn played a much more active role than Helen. He helped establish the Motion Picture Artists Committee to Aid Republican Spain and the Hollywood branch of the Joint Anti-Fascist Refugee Committee, both pro–Spanish Republican groups. His most sustained involvement came with the Motion Picture Democratic Committee, organized in the early summer of 1938. In June 1938, Melvyn sent a letter to the entire industry reminding individuals of the "Great Humiliation of 1934" when studio heads had pressured actors, screenwriters, directors, and producers to contribute one day's salary to Merriam's campaign. The organization held rallies, raised funds, printed pamphlets, and produced radio shows. Pick wrote De Sola that Melvyn had become "a great force within the Progressive ranks in California. Last night he spoke at a tremendous mass meeting . . . sponsored by the Anti-Nazi League and held as a challenge to Martin Dies and his investigating committee. Mel spoke so brilliantly and with such great intensity and directness that the 2700 people who were there applauded with such enthusiasm as I've never before heard." Pick closed with a tongue-in-cheek comment: "The Dies Committee for some reason neglected to stamp Melvyn a red—he is hurt because he was so forgotten." That fall Melvyn shared offices with the young politician Jerry Voorhis, who was later elected to Congress from the Los Angeles area. Although historians have mixed opinions about the importance of Douglas and the Hollywood vote in Culbert Olson's election, the new governor considered him the key to his Hollywood support, and New Dealers outside of California took note of the actor's political skills.[7]

During the months that Melvyn was immersed in the primary, Helen remained on the sidelines. After her Toronto concert in April, she cut back on all her activities. A baby girl, whom Helen and Melvyn named Mary Helen, was born in August 1938. Pick's amusing recollections of the day Mary Helen was born reveal Helen's uninhibited side, her flair for the dramatic, and enjoyment of being center stage. She planned to have labor induced. At the appointed time, the Douglases, Chavoor, and Pick arrived at Huntington Memorial Hospital in Pasadena. Helen had dressed in a velvet dressing gown with mink tails. The group had first stopped off at Occidental College to visit close friend and university president Remsen Bird. They made quite a stir in the hospital as they all trooped in. Several hours later, Mary Helen was born.[8]

The arrival of Mary Helen did not stop Helen from an unexpected move into the political arena. A newly created Hollywood group headed by Carey McWilliams, the John Steinbeck Committee to Aid Migratory Workers, held a meeting on the Douglases' patio in the early fall of 1938. This group had organized to arouse public awareness about the migrant problem. Although The Grapes of Wrath had not yet been published, author John Steinbeck was already known for his sympathetic treatment of the downtrodden. Helen, still recovering from childbirth and unpleasant back pain, did not attend the meeting. But at Pick's urging, she came to the patio door and listened to the lurid descriptions of the California migrant's conditions. These images reminded her of the 1931 cross-country trip when she and Melvyn followed a migrant train. Although she did not realize it then, she later recalled, "that afternoon I took my first step into politics."[9]

She accompanied Melvyn to another Steinbeck Committee meeting where discussion revolved around how to raise money for a Christmas party for migrant children. When she suggested soliciting donations from merchants, she ended up in charge of the party. Over the next few months Gahagan became better informed about the migrants. She found herself fascinated, and her initial curiosity evolved into a serious commitment to action. She began visiting the camps and attending meetings of people trying to demand state and federal support. When Governor Olson appointed Carey McWilliams chief of his Division of Immigration and Housing in early 1939, Gahagan replaced him as the committee's chair. She pursued the same goals as McWilliams: publicizing the problem, soliciting money, and encouraging the public to push for labor laws and social security that would include the migrants. She also urged improvements in housing, health services, and food distribution centers. Although Melvyn also participated in the committee's work, he concentrated on anti-fascist activities and Democratic Party politics.

In time Helen found herself in demand as a speaker. Drawing her information from the experts around her, such as McWilliams or Paul S. Taylor, professor of economics at the University of California at Berkeley and the leading academic expert in the country on agricultural labor, she articulated complex ideas and conveyed detailed information in a succinct and effective manner. She eventually drew the attention of migrant experts in Washington, including Arthur Goldschmidt, who worked for the Interior Department under Harold Ickes; and Aubrey Williams, head of the National Youth Authority. As Goldschmidt described his first encounter with Helen: "I found myself subjected to an intense cross-examination—grilling might not be too strong a word. She accepted no vague generalities. . . . Her questions were not naïve; . . . I came away . . . enchanted with a sense of wonder at Helen's display of energy—at the physical, emotional and mental drive of this beautiful and glamorous person." David E. Lilienthal noted in his diary after meeting Helen that she was "remarkably clear-headed and clear-spoken, and with such intensity, using a beautiful voice to accent her points."[10]

Helen found this new involvement stimulating. While she did not consciously decide to stop singing or acting, performance opportunities were scarce. She did not say whether having a second child affected her move into politics, but most likely it did not. The pull to politics evolved like the pull to singing—an exciting new adventure to replace an unsatisfying life outside her home. As the Douglases' political activities changed, so did their social life. They did have some close film friends, including Herbert Marshall, Ernst Lubitsch, and Edward G. Robinson and his wife Gladys, but they expanded their circle considerably when they entered the political scene. They became particularly close during this period to their first academic friends, Remsen and Helen Bird, a couple they met through Elinor Remick Warren, a close composer-and-pianist friend of Helen's. The Birds enjoyed mingling with people who were both intellectually stimulating and glamorous, and the Douglases fit that description. Although a political conservative, Remsen Bird had become a Roosevelt enthusiast and was drawn into the politically liberal Hollywood circles that centered around the Douglases. The Birds were also part of a small cluster of intellectuals in Carmel whom the Douglases became close to after they built a small but enticing retreat overlooking the Carmel Mission grounds in 1938. In addition to the Birds, and Totheroh when he was in Los Angeles, who also socialized in the resort town, their group of friends who lived in Carmel included writer Noel Sullivan, poet Robinson Jeffers and his wife Una, and actress Cornelia Clampett and her husband, playwright and novelist Martin Flavin.[11]

Melvyn's political work hurt him at MGM. In 1939, Louis B. Mayer, head of the studio, called Melvyn to his office for their first conversation outside of routine formal greetings. Melvyn's most recent film, *Ninotchka*, had been a box office hit and gained critical acclaim. In this movie he played the part of a gigolo who converted a tough Soviet Communist Party official, played by Greta Garbo, to capitalism. While a comedy, the movie also sharply indicted Communism. Melvyn did the film in large measure to demonstrate his anti-Communist political stand, but that carried no weight with Mayer. Mayer made it clear to Douglas that actors should stick to acting, since political activities "hurt the studio." Douglas responded that given the current world situation, participation was critical. He refrained from reminding Mayer that it was liberal politics that the studio moguls did not like, not politics *per se*. When Mayer realized "he wasn't getting very far," Douglas recalled, Mayer "suddenly said to me, 'Your wife's an actress, isn't she?' I said 'yes.' So he looked up at me rather cutely and said, 'Don't you think she would like a nice contract with MGM?' " This comment infuriated Melvyn, and he suggested that he break his contract. Although Mayer backed away from Melvyn's threat, Douglas's relationship with the studio cooled perceptibly, despite the huge success of *Ninotchka*. He became convinced that after that point MGM went out of its way to prevent him from getting any "plums."[12]

In the summer of 1939, Aubrey Williams brought the Douglases and their California political activities to the attention of the Roosevelts. The President had recently signaled his determination to address the migrant issues by ordering a federal investigation. Both Roosevelts had read *The Grapes of Wrath*, published in April 1939, which had aroused both public concern and controversy. Two other books furnished additional persuasive documentation—Carey McWilliams' *Factories in the Field* and the moving pictorial study *An American Exodus* by Paul Taylor and his wife, Dorothea Lange, an acclaimed photographer noted for her stunning Farm Security Administration photographs of rural conditions. In addition, the publicity surrounding the findings of the United States Senate La Follette Committee investigating the deprivation of migrant civil rights added to the swell of public outrage.

Williams was aware of Melvyn's rising stature in the California Democratic

Party. He was not only well informed but, like Helen, very articulate. Lilienthal commented about Melvyn, after meeting him at a dinner, that he had "hardly expected to come to Hollywood to hear one of the best expressions of the New Deal philosophy I had ever heard." Williams wrote Roosevelt that Melvyn thought movie people could play a larger role in preserving and extending the New Deal, support the President sorely needed, given the general decline of New Deal programs and the rise in conservative political strength after the 1938 congressional election. Melvyn had told Williams that he wanted to meet the President. "You will remember [he] is one of the top flight motion picture people," Williams reminded FDR. Williams also knew that both Roosevelts would profit from hearing Helen's first-hand account of some migrant camps. Eleanor Roosevelt responded quickly to the suggestion. She wrote Helen: "The President and I hope very much that you and Mr. Douglas can come to Washington on November 30 to dine and spend the night with us. [We] would so much like to see you." When the Douglases accepted, the First Lady inquired about the time of their arrival so that "we can have a White House car meet you." The Douglases, logically, felt both excited and a bit overwhelmed. Helen revealed her discomfort to Melvyn that night. The two had been given separate bedrooms, as they had at home, but Helen insisted that Melvyn join her for the night. The next morning Melvyn went to his bedroom and "rumpled up the bed so the maid wouldn't think that they couldn't stay away from each other at least in the White House." [13]

That evening and over the next few days, the Douglases met a large group of high-ranking New Dealers who were as eager to rub shoulders with the bright, articulate, enthusiastic, and glamorous Hollywood couple as the Douglases were to meet Washington's political élite. Those who met the Douglases on this first visit included Attorney General Frank Murphy (soon to be appointed to the Supreme Court); Secretary of the Interior Harold L. Ickes and his assistant, Oscar Chapman; Judge Francis Biddle, who became Attorney General in 1941; and Secretary of Labor Frances Perkins. Several, including Ickes, Perkins, and Dorothy McAllister, head of the Democratic Party's Women's Division, entertained the Douglases. Helen and Melvyn left Washington exhilarated. Williams' intuition had proven correct. Melvyn had promised that the Motion Picture Democratic Committee (MPDC) would do all it could for the floundering New Deal. The Roosevelts were drawn to the Douglases, and a special friendship, from which both couples stood to benefit, took shape almost immediately. Melvyn and Helen both became close to the President and First Lady, an unusual friendship for the Roosevelts, who generally maintained their separate circle of friends. [14]

While both Douglases felt committed to promoting Roosevelt's goals, the reasons for their commitment differed. Melvyn's dedication to FDR and the New Deal grew out of twenty years of acquaintances with liberal thought, an interest that drew him into Democratic Party activity in the 1938 race for California governor. Helen's political awareness was recent and grew during her trip to Europe and afterwards with her migrant work. She channeled her concerns into the Democratic Party once she met the Roosevelts. Her commitment to FDR's policies emerged from her effusive affection for the Roosevelts. While Helen was certainly aware of the political benefits of the Roosevelt connection, her motivation in cultivating the relationship had to do principally with her personal feelings. She regarded ER, as the First Lady was often called, as a warm friend and a political role-model. The President loomed as an awesome figure whose interest in her welfare flattered and inspired her.

After the whirlwind week in Washington, Helen turned her attention to her second migrant Christmas party. She wrote details to Eleanor Roosevelt's secretary, Malvina "Tommy" Thompson. Although local Imperial Valley conservatives thought the Steinbeck Committee had "a red flag in one hand [and] a bomb in the other," the party attracted over 8,000 migrants. Shortly after the party, however, Helen decided to resign from the committee. Neither she nor Melvyn knew how to deal with Communist Party members on their committees who had become identifiable when Russia signed the Non-Aggression Pact with Germany in September of 1939. American Communists suddenly began objecting to the anti-fascist stands of the liberal organizations. The Popular Front fell apart quickly as non-Communist liberals dropped their membership. Helen officially resigned in March 1940, although two months earlier she had essentially abandoned her responsibilities on the grounds that "dissenting spirits" made it difficult for her to be an effective chair. She wrote Congressman Jerry Voorhis, with whom she had begun to correspond regularly about their mutual interest in migrants, that she found herself in the "absurd position of most liberals today. The Communists call us reactionaries and the reactionaries call us Communists!" Despite her departure from the Steinbeck Committee in January 1940, she promised that she would continue to work on the migrant problem.[15]

Melvyn dropped out of the MPDC after harassment from certain Communist members. He was convinced that key motion picture industry people could make a difference in electing a Democratic president in 1940, and he worked hard to get the Communists out of the group. "There is little doubt in any quarter as to our possible value. . . . I talked to most of the Washington 'glamor boys and girls' . . . and I stressed the fact that we needed them to attract the 'glamor crowd' in Hollywood and I have their assurances of real cooperation." But when he realized that he could not persuade the Motion Picture Democratic Committee to support FDR's stand opposing Russian aggression in Finland, he resigned.[16]

The Douglases next threw their energy into organizing the California Citizen's Council to provide a forum for non-Communist liberals to discuss issues.

The initial group included the Birds; producer Walter Wanger; lawyer John Packard and his wife, both former Socialists; active Democrat Mary Workman; and the editor of the liberal *Los Angeles Daily News*, Manchester Boddy. At the same time that Helen worked with Melvyn to draw together southern California liberals, she took her initial steps into the Democratic women's organizations, steps that not only linked her more closely to Eleanor Roosevelt but also provided her entrée into Democratic politics. Her first exposure was to the politically conservative Democratic Study Clubs, organized nationally at the end of the nineteenth century to study political issues. The clubs did not have much political power and did not play an active role in party politics. The state club head, long-time Democrat Nettie Jones (who generally went by "Mrs. Mattison Boyd Jones"), had asked Helen to speak on migrants at the group's state convention, which she was organizing for mid-February.[17]

Two weeks before the convention, Jones found herself in the middle of squabbles in both the San Francisco Bay area and southern California over her handling of convention arrangements. The hostility erupted initially over the plans for the convention keynoter, Secretary of Labor Frances Perkins. Jones, who also headed the more liberal Democratic Party's Women's Division in southern California, a national group organized in 1933 by Eleanor Roosevelt as an official arm of the party, had apparently reneged on her promise to include the liberal Democratic women in the convention planning. But the feuding had deep roots in the clashes in Sacramento between Olson liberals and conservative Democrats over legislative policy and accusations of corruption and Communist infiltration of the State Relief Administration, the agency that provided aid to migrant workers. Three recall movements mounted by various conservative citizens' groups against the governor had further complicated the issues. The fight also revealed deep, bitter schisms among women in the north and south, and between the Women's Division, the Democratic Study Clubs, and nonpartisan groups such as the League of Women Voters.

Gahagan, not yet a member of any group of Democratic women, kept out of the fighting. Capitalizing on her personal relationship with Perkins, which had begun in Washington the previous November, Gahagan and Remsen Bird planned a small dinner and larger reception for liberal and conservative Los Angeles civic leaders plus some Hollywood figures to add glamor. They hoped that the meeting might lessen conservatives' hostility to Roosevelt. Her dinner list included Manchester Boddy, the Birds, Carey McWilliams, and George Martin, a bank vice-president. At the reception that followed, she included Mayor Fletcher Bowron and his wife, prominent members of the conservative Associated Farmers and the Chamber of Commerce, and a wide cross-section of liberals, including academics, lawyers, businessmen, and political organizers. Helen's notations accompanying her guest list reveal her style. Beside one name she wrote, "wholesale groceries, a darling, Jewish. Was head of Merchants and Manufacturers for 60 yrs in California." None of the people involved in the women's fight were invited; not even Jones. Gahagan planned to cement her relationship with Perkins without competition from other political women. Her gesture to Perkins paid off. Walter Pick recalled that it "turned out to be an extremely successful evening. . . . It was the beginning of Helen and Mel being really tied into the community . . . and Remsen was responsible for all that." The Secretary of Labor wrote Gahagan a warm, friendly letter: "The evening at your house was of great importance and help to me . . . in comprehending the fears, the hopes, the doubts of the influential Californians, who are conservative but not irresponsible. . . . I am very grateful to you for the effort, the discrimination, the warmth and the taste with which you gathered together that particular group for my edification. . . . I hope that our friendship has only just begun. . . . Please always look me up when you are east." Helen responded that Perkins' visit to California had been a "real triumph" and had opened conservatives' eyes to the New Deal so that "a little light may reach into the dark places." Gahagan added that she did plan to be in Washington in April and perhaps Perkins might "have a moment to spare me."[18]

Also in February 1940, Gahagan gained some national visibility from an article she published on migrants. Dorothy McAllister, head of the National Democratic Party's Women's Division, had asked her to write the piece for the February issue of the Division's widely read monthly magazine, *Democratic Digest*. Douglas drew from her research material and first-hand knowledge of migrants from her visits to the camps to review briefly in a well-written article the history of the migrant problem in the Southwest. She graphically described the daily life of the migrants in the Farm Security Administration camps. She urged state and local governments to respond to the physical and emotional needs of migrants. Communities must assimilate the migratory worker, she argued, and most important, must "recognize him for his true worth—a vital and necessary element in the agriculture structure [and] a human being whose mental, physical and spiritual welfare affects the community and the country at large." McAllister thought the article one of the best treatments of a complex problem ever to appear in the *Digest*, and both she and Gahagan received complimentary letters on it. Even United States Supreme Court Justice William O. Douglas took the time to jot a note to Helen saying that he found the article "*most* interesting." McAllister, seeing Gahagan as a woman worth cultivating, invited her to speak on migrants for the Women's Division's first National Institute of Government in Washington. McAllister intended this conference as a forum to educate party women about campaign issues and the techniques for effective party organization in time for the fall campaign.[19]

As Helen began to involve herself with organized Democratic women, she continued to develop her relationship with Eleanor Roosevelt. Helen wrote her new friend that she had learned that the First Lady, who planned a trip to California in April, hoped to visit some migrant camps since FDR had urged his key advisors to gather first-hand information about the migrant problem. Gahagan asked if she might offer her "services . . . in arranging as comprehensive a tour as possible?" Roosevelt accepted. Helen planned the visit carefully. She contacted Taylor and Lange for advice as to the best camps to tour. Helen chartered a small private plane, and in early April she and Melvyn flew with Eleanor Roosevelt to the lush San Joaquin Valley, where the Federal Housing Administration's regional head, Lawrence Hewes, met them and served as their guide through several camps. The tour reassured the First Lady about conditions in the government camps and convinced her that Steinbeck had accurately portrayed the crisis in *The Grapes of Wrath*. She filled her *My Day* column for three days with enthusiastic comments about the trip. She wrote Helen, "I know the President will be enormously interested in what I have to tell him." She continued, "I am counting on having you stay at the White House when you come to Washington for the National Institute of Government." Helen answered that while she had "promised not to write . . . I felt guilty not letting you know how much your trip meant to the people we visited." She also accepted the White House invitation, as long as it did not "inconvenience" the First Lady. Two weeks later, Roosevelt asked Gahagan to become a member of a National Advisory Committee for Community Service Projects to advise the Works Progress Administration on extending its programs.[20]

Gahagan was on her way up. To some it may have appeared that she had her sights set on attaining political power as quickly as possible. But that was not the case at this stage. She had a new direction in her life, and she rushed into it as she had into acting and singing in the 1920s. After her visit with the Roosevelts she became a New Deal convert. She held both Eleanor and Franklin in the highest regard, with a reverence that suggested almost a religious conversion. She again had a "fairy godmother" to ease the way. Eleanor Roosevelt, like Grimball and Cehanovska before her, took Helen by the hand to encourage and instruct her. Just as Helen was able to avoid knocking on theater doors, so was she able to bypass the tedious trenchwork generally required of women entering politics.

How drastic a change was Helen's move into politics? The parallels between acting and politics are interesting. Both actors and politicians use a stage; they play roles; they strive to persuade their audiences; they both have scripts. Helen excelled from the beginning in political life because she could speak effectively before an audience. She presented her message—her script—in a persuasive manner. She was very attractive and engaging, she had a maturity that lent strength to her persuasive manner, and she had a contagious enthusiasm. A director of the Town Hall Forum of the West wrote Melvyn about a speech

Helen gave for his group. He commented, "I have seldom heard a more magnificent woman speaker than your wife—they are rare on the American platform. The forceful woman is usually the straight Feminist or Careerist—and
that in itself blocks the audience's sympathy—but your wife has the rare combination of intelligence and spirituality . . . that still spell WOMAN."[21]

Gahagan's trip to Washington for the Women's Division National Institute of
Government in May 1940 proved yet another steppingstone in establishing her
credibility as a new but effective New Dealer. The Women's Division played
up Gahagan's participation prominently in the pre-Institute publicity. She and
Molly Dewson, one of the most prominent Democratic women of the Roosevelt administration and a Roosevelt intimate, were the only two delegates invited to stay at the White House. Gahagan arrived a day early to attend a
dinner Frances Perkins gave in her honor. McAllister and her staff prepared an
excellent program: seminars with Cabinet members and other administrative
officials and a tea hosted by the Roosevelts on the White House lawn. Mc-
Allister had asked all Democratic members of Congress to encourage their state's
best women to attend the Institute and to entertain them when they were in
Washington. Much of the careful planning disintegrated, however, when five
thousand instead of the expected five hundred women poured into the capital.
Despite the problems, McAllister was euphoric over the response to the Institute and resulting press coverage, for it offered concrete evidence that women
had both the interest and the ability to play a significant role in the fall election. Official Washington's response also demonstrated that, in some sectors at
least, the party power structure took women seriously.
    After the conference, Gahagan stayed on at the White House and enjoyed
more parties in her honor. Perkins' assistant, Mary LaDame, gave her a tea;
Supreme Court Justice William O. Douglas and his wife and other prominent
New Dealers had dinners for her. Eleanor Roosevelt and the Ickes both entertained Gahagan at lunch. She visited with Secretary of Agriculture Henry A.
Wallace, conferred with Representative John Tolan from the Berkeley area about
the creation of a special House investigating committee on the migrants, and
testified before a Senate subcommittee. She also attended a meeting of the
White House Advisory Committee on Community Services. Before returning
to Los Angeles she traveled to McAllister's home base, Grand Rapids, Michigan, as well as to Chicago and Oklahoma, to speak on the migrant situation at
conferences of social welfare professionals.[22]
    The trip left no doubt that Gahagan had established herself as an attractive
political newcomer. She had gained national attention for her publicity of the
agricultural labor issue and had also considerably expanded her contacts in
Washington. Despite her apparent success, however, she needed reassurance.
She wrote Eleanor Roosevelt about her appearance before the Senate subcom-

mittee shortly after returning to Los Angeles. "I hope I said the right things. One gets kind of panicky. Sometimes it seems as though one is swimming in a sea of words—empty and inadequate words that convey no meaning—just frothy, foamy things that make a loud noise but in no way . . . pave the way for a better understanding. I think maybe we should invent something else to take their place." She also thanked her for her "kindness and generous hospitality. But thank you most for being you. I could go on and on about how Melvyn and I feel about the President and his beautiful wife but you are so wise in so many things that I am sure you know and understand all we would like to say. . . . [but] thank you for letting me be so close to you for so long." Roosevelt wrote back not to worry. She had heard that Helen had done a "marvelous piece of work" testifying before the committee. "Everyone said you were exactly right and that you touched everybody there and yet were very restrained." She added that she had also learned that Helen had made an excellent presentation at one of the social-worker meetings "so you can feel that you are doing very good work." In closing, she sent "kindest regards" from the President. "Do not [overdo] and kill yourself, because we need good people alive."[23]

Gahagan returned to a tense political situation in California, exacerbated by the national concern over Hitler's successes in Europe and Roosevelt's shifting policy on neutrality. Melvyn was part of the current uproar. Olson had appointed several prominent Californians, including Melvyn, to the honorary position of Lieutenant Colonel of Intelligence in the National Guard without consulting any of the appointees. Melvyn learned of the appointment in the newspaper. Shortly after the press release, conservative Democrats Assemblyman Chester Gannon and Assembly Speaker Gordon Garland attacked Melvyn as a "Communist linked with subversive activities," and introduced a resolution opposing his appointment and requesting an FBI investigation. Melvyn was furious at Olson for not consulting with him prior to making the appointment. He agreed with the American Legion, which had joined in the attack, that he was not qualified for the job. But the "insinuations as to my Communist activities are not only baseless but vicious." As he told the governor, people have "taken advantage of this incident to make me their victim . . . for sheer political reasons or because of their complete misunderstanding of my activities." Any investigation, he went on, would establish that he had no regard for Communists. Some people freely called people subversive when their views did not agree. "In these perilous times, such hasty and unfounded condemnation is an attack upon the very foundations of all that we as Americans hold dear." He requested that the governor retract the appointment. He also asked both Attorney General Robert H. Jackson and Martin Dies, chairman of the House Un-American Activities Committee, to investigate him to prove his innocence. Jackson replied that he did not have time and it would not serve a useful purpose. Dies said he had no evidence that Douglas was a Communist but he was welcome to come to a hearing. Melvyn declined that invitation. The worst part of all to Melvyn was the widespread adverse publicity, including a "crack" in *Time* magazine that he considered exceptionally insulting.[24]

Helen wrote ER that the attacks upset her, both on Melvyn's account and because it would affect her own political activity. The First Lady, a long-time target for Red-baiters, told Helen that the publicity would not harm her in the long run. In the letter she addressed her as "Helen" for the first time, indicating a new level of closeness. "I loved your letter and I wanted to send you a wire at once to tell you not to be worried when they accuse you and Mr. Douglas of being Communists." Other astute political friends thought the Douglases had cause for concern, however. Margaret Workman wrote McAllister that although the Douglases had made a fine political contribution, "the recent episode . . . has unfortunately lessened their influence with public opinion to a marked degree. It will take some time to overcome the fear that has been produced by all the publicity." They were vulnerable because they had not been associated with the Democratic Party for any length of time. "I feel but cannot prove," she continued, "that this whole situation was planned and executed by reactionary forces within our own Party." Although the attacks did not noticeably damage the Douglases at this point, they both were targets of Red-baiting all during the 1940s. Liberals in California had been targeted as un-American throughout the 1920s and 1930s, particularly in Los Angeles.[25]

McAllister seemed unperturbed. She held Helen in increasingly high esteem, appointing her as one of eighteen prominent Democratic women to serve on a Women's Advisory Committee to draft legislation for the Platform Committee of the upcoming national convention. New Jersey congresswoman Mary Norton chaired the committee; other appointees included former congresswoman Nan Wood Honeyman from Oregon, Utah's national committeewoman, Carolyn Wolfe, Molly Dewson, and Virginia Gildersleeve, dean of Barnard College. Since the 1940 Platform Committee followed for the first time a "50-50 Rule" that required one man and one woman from each state and territory, McAllister anticipated that the Women's Advisory Committee would carry some weight.[26]

In June, Helen took advantage of a couple of weeks to relax and enjoy her children. She had been away from Peter, almost six, and twenty-month-old Mary for over six weeks. She wrote Perkins: "Two days ago I arrived home. I was very glad to get here and haven't been able to do much of anything but play with the children. How quickly they grow. Little Mary Helen is starting to talk which fills me with delight but also with unhappiness at the thought that I am losing my baby."[27]

As the date for the 1940 Democratic Convention grew closer, tensions among the splintered California Democrats continued to increase. At the primaries in

May, party members chose between four slates of delegates, each pledged to a different candidate. Dissension even extended to the Roosevelt supporters. FDR sent Ickes out to investigate. He held a meeting of key Roosevelt-slate Democrats, which included the principal organizer, Governor Olson; and Melvyn Douglas. The *Los Angeles Times* wrote: "California's Democratic party has become the New Deal's problem child," and Ickes was about to give it a "good, old-fashioned spanking." Despite his efforts to force reconciliation, however, he could do little to rectify the unhealthy condition of the party. The Roosevelt slate won.[28] In June, the convention delegates began talking about their selection of a national committeeman and committeewoman, which would occur at the national convention. The outgoing holders of those positions, the influential former senator William Gibbs McAdoo and San Franciscan Lucretia Grady, wife of Assistant Secretary of State Henry Grady, had the respect of their colleagues. Many felt that Olson, who wanted to be nominated national committeeman, deserved the position. Some delegates wanted Grady replaced with a woman who lived in California, not Washington. In addition, many believed the positions should rotate between the north and south.

Three candidates surfaced for committeewoman: Grady, Nettie Jones, and Helen Gahagan. In Washington, McAllister, serving as a sounding board for the various factions, kept in close touch with the women. Grady gradually faded out of the competition, leaving the field to Jones and Gahagan. Jones badly wanted the position and she had considerable support. Hundreds of southern California women she had worked with over the years signed a petition that stated that Jones deserved this position after her years of service to the party. Although Gahagan had only entered the political scene six months before, she drew grassroots support from women who still resented the way Jones had failed to include the Women's Division in the Perkins visit in February. Gahagan also appealed to those who found her more likeable than the older, heavyset Jones, who had a prickly personality and a conservative outlook. Gahagan later reflected that she was not seeking the position of national committeewoman; she did not even know what one was. She did recall, however, that her friend George Creel, a prominent California Democrat who had been active in the Woodrow Wilson administration, urged her to accept the job if she won it. Various contemporaries' reports also suggested that she was indeed interested.[29]

Jones logically regarded Gahagan as a threat and had become increasingly wary throughout the spring of 1940 as Gahagan became more visible in the state and nationally. Jones's husband, a prominent Los Angeles lawyer and an active conservative Democrat, seized an early opportunity to discredit Helen. He wrote Olson in March that he had heard Gahagan give a speech in which she had "revealed herself unquestionably to me, my wife, and the [large] audience that she was a Communist. . . . I hope you will not consider this a letter written with any motive other than in the interest of our Party and our country." Nettie Jones was convinced that Melvyn Douglas had shut her out of the intraparty fighting over the Roosevelt slate. Although Jones was finally selected as one of four women on the Roosevelt slate, she did not get invited to the Ickes meeting. She blamed her exclusion from the Executive Committee of the Roosevelt delegation campaign committee on Melvyn, who helped appoint the committee. The head of the Women's Division in the south, she wrote McAllister, should certainly be on the Executive Committee "by virtue of recognizing organization work rather than personalities." As a further blow, she told McAllister, she had not been permitted to visit with Eleanor Roosevelt when she came to see the migrant camps in April. When McAllister appointed Gahagan, not Jones, to the Platform Committee's advisory committee, Jones felt further insulted.[30]

The friction intensified as the convention date in early July neared. The *San Francisco Chronicle* called the problem an "acrimonious row over the selection of a new national committeeman and national committeewoman." Although many felt Melvyn Douglas deserved the nomination, Olson wanted the position, and as titular head of the party had a right to the job. In the end, Olson and Helen Gahagan won the nominations. Many interpreted Helen's victory as a trade-off to appease Melvyn. The argument continued that Helen had little political standing in July 1940; only in the fall did she begin to build a base independent of her husband. This theory, however, failed to take into account Helen's activities during the first six months of the year. The many contacts she had made, primarily through her close association with Eleanor Roosevelt, combined with her personal assets, made Helen a viable alternative to Nettie Jones. In Helen's words, support for Jones "just washed out."[31]

Winning the office thrust Gahagan into the center of Democratic National Committee (DNC) activity at the Chicago convention. Her appointment drew national attention. She seemed to feel at ease in her new role, enjoying the publicity that she and Melvyn attracted and feeling quite comfortable mingling with the top Democrats. She also witnessed an exciting convention for women. McAllister addressed the convention, the first such speech by a woman. Women participated in the Democratic Resolutions Committee, also a first. Almost all the Women's Advisory Committee recommendations were incorporated in the final platform and several of the planks adopted verbatim. After the convention ended, the exhausted Gahagan took a break and resurrected her part of the prima donna singer in *Tonight or Never* at Maplewood, New Jersey. She did a week of performances, and then announced that she would not return to the theater until after the election. "I want to get into this campaign." She returned to Washington. After a few days in Washington staying with the Ickes, she returned home to face a busy schedule in the political campaign.[32]

Democratic women formally launched the campaign in southern California on August 12 with a well-attended luncheon in Gahagan's honor at the Hollywood Bowl. She began working with dozens of local clubs and Democratic leaders throughout the state. In her speeches to women, she generally discussed why she entered politics and what the New Deal and FDR had done for the country. Jones and her supporters continued to resent the new committee-woman. Jones grumbled that Gahagan had won the post because of her legs. One prominent active Democrat commented, however, that Helen certainly was not a "sex pot," and actually, "her legs weren't all that attractive." Complaints from Jones and her camp crossed McAllister's desk and reached Eleanor Roosevelt and Frances Perkins. "To the utter amazement and chagrin of all of us," one wrote to Roosevelt, Helen Gahagan had become the new committee-woman. She "may be an estimable woman and a leader in her chosen profession as a singer and actress," but, she legitimately complained, "she is utterly unknown to the loyal, faithful women who helped to make a Democratic victory possible in this normally Republican State in 1932, and 1936." The writer alluded to newspaper reports on Gahagan's alleged "close association . . . with extremely radical groups in our community," and argued that "the party needs the help of those women who have friends and neighbors who will vote with them but have no great interest in the glamour of movie or stage stars." She expressed hope that Eleanor Roosevelt could "alleviate the harm done to the Party here." Jones complained that Helen had not consulted her about any of the women's activities for the fall. "I honestly thought that when Miss Gahagan assured me that I would have full charge of the Women's campaign that she meant what she said." McAllister downplayed the protest. She wrote Helen that she had received only one protest letter and many complimentary ones. "The women are enthusiastic over your leadership and appreciate your intelligent grasp of the issues and devotion to the New Deal cause. You have accomplished more in the short time since you have been National Committee-woman than anyone else has in the state in years."[33]

Despite McAllister's apparent lack of concern, the animosities and jealousies were destructive to California's Women's Division activities because the program had no director. Jones resigned the position officially and no one had replaced her. Gahagan apparently gave her free rein to work with the women, yet Jones complained (probably justifiably) that Gahagan ignored her. Helen had no clear directives for action as national committeewoman except that McAllister urged her to present the factions as united. Part of the confusion resulted from poor organization at the state level. Secretary of State Paul Peek headed the statewide campaign efforts, but he did not organize at the precinct level in most cases. One astute observer said that Peek did not know "what it's all about," and Gahagan might know a lot about migrants but she did not know "what a precinct looks like."[34]

Gahagan tried to rise above the friction by concentrating on the big issues and leaving the bickering and detail to others. She helped organize the visit of

Henry Wallace, FDR's running mate, which she termed "triumphant." Wallace spoke before 18,000 in the Hollywood Bowl and received good coverage from all the papers. Over 1,400 came to the luncheon in his honor and hundreds of others had to be turned away. Gahagan also managed to get Eleanor Roosevelt to come to southern California for a campaign speech in October. Gahagan introduced her to the gathering of 1,500 women, thus clearly establishing her closeness to the First Lady. During the critical pre-election week of October 19 through 25, the DNC sent Gahagan on a speaking tour of key Midwestern states. The National Committee Speakers' Bureau told her later that her "presence and message inspired many of our people to greater activity." In all, she made over 250 speeches during the campaign, an impressive and exhausting accomplishment, especially for a novice politician.[35]

Melvyn also played an important role in the Roosevelt campaign. He concentrated his efforts, coordinated out of the DNC office in Washington, on large rallies that used Hollywood personalities to attract the public. He also worked to win support in the movie capital. "Hollywood is not all glamour . . . neither is it very damned dumb," he contended at the Hollywood Bowl rally with Wallace. The community clearly realized that "the driving force behind New Deal legislation . . . has been a deeper concern for the rise and the welfare of the average American citizen." Both Douglases worried about Roosevelt's chances in California, despite a two-to-one Democratic lead in registration. Helen wrote Ickes in mid-October that she was, like him, scared. She would "wake in the night with cold chills. There is division in the Democratic ranks and there are those who call themselves Democrats who belong anywhere but in our ranks. . . . We just have to pray that there are enough of us who are using elbow grease and trying to get around in time to make them all realize the vital necessity of getting to the polls." She spoke directly to Ickes' feeling of impotence in the campaign. "Don't let them push you out of this campaign. I am sending today a telegram to the President, asking him to send you out here. We need your fire and your mental clarity. It is a way of life that is at stake this November and that must be made clear to the people in power who do not care." She also agreed with him that Edward Flynn, the DNC head, was a "dud."[36]

During the campaign, life at the Douglas household was even more chaotic than usual. Pick described the situation to De Sola. "If you could see us these days you would think you were in Grand Central Station at the noon hour rush or, if you prefer, take Times Square on New Year's Eve. It is a madhouse." If Melvyn was not at the studio he was "either writing campaign speeches or making them, 'ditto for Helen.'" All three phones rang constantly, two typewriters were in continual use, and a "stream of telegraph boys and people to interview" came to the house constantly. And one afternoon "the devil or something appealed to Mary Helen's destructive nature during what should have been her sleeping period, resulting in giving her room the appearance that a hurricane had struck it. I guess psychologists call this the inquisitive age. She sampled everything from tooth paste to nail polish, and the debris remaining from an afternoon of adventure was scattered everywhere."[37]

Despite concerns, Roosevelt took California by a landslide. Party officials recognized both Douglases for their contributions to the victory. Helen's speaking ability surpassed that of more seasoned politicians, and she had proven that she had the power to draw a crowd. Together the Douglases had led the campaign efforts of Hollywood Democrats. Melvyn made good his promise to involve, for the first time, the talents of numerous film stars in the campaign, a practice continued in subsequent campaigns. Ickes wrote the Douglases that they had both done a "great job. By the time that 1944 rolls around you will be seasoned campaigners. In that year of grace, I am going to sit on the sidelines and watch how younger and more competent people can do it." Once the campaign ended, the Douglases tried to slow down, although Helen had committed herself to organizing a third migrant Christmas party. She wrote a friend, "We are up here in Carmel trying to recover from post-campaign pneumonia, flu and God knows what all. Everybody in the family was sick (with Xmas for 11,000 migrants sick or no sick)."[38]

But Helen and Melvyn recovered by the time of the inaugural and flew to Washington on January 17. Their arrival elicited considerable publicity. "Melvyn Douglas Leads Influx of Film Stars for Inaugural" said one headline, with a photo of the Douglases debarking from the plane. Hollywood notables Mickey Rooney, Charlie Chaplin, Ethel Barrymore, Douglas Fairbanks, Jr., and Edward G. Robinson also attended. During the festivities the Douglases stayed with the Ickes and attended various functions at which the Roosevelts were present. After the inaugural events, Melvyn returned to Los Angeles, but Helen stayed on, moving into the White House for a few more days of parties. At one event the press noted that unlike most of the wives, "pretty Helen Gahagan . . . was deep in political discussion with a group of 'big wigs.' Incidentally she wore one of the best looking tailored costumes—a narrow maroon hip-length striped jacket on black over a black skirt and a severely tailored blouse." Helen attended the National Theatre with ER one evening and lunched with her on another day.[39]

Gahagan returned to a busy household in California, including sick children. She wrote a friend that she had been "literally standing on my head ever since I have been home with nurses, doctors, the Democratic Central Committee, my brother and his wife who are here from the East, Flynn who chose this moment to come to California and countless other things that I don't want to worry you with." She thanked Eleanor Roosevelt for the "beautiful visit at the White House . . . [and] for all your kindness to me. My visits with the President and you are something that you must know I prize very dearly." She also said that Peter, who was still ill, was happy with the presents the First Lady sent him. "He sends you his love and says that he will write you as soon as he is able to sit up. We are all looking forward to having you with us in California in April."[40]

She also answered the young and pretty Jane Ickes, who had asked her for her "beauty secrets." In a rare disclosure of her thoughts about her personal appearance, Gahagan wrote Ickes that she really did not know any secrets, and Ickes did not need advice. But Helen did think that the best skin lotion was Squibb's odorless mineral oil and Squibb's odorless castor oil. She thought them much better than cold creams, which did "more harm than good." She also sent Jane some lipstick and brown mascara. "I don't think that brown kind of lipstick you are using is any good. When you use the mascara don't use too much and make sure it does not drip off under the eye so as to make you look as though you were about ready to die. When you have it on, you have to look into the mirror every now and then during the evening to see that this does not happen. I haven't found any other way. In conclusion, let me say that no one should ever buy a hat or dress just because it is stylish. They should be bought for the simple reason that they are becoming." She also added that she had followed advice she received once from an Englishman who appeared much younger than his age. He had told Helen that people should stretch their necks to counteract the tendency of the neck tendons to shorten. "I have always pulled my chin up in the air ever since. Mostly because it felt good. I haven't any idea whether it has any beneficial effects or not."[41]

After the excitement in the capital, Melvyn plunged back into his studio work. The month before, with encouragement from leading Democrats, he considered entering politics full-time. Some even spoke of him as a possible gubernatorial candidate to run against the Democratic incumbent, Culbert Olson, in the 1942 primary. Remsen Bird wrote Eleanor Roosevelt about Melvyn's dilemma. "Last night we had dinner with Melvyn and Helen and had an exceedingly interesting conversation. I wish you had been present. The studios are making a new contract for Melvyn for the next seven years and last evening was a time of very momentous decision." Bird had advised Douglas that he could be of more service through his profession and the "gift of his funds and counsel rather than to withdraw from the world of his specific training and enter public office." ER answered that she and the President agreed with Bird.[42]

Melvyn had ambivalent feelings about his decision against a deeper commitment to politics, which at that point meant running for political office. His choice may well have encouraged Helen to become involved, particularly if she were searching for a new arena in which she could excel. Helen also had a need to feel professionally equal to Melvyn. The decline of her theatrical career in the 1930s had, to a degree, disturbed that critical balance in their relationship. Politics offered an opportunity to regain the equilibrium. Unlike

Douglas's previous careers in theater and opera, she did not initially approach politics with the intention of rising to the top. As she later observed, "I *decided* I wanted to be an actress; I *decided* I wanted to be a singer; I *didn't* decide I wanted to get into public affairs. . . . The current of the times . . . carried me."[43]

The Douglases' relationship was further complicated by an affair Melvyn had during this period, a situation that hurt Helen deeply and created emotional strain in their intimate life. Years later, Helen wrote Melvyn and explained why she had not divorced him at that point. "1. I loved you. 2. the family, brought up as I was the thought of breaking up the family was like considering murder. 3. I could not believe what had happened so I just suffered dumbly." These feelings may have increased her desire to explore new avenues. She certainly moved quickly into the party structure after the election. In December, state party chair William Malone appointed her to two positions, vice-chair of the state party and head of the Women's Division for California. He said later that he gave her these positions so that he would not have to deal with more than one woman and because he did not view her as a threat to the existing power structure, but he admitted later that he underestimated her abilities. With the authority of the three top positions for women in the state, good connections with the national party structure, a talent for speaking, a fervent commitment to Franklin Roosevelt's domestic and foreign policies, Eleanor Roosevelt as her political "fairy godmother," and Melvyn withdrawing from participation in the party structure, Helen had a good start up the political ladder. But she made these choices at the expense of time spent at home. While she still had a well-organized household, her activities absorbed her energies in a new, intense way. And her marriage to Melvyn was never the same. While they remained friends and continued to keep the structure of their marriage functional, the romance had died for Helen, and perhaps for Melvyn as well.[44]

7

Rise to Political Power

FROM 1941 TO 1944, Helen Gahagan gained considerable power within the Democratic Party by masterfully taking advantage of the opportunities offered by her three party positions, the top women's jobs, and honing leadership skills she had developed in college. In 1942, she briefly considered running for Congress. Two years later she had acquired more power than any woman in California politics, and she did run for Congress, winning the race from the Fourteenth Congressional District, located in downtown Los Angeles. She was the third California woman to win a congressional seat, and the first to run on her own merits rather than as a widow of a deceased congressman. In addition to learning about politics, she had to deal with challenges at home. In 1942, Melvyn, who changed his mind about political involvement after the bombing of Pearl Harbor, moved to Washington D.C., to work as a volunteer for Eleanor Roosevelt in the Office of Civilian Defense. Several months later he joined the Army and was stationed in India. Helen had to learn to manage the complications of a wartime household alone.[1]

Political activity in 1941 took place against the backdrop of America's increasing involvement with the war. The fall of France to Hitler in June 1940 had brought the war closer to Americans than at any other time, but Roosevelt remained cautious throughout the fall of 1940 to offset charges of warmongering from isolationists and his liberal opponent, Wendell Willkie. Once he had the election behind him, Roosevelt moved towards a more forthright position of aiding the Allies. As Hitler extended his empire, Americans became increasingly active in groups such as the Committee to Defend America by Aiding the Allies, organized by journalist William Allen White in 1940, and a similar group formed later, the Fight for Freedom Committee. These organizations also worked to combat the influence of the isolationist America First Committee. As tensions increased, so did conservative Red-baiting of Roosevelt liberals.

Gahagan took on the challenge of her new milieu with a zealous intensity. She wrote the Women's Division's national headquarters in January 1941 that she felt quite "foggy" about how things ran and spent the spring becoming more acquainted with California Democrats and energetically reorganizing the Women's Division. This suborganization of the Democratic Party at the national level and in certain states had become an important part of the Democratic Party structure by the 1940 election. Although national Democrats could not evaluate the precise impact of their highly organized women, the Women's Division confidently took credit for Roosevelt's 1940 victory. Even pollster George Gallup admitted that he had not predicted the results as accurately as he had hoped because the women had voted in larger numbers than he had expected, and they voted for FDR. After the election, the national office surveyed their national committeemen and committeewomen plus state and county party heads. The general consensus gave credit to the women, who did "the most energetic and effective work" of the campaign.[2]

The creation of a separate Women's Division within the Democratic Party in 1933 was a result of the Roosevelt partnership. FDR believed that it was critical that the maximum number of women become involved in "free, full and fearless discussions of public questions." As governor of New York he had witnessed the impact of the party's Women's Division at the state level that his wife had helped organize. In 1933, at ER's urging, FDR instructed DNC chairman James Farley to work with Molly Dewson and Eleanor Roosevelt to set up a Women's Division within the national party structure. The two women believed that people should vote first on issues, not personalities. As ER said in *It's Up to the Women*, "A vote is never an intelligent vote when it is cast without knowledge." The two women viewed the Division as the means to educate both women and men about New Deal policies, to open up the political system to women, and to train women to assume leadership roles in politics. In addition to setting up an organizational structure to achieve these goals, Dewson and ER expanded the party's *Democratic Digest* and developed it into an important publication for the entire party. Douglas learned in 1940 when she published her article on migrants how widely read the magazine had become.[3]

Gahagan relied principally on the Division's new director, Gladys Tillett, a prominent North Carolina Democrat who replaced Dorothy McAllister, for training in her Women's Division job. Helen also became close friends with the newly appointed executive secretary Lorena Hickok, a former Associated Press correspondent and a politically savvy personal friend of Eleanor Roosevelt's. Gahagan also consulted frequently with the First Lady. Although Helen had had little administrative experience outside of her work with the Steinbeck Committee and membership on two New Deal advisory boards, she learned quickly. She faced a formidable challenge, however. State laws governing party structure, apportionment, and elections, including the cross-filing rule, resulted in weak party organization in the state, and particularly within the historically divided Democratic Party. Cross-filing permitted candidates to file on more than one party ballot without identifying their own party affiliation. Both the press (particularly the conservative Hearst papers) and lobbyists wielded unusual influence. Women had made almost no inroads into the power structure; not only because of the disorganized and divisive nature of the party system, but also because women themselves had not been effectively organized.[4]

As Gahagan began to find her way, she relied on Women's Division philosophy and her view of gender relations. She told women who complained about how men ignored them that she had grown up with three brothers and a strong-willed father. There was *"no way* to make men listen to you," she said. "The only way to have a voice in politics is to build strength at the grass roots. Now, I don't know how we're going to go about that, but that's what we've got to do." She did not completely ignore the men, however. While reaching out to women, she also built a base of support among liberal male party officials and congressmen in the southern part of the state. As a political newcomer, she had the advantages of no obligations, fresh ideas, a habit of working outside of channels, and high-level connections. Gahagan first selected her principal assistants. She asked Julia Porter, president of the San Francisco League of Women Voters, to take charge of northern California, along with Catherine Bauer as her assistant, a woman known for her work with the California Housing Association. Although neither had worked with the Democratic Party, Gahagan turned over the north to them, and she assured them that she had confidence that whatever they did would be fine with her. She selected lawyer Leisa Bronson as her assistant in southern California. Bronson headed the party organization in Voorhis's Los Angeles congressional district around Claremont and Pomona. As Gahagan worked her way through her county appointments, she took the time to talk with party leaders to learn about leading women in their districts as well as about broader state and national problems. She quickly became aware which men were willing to listen to women and often accepted the advice of those men in appointing women to party positions. This made it easier for the women to function with authority. Her appointment of Bronson, for example, was, as Gahagan told Porter, a "bow" to Voorhis's "integrity and worth."[5]

Porter, Bauer, and Bronson typified Gahagan's appointments: bright, capable, and professional women, many of whom had never before been active in the Women's Division. By selecting women who had had no previous experience, Gahagan could partially bypass the rampant factionalism she had encountered during 1940. She wrote Hickok that the appointment process "would all be so much simpler if we had a serum which would do away with all the allergic reactions that some of the Party factions have towards each other!" Tillett, pleased with Gahagan's work, wrote Molly Dewson, who still remained the titular head of the Division even though she had been retired for six years, that Gahagan was "picking able leaders all over the state, and I believe she is going to build a good women's organization." Helen felt satisfied but exhausted. She wrote Ickes, "I have made so many trips up and down the state that I feel I now know every acre of ground!" Ickes answered that she seemed to have covered "more territory than a migratory bird." She was methodical and well organized, a skill she had developed managing her household. She had never had much more than negative control, or the right of refusal, over her acting and singing opportunities.[6]

Once Gahagan had appointed all county heads, she turned the job of organizing the Division according to the "6 Point Plan" prescribed by the national office to Porter, Bauer, and Bronson. Six women from the north of the state and six from the south headed each segment of the structure—Reporter Plan, Publicity, Radio, Speakers, Finance, and *Democratic Digest*. These women in turn coordinated the county organization down to the precinct level. Gahagan developed warm friendships with many of the women she appointed. Most women, as William Malone recalled, found her capable and "full of life and vitality with a winsome appearance." Her approach to organizing resulted in both a cadre of loyal women and a group of alienated Democrats who thought they deserved appointment by virtue of long-term service to the party. While her system undercut existing networks among Democratic women, it was effective as long as she kept in close touch with her people. Enjoying these new women friends was a different experience for Gahagan; while she had the loyal friendship of De Sola and a few others, she had few close male and even fewer female friends.[7]

Also during this busy spring, as a member of California's State Advisory Committee to the National Youth Administration, she hosted a youth orchestra performance at her home and invited Eleanor Roosevelt to come, an invitation she accepted. She and Malvina Thompson spent several days in Los Angeles as guests of the Douglases. The guests at the concert, held outside on the Douglases' patio, included top political people from the north and the south, even Governor Olson. Gahagan also skillfully arranged a variety of other events that enhanced her own political stature, such as a tea for the State Advisory Committee, another tea for some of her new Women's Division appointees, two intimate dinners with close friends, and a luncheon to thank key members of the Hollywood for Roosevelt Committee, which had been active in the 1940 campaign. Walt Disney and his wife, guests at one dinner, gave the First Lady a personal tour of Disney Studios.[8]

With her Women's Division in place, Gahagan turned her attention to home-front defense plans. As America moved closer to a position of undeclared war in 1941, Roosevelt created the Office of Civilian Defense (OCD) in the summer of that year in an effort to increase awareness of the problems of home defense and to coordinate volunteers. He appointed New York mayor Fiorello LaGuardia director and ER as LaGuardia's assistant. In July 1941, the President appointed Gahagan to a forty-five-member Volunteer Committee created to help LaGuardia organize volunteers for possible crises like air raids, damaged transportation lines, or fire. The committee's membership included some of the "big Democratic gals," such as Gahagan, McAllister, Daisy Harriman, Ellen Woodward, and Anna Roosevelt Boettinger, the President's daughter. Some of the better-known male appointees included Barry Bingham, publisher of the *Louisville Courier Journal*; Adlai Stevenson; James Patton, president of the National Farmers' Union; and C. J. Haggarty, president of the California State Federation of Labor. Both Roosevelts spoke to the group. Americans had little idea of the meaning of modern war, FDR warned, for the war had become a "war between populations, and not alone between armies." The committee was responsible for organizing every county in the nation. ER stressed her approach to mobilizing citizens through local organizations. Personal involvement could not be "theoretical" but must be "tied to something they [the citizens] can see," she stressed. Mrs. Smith might donate home-canned vegetables to ship to England, or Mr. Jones could drive people to work in defense factories. She emphasized the potentially significant role of women.[9]

Gahagan's OCD responsibilities overlapped with her job as head of the Women's Division in California. Gladys Tillett had shifted the Division's energies to the civilian defense movement. Douglas rented an office in Los Angeles at her own expense, which provided a central location for women to come to discuss problems and share ideas. She spoke to groups of women throughout southern California suggesting ways that they might help home defense. She organized busloads of women to visit problem areas like public housing developments, migrant camps, and inner-city slums. In order for her women to function more independently from the Democratic National Committee, she held fund-raising teas in her home, affairs that often drew from 1,500 to 2,000 women.[10]

In addition to the activities Gahagan developed on her own, she coordinated two Women's Division functions that further enhanced her reputation. The first, a luncheon, provided an opportunity for women from the southern California counties to talk about their county's defense preparation. Over seven hundred women came, an attendance that impressed Tillett. But the luncheon proved simple compared to the challenge of organizing a regional conference in California for September. In 1938 the Women's Division had begun sponsoring regional Institutes of Government. These educational gatherings, models for the National Institute held in Washington, D.C., in May 1940 that Gahagan attended, brought women together for workshops on such topics as public speaking, producing radio programs, writing newspaper releases, organizing precincts, and fund-raising. The Institutes also built communication networks, created a spirit of cohesiveness, and offered leadership opportunities. The fact that leading Democratic men often attended made the sessions all the more significant. In 1941, Tillett wanted the regional conferences to emphasize support for FDR's foreign policy and heighten awareness of home defense responsibilities. [11]

Gahagan hoped to draw a major gathering of Democrats from the eleven-state Western area. She capitalized on the contacts she had been cultivating since first becoming involved in politics and persuaded male state and national leaders to help generate attendance. She asked Governor Olson to issue the call to the conference with accompanying messages from Los Angeles mayor Fletcher Bowron, herself and Melvyn, and other state party leaders. At Gahagan's request, DNC chairman Flynn sent the invitation to the eleven state chairmen to bring their leading women. Gahagan invited labor leaders from throughout the state to meet with one of the Institute speakers, Congresswoman Mary Norton, in hopes of stemming the wave of strikes and walkouts in defense plants. Helen also asked Melvyn to organize an event using film stars. Tillett commented that all "the Democratic girls would get a tremendous kick out of the appearance of a few movie star Democrats. I am afraid that it will take them some time to get back to precinct work after two or three days with the Melvyn Douglases!" [12]

Gahagan faced numerous touchy problems. For example, she decided to introduce the governor at the banquet and then turn the program over to Melvyn to prevent the women from complaining that the men were completely "stealing the show." She also asked Malone to introduce Tillett to indicate "the men and the women are working closely together." Another problem concerned dress for the banquet. Hickok suggested that the men wear business suits, as many could not afford a dinner jacket. "The women will dress, of course, but Mrs. Tillett and I never wear anything more elaborate than a dinner gown to those banquets. We also do not want to feel too far away from the women we are most anxious to reach. I guess you get the idea." Another complication concerned the treatment of Nettie Jones. Hickok felt Jones deserved some recognition. Gahagan agreed but reminded Hickok that "we don't want to blow her up into a position of importance. . . . She is going to continue to be a thorn in the side of democracy" as long as she lived in California. While the funding for the Institute came partially from the Washington office, Gahagan had to get additional money from the state party. She pressured Malone, reminding him that she had flown to Washington to persuade Agriculture Secretary Claude Wickard to be the keynote speaker. Flynn thought that the Institute was "going to be one of the most important conferences yet to be held," she wrote Malone. "I hope I have proven myself a good saleswoman, have broken down your resistance, and that the check for the Conference will be on its way." Malone sent the check.[13]

The Institute opened the night of September 11 with dinner at the Douglas home, where leading state and national Democratic leaders mingled with Hollywood luminaries, among them Robinson and Fairbanks. The next morning Governor Olson officially opened the Institute. He proudly, if erroneously, termed California a " 'successful training ground for many of the New Deal policies.' " Nan Wood Honeyman, a close friend of Eleanor Roosevelt's and a former member of Congress from Oregon, sounded the conference theme: all-out support for the goals of the President and his wife. Tillett urged the women to lead the efforts to prepare the public for sacrifice and service to the war effort. Gahagan, introduced as the " 'spark plug of Southern California,' " emphasized the need for training speakers " 'to back important bills, help fight for issues and teach persons to shoulder the responsibilities of a free people.' " In the evening, the delegates were treated to a gala banquet. One reporter observed: the evening "brought about a change of scene as glamorous as in any of Hollywood's most extravagant film fantasies. The corridors filled with women in bright evening gowns, and long limousines [delivered] stars of the stage, screen and radio." More than 1,000 men and women gathered for the dinner. Gahagan had arranged for a national broadcast of Secretary Wickard's keynote address, in which he discussed food production goals for 1942. A group of stars including Douglas, Jackie Gleason, Beulah Bondi, Sidney Blackmer, and Fairbanks provided the evening's highlight, a dramatic reading of Stephen Vincent Benét's poem, "Listen to the People." The Democratic Digest reported that "actors and audience were drawn together in one common impulse [that] brought them to their feet singing 'America.' "[14]

The nationally broadcast sessions the following morning closed with Norton's speech. "Talk to them like a Dutch aunt," Gahagan had urged the congresswoman. Norton appealed to the labor representatives to unite and back the administration's policies. She warned that continued strikes would only increase the possibility of anti-labor legislation. Afterwards labor leaders met with her and passed a resolution forming a United Committee to back Roosevelt's policies, promising to carry the endorsement to their union membership and the press. This portion of the program alone set the conference apart from others, Eleanor Roosevelt wrote in her essay on Gahagan in Ladies of Courage. Although some "backsliding" occurred, "the situation never got so bad again."

While labor leaders met with Norton, the rest of the participants toured homes of well-known actors and actresses and ended up in Chinatown for tea.[15]

Helen felt exuberant after the Institute. People showered praise on both of the Douglases; on Helen for the "masterpiece of efficient organization and showmanship" and on Melvyn for the Benét performance. Tillett and Hickok wired her that "we just want to tell you how much we admire you and appreciate your unselfish devotion to the things we all believe in. We love you very much, Helen." Tillett followed up with a letter. "You have set such a high standard for Regional Conferences that all of us are a little low spirited over whether we can ever attain such heights again. We shall have to place you apart as the standard among National Committeewomen toward which others can work." All of the national speakers were acting like seventeen-year-olds as they went about "looking for opportunities to burst into praise of the movie folk," she continued; many left surprised at their "intelligent outlook and old fashioned character." Tillett also commented that Gahagan's recruits into the Women's Division were "going to make it one of the strongest organizations in the country." Norton found it hard to express her gratitude for all Douglas had done to bring about "the most successful conference held so far." The congresswoman said that while she had heard much about Gahagan, that had not prepared Norton for her "charm and efficiency." "The consensus of opinion was that if all the states had half the leadership of California the work of the National Committee would be a thing of joy. So, my dear, your ears should have burned."[16]

While Helen worked with the women, Melvyn began organizing rallies for the Fight for Freedom Committee and groups helping Jews escape from Europe. This offered him a satisfying change of pace from filming. He continued to co-star for MGM, United Artists, and Columbia, working with stars like Myrna Loy, Rosalind Russell, Joan Crawford, and Greta Garbo. He received consistently good reviews. His salary had climbed each year, particularly after *Ninotchka*, so that by 1941 he earned $200,000 annually, placing him among the top income group in Hollywood. But the scripts were superficial and his roles unchallenging—"frivolous fluff" as the *New York Times* called *That Uncertain Feeling*. After the United States entered the war, following the bombing of Pearl Harbor on December 7, 1941, Melvyn decided to become involved full-time with the war effort, a decision that both he and Helen knew would require adjustments at home. He was particularly interested in the area of civilian defense. He thought that the talent of Hollywood's writers, artists, actors, and entertainers could help information agencies such as the Office of War Information (OWI) and the OCD broaden their scope. He envisioned, for example, writers helping the Army produce pamphlets, or artists designing posters. A letter to this effect made the rounds of Washington offices and, in January 1942, ended up in the hands of James M. Landis, dean of Harvard Law

School and LaGuardia's successor as the director of the OCD. After consulting with Eleanor Roosevelt, Landis wired Douglas, asking him to join the OCD to implement his suggestions. Douglas accepted immediately.[17]

The early February 1942 press release announcing his appointment brought a sudden and unexpected congressional uproar, a protest intensified by dismay at a simultaneous OCD appointment by Eleanor Roosevelt. She had asked a close friend, dancer Mayvis Chaney, to be coordinator of children's physical fitness activities. The appointments offered congressional conservatives an ideal opportunity to vent frustrations about the liberal leanings of Landis and Eleanor Roosevelt in particular and others in general, as well as to criticize rising government expenditures. Members called Chaney an incompetent night club dancer and attacked Melvyn from various angles. They not only viciously Red-baited him, they also brought up the frequently raised charge that movie people, particularly actors, did not have the qualifications for political activity. As one paper put it, Congress dragged out the old argument, "Are actors people?" Critics also brought up Helen, "another star of great fame, charm, and personality [who] doubles as democratic national committeewoman" and who also had a dubious past as a Communist Party "fellow-traveler." Finally, despite the fact that Melvyn was only to be paid a *per diem* allowance, debate went on at length about his non-existent high OCD salary.[18]

Leland Ford, the Republican congressman from the Los Angeles Sixteenth District, led the week-long attack on Melvyn Douglas. He laced his attacks with anti-Semitic overtones by endlessly reminding his colleagues that Melvyn's real last name was Hesselberg. He asked, "Do we always have to have men who have changed their names . . . in high places in Government?" Douglas's history of " 'pink' and 'red' activities" duplicated those of other OCD employees who were linked to "interests which would destroy the American form of government." Another southern Californian, Republican Carl Hinshaw, took up where Ford left off, reviewing in detail Douglas's activities with alleged Communist-front organizations. One reporter added that such "fine appointments" should be followed with equally important directors of flower arranging, hobby culture, or quiz programs. Melvyn's House defenders ridiculed the Communist affiliation implications and saw the debate as a foolish diversion from the critical issues facing Congress as the country moved into full-scale warfare. Jerry Voorhis pointed out that the Communist Party had organized a boycott of Douglas's film *Ninotchka* because of its anti-Communist character. Mary Norton praised his patriotism and willingness to give up his high movie salary.[19]

Although the debate finally cooled, both Chaney and Eleanor Roosevelt resigned from the OCD. The First Lady announced that she was determined to save a program from criticism that came from the " 'age old fight for the privileged few against the good of the many.' " But Douglas did not back off. "I thought to cave in, to give up, to retire from the scene would be not only a confession of weakness but in a curious way an admission that maybe there was some truth to these attacks." But it was not pleasant. Norman Littell wrote Helen, "Melvyn has had a rotten time of it here. He was simply the victim of pent-up forces of spleen and the best opinion all recognizes this. He has not been very apt or quick enough on the trigger about his public statements, but that is a matter which takes practice or natural facility." [20]

Before moving to Washington to begin his new job, Melvyn returned home briefly to make some quick money in a film *He Kissed the Bride* with Joan Crawford. He found his household in chaos. Helen had entered the hospital with strep throat, Mary Helen was suffering from a broken collar bone from an automobile accident, and Gregory, his sixteen-year-old son by his first marriage, who was visiting, had suffered a skiing injury. Despite feeling physically drained, however, Helen was furious over the Red-baiting. She decided that Leland Ford, whom she deemed the worst of the congressional "bad guys" who opposed labor, public power, and public housing, had to be defeated in the fall election. She wrote Littell, "if we don't clean some of the people out of Congress, this program for a better world is never going to take place." If it meant she had to run for Ford's seat, she would do it. [21]

At the same time, however, she felt uncertain about the right course to follow to get Ford. Melvyn questioned her running because he did not think that she would win. Helen told Molly Dewson that even the powerful oil man and conservative Democrat Edwin Pauley, who disliked her, wanted her to take on Ford, thinking she was the only one who could beat him. Dewson, in turn, asked FDR his opinion, who responded that Douglas should "go ahead and work like fury [and] not to mind the hard treatment" she inevitably would receive. She should not run, however, unless she knew the men would support her. Julia Porter's reaction from the north reflected that of many of her Women's Division workers. "This is tremendously exciting and my love and every good wish if you decide to take the plunge." But she would regret Helen's leaving her post with the Women's Division and as national committeewoman. "Your influence has been so important and your vision and enthusiasm have been so stimulating, that the loss will be almost irreparable. You are the star by which our course is steered." [22]

By early April, Douglas, still ambivalent about running, wrote Hickok and Tillett that "the more I view the whole picture, the more concerned I am about the Women's Division. . . . It is just beginning to mean something, and in another two years it will really be a power to be reckoned with. If the President needs support now, he is going to need it more in two years. In other words, I have not decided definitely to run. . . . I don't want to, as you know, because it would mean a real sacrifice to me. But also, I don't want the district to go by default." In mid-April, the district's Democrats endorsed the liberal candidate, Will Rogers, Jr. Melvyn wrote Helen from Washington that he had seen Eleanor Roosevelt, Tillett, and Hickok, and all were glad Helen had decided not to challenge Rogers for the endorsement. The women "had hoped right along that you would read between the lines in their letters and gather that they were not too happy about it." They knew Helen would have had an uphill battle, and they felt she should concentrate her talents where they were badly needed: mobilizing the Democratic women for the 1942 campaign. Douglas had yet to demonstrate that she held significant power within a male-dominated, fractured party structure, particularly given her attitude towards politics. "I wasn't really interested in the machinations and the maneuverings of politics," she later recalled. The fact that she even considered running for Congress, however, illustrates her recurrent pattern of restlessness, emotional reactions to situations, impulsive behavior, and remarkable self-confidence.[23]

Nationally, the picture looked gloomy for Democrats. The congressional coalition of Republicans and conservative Democrats had continued to grow in strength since the 1936 election. After the American entry into the war, hostility towards the extension of federal controls and additional social reforms had intensified, and Democrats feared losing their congressional majority. Gahagan was concerned about all the southern California seats, but she set her sights on six in particular. In 1940, the Democrats held seven congressional seats and the Republicans two. The Republicans had won three new southern California districts created after the 1940 reapportionment. The women in Gahagan's well-organized counties worked diligently to educate and get out the vote. They had to contend with California's bizarre cross-filing system, which allowed a candidate to file for both the primary and the final campaign on any political ticket. This practice had numerous repercussions. Often voters did not know the party the candidate belonged to, which helped incumbents. A person running in the primary could, and frequently did, win a majority of votes in the two major parties, thus avoiding a runoff in the fall. In spite of this possibility, Democratic candidates won their party's nomination in all of the districts Gahagan had targeted as critical.[24]

But the California Democratic Party had a pessimistic outlook for the fall campaign, reflecting the party's national mood. As a group they were disorganized because they lacked effective leadership at the top. The party had been splintered since 1934, during the Upton Sinclair campaign, only two years after it had become the majority party. The election of Sheridan Downey as senator and Culbert Olson as governor in 1938 should have helped the party's structure, but neither man provided the necessary leadership to pull the party together. The party did not get adequate recognition from the White House or the Democratic National Committee. State chairman Malone never called the Democratic State Central Committee into session. The Women's Division reorganization that Gahagan mobilized in the spring of 1941 worked well in southern California but finally fell apart because of bickering in the north. Despite their commitment to helping Gahagan, Porter and Bauer resigned after the primaries because of the lack of cooperation from other women.[25]

Undaunted, Gahagan moved optimistically into the fall campaign. By keeping the Women's Division separated from the regular party organization, which was running Olson's campaign, she organized the women effectively, Women's Division style, to distribute information about the candidates, raise money, and get out the voters. The Democrats won three of the six critical districts and six other southern California seats despite Governor Olson's loss to Earl Warren and a Republican sweep nationally. Most satisfying to Gahagan personally was Will Rogers, Jr.'s defeat of Leland Ford. But she was delighted with the other winners as well, including George Outland in Santa Barbara; Chet Holifield, Voorhis, and Thomas Ford in Los Angeles; and San Diegan Ed Izac. Democrats were disappointed, however, that only one Democrat won out of ten congressional races in northern California. Democrats praised Gahagan for her organizing efforts. Hickok sent a wire to Washington making Gahagan sound as if she had engineered these victories singlehandedly. "What you accomplished in California was the one bright spot in our lives last week. We think you did wonders. Leland Ford out of Congress! Particularly significant because of national race." Even Pauley wrote that she "did a magnificent job. At least we could have come out much worse in our Congressional Districts and where we did come out successfully I am sure the results were due to your efforts. I want you to know that all of us in Washington appreciate this immensely."[26]

During the campaign months, Melvyn lived in Washington, working for the Office for Civilian Defense. He and Helen spent very little time together but kept in touch by phone and mail. He enjoyed his work, but he also found it frustrating. He felt internal dissension in the agency resulted in intra-office confusion. By September, after he had established his own smoothly running program and the "snipers," as he termed them, could no longer find anything to criticize, he turned for advice to Eleanor Roosevelt, with whom he had become quite close, about whether or not he could join the Army. He believed that whatever he did could have implications for the Roosevelts and the administration because his FBI record listed all his various activities with alleged front organizations. He saw the only alternative as enlisting as a private, assuming that if he trained as an officer he might have to undergo unpleasant investigations. He knew that as a private, because of his age and minor health problems, he could end up at a boring desk job, but he reasoned, "the very fact of my enlistment as a private might have excellent repercussions in many directions." ER encouraged him to join. Throughout the fall he had discussed his feelings with Helen. She urged him to do whatever he felt was best for him.[27]

He enlisted on December 7, 1942, the first anniversary of the attack on Pearl

Harbor. The wire services quickly picked up the news, as they had with other film stars who had joined that year, such as Henry Fonda and Tyrone Power. Liberals from all parts of the country sent Melvyn their congratulations. As Voorhis put it, "This example will be an inspiration to millions of Americans." Helen wrote Melvyn of the reaction of the Los Angeles newspapers. As to be expected, she reported, the only "factual" report appeared in Manchester Boddy's liberal *Los Angeles Daily News*. The others "could not help but give a few twists,"and the *Los Angeles Times* and the *Herald Express* gave the impression that he had resigned after the OCD ruckus. "What bastards they are," she said. Some of Melvyn's Hollywood friends appeared to regret his enlistment because, she assumed, "it seems to challenge their own position." But most felt that enlisting was the "honorable" thing to do. She could not resist adding, "and darling, I still feel the exercise is going to do you good." [28]

After six months of basic training in several locations, Melvyn realized that his FBI record was preventing his efforts to secure a good assignment. The delaying tactics also disturbed Helen. He turned to Eleanor Roosevelt in the summer of 1943, and moved quickly. She went to the President, who persuaded the War Department to remove the FBI information from his record and to recommend promotion to captain. All papers progressed through usual channels to avoid special attention. Within days, Melvyn learned of his promotion and the promise of an overseas assignment. Despite efforts to keep the procedures confidential, the press found out about the advancement. Once again, Melvyn became a target for criticism. "Douglas, whose real name is Melvyn Hesselberg, held what Army authorities here said might be a world's record for advancement," one paper reported, as he "bounded lightly over the heads of an estimated 1,250,000 officers." Louisiana Democratic congressman James Morrison demanded that the War Department "make public this streamlined recipe for high rank." Surely, he commented, it could not be his friendship with Eleanor Roosevelt or Harry Hopkins. ER felt sad. She wrote Melvyn: "I do not mind any kind of nastiness and I hope you and Helen do not mind either. Evidently any friend of mine has to go through [such criticism], and I hope the effect will be strengthening of our friendship rather than the lessening of any bond that may exist." Fortunately the crisis passed, and Melvyn prepared for an interesting assignment as an entertainment coordinator in the Burma–China–India theater. After a happy visit with Helen and the children, he left for India in late fall of 1943. [29]

Helen's letters show continual support. "How we miss you," she wrote, "but how happy I feel about everything. I am very sure you have done just the right thing." She wrote Eleanor Roosevelt, "It is strange . . . how near I feel to him and how lighthearted I feel about his going." She commented, however, that since she would be writing so many letters, she would have to learn to spell. In December 1943, Helen wrote Melvyn that while she missed him, she knew he would get satisfaction from what he was doing. "I have such a *fierce* pride in you. I always had a sneaking [*sic*] suspicion that I did but never realized how fully until now." She found herself furious about anyone who criticized him. "My muscles seem to be getting ready to spring at the next person . . . who opens his mouth." She never expressed anger for being left alone. She would have considered it disloyal to Roosevelt to ask Melvyn not to participate in the war effort. It is also likely that their intimate, sexual relationship continued to be tense, and it was easier to be supportive when they were separated. The passion of their letters of the 1930s had clearly given way to a tone of a close, concerned, loyal companionship. [30]

While Helen's problems in maintaining a wartime household were, relatively speaking, less disruptive than for many other women, she nevertheless found the pressures difficult and sometimes overwhelming. She wrote Melvyn at one point: "What with Democrats and Hearst papers and sick children and everything else, life begins to look a little confused." She had other problems as well. After Melvyn left in March 1942 for Washington for the OCD job, the two used Melvyn's savings to support the two households. Helen had difficulty deciding where to cut back on spending; she had never had to budget money. In early 1942, she let all the household help go. Pick had already joined the Army, and Chavoor, who had been working full-time caring for the children for several years, had taken another job. Helen finally resorted to hiring help occasionally, although she had trouble finding responsible people. When she fired her help, she put both Mary Helen, age three, and Peter, age nine, in boarding school. They came home for monthly weekend visits. By the end of 1942, she had "only" $18,000 left plus whatever Melvyn sent home from his monthly salary. [31]

Another problem that constantly concerned her was whether or not to stay in the Outpost house. Initially, when Melvyn went to Washington, she considered moving to a smaller house to save money. She even thought of leaving Los Angeles because of rumors that the city, a major center for munitions and aircraft production, would be bombed. She toyed with the idea of moving to New York to be with her mother and family as her brother Fritz was dying of cancer. Yet while she felt she should be there, she also realized that she would probably not be much help, and she needed to follow through on her political responsibilities. Towards the end of 1942, the Navy offered to buy the house as a recovery spot for injured soldiers. Ultimately, however, she stayed in their Outpost home and kept her office open in downtown Los Angeles. Helen was also frustrated by government controls and the lack of available service people to fix things around the house. In mid-1943, she wrote Melvyn and ER that she was getting tired of the war. "What really gets me down are all the *little* things, window cords broken, plumbing broken. I suddenly understood how people feel about OPA [Office of Price Administration] and rationing" she told

Melvyn. To the First Lady she commented: "The other day I sat down in my living room and almost wept" because so many things did not work. "I just couldn't take it." The household had also grown considerably: Gregory, Melvyn's brother George, his wife and two children, and Melvyn's mother had moved in. The additional family made Helen less lonely but complicated running the household. [32]

She also had ambivalent feelings about placing such young children in boarding school, a rarity in the United States, although their school, the Buckley School in Los Angeles, did have a number of Hollywood children both as day students and as boarders. But as she saw it, if she could not get adequate help at home, boarding school was the only solution. She never gave serious consideration to setting aside her own work. She felt lonely and missed the children, she wrote Alis De Sola, but this left her "free to do a lot of good hard work." If she left for a long trip, as she did in early 1943, she took Mary Helen with her and left Peter in school. She found her daughter delightful, as she mentioned in almost every letter to Melvyn. Her enchantment with Mary Helen paralleled her feelings about Peter at approximately the same age. Mary Helen was "good," "beautiful," and a "pure delight," she wrote. When Helen gave Mary Helen a doll for her birthday, the child not only washed the doll's hair immediately but poured "a full cup" of vinegar on it. It was "adorable," Helen wrote. "It is too cute to listen to the running conversation Mary Helen carries on with her doll." [33]

In contrast, she found Peter a constant strain. She wrote Melvyn that Peter "has never been an easy child. He wears me out more in ten minutes than everybody and everything else put together for a week." After all these years, "I am still hunting for the key as to how to manage him. He still wets his bed. There simply must be some cause for it. Well, I shall keep on struggling." She never raised the issue of whether Peter might have been emotionally distressed. Various factors must have been at play—a feeling of abandonment at being sent to boarding school at such a young age, anger about his father's absence, resentment about his mother's frequent travels, pressure to perform well academically, and the frustrations resulting from life as a child of public figures. When Peter refused to return to school because the children teased him about his bedwetting, Helen told Melvyn that she was looking for another school but it had to be one with a lot of discipline because she felt Peter needed that sort of environment. [34]

In addition to her worries about Peter, Helen also became involved with Melvyn's son Gregory, who had been living in the Outpost house while a student at nearby Occidental College. For the first time, Helen felt comfortable with him around. In the summer of 1943, Greg decided to enlist in the service. He wanted to join the merchant marine. Melvyn, who had had little contact with Gregory as he was growing up, tried to get Helen to persuade Greg to go into the Navy instead. At one point Helen offered Greg a vacation trip of his choice if he would join the Navy, and for a brief time, she thought that he planned to do his father's bidding. Ultimately Greg joined the merchant marine, perhaps more out of rebellion than for any other reason. [35]

Although Helen kept herself together emotionally during the long separation, she often found Melvyn's absence difficult to endure. "It is strange," she wrote in a moment of feeling particularly sorry for herself, "how up-rooted I feel out here. You have been the only contact with the community and a conventional life. The moment you leave me there don't seem to be any real ties at all." While Melvyn was still in the United States, she hungered for Mel's calls and became distraught when she missed one. She wrote him after she learned he had called while she was out that she felt like a "small child again and that somehow I have been left out of a party, a party that I had waited for for a long time." [36]

Melvyn constantly worried about Helen's tendency to overdo and become exhausted. "I tremble lest you run into a series of nerve-wracking complications." She was doing her job magnificently, but "use your energy and your resources with care. Don't let the Democrats or the children or the economic problems wear you out." But if things did become overwhelming, she must exert her "utmost effort to remain calm and coordinated. When you feel yourself flying apart, walk away from it up onto the hill or into the pool. You might as well use the luxuries to a good purpose." Above all, he urged, she should find time to be alone. He reassured her: "I wonder, darling, if you realize how tremendously you have matured during the past year. . . . You have always been an alive and fascinating person but you have recently developed into real stature. It is a very thrilling thing to see and to feel. Bless you." He felt grateful that she was willing to help with Greg. In response to one despondent letter from Helen, Melvyn wrote that they must all keep in mind "how fortunate we are to be part of such a beautiful family." [37]

He missed Helen and hoped that both of them would get something out of the experience. "You, like me, are an absorbing sort of person," someone who got something out of whatever she did. Yet these experiences that would surely add to their "store of life" still were not the "full and beautiful thing we have together. That is what I shall miss dreadfully." Writing her on the voyage to India, he reminisced about the wonderful visit they had together just before leaving. "Christ, if we can only make a world where such a life is generally possible." [38]

The emotional stress of the separation and the complicated home situation most likely intensified Helen's involvement in her political responsibilities. She worked to rebuild the organization in the north of the state and had to replace Bronson in the south when she left to look for a job in Washington. Helen coordinated the women throughout the state in working out a program of education, particularly about postwar reconversion to a peacetime economy. She kept her office open daily as a communications center staffed by volunteers and held regular office hours two days a week. Gahagan felt that in order to keep well informed she had to continue to cultivate her contacts in Washington, particularly with the southern California congressional delegation. Her ability to develop these relationships was not typical of Women's Division leaders. Gahagan had time, resources, and access that most others lacked. In early 1943, for example, shortly after Melvyn began his basic training, she went east for an extended trip. She had two purposes in mind: to get a better feeling for what was going on in Congress and to spend time with her family in New York. She took Mary Helen with her and headed, as usual, for the White House. She wrote De Sola just before leaving: "I am actually on my way with my little Mary Helen under my arm." While in Washington she visited with each of the nine southern California Democratic congressmen, a delegation she called the "best in the country," to get their assessment of where Congress was headed during the Seventy-eighth session. She visited each individually and also called them together to discuss problems and strategy. She had already developed a close relationship with Voorhis. He often sent her materials to get her opinion on issues, and they consulted regularly when he visited his Los Angeles district. Holifield also respected her. He wrote her in 1943 that his decision to support her in 1940 for national committeewoman was one of his "most important contributions to the welfare of the Democratic Party in California." She had given of her time, energy, and money "unselfishly and at a great cost." In less than two years, she had developed "the ability to evaluate political situations and persons to a remarkable extent." Her influence had given the Women's Division "life and vigor." During this visit to Washington she became closer to Thomas Ford, who represented the Fourteenth District in Los Angeles, and his wife Lillian. Eleanor Roosevelt helped the getting-acquainted process along by inviting the Outlands, the Voorhises, the Fords, and Will Rogers, Jr., for lunch and a personal tour of the White House. "They were very thrilled," Helen wrote Melvyn.[39]

After her meetings with the congressmen, she wrote Melvyn that she was "much the wiser for having done so. There is no leadership in the House or Senate. [John] McCormack and [Sam] Rayburn just lack what it takes. . . . There is much that can be done but some one must take the initiative. . . . Everything is too awful. We are certainly paying a heavy price for the loss of our good men in Congress, but then we get what we deserve in a Democracy. . . . I feel that I have been of service in many ways here," particularly by impressing on the congressmen the importance of their working as a team. Gahagan also spent time at the Democratic National Committee offices consulting with Frank Walker, the new DNC chairman, and Tillett and Hickok about the impact of the war on party organization in California and prospects for the 1944 election. Polls showed that women might represent close to 65 percent of the registered voters in 1944. Drastic budget cuts had diminished DNC staff and facilities and put more responsibility on organizations in key states like California.[40]

In addition to broadening her political contacts, Gahagan spent much of her free time socializing with the First Lady. During the more than two years since they first met, the two women had kept in close touch by mail and had visited each other. Helen and Melvyn had standing invitations to stay at the White House when business brought them to Washington, and Eleanor began a practice of visiting and often staying with them on her trips west. Neither Douglas hesitated to contact the Roosevelts or the Cabinet members they had met concerning their political activities. Helen occasionally sent flowers and words of encouragement. In August 1943, for example, she wrote ER that she had so much enjoyed seeing her in New York; the First Lady looked so good. "I don't know how you do it, with the whole world pulling at you." She urged her not to be upset by criticism from the columnist Westbrook Pegler. "You are utterly good, brave, simple and beautiful, and don't say no—that you aren't." Millions felt the same way, Helen added. On this visit, Eleanor and Helen attended plays and had breakfast or lunch together. Helen also occasionally attended formal White House functions, such as the banquet for Madame Chiang Kai-shek. "The evening will be thrilling," she wrote Melvyn, "because the President is sure to be present too."[41]

Gahagan left Washington aware that she had a major job ahead of her. She felt, somewhat immodestly, that the prime responsibility for electing Democrats in 1944 fell to her, and that she could make a difference. For example, she went to San Diego in June 1943 and "talked to everyone about Izac—it did a lot of good. Support must be built under Izac or we are going to lose him in the next campaign." She continued her fund-raising events. In August, she had a tea in her home for Democratic Women's Day, planning for 1,400 women. Although she "dreaded" the event, she knew it was important. She wrote Melvyn that she expected all the "*Good*" congressmen to come and hoped to raise $1,000. She also became involved in patronage fights, which did not endear her to the men trying to control the party. She lost one of her early causes, the appointment of former Socialist and friend John Packard for a federal judgeship in southern California, although she made the party regulars like Malone and Pauley realize that she did not intend to be pushed around. Gahagan won her second fight in 1943, the appointment of a woman as the Los Angeles postmaster, despite tremendous opposition from Pauley and others. When the appointment finally went through the Senate, it was generally considered Gahagan's victory.[42]

*

Although Gahagan felt that she had made some positive contributions in 1943, the job increasingly frustrated her. She wrote Melvyn: "I was out trying to save the world, to wake people up about the whole inflationary threat, and . . . very suddenly I am very tired of everything. We have tried so hard to be good, honest, and unselfish citizens and we get bricks. But then so does the President." Sometimes she wished she could go back to singing or acting and let everything else go, or at least be able to perform occasionally. "But then I realize I can't. The constructive work the Women's Division has done makes it impossible. We have assumed leadership in the state and we can't shirk our responsibility. . . . The realization that I can't let go gives me claustrophobia." At least, she assured Melvyn, she had decided to prepare a group of women to take over the leadership for the 1944 campaign to lessen her responsibilities.[43]

This restlessness reflected similar feelings from a year before when she considered running for Congress. Throughout her life, she had decided to quit what she was doing either out of loss of interest or when the next step appeared to be too much of a challenge. She left the theater and began singing lessons in 1927 when she felt her work becoming tedious. She left opera and returned to the theater in 1930 when she decided she did not want to learn German. She went into politics in 1938 when the reality of her sliding theatrical and singing career set in. In 1943 she felt both overwhelmed and bored by what she perceived her responsibilities to be in the 1944 election. Thomas and Lillian Ford understood her feelings, and they felt that Gahagan was not using her political talents to the fullest. She had made an excellent contribution as Democratic national committeewoman, in their opinion; in fact, she had accomplished more than any other person in a similar position. They wrote her that she had "planned and worked and suffered and been insulted and refused to be discouraged." They felt she was the only "disinterested, unselfish leader" in California. "But California is still in a hopeless state, with workers too indifferent to vote. . . . Only a great wave of enthusiasm will awaken our voters and no one can create this. It will come or it won't." Meanwhile, Gahagan had to contend with the pettiness of power-seekers. "If ever the biblical 'casting pearls before swine' was warranted, it is in your case."[44]

Maybe, Lillian suggested, Helen should carry out "her own destiny" by returning to the theater, since Melvyn was away and the children were in boarding school. "Mary can be tucked in some place and you can be her guardian angel." But, Helen explained, despite her desire to get out, she felt she could not abandon the Women's Division until after the 1944 election. When the Fords realized that she intended to stay in politics at least for the time being, they suggested that she run for Thomas Ford's congressional seat. Although he had not made his decision public, he had planned to retire at the end of 1944 after six terms. Helen seemed to him the perfect replacement. She and Ford shared a devotion to FDR, and he felt the district would like her as a candidate.[45]

Unlike 1942, when Gahagan thought about running for Leland Ford's seat, the circumstances were entirely different, and she found the prospect appealing. She certainly had no interest in following the traditional route to female political power pursued, for example, by Women's Division heads Dorothy McAllister, Gladys Tillett, and a bit later, India Edwards. Although she liked working with women, she did not feel committed to the "separatism as strategy" tactic of the Women's Division as a long-term commitment. The experience simply added challenge to her life. Although she remained undecided, just the idea of running for Congress gave her renewed incentive in her Women's Division work. She needed activity to take her mind off her personal life. Her brother Fritz had died, and Melvyn was gone. "I was in a state of agony and loss," she recalled. In October she organized a meeting to discuss the formation of a Roosevelt slate for the primary. Concerned about possible defection of liberals to another candidate, the group supported Gahagan's proposal to create an advisory committee that would, they hoped, control the direction of the ticket. This action caused a minor furor at both the state level and in the DNC office. Gahagan also worked on generating public enthusiasm for the renomination of Henry Wallace as vice-president.[46]

Gahagan faced substantial odds as a congressional candidate. Not only was she a woman, her credentials did not in any way resemble those of other congressional candidates, male or female. In addition, she did not live in the Fourteenth District but in the affluent residential hills of the adjacent Fifteenth. She was, in fact, a total stranger to the Fourteenth, which encompassed the downtown core of Los Angeles. Although she had lived in the city since 1930, she had frequented Hollywood and the wealthier suburbs. Even her Women's Division work had not taught her much about the district, other than the fact that it was traditionally Democratic. As she put it, "Tom Ford was so admired in his district, he had needed very little help from the women's division to get elected."[47] The Fords reassured her that residing outside of the district would not make a significant difference because she had sufficient political experience and the right philosophical outlook to win. Nevertheless, she did not know the district, nor did the district know her. Other than Ford, she knew only a few labor leaders and Augustus Hawkins, a black state assemblyman representing one of the four assembly districts in the Fourteenth. Gahagan's rearing and her lifestyle bore little resemblance to those of the people she sought to represent, which complicated the challenge of convincing the voters that she not only could identify with their problems but could help them.

She also faced a possible challenge from Hawkins, who had waited patiently for Ford's retirement so he could run. Hawkins held a distinguished record in his fight for labor and civil rights. During the war years, the Los Angeles black population, which concentrated primarily in the assembly district that Hawkins represented, grew substantially, and Hawkins had become an increasingly powerful voice in the community. The Fourteenth Congressional District lay in the heart of downtown Los Angeles. Its constituents ranged from the poorest of minority families in Los Angeles County to some of the wealthiest. Pockets of ethnic groups nestled next to each other and in between commercial districts. By 1945, 86,000 blacks lived in the district, making up almost 25 percent of the district's total population of 346,000. Blacks had swarmed into the city first to work for the railroad. They later secured factory jobs, particularly in the numerous defense factories with the implementation of Fair Employment Practices Commission (FEPC) regulations after 1941. During the war years, in fact, blacks accounted for the entire population increase of the district. Indeed, the white population had dropped by a total of 2,700 between 1940 and 1945. Sunset Boulevard formed the northern boundary over to Elysian Park. The line then dropped south along the Los Angeles River to Twenty-sixth Street, turned west along Twenty-sixth, and north at Main Street up to Sunset. Four longtime Democratic state assembly districts, the Forty-fourth, Fifty-fifth, Sixty-second, and Sixty-fourth, made up the Fourteenth.[48]

The Fifty-fifth, long the district of liberal Vernon Kilpatrick, was principally occupied by poor whites who lived in old mansions turned into boardinghouses or other decaying slum areas. Douglas once described the slums in her district as areas where a "chicken coop would be considered a high-priority dwelling—especially if you could have it all to yourself."[49] Around 400 blacks lived in the small area between Maple and Main. To the north of the Fifty-fifth was the Sixty-fourth, the district of Sam Yorty, former chairman of the state's Un-American Activities Committee, a district that included the most affluent residential neighborhoods of the district as well as some commercial zones. Two politically conservative, wealthy areas surrounded LaFayette Park and ran along Wilshire Boulevard, a main city thoroughfare that also included businesses and professional offices, and more old mansions converted into boardinghouses. A sizable middle-class Jewish population had grown up along Sunset. Only about 1,700 blacks lived in a small area bounded by Third Avenue, Beverly, Hoover, and Main. A tiny section of Hollywood intersected the Fifty-fifth at the northwest corner.

The Forty-fourth, John Pelletier's district, was often termed the "river bottom" district because it included the Los Angeles River, which ran east of the huge Elysian Park. This district comprised the commercial downtown core, which included retail and wholesale stores, long blocks of warehouses that were often abandoned and rat-infested, fertilizer factories, retail and transient hotels, and Skid Row. Railroad yards ran north and south alongside the train station on Alameda Boulevard. Northwest of the train station were three major ethnic pockets: Chinatown, Little Tokyo, and, around Olivera Street, the city's oldest

Mexican district and the location of the famous zoot-suit riots of 1943. Blacks moved into the housing in Little Tokyo after the wartime evacuation of the Japanese to concentration camps, and the area became known as "Bronzeville." Most of the congressional district's smaller clusters of more than two dozen racial and ethnic groups also lived in the Forty-fourth, including Italians, Russian Jews, Hungarians, and Slavs. The Sixty-second, Augustus Hawkins' district, encompassed the majority of the district's blacks, with the highest density along Central Avenue, also a former Japanese ghetto. In this assembly district, the black population increased from 45,000 to over 73,000 between 1940 and 1945. Some of the census tracts showed an increase of black population of several hundred percent.[50]

In December, a "Helen-for-Senator" boomlet occurred. Esther Murray, Gahagan's replacement for Bronson as vice-chair of the Women's Division in southern California, wrote Thomas Ford about the flurry of interest. He responded that Gahagan would be good in the Senate, for "we need her fearless, outspoken support of what is right and her ability to analyze and uncover what is bad. We need her compelling personality, her tact and cleverness in handling people; her sweet reasonableness and her unwavering sympathy with the underprivileged." But she could never get elected to the Senate. "A state-wide campaign is fearful. All sorts of groups get together and work for one's opponents, bringing out light and heavy artillery that the unsuspecting did not know existed." There were so many conservative groups in California that "the sensible thing to do" was to run in the Fourteenth District, for it would be almost "handing it to her on a platter." The boomlet died quietly.[51]

In late January of 1944, Ford began to orchestrate his retirement announcement. He wrote his key labor supporters, including left-winger Phil Connelly, head of the pro-Stalinist Los Angeles Congress of Industrial Organizations (CIO) Council, and C. J. Haggarty, the conservative Democrat who was secretary-treasurer of the California State Federation of Labor, outlining the problems the next Congress would face and telling them that he wanted Gahagan as his successor. Although she lived outside the district, he argued, "no likely candidate in the 14th . . . has the background, the prestige and ability of Helen Gahagan. She understands domestic and international problems and she has the personality and ability to put up an effective fight for what she is supporting. I need not tell you that labor needs such a voice as hers in the House right now. She can do more to offset the Howard Smiths and the Clare Luces than ten or a hundred other members." While Smith, a popular Virginia conservative in Congress, seems a rather odd comparison, the reference to Luce was not. Luce, a first-term member of Congress noted for her flair and physical attractiveness, had previously made a name for herself as a playwright, journalist, and wife of the prominent Henry Luce, publisher of *Time, Life,* and

Fortune magazines. Ford also stressed the friendship Helen enjoyed with the Roosevelts and pointed out that she stayed at the White House or with the Ickes when she visited Washington.[52]

In addition, Ford wrote a general letter addressed to his "dear friends" inviting them to join him in a "draft Helen" movement. In a letter to a close friend, he elaborated on his reasons for retirement, saying that he felt like little more than a "no" vote with fifty Democrats siding with the Republicans. On the other hand, Gahagan's sex made her an ideal replacement. She would be "invaluable in combating La Luce, who is just a wise-cracking nit wit, but a man can't take her on without being too rough. Helen could take Clare down the line and make a fool of her with ease." The Democrats also needed another woman to join Eleanor Holmes Norton, the "grand lady from New Jersey," to help balance the six Republican congresswomen.[53]

Ford got a mixed response. American Federation of Labor (AFL) representative Neal Haggerty felt labor would find Hawkins a more attractive candidate. Ford responded that however well qualified the assemblyman might be and possibly capable of getting the Democratic nomination, he could never win the election. In Ford's opinion, the district would not elect a black, "however light-colored he may be." Therefore, if Haggerty wanted a Democrat in Congress, he should "move Heaven and earth to call Hawkins off." CIO official Philip M. Connelly opposed Gahagan because he was unconvinced of her stand on labor issues and saw her as a "silk-stocking candidate." The national CIO, however, disagreed and urged labor to rally behind her. Manchester Boddy, editor of the *Los Angeles Daily News*, commented that while he personally was "very fond of Helen" and agreed that she had many friends in the Fourteenth, many opposed her because she "personifies the many phases of the New Deal administration that are most vulnerable." He also questioned her strength against the promise of a well-financed Republican campaign. Still others thought she would be a better candidate for the Fifteenth or Sixteenth Congressional Districts; Ford disagreed.[54]

Amerigo Bozzani, head of the American-Italian Democratic Headquarters in Los Angeles and an influential campaign worker in the Fourteenth, backed Ford's choice. But he warned Ford that, in a meeting of district Democrats to discuss Ford's "draft Helen" request, a few of the women whispered their disapproval. They gave no reason, "except perhaps hinting their personal jealousy of this grand leader." He figured that the "underground opposition" was instituted by powerful politicos such as Congressman John B. Elliott, Ed Pauley, Bill Malone, and Attorney General Robert Kenny. Although Kenny philosophically agreed with Douglas, he did not like her challenging male-controlled federal patronage. These men had not forgotten Gahagan's success in the fight to get a woman appointed head of Los Angeles' postal service. They also realized if Douglas ran they might well lose even more control because, in Bozzani's words, of the "great influence and respect which this grand lady enjoys with the President and the Party leaders in Washington." Bozzani had good reason for concern about Gahagan. The chairwoman of the Fourteenth Assembly District led the fight against Gahagan on grounds of incompetence, the " 'plot of forces outside the district to foist the ex-actress on them as a candidate . . . and an 'attempt to establish the Hollywood Follies on the Washington stage.' "[55]

Although the ambitious Hawkins had a sizable group of supporters, it was not enough to combat the Ford forces. Hawkins did not command support from all the black activists, and in the end he did not file. Juanita Terry Barbee, whose mother was a leading black in the district, recalled that many in the black community resented "the fact that this glamorous actress should run for Congress in the district when we had qualified people. . . . It hurt Gus very much because he really worked for [the congressional seat]. My mother, [however], was a Douglas fan." Although Hawkins was talented, he was young and "for the things we [blacks] wanted to accomplish, it probably was a good idea to have somebody who did have the backing and the contacts."[56]

While Ford worked enthusiastically to gain support for Douglas, she felt anxious about taking the final step of filing. She had written Melvyn in August 1943 about the decision but had not heard from him. She assumed Melvyn would support her, as he always had, but she must have wondered what the impact would be on their relationship and the children. In her letter Helen expressed concern about the future of her acting and singing, despite the fact that she had done neither for four years. Madame Cehanovska was "furious at the mention of Eleanor Roosevelt, who she believed had lured me from greatness on the opera stage," she commented.[57]

Lillian Ford wrote her in early February 1944. "Take it for granted that you are going to be a candidate, because a lot of people want you to be." But she should "stage" her announcement and not allow any residents outside the Fourteenth—specifically Hollywood types—to take an active part in the campaign until after the filing deadline of March 7. She should also make it look like Ford was drafting her. Gahagan wrote Eleanor Roosevelt for advice February 21, two weeks before the filing deadline. "Tom Ford wants me to run in his district," Helen said. "He will come out for a month before the primaries and campaign for me. I am in a terrible quandry [*sic*] to know what is best to do. . . . The campaign doesn't frighten me at all, but when I think that I may be elected and that I would have to look and listen to some of those monsters in Congress I get perfectly sick to my stomach. Oh, dear, I wish I was near you so I could talk to you." ER tried to calm her friend down. Both she and the President felt the time and conditions were right for her to run, she wrote on February 28. "I am sure you can weather anything the Republicans say about you. After one has been in the public eye long enough, one learns to be impervious." With this final encouragement, Gahagan filed. If she could help the President by running for Congress, then she figured she could overcome any hurdles. Her concerns appeared to be less for her family and the campaign itself than for the reality of confrontation if she reached Washington. FDR reinforced her decision. "I do not need to tell you how much I have always thought of Tom Ford," he wrote, "but if he has to leave the Congress I can ask nothing better than to have you in his place." The challenge had become exciting. [58]

8

An Actress in Congress

THE FOURTEENTH District congressional campaign got off the ground in mid-March. Fortunately Ford passed on to her a strong campaign structure. The principal figures included Ford's manager, Ed Lybeck; his wife, Ruth Lybeck; and Florence Reynolds, who had coordinated Ford's Los Angeles office. The three had run several of Ford's campaigns "with silky efficiency." Ed Lybeck, a noted mystery writer, had grown up in New York. He first became involved with political campaigning in Al Smith's run for the governorship of New York in 1926. In the early 1930s, the Lybecks moved to California and lived on Shatto Street, a low-rent area in the Sixty-fourth Assembly District. They immediately involved themselves in California politics and in 1938 began working for Ford, using their house as a campaign headquarters. Lybeck knew the area "like the palm of his hand" and took his responsibilities seriously. Florence (Susie) Clifton also joined the campaign team for the 1944 race. An active Democrat in several elections and an astute campaign strategist, Clifton had been closely connected to the Olson administration through her husband, Judge Robert Clifton. Helen was also fortunate to have Evelyn Chavoor, now twenty-five, working for her again as both a personal and professional assistant. Evie, who had been a full-time nanny for the Douglases from 1938 to 1941 after she had taken classes at the University of California at Los Angeles, had left the family for a civil service job. But when Helen ran for Congress, she persuaded Evie to return to help in the campaign and then to go to Washington.

Ford, the Lybecks, and Clifton ran a tight campaign. Before the filing deadline, Ford put pressure on his inner circle of key supporters to back Helen, rather than promote another strong candidate, and to provide funds. For example, he asked Congressman John Elliott, who had received crucial support from Ford in the past, not to oppose her or to support her opponents, even though Elliott did not like her. Although Hawkins was not in the race, another prominent black in the district, lawyer Loren Miller, filed, as did two other Democrats and three Republicans who cross-filed. Once the campaign was in full tilt, Lybeck used the same strategy as Ford's campaigns, which included writing flyers and brochures targeted for different socioeconomic and ethnic populations. Lybeck decided Helen should use her full name, "Helen Gahagan Douglas," to capitalize on Melvyn's Army duty and the image of family. From that point on, she never used "Helen Gahagan" as her public name. Brochures generally included a family photo of Helen, Melvyn in his Army uniform, Peter, and Mary Helen. The team also moved into key neighborhoods to organize volunteers to pass out literature. Clifton implemented Women's Division–type campaigning with detailed instructions for every street within each precinct, a strategy she had used successfully in the 1938 Olson campaign in Los Angeles County. There is no evidence to suggest that Lybeck worked closely with the Women's Division. As the district had always been a safe Democratic seat, this sort of cooperation had never been necessary: although this time, Lybeck needed all the support he could find.[1]

Vicious Red-baiting and anti-Semitic literature, with ample references to both Helen's and Melvyn's ties with Popular Front organizations and Melvyn's Jewish background, circulated from the beginning of the campaign from other candidates, although no single individual emerged as the principal opponent. One flyer reminded voters that Douglas's real name was "Hesleberger [sic]." "She is a communist. Has filed out of her district . . . 12 years of communistic Tom Ford is enough." Another pamphlet claimed that Douglas had been married four times and "lives in wonderful Hollywood mansion. Has never had business or executive experience." Douglas wrote Eleanor Roosevelt, "Well, I am really in the campaign and I never knew anything could be quite so repulsive. I hope I'm not deluding myself in thinking that I can be of some help if elected." The *Los Angeles Times* accused her of Communist ties because the allegedly Communist-run national CIO backed her and because of her friendship with Henry Wallace. A poster from a Democratic opponent pictured Douglas, labeled "Lady Bountiful," coming down out of the hills of the Fifteenth and asking a passerby, "Where's the Fourteenth District?" None of this criticism bothered Ford. He figured that when he came out to campaign, "all those little eggs [including] Hawkins . . . will be put in their places." Douglas would "carry on in the tradition of *Stand by the President* [and] put the 14th on the map."[2]

Douglas, conducting an issue-oriented campaign, championed the New Deal record and emphasized her confidence in Roosevelt's leadership. She went armed with figures and simple language and refused to run down her opponents. What was good for the country was good for her district, she argued, for its problems mirrored the challenges facing America. In her speeches and campaign literature she followed the Democratic party line, arguing that only President Roosevelt and a Democratic Congress were qualified to handle postwar challenges of reconversion and the securing of social and economic justice for all Americans. She emphasized that Republicans opposed measures to improve the life of the average American. She went beyond Roosevelt's position on blacks as she played to her district, urging the establishment of a permanent Fair Employment Practices Commission (FEPC), abolition of the poll tax, better housing, job training for wartime workers, respect for the rights of organized labor, full protection for small farmers and small business, government support for the physically handicapped, and veterans' benefits.

Douglas set up a series of meetings early in the campaign to talk with women in neighborhood homes about their perceptions of neighborhood problems. As few as ten to as many as a hundred came to meetings throughout the district. She liked communicating with small groups on their "own territory," a technique she eventually developed into a refined skill. Despite Ford's advice to the contrary, as he downplayed the power of the black voter, she spent the majority of her time in the heavily black Sixty-second Assembly District. She particularly liked visiting black churches. Her personal contact helped dissipate some of the hostility from women who could not envision a woman in Congress and from some blacks who wondered if she would fight for their needs. The key to this success, however, lay both in her message and in the way she communicated. Her long years of acting experience paid off. As an actress, Douglas had learned how to read her audience and then reach out and emotionally charge the group. She used this skill in a powerful way during her campaign. Douglas did not let the campaign stop her from continuing her Women's Division work, however, including campaigning for other congressional candidates. She spent four days in March working in Santa Barbara for George Outland. In April, she held the annual Women's Division tea in her home, which drew over 1,000 women. She wrote Dewson, "I feel sometimes that with the weight of the entire state on my shoulders, as well as my personal campaign, that I'm not going to quite last the day or night, and I begin praying for strength."[3]

Douglas won the primary, gaining over 14,000 votes to her closest competitor's 5,200. She was "replacing the Dean of the delegation," she wrote De Sola, and they "threw everything at me they could get their hands on." The Fords were jubilant. "It makes us so happy to think that you will be the mother of the 14th." They had no doubt that her Republican opponent, William Campbell, who had lost three times to Ford, would lose again, although he had come very close to taking both party nominations through cross-filing.

Douglas had a victory party at her house following the campaign. All went except Lybeck, who stayed at headquarters out of principle. As Clifton recalled, Ed "wasn't going to hobnob . . . in the Hollywood Hills. He belonged down in the district." In fact, he criticized everyone else for going. Although he had respected Ford's choice of Douglas and worked hard for her, he was turned off by her glamorous image and her wealthy lifestyle. He also was turned off by what he and the staff considered her constant "role-playing." The staff who knew her best would say, " 'Helen's playing this role . . . or that role today. And she was . . . always being an actress. . . . Ed wasn't overly impressed.' "[4]

Although pleased with her victory, Douglas was also nervous. But a letter from Melvyn, dated May 29, about her decision to run for Congress—the first response she had had from him concerning her campaign—offered some comfort. She realized the sagacity of Melvyn's eloquent and thoughtful observations when he wrote that though her chances to win were good, "what a job you will have. The war congress will seem tame as compared to the peace congress." It would have to contend with the old pressures for special privileges and new ones from veterans wanting their share of material goods. "I wonder if they can be convinced that without a well-defended moral basis to world society the possession of things will only be fleeting and life itself will be in constant danger." Creating such a moral base was difficult, though, since the American standard for decades had "largely revolved around the accumulation of *things* rather than the building of a humane and well-balanced society." Nowhere in the letter, however, did he make any reference to their personal life. While Melvyn wrote with a warm and supportive tone, the letter clearly indicates the detachment he felt. Three years away from home had taken its toll.[5]

Douglas temporarily put aside thoughts of the fall campaign and the possible reality of a move to Washington to plan for the Democratic national convention, where she was to play a key role. The DNC had ticketed her to be the most prominent woman among the convention speakers. Tillett also delivered a principal address, the first time that two women played such visible roles at this event. The press played up the decision to include the glamorous Douglas, claiming that the Democrats were trying to copy the Republicans, who had placed the flashy Congresswoman Clare Boothe Luce in a prominent spot in their June convention. Much to the press's disappointment, neither woman had any interest in a "catfight." Luce commented that she had no intention of getting "into any hair pulling contest with any woman—regardless of what side of the fence she's on. . . . I am for women making greater . . . strides in politics in both parties." Helen also responded angrily to the press's insistence on playing up a glamor-girl competition. She hostilely answered questions about nail polish, kissing babies, her height, and her weight. She was "neither a wit nor a fencer," and she was in Chicago only because she thought Roosevelt was the "greatest man in the world. . . . 'If I go to Congress it won't be to spar with anybody, man or woman. . . . It's all nonsense and an insult to the American people. . . . I'm in politics because there's a world and I just hope that I can be of some help.' " Her brother Walter wrote her that he knew she was not interested in a "bicker" with Luce and that she should remember some "wonderful words of wisdom" that their mother Lillian had said after Helen criticized isolationist Charles Lindbergh. If you have to attack other people in a fight, Lillian said, get out. Fight on issues, not personalities. Ford's fantasy of Douglas taking on "la Luce" quickly faded.[6]

Douglas stayed with her family in New York to work on her convention speech. Walter provided her a stenographer whom Douglas kept busy with revisions as she constantly consulted with various Washington people, including Eleanor Roosevelt. Family friends served as critics, suggesting phrasing and sentence construction, but, as Walter wrote Melvyn, "the final product is, I feel, exactly what Helen believes and wants to say," a spirited presentation of the meaning of the Democratic Party and FDR. Walter added that although Helen felt physically tired, he was relieved that she did not appear to be under the strain that he had previously observed when she was attempting to do too much. "It has been inspiring having Helen here. . . . Her enthusiasm is infectious." Before leaving for Chicago, Douglas went to Hyde Park to review her final draft with the First Lady. ER wrote Walter Pick that Helen was doing "the big woman's speech for the Democratic Convention—not answering Clare Boothe Luce, but doing a better speech than she did." The First Lady thought the talk was so good that the DNC should allow her more time.[7]

At the convention on the night of Douglas's speech, fans had stretched a huge banner across the platform that read "Our Helen," and the audience gave her warm applause. She enjoyed the attention, but moved right into her pragmatic speech, opening with a brief discussion of the responsibilities of a free country—"self-discipline, sacrifices, and a high choice of leadership." She described the Democratic administration as the "instrument of the people," one that had to be at one with the "people who must pay the price for food, clothing, and shelter." She continued: "The Democratic party is the true, conservative party [since it has] conserved hope and ambition . . . rescued banks and trusts [and] insured crops and savings. . . . We reject the hazy Republican dream that this country can get along with its government dismantled, its housing programs destroyed, its wage and price controls thrown out the window." She then proceeded, clearly and succinctly, to compare the two party platforms, point by point. Douglas's hard work on the speech paid off. Her comparison of the party platforms was later quoted frequently by politicians, and one commented that "she's put the phrase 'double talk' into the campaign to stay." Not all political observers, however, liked her address. The *Los Angeles Examiner* correspondent, who thought the entire convention reeked of disillusionment, called her speech "dull" and delivered in an "overloud, almost shrewish voice." Even her admirers felt that her voice came through on the radio in an unflatteringly high pitch. Melvyn wrote a very emotional letter after reading a copy of the speech, suggesting, perhaps, that he had begun to face the personal implications of Helen's new life. He felt frustrated being so far away, he told her. "You can imagine how intensely I wanted to hear [your speech] from your own lips." As he read it aloud to his roommate, "it was with difficulty that I controlled my voice. Pride and tears insisted on creeping in."[8]

In addition to delivering a principal speech, Douglas also became involved with those pushing Wallace as the vice-presidential candidate. Wallace supporters initially lacked strong leadership at the convention. Finally Roosevelt sent a letter to the convention delegation in which he indicated that he would leave the choice up to the convention, although if he were a delegate, he would vote for Wallace. The letter, though lukewarm, rekindled the Wallace movement, and Douglas called an unofficial meeting of delegates from Western states to discuss strategy. The strategy included California's passing to Iowa on the first ballot. California split 3–2 for Wallace on the first ballot. On the second balloting, only ten out of fifty-two California delegates, including Douglas, remained with the vice-president. This forlorn group became the focus for cheering pro-Truman delegates, who "milled around" their California colleagues and "draped them with Truman banners." ER, who had worked hard for the vice-president's renomination, wrote Pick: "I feel sad over Mr. Wallace's defeat and I know that Helen worked very hard for him with her delegation. I would have liked very much for him to win, but I am told that Truman is a good man, better than many we might have pushed through the Convention. I suppose we ought to be grateful, as the President made up his mind he could not be a dictator on the subject." She added that she knew she was going to hate the campaign. "If the President is elected, as I suppose we must hope he will be, I am not going to like another four years in Washington. However, if this is for the good of the country, we will have to accept it philosophically."[9]

Although many liberal Democratic women shared the disappointment of the Wallace defeat, they felt pleased about the progress and visibility of women at the convention. About 1,500 women attended a breakfast honoring Mary Norton's twenty years in Congress. A *Democratic Digest* reporter wrote that "the charm, warmth, and intelligence of Helen Gahagan won over the newspaper girls, to say nothing of the newspaper men." Another *Digest* writer commented: "Gone are the days when women's publicity in politics consisted of a description of the lady's pet recipe." The success of women lay less in statistics or the "stars" than in individual stories of "women who spoke with force . . . in their own delegation caucuses . . . who won their points in committee meetings. . . . The Democrats did not have all their eggs in one basket but had lots of capable women." Dozens of women had spoken on local radio stations and the four national networks. In short, "real recognition was given to Democratic women and . . . the women measured up to that recognition." The major urban papers, however, did not indicate much interest in women's political advances. Tillett wrote Dewson that all major committees had 50 percent women and a co-chairwoman; "I would give anything if you were here to see our accomplishments for women at this convention. . . . I have been trying to think of something else to ask for but I have about run out of 50-50 requests."[10]

The fall campaign got off to a slow start both in California and across the nation. "This campaign seems to be apathetic," ER commented in a letter to Pick. "I think people are so much occupied in war they cannot give very much thought to the political activities. I do not know how the campaign will come out, but I know the President certainly can not follow Mr. Dewey around the country." Both women and labor, however, worked hard to combat voter inertia. Although the Women's Division was hampered by a lack of funds, it continued to play an active role in registering and educating voters, convinced that the woman's vote would be a critical one in November. Labor also felt that its vote was important. The more conservative mood of the Seventy-eighth Congress and the passage of the irritating anti-labor Smith-Connolly Act encouraged Sidney Hillman, president of the Amalgamated Clothing Workers Union, to persuade the CIO's executive committee to create a well-financed political action committee, CIO-PAC. The policy that "what was good for the country was good for labor" reflected a shift from previous thinking that labor should only look after its own special interests. Like the Women's Division, CIO-PAC saw its role as one of educating voters, publicizing the records of liberal candidates, and making certain that people both registered and voted. They had more money than the women, however, to accomplish their goals.[11]

Douglas's congressional race generated considerable interest around the country. This was due in part to labor's support, which proved stronger than that from women. As Lybeck said, "the hardest thing about Helen was selling her to women." It was one thing for a woman to educate and organize women as voters, and quite another to run for national office. Furthermore, Douglas was very attractive, wealthy, and unpopular among conservative Democrats, men and women. She did win the support of many of those who had been in the inner circle of Ford's support group but who had held out during the primary. Douglas got considerable publicity from her Hollywood friends, such as Walter Huston and Eddie Cantor, who spoke for her or gave money. The active Hollywood branch of the left-wing Independent Citizens' Committee on the Arts, Sciences, and Professions (HICCASP) also supported her. This local group had first organized Olson campaign workers in 1938 and had a membership of over 2,000 by 1944. Its executive committee included screenwriter Dalton Trumbo and John Howard Lawson, scientist Linus Pauling, actor Ronald Reagan, and politician James Roosevelt, the President's son. Lybeck, however, tended to discount Hollywood support because it came from outside the district and represented what he considered the least appealing quality about Douglas.[12]

As in the spring, Douglas's literature emphasized that Roosevelt and Ford backed her. Pamphlets aimed at blacks mentioned the endorsement from Mary McLeod Bethune, the leading black female in political life in the country, and from labor leader Phil Connelly, who had finally swung to supporting Douglas. She mentioned Melvyn's overseas duty with the hopes of combating the ever-present Red-baiters who relished challenging her loyalty. She also probably assumed she could capitalize on Melvyn's popularity as a film celebrity. Lybeck worked hard to get her out into the district. As in the primary, she used the house meeting as her key means of meeting the voter, but she also spoke at many labor union meetings, black churches and social clubs, ethnic organizations, and some large rallies. Once again Clifton coordinated massive registration efforts and carefully organized precinct campaigning.

William Campbell, Douglas's Republican opponent, tried to exploit her endorsement by CIO-PAC by stressing Hillman's alleged Communist leanings. He also played up the HICCASP endorsement, again insinuating Communist ties. One advertisement read, "Which will you have? Communist or American. A Vote for HGD is a Vote for Hillman and [Earl] Browder." He called her a carpetbagger and implied that she was incapable because she was a woman. At the same time, Campbell constructed his platform to parallel Douglas's so that the two candidates would appear almost identical philosophically. Douglas and her supporters were undaunted by Campbell's tactics, although they did not ignore them. A Douglas pamphlet in reply read, "Don't be misled by desperate last-minute political slanders and misrepresentations." The *Los Angeles Daily News* assured its Democratic readers that Douglas was too good to let these criticisms pull her down. What mattered much more, of course, was that the district had gone Democratic for years. It had the highest percentage of registered Democrats in the state.[13]

Douglas not only worked in the field but at headquarters; at these times she often brought Mary Helen with her. But once there, she left it to the staff to entertain the six-year-old. Susie Clifton recalled that the staff would set up Mary Helen with projects, often paper and crayons. On some days Bob Clifton would wait at headquarters for Susie, and he and Mary Helen would play imaginary games. One time, "Mary Helen asked Bob, 'Would you mind if I call you Daddy?' Which we thought was pathetic, so I tell it only to reflect what she [Mary Helen] was feeling." In general, however, Helen relied on full-time help to take care of the children.[14]

Although Douglas spent most of her time on her own campaign, she felt so confident of victory that she accepted speaking engagements in southern California and nationally. She even began to look into housing in Washington. Her greatest triumph turned out to be a speech she gave in a debate in October with New York Republican governor Thomas E. Dewey, Luce, and movie director Orson Welles, sponsored by the New York Herald Tribune Forum in October. Initially the DNC and Roosevelt opposed her involvement on the grounds that the forum was not bipartisan, but at the last minute they changed their minds. In her speech she outlined Roosevelt's foreign policy as far back as 1933, and credited his vision with forging the alliance that proved critical for the United States in World War II. "The people of this country will vote for those whom they believe best qualified to guarantee a world [in which] Fascism and aggression will never again threaten us. . . . I believe there is no man or woman alive who is indispensable. But there is something that is indispensable, and that is a certain point of view, a way of thinking. . . . That philosophy holds that our security is identical with the security of our neighbors in England, Russia, China . . . and that we can never stand apart in isolation. Franklin Roosevelt has long understood the importance of the philosophy. . . . That we do not stand alone in the world today, hemmed in by our enemies, is due to his vision."[15]

Helen wrote Melvyn and Walter Pick after the speech: "What a time we had through all of it. When [the DNC] decided that I wasn't going to do it, we stopped working on the speech and as a result it wasn't completed when I arrived in New York. The night previous to departing neither Evie nor I took off our clothes." In fact, "Bocky says the next time I leave an important speech to the last minute, he will put me over his knee and spank me." Now that it was over, she felt very relieved. "It went off beautifully. . . . Luce when she can't be vindictive, is no good." DNC chairman Robert Hannagan wired telling her that her speech was "tremendous." The headquarters had been getting calls from all over the country "advising that your speech is the greatest in the campaign. I listened to your speech together with a group of friends and cannot tell you how delighted we were. You really did a marvelous job." Eleanor Roosevelt was "terribly pleased," as was the Women's Division, which was receiving hundreds of requests for mimeographed copies and recordings. Hickok wrote that the agony of preparing the speech was worth it. Norton had called up the Women's Division the day after the speech and "raved about it. . . . My pet, you really did a job."[16]

Once back in California, Douglas re-entered her whirlwind of campaign speeches. Her campaign results were carefully monitored all over the country. The Democrats in Utah, for example, showed a "remarkable intense interest," reported the national committeeman from Utah. More important, her Washington friends watched with concern. The national election was as close as Douglas's, and the results were not clear until early the next morning, although Douglas remained confident throughout the evening. Lorena Hickok wrote

Douglas that she had worried terribly. When she finally learned that Douglas had won, she said, "I was so relieved and so weary that I went home and celebrated all by myself, in bed, with a bottle of brandy. It took only three drinks to put me out for the night." FDR, who had watched the campaign closely, wrote that he had been very concerned because at about two o'clock in the morning, she was still five hundred votes behind. "I was afraid that this included the counting of the soldiers' vote. However, the next morning everything cleared up nicely and now you are to be a real Congressman and not just a beautiful cloak model to outdo the Luce woman. We are, of course, awfully happy." ER was "thrilled" over the election and invited Helen to stay at the White House until she found a place to live. Mary Norton wrote how she had "rejoiced with you in my heart. I have been lonesome all by myself on the Democratic side."[17]

The vote was, indeed, very close. Douglas won by a margin of less than four thousand votes out of approximately 137,500 cast. But she entered election day with enormous confidence. In fact, she felt so assured of victory that she bought expensive watches for Lybeck and Clifton for their help and gave them their presents before she knew whether or not she had won. Clifton remembered that she and Lybeck, less sure of a victory, said to each other, "What do we do with the damn watches if she doesn't win?" Douglas did acknowledge the "bitter, cruel" nature of the campaign, as she phrased it in a letter to the President. "We were so near the precipice [but] people, largely the inarticulate ones, the honest and believing, the silent ones, carried the victory." She told him again how much he and his wife had changed their lives. She cherished their friendship.[18]

Douglas's win was part of the tide of victory that Roosevelt enjoyed in California in 1944. The state's Democrats increased their congressional representation from twelve in 1942 to sixteen. Nationally the Democrats added twenty-five seats, making the total 243. Despite this coattail effect, however, it was still unusual that Douglas won if one looks at the pattern of female congressional victories. The pattern of success suggested that women running for office needed substantial financial backing, family political connections, professional training, and political experience. Most women who won electoral offices grew up in an environment of political or social activism. Douglas did not fit this profile. Most likely the backing she received from the popular Ford and Roosevelt, the Democratic swing, her glamorous image, and her effectiveness in relating to people gave her the edge she needed to topple three-time loser Campbell.[19]

Douglas wrote Eleanor Roosevelt after the campaign that she felt overwhelmed with all she had to do, but typically she figured "somehow things will work out." The Women's Division had given her a desk set, she wrote, and she "didn't know whether to laugh or cry. . . . How I hate letters—mail, meetings, everything that goes with Desk Sets. And here I am a Congress-woman. It's really very ironic. I suppose I shall even have to learn to spell before I die." She closed with the message, "I love you. I love the President," leaving no doubt about what motivated her to political action. Douglas had cleanup activities from the campaign and final jobs with the Women's Division. She also had to face the realities of a move. At least she could stay at the White House until she found a place to live. She needed to find renters for the house, decide what to do with the children, and find a place for Melvyn's mother to live. She had been living with Helen and the children for two years.[20]

By mid-December, Helen had solved most of these problems. She wrote Melvyn that she had found good renters, a young New York couple with two children who "appear to be very clean." They had a cook and a nurse. They agreed to pay $1,000 monthly rent with Douglas paying to maintain the garden and the pool. She decided to send Mary Helen, who had just turned six, back east with her grandmother Lillian, who had been helping to get the Outpost ready for renting. Douglas arranged to leave ten-year-old Peter with a friend until his school term ended. Once she was settled, she planned to have the children join her in Washington. Although she originally thought she would leave for Washington in mid-December, she decided to wait until after Christmas so she could be with Peter. "Mary Helen won't mind nearly as much as Petie would if I weren't to be with him," she wrote Melvyn. She found an apartment for Melvyn's mother, not an easy task at the end of 1944. Helen wanted Lena to live in the Fourteenth Congressional District so Helen could use the address as her permanent residence to defuse the "out-of-district" issue. She found a place on Wilshire Boulevard, "thereby establishing a residence in the district. Whenever I need to return to California during the next two years," she wrote Melvyn, "I will stay there with her and register."[21]

In between packing, sorting, and planning, Douglas worked at social obligations and going-away parties. She hosted the annual Women's Division fund-raising tea for 1,600 women, which meant "working frantically . . . to get out the thousands of letters and cleaning in preparation." Evie arranged a surprise party for all the Douglas friends who had helped get the family ready to leave. Douglas told Chavoor that if she had thoughts of "any tom foolishness such as a party" the day before the tea, "I'll slit your throat and mine too." Evie finally confessed, Helen wrote Melvyn. "She's such a poor liar. The next day I had to act surprised. . . . Everyone had been told what I needed in the way of clothing [and] I was clothed from my skin to my slip including night clothes." Many of the outfits had been made from her old theater costumes. "Our first toast was to you, darling," she continued; and then "we played charades until one in the morning. . . . The greatest part of the helpfulness comes because you are in India. It is everyone's way of thanking you."[22]

The day after Christmas of 1944, Douglas set off by car for Washington, accompanied by Chavoor and an actress friend, Jarmila Marton, wife of a Hungarian director. Although Douglas had visited there many times, this was different. As a member of Congress, her new job would bear no resemblance to that of a volunteer. She had only a vague sense of the contours of her new job, although she knew she had taken on an awesome responsibility. But she approached this new undertaking much as she had new challenges in the past, by taking it one day at a time. She knew that the car trip east presented an opportunity to let down, which was hard for her to do, and she spent most of the trip sleeping on the back seat while her friends drove. They planned no visits with friends except the David Lilienthals in Tennessee. Lilienthal, director of the Tennessee Valley Authority, had promised to fly Douglas over the project. Otherwise, the trip proved uneventful. They were amused, however, when they heard on the radio that Helen had been named one of the best-dressed women in the country, apparently defeating Clare Boothe Luce. As Douglas recalled, "We all howled. I hadn't bought any new clothes since Melvyn joined the army. My best outfit, a black velvet suit, was made from a costume I wore in *Mary of Scotland*." Chavoor remembered the incident with as much hilarity. When they caught the announcement at about five o'clock in the morning, she looked at Helen in the back seat "with terribly sloppy pants on, and some warm hose . . . huddled in a blanket, her hair all streaming down." Helen also had just broken a front tooth. Evie laughed and wondered what the photographers would think if they could see her at that moment. From then on, the ladies primped the star to make her look glamorous before stopping for the night. The "fixin' " for the tooth had been mailed to the Lilienthals so that David's dentist could "fix her up for the Washington photographers." After the visit, Lilienthal joined the group and drove to Washington, arriving on January 2, just in time for the first congressional caucus and the swearing-in. Rather than staying at the White House, they moved into a hotel. Shortly after, Douglas found a house in the suburb of Chevy Chase, Maryland, large enough for herself, Chavoor, and the two children.[23]

The Seventy-ninth Congress was a "good, average, American-way-of-life Congress," said the *Washington Post*, with "Democrats still insecurely at the controls." The Southern Democrats and Republicans still formed a majority. Liberals assumed this would preclude any major Democratic Party legislation. Douglas felt particularly encouraged about several of the new Democratic House members, especially two outstanding women, Emily Taft Douglas from Illinois and Chase Going Woodhouse from Connecticut. The three new women provided a strong liberal complement to Mary Norton.

The liberals faced the same problem of political balance in the Senate that they found in the House. The Democrats had lost one seat, giving them a total of fifty-seven members; Republicans held thirty-eight seats, and the Progressive

Party, one. Two new Democratic senators, Brien McMahon of Connecticut and Washington's Warren Magnuson, soon became close associates of Douglas's. Democrat William Fulbright from Arkansas, who had distinguished himself in the House as an internationalist, replaced the Senate's only woman member, Hattie Caraway. Senate liberals were also encouraged by the addition of two liberal Republicans, Oregon's Wayne Morse and Leverett Saltonstall from Massachusetts.[24]

The three new Democratic women brought the number of women in the House to nine. As a group, they set a new tone for the second generation of congresswomen. Norton, the "dean of women Representatives" in her eleventh term, still head of the House Labor Committee, felt elated that she had female support to help battle the conservatives. She had entered the House with substantial experience in welfare work and powerful statewide influence within the New Jersey machine of Frank Hague. While most women elected to Congress before the war were either widows of deceased congressmen or unmarried, all three new Democrats came to Congress on the merits of their own activities and had family responsibilities. The *Democratic Digest* called the election a victory of women who won without significant help from the men in their lives. Woodhouse, the most experienced, was, at the time of her election, Professor of Economics at Connecticut College. She had held the office of Connecticut's Secretary of State and served on government war boards. Emily Douglas's political experience included a long involvement with the Illinois League of Women Voters. She initially became involved in politics with her husband, Paul, an economics professor at the University of Chicago, when fascism grew in Europe in the mid-1930s. Like Melvyn, Paul had enlisted in the service in 1942. On the Republican side, Edith Nourse Rogers from Massachusetts, noted for her work with World War I veterans, was elected to Congress in 1925, the only Republican woman to survive the early New Deal years. Maine's Margaret Chase Smith and Frances P. Bolton from Ohio came to Congress early in 1940. Smith, a congressman's widow, had been her husband's secretary prior to her election. The wealthy Bolton, a nurse by profession, had played an active role in civic and philanthropic activities before her election. The two other Republican women in the Seventy-ninth Congress were second-termer Luce and Illinois's Judge Jessie Sumner, elected in 1940. Although these women periodically gathered together to be photographed or honored at a tea, it did not occur to them to work together as a group; they did their best, in fact, to downplay their differences from their male colleagues.

For all members, the beginning of a new Congress meant the rearranging of committee assignments, an important and complicated activity controlled by the House Speaker. Committee work absorbed more time than any activity other than responding to constituents, and played a principal role in shaping the member's relationship to the House. Members could request a particular committee, but they often did not get their first choice. Some sought more influence in their district through a "bread and butter" assignment; others wanted to gain more power in the House. Still others, like Douglas, hoped to help shape national policy. For women, the doors were virtually shut to committees in the first two categories. In the third category, the most prestigious committee available to women was Foreign Affairs, the committee Douglas was determined to get appointed to. The House Foreign Affairs Committee had a new-found prestige in 1945.[25]

The Constitution had placed power over foreign-policy formulation in the hands of the President and the Senate. Thus the House Foreign Affairs Committee had always been considered a political graveyard. But as the war ended and the United States assumed a new leadership role in maintaining world peace and attempting to keep the superpowers in balance, the House began to play a more important role in shaping policy. Even before the war ended, it seemed clear that Americans would have to provide monetary aid to assist European countries in restoring healthy economies. Once the war was over, some also thought it essential to provide funds for military aid to prevent Communist takeovers in politically unstable countries. When foreign policy began to involve questions of money, the House, the originator of money bills, became an active partner in shaping foreign relations. Although the House committee never approached the power of the Senate Committee of Foreign Affairs, it suddenly became a popular and prestigious House appointment. In addition, various other House committees, including Appropriations, Agriculture, and Armed Services, became involved in foreign policy, diluting the new power of the Foreign Affairs Committee and resulting in the duplication of efforts of the committees.

None of these concerns dampened Douglas's enthusiasm for working closely with foreign-policy issues through her committee assignment. She carried enough weight, probably through FDR's influence, to secure an appointment, "a post which the Republicans refused to give to their beauty and brains trust, Clare Boothe Luce," one paper quipped. Emily Taft Douglas was also appointed to Foreign Affairs, balancing the two Republican women on the committee, Bolton and Rogers. The Democrats, in fact, added two positions to the committee in order to accommodate the two Douglases.[26]

Douglas had to organize her office quickly so she could move into the work routine of the House. The adjustment process also included the time-consuming business of getting to know the other members, learning the House rules, setting up an efficient system to handle constituents' problems, and becoming familiar with committee work. She was assigned an office in the Cannon Building, or the "old Office Building." She liked the wide corridors, high ceilings, railroad carpeting, and old furniture. From her two rooms on the first floor, she could look across the lawn to the Library of Congress. Her outer office had three desks, a work table, chairs, and a row of filing cabinets, "regular congressional stock, House of Representatives' style," a *Baltimore Sun* reporter commented. To this furniture, Douglas added large old overstuffed leather chairs, "bilious" green rugs (the *Sun* reported), a mahogany desk, bookcases, and plain linen drapes. When the *Sun's* representative inquired if Douglas planned to decorate the office, "she looked puzzled. 'I think it is wonderful,' she declared. 'You should have seen my office in California.' " Her inner office included an enormous desk, a swivel chair, a black leather couch, and several armchairs. [27]

Douglas enjoyed unexpected assistance in organizing her office from the lanky, suave, handsome, and flirtatious New Dealer from Texas, Lyndon B. Johnson. Johnson, elected to his fifth term, had moved more quickly than his colleagues into the informal power networks in the House, both because of his approach to politics and because of his close relationship to House Speaker Sam Rayburn, a fellow Texan. Douglas met Johnson shortly after arriving in Washington. Soon after the term began, he dropped by her office to see how it was run. As Douglas later recalled, "he draped his long frame in one of my easy chairs" and listened to her explain her day. Unquestionably attracted to Douglas and convinced that he could teach her many things about how Congress functioned, he invited her to visit his office to see how it was run. Although Douglas found Johnson's suggestions instructive to a point, her personality, style of learning, and approach to problems ultimately dictated the rhythm of her day, the organization of her office, and how she spent her time. The result was frequently chaos. [28]

The responsibility of having Peter and Mary Helen in Washington added to the already enormous demands made of all members of Congress, especially a new one. Also, unlike most of her male colleagues, Douglas did not enjoy the luxury of a wife who assumed responsibility for a stable household, which included entertaining, organizing children's activities, and often assisting in the congressional office. Although Melvyn had never played the "wife" role, he and Helen had organized home activities together, and they had enjoyed ample house staff. Melvyn also provided occasional companionship for the children, and most important of all, served as Helen's sounding board and her emotional support system. In place of a "wife," Douglas expected the twenty-five-year-old Chavoor, who ran her congressional office, to assume the responsibility for organizing the household and providing the stability all three Douglases needed. Douglas did hire some supplementary help—a maid, a housekeeper, and a teacher who cared for the children after school. But Chavoor ultimately played the "wife's" role. On the frequent occasions when Douglas left town, Chavoor had charge of the house, the children, and the office. [29]

Chavoor often found her responsibilities overwhelming. She vented her frustrations to the Lybecks. In early February 1945, she wrote: "Please forgive me for not answering [your letters]. It's a plain unadulterated fact, I just don't know whether I am coming or going. We moved from the hotel yesterday into our house, finally. It was a holy mess and I have been going around in circles . . . trying to get a little bit of order out of chaos." Although Chavoor often felt overwhelmed with her responsibilities, her loyalty was so strong that she customarily did more than was expected, even passing up vacations or, when on vacation in Los Angeles, helping in Douglas's district congressional office.[30]

Douglas described a typical day early in her congressional term to a reporter from *Redbook*. The day began early, generally at "the unthinkable hour of 4:30 when my 6-year-old daughter Mary Helen crawls in bed with me. I may manage to stay there until 6:30, muttering . . . 'can't you possibly lie still?' but real sleep has departed." Once up, Douglas and Chavoor got the children ready for school. Mary Helen insisted that her mother, not Chavoor, braid her long, golden-blonde hair. At breakfast, Douglas went on, "I hear myself chanting, 'Peter you can't have eggs every day—you must eat your cereal, it's good for you.' I hand him the funnies while I try to find out what has happened overnight in the world." Once the children left for school, Douglas and Chavoor reviewed last-minute instructions for the household help, and took off for Capitol Hill.[31]

Douglas drove so she could dictate letters to Chavoor. Often the two continued to work undisturbed in the parking lot. Once in the office, Douglas retreated to her inner office, and Chavoor began to open the day's mail, dividing it into voters' inquiries requiring referral to agencies for answers, constituent comments about legislation, hardship cases, speaking invitations, and requests for Douglas to sponsor organizations. Phone calls and supervision of the two secretaries constantly interrupted Chavoor's attention to the mail. Although most members of Congress managed with two or three secretaries, Chavoor felt that they needed more help in the office. "Helen's engagements and appointments and telephone calls are enough to drive anyone crazy," she wrote friends. "The office is a bee hive of activity. There are always people waiting to see her and the two telephones and the two girls in the office, plus me, are always on the hop, skip, and jump."[32]

By mid-morning, Douglas generally left for the Foreign Affairs Committee meeting, and by noon she had assumed her seat in the House chamber. She quickly became restless, she confessed, because she found the seats "sheer physical torture. It is doubtful if any theater could prosper if it provided such seats for its patrons." Members had no desks, which made it difficult to write. "Perhaps," she quipped, "if there were more women in the House, something might be done about this." When the House recessed for the day, she returned to the office to sign "piles and piles of letters." Towards late afternoon, the children began calling the office to find out when their mother planned to come home. Although she tried to have dinner with her children each evening, she occasionally would dine with close friends such as the Ickes. She rarely attended the evening round of official social events, the sort of socializing she abhorred. After putting the children down for the night, she collapsed into bed, her first time alone for the day, reading late into the night to prepare for the following day. She found that one of the most difficult adjustments to congressional life was finding time to concentrate without interruption. The only previous time in her life that she had studied so hard was when she learned to sing. During that period, she had the luxury of living alone with no responsibilities other than herself.[33]

Like all new members of Congress, Douglas had much to learn in Washington. Her several years of contact with Washington politics had little relevance to her new job, where she faced not only unfamiliar rules but new standards of performance on a different stage. Early on, nevertheless, as she acquired a feel for her job, she began to develop what was to become her own congressional style. A variety of personal characteristics played a part in shaping this style. Her ideas of how American government ought to function and how postwar American domestic and foreign policy should be formulated provided the content of her speeches. The barriers to effective action facing all new members of Congress (which lowered only slightly for women as they gained seniority) plus Douglas's impulsive and impatient approach to solving human problems through the "right" legislation led Douglas to take her message not only to the legislative floor but to people all over the country. Her talents as an actress, her psychological needs to be at center stage, her physical attractiveness, and her association with Hollywood made people listen and often take action.

As Douglas's view of national and world problems broadened, shaped by Roosevelt's rhetoric and later Truman's Fair Deal liberalism, her purist theoretical notion of representative government became clear. Confusing politics with ethics, she saw political issues in terms of right and wrong. She did not want to understand that what she believed "ought to be" could rarely occur in the real world of politics. She had faith that government, run for and by the American people, could and should be improved through the power of the voter. In her mind, only one set of "right" moral values existed. Believing Roosevelt's dictum that "the greatest duty of the statesman is to educate," she assumed that the well-informed voter would elect legislators who would vote for the "right" programs. She carried this idea one step further by refusing to acknowledge that even if all "right thinking" representatives were elected, the spirit of compromise would still prevail in the legislative arena. She assiduously followed a dictum well expressed by Adlai Stevenson: " 'It is the urgent duty of a political leader to lead, to touch if he can the potentials of reason, decency and humanism in man.' " This type of approach was not gender-based or in particular a liberal outlook; some conservatives had an equally close-minded attitude towards political issues. In Douglas's case, this view may have developed because of her relative inexperience in politics and her uncritical view of the Roosevelts. Also, idealists tend to draw an enthusiastic audience; those who do not want to listen stay away. She also knew that she did not have to stay in electoral politics; she had Melvyn as a provider.[34]

Douglas believed that America had to bear the major responsibility of creating an international structure to prevent a third world war. Secondly, she thought that the government had to guarantee every American the right to a decent way of life. One objective could not be achieved without the other, and it was the duty of Congress to accomplish these goals. Two speeches she gave in early March 1945, one at a World Unity Rally in Madison Square Garden and the second at a dinner in New York for the Liberal Party, illustrate this general philosophy in a more coherent fashion than her campaign platform. She asked why people seemed to demonstrate more creativity when they sought destructive rather than constructive ends. Perhaps, she suggested, because "survival is obviously at stake. . . . But if for war, why not for peace?" Defining a liberal as one who was free and open-minded, "capable of facing facts however disagreeable they may be" and "capable of mental reflexes," she declared that only liberals could accomplish creative peacetime goals. Liberals in the United States had two tasks, to "make all understand that this half-shattered world cannot survive the shock of another war" and to help the nations of the world "find a common ground for peace."[35]

In order to ensure world peace, she continued, Americans had to have a "prosperous and healthy" country—which meant jobs. "Jobs mean happy people—hopeful people. Just as we have made the struggle against fascism a people's war, just as we are resolved that it shall end in a people's victory, so must we also support and insist upon a people's peace." Securing such a peace required a plan, she argued. "A home is run on a plan, budgets are worked out by plan, we make plans for our children, . . . a business works by plan, any shop or factory has a plan." Such plans existed in Roosevelt's program. Preliminary meetings in the latter half of 1944, taking place at Dumbarton Oaks, a lovely Washington, D.C., estate, formulated an outline for an international peace organization. The United Nations conference in San Francisco, opening in April 1945, would refine these goals. At home, the beginnings of the right sort of plan existed in the Murray-Patman bill for full employment, Douglas argued. All these proposals deserved full support.[36]

When Douglas entered Congress, she did not know exactly what her role would be in helping accomplish these goals. She did, however, assume quite unrealistically that she would make a difference, and right away. Otherwise there was no point in being in Congress. After her election, she wrote Eleanor Roosevelt with assurance: "Perhaps I can go around kicking Congressmen when

they get ornery. I shall kick ours, you may be very sure, if *they* get out of line."
Once in Congress, she explored various avenues of influence; when she found
the way blocked, she tried other routes. Douglas discovered quickly that in
order to have any sort of impact as a new member, she would have to play a
nontraditional role. She was too impatient to wait the necessary length of time
dictated by the behavior norms of the House for new members wishing to
assume a position of power. Without question, the tenure in office for a member of Congress, no matter the sort of previous qualifications, essentially determined the member's position within the House. One close observer of Congress in these years noted that the seniority system "is a spirit pervading the
total behavior of Congress." Emanuel Celler, one of Douglas's senior colleagues, called a freshman member of Congress "a lost soul. He cannot find
his way. . . . He does not know the rules and nobody bothers explaining
them." In the process of gaining seniority, those who obeyed the rules got
ahead faster.[37]

The first basic rule—to specialize—did not interest Douglas. Although in
time she did become more committed to certain issues, she essentially considered herself a generalist fighting for an overarching plan for America. Nor
did she have any inclination to learn the intricacies of legislation. Speaker Sam
Rayburn's dictum that new members should "go along to get along" did not fit
her style. She had no intention of ingratiating herself with her colleagues. She
worked to get along with those who thought about issues as she did; otherwise
she saw legislators as her enemies or simply incompetent. Even if Douglas had
had the temperament to follow the time-honored traditions of the House, the
result would have been far less satisfying for her as a female member than for
her male colleagues, a fact Douglas undoubtedly realized. One role that did
work for Douglas was that of the idealistic harasser, the goader, the one who
urged voters to action and persisted in lecturing those of her colleagues whom
she considered immoral and irresponsible; in other words, a self-appointed whip.
Such a role was open to women, but few men or women had the talent to play
the part as well as Douglas. The script dictated that an emotional, convincing,
and effective actor take an uncompromising philosophical stance, and Douglas
had the necessary skills. As political scientist Richard F. Fenno, Jr., commented, "Dramatic analogies are appropriate to politics because politicians,
like actors, perform before audiences and are legitimized by their audiences."[38]

Modeling herself after Eleanor Roosevelt, Douglas concerned herself with
developing new policy for a national and international constituency of "ordinary people" rather than concerning herself exclusively with the needs of her
district's constituents or with legislative procedures. In many cases, her personal
views rather than direction from her district guided her decisions. She believed
her philosophy would ultimately benefit her constituents. Indeed, the economic interests of the national groups she deemed important, particularly labor

and blacks, were similar to the key groups in her district. In foreign affairs, she saw herself speaking for every American who wanted peace. What was good for the world, therefore, was good for the country and for her district. For without world peace one could not have economic prosperity. She often sounded more like a senator than a member of the House.[39]

Douglas played her part with a distinctive flair, setting herself apart from her colleagues; yet her style was not a role entirely unknown to the House or Senate. Political scientists have variously typed these legislators as outsiders, mavericks, gadflies, crusaders, or agitators. Generally, the fewer rules that legislators followed, the faster they became cast in this nonconformist role. One close observer of the political scene described this type in words that fitted Douglas precisely. Unlike typical legislators who saw themselves as bargainers, an art very finely honed by Douglas's colleagues Everett Dirksen and Lyndon Johnson, outsiders felt "impelled to stand for principle absolutely, preferring defeat on those items to half-a-loaf. [They like] to tell people what they should and frequently do not want to hear." These types took themselves very seriously, and were often lacking a sense of humor. More often than not liberals, who believed they could not accomplish liberal goals if they followed the rules, these legislators felt free to criticize even their own party leadership. The more non-conformist their position, the less effective they were at pressing for their legislative objectives. This stance rarely won them regard from the majority of their colleagues, who tended to cast an ideologue aside as a demagogue or "showhorse." This style either generated enthusiasm and loyal devotion from followers or hearty dislike. These legislators looked outside the House for support, to "ideological allies across the nation." And "demagogue" described Douglas well. She sought center stage and wanted credit for what she did. She felt confident that if she could communicate the urgency of the crisis facing America's future to enough voters, she could make a difference in the direction of American politics.[40]

Thus, although Douglas's political ideas duplicated Roosevelt's and later generally reflected Truman's goals, Douglas's personal style as a legislator and speaker set her apart from her colleagues. As she communicated her ideas persuasively and emotionally on the floor of the House and in speeches to public groups all over the country, she developed a following many were envious and others resentful of. Although she would sometimes address a single issue when she spoke to a special-interest audience such as Jews, blacks, labor, or veterans, she more frequently spoke dramatically and emotionally of the overall dilemma facing postwar Americans. These more-general speeches frequently gained her the national spotlight, attention she enjoyed.

Although many political scientists see little value in the role of the outsider, these critics define political power too narrowly. They tend to measure a member's contribution by the passage of specific legislation. Journalists and lobbyists, however, often rank outsiders at the top of their list when they evaluate congressional effectiveness, because as political scientist Ralph K. Huitt has argued, legislation is only one function of members of Congress. Even with legislation it is difficult to evaluate who deserves the credit for the passage of a bill. The political system needs outsiders to represent those who hope to change the political system. Protest groups seek outsiders to gain a hearing inside Congress. Those who seek moderate change find that outsiders who stand for the extreme position can play an important role in eventually securing compromise. Although Huitt cites only male politicians as his examples, such as postwar senators Wayne Morse, Paul Douglas, and William Proxmire, his argument can persuasively be applied to Helen Douglas. Early on, certain lobbyists found her an important legislator for their causes, and by the end of her second term they saw her as critically important to their program. In 1948, labor considered her one of the two most important members of Congress to re-elect, and, conversely, Republicans saw her as one of the most important people to unseat. She was consistently ranked by liberal journalists among the most valuable members of Congress.[41]

Just as Douglas had been a popular speaker during her years with the Women's Division and as Democratic national committeewoman, many people continued to love her speeches. Chavoor, an obviously biased source, wrote Ed Lybeck that "everyone went wild" over her March speech at the World Unity Rally. "They clapped, cheered and whistled and practically brought the house down. And during her speech, you could hear a pin drop—which certainly is a lot more than can be said when others were speaking." A Pittsburgh Democrat wrote DNC chairman Robert Hannegan after Douglas addressed a United Jewish Fund rally that she had been "flooded with telegrams and calls telling me what a magnificent speech" Douglas had made.[42]

Douglas felt increasingly comfortable in the outsider's role. Not all actors could translate their skill to public speaking. But Douglas could capture an audience as effectively as a political speaker as she could as an actress in a play. Indeed, since childhood, Douglas had learned how to hold the attention of others, whether in family council, in a Barnard classroom, among friends, or in a meeting. As a public speaker, Douglas applied actors' techniques of arousing in their audience the emotions they felt. She knew the importance of vocal techniques, timing, and the power of body movement, including her face, hands, arms, and legs. She had learned the importance of relating her body movement to what she said as she communicated a message.[43]

Douglas's reputation grew rapidly as an articulate and well-informed speaker proposing solutions for postwar problems while demanding responsible action from voters. Early on, the new congresswoman received dozens of speaking invitations from liberal groups all over the country. She accepted as many as possible, often ten to twelve talks per month. Although some of these speeches were in the New York–Philadelphia–Washington, D.C., area, a considerable number were some distance away. This schedule gave a frenzied pace to her already crowded schedule and home responsibilities. She claimed that she had to accept these time-consuming speaking engagements to augment what she considered an insufficient $12,000 congressional salary. Melvyn and she had liquidated all their savings from the 1930s. She also found these opportunities an ideal chance to urge grass-roots pressure on Congress, to increase her sense of effective leadership, and to enjoy the limelight around the country. She revelled in the flood of letters that followed each of her nationally broadcast speeches. In addition to speaking, she helped organize rallies and let pressure groups use her office as a base of operations.

Douglas enjoyed considerable press attention, more than most other congresswomen and more than many male newcomers, as a result of her popularity as a speaker. Although the attention frequently came from women, male journalists from liberal newspapers also found that Douglas made a good story. Prior to 1945, journalists generally regarded congresswomen as "oddities" on the political scene, objects of curiosity more than individuals of political significance. The work of the Women's Division in the 1930s had helped dignify news stories about women in politics. Furthermore, the quality of women elected to Congress improved after the war. While Douglas benefited by increased press respect, she was set apart from other women because of the combination of her dynamic personality, her good looks, her association with the glamorous entertainment industry, and her quick mind. One journalist wrote that official and social Washington had prepared for her tall, stately, and gracious beauty, "but they weren't prepared for her brilliance, in short, her brains." While her intelligence would not have been so singled out had she been a male, journalists seemed surprised to find a bright woman in politics, particularly one who was physically and personally attractive. People gravitated to her, drawn by her enthusiasm, vibrancy, and "quick, infectious laugh." She spoke with a "low and well modulated" voice, even when she interacted informally. "Talking to her," a Louisville Courier-Journal reporter said, "you get the full impact of her unusual amalgam of physical beauty, bigness of spirit and mental stature. You sense that before you is a fine American with a conscience and the wisdom and courage to act upon it."[44]

Despite Douglas's efforts to the contrary, the press continued to try to pit her against Luce as it had during the 1944 convention. At a party for congresswomen, the two shook hands on their agreement to get along with the hope the press would drop the issue. "Report of this gesture of amity will disappoint citizens who anticipated some special fireworks when these two talented ladies clash in debate," the Dallas Morning News wrote. "Both are endowed with personality, gift of tongue, a liking for argument and strong convictions. . . . Before this session ends, Mrs. Douglas and Mrs. Luce may be calling each other Helen and Clare. Still, they shouldn't deny expectant admirers a few exhibitions of their ability to dish out the tabasco on timely occasions."[45]

Douglas generally dressed in a dignified manner, a look enhanced by her trim figure. She recoiled from publicity about her beauty. She wore her hair pulled back from her face, generally rolled softly at her neck instead of the more feminine look of large, soft curls around her face that she often wore at home. She bought tailored suits, generally navy or black, with which she occasionally wore exotic pastel blouses. She wore little jewelry, except for a simple family heirloom pin on her lapel; no makeup, except for bright shades of lipstick; but she did wear perfume. But none of this detracted from her charisma. Douglas commented naïvely, " 'I just forget I am a woman and everybody else seems to, too.' " She was not entirely successful, however, at taking the focus off her looks, and maybe she really did not want to do so. One journalist said that "the House gallery visitor most any session can look down on Helen Gahagan . . . and see her surrounded by attentive male colleagues." Another commented that somehow, despite her compulsive determination to change things, journalists could never stigmatize Douglas with the " 'jutted jaw' characteristics which cartoonists and others attempt to pin on women who feel that they have a job to do." Although good looks can tend to make public figures inaccessible, this was not true in Douglas's case. But it did change the nature of her interaction with men and may well have made certain other congresswomen uncomfortable.[46]

While Douglas worked to gain attention quickly, she also concentrated on establishing good relationships with the liberal members of Congress, particularly the newcomers, although some of the more senior people also welcomed her election. She soon found herself with the job of organizing the freshmen Democrats when she suggested they have a dinner to meet the party's congressional leaders. Chavoor reported to the Lybecks that "the idea . . . went over with a bang." The meeting turned into a "quiz program with questions and discussion popping from all over the floor. . . . As a result they have organized a 79th Congressional Club to meet and hold discussions with important speakers" addressing critical problems. "Of course Helen immediately was made chairman." This appointment meant "more work for our office but I mention [it] to give you an idea just how effective she is being here." She also confirmed that in general "our girl friend has been doing very well. Everyone is crazy about her and she seems to have caught fire as a real leader. Of course, that we knew." Douglas also met often with the southern California Democrats who formed an informal but often important lobby group on issues of mutual concern.[47]

Of all her House colleagues, however, she spent the most time with Lyndon Johnson, particularly during her early years. Their initial attraction to each other developed into a very warm and important friendship. As one Texas politician commented, "Helen and Lyndon were always together on the [House] floor." They often carried their discussions on into the evening, when he was a frequent visitor to Douglas's home. The exact nature of the Douglas–Johnson relationship is not clear. Observers agree they were very close friends. Some suggest the relationship became quite intimate. A Texas lawyer friend of Johnson's who worked in Washington during this time, commented that the two essentially "lived together" for a period. "It was an open scandal in Washington because Lyndon would park his car in front of the house, night after night after night and then would get up in the morning and drive off at 6:30. . . . There were all sorts of people, I know, who talked to Helen and said, 'You've got to stop Lyndon from doing this.' " Walter Pick, who worked in Douglas's office after he returned from overseas, evaded the question in an interview. He acknowledged that Johnson visited Douglas frequently, but he would not comment on whether Johnson spent the night.[48]

The relationship that opened the most doors, however, was Douglas's friendship with the President. He was in Yalta much of the time during her hectic first two months in office and Douglas had trouble finding time to visit much with Eleanor Roosevelt. ER wrote Pick at the end of January that she had not seen Douglas much since she arrived in Washington, and she was looking forward to visiting with Helen "under more leisurely conditions." Some of Douglas's colleagues resented the friendship and suggested that she talked so much about the Roosevelts that it worked to her detriment. The euphoria of the friendship, which carried over into Douglas's work, ended abruptly on April 12 with Roosevelt's sudden death. Douglas had last seen the President a few weeks before, on the day he addressed a joint session of Congress to discuss the Yalta agreements. She recalled later that she was struck that night by his "haggard appearance." He spoke from his wheelchair, unable to use the iron harness that helped him stand for certain occasions. "As the double doors closed behind him after his address, I had a premonition that I would never see him again. I left the chamber and ran down the hall to a back staircase I knew he would have to pass on his return to the White House. When he came into view, I called out: 'Good-bye, Mr. President!' He looked up, smiled, nodded his head, and waved."[49]

On April 12, Douglas was flying to Milwaukee to deliver the annual Jefferson Day address when she learned of FDR's death. "I cried out, 'No! No!' and tried to stand, forgetting I was buckled in," she recalled. She looked down at the magazine she was grasping in her hand, one which often took an anti-Roosevelt stand. She suddenly recalled a dinner at the White House when FDR had "read aloud a vitriolic criticism of himself" from an issue of that magazine and laughed. " 'Isn't that *wonderful?*' I wondered when we again would have a President in the White House who could laugh at himself." When Douglas reached Wisconsin, she held a press conference where she de-

A composed Helen *(right)*, around age 10, with her younger sister Lilli, who was, as usual, frowning in photos—at home in their posh Brooklyn neighborhood of Park Slope. *Courtesy of Peter Douglas*

Gahagan in 1927 with Glenn Hunter *(center)* and Herbert Bunston in the popular *Young Woodley*. As the unloved wife of a prep school headmaster, she has an affair with a lonely, needy student, only to be discovered by her husband in his study. *Courtesy of the Carl Albert Congressional Research and Studies Center, University of Oklahoma*

Late in 1927, the restless Gahagan left the theater, despite critical acclaim, to train as an opera singer. After two intense years training with Sophia Cehanovska, formerly an instructor at the Imperial Conservatory of Petersburg, Helen debuted in Europe. *Courtesy of the Albert Center*

Gahagan, tired of Europe, accepted David Belasco's offer of the lead role in *Tonight or Never* in 1930. She married her leading man, the handsome Broadway newcomer Melvyn Douglas. The real-life romance translated well to the stage. *Courtesy of the Albert Center*

In 1931, the Douglases moved to Los Angeles so that Melvyn could begin his film career. Two years later, Melvyn, tired of making second-rate films, and Helen, frustrated away from her base in New York and Europe, took a nine-month trip around the world, ending in the Far East. *Courtesy of the Albert Center*

In 1934, Helen and Melvyn were thrilled to work together again on Broadway in *Moor Born*, about the Brontë sisters. The play failed at the box office, but Brontë fans loved the production. Helen *(center)* played Emily with Frances Starr *(right)* and Edith Barrett; Melvyn directed. *Courtesy of the Albert Center*

In her only movie, Gahagan played the cruel, sensual goddess of the Kingdom of Kor in RKO's 1935 production of *She,* based on the H. Ryder Haggard science fiction book. Panned by the reviewers, the movie enjoyed a revival and won awards as a horror movie in the 1970s. *Courtesy of the Albert Center*

Helen poses with her and Melvyn's first child, Peter, in the mid-1930s. Their second child, Mary Helen, was born in 1938. Neither let parenting interfere with their professional lives. *Courtesy of the Albert Center*

Gahagan sang a concert series in Europe in 1937, culminating with the Salzburg Festival. She had two piano accompanists, noted German composer Joseph Marx *(left)*, and Fritz Kuba. She became aware for the first time of the growing Nazi threat. *Courtesy of the Albert Center*

The Douglases took Eleanor Roosevelt, a new friend, on a tour of California migrant camps in early 1940. Helen stopped seeking theatrical and singing engagements to move full time into the political arena to join Melvyn, already active in party politics. *Farm Security Administration, courtesy of the Albert Center*

Helen and Melvyn, certainly a glamorous Hollywood couple, take time out from their busy lives to attend the opera in 1941. *Los Angeles Examiner, courtesy of the Hearst Collection, Dept. of Special Collections, University of Southern California*

As Democratic National Committeewoman and head of the Democratic Party Women's Division in California, Gahagan became involved in a broad spectrum of volunteer political activities. Here she arrives to promote the sale of war bonds. *Courtesy of the Albert Center*

In 1944, retiring New Deal congressman Thomas F. Ford and President Franklin D. Roosevelt urged Douglas to run for Ford's seat, the Fourteenth Congressional District, representing downtown Los Angeles. She ran as "Helen Gahagan Douglas" to capitalize on Melvyn's military service and the image of family. *Courtesy of the Albert Genter*

A triumphant Douglas and Samuel Jackson, 1944 Democratic National Convention chairman, acknowledge the enthusiastic crowd as Helen waits to deliver a major address. A huge banner stretched below the podium read "Our Helen." *International News photo, USC*

Douglas chats with United Auto Workers Union supporters during her first campaign. Her district included a socio-economic, racial and ethnic mix. Over twenty-five percent of the population was black, the largest black district west of Chicago. *Courtesy of the Albert Center*

In a rare unposed shot, Douglas, justifiably concerned, listens to returns on election night in the 1944 campaign with friends, including Esther Murray (left). *Lucille Stewart photo, courtesy of the Albert Center*

Douglas writing to Melvyn, stationed with the Army in India, to let him know that she is a new member of Congress. Along with a photo of Melvyn in uniform is an autographed picture of FDR. *Associated Press photo, Albert Center*

The leading Democratic Party women at a tea in early 1945, honoring the Democratic women of the Seventy-ninth Congress. From left: Gladys Tillett, director of the Democratic Party Women's Division; Eleanor Roosevelt; Mrs. Henry Wallace; Mary Norton; Emily Taft Douglas; Chase Going Woodhouse; and Helen Douglas. *Harris and Ewing photo, courtesy of the Albert Center*

President Harry S Truman appointed the new congresswoman to the 1946 American delegation to the fledgling United Nations. *(Left to right)* Representative Charles A. Eaton, Charles Fahy of the State Department, Eleanor Roosevelt, Representative Sol Bloom, Senator Warren R. Austin, Adlai E. Stevenson, and Douglas. *United Press International photo, Albert Center*

During her years in politics, Douglas found it difficult to escape to Cliff Mull, her beloved family home in Fairlee, Vermont, where she had spent summers from the time she was a teenager. Here she enjoys a quiet moment on the porch. *Courtesy of Peter Douglas*

Douglas spoke frequently, and always dramatically, before her colleagues in the House of Representatives. For her 1947 "Market Basket" speech, she strode before the House with a basket of groceries to complain about spiraling inflation. *Harris and Ewing, courtesy of the Albert Center*

Douglas in earnest consultation with California politicians Jimmy Roosevelt and Allen J. Carter at the 1948 Democratic National Convention. (Unlike in many similar photographs, she does not have one eye on the camera.) *International News photo, Brooklyn Public Library—Brooklyn Collection*

Douglas gained a reputation as a leading member of Congress fighting for the rights of ordinary Americans, particularly blacks and labor. 1948 Democratic National Convention delegates welcome her as she prepares to speak. A group also nominated her for vice-president. *Associated Press photo, USC*

Douglas with campaigners in front of a sound truck during the 1950 Senate campaign. Hollywood friends provided important support, particularly money, for her race. *Courtesy of the Albert Center*

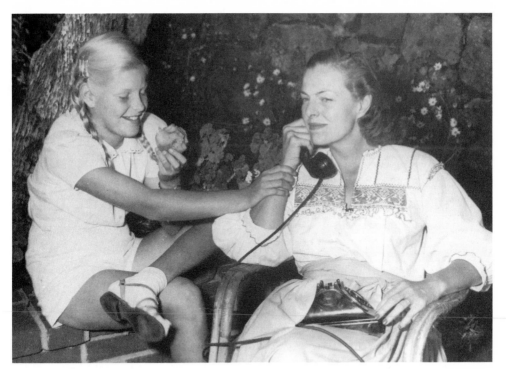

Douglas had little time with her family during her congressional years. When possible, she took Mary Helen with her to meetings and campaign headquarters. Here the two are in the garden of the Douglases' lovely home, high above the Hollywood Bowl. *Courtesy of the Albert Center*

The jubilant Douglas emerges from a voting booth on election day after a hard-fought Senate primary. She won, only to encounter an even more vicious campaign run by her Republican rival, Richard Nixon. *Courtesy of the Albert Center*

Douglas zealously delivering an address over the radio during the 1950 campaign. *Courtesy of the Albert Center*

"*Today we face a violent and cynical attack upon our Democratic faith . . . Those who support this evil purpose are prepared to back it to the limit with every device . . .*"
PRESIDENT TRUMAN . . . *San Francisco, October 17, 1950*

Is Helen Douglas a Democrat?

THE RECORD SAYS *No!*

"*Mrs. Douglas gave comfort to the Soviet tyranny by voting against aid to both Greece and Turkey. She voted against the President in a crisis when he most needed her support and most fully deserved her confidence.*"
DEMOCRATIC U. S. SENATOR SHERIDAN DOWNEY . . . *May 23, 1950*

Nixon developed a variety of campaign materials designed to confuse voters. This piece is one example illustrating his determination to convey the impression that Douglas was a Communist. *Courtesy of the Albert Center*

After the 1950 campaign, the Douglases moved back to New York City. Helen became involved in a host of activities, including a trip to Russia in 1964 with the Women's International League for Peace and Freedom. *Courtesy of the Albert Center*

In the early 1970s, Watergate and the push to elect women to public office brought Douglas back into the national limelight. Here she reminisces with Jerry Voorhis, Nixon's first "victim," at a 1974 Democratic Women's Forum luncheon in Los Angeles. Voorhis's button reads "Don't Blame Me. I Voted For Helen Gahagan Douglas." *Courtesy of the UCLA Dept. of Special Collections and* Los Angeles Times *Archives*

After leaving politics, Helen was finally able to spend long summers at Cliff Mull. She and Melvyn are standing on the long staircase leading down to Lake Morey. *Courtesy of the Albert Center*

Despite a recurring battle with breast cancer after 1972, Douglas continued to be active and vibrant up to her death in June 1980. *Courtesy of the Albert Center*

veloped a theme she repeated over and over during the next year. "President Roosevelt lived long enough to get the game started and set the rules; he has passed the ball to the people, and it is up to them to see that we win the peace as well as the war." She joined her southern California Democratic colleagues to send a moving message to their constituencies. When Douglas returned to Washington, Lyndon Johnson, also close to Roosevelt, sought out her support. [50]

The Lybecks worried about Douglas's emotional stability after Roosevelt's death. Chavoor reassured them: "The shock is terrific but she seems to have taken hold now and is feeling much better. I tried to get her out as much as I could. We went visiting to the Outlands, then to Lyndon Johnson's home. . . . She saw Eleanor Roosevelt before she left for Hyde Park. Really that woman is truly magnificent. If our Helen becomes near as great as she, it will be enough. As it is, she is practically her ghost. No wonder we all love her." [51]

Douglas had lost another mentor, her stage director. The Roosevelts had drawn her into politics, motivated her to run for political office, inspired her, and provided her with her ideology. Like many New Dealers, whose relationship to President Roosevelt had a religious fervor, Douglas viewed FDR as bigger than life, a godlike figure who provided her with a cultist absorption into the New Deal. While she had Lyndon Johnson and a deeply loyal and loving staff to guide her and give her support and direction in the early months of her first congressional session, Roosevelt's death forced her to make major adjustments, to grow beyond her dependence on a key male figure. Although in time, Eleanor Roosevelt would again become an articulate model for Helen, and Melvyn would return to offer emotional support and political advice, in April 1945, Douglas had to cope essentially on her own. She showed no signs of wanting to drop out of politics as many New Dealers did; she dealt with the loss in part by continuing to use Rooseveltian language in her speeches and referring often to carrying on the Roosevelt legacy. She frequently inserted emotional poems about Roosevelt in the *Congressional Record*. But ultimately she had to develop a new rationale for political activism and adjust to the realities of a new administration.

9

The Challenges of Postwar Conversion

MILLIONS OF AMERICANS wondered what kind of president Harry S Truman, the unsophisticated, relatively unknown man from Missouri, would be after twelve years of a charismatic president who had guided the country through the Great Depression and World War II. Roosevelt died as the war was ending and the country faced the challenge of reconversion to a peacetime economy. Germany surrendered in May of 1945. In July, Truman met with Stalin and the new British prime minister, Clement Atlee, in Potsdam to discuss the defeat of the Japanese. During the conference, Truman received word of the successful testing of the atomic bomb, the secret "Manhattan Project" that had been developed during the war, and he made it clear to the Japanese that the United States had the power to end the war quickly. In early August, Truman ordered the bombing of the Japanese cities of Hiroshima and Nagasaki, which brought an almost immediate surrender from Japan. Shortly afterwards, he dismantled American troops and brought the soldiers home.

Congress and Truman faced two major responsibilities when the war ended— to reconvert the wartime economy to a peacetime one and to formulate policy to guide the country as a major world power. Truman hoped to make a transition to his own brand of liberalism, based on the extension of New Deal ideals but shaped by postwar realities. Questions on the home front centered on government's role in providing jobs and affordable housing for veterans and other Americans, controlling the cost of living, and meeting the demand for consumer goods by reconverting factories to domestic production. Blacks made demands that a country that had fought for freedom abroad should guarantee equality at home. Many women had developed a new consciousness of their own abilities and a sense of independence resulting from maintaining a household while their husbands served overseas and working in wartime factories.[1] Women, blacks, and the returning veterans demanded the right to economic and personal equality. On September 6, 1945, Truman articulated his goals for reconversion at home in his "Twenty-one Points" speech. He called for the government to assist in providing jobs and housing for all Americans, government aid to farmers and to public schools, the extension of Social Security, an increase in the minimum wage, federal health insurance, and other programs maintaining and extending the New Deal.

The country also faced new responsibilities abroad. The United States could not return to an isolationist position as it had after World War I. It took the major role in developing the United Nations (U.N.), an international body to preserve world peace. The American government also felt obligated to rebuild its European allies, who emerged from the war with weakened economies and massive physical destruction. The United States had to develop guidelines for dealing with Russia, also a new world power. While some Americans trusted Russia, our wartime ally, others worried about Stalin's possible plans to expand. The wartime allies reverted to the adversarial relationship of the 1920s and the beginning of World War II. Anti-Communism, which had not died during the war, became more widespread. Americans had to make decisions about atomic energy—whether it should be controlled by the military or civilians or both; whether we should share any of our knowledge with other countries, specifically Russia; and how this new source of energy should be developed. Helen Gahagan Douglas saw each of these problems as critical. Rather than attempt to specialize in one area, as did some members of Congress, she considered herself a generalist, never hesitating to try to influence the resolution of every major postwar problem. But some issues did take more of her time than others, among them, civil rights.

Although civil rights captured Truman's attention by the end of 1946, only a handful of members of Congress considered the issue a priority in 1945. Douglas was one. The importance she gave the problems blacks faced was due both to the fact that the concern was part of her liberal agenda and because blacks represented twenty-five percent of her constituents. Douglas was a civil rights advocate in the style of her political model, Eleanor Roosevelt. Just as the First Lady had grown up insensitive to racial prejudice, Douglas's Republican family in upper-class Brooklyn society had never mixed with blacks socially; they never even saw blacks in their daily activity. Not until Douglas's late twenties did she experience her first social encounter with blacks. She attended a racially mixed theater cast party given by Harry Gribble, a gathering "highly unusual in theatre at that time," Douglas recalled. "I was appalled to find myself unaccustomedly awkward and self-conscious." When a black actor asked her to dance, she felt obligated to accept. "We circled the floor once and he led me back to my seat. He said kindly, 'Thank you, Miss Gahagan. I appreciate what that cost you.' I waited a decent interval and then asked Harry to take me back to my hotel. I was ashamed of my feelings. I hadn't been taught prejudice against blacks, or any minority, but apparently I had picked it up unknowingly. I lay awake a long time that night appreciating for the first time the humiliation that black people endured."[2]

Douglas's attitudes about blacks changed as she became involved with politics. In particular, Eleanor Roosevelt, the leading white civil rights advocate among New Dealers, helped her. During Douglas's frequent visits to the White House in the war years, she met numerous national black leaders. ER encouraged Mary McLeod Bethune, the most important black female political leader and head of the National Council of Negro Women, to regard Douglas as a potential friend of blacks. Douglas's stint as national committeewoman and head of the Women's Division offered experiences with blacks that provided some preparation for representing the large black population in the Fourteenth Congressional District. She worked to end the Division's practice of excluding all minorities, not only blacks, but also Mexicans and Asians, from functions held in private homes. The first big tea that she organized was held in Long Beach. The hostess became distraught when she learned that blacks would be attending. She wondered if the prominent Democratic men would come if black women attended. If they would not, Douglas told her, "we'll simply have it without them." Douglas later recalled (with distorted memory), "It wasn't long before it was accepted as natural that all minorities would be present whenever Democrats met." Another incident that amused Douglas occurred at a reception in her home attended by some visiting Democratic women from Georgia. The ladies arrived, Douglas remembered, voicing their delight at the idea of visiting a movie star's home; they "exclaimed about [Melvyn's] handsomeness . . . and our home with an equal degree of rapture." But when they got inside the house "where the first sight to greet them was a room full of black people," they quickly exited.[3]

Despite an increased awareness of black problems and "good instincts," as one associate said, it took Douglas, like Eleanor Roosevelt, years to become genuinely sensitive to the feelings of blacks. One of her civil rights advisors during her congressional years recalled an occasion when Douglas spoke at a black church where a large and enthusiastic crowd had assembled. "Helen got all keyed up, and after her grand introduction she strode up to the rostrum there and held her arms out and said, 'I just love the Negro people.' . . . The people considered that to be patronizing. . . . The whole audience reacted, and she could feel it [but] she had no idea she had done anything wrong, you see. She was completely . . . spontaneous, and that's the way she felt—she just loved them." After the meeting, her friend told her "some of the facts of life, and from that point on she never made that kind of mistake again. She was a quick learner [especially] when you consider her beginnings."[4]

As a new member of Congress, Douglas lacked a lengthy track record in civil rights, but she had begun to learn about their needs and felt committed to civil rights legislation. Blacks, who had few friends on Capitol Hill and saw no legislative success during the war, welcomed her to Washington. With the headlines "Glamour Girl in Congress Backs Equality for All Races," the *Chicago Defender* wrote that "the cause of liberalism on Capital Hill won a new champion the day Los Angeles' east side sent charming and intelligent Helen Gahagan Douglas to Congress." Douglas came from a "virtual racial melting pot," the paper declared, and she came with "dead earnestness and sincere determination to call 'em as she sees 'em."[5]

Douglas's views on racial equality paralleled those of white civil rights advocates of the period who urged blacks to be patient. Like other white reformers, Douglas naïvely believed that rational white people would eventually solve the problem of racial prejudice. She elaborated on her views about blacks and political action in various articles. In an essay entitled "If I Were a Negro: Racial Progress with a Plan," for example, Douglas wrote that if she were black, she would try to "quiet the righteous wrath of my indignation." Though she would realize that whites had exploited her, she would also try to be aware that "no people has gone so far up the road from bondage in a short fourscore years." She would try to sacrifice "momentary comforts for my children's education" and join with "liberals of all faiths, all shades." She would "reject him who solicits my help, my contribution, and my vote as a Negro. I would heed him who approaches me as an American and as a citizen. I would realize that progress to be sound must be orderly and . . . slow. I would therefore seek progress with a plan and with a technique." She also argued that she would support constituted authority, not because it was white but because as bad as it was in some places, "in the end it is my protector. . . . Above all, I would realize that there is no Negro problem. Only a white problem which, in the final analysis, must be solved by whites."[6]

Douglas became involved with civil rights groups as soon as she moved to Washington in January of 1945, particularly the National Council on Negro Women, the National Council for a Permanent Fair Employment Practices Committee, and the National Association for the Advancement of Colored People (NAACP). In March, Bethune asked Douglas at Eleanor Roosevelt's request to join the two of them and a "few thinking white and Negro women" in a confidential meeting at the White House to study ways to improve the effectiveness of the National Council on Negro Women. Later that spring, Bethune appointed Douglas vice-chair of the organization's fund-raising advisory committee along with several others, including Congresswoman Emily

Douglas and Eleanor Roosevelt. Douglas leaned on her liberal Hollywood friends to support the fund-raising effort. In February Douglas introduced a bill to abolish the poll tax and to make the FEPC a permanent rather than a temporary agency. She began cultivating friendships among the small but committed civil rights group in the House, which included Mary Norton; New York's Vito Marcantonio, a member of the American Labor Party; and the two black congressmen, newly elected Adam Clayton Powell from Harlem and second-termer William Dawson from Chicago. She began speaking to various civil rights groups.[7]

A second issue Douglas became identified with early in the session concerned the restrictions the British had imposed on Jews migrating to Palestine during the 1930s. The issue was a natural outgrowth of her indignation at the Nazi persecution of the Jews, Melvyn's Jewish background, and the Douglases' trip in 1933 to Palestine. American Zionists, including Douglas, protested the policy, as did the British Labour Party, British prime minister Winston Churchill, Roosevelt, and the League of Nations. The executive council of the American Christian Palestine Committee, chaired by Senator Robert F. Wagner, appointed her to a bipartisan committee along with other members of Congress, such as Democrats House Speaker John W. McCormack and Senator Claude Pepper, and the Republican Senator Arthur H. Vandenberg. In May 1945, she, as the group's secretary, sent a letter along with the co-directors of the committee requesting every member of Congress to sign a letter to Truman urging the restoration of Jewish immigration to Palestine. This letter elicited numerous responses from her colleagues.[8]

Douglas wrote various magazine articles on the topic, including "Back from Babylon," for the Unitarian Church's *The Christian Register*. In this she argued that the problem was "more a Christian than a Jewish problem. Upon us rests the responsibility for its solution." The world had to "rebuild what has been shattered, and to make justice and decency grow where iniquity and hatred flourished before. . . . Palestine is a test of the ability of mankind to establish this brave, new world. [Jews] are entitled to have their chance for a normal existence in a land where they are welcomed." Douglas's stand brought enthusiastic approval from numerous Zionist Jewish organizations and individuals. Max Nussbaum, a Hollywood rabbi, wrote her that "many of us who have known you in this city worked for your election because we had great hopes in your career as a Representative. . . . Your fight for every liberal cause on the American scene and the stand you have taken on the problem of Palestine wholly fulfills our greatest expectations. I was pleasantly surprised at your knowledge of the Jewish problem and the forthright way in which you defend the Zionist cause." The Los Angeles Emergency Committee thanked her on behalf of the 10,000 affiliated Los Angeles members for her "untiring efforts" in pushing the Senate resolution favoring a permanent home for Jews through the House. A constituent wrote that he understood that Douglas was "instrumental in bringing about the favorable passage of the Wagner-Taft resolution" supporting Jewish entry into Palestine. "It is gratifying to know that there are still leaders of your caliber who would go out of their way to alleviate the suffering of the underprivileged." Hadassah, the Women's Zionist Organization of America, and the New Jersey B'Nai B'Rith selected her for their annual awards in 1945.[9]

Although congressional action on civil rights and Palestine were important to Douglas, her schedule just in the first six months of 1945 documents her exhausting attempt to speak out publicly on many issues, study problems, and to be as available as possible to groups for speaking, for which she often received several hundred dollars. She wrote Ed Lybeck that while she loved being a congresswoman, it was a "day and night job. . . . Poor Evelyn seems to be doing nothing but turning down invitations. I am sure we turn down thirty a day." Chavoor reiterated the same to Lybeck, lamenting how often Helen was away. "What in the blazes did they do before when she wasn't here anyway?" Douglas spent January and February in 1945 trying to "catch her breath" and get a sense of her job. But by March she was ready to begin traveling. On March 12 she spoke at the Women's Club in New York on the women's view of the Dumbarton Oaks agreement to set up a United Nations, and also gave her World Unity Rally talk in Madison Square Garden. Four days later, on the sixteenth, she talked to the Thirty-third Congressional District Democrats in Pennsylvania. She made three more trips to New York—on the eighteenth to speak with the New York Metropolitan Council of the National Council of Negro Women, the twenty-first as a principal draw for the World Youth Rally at Carnegie Hall, and the twenty-third at the New York Liberal Party dinner. Although she spoke around the Washington area continuously, she did not travel again until April 7, when she attended a forum sponsored by *Mademoiselle* magazine at Vassar College. She gave two speeches, one on postwar economic and social problems and another on the importance of women in politics.[10]

She slowed down a bit after FDR died on April 12, but by the end of April, Douglas was back on the road, speaking at a Dumbarton Oaks rally in Hartford, Connecticut. She flew to the West Coast in early May for two weeks of speeches in San Francisco and Los Angeles. She left four days after she returned for her commitment as commencement speaker at a black school, Alabama College. Back in Washington, she wrote Los Angeles labor leader Jerry Posner that she was busy fighting on the House floor for the reciprocal trade agreement, the extension of price controls, and then the U.N.'s Bretton Woods agreement on international monetary and financial policy. Douglas had a hectic schedule in June also. She intended to take the children to Vermont in early June, but she could not take them to Lake Morey until the end of the month because of legislation on the House floor. She took time on June 15 to fly to Wichita, Kansas, at the request of the Democratic National Committee to speak at their Jefferson Day dinner; her topic—"The World and Wichita After the War." She did turn down an engagement the day before she left for Kansas because Mary Helen was sick. She returned to action to get civil rights legislation out of committee and to join a floor fight on the Equal Rights Amendment (ERA).[11]

June also proved to be a special time because Melvyn returned to the United States. During the first six months after Helen had moved to Washington, Melvyn was still in India. In addition to Chavoor, Helen depended on her mother, sister, and brother Walter in New York for support and diversion. She visited them often, wrote letters, and called frequently. But she was very anxious for Melvyn to come home. Judging by Melvyn's letters, he felt the same way. After receiving a letter from Helen telling about Mary Helen shortly after moving to Washington, Melvyn answered, "The descriptions of Mary are too good to be true. How awful it is to be missing her during these times. For God's sake don't let them teach her to curtsy and all that stuff." Later in the spring he wrote: "Tell Mary Helen that I dance with her in my dreams. Tell Peter that I long for the day when we can walk and swim and talk together, once more. Tell Greg that I am joyful in his awakening manhood. And tell Mommie that her beauty, inside and out, is a guiding star." He had begun to feel, at age forty-four, like he had aged. "Do you feel awfully old, these days?" he asked Helen. "I have increasingly frequent moments of feeling that old age had really settled on me. . . . Take care of yourself, darling. My arms are around you and my thoughts enfold you." Just before he returned to the States, he wrote again that it was a "God-damned shame" he had not been around the children, particularly Greg who as a young man "doesn't know quite which way to turn and he's reaching out desperately for love and guidance." He hoped to make it up to all the children when he returned home, if they wanted it. He worried that Peter and Mary Helen might soon be more interested in their friends than their family. If that were the case, Helen and Melvyn could only "be there when they reach for us. But that's something!"[12]

Melvyn did not tell Helen exactly when he planned to come home; he wanted to surprise her. Although he had not yet been discharged, he had come back to the United States to be reassigned to the West Coast. Helen was stunned when she picked up her office phone and a voice inquired, " 'Is this the Honorable Helen Gahagan Douglas? It is? Well, this is your husband.' " Chavoor reported to the Lybecks, "Just imagine the rest. Helen just screamed! The rest of the day was bedlam. You never saw anyone so excited in all your life." Helen flew immediately to New York to spend two days alone with Melvyn. The two then hoped to get to Vermont to visit the children. Mary Helen was staying with Grandmother Lillian at Lake Morey, and Peter was at camp. But

Melvyn did not have sufficient leave time to make the trip. In fact, Helen and Melvyn had very little time together that summer. She stayed in Washington to work until Congress recessed in mid-July for two months. She flew home to work in her Los Angeles office and visit with Melvyn, but in early August returned to the East Coast. She had a chance to see Eleanor Roosevelt and also enjoyed four days with her mother and siblings in New York, but then she returned to her congressional office. Not until mid-August did she finally get up to Vermont for a "much-needed rest." She was distressed that her vacation had dwindled to two weeks, but fortunately Melvyn could join the family for a few days.[13]

The Douglases had undoubtedly assumed that once Melvyn returned they could rebuild a family structure that had been ruptured by three years of separation. Yet, despite the initial excitement, the summer did not prove a productive time for Helen and Melvyn to rekindle their relationship, nor could they spend much time with Mary Helen and Peter. This resulted in part from busy schedules, but it also may have grown out of the emotional distancing that had resulted from the long separation. Over the next several years, the relationship between Helen and Melvyn continued to deteriorate. Also at this point, plans were unclear about where the children would live. Helen and Melvyn had decided that if Melvyn moved back to Los Angeles, the children would return to California; until that time they would stay in Washington. But as Melvyn did not have a clear picture about what he was going to do, the couple decided that Peter and Mary Helen would remain in Washington for the upcoming school year.

Initially Melvyn chose to continue with the military during the rest of 1945, and then decided he had had enough. As he anticipated his discharge at the end of 1945, he decided he wanted to sever his Hollywood connections. He knew he had to work because "the finances of the Douglas family were somewhat in disarray," he recalled later. But "the idea of getting back into a restrictive situation again was abhorrent." But when he investigated the status of his seven-year contracts with Columbia and MGM, he learned that neither studio would count his three years of military service towards his contract fulfillment; to his dismay they were anxiously awaiting his return to Hollywood. Chavoor underscored the financial problems in a letter to Ed Lybeck. "Melvyn will be out on the Coast probably within a month to make some pictures. That's good too because the money won't hurt us any. Not the way la Gahagan spends money." But during 1946, before returning to Los Angeles, he co-produced a review about life in the military, *Call Me Mister*. After several extremely successful months in the New York City area, Melvyn helped organize a traveling company that enjoyed a long run. Chavoor wrote the Lybecks: "You are right about the head of the House of Douglas having a hit on his hands. The notices have been raves and it will probably run a long time."[14]

*

By early September 1945, Douglas was back in her Washington office working on a variety of bills, particularly ones designed to help keep inflation down and provide affordable housing, and participating in discussions on the new issue of atomic energy. She was convinced that whoever controlled atomic energy would control the direction of American political power. She left briefly near the end of the month to fly to Los Angeles for a major speech to her district in which she focused on child care centers, a permanent FEPC, and the atomic bomb, but returned immediately to immerse herself in the heated debate on atomic energy. Truman encountered sharply divided opinion over the role of the military, the sharing of information with the Russians, and the direction of research. The discussions did not include those best informed—the scientists who had developed the bomb. They feared any military involvement, shuddered at the thought of government-enforced security measures, and rebelled against any notion of secrecy. They began organizing themselves as a variety of bills were submitted to Congress.

On October 3, 1945, Truman went before Congress to urge legislation to create a commission to control atomic energy, a group that would include military personnel. On the following day, Douglas, in a major speech entitled "The Atomic Age," sharply criticized the President's failure to discuss the issue of sharing scientific information with Russia. The President was already suspicious that Russia had expansionist designs on Eastern Europe and was not interested in cooperating with the West. Douglas began her statement in typical style, with a lecture to her colleagues. "When I returned to Congress this fall," she said, "I wondered if we would begin where we had left off, as though nothing had happened. Or would we demonstrate to the world that we did understand that a new age had begun?" Would Americans recognize that "we are the problem—not atomic energy. . . . Would we live up to our responsibilities? Would we realize that the first order of business of this Congress and of the peoples of the world is the question of the survival of mankind?" There was no way, she argued, that Americans could keep secret the information necessary to produce a bomb. This argument was "based upon the fallacious premise that there is a secret which can be kept," for everyone knew the atom had been smashed. Thinking we had a secret would only give Americans "a false sense of security and a false sense of our own power"; words she quoted from Walter Lippmann. Again using Lippmann's ideas, she pointed out that international control was impossible if scientists themselves, who would share their research findings, did not supervise that control. In sum, "our faith in the future cannot be built upon the sands of isolationism, or on the false security of any secret weapon. It must be built upon the rock of international good faith, upon the brotherhood of man." [15]

In order to get the bill reflecting Truman's request through committee quickly and onto the House floor, Speaker Sam Rayburn sent it to the Military Affairs

Committee chaired by Representative Andrew J. May. Senator Erwin Johnson submitted a similar bill that became known as the May-Johnson bill. But pressure from the scientists and others supporting civilian control dashed hopes of quick passage. On October 9, May's committee held a one-day, unpublicized hearing, an action that startled even the Truman administration, who feared an angry response from the already agitated scientists. But no one expected the extent of the uproar that was to occur in Congress. In the House, Douglas and her southern California colleagues Chet Holifield and Jerry Voorhis became the principal organizers of the protest movement against the May-Johnson bill. Douglas's involvement with this issue demonstrated her style of politics—working to build the public's awareness so they would lobby Congress. When she learned that May's committee had not held public hearings on the bill, she moved immediately into action. She called her brother Walter in New York to "collect some of his lawyer friends who had expertise about constitutional and legislative matters." The group concluded that further hearings were appropriate. Douglas then contacted the national media, declaring that it was "unbelievable that the House Military Affairs Committee has already closed hearings. . . . It is disturbing to see strong men propose to legislate in a spasm of hysteria. . . . At present the scientists are forbidden to speak. Yet they are the only ones who can tell us fully what is in store." She attached a list of the leading scientists who wanted to testify, including Nobel prize–winner Harold Urey and Karl T. Compton, president of the Massachusetts Institute of Technology. [16]

The response to Douglas's call, as well as protest from other members of Congress, was overwhelming. A barrage of letters, telegrams, and phone calls between the scientists, the non-scientist liberals who opposed military control and favored sharing information with Russia, the news services, members of Congress, and the Administration spilled forth throughout the next few days, a sign of the drama that, for the next nine months, became a "confused jumble of motion," as one member of the administration commented. A telegram from the editor of *The Nation*, Freda Kirchwey, to California's attorney general Robert Kenny typified the anti-military response. She wired: "Public hearings on atomic bomb control bill prematurely closed. Danger will be rushed through in present form despite fundamental differences of opinion publicly expressed by scientists responsible for its development. Urge public hearings be reopened immediately." The Manhattan District Scientists, among many groups who contacted Douglas, wired that they "heartily" endorsed her protests. Friends wrote that she was "one of the apparently very small number of sane people left in Washington." [17]

Douglas's efforts to reopen the hearings finally paid off. Chavoor wrote Hickok: "Helen's new name is the A.B.—in other words, the Atomic Bomb. She can't kid me. So glad Mrs. Roosevelt thinks she is hitting it on the head. The newspaper publicity and the letters we have gotten in are enough to make you want to cry with joy." Douglas's office also became a center and clearinghouse for the dozens of scientists representing groups, such as the Association of Los Alamos Scientists, who came to testify before committees and talk to members of Congress. She also helped coordinate efforts for meetings November 16 and 17 that resulted in the creation of the Federation of Atomic Scientists and two citizen support groups. Yet all this activity did not keep Douglas in Washington. In early November she left for a ten-city Midwest tour including Ann Arbor, Dayton, and Cleveland to talk about the FEPC, atomic energy, and general postwar problems. She returned November 16 for the atomic energy meetings, and on the eighteenth sped off to New York for a speech, "Art for the Average Person," at the Conference on American–Soviet Cultural Cooperation.[18]

Also in mid-November, Douglas worked on a resolution to include Russia in discussions about international cooperation, which she planned to introduce in the House. She directed her statement at Truman, who had met with the British and Canadian prime ministers on November 10. The three had called for the exchange of scientific information and the development of atomic energy for peaceful purposes only, with control by a United Nations Commission; they did not mention Russia. Douglas, hoping this statement would "represent the best thought of the atomic scientists at the time," called for Russia to be included in all discussions with the United States, Great Britain, and Canada. She circulated it to scientists and friends, including Eleanor Roosevelt, and to wire services, liberal magazines and organizations, and sympathetic major city newspapers—such as the *Philadelphia Inquirer* and the *Washington Post*, and the papers in her district. The resolution solidified Douglas's position within the group of liberals who wanted Russia included in postwar discussion of world issues. Douglas's final version called for a "world-wide system of international cooperation and control of atomic energy" to prevent a competitive arms race and preserve peace. She requested a meeting of the Big Three—the United States, Great Britain, and Russia—to discuss the issues before the matter went before the United Nations. She had gathered an impressive list of signatures to the resolution from individuals at various labs and universities, as well as endorsements of groups of scientists, among them the Federation of Atomic Scientists.[19]

She introduced her resolution on the House floor on November 23. The critical question, she said in her prefatory remarks, was not the control of the bomb, but the "control of the relations between men. . . . We can afford to split the atom, but we cannot afford to split the Big Three. . . . If man is to survive, international collective bargaining must replace international anarchy and lawlessness." The resolution, with all the accompanying publicity, added to the unease the Truman administration felt about resolving the question of

approaching Russia; particularly after talk circulated in the Senate about sub-
mitting a similar resolution. But when Secretary of State Byrnes negotiated an
early December meeting with Russia with atomic energy high on the agenda,
Douglas felt that the resolution had made an impact. Douglas was in such a
frenzy at this point that she voted for a tax-cut bill because of her confusion
about what was up for a vote. She wrote an angry labor supporter, "The bells
rang calling everyone to the floor. I dashed through the tunnel, and thinking I
was voting for the Navy bill, voted yes." She did not discover what she had
done until later in the day when she responded to another vote call and discovered that this time the Navy bill was up. "The whole thing is stupid, and I
can tell you that Evelyn and I are more upset than you could possibly be. . . .
You know, of course that I was one of the 13 who signed the statement de-
nouncing the original tax bill. Not only did I sign it . . . but I instigated it."
Nevertheless, she incurred so much criticism in her district that Lybeck had to
work to quell the uproar.[20]

With the administration finally pressured into working with Russia as it prepared for the United Nations General Assembly meeting in January 1946,
Douglas returned to working with the energetic campaign of scientists and liberal groups to educate the public about atomic energy. Douglas helped organize two early December 1945 rallies in Washington—one sponsored by *The
Nation*, which brought together the scientists in Washington; and a second
massive gathering in Madison Square Garden backed by the Independent Citizens' Committee of the Arts, Sciences and Professions (ICCASP). A week
later, she spoke at a rally sponsored by the Hollywood branch, HICCASP.
Scientist Linus Pauling and actor Ronald Reagan, who delivered a dramatic
reading of Norman Corwin's "Set Your Clock at U-235," joined Douglas on
the speaker's platform in Los Angeles.[21]

Douglas also had her office staff and Lorena Hickok busily working on a
civil rights project. Despite being absorbed with the atomic bomb question, she
never neglected civil rights questions. The NAACP pinned their hopes on a
"militant group of freshmen," including Douglas, for the "battle against blind
conservatism." She participated in a radio debate on the FEPC, fought to get
the FEPC out of committee, and protested vehemently the DAR's refusal to
permit singer Hazel Scott to rent Constitution Hall. In December 1945, she
was working on the final stages of a report she entitled *The Negro Soldier*. The
report consisted of a partial list of the contributions black soldiers had made
during the war. The incentive to conduct this time-consuming research came
from an exchange on the House floor with Congressman John Rankin. Rankin
had read into the *Congressional Record* a list of recent American casualties and
placed much of the blame for these deaths on American black soldiers. Douglas, who had already developed an intense antipathy for Rankin, became so
angry that "I surprised myself by hissing loudly. I'd never hissed before in my

life." She was particularly embarrassed when she learned the press had heard her. She stayed in Washington for the Christmas holidays to work on this and other projects. So she and Melvyn gathered on Christmas day in Washington with Mary Helen and Peter. In January Douglas read her list into the *Congressional Record* for eight evenings in a row. Her material filled fifty-four pages in the *Record*. Although after the first day she did not have much of an audience, her colleagues stayed to hear her opening comments about "the Negro soldier" mainly out of curiosity. As she began to speak, Rankin's temper flared and, according to Douglas, the man had to be physically restrained from interrupting. She received considerable newspaper publicity and blacks' commendation for this effort.[22]

The debate over who would control atomic energy continued to build in the early months of 1946. In November 1945, a special committee chaired by the new senator from Connecticut, Brien McMahon, conducted information-gathering investigations on atomic energy. In December he submitted a bill favoring civilian control, which Truman supported; the President had backed away from the idea of military control. Douglas submitted an identical bill on the House side in February 1946. The McMahon bill, or McMahon-Douglas bill as some called it, emphasized the peaceful uses of atomic energy, stressed the need for international cooperation between scientists, called for international control, encouraged the free exchange of scientific information, and most important, prohibited military personnel on the commission. Both Douglas and McMahon relied heavily on James Newman for advice on the bill. Newman, a lawyer with a strong background in science, headed the Science Division of the Office of War Mobilization and Reconversion, which supervised the drafting of legislation after the uproar over the May-Johnson bill. He then became White House advisor on atomic energy legislation. Douglas later recalled that she "learned from the best teacher in the country what atomic power was all about."[23]

In March, Senator Vandenberg proposed an amendment to the McMahon-Douglas bill creating a Military Liaison Committee, a move that caused a furious debate. Douglas intensified her efforts to arouse the public. She wrote a flyer, "What You Can Do About Civilian Control of Atomic Energy," and helped organize dozens of groups to fight the Vandenberg amendment. Douglas and several other members of Congress worked with representatives of over 350 groups to prepare for a mass rally. When Douglas spoke, she urged women to take the lead in the fight for peaceful development of mankind because "women are the givers of life." She also organized a rally of women's groups where she pointed out that civilian control of atomic energy was the greatest challenge that had ever come to women. If they failed, there was "a very good chance that this globe will go back to the molten mass of gas and flames it was before any life existed on it." She and McMahon joined Senator Johnson, co-sponsor of the May-Johnson bill, and a member of the military for a public debate on the issue on America's Town Meeting of the Air.[24]

The many efforts were effective. Over 400,000 letters and telegrams came to McMahon's Senate committee urging the passage of the McMahon-Douglas bill. Individual congressmen also received hundreds of letters. An historian of the Atomic Energy Act commented that "the effects of the Washington groups brought quick results. . . . By the last week in March, there were signs that the atmosphere was clearing. Tempers had cleared. McMahon was beginning to feel the ground swell of public support." Both McMahon and Vandenberg showed signs of compromise; Vandenberg agreed to soften his amendment, and the bill moved fairly smoothly through the Senate. The prognosis appeared less hopeful in the House when the Military Affairs Committee proposed amendments designed to include the military on the commission, permit the Army to continue manufacturing bombs, and reduce the commission's regulatory powers. Debate continued into July, and much to Douglas's dismay, the House passed all of the debilitating amendments.[25]

After the House vote, scientists and their liberal supporters pinned their hopes on the House-Senate conference committee that was working on a compromise measure. Douglas wrote a scientist friend: "We fought a losing battle on the House floor. One after another of the Congressmen admitted they were utterly confused. It was a shameful exhibition of the inability of the people's representatives to cope with the most urgent problem of our time." While the opposition might have had a fuller rebuttal, its leadership feared that stretching out the debate would only increase the provisions for military control. Perhaps in the conference committee, where the senators "know something about atomic energy," the House amendments could be eliminated. *PM* magazine, disgusted at the House debate, commented that the months of testimony "by the most eminent scientists and political leaders in the country went for nothing. Only here and there were men and women—one of them, Helen Gahagan Douglas, was particularly effective—who had ever read the testimony, who had some real feeling for the issues at stake." The joint committee did delete most of the House amendments, and the final bill was essentially in the form in which it had left the Senate. McMahon, Douglas, the other legislators who had worked hard for the victory, and the scientists were delighted. They believed that this law would ensure that the world could use atomic energy for peaceful means with international cooperation. The subsequent history of the Atomic Energy Act, however, did not fulfill these idealistic dreams.[26]

Scientists, the press, and lay people praised Douglas for her role as a principal organizer of the protest movement. The UAW-CIO Washington lobbyist wrote that Douglas was "doing a great service in exposing the ballyhoo about the artificially inspired hysteria over atomic secrecy." William A. Higinbotham, head of the Federation of Atomic Scientists, thanked her for her "outstanding contribution." Few others, he wrote, had been "so keenly aware of the crisis which faces us and the world. None has been more courageous in assuming public responsibility." Scientists recognized her as one of the best-informed and "few outspoken champions of an intelligent atomic policy in the Congress." Newman and Bryon S. Miller, a lawyer who helped draft the Atomic Energy Act, published a book in 1948 about the Act and the early days of the Atomic Energy Commission. The authors dedicated the book to Douglas and McMahon, "two of the people's representatives who saw far and who saw clearly." Newman's personal dedication in Douglas's copy of the book told more: "For Helen, who is the best of us in heart, in spirit, in courage, in integrity, in sympathy, in forbearance, in vision, and in purpose. She evokes our love, commands our admiration, and earns our fealty."[27]

Forty years later, Albert Cahn, head of the Citizens' Committee for the Control of Atomic Energy, and Congressman Chester E. Holifield reflected on Douglas's role. As a lobbyist, Cahn found Douglas and Holifield the most helpful members of the House. "Helen felt very deeply about it" and worked hard. But in terms of their overall commitment to the problem in relationship to other critical issues in late 1945 and 1946, Holifield worked harder, perhaps because he "saw a career for himself in it. . . . I think he saw very early that he wanted to become an expert on atomic energy." He hoped to stay on in the House and make a career of being a congressman; Douglas, Cahn felt, had senatorial ambitions very early. Holifield eventually became head of the joint congressional committee on atomic energy, created by the Atomic Energy Act. He commented that Douglas was not influential. He downplayed the role of public opinion. "She was very enthusiastic so that I don't mean this in a derogatory sense." But no new members, including himself, had much power.[28] Douglas believed that she was very effective in representing the scientists in Congress during the intense buildup towards the passage of atomic energy legislation, and she was proud of this final piece of legislation, in which she had played an important role. Yet when the Act passed in July 1946, she moved on to other things. She did not lose interest in atomic energy, but the problem no longer consumed her. The fact that she was not appointed to any committees dealing with the development of atomic energy may have affected her shifting directions. More likely, however, she was ready for something new.

As early as 1945, Douglas developed a variety of emotional statements calling, for example, for the careful shaping of the United Nations and a full employment bill. In 1946 she called for a better world for America's children; warned of the problem of inflation; urged the continuation of wartime rent and price controls; pressed for additional funds for daycare programs, school lunches, and farm loans; spoke out in favor of an increase in the minimum wage and an extension of social security; and pushed for cancer research funding. She called the economic needs of the veterans a crisis, struck out against the House Un-American Activities Committee, began a long-term investigation of the problems of water in California's Central Valley, demanded attention for the problems of migrants, and opposed state control of tidelands oil. In foreign affairs, she supported UNESCO, opposed Argentina's entry into the United Nations, and spoke on food rationing in Europe. In July she was thrilled when President Truman appointed her as an alternate to the United Nations Assembly meeting in the fall of 1946.

Douglas made several major addresses in Congress during 1946; one in March she entitled "My Democratic Credo." Another tangle with Rankin stimulated her to write this statement. According to Douglas, Rankin "was tirading about some liberal issue, at the high point of which he turned to where I and a group of freshmen Congressmen were sitting, waved his arm in our direction and said, 'These Communists.' " Douglas tried to get Rayburn to demand an answer from Rankin as to whether or not he was calling her a Communist. Someone told Lyndon Johnson, who was eating lunch, that Douglas was having trouble with Rankin. He raced up to the House floor, went to the podium, and asked Rayburn if he were going to let Rankin run the House. "Rayburn scowled" and finally forced Rankin to address the question; he denied that he was referring to Douglas. This situation so infuriated Douglas it prompted her to write down her thoughts on democracy. On March 29, she delivered her speech. She opened by saying that "we all know that communism is no real threat to the democratic institutions of our country." While there were undoubtedly Communists in the United States, they did not present a problem. And cooperating with Russia for world peace did not present a security threat. But the way certain individuals falsely labeled people who favored the democratic system, and the system itself, as Communist, resulted in hysteria and fear. Accusations that measures to pay for school lunches, money to raise teachers' salaries, assistance for day-care centers, funds for better housing, and full employment were communistic were ridiculous and dangerous. Underfed, poorly clothed, poorly housed people were the real danger to democracy. She had seen children with "sore eyes and swollen bellies" held by their "despairing parents." "Our fight is not against the windmill of communism in America. Rather it is against those who would make a treadmill of democracy through special privilege, bigotry, and intolerance."[29]

Douglas emphasized that she believed in the free enterprise system; she was the product of a successful business family and had enjoyed all the financial benefits. But monopolies stifled the free enterprise system. Americans had to stop the trend to monopolies and enlarge opportunities to provide new security, hope, and well-being for everyone. We had to recognize our real enemies, of which one of the most dangerous was "intolerance born of fear and loss of faith in America." Douglas closed with a flourishing final statement written by Lyndon Johnson. He felt it would help, and "he'd been so kind and supportive, I accepted his closing statement although I thought it a little more picturesque than necessary." The members of the House, LBJ wrote, "do not believe that Capitol Hill is a hill on which to kindle a fiery cross but rather one on which to display the shining cross which . . . has been to all the world the symbol of the brotherhood of man."[30]

Douglas was so busy with her work on the House floor and a continued schedule of speeches all over the country in the spring that she did not return to Los Angeles during this time. She had been home for a few visits, the last in January 1946, for several days. Yet despite her absenteeism, she had by this time won widespread support among her constituents. She was a popular speaker and she had the loyal support of her key group of campaign workers. Unlike some members of Congress, she did not develop close personal ties with many individuals. She certainly did not keep track of birthdays, deaths, and weddings like her friend Lyndon Johnson. Instead, she related to individuals and groups with an emotional fervor on the basis of shared values. Her energy and manner inspired confidence, familiarity, and support, whether in an informal small-group setting, a larger gathering, or at a rally of thousands. She used the same techniques of relating to people whether she was talking to a group of striking automobile workers in Detroit or to Chinese-Americans in her district. The vast majority in her district—low-income and poorly housed—fit the profile of her "national constituency" and generally agreed with her position on veterans, housing, unemployment, inflation, and civil rights. The strong emotional ties that people developed to Douglas were intensified for some by the fact that she was a woman. She fulfilled Lillian Ford's prophesy of becoming the district's "mother," a caring provider. Many, particularly black congregations, called her "Our Helen," an affectionate phrase that would never have been used for her male colleagues. The support of two powerful local black women, Charlotta Bass, the well-known and respected editor of the liberal black paper the *California Eagle*, and Dr. Ruth Temple, a physician who headed a medical clinic in the center of the black district, added to the respect blacks held for Douglas.

But despite Douglas's ability to engender enthusiastic support among her constituents, she alone could not reach enough voters to warrant re-election. Ed Lybeck and the staff who worked with him were of critical importance. Although he had a full-time position with the Los Angeles Housing Commission, his work for Douglas was almost a second full-time job. He established an election strategy based on precinct analysis and shrewd political judgment that resulted from years of working closely with the district. Lybeck also monitored the feelings of the various constituencies within the district between elections. He distributed thousands of copies of congressional speeches to target groups, and press releases to the local neighborhood newspapers. He fed detailed information to Bass for the *Eagle*, kept in touch with the four assembly district offices, wrote newsletters, arranged and publicized radio talks, and maximized Douglas's time during her visits. He often suggested appropriate timing for the sponsorship of bills, urged Douglas to keep blacks and veterans at the top of her priority list, criticized a vote when he felt it would hurt her at home, and commented freely on her speeches. In short, he took Douglas's national image and shaped it to the district, constantly keeping her in front of the voters. The awkward distance he had felt between himself and Douglas in the 1944 election vanished in 1945; he became singleminded in his personal devotion to her and his dedication to her re-election. Equally committed to Douglas was his wife Ruth, although she remained less publicly visible than Ed. Neither Lybeck received salary; only the secretary, Florence Reynolds. Douglas had funds to reimburse the office for printing, duplicating, and mailing expenses. Several other people were also instrumental, particularly during the 1946 election—such as Susie Clifton; Esther Murray, who replaced Douglas as Democratic national committeewoman; and Jessie Terry.

While Douglas was too independent to follow Lybeck's advice all of the time, she valued his help enormously. Douglas often made suggestions, some of which Lybeck found naïve. For example, she asked him to send out one of her statements to the doctors in the district. He thought this impractical because almost "every croaker in LA has an office in our District, while practically none of them live in it." Lybeck also cautioned Douglas that foolish mistakes in campaigning techniques would hurt her more than her male colleagues. "You are somewhat in the same position as a one-armed guy in a machine shop," he said. She had to be "at least five times as good as the average machinist to hold his job, and you have to be at least five times as careful as your average male colleague not to appear in a position that is even faintly ridiculous. Where the average run-of-the-mill Congressman pulls something at least once a year that belongs strictly in the comic strips, you can't EVER do it." If she did, he went on, "ten thousand people, including all the trained seal columnists, will jump up and scream that that's what you get for putting a woman in office . . . but what can you expect of an actress who is trying to make laws between engagements." Therefore, before she sent out any letters, she should always look at all the angles "just to see if it really is as goofy as it looks from here."[31]

Lybeck frequently took Douglas on walks through her district. They trekked through dilapidated housing areas, particularly in the Sixty-second Assembly District. These visits provided concrete examples for Douglas's speeches and generated good material for local publicity. Lybeck asked the press to photograph Douglas "pushing doorbells." In time, the argument that she was not a "local" faded as an issue because most grew to like Douglas and felt she had the critical interests of the district at heart. Her closest advisors, however, were often amused by the awkwardness that resulted from her naïveté about inner-city street life. Douglas had no fear of people, no matter the area or the time of day or night. At night, driving to a meeting wearing her fur coat, she would frequently pick up hitchhikers. On one occasion, Lybeck had planned for Douglas to take the streetcar into the heart of the district to visit the headquarters of the *Los Angeles Daily News*. Douglas felt extremely uneasy, as one close associate remembered. She "had never been on a streetcar in her life. She had to ask which end you got on. And we had to get the money for her. She didn't know how to pay the fare." She also panicked because she was not accustomed to wearing panties. Fearing her skirt might blow in the wind, she rushed a staff member to a nearby department store to buy a pair. The public, however, only saw pictures portraying a representative out among the people. [32]

Douglas catered more to her black constituency than to any other group. While she concentrated on orchestrating public pressure on Congress to pass legislation to help blacks rather than bringing federal monies into her district, she did not neglect the need for increased services benefiting her black constituents. She investigated citizens' accusations of housing discrimination, such as those of a group in West Hollywood who were very upset with a local housing association that drew up restrictive covenants. She, Holifield, and colleague Clyde Doyle persuaded Governor Earl Warren to halt construction of the Hollywood Freeway until the acute housing crisis had passed. In her district the proposed freeway cut across the northwest corner where 1,000 low-income minority families, in the area of the "most critical housing shortage in the United States," faced eviction. She worked with the Committee for Interracial Progress, a coalition of fifty organizations, to direct federal housing funds into Los Angeles County, particularly into her district. After a long struggle, she secured funding to expand post office facilities in the center of the black district. She donated personal funds to local black causes such as Dr. Temple's medical center in the Sixty-second District or the church building fund of the black St. Paul Baptist Church. She invited local whites and blacks to meet Mary McLeod Bethune when the black educator visited Los Angeles seeking funds for her college. Douglas assisted a group of black businessmen headed by one of her principal supporters, H. A. Howard, in securing permission for a federal savings and loan bank in the black district. The Federal Home Loan Bank Commissioner's office had initially denied the group's application but reconsidered favorably when Douglas intervened. The loan company, in strong operation forty years later, was the first such black company west of Chicago. [33]

Lybeck and Chavoor together worked to get *Congressional Record* statements about various key issues out to blacks. When Douglas gave a speech in Congress supporting the FEPC in June 1945, Chavoor reprinted 10,000 copies for Lybeck to send out to the blacks on a special district mailing list. "It does look as if the FEPC will die a slow death," Chavoor wrote Lybeck, "but in the meantime the issue is hot and I think it is a good idea to get the mailing out." The office also reprinted tens of thousands of copies of "The Negro Soldier" to circulate throughout the district and to all white and black liberal newspapers and journals. Lybeck also capitalized on unexpected opportunities to publicize Douglas's pro-black stance. For example, when she administered a standardized test for West Point candidates, a black youth, David Carlisle, received the highest score. Lybeck publicized the appointment extensively, praising her for appointing the first black cadet west of the Rockies to the Academy. Lybeck also encouraged Douglas to gain appointments for blacks. Blacks credited her with encouraging the United States district attorney for Southern California to select a young black local lawyer, George E. Cannady, an honors law school graduate from Howard University, as an assistant district attorney. Lybeck also insisted that Douglas recognize dedicated black campaign workers such as Fay Allen. He reminded Douglas that Allen could be an advisor in racial relations. If Douglas did this, he wrote, it would "really go through the 62nd like wildfire. . . . The word about you would be: 'Jesus, does she pay off.' "[34]

But Douglas also kept track of many other issues, making speeches, urging voters to put pressure on their representatives, and working within the government to put pressure on certain offices. She continued to speak out against the Equal Rights Amendment, for Farm Security Administration rehabilitation loans, for child care centers, and for public power development. She also got quite entangled in a ruckus over the impending release of Nazi propaganda films confiscated in 1938 by the Alien Property Custodian Office, a ruckus that illustrated both her style and her staff's admiration. She opposed the release of any more Nazi propaganda than what already was in the country before the Nuremberg war criminals' trial. According to a draft of a release from Lybeck, Douglas's threat to bring this to the attention of Congress "was enough to avert the [flood of propaganda] upon an unsuspecting American public." In Washington, he continued, "they know that when 'our Helen' speaks, people pay attention." Chavoor wrote Lybeck that Douglas and her colleague Emanuel Celler "started the ball rolling—the rest just followed along and took all the credit. But that is nothing new. Helen does many things on the QT that no one else knows about." Douglas caused considerable congressional turmoil in early 1946 when she spoke out briefly but vehemently against HUAC. She accused the Congress of permitting HUAC "unlimited power," resulting in "thoroughly un-American" acts and encouraging its employees to "feel free to run wild and in any direction" in its search for Communists. This set off almost a "brawl," in the words of the *Detroit News*, between John Rankin and John McCormack, resulting in an "uproar" in the House. Both men were ordered to their seats; "Douglas had long since made a discreet exit."[35]

*

In the 1946 spring primary, Douglas ran against three Democratic candidates and four Republicans who cross-filed, including Fred Roberts, a black businessman who had served sixteen years in the state assembly. Roberts had a liberal record on civil rights but a conservative outlook on other political and economic issues. In 1940 he had challenged Ford for the congressional seat. The Republicans, hoping to unseat Douglas, worked hard for Roberts because they felt that a black candidate was the best hope for removing her from office. An unexpected flurry of opposition came from a group of women who threatened to campaign against Douglas because of her stand against the ERA, a hot issue in Washington. While labor and the NAACP retained their traditional stance of neutrality during the primary, HICCASP campaigned hard for Democratic liberals in the Los Angeles area. One American Legion officer accused Douglas of membership in the Communist Party, information that spread quickly through the Legion posts. But unlike past Red-baiting experiences, this rumor was not blown out of proportion. The *Eagle* and the *Daily News* gave her good coverage. As the *Daily News* put it, Douglas was one of the few who "really got in there and pitched for the common man." Despite a relatively low-key campaign, however, Lybeck did not take any chances, particularly since Douglas was not available for appearances. He knew that while he could count on the support of some blacks, others watched from the sidelines to see how Roberts would fare. Gus Hawkins still resented Douglas and did not work for her; Douglas did not trust him either. In the summer of 1945, for example, Douglas was asked to support Hawkins as a candidate for the position of Minister to Liberia. She agreed, but wrote Lybeck, "No wonder Hawkins was so friendly. There is always a reason it seems." During the primary, Hawkins apparently told Douglas that she "went out and did too much talking around the country and should stay more on the job in Washington." [36]

Douglas's total primary tally amounted to over 41,000 votes. Roberts led the Republicans by about 10,500. Douglas's Republican vote was just under two thousand short of Roberts' total. She wrote Hickok, exaggerating the closeness of the race: "The election was wonderful but everyone is blaming everyone else now for not stealing the Republican nomination. I lost, you know, by only twelve to fourteen hundred votes. But that's always the way." If they had blanketed the Republicans with reprints of "My Democratic Credo," she continued, she undoubtedly would have taken both party nominations. Lybeck was pleased with the heavy black support and hoped it would remain stable for the fall campaign. Jessie Terry felt optimistic, but she cautioned that a "heavy race plea would be put on." Lybeck conferred about Roberts with another key black supporter, lawyer Gilbert Lindsay, who also felt Douglas would win. When Lybeck reminded him that Roberts had taken the black district against Ford, Lindsay remarked that the blacks had never liked Ford. They felt that Douglas was their friend. "This struck me forcibly," Lybeck wrote Chavoor, "because it's the special way that Gilbert speaks about Roosevelt." Lybeck also told her that Douglas should work for a "splash appointment" for a black. He suggested lawyer Loren Miller. Even if Miller turned down an offer, Lybeck reasoned, it would be important.[37]

In April 1946, Melvyn moved back to Los Angeles to begin filming. Although he was not enthusiastic about fulfilling his studio contracts, he was happy to be back in the Outpost house, which had been fairly well cared for during the two years the Douglases had rented it. During the filming of his first picture, *Sea of Grass* with Spencer Tracy and Katharine Hepburn, he had an unexpected break. A lawyer friend, apprised of Melvyn's contract problem, offered to take the studios to court, and won the case. Melvyn was free to return to the stage. He did sign on with RKO for an optional single film a year to guarantee the family a base income. At that point Helen decided not to pull the children out of school but rather to take the youngsters with her and join Melvyn in Los Angeles in early June. Chavoor was dismayed by Helen's decision to let the children complete the school year. The responsibility of taking care of them was more than she could handle. Mary Helen had missed two months of school with flu, colds, and the measles, she lamented to Lybeck. "My hands have been more than full. Oh, Ed, sometimes I wonder if we will live through it all." But Helen felt that the kids "had been dragged from pillar to post too much. . . . She won't have any peace of mind until she knows that all is well with them. . . . I guess I will have to take the medicine and not make any complaints." The housekeeper was "ready to give up the ship any minute. Every other day when the kids get obstreperous, she says she's gonna leave. Well when that happens we are always in the soup and I have to pitch in." Looking back on those years, however, Chavoor's frustrations had mellowed. "We had some merry times," she recalled; "Peter was something else again. He'd get into mischief." She particularly remembered an evening when pre-teen Peter did not get home until after two o'clock in the morning. Apparently he had been out " 'having a beer with my buddies,' " some Navy men from the Naval Hospital nearby. "I just broke down," Chavoor recalled, but she did not call the police. "I could envisage headlines, 'Where is the mother?' " She also did not tell Helen, for "I was the mother enough."[38]

Douglas postponed her trip west with the children, however, when she was hospitalized from overwork. Doctors discovered that she suffered from high blood pressure and an enlarged heart, a problem that became recurrent. While Douglas tended to ignore most physical problems, the heart situation worried her. Chavoor wrote the Lybecks even before Douglas was hospitalized: "You undoubtedly know that Helen is quite a tired girl. . . . I might as well tell you that her ticker has become enlarged. . . . It has all happened I am sure through . . . hard work with no thought of self—no rest—no nothing." Chavoor had been "beating herself out trying to do things for her" while continuing to play the mother role, which included staying with Mary Helen in the hospital for a tonsillectomy. When Douglas finally ended up in the hospital, Chavoor wrote, "please say some prayers for me to last these next two weeks. . . . I don't mind the work . . . but the children really get me down . . . and it is almost more than I can bear. But it is all for the cause and that's the only thing that's going to help ease her mind." She pleaded, "If I miss the boat here and there . . . please don't be too hard on me. I know a better job can be done . . . but with the kind of boss we got and the way she operates together with the added burden of children and the house, I can do no better." Within two weeks, Douglas was back in her office, involved in the final days of the atomic energy legislation and fulfilling various speaking engagements including a nationally broadcast speech at a rally to continue the Office of Price Administration (OPA). The children finally went to the West Coast without her, and Melvyn took over the principal-parent role for the summer. Chavoor told the Lybecks, "You don't know what a relief it is not to have Mary Helen and Peter here—as much as I love Mary Helen and can even tolerate Peter."[39]

Peter spent much of his time with a tutor, making up for academic problems he had encountered in his Chevy Chase, Maryland, school. Helen sent Melvyn Peter's grades. She commented that he had worked hard, but his efforts were intermittent. "He did break his neck staying up practically all night working on a special project, like his mother, and then would put off for two or three days any other work which had to be done—which is done by so many children." He had a wonderful imagination, she told Melvyn, that was important to cultivate. The tutor should "fill his mind with interesting images." Peter also had a wonderful comprehension of current events, far more than other sixth graders. As for the D in behavior, Helen continued, that did not "reflect bad classroom habits" but rather problems with his peers on the playground and in the cafeteria. As a family friend had pointed out, Peter was "desperately lonely. He is suffering from the kind of loneliness that hits people late in life. He needs to feel that he is loved. Whatever you plan for him be sure that you don't make the mistake that I made. I think you can do anything with him and be as severe as you want if he feels that you love him and want to be with him." If he sensed that it was an effort, "he will respond badly and feel as though he doesn't want to do anything with you." Melvyn answered that he had found a good tutor, one who was "friendly and sufficiently casual in his approach to intrigue Pete rather than cause him to hold back." Melvyn also scheduled the tutoring for mornings so Peter would have the afternoons free, although "I have made it quite clear to him that various things which he is anxious to do, both on his own and with me, will depend upon the progress which he makes in his work as well as in his manners and general attitudes.

He is really an awfully sweet kid, and I have no doubt but what with patience and persistent effort we will get him through." [40]

Although Helen had been relieved of the daily care of Peter and Mary Helen, she still suffered from stress-related health problems, and in July she was hospitalized a second time and ordered to take a long rest in Los Angeles. She finally left Washington in August to join her family before her two-month assignment as alternate delegate to the United Nations. She did very little except rest, but this required break gave her time to think about things at home and spend time with the children. She even resisted working the district in preparation for her fall campaign. In September, after looking over various options for the children's schooling, Helen and Melvyn decided on Chadwick, a reputable school popular with wealthy families, particularly those from the Hollywood community. The school also had boarding facilities, which the Douglases believed would provide the most stable, structured environment for Peter and Mary Helen since Melvyn would be in and out of Los Angeles and Helen in Washington. Once the children had moved into the school, Helen had some totally uninterrupted time as she prepared for her work at the United Nations.

10

Postwar Politics

DOUGLAS, exhilarated and rested, left home for New York on October 16, 1946, to prepare for the opening of the U.N. General Assembly a week later. The assignment was taking her to the heart of a peacemaking action, closer than she would ever be during her political career. Using analogies learned as a child, she called the United Nations the "greatest engineering project ever undertaken by man. It is building bridges to people the world over." The American delegation stayed at the Pennsylvania Hotel; Secret Service men and police surrounded the hotels and meeting places. She wrote Melvyn two days after her arrival that the American delegation was meeting constantly; in between she was trying to read as much as she could. "They send the stuff up here by the bushel, most of it marked 'secret' or 'very secret' or 'top secret' " with memos ordering delegates to lock up the materials. She could not really understand why it was all so secret, though she was stuffing it all on the top shelf of her closet. Melvyn hastily answered, "For God's sake don't talk too freely about those secret documents, even though they don't add up to much in your opinion. It wouldn't help your campaign any if you were suddenly accused of discussing State Department Secrets."[1]

Secretary of State James F. Byrnes headed the bipartisan American delegation, which included a group of distinguished men and women noted for their knowledge of foreign affairs: senators Warren R. Austin, the United States delegate to the Security Council; Arthur Vandenberg, the ranking Republican on the Foreign Relations Committee; and Tom Connally, chairman of the Senate Foreign Relations Committee; also Representative Sol Bloom, chairman of the House Foreign Affairs Committee; and Eleanor Roosevelt. Alternates included representatives Charles A. Eaton, John Foster Dulles, Adlai Stevenson, and Helen Douglas. Only six countries out of fifty-one had women on their delegations; the few women delegates attracted considerable press attention. The *Brooklyn Eagle* commented about Douglas: "A tall, well-tailored woman, she swings along through the U.N. corridors, her black topcoat tossed over her shoulders, the sleeves flying behind." As she saw people she knew, she greeted them "with a breathless hello, an impulsive toss of her dark long hair, and a large grin."[2]

Delegates were divided among various committees: Roosevelt, for example, was assigned to the Third Committee, Social, Humanitarian, and Cultural, where her focus was human rights; and Douglas and Stevenson to the Second Committee, Economic and Financial. The principal issues addressed by the committee included the world shortage of cereals, the United Nations Relief and Rehabilitation Association (UNRRA), and the economic and social reconstruction of war-devastated areas. Committees met almost daily; Douglas deferred to Stevenson to speak for the United States within the committee, but she found it hard to keep quiet. "I am trying to keep calm," she wrote Melvyn. "It is hard at times. . . . Our position is wonderful but . . . real *statesmanship* is badly wanted at the 'top.'" She also attended plenary sessions that were held almost daily, American delegation strategy meetings, and banquets. She had one chance to speak before the General Assembly on the closing day of the session, December 15, when she addressed the question of American opposition to the Soviet Union's resolution on the World Federation of Trade Unions to elevate the organization above other groups in terms of access to the Economic and Social Council. She received only perfunctory press coverage. Douglas also spoke to various New York groups, including one called the "Unseat Bilbo" dinner on October 17. Always sensitive to potential Red-baiting, she wrote Melvyn, "The dinner turned out to have the left-wing boys I thought would be present. I hope I do not get a kickback from having spoken there." She presided over the World Friendship dinner, attended by over a thousand people, an affair organized by the United Nations Secretariat and the American delegation to educate the young people about the dangers of war, to "teach children to be good neighbors." Twenty children from New York City acted as banquet hosts.[3]

Lorena Hickok moved in with Douglas to help her out with secretarial needs, which included writing Melvyn to keep him abreast of daily events. One evening after "three brandies and soda," Hickok reported that a recent health exam showed that Helen's heart swelling had gone down and she seemed in good condition. The doctor, however, had told Helen he did not like giving her good news, for fear "that she would take advantage of it!" Helen was working hard, and "Mrs. R says she is doing a magnificent job." Hickok then recounted several of her favorite recent "Helen stories." Her favorite detailed one evening session, after almost all the delegates had gone. Roosevelt and Douglas were among the few who were left, she wrote Melvyn, "surrounded by acres of empty seats while some guy droned along in Spanish. . . . they were calm and, apparently, listening intently. Don't you love it?"[4]

Meanwhile, while Douglas was enjoying the excitement of the United Nations, Ed Lybeck was managing the 1946 re-election campaign without his candidate. Although Douglas did not leave Los Angeles for New York until mid-October, she was exhausted and spent what energy she had during the congressional recess preparing for the General Assembly. Lybeck's major concern was the split in the black community between Douglas, a white liberal Democrat; and Roberts, a black Republican. Roberts based his race on the argument that "blacks should send blacks to Congress." He presented himself as a liberal with a platform identical to Douglas's, favoring the FEPC, anti-poll tax and anti-lynching bills, rent control, reduction of income tax for the poor, the extension of social security, the Wagner-Ellender-Taft housing bill, and labor union power. The Republican National Committee, overlooking its antipathy to blacks in its determination to defeat Douglas, helped Roberts financially and even sent Joe Louis to the district to campaign. Philip Connelly, head of the Los Angeles CIO Council, warned Douglas early on that already "a clever job is being undertaken" for Roberts by those who used southern Democratic representatives Rankin and Bilbo as examples of the "Democrats' disregard for the Negro voter." He also warned her that some of her supporters had much too "serene" an attitude towards the campaign, assuming her victory was "in the bag." While Douglas insisted that the campaign message never mention race, only qualifications, she finally told Lybeck to conduct the campaign "as though we were fighting for our lives."[5]

Black newspapers reflected the division among blacks. The *Los Angeles Tribune*, a conservative paper, came out early for Roberts. The *Los Angeles Sentinel* initially remained neutral as it had during the primary but viewed Roberts as a strong opponent. Many blacks had voted for Douglas, the paper pointed out, because they did not think Roberts had a chance to win. The campaign, therefore, might well turn on the "legitimate desire" for black representation in Congress, despite party loyalties. This "general skittishness" disturbed Lybeck. He wrote Chavoor, "we haven't gone quite far enough along the road with [the black brethren to] know where we have them." By October, the *Sentinel* editor, Leon H. Washington, Jr., had come out strongly for Roberts, although he otherwise supported the Democratic slate. He did not, however, criticize Douglas. The paper scored liberals who voted only for white candidates and never for blacks, mocking Douglas's argument that race was not an issue; "race is an issue in every aspect of American life." Despite Leon Washington's disagreement with Roberts on some issues, he declared "a vote for Roberts is more than a vote for a candidate. It's a vote for a principle . . . a vote against Lily-Whiteism in government." Roberts' victory would "lift the morale" of blacks all over the country. As expected, the *Eagle* provided solid support for Douglas. Editorials championed Douglas's civil rights record in every issue, and editor Charlotta Bass published frequent articles on Douglas's United Nations activities.[6]

Lybeck leaned heavily on target mailings and handout literature, mailing out over half a million pieces in all. He urged Douglas to get statements from national black leaders like "Powell, Dawson, White, Randolph, et al.," as well as from the Washington party powers, which he incorporated into the campaign literature. Washington folks complied; Rules Committee chair Adolph J. Sabath said that in his forty years in the House, "I can recall no Member who, in the short space of a single term, has attained such a standing." Senator Robert Wagner singled her out as "the outstanding first-termer in the Seventy-ninth Congress." Lybeck also mailed thousands of copies of a handwritten postcard from Douglas. The names of the American delegation to the U.N. were around the edge of the card; the message read: "Dear Friend: I trust that my conscientious efforts in your behalf both in the Congress and as your delegate in the Assembly of the United Nations will merit your support for my reelection to Congress, November 5th. Sincerely Helen Gahagan Douglas." Helen also prepared numerous radio recordings.[7]

Liberal newspapers both locally and around the country also provided grist for handouts: "You could count on your fingers the Congressmen better versed in world affairs and social economics," the little-known *Liberty Magazine* said. The *Louisville Courier-Journal* called her "one of the most world-minded members of Congress," and *Collier's* wrote that there were "not twenty men in Congress who know more of international affairs" than Douglas. A poll taken of eighty Western reporters who regularly covered the House was released close to the election. It ranked members of Congress according to their ability to debate, presentation of critical issues, committee work, and leadership and conscientiousness. Voorhis came in first, with Douglas a close second. Douglas begged Harold Ickes to mention her in his "beautiful column" because "everyone here loves you so and believes you are one of the few honest men in the world. It would help a great deal. If you can't, I'll understand." Ickes amiably agreed, and Douglas wrote back, "Thanks a million. They're really bringing the guns into my district, oil interest, real estate, home loan, etc." Ickes devoted his October 9 column to the California elections. Few had as "enviable" a voting record as Douglas, Outland, Voorhis, and Healy, he began—all of whom had voted against state control of tidelands oil early in 1946 and supported cheap public power. "It would be a particular tragedy," he concluded, "if Helen Gahagan Douglas should fail of re-election. Think of the House of

Representatives with John E. Rankin screaming with sweating and distorted face with Mrs. Douglas not there to whom one might turn with gladdened eyes for welcome relief."[8]

The Democratic Party and individual contributors provided financial support. The Democratic National Committee gave Douglas $3,500 for the fall campaign. The remaining $4,000 came from various friends. Jimmy Roosevelt, the newly elected head of the California Democratic Party, joined with organized labor to bring national figures to California to campaign for a short list of key Democrats that included Douglas. The party had already lost the gubernatorial race, as the popular Earl Warren won both the Democratic and Republican primaries. Although Roosevelt could not persuade Truman to come, several agreed to, including the controversial Henry Wallace, recently dismissed as Secretary of Commerce because of his opposition to Truman's foreign policy, who drew enormous crowds. Organized labor, particularly the CIO, worked for Douglas. Leaders had no doubts about where she stood on key issues. She had voted 100 percent with labor on economic issues, frequently appeared as a keynote speaker at large union rallies, and testified before labor subcommittees, particularly on protective legislation for women.[9]

In mid-October, just as Lybeck began to feel fairly confident, the Fourteenth District League for the Preservation of the American Way of Life circulated tens of thousands of copies of a flyer printed on red paper in hopes of boosting Roberts' sagging campaign. The broadside asked Douglas why she had made a "secret trip to Moscow" the previous year, visited Stalin and other Russian leaders, and attended "political and social functions of Joe's?" The furious Douglas, threatening "vigorous prosecution," protested to the Department of Justice and turned the case over to the district attorney, the FBI, and Post Office officials. Although the *Eagle* accused Roberts of instigating this flyer, Douglas did not. As she wrote one friend, she was certain that Roberts "disliked the kind of campaign the Republicans waged."[10]

Despite this setback, Douglas emerged with a solid victory, winning in every district. The Douglas forces were jubilant. Lybeck wrote Douglas, "You are practically the leader of the Democratic Party in California, right now. Your name is on everybody's tongue." She should "stand back while I bump my head three times on the ground before the new leader of California Democracy. Bump, Bump, Bump. There—and we all love you besides." Everyone was excited, and "Ruth and I have been congratulated until we almost ain't got no hand left to be shooken." Her black supporters deserved particular credit for combating the "nationalistic race-baiting campaign," which "took guts— because Central Avenue [the heart of the black district] was so God Damned hot the pavement burned your feet." Her opposition "were traitors and betrayers" as well as "Uncle Toms and Christ knows what all . . . who whooped and hollered and snowed down crap on us until they couldn't see us any more."

It was a good thing, Lybeck concluded, that Douglas had not been around. While she did lose the precincts right around Central Avenue, probably from newly arrived Southern blacks who voted Republican, she got more votes in the Sixty-second than in 1944 running with Roosevelt.[11]

While Lybeck had not been that impressed with labor's organization (all they really did was "sit on their hands"), he realized that she could not have won if labor had actively opposed her. In the northwest corner, the Sixty-fourth, Lybeck attributed her victory to her role in stopping the freeway construction. She also got the Mexican and Italian votes and the retirees on Bunker Hill. "Someday you'll get over being gun-shy of the Senior Citizens" and introduce a strong pension bill. Then she would see what Bunker Hill could "REALLY do for you." To his knowledge, her victory represented the first time that a white had carried a black district against a black in a major election, something the "well-meaning hot-shot guys didn't think for a moment could be done." So he and Ruth were "very busily suggesting to people that, of course, if you had run for the Senate. . . ." The *Sentinel* blamed Roberts' defeat on the black split; Douglas supporters had "left no stone unturned to defeat him." Douglas was particularly delighted that she had taken the Sixty-second. To her this meant that she had made her "first really concrete contribution" since entering Congress. It proved "the fundamental principle for which I have been fighting—the principle that is very important in the international pattern of human relations. I have long felt that the oppressed had a potential of loyalty far beyond anything you or I could feel or understand."[12]

Statewide, the Republicans enjoyed a landslide typical of the rest of the country. In southern California, the Democrats lost six congressional seats, reducing the ratio of Democrats to Republicans from 10–3 to 4–9. Critical Democratic losses included Voorhis's loss to Richard M. Nixon, Outland from Santa Barbara, Doyle from Los Angeles, and Izac from San Diego. Douglas found all these defeats tragic; they demolished the power of the southern California liberal coalition and left Douglas essentially on her own. Jimmy Roosevelt blamed the results on "war weariness," the "burdensome administration of federal agencies," and Red-baiting in some congressional races. California Democrats began raising money immediately for the 1948 election, coordinating their efforts rather than running costly individual campaigns, and disassociating the party from any left-wing elements. Lybeck had a much simpler explanation for the Democrats' defeat. The party was "scared to death." "Every damned one" of the candidates "hunted a hole and crawled in it and their campaigns dived right in beside 'em." Voorhis crumpled under Nixon's carefully crafted Red-baiting campaign, Lybeck commented; the least Voorhis could have done was to "stick his chin out and say 'Well, nuts to you!' " Douglas agreed. The issues had simply not been "carried to the people. That is the great tragedy because this next Congress has been given no mandate. They are footloose and fancy free." Eleanor Roosevelt tried to reassure the losers in "My Day." "From my own point of view, being out of office had always been a pleasant situation." The best of politicians in a democratic form of government would find ways to serve in other occupations. But, she continued, some important victories did occur, particularly that of Helen Gahagan Douglas.[13]

Overall, the liberals felt overwhelmingly depressed. It had been bad enough when the minority Republicans teamed with Southern Democrats to defeat their legislative proposals. Now, for the first time since 1930, the Republicans had a majority. They had gained fifty-six members in the House, resulting in a balance of 256 Republicans to 188 Democrats. The conservative tilt also affected the number of women elected, which dropped from nine to seven. Republicans Luce and Sumner had decided not to run again, and Democrats Emily Douglas and Woodhouse lost their races. Two new women joined the House: Democrat Georgia L. Lusk from New Mexico and New York Republican Katharine St. George, a first cousin to Franklin Roosevelt.

Despite the gloomy prospects for Democratic successes, Douglas's prominence and popularity grew enormously during this congressional session. While the black-clouded prospects of the Democrats made Douglas increasingly angry, frustrated, and disgusted, she emerged as a leader of the dispirited, a cheerleader urging on the Democratic team despite overwhelming odds. Her success resulted in part from her ability to make the transition from her deep loyalty to the Roosevelts to the reality of the Truman administration. Unlike other New Dealers who fell by the wayside as the years passed after Franklin Roosevelt's death, Douglas achieved a relationship of mutual respect, if not power and affection, with Truman. Douglas's friendship with Eleanor Roosevelt seems the obvious explanation for Truman's initially taking note of the flamboyant Helen. He held the former First Lady in the highest regard; it seems only logical that it was Roosevelt who persuaded Truman to nominate Douglas to the United Nations delegation. Thus, once again, Eleanor Roosevelt had helped Douglas move from the periphery to the center of political action. The U.N. experience clearly added to Douglas's measure of knowledge on matters of foreign policy and also helped make her feel very much a part of the postwar administration. Her successful campaign, without FDR by her side and at a time when numerous talented and popular liberals lost, also buoyed her confidence.

Within the first six months of the Eightieth Congress, Douglas made clear her position on the issues facing the session, a position that usually reflected Truman's goals. As she had argued in the Seventy-ninth Congress, America had a responsibility to provide its citizens a decent life through international peace and the ability to buy food, clothing, and adequate housing. If voters had the facts (and she was always prepared to supply them), it would be obvious that the proper use of the United Nations and appropriate domestic legislation would provide this security. On the home front, Congress's principal job was to control inflation by continuing wartime rent and price controls, changing the tax structure, and, above all, providing low-cost housing. Along with these guarantees, legislators had to protect the hard-won rights of labor, further civil rights, increase the minimum wage, extend social security, provide proper health care and insurance, guarantee women equal pay for equal work, improve conditions for migrant labor, and protect First Amendment rights. Abroad, the United States had to participate in developing a plan to maintain a balance of power between the East and West, protect the new Jewish homeland, provide for helpless refugees, and rebuild Europe. She made it quite obvious that she would fight the Republicans every step of the way by constantly monitoring and publicizing conservative activity and by speaking up on the floor and in committee hearings. She inserted letters, speeches, and newspaper editorials in the *Congressional Record*, pushed the Democrats' program, and proposed modifying amendments to Republican bills.

By this time, Douglas saw herself as the leading protester in Congress, the bright light for the working class. Chavoor wrote the Lybecks that everyone had the idea that Douglas "is God and can move this damn reactionary Republican Congress [but] what the hell else [she] can do or thinks she can do except support the [right] bills is beyond me." Chavoor later commented that her boss was "up all hours of the day and night here studying and probing and speaking out whenever the cause so necessitates. It seems she is practically the only whip left of any kind."[14]

Douglas's style captivated liberals everywhere. They inundated her office with requests for speeches and endorsements. She responded to this clamor with a stepped-up speaking schedule, using the National Concert and Artists Corporation to increase her engagements. "Unless a few real leaders went around the country arousing the people to the issues facing them and telling them what was wrong in Congress," she argued, none of the programs that she favored would get passed. "It was just as important to do a job rallying support as it was to just cast a vote" on the floor. The outspoken Bella Abzug, a member of Congress from New York in the 1970s, reflected Douglas's approach. She saw her role as being "among the people," organizing them politically on the outside and fighting for them on the inside. Both women believed that if they could not struggle for what they believed in, they did not want to be re-elected.[15]

Douglas's style increasingly set her apart from her colleagues. She began to sound more and more like a member of the Senate than of the House. Although if requested to do so she would limit her remarks to a single issue, her basic stump speeches addressed the overall dilemma facing postwar Americans, speeches that gained her the coveted national spotlight. She always reminded her audience of their number-one responsibility: to be informed and write their representative or senator. She wrote one of her constituents that she worried that "Republicans will . . . continue to confuse the issues"; this "blind apathy" led Americans to swallow "hook, line and sinker . . . paid Republican advertising." Douglas and her staff were convinced that the Republicans viewed Douglas as a threat. Chavoor wrote Lybeck: "This is strictly on the QT but during one of the caucuses of the hierarchy of the Republican strategy committee, [they] really blew their top about not having defeated the gal." Conservative newspapers panned her—"Hysterical Helen," one writer called her. When stories circulated early on in the session that she did not plan to be a candidate in 1948, she accused Republicans of initiating such scandalous remarks. "I know that it is rumored around the Capitol that I am the most irritating thorn in the side of the corporate Republican body and that every effort will be made to destroy me in this next election," Douglas wrote Lybeck. "But I did not think they would try such childish tactics as this." [16]

Douglas established her frenzied and chaotic pattern of activity in the Eightieth Congress early on. Her pace was even more intense than during the Seventy-ninth Congress as her sense of urgency about the state of the world and her self-importance increased. Relief from child-care responsibilities gave her more time. She was constantly on the move, combining her office responsibilities and floor work with keeping on top of issues before the Foreign Affairs Committee; testifying before other committees, both congressional and in Los Angeles County; traveling nationally to speak to a wide variety of organizations; participating in roundtable discussions at universities, conferences, and on the radio; and keeping in touch with Melvyn, Peter, and Mary Helen, and her family in New York. Her main means of taking needed rest proved to be pushing herself to the point where she would end up in the hospital, generally for the persistent enlarged heart problem, back pain, or total exhaustion. She usually stayed two weeks, periods that proved critical for her to regain her strength. In fact, she began the Eightieth Congress with a two-week stay for treatment of a severe case of poison ivy and fatigue. She always continued to direct her office staff from her hospital bed.

At the opening of the session, Douglas submitted bills against the poll tax and lynching and for the establishment of a permanent FEPC. Lybeck had urged her to time her sponsorship of civil rights legislation carefully. "Pick yourself out a couple of nice [civil rights] bills and introduce 'em," he wrote, "before this nice respectable Republican Congress can even get its fat rear ends into their new chairs, so they'll have something to play with. Then sit back and enjoy the show. Don't beat your brains out on the bastards. Just point out their mistakes every time they make a fresh batch, plug your own bills, sit back and make the *Record* and—in general, act like the Senator-to-be. In the meantime, pay lots of attention to your own district." [17] Douglas also submitted a bill for funding cancer research, a reflection of her losses of her father and a brother to the disease and her keen awareness of the need for basic cancer studies.

After two weeks in Washington, however, she returned home briefly to work with Lybeck on district concerns. She also enjoyed being at home again after the exhausting U.N. session. The Christmas holidays had been too short. She played a key role in the Citizens' Housing Council Conference in Los Angeles, which brought together veterans, labor, and church and civic groups. The *Los Angeles Sentinel* called the meetings a real effort to see how the city could get out of a "near tragic" housing dilemma. For Douglas, the issue of housing was, like civil rights, a good vehicle to connect the needs of her district with her concerns for a national working-class constituency. She considered inflation the most pressing domestic problem and argued that the high rents and the lack of inexpensive houses on the market were the principal causes of inflation. Douglas developed her emotional involvement with the issue from her acute awareness of housing shortages and poor living conditions for veterans in her district. In one speech she declared that building costs were caught in an inflationary spiral and "housing for veterans is our No. 1 problem inside the over-all No. 1 problem of housing." Our veterans fought from "Guadalcanal to Tokyo and from north Africa to Berlin," but they were daily "defeated by the bitter home-front battle for a decent place . . . to live" except in " 'hand-me-down houses for heroes.' "[18]

Douglas also spent time with her black constituents during this two-week window at the beginning of the Eightieth Congress. One matter of considerable discussion concerned hiring a black staff member. Lybeck, black district leaders, and Bethune had pressured Douglas to hire a black secretary either for the Washington or the Los Angeles office. Lybeck told Douglas, "it's silly as hell to deliberately set ourselves up for that chauvinistic 'lily-white office' sneer. And our good friends among the Negroes would really enjoy it; it would be one more thing they could slap the opposition in the puss with." Douglas was enthusiastic about the idea, despite the fact that the young woman's salary would have to come from Douglas's personal funds. She had used up her staff funding and did not want to replace any of her existing staff members. Douglas also knew that a black would have to deal with the segregation in federal cafeterias and hostility from other secretaries; no white member of Congress had yet employed a black secretary. But in typical fashion, Douglas figured they would "work it out."[19]

Hiring someone for the Washington staff seemed less difficult than one in Los Angeles, as Florence Reynolds could not cope with supervising a black person. Chavoor wrote Lybeck that it would never work, "knowing how Florence feels and how she washes her hands after she has to shake hands with one of them." Lybeck and Douglas eventually selected Juanita Terry, the daughter of active campaign worker Jessie Terry. Douglas offered Juanita $200 a month, which the girl thought quite generous; her previous monthly salary was $135. The Douglas staff made her feel welcome, except for one Southern girl who quit as soon as Terry arrived. Terry's office responsibilities were primarily basic secretarial tasks—dictation, filing, typing, and drafting routine letters. She never dealt with civil rights problems or black constituency questions. "I was purely a clerical assistant," she said later. Helen had others to advise her on political issues. Because neither Douglas nor Chavoor had much time to orient her either to her job or to life in Washington, Terry found herself depending on the black secretaries of congressmen Powell and Dawson. "I could probably not have made it had it not been for them showing me the ropes," Terry recalled. But Douglas treated Terry in a warm and sensitive fashion. She successfully pressured the staff of the House cafeteria to integrate. "I never really understood why either Powell or Dawson hadn't done something about that," Terry commented. "And it opened up a whole career—not only for me, but actually for other Negroes up here on Capitol Hill." Terry and Chavoor helped Douglas hostess formal parties, and the three occasionally relaxed with an evening of charades or bridge. The parties gave Terry opportunity to chat informally with Douglas's Washington friends, and she became acquainted with the Gahagan family members when they came down from New York to visit. [20]

On January 31, 1947, after this hiatus in Los Angeles, Douglas returned to Washington. She submitted additional bills, including one reflecting her growing awareness of the importance of taking a more active stand on women's issues—a bill to establish a commission to study the status of women that the Women's Bureau in the Department of Labor had helped her frame. Later in February she submitted a bill supporting equal pay for equal work and another providing more funding for nursery schools and kindergartens to assist working mothers. Douglas had become increasingly conscious of the special interests of the working women through her close contact with organized labor. Women in the labor movement were concerned in large measure with economic status, particularly equal pay. Douglas did not, however, cultivate women's friendships in the same way she had during the early 1940s and did not go as far as Eleanor Roosevelt in immersing herself in women-related issues. In Congress, she was friendly with her female colleagues on both sides of the aisle. But few of the women felt bound to one another because they were women or because they felt that power would result from unifying. As Margaret Chase Smith put it, the "women did not function as women but as members of Congress." Douglas, in fact, denied that she was treated any differently than a man. Nevertheless, the fact that congresswomen led in sponsoring legislation supporting women's needs suggests their sensitivity to women's second-class status in many areas of American life. [21]

Douglas's comments commending the newly formed United Nations Commission on the Status of Women and in an article she wrote for the *Woman's Manual*, on women in politics, typify her view. "Any restraint on the progress of women is a restraint on the total national progress. Theoretical equality is not enough." She pointed out that women understood better than men what their money would buy at the grocery store, how to educate and care for their children, and how to secure peace "so that their children will not have to be blown to pieces in a new war." Women, however, could accomplish this only through teamwork. She pointed to women in the labor movement who set a "fine example [for] their more disorganized sisters." She made the following suggestions: women should build up the morale of their fellow workers, accept responsibility as voters, study issues and candidates, and demonstrate ability in policy-making. But women should not take their disappointments or frustrations too seriously.[22]

When Douglas spoke to women about political involvement, she generally compared housekeeping to national and world politics. She used this language, initially used by women reformers during the Progressive period and picked up later by the Women's Division, because she believed the average woman could relate best to housekeeping analogies. As she said in a message she was asked to send to Japanese women on the importance of female suffrage: "Since government is only housekeeping on a large scale, it seems to me that women can play an important and constructive part in building world peace and healthy, sound communities at home. Who knows more about running the home than the mother? And who in the home works continuously for harmony? Again the mother." Women could see that world peace was essential for prosperity at home, and they were willing to do something about it. In fact, women had no choice; they had to be more interested because of the atomic age. And on another occasion she commented that "from the time she is born, a woman is a politician. At home she must be housekeeper, mother, teacher, judge, and sometimes even jury." She also spoke often on her perception of how women interpreted current policy issues. At a luncheon of the Philadelphia branch of the Foreign Policy Association, for example, where the topic was world security, Douglas spoke on "a woman's view"; other speakers included the Danish Minister to the United Nations, Senator Joseph H. Ball, and Attorney General Francis Biddle.[23]

The Equal Status bill that Douglas submitted was labor's answer to the Equal Rights Amendment. In the Seventy-ninth Congress, Douglas had helped Dorothy McAllister, the former director of the Democratic Party's Women's Division and now the head of the National Committee to Defeat the Un-Equal Equal Rights Amendment (later renamed the National Committee on the Status of Women). When ERA supporters launched a major push to get the amendment through Congress, McAllister's committee mounted a massive protest by heavy mailings to members of Congress and the President and work on the state level. Over forty major organizations, mainly labor unions, and numerous noted lawyers supported these efforts. Anti-ERA forces argued that the amendment would not end discrimination in state laws and would invalidate the important protective labor legislation, much of which dated back to the first twenty years of the century. This special-interest legislation included the regulation of hours and wages, the employment of young girls, exposure to hazardous substances, carrying heavy weights, and providing seats for certain jobs. Opponents also felt that the ERA threatened family life by challenging important family and property laws that regulated family relations. If men and women were considered equal, laws requiring the husband to support his family, protecting the wife's separate property when living away from her husband, or providing widows' allowances, would be eliminated. Differential treatment in social security and workmen's compensation would disappear. Finally, opponents argued, even if safeguard provisions protecting this special-interest legislation were attached to the ERA, the process of passage, securing ratification in three-fourths of the states, would be lengthy. The Fifth and Fourteenth Amendments constituted sufficient legal ground for equality, and what was necessary was a close examination of legislation at the state level where true discriminatory legislation existed. The bill for the ERA died in the Seventy-ninth Congress.[24]

Douglas was joined by Norton and Rogers in co-sponsoring the Equal Status bill, and all seven congresswomen supported the bill. Margaret Chase Smith joined Douglas in introducing the Equal Pay bill. The Equal Status bill captured public attention. The idea behind the bill was to prevent "unwise" legal discrimination but still satisfy those who believed that differences between women and men in their physical structure and biological and social functions warranted differential treatment in the workplace. The bill proposed the establishment of a Commission of the Legal Status of Women to prepare for the President a "complete study of the economic, civil, social, and political status of women and the nature and extent of discriminations based on sex." In addition to state laws, the commission would examine all government agencies and departments for discrimination. Anti-ERA lawyers applauded the bill, saying that it would avoid the principal problem of the ERA, the elimination of "all distinctions in legal treatment . . . even where their fundamental resonableness and common sense is apparent." Douglas introduced Eleanor Roosevelt's blessing in the *Congressional Record*. Roosevelt's opposition to the ERA emphasized her belief that it would be easier to attack discriminating laws on a state-by-state basis and still retain "such labor laws as are still needed for the protection of women in industry." Despite the efforts of Douglas and others, both the Equal Status and the Equal Pay bills died in committee.[25]

Work on her bills did not interfere with her travel. A week after returning from Los Angeles, she left for a speaking tour that included Emory University in Atlanta, the United Jewish Appeal in Richmond, and other stops in Orlando, Dallas, Fort Worth, and Columbia, Missouri. She returned to Washington on February 17 for eight days and then left again. But Douglas constantly kept visible in Congress, always voting on bills and speaking up regularly. On March 13, 1947, she delivered her most dramatic and memorable address to the Eightieth Congress, her "Market Basket" speech to call attention to the rising spiral of inflation. Her staff had selected groceries at a store close to Capitol Hill and arranged for national press coverage of Douglas buying the food items. With her basket over her arm, she strode to the front of the chamber and announced that she had just come from the "lowest-price chain store in the city." It took fifteen dollars, she exclaimed, to buy the same items that cost ten dollars in June 1946, shortly before the lifting of price controls. She itemized her groceries. "Mr. Speaker," she said, "the food-buying power of a $10 bill is very important . . . as important and disturbing and as full of economic and political implications and consequences as any weighty, complicated matter that will come to the floor of this House." The National Association of Manufacturers promised Americans nine months ago, she claimed, that if Congress lifted controls, future goods would sell at prices all could afford. "Well, gentlemen," prices had risen 50 percent; "that is the way it has worked out." Congress had a responsibility, she charged, to keep a healthy balance between prices, wages, and profits. The 1946 Employment Act was passed to achieve this goal. But the Republicans claimed that the joint congressional committee assigned to implementing this act had not had adequate time to carry out its job. "If General Marshall and General Hershey had assembled the Army with the same speed now being displayed by this . . . committee, the war would still be on—assuming we had not been beaten." The Republicans had found time, however, to remove rent controls and go back on their promises to veterans to provide them housing. She wanted to put her basket "where it belongs—squarely in the lap of the Republican Party."[26]

Not surprisingly, her speech irritated some of her colleagues. She had hardly begun talking when Republican congressman Frank B. Keefe from Wisconsin interrupted to ask a question. She refused to yield, and Keefe protested disgustedly that "it would be perfectly impossible to ask a question pertinent to this point at the end of the lady's speech, which is listed for an hour." But she would not give ground, forcing Keefe to wait until the end; at that point, he proceeded to call her speech unintelligible. What exactly did she want Congress to do, he asked? She responded tersely, shifting her focus from food to housing: "I am trying to sound an alarm before it is too late on the question of rent control." The rent control bill under consideration, she claimed, could not possibly control rents since the Republicans had removed supervisory controls. She accused Keefe of failing to support real controls, and he retorted that she had made an "impassioned statement." She answered: "It is an impassioned statement, and if the gentleman will go with me out to the grocery stores . . .

he will be impassioned too. I am impassioned. I am not making this speech for political capital," but rather in the "vain hope, perhaps, that the majority party will do something before it is too late." The key House Democrats, particularly McCormack and Rayburn, expressed delight at her Market Basket speech, and her office received an overwhelming mail response. Newspapers in small towns across the country picked up the speech, prompting people to write letters. Douglas inserted many of these in the *Congressional Record* with the hope that some legislator might change his mind. One letter told of an eighty-year-old woman who had just died—she had been "tramping the streets" for three weeks looking for a room because she could not pay her rent increase.[27]

Douglas continued to link the problems of inflation, rent control, and housing, and kept herself abreast of bills in committee and in the forefront of floor debates. She considered housing a most urgent problem in her district. As she said to a group of national housing officials, the only "spot on earth that needs housing worse" than the Fourteenth Congressional District "must surely be Hiroshima." She had worked closely with Wilson W. Wyatt, Truman's housing administrator during 1946, and backed a comprehensive bipartisan Senate bill co-sponsored by Ohio Republican Robert Taft and Democrats Robert Wagner from New York and Allen J. Ellender of Louisiana. The bill, generally referred to as the TEW (Taft-Ellender-Wagner) bill, provided for liberalized Federal Housing Agency mortgages, rental housing, new construction of 1.2 million housing units each year for ten years, low-interest loans to construct 500,000 units for a four-year period, and other grants for slum clearance and farm housing. While Douglas approved of the bill, she did not feel that it adequately responded to veterans' needs for inexpensive housing. She submitted a bill that she felt would provide for this omission. And the *New York Post* commented, Douglas had "bravely gotten underway" a discharge bill to get the TEW bill out of committee. She also submitted a bill to investigate the real estate lobby, which she and others were convinced was at least partially responsible for blocking the TEW bill. The TEW bill passed the Senate more than once but was continuously blocked in House committees.[28]

On the House floor, she declared repeatedly—generally to deaf ears—that if Congress lifted rent controls, economic chaos would ensue. She introduced a bill to extend current rent rates until 1948, but it died in committee. During one debate on terminating rent controls, a journalist commented that the House was in "uproar and confusion." Douglas called the bill hypocritical and complained that one of her amendments had not even been read. With that, "meows were heard from the floor." On more than one occasion, she pled with Congress to help the vets. Stories of veterans living in chicken coops and rabbit hutches were not exaggerated "one iota," she commented, and almost half of them had to double up in already cramped quarters. Ninety percent of these men could afford only between thirty-eight and fifty dollars per month on housing costs.[29]

Douglas also stepped up her work with labor in the spring of 1947. Unions, led by the CIO, began major internal restructuring immediately following the disastrous 1946 campaign so they could lobby in Congress and significantly affect voters. Union leaders had finally confronted the reality that their ability to improve wages and working conditions related directly to the success or failure of pro-labor congressional and state legislature candidates. Newly reorganized political action committees began to keep a careful watch on congressional voting records, which they continuously published in their national and local newspapers and in liberal periodicals, such as the *New Republic*. Unions also began implementing a complex plan for fund-raising, voter registration, and securing one million volunteers from their ranks to work on the 1948 campaign. The pace of these efforts intensified in February of 1947 with the introduction of the Taft-Hartley bill, which labor called the "greatest travesty" of the Eightieth Congress. The bill, which reflected the conservatives' fear of the postwar strikes and labor's increased power, declared certain practices illegal, including secondary boycotts. The measure also gave the President authority to delay a strike for eighty days if he felt it threatened the national interest.

Douglas responded angrily to the Taft-Hartley bill, commenting that "binding the hands and feet and gagging the mouth of labor doesn't put milk or eggs in the icebox." Douglas wrote Lybeck that the bill threatened to "completely destroy all labor unions. . . . Maybe the labor boys now will understand what some of us have been saying for a long time. If they want to protect themselves they had better really get active politically." While she acknowledged that some unions abused their privileges, she blamed these "bad habits" on the anti-union employers. She believed that the remedy for abuse was reform within the union, not "punitive labor legislation." She constantly consulted with Paul Sifton, the head of the newly formed CIO-PAC lobbying office in Washington, and contracted with him to write her position papers and speeches on labor issues.[30]

Despite well-organized efforts from labor and support from the Hill, they had no effect on the congressional majority. So when the bill reached Truman's desk in June, labor mounted another protest, helping to generate the greatest flood of mail that Truman had received in the White House. Labor delegations from all over the country arrived in Washington as a "veto caravan." Douglas helped organize a massive "oratorical pep meeting," which opened with the singing of the "Star Spangled Banner" and labor's "Solidarity Forever"; the crowd then enthusiastically welcomed their congressional supporters. One paper reported that Douglas got a "great ovation" when she cried out: "labor did not break under the goon squads and tear gas of the 1920s, and it won't break now."[31] Although Truman did veto the bill, hoping to gain important support for the 1948 election, the bill immediately passed over his veto as he had predicted. But at least the new anti-labor law gave the Democrats a major theme for the 1948 election and strengthened labor's resolve to overthrow the Republican majority in Congress. The debate also provided an opportunity for Douglas to cement her bonds with both national and local labor officials. These efforts paid off, particularly in her 1948 campaign.

Also in the spring of 1947, as the Eightieth Congress took shape, the House Foreign Affairs Committee became more involved with diplomacy questions as the Truman administration initiated a program of foreign aid. Douglas felt more self-assured in her knowledge of the finer points of foreign policy questions, which resulted in her becoming more outspoken in committee hearings. Truman's suspicion of Stalin had increased in late 1945 and early 1946 as the Russian leader seemed to give no signs of interest in peaceful coexistence. In April 1946, the former British prime minister Winston Churchill gave a speech in Fulton, Missouri, in which he stated that Stalin's "iron curtain" was "descending across the Continent." At this point, Douglas still urged Big Three cooperation. But by early 1947, she, too, became concerned about Stalin's apparent interest in territorial expansion. The first big crisis involving direct American action to prevent the spread of Communism arose in early 1947. Great Britain announced its withdrawal of military and financial aid from Greece because of shortage of funds. Truman worried that the Communists would soon move into Greece. The Turkish government, a military regime, feared that Russia had plans to annex one of its provinces and perhaps eventually the entire country. In a March 12, 1947, speech that set forth what became known as the Truman Doctrine, the President proposed a 400-million-dollar aid package to help the Greek and Turkish governments, the first request for action on his "get tough" policy.

Douglas supported the concept of the economic and military aid package to Greece in principle, but she questioned the intent of the current Greek government and wondered whether the money would get into hands of the people who needed it. If not, the Greek people would become alienated from the United States. She did not like the link to Turkey because of its military government. She felt the two situations were different. In Greece, a power vacuum would be created when the British pulled out, she argued, but in Turkey, the challenge came from outside and appeared vague. The proper approach to the Turkish situation, she pointed out, was to turn the Greek and Turkish problem over to the United Nations Security Council; the United States should not furnish military aid in a unilateral move. The country needed to explore the existing international machinery that the United States had helped establish. She considered it presumptuous and morally questionable for the United States to try to settle international problems independently of other nations.[32]

On May 7, Douglas presented three amendments to the Greek-Turkish aid bill. The first prohibited the United States from sharing atomic energy information with Greece; the second required that the United Nations have six months to investigate the Turkish situation, after which Congress could take action; the third stipulated that six months after sending aid to Greece, the United Nations or the United States would supervise free elections. The amendments were discussed at some length, but Congress voted each down. Douglas had coupled her argument on Greek-Turkish aid with her opposition to a bill to discontinue the Office of International Information and Cultural Affairs, created in mid-1946, to spread information about American life to foreign countries. This bill would in part close libraries and terminate the radio network "Voice of America." When the final vote on Greek-Turkish aid came up, only a few joined Douglas's protest. Truman was most displeased at Douglas's lack of support. Evidence suggests that he did not reappoint her to the United Nations 1947 General Assembly because of her opposition to the Truman Doctrine.[33] She did enthusiastically back the administration, however, in the development of the Marshall Plan, a proposal by Secretary of State George C. Marshall (who had replaced Byrnes) of massive American aid to rebuild Europe.

Douglas also set herself apart from mainstream Democrats with her stand on loyalty issues, which further rankled Truman. In March 1947, during the same weeks that Congress was debating the Truman Doctrine, the President issued an executive order for employees of the executive branch to take a loyalty oath. Douglas came out strongly against this move. When the bill for implementation of the order came before Congress, Douglas launched into a discussion of democratic principles and charged that the bill, which she deemed unconstitutional, struck "at the very root and fiber of democratic life." The bill passed with a large majority, but she voted against it. She also voted consistently against funding for HUAC, fought the citation of the Hollywood Ten for contempt of Congress, and all bills outlawing the Communist Party. Her willingness to defend the civil liberties of accused Communists and fight against bills she felt would only create hysteria attracted local support, both volunteer hours and financial contributions, from the more élite pressure groups, including Jewish associations, Hollywood political groups, and university faculty. But these views obviously hurt her with more conservative groups.[34]

Douglas allowed herself little time to relax during this first congressional session. But occasionally she did let down, and everyone enjoyed the breather from the pressure. She and Chavoor would have guests for dinner, ending the evening with their favorites, charades or bridge. Chavoor particularly found bridge relaxing because it shut out all the "unanswered mail or fifty-seven other problems in the district." A rare visit from Douglas's mother and another relative in the spring of 1947 proved delightful. Chavoor wrote Ruth Lybeck that they were having a wonderful time, especially because instead of going immediately to bed and reading or discussing politics, "we have had dinner and played bridge. . . . It has been fun. Matter of fact, I hate to see them go. Which isn't what I can say whenever Melvyn's mother is around (Meowwww!!!!)." Hickok taught Douglas how to play double solitaire, which she found so relaxing that she and Chavoor frequently played just before bedtime. "You should hear Helen swear," Chavoor wrote Hickok. "Calls me a bitch and what not just because I get a card up before she does." Chavoor usually won, although "every now and then [Douglas] really goes to town and gives me a real lacing."[35]

Douglas saw very little of Melvyn and the children during the first session of the Eightieth Congress, but the family remained in close touch by phone and letter. Sometimes Helen and Melvyn were both invited to give speeches at the same event. Very occasionally they planned a weekend away from any work. The children continued as boarders at Chadwick, coming home on weekends. Helen's speaking trips, which were not essential to her congressional work but necessary to her self-esteem, cut down on her opportunities to fly home. And home visits were pressured because she had to split her time between the Lybecks and district demands, her family, and resting in bed, trying to regain her energy. Although the marriage became increasingly shaky, Helen and Melvyn still cared for each other. Melvyn wrote her at one point: "I miss your intelligence, your quiet understanding—and I miss, too, the meaningful noise and restless activity with which you sometimes disturb the atmosphere. It all adds up to a chunk of my existence which is irreplaceable." A librarian who worked in the Library of Congress during the postwar years recalled the poignant sight of Melvyn wandering around the Library's main reading room, patiently waiting for Helen to break away from her congressional activities.[36]

Summers were more complicated because the children were out of school. Melvyn (with Helen offering long-distance advice) arranged a combination of tutoring, camp, and a long visit to Vermont when the family generally was together. In the summer of 1947, for example, Melvyn planned a busy day for nine-year-old Mary Helen, adding daily piano lessons and ceramics classes to her tutoring. She would have rather gone to camp, Melvyn reported, but the school had encouraged tutoring. He also hired a young woman to be with the nine-year-old, as a "sort of social companion and planner" during the time Melvyn was at the studio. Peter, now fourteen, had tutoring as well. He also took a trip with his stepbrother Gregory to Lake Tahoe, the first such venture he had taken. Peter had lost weight and grown much taller, almost approaching his father's height of six feet. Evie wrote Hickok that Peter had become very handsome. And, of even more importance, "his whole attitude towards life has changed. He is one of the most polite, best behaved young men I have ever

known. You just wouldn't recognize him. When Helen told me all this on one
of her return trips, I couldn't believe it. . . . Well—now I have seen and I
believe." Helen did have a block of time in Los Angeles from the beginning of
August 1947, when the congressional session ended, until November when she
was called back to Washington for a special session that included numerous
Foreign Affairs Committee hearings. But travel and district work filled these
weeks. Chavoor wrote Hickok that "August, with the children here, was, of
course trying." Sometimes Helen took a week off from work just to see Mary
Helen, refusing to work with the district office. Melvyn combined acting with
renewed political activity, working closely with the American Veterans' Committee and helping to found Americans for Democratic Action. But he had no
interest in running for office. With Helen in Congress, he commented, "our
political interests are in very competent hands." [37]

As Douglas moved into the activity of the second session of the Eightieth Congress, an election year, she felt she could count on her black constituents as
well as solid labor support. Labor regarded California as a critical state, particularly the southern California liberals. And Douglas stood out in this group.
Despite this solid support, Douglas faced two unknowns. She and Lybeck did
not know how seriously the Republican National Committee would work to
defeat her. Also, no one knew the implications of Henry Wallace's shift to the
left. After he left the Truman administration in 1946, liberals still found him
an appealing speaker. But in late 1947, as he began to organize a new political
party, which he called the Independent Progressive Party (IPP), his mainstream
liberal support quickly vanished because of his open courting of support from
members of the American Communist Party. Some liberals argued that this
new party might drain off liberal votes; but it was also possible that voters would
realize the party's association with the Communist Party and discount it. Initially, Douglas worried more about Republican opposition. She suggested to
Lybeck before the March 1948 filing date: "I think we should do what Chet
Holifield did in the last election . . . namely to put a Republican of our own
into the primary in the hope that we can split their vote and maybe capture it
ourselves." Lybeck disagreed. The Republicans, he felt, were convinced that if
there was an IPP candidate on the ballot, they would win both the Republican
and Democratic primary vote. Numerous Republicans, therefore, had filed.
To Lybeck, the big question was whether or not Douglas should cross-file on
the IPP ticket. [38]

The IPP had urged her to cross-file, promising that they would not run an
opposition candidate. But if she did cross-file, Lybeck reasoned, she would
invite a smear campaign from the right. On the other hand, even if she did
not cross-file, she probably would be Red-baited anyway, as she had been since
she entered politics in 1939. He cited a recent meeting of Republicans when

they "gratuitously characterized you as the 'outstanding disgrace to Southern California, that must at all costs be defeated.'" The goal, of course, was to avoid a three-way contest in the fall. He also was not as sanguine as Douglas about taking either blacks or the Jewish vote for granted. Many new blacks, migrants from the South, would vote Republican as in the 1946 election; and numerous Jews, no matter their support of Douglas, would vote Republican or even IPP to protest what they considered a Democratic Party "sell-out" on the Palestine issue.[39]

When finally pressured into a decision several days later when she had to file, Douglas did not cross-file on the IPP ticket, just the Republican. When the IPP immediately entered a candidate, county labor leaders became concerned. The United Auto Workers (UAW) called the IPP a "Communist Party maneuver designed to advance the foreign interests of the Soviet Union at the expense of democracy and freedom throughout the world." One labor leader wrote to Jack Kroll that the "commies" and the IPP "have finally shown their true colors" and endorsed candidates against Douglas, Holifield, and Cecil R. King. Their scheme was "out in the open"; they planned to "defeat these liberals." Jerome Posner of the Amalgamated Clothing Workers in Los Angeles and head of the union's PAC activities in California wrote Kroll, "You know the situation in California and it will require every second of our time and the right people to do the job." Kroll wrote UAW leader Walter Reuther that the California election was unusually significant and difficult because of the fight against the IPP. Yet Lybeck initially downplayed the threat of the IPP candidate. In a note to Douglas referring to Wallace's critique of American foreign policy, he wrote that "Wallace is not going over. The Communists, of course, are plugging his speeches, but the average voter just doesn't seem to think that it's cricket to gallop off to another country and pan the hell out of your own."[40]

Despite the concerns, Douglas did well in the primaries, although once again she had no time to make personal appearances in the district. She won the Democratic nomination easily, and took the Republican by a slim majority. But the Republicans demanded a recount, claiming that certain precinct returns had not been reported. The recount, which Lybeck never believed accurate, gave businessman William Braden a 300-vote lead over Douglas. As Lybeck put it, the "Republicans were out to get Congresswoman Douglas in this election." They were apparently basing their campaign on two principles: "expense was no object" and the "maxim that 'the Truth is a valuable commodity and should not be wasted.'"[41]

The congressional session ended shortly after the campaign, and Douglas turned her attention immediately to the Democratic National Convention. She had joined a small group of liberals who approached General Dwight D. Eisenhower as a candidate to replace Truman. When he declined, Douglas decided to support Truman. As at the 1944 Democratic convention, Douglas was slated to make a major speech. She also enjoyed a groundswell of interest in her nomination as a candidate for vice-president. Although she quickly quelled the interest, she was flattered and received a flurry of publicity. The *Washington Post* commented that this was the "first genuine boom in history for a woman for vice-president [and] heralded what may happen sooner than we think, even possibly in 1952."[42]

In September, the campaign picked up momentum. The CIO and UAW PACs worked out an organized work schedule by precinct within each congressional district. Douglas received the largest labor contributions of any congressional candidate nationwide. Initially she got a total of $4,500 from labor PACs, including $2,000 from the CIO-PAC. In California, by contrast, other liberals received between $500 and $1,250. The amount in part reflected the nature of the race; rumors suggested the Republicans had allocated more than $500,000 for Braden. The IPP candidate withdrew in September, leaving Douglas with only Republican competition. Wallace made some unsolicited and certainly undesired comments in late September urging Douglas's election. But he was not overly enthusiastic about a person who only four years prior to this had pushed vainly for his vice-presidential candidacy. As one newspaper reported his speech, Wallace said that he still didn't know exactly "how Helen Gahagan *Dulles* (laughter and applause)—I don't know how she stands on the Truman Doctrine. But I suppose she'll do better than her Republican opponent." Michael Straight, editor of *The New Republic*, supported her, Wallace continued, as well as numerous labor union people who were IPP supporters. "But it comes hard when she doesn't want our support—or does she want our support? I guess our friends will vote for Douglas and Holifield but I suspect for fear of offending them they won't ring any doorbells."[43]

The Republicans, for their part, embarked on the expected Red-baiting and other well-worn tactics from past campaigns. "Doctors for Braden," for example, implied that Douglas was part of the left-wing influence in Congress. The right-wing *Jeffersonian Democrat* brought up the "trip to Moscow" again. A pamphlet out of Braden headquarters played up Douglas's Fifteenth District residence. It referred to her as the Hollywood representative who lived in the "hotsy-totsy area of Hollywood" as contrasted with the "modest home of our good neighbor and friend" who lived in the district and was not ashamed of it. Lybeck repeated the techniques he had used in the 1946 campaign—widely distributed speeches and various pamphlets tailored to different constituencies. Once again he had to run a campaign without Douglas in town. He cultivated a new group, public school teachers, who appreciated the congresswoman's support of more funding for public education. He publicized her endorsement from the California State Colored Republican League. He helped sponsor a mass rally at a local high school featuring prominent Hollywood actors' support for Douglas. Film industry friends, led by Melvyn, Rita Hayworth, and Harpo

Marx, also arranged a "Star Parade" and marshalled financial donations. Douglas commented after the election that she was "in no position to report on the part played by Hollywood in this campaign. [But] I know that Ronald Reagan and my husband, Melvyn Douglas, were kept pretty busy."[44]

Despite Republican attacks and the lukewarm IPP support, Douglas took each precinct by a stunning 2–1 margin. The most significant change came in the conservative Fifty-fifth Precinct where she beat Braden with a vote of over 22,000 to his 17,000. In the black Sixty-second, the count was 31,000 to 4,000. In toto, she won approximately 89,000 votes, while Braden garnered only 43,500. Democrats nationally hailed her victory, calling it the dirtiest campaign since 1934, when Upton Sinclair was defeated. Supporters and skeptics alike realized that in four years, she had developed the Fourteenth District into as safe a seat as Thomas Ford had enjoyed. She could rest comfortably, knowing that she had control over that district and could retain the seat for as many years as she wished.[45]

11

The 1950 Primary Campaign

HEARTENED BY the 1948 election results, the Democrats returned to Congress with cautious optimism. Truman, buoyed by the unexpected returns and feeling more self-assured, attempted once again to pressure Congress to support his Fair Deal program. On the domestic front his requests included demands for more low-cost housing, extended social security, civil rights legislation, and, to help curb the inflationary spiral, the continuation of some rent and price controls and increased taxes. The President also asked for the continuation of monies for European recovery and defense funds for NATO countries. Labor, self-congratulatory about its role in the campaign, looked forward to a more favorable legislative session than the Eightieth Congress, particularly hoping for the repeal of the despised Taft-Hartley Act. But despite the Democratic victory, congressional control rested, as in the Seventy-ninth Congress, with a conservative coalition of Southern Democrats and Republicans. Nine women won their congressional races, four Democrats and five Republicans. Judge Reva Beck Bosone from Utah and Connecticut's Chase Going Woodhouse, who had served in the Seventy-ninth Congress, joined Norton and Douglas on the Democratic side of the aisle.[1]

Douglas's 2–1 victory added not only to her political self-assurance but also to her visibility. She initiated a well-received weekly series of radio talks aired in Los Angeles that she continued throughout the Eighty-first Congress. She reviewed the week in Congress, explained how Congress worked, and interviewed key politicians. Her first speech, for example, targeted blacks; she described the festive and large reception honoring Representative William Dawson from Chicago, the first black to head a congressional committee. She highlighted political women in another in a lively conversation with India Edwards, national director of the Democratic Party's Women's Division. Lybeck wrote Chavoor in March that he thought Douglas was doing an excellent job. "That sort of stuff, about make-up of Committees, descriptions of how they sit and what they do, etc., is just the kind of thing people really go for. . . . She's coming off the record [disk] in a black lace negligee. Intimate, is the word." If she continued in this fashion over enough stations and made numerous personal appearances, "she can be elected to ANYTHING!" he exulted. Although Douglas probably would not have liked his bedroom language, Chavoor was glad to hear Lybeck's positive response; she commented that while Douglas was "improving by leaps and bounds," she did not have enough time to prepare and sometimes "the darn script isn't written until just before recording time."[2]

Also in the early months of the Eighty-first session Douglas submitted over two dozen bills reflecting her increased self-confidence about proposing legislation. Her bills included some new issues—investigating the procedures of House investigating committees, establishing a New Deal–style Civilian Conservation Corps, studying the employment problems of middle-aged people, providing relief for grain growers, creating a federal commission to set up services for the physically handicapped, developing the Franklin D. Roosevelt Redwood Forest, and extending development of California's Central Valley water resources. She wrote Ed Lybeck that the White House had asked her to introduce a housing bill proposing federal loans with lower interest rates for low-income families. She had responded with a full employment bill that included funds for middle-income housing, and spearheaded House efforts to pass these bills. She periodically visited Truman to secure his support for a particular bill and persuaded the President to appoint an investigatory commission on migrant labor. Douglas also introduced several bills, similar to those submitted in the Eightieth Congress, reflecting her continued concern about women. These bills allowed, for example, tax deductions for household help and provided funding for nursery schools and kindergarten. Two bills required equal pay for equal work and requested minimum wage for telephone operators. The most important, a bill generating considerable adverse mail, proposed the establishment of a presidential commission to investigate fully the status of women. The commission's charge included identifying discriminatory laws. As she and others had emphasized in the Eightieth Congress, she felt the ERA would only delay equal status because of the long ratification process and it would remove protection legislation for women workers. She distinguished between what she called equal treatment and identical legal treatment. The former, she argued, would deny the critical differences between the sexes. But equal legal treatment was necessary in such areas as control of property.[3]

As in the previous two congresses, Douglas lectured colleagues at committee hearings and on the floor and inserted speeches and editorials in the *Congres-*

sional Record. She justified one lengthy speech on military aid on the grounds that she was a woman: "I think a little more directly than some of my distinguished male colleagues." She continued to work to secure funds for her district's Station K post office, the only specific federal funding she ever sought for her constituents. She had Ed Lybeck print thousands of copies of her various speeches for circulation. She testified for the establishment of Children's Day suggesting that it would give parents a chance to "evaluate their children as people," to think about their needs, observe advances in science and education, and be "grateful for democracy." While none of Douglas's bills passed, she felt fairly satisfied with the results of the first session and believed she played a part in the passage of a decent housing program, a modified rent control bill, and a measure increasing minimum wage from 40 cents to 75 cents an hour. Other Fair Deal bills had passed the Senate or House and were waiting for action. The conservatives managed to prevent repeal of Taft-Hartley and the passage of civil rights bills as well as cut down on the effectiveness of various other Fair Deal proposals.[4]

Douglas also spent a large part of her day in the Foreign Affairs Committee working out the fine details of bills. The March 1949 death of the committee's chair, Representative Sol Bloom, was a blow. Douglas's comments in the *Congressional Record* reflected the emotional attachment she felt, not only to Bloom, but to the whole committee. His death, she commented, made her ever more conscious of the "quality of the friendships that exist around the Foreign Affairs Committee table," which both Bloom and Representative Eaton made possible. She felt their committee overrode party differences more than any other House committee. "We could disagree, and we did, but we remained friends" because of the atmosphere that Bloom created. The committee worked hard to continue the spirit of cooperation, working diligently on critical legislation. Douglas tended to focus on the fine points of bills and often persuaded her colleagues to make small changes. Major bills that passed during this first session included the Atlantic Pact, bolstering the mutual support system between the allied countries and providing for the extension of both the Reciprocal Trade Act and the European Recovery Program (ERP), and a military aid program. The ERP administrator wrote Douglas that she had a thorough understanding of the legislation, and her hours of hard work along with the rest of the Foreign Affairs Committee were responsible for the success of the ERP bill.[5]

Lybeck worried, however, over the lack of news coverage of Douglas's activities, particularly with domestic issues. In 1948, she was "all over the paper; this year, they wouldn't even know how to spell her name if it wasn't for the Fashion Academy, God bless 'em," referring to a front-page illustrated story on the way she dressed. Chavoor tried to calm him down; the work Douglas was doing—"in committee; with the White House; on the Floor with members"

Chavoor explained, did not typically get coverage unless "you constantly toot your own horn. And you know our gal when it comes to that." But Douglas certainly was working hard. "She has grown so in stature" with her colleagues; even the "worst die-hard Republicans and the Southerners" had "grown to respect and admire her for her courage and her ability." Douglas had "practically been running" the Foreign Affairs Committee since Bloom died and representing the committee before the Rules Committee. "She had such a firm hold of herself and is so calm and matter of fact, she swings them all over. . . . Everyone else screams and pounds their fists [and] she just gets up and with a calm voice soothes the whole bloody mess of them." Douglas had become much more tense, Chavoor reported; the congresswoman wanted things done her way, and she had become increasingly inflexible. When things did not go right, "it seems she is always scolding me. . . . She fairly shouts and I have to tell her that I'm standing right next to her." Then she always apologized afterwards. Chavoor also tried to protect Douglas. "I am getting one hell of a reputation around Capitol Hill about what a bitch I am." But Chavoor was "determined to save the girl a little bit." An article in *Fortnight* confirmed Douglas's intense activity. The office of "the superanimated whirlwind," it reported, was "one of the busiest—if not always one of the most effective" on Capitol Hill. Douglas continued to be a "center of controversy," a person with "firm friends and bitter enemies," just as she had since first elected to Congress.[6]

Despite Douglas's continued bustle of activity in the House, however, and her old pattern of making speeches outside of Washington, she was constantly preoccupied with a major decision that would have great consequences both politically and for her family: whether to run for the United States Senate in 1950. She had thought about the big jump before; this time, however, the possibility was real, which made her feel both excited and scared. The immediate motivation stemmed from her increasing disgust with the senior senator from California, the heavyset, sixty-six-year-old lawyer, Sheridan Downey. In his early years, Downey had supported Progressive politics; in 1934 he ran with socialist gubernatorial candidate Upton Sinclair for lieutenant governor. After losing that race, Downey became the lawyer of the radical Dr. Francis Townsend, whose pension plan for the elderly provoked much controversy. In 1938, Downey ran successfully for the United States Senate on a left-wing ticket. He expressed concern during the war that American efforts were draining labor and industrial resources; after the war he supported Truman's reconversion proposals. Despite this liberal record, during the war Downey increasingly began to side with California oil interests and corporate farmers; supporting, for example, state, not federal control of tideland oil, and the exemption of the massive Central Valley project from the 1902 Reclamation Act, which required the limitation of water from federally funded projects to 160-acre farms. After the war, ending this limitation and a personal vendetta with the Bureau of Reclamation and Harold Ickes became all-consuming issues. He developed his stand in his book, *They Would Rule the Valley*, published in 1947, and two years later demanded a Senate investigation of the Bureau and the Department of the Interior, which became a messy affair.

Douglas viewed Downey as a "menace" to society, sold out to the oil powers, and a threat to the heart of California's past and future, the small farmer. She made no effort to deny rumors early in 1949 that she might challenge Downey. Harold Ickes wrote in his column "Man to Man" that the senator had not only been invisible during the 1948 Truman campaign, he was generally inept. He mentioned that the beginnings of a "Douglas for Senator" movement were underway; "the sentiment for Mrs. Douglas is very strong." A board member of the California Business and Professional Women's Clubs wrote Douglas in January 1949 indicating that the state organization was considering endorsement of her Senate candidacy, but they needed to know her views on women's rights. Walter Pick wrote Ruth Lybeck in early February that the office was already receiving dozens of letters about the race. Douglas realized quickly, however, that the party's power structure and her political friends, including labor, had mixed reactions to her candidacy. Alvin Meyer, a long-time friend and political advisor, took a trip up and down the state, meeting with party leaders. He found most to be Downey supporters. Some could not envision her as a senator, and others simply did not like her. Meyer advised her not to run. Another group, including her former congressional colleague George Outland and India Edwards, did not think she could win and did not want to see her lose her congressional seat.[7]

Mille Logan, a black leader in San Francisco, wrote Douglas that large numbers of people were "inspired" by the thought of her candidacy. "But when I went into Democratic headquarters, the atmosphere was damp with pessimism, except for Howard McGrath [chairman of the Democratic National Committee]. They are flattened by the unorthodoxy of such a project." The size of the state, her sex, and Downey's machine "bog them down." Some telling comments came in from Bert Falconer, a Democrat fond of frequently writing Douglas lengthy opinions. Although he generally wrote newsy and supportive letters, this time he reported rumors critical of her style that he argued would hurt her in a Senate race at all levels of support. Many felt, he reported, that she was a "good showman but not a good politician"; that she voted correctly but had influenced little legislation; that she was surrounded by a "little coterie" who unduly influenced her and who alienated certain other supporters, and that many were hurt who had worked hard in the 1948 campaign and got no personal recognition from Douglas.[8]

While labor groups valued Douglas as one of the most important Democrats in Washington, most were very surprised that she was considering running.

CIO leaders were not at all sanguine that she could win, particularly because they doubted she could gain AFL support, and they did not want to lose her in the House. Douglas wrote Lybeck that her key labor supporters at the national level were "very nervous about losing me and are not at all certain we should make the race. [And] as for money, I don't know where it's coming from." Some had assumed she planned to challenge Republican senator William Knowland in 1952. But as she told Al Barkan, director of the Political Action and Legislative Department of the Textile Workers Union of America (TWUA), that idea was out because another Democratic candidate had been promised key support. Besides, she was after Downey. Ed Lybeck made it clear that while he would support whatever decision she made, he did not want her to run for the Senate. He knew she could continue to win in her district, and eventually she would become chair of the Foreign Affairs Committee. "We'd just concentrate on keeping you in the House and . . . suddenly everybody would wake up and realize that you were the outstanding law-giver in this part of the woods and why the hell weren't you a Senator." But on the other hand, he would rather she ran for the Senate than "lose you just because you got bored and nobody would do anything to alleviate the boredom." But she needed to know that she was in the process of "building a distinguished political career—a guy who leaves an indelible imprint on the political philosophy of the country." But it took fifteen to twenty years to get into that "league."[9]

As the spring of 1949 progressed, however, the flow of letters to and from constituents made clear that Douglas really wanted to run and that growing grassroots enthusiasm buoyed her confidence. In May she answered a young San Francisco man who offered his support. She told him Downey weakened the Democratic Party with his "outrageous" attacks on the Democratic Party platform, and his Central Valley stand certainly did not benefit the best interests of California. Her final decision to run would depend on how much support she seemed to have. "I will have oil money, utility money, Associated Farmers money, plus real estate and NAM [National Association of Manufacturers] money poured in against me. This doesn't frighten me one bit, but we will need to have communities mobilized. Young people will be needed as never before. You can be of very great help in such a campaign." Another fan noted the enthusiasm of Bay Area small business and working people. He praised Douglas's "uncompromising and unflinching fight" for the average American, which had given her "a place of preeminence among leaders of the liberal forces." Judging by the quality of her speechmaking for candidates outside her district, she obviously had the ability to conduct a "fighting campaign."[10]

Evie Chavoor felt overwhelmed at the thought of coping with a Senate race. In May she wrote Ed Lybeck that the "likelihood of Helen's running for the Senate has placed additional work on my shoulders and I just don't seem to be able to meet the challenge and take on the responsibility." The office needed a full-time person just to handle the activity generated by the Senate "business," including countering "all of the latest 'trash,' " mainly Red-baiting comments. Douglas had told her to send out the "Democratic Credo" speech she had given in March 1946 to leading state Democrats to see if she could stem some of the negative publicity. Lybeck, also hopeful Douglas would change her mind, warned Chavoor to stop Douglas from writing anti-Downey comments to constituents until she had made her decision. In the event she decided not to run for the Senate, it would look bad for her 1950 House campaign because she would have to support the entire Democratic ticket. He also jumped on Douglas for what he considered a terrible appearance in July 1949 on Jimmy Roosevelt's weekly radio program. "Don't you guys have ANY appreciation of the rudimentary delicacies of Public Relations?" Douglas had made no mention at all of Roosevelt; "for God's sake, when you go on a man's air, recognize the existence of the man who's supplying the air," particularly since the relations between Douglas and Roosevelt, the principal Democratic candidate for governor, were fairly tense. In fact shortly after this incident, Lybeck warned Douglas not to associate at all with Roosevelt for a while because of rumors concerning his illicit financial dealings.[11]

Douglas initially targeted July 15 as her decision date. But she finally acquiesced to Lybeck's plea to wait until Congress had recessed and she had had some vacation time. Congress finally recessed in August. Chavoor wrote Lybeck that "the boss" was in Vermont with Melvyn and the children. Melvyn's current filming had been postponed and he felt lonesome, so the two took "*my* car and drove up to Vermont to spend what little time they would have together." Helen planned to go to California in September to settle Mary Helen and Peter in school and make several speeches. All this left Chavoor feeling as if she was "sitting on a keg of dynamite that will explode one day. . . . It sure is hell living through the uncertainty." She could not even leave the office, despite her sister's impending wedding and a sick mother who wanted her to come home. Lybeck continued to brainstorm about the Senate race, particularly Douglas's relations with labor and her campaign structure. "What about a guy for a State-wide front . . . like Ronald Reagan?" He figured that a person who would be a "stellar attraction on his own" and could make good speeches would be critical.[12]

Helen's time with Melvyn in Vermont gave the two an opportunity to discuss the Senate race, and at that point she made the final decision to run. While Melvyn felt their relationship and the family would suffer (they were already fighting rumors of marriage problems), he, as always, backed her professional decisions. Nothing suggests the insecure wavering that characterized her decision to run for the House in 1944. The issue revolved around whether or not she believed she would win; once she decided that she would, she moved ahead swiftly.

A tired Douglas finally announced her candidacy on October 5. She declared that she was running "in response to a growing insistence from people in all parts of California" and because of the inadequacy of California's Senate representation. She made it clear that her decision was hers alone, one made "without obligation to any special interest." The people of California had a right, she continued, to leaders who were free from "any private commitments"; dedicated only to serving the public interest, to "laying the solid foundations upon which a peaceful world can be built." She reminded her audience of the daily barrage of socialist accusations and the implied link with Communism. "I will be especially a target for these attacks," she acknowledged, because of her fight for low-cost housing, the farmer, social security, civil rights, and other programs designed to improve Americans' lives. She reviewed Downey's alliance with oil interests and corporate farmers, accusing him of opposing all the issues she supported. Paraphrasing Roosevelt, she reminded Californians that many citizens "were poorly clothed and undernourished and ill housed. . . . Are we to remain indifferent to such evils [which] are the enemies of freedom?" On the same day, she issued a press release claiming that California lost out on the power program in the Senate because neither senator had fought to restore cuts for California in the appropriations bill to fund dams, canals, and other reclamation projects. She listed the items that were cut from the Central Valley Project. California, she summed up, had had the greatest increase in population in the country, but in the power-development appropriations bill the state had been relegated to second-class status.[13]

No concrete evidence suggests what finally made up her mind, so one can only surmise. Few close to her felt confident that she could win a statewide campaign, although they pledged loyal support. But Douglas believed she could win. Many idealistic Democrats throughout the state agreed. Her decision to take on the campaign said a great deal about her need for a new stage as well as her increasing ability to shut out family needs from her mind or at least deny them. She was restless in the House; she did not have the patience or the personality to become a major player in the tedious legislative business in the House. She certainly had contributed sound opinions and spurts of energy on bills. But she generally preferred to cast herself as a spokesperson for a wide range of topics with the goal of energizing and educating the American voter, rather than build relationships on both sides of the political aisle. While her long-term antipathy towards Downey cannot be discounted, it is also critical to recognize that to become a United States senator held enormous political appeal for her. The 1950 campaign would prove her biggest challenge in her public life; this time, however, she had neither an influential and powerful mentor nor money. She was on her own, a "people's candidate." As she wrote Ickes, "You don't know anyone who has any money, do you? We have a campaign on and no money—and I mean *no* money."[14]

Doubting friends continued to express their opinions, but Douglas put any nagging second thoughts aside. Amerigo Bozzani, a long-time active Italian-American campaign worker, wrote her that he was nervous. She reassured him that the best service she could render the state was to "highlight the basic issue of reclamation—cheap power and land for the people. Believe me, Downey is done for—and should be. He has turned his back on the people of California. . . . We are going to win this fight and it will be the first fight of its kind since Hiram Johnson ran against the Southern Pacific Railroads. It will be in the great Western tradition." Another close friend, Allen Rivkin, part of her Hollywood circle, wrote her of division within the film industry, because aside from the reclamation issue, they considered Downey an acceptable liberal. She tacitly acknowledged that on many liberal issues, Downey had at least voted right, but he was not a fighter. A case in point was the Taft-Hartley repeal. Nor had he fought for rent control, federal aid to education, an increased minimum wage, low-cost housing, Palestine—"I could go on down the list." He did not get involved in the 1948 election "when labor was fighting for its life . . . he had already condemned the Democratic Party to the ash heap." Furthermore, she argued, the Central Valley issue was not one to dismiss lightly. Downey spoke for the corporate farmers, which automatically made him against labor. *Pageant Magazine,* she continued, had published a press poll on the quality of senators and Downey was "practically a non-entity." In sum, a "great liberal party cannot be built with such men as Sheridan Downey. . . . A prairie fire has been started [to turn Downey out] and nothing can stop it."[15]

Liberal labor leaders had by this point become more sanguine about Douglas's campaign. Jack Kroll, national director of CIO-PAC, sent Emil Mazey, secretary-treasurer of the UAW, a summary of Kroll's trip west to assess the political situation. In his opinion, Downey was "weak in all parts of the state." Douglas had received an "excellent reception" at the Democratic Conference in San Francisco. In fact, "our people are very enthusiastic about her as are many of the officials of the Democratic Party." Although the CIO did not tag the California Senate among the top seven "critical" campaigns, it was included among the next seven that needed "considerable work."[16]

Douglas wasted no time in getting her campaign underway. She in fact had written Helen Myers, a Los Angeles Democrat, in June 1949, four months before she declared her candidacy, that it was not too early to begin organizing. She indicated her intention to "carry the fight into every county, city, town and hamlet in the state," and while she knew she would win, it would take a great deal of help. She asked Myers to begin gathering information on the leading Republican candidate, Representative Richard M. Nixon from the Los Angeles suburb of Whittier. To numerous others she sent the message to begin organizing "Douglas for Senator" clubs; most response at this point came from some of the large urban counties, such as Alameda, Sacramento, San Jose, and San Diego. As her office compiled Downey's complete record, Douglas resumed her biting comments about his views in press releases and in letters to constituents.[17]

While Douglas capitalized on labor and considerable local support, Downey retained the enthusiastic support of the powerful conservative wing of the party, which included Malone, Pauley, and Elliott, as well as some prominent liberals. Downey selected southern California liberal Will Rogers, Jr., the 1946 Democratic candidate for the Senate, to head his campaign, an astute choice; Douglas had presumed she had Rogers' support. Nettie Jones, who had never lost her strong dislike of the congresswoman who had beaten her for the position of Democratic national committeewoman in 1940, eagerly agreed to organize women for Downey. Manchester Boddy, editor of the Democratic *Los Angeles Daily News*, who had supported Douglas as a congresswoman, was showing signs of using his paper as a vehicle for the more conservative Democrats. Rumors even circulated that it had become controlled by the Hearst papers. He, too, supported Downey for senator, another blow to the Douglas forces.[18]

Downey began to respond to Douglas's vituperative comments in December 1949. In a speech to southern California Democrats, Downey presented himself as a liberal Democrat, a gesture indicating the importance of courting this wing of the party. He even stated that he favored the 160-acre limitation where it could be enforced. He simply did not think that was possible in the Central Valley project. He made a pitch to labor, emphasizing his opposition to Taft-Hartley. He criticized Douglas for limiting the campaign issue to water control, commenting that while she was charming and a good congresswoman, she did not know anything about reclamation issues. He ended by challenging Douglas to a debate. Douglas refused his offer, but she did broaden the field of issues beyond 160-acre limitation. She began sending telegrams to Downey asking his opinions on various questions. When she wired him on some pension issues, he responded that her telegram was so "garbled, ambiguous, and incomprehensible" that he could not answer it, and he had no desire to enter into any argument on important issues through an exchange of telegrams. He challenged her a second time to a debate, but again she refused. Debating was not the way "to bring all the facts to the voters in this campaign." Downey retorted that Douglas had obviously decided to "indulge in a campaign of personal bias and prejudice rather than a broad and objective discussion and consideration of the many problems" in California.[19]

The national media watched the developing California campaigns with interest and curiosity, particularly the Senate race. As columnist Marquis Childs put it, "Nothing that California ever does is on a scale less than super-colossal, whether it's movie spectacles or weather, good and bad. That goes double for the political campaign just coming up." Douglas, who was after Downey, "brings to politics the intensity of a highly dramatic temperament and an energy that could have developed only in the atmosphere that produces those giant geraniums and sunkist starlets." [20]

Douglas took a brief Christmas break with Melvyn, Peter, and Mary Helen and then moved immediately back into her campaign. As if to deny a rumor started by Earl Behrens of the *San Francisco Chronicle* that she had decided to quit because of lack of funds, Douglas immediately opened her principal offices in San Francisco and Los Angeles, and at the end of February 1950, she made her speech officially opening her campaign. Supporters organized fund-raising parties throughout the state for the night of her address. Her message rang clear: she was the champion of the people—veterans, workers, small farmers, women, blacks, middle and lower-middle income people—it was their campaign. She emphasized her alignment with Truman and "the platform that the American people endorsed in 1948." She informed her statewide audience how popular she was in her district. California, the second most populous state in the country, was represented in the Senate by a little-known man, she continued; he had never sponsored constructive legislation, assumed any position of leadership, or established a reputation of fighting for public welfare. But he had "waged a continuous and unrelenting fight for the corporation farmers and the private utilities." She reviewed her record, pointing out that while she represented a city district, the issues she had fought for, all critical for a healthy economy in California, the West, and the nation, and a free and peaceful world, affected both farm and city people. She assured voters that there would be no secret platform or secret commitments to a few powerful campaign contributors. "I do not know if we will have many billboards. I do not know how much radio time can be bought, or how much literature we can afford. I do know that this will be your campaign, your fight, and that when I am elected I shall be your Senator," elected on their platform, which was drawn up to promote the general welfare at home and peace in the world. In short, she hoped to establish herself as a penniless model of uncompromising purity dependent on thousands of committed volunteers. [21]

Before Douglas could get her campaign under way, however, she had to select someone to coordinate the dozens of volunteer groups throughout the state, a coordination that took place independently of Jimmy Roosevelt's gubernatorial campaign. Douglas and Roosevelt viewed each other more as liabilities than benefits to their own election prospects. Ed Lybeck, who had so masterfully managed Douglas's congressional races, did not head the senatorial campaign. Evie Chavoor remembered considerable discussion between the various factions in Douglas's inner circle about what sort of person should be selected. Many, particularly northerners, thought the person should have "glitz and gloss"; while Lybeck was talented, warm, and down-to-earth, he lacked "polish." Sharon Lybeck Hartmann commented later that her father did not really want to head the campaign. He had tied his success to knowing the Fourteenth District; taking on a precarious statewide campaign along with a full-time job was more than he wanted to handle. Initially Douglas hired a Los Angeles public relations firm to manage the campaign; when that relationship turned sour, she hired Harold Tipton, who had been working for the campaign. This appointment seemed strange and naïve; Tipton, a newcomer to California, had no knowledge of the complexities of the state's Democratic politics. Possibly Douglas thought a totally neutral figure would prevent typical Democratic factionalism. Tipton did have some political campaign experience; he had managed the campaign for Helen's friend Representative Hugh B. Mitchell from Seattle and had served as campaign advisor to Senator Harley Kilgore from Virginia. In addition to being a nice person, he had both polish and earthy qualities. In fact, Chavoor reminisced, "I fell in love with him." Not that anything happened, she laughed; no one had time for romance during the campaign. The appointment surprised Tipton, as he wrote Mitchell early on. "I'm scared to death, but ain't showing it. If things weren't so screwy in this state it wouldn't make a nickel's worth of sense for an outsider to come in and take the top spot. . . . I'm going to be rough on everybody, including Mrs. D." Nobody had any sense of the sort of political "pitch" needed; "one group advocates comic books—the other advocates a 43-page treatise on the 160-acre limitation. Personally I'm bored by both." Tipton asked Mitchell to "tell Mrs. D. that I'm a mean S.O.B. . . . but that generally speaking I know what I am doing."[22]

Ruth Lybeck became assistant state coordinator, and Ed remained a very involved member of the team. The Los Angeles office Ruth operated out of served as a clearinghouse for the loosely structured campaign operations. In mid-March, she organized an Advisory Committee to help the campaign "attain maximum efficiency and suffer as little as possible from tangled public relations and impolitic moves," an admission of earlier organizing problems. Lybeck also spearheaded the haphazard growth of various interest groups— labor, black, professional, religious, ethnic, farm, youth, women's, Hollywood, and patriotic. Her office also kept track of finances, coordinated the use of national figures, planned state and regional radio programs, printed campaign materials, circulated records of speeches, and scheduled Douglas's southern California speaking engagements. Lybeck also began a weekly newsletter, with the motto to elect a "fighting conscience," which eventually had a circulation of 20,000. Tipton operated very differently. He considered the north his territory, despite his title of statewide campaign coordinator, and left the responsibility for organizing offices to women. He worked loosely out of the San Francisco office, moving elusively from event to event, often making it difficult for people to contact him. His style really frustrated Lybeck and others trying to work with him. As time went on, most groups relied on Lybeck for organizational advice and materials.[23]

As the central headquarters slowly became sorted out, enthusiastic Democrats continued to organize "Douglas for Senator" offices on their own initiative. County organizers set up offices and reported to Lybeck. Some received campaign literature from Los Angeles; others raised money to print their own. These offices, in turn, helped coordinate the efforts of small clubs like Assembly District or town clubs. Other groups such as the ADA "Office for Douglas" in San Francisco, the Los Angeles Attorneys "Committee for Douglas," the Young Democrats, and the Veterans' Political Council linked themselves to the informal structure. One wrote Lybeck from San Jose that Douglas clubs were "popping up all over Santa Clara County." From the start, these offices were separate both from state party headquarters and from the campaign offices of other candidates running for statewide office, particularly Jimmy Roosevelt, who was challenging the well-liked Republican gubernatorial incumbent, Earl Warren. The decision to remain independent stemmed principally from the view that Roosevelt was a political liability because he had angered hundreds of Democrats while head of the state party. In fact, many Downey supporters, including Manchester Boddy, opposed Roosevelt. Douglas obviously cut herself off from any conservative groups that would require her to change views, and she also proved wary of the left. She told Tipton to shy away from the San Francisco CIO because of the high percentage of Communist Party membership; "for my money we don't want their endorsement."[24]

The strength of each county organization rested with the individual in charge. Helen Lustig in San Diego quickly became recognized statewide as an effective organizer. Sacramento County had early troubles. Bea Stern, an important advisor from the start and one of the frankest about pointing out management problems, wrote Lybeck about the disorganized campaign in Sacramento, a letter that sensitized Lybeck to the demands of the campaign. Stern said she had finally gotten the office underway in a "bare and unsung headquarters." She did not know where to go for information; Tipton tried to be helpful but was hard to contact. She needed to know who paid for radio time, where to get buttons, glossies for ads, posters, and campaign materials. The office had no money. But she ended on a note reflective of the typical campaign worker. "Our hopes are high, and we have made a real start. If our beloved candidate can do the kind of personal campaign she must do, and if we can all click together to help her, we have better than an even break." As funding finally began to come in, Stern eventually organized a model county office, carefully coordinated down to the precinct level. By April she finally felt ready for a "positive, aggressive campaign."[25]

Prickly problems existed in Fresno County because of a nasty liberal–conservative split in the county officials. A ruckus arose around Douglas's early firing of Iva Blank, the liberal county head. Accusations circulated that both Downey and Douglas people were involved in the shakeup. One Blank supporter cattily asked Douglas if her removal of Blank "could have been unconsciously influenced by the fact that she too is a dominant personality and an attractive woman." Eventually reinstated, Blank set up an organization that ran as smoothly as the one in Sacramento. She, too, jumped on Ruth Lybeck when Blank saw inefficiency. For example, she wrote in March that duplicate and triplicate newsletters from Los Angeles had reached many campaign workers; this wastefulness only hurt morale. Some Democrats, especially in rural areas, no matter how supportive, needed time to adjust to the curiosity of a female candidate. A columnist for the *Mountain View Register* in Santa Clara County commented at how young and relaxed Douglas seemed, "without reliance on any of the useful artifices of make-up, hair retouching, trick millinery, flattering colors, corsages." She dressed in simple, handsome dresses and suits with little jewelry and no hats. After one luncheon talk, she could not resist taking a spray of lilacs from the centerpiece.[26]

Counties set up strenuous schedules. Only in mid-March did she cancel engagements to fly back to Washington to "lead the fight" to keep the middle-income housing program. She spent a nine-day blitz in Los Angeles County expanding her contacts beyond her own district. She visited with city councilmen, made a radio broadcast with black lawyer Loren Miller, visited the black engineers at Exposition Park, lunched at Universal Studios, met with representatives of the Filipino community, brainstormed with her finance committee, toured the Twelfth Congressional District, gave a nonpolitical broadcast on women in public life, attended a tea in Pasadena and a fashion show sponsored by a Business and Professional Women's Club, talked with the CIO oil workers and women's auxiliary, and lunched with a Jewish women's organization. She consistently drew good crowds. On street corners she always attracted at least 250 to 300 people; at more organized events she often drew thousands. Her pattern varied when she visited Kern County, a farming area with a sizable population in the San Joaquin Valley, where the largest town was Bakersfield, with 35,000 residents. She made numerous sidewalk appearances in small towns such as Delano, Oildale, and Porterville. She met with small groups and spoke on the radio about Central Valley and its importance to the state's economy. In Bakersfield a well-attended evening rally, a private reception with the World Federalists, and an appearance at the Bakersfield Policemen's Ball completed that tour.[27]

Douglas's speeches focused on a variety of themes, but she found it almost impossible to get away from claiming Downey's basic incompetence plus his stand on 160 acres and a review of her congressional record. Al Meyers commented that she rather overdid the 160-acre problem; she simply could not understand that workers streaming out of a factory in Los Angeles, for example, had no interest in water reclamation. But she had the attitude that workers ought to be concerned about the small farmer. When she spoke on anti-Communism, she pointed out the irrational fear in America, a fear that was "being deliberately used in many quarters to blind us to our real problems. The spreading of this fear is in fact propaganda for communism." She frequently defended her position on the Hollywood Ten, explaining that neither she nor Melvyn had defended the group; they opposed the contempt citations because they abridged America's "principles of justice." In one speech, "Women's Status in a Changing World," she revealed personal vulnerability. A woman in Congress, she pointed out, is viewed as "sufficiently odd to warrant a place in a zoo or a museum . . . but the mere fact that I am a woman has made no difference at all . . . in the performance of my duties." She admitted that her political life had brought on family problems. She hastened to argue, however, that her problems were no different than a married businesswoman's except for the long absences from home. For her, the family sacrifice had been worth it because of her faith in the principles she had fought for in Congress and because as a woman, she brought a "special viewpoint" to issues. She predicted the day would come when a woman would be a serious contender for the presidency, but this would not happen until women were willing to compete equally, expect no favors, and have their own principles.[28]

As a rule Douglas took every appearance with the utmost seriousness—generally lacking a light touch and a sense of humor, which she defended by saying that the issues were too serious for jokes. But she occasionally surprised people. At one stop in a Los Angeles motorcade she sang (upon request) "God Bless America." When her car broke down in a mad dash to Watsonville, near Santa Cruz, she felt no qualms about hitching a ride. To help in situations with no available public address system, she hooked a small, one-wheeled, three-sided box equipped with a microphone onto her car, which looked peculiar; but it worked. She did draw the line at endorsing the "superburger" at a host restaurant despite the owner's plea. At the University of Southern California, members of an honor society at the height of their initiation pranks bombarded Douglas with hay and seltzer water, a prank that brought humiliated apologies from the university president. Douglas, far from upset, answered that she did not mind; she only wished that she had had something to squirt back.[29]

Fund-raising never ceased to be the most serious problem. She knew she could not expect money from the party until the fall campaign; she had no clear idea of what labor would give her, and she was obviously unwilling to accept the sort of money that streamed into Downey's office. But eventually funds began to come in, initially from outside the state. In fact, if it had not been for these early contributions, her campaign efforts would have been seriously hampered if not over. Eleanor Roosevelt was the first to come to Douglas's rescue. Towards the end of February, she and a wealthy New York friend invited over four hundred people to a cocktail party. The invited guests included the Bloomingdales, the Carnegies, Bennett Cerf, Barry Bingham, the Marshall Fields, Lillian Gish, Myrna Loy, and Franklin Delano Roosevelt, Jr. The women raised about $5,700. Roosevelt also featured Douglas in one of her "My Day" columns, which she entitled "A Fearless Woman." ER argued that Douglas deserved the support of women outside her state because her record in Congress reflected devotion to public interest across the nation. "Mrs. Douglas is fearless, and no one questions her integrity." But, she continued, "at times I worry about her because I think she feels so intensely about some of the principles she upholds that she will wear herself out." Douglas wrote her friend: "You are an angel. Your column has impressed everyone." She had even recently received offers of "big money" that she had turned down because they were "conditioned on a slight reversal of my thinking on certain subjects."[30]

Daisy Harriman in Washington, D.C., mounted a fund-raiser targeting Democratic women nationally. She raised around $700, including contributions principally from sources like Mary Norton and other women who had worked with Douglas during her Women's Division years. But some, including Emma Guffey Miller from Pennsylvania, refused to contribute. While she was "personally very fond of Helen Gahagan and know she is an able woman," Guffey wrote Harriman, she could not "in good conscience" support Douglas because of her opposition to equal rights for women. The Women's Division in Kentucky and other states also held fund-raisers. Finally, in late March, California groups began to raise funds. An ADA chapter in the Bay Area raised over $2,000 at two private parties. The movie industry began to get mobilized; the Motion Picture Committee for Douglas developed an extensive sponsor list that included support from Myrna Loy, Lena Horne, Eddie Cantor, and Ronald Reagan.[31]

While it was hard to get an early reading on the possible success of Douglas's challenge of Downey, he certainly could not ignore her. One Douglas fan told her that at a recent Jefferson-Jackson Day Democratic banquet with 2,000 in attendance, the audience had cheered far more vigorously in response to Douglas's greeting telegram than to that from Downey; "I noticed some of the old San Francisco Boys looking at each other in a kind of wonderment over the demonstration for you." As early as January, rumors began to circulate that Downey was considering withdrawing from the race. James Walker, head of the Santa Ana County office for Douglas, wrote Helen that many previous Downey supporters and personal friends were favoring Douglas. The press played up the rumors. Kyle Palmer, the conservative political columnist for the *Los Angeles Times*, called Downey a "fish out of water"; his colleagues did not take him seriously, he was "never quite in harmony" with the Truman administration, and "organized Democrats never particularly supported him." In this race, however, the state Democratic power structure clearly favored Downey over Douglas, Palmer continued, although Downey had "no stomach for the kind of strife he will encounter . . . with sharp-tongued, rabble-rousing . . . Douglas. Helen is a scolding woman in politics. And she is not at all averse to campaign brawling." He continued: "Her skill as a really great actress has never shown to more dramatic advantage than in her political speeches which are marvels of diction, elocution and declamation. There are a few male demagogues scattered around here and there, but HGD has no female challengers for her supremacy in that category. She's tops."[32]

Downey continued to vacillate during March as he coped with the prospects of a hard campaign complicated by influenza and stomach problems. Finally at the end of the month, he decided to withdraw. In his announcement, he stated that his doctor had urgently advised him to take this action because of two peptic ulcers requiring considerable medical treatment and a curtailed schedule for a year that would prevent him from waging a "personal and militant campaign against the vicious and unethical propaganda of one of my opponents." Some skeptics like Harold Ickes suspected that Downey was troubled more by the fear of defeat than he was by peptic ulcers. Ickes had been told by an inside source that Downey's doctor had said "off-the-record that he does not have any peptic ulcers" and that "he would be able to go to work again in a week." But ill health certainly played a part. Downey entered Bethesda Naval Hospital for treatment in early April and remained on sick leave from Congress for several months.[33]

Downey's key men—Rogers, Malone, Elliott, and Pauley—initially considered backing Douglas. Bea Stern recalled that after Douglas had made a speech in Sacramento, she said, " 'take us to a place where absolutely no one can hear what we say.' So we went to the capitol grounds which were deserted at 1:00. She'd had two calls from Bill Malone saying he wanted her to give him control over northern California patronage in return for his financial support." While Douglas had already decided she should turn him down, she wanted Stern's advice; Stern concurred. With this rejection, Malone immediately decided to look for a substitute candidate; in consultation with Downey, they decided on Manchester Boddy, editor of the *Los Angeles Daily News*. "Clearly the Democratic machine did not want Douglas in Washington," the liberal statewide magazine *Frontier* commented, because they would have no influence through her office. Douglas agreed: Malone and the others "don't like the idea of having a woman in the Senate with whom they can't make deals."[34] The choice of Boddy was in some measure puzzling. While people throughout the state knew his name and he edited the only widely circulating Democratic newspaper daily, he had had no political experience. Though he had long supported Downey, he also generally liked Truman. Because he lived in Douglas's district and had covered her congressional career in a favorable fashion for five years, Boddy obviously knew Douglas and her record well, including her vulnerable spots. He apparently had no qualms about turning against Douglas. Boddy had also suddenly changed his position on the 160-acre limitation and declared himself in favor of state control of tideland oil.

While many Downey supporters shifted their support to Boddy because they either disliked Douglas or did not believe she could win in November, others switched camps. Ellie Heller, California's Democratic National Committee-woman, thought Boddy made a "lousy candidate," although her political husband worked for Boddy. Downey and Boddy supporters "just had *no taste* for the way [Douglas] was campaigning or the people she was attracting," she recalled, although obviously not all Douglas supporters were fanatics. She had some "very nice people" supporting her, but she also had some radical "fringe people." Douglas did often bore her audiences, had "no terminal facility" when making speeches, and was too emotional and idealistic for many.[35]

Douglas hoped that the Downey withdrawal would not diminish her press support. Frank Clarvoe, editor of the *San Francisco News*, wrote her that the switch "may make a difference," but he planned to watch how the primary proceeded. He admired Douglas, but since his goal had been to get Downey out of office, he had not decided his new position. She also courted the three McClatchy papers, the *Sacramento Bee*, the *Modesto Bee*, and the *Fresno Bee*. With all three editors she stressed her position on the water resource question. She evidently feared the *Sacramento Bee* editor would switch to Nixon; she warned him that this endorsement would not serve the "liberal, intelligent, freedom-conscious policy of the *Bees*." But ultimately these efforts failed.[36]

Few Douglas Democrats seemed concerned, however, about Downey's withdrawal. Douglas supporters felt relief; they saw Boddy as an easier challenge than Downey. Ickes wrote that the people he had talked with felt that Boddy would not be able to "get up enough steam" to beat her at the primaries. His friends had money but no organization. On the Downey side, Michael Fanning, the Los Angeles postmaster and a long-term Douglas supporter, wrote Downey: "I am damn glad that you are not going to run." He was afraid he would stay in "just because a lot of people with axes to grind wanted you to stay in." Downey's friends could not feel anything but happy because they knew that his "heart wasn't in it." Fanning had wired Boddy to congratulate him for "picking up the torch" and to offer "whatever help" he could. Rogers wrote Downey that California was losing a "great leader," but maybe it was just as well he was not running because the campaign would take "such boundless energy, such driving ambition, and a shamelessness and thick hide of an elephant." While Rogers reassured Downey that his old friends would be supporting Boddy, he did express concern that Boddy had some advisors and friends who were "not well-known for their ability to . . . work with the divergent and disputative elements that make up the Democratic party." Several AFL unions expressed their regrets to Douglas but planned to support Boddy. One Democrat however, wrote Downey saying that he felt that while the senator could beat Douglas, a "self-seeking, highly perfumed, smelly old girl but pretty intelligent," Boddy could not. Margaret Workman, a friend from the late 1930s, wired Downey that although she had nominated Douglas for Democratic national committeewoman in 1940, she was "terribly disappointed at her record" as a member of Congress and "amazed" that she thought she could run for the Senate on this record.[37]

With Downey out of the race, Douglas's original reason for running vanished. But she had no intention of backing out; the underlying reason clearly the lure of the Senate. Douglas did not shift gears with Downey's pullout. "The plot is the same. It is only the leading man that has been changed," she wrote Tipton, Clarvoe, and others. Boddy essentially agreed with Douglas on most issues. Douglas charged that he did not believe in the "full development of water and power resources of this state in the interest of the people." He had recently changed his views on tideland oil and had editorialized against certain labor legislation and the extension of the Fair Employment Practices Commission. She wrote India Edwards that the "picture looked better now that Downey was out of the race. . . . I know I am going to win." Malone was "fighting for his political life" and would not stop at anything to "bludgeon people into line. . . . When we are finished winning this campaign, it will go down in history as a campaign run on hardly any money at all." She told Tipton not to even bother mentioning Boddy's name; "just take it for granted that I am going to win the Democratic nomination and that the Republicans ought to vote for me too." In fact, she went on, "there is just a very long chance that I can win the Republican nomination" especially if Tipton would "do a job" on Senator Joseph McCarthy and the Republicans. Tipton shared Douglas's optimism. He wrote Mitchell on April 20: "This is a mad-house. I think it's in the bag, however. She is a wonderful gal but you can stand only so much evangelism. She is a swell candidate but too intense—swell for voters and audiences—tough on associates." Mitchell answered that the California congressional delegation was "maintaining its watchful waiting attitude." Only Cecil King thought she just might pull off both nominations.[38]

While Douglas did not change tactics, headquarters had to find funds to print new campaign materials. The *Los Angeles Times* reported with amusement that Douglas's first brochure out after Boddy replaced Downey quoted Boddy from the *Daily News* stating that Douglas was "not only one of California's great women, but one of its ablest representatives." Stern wrote from Sacramento that "as far as I can find out, everybody up here wants the Boddy record. Why can't we have it?" Lybeck responded that they were working on Boddy's record, but "we do not intend at this time to engage in any campaign of either ridicule or vilification." There was material, but because there was little to Boddy it was better not to call attention to him. Besides, Boddy was "treating Helen with kid gloves." The Douglas group did not want to cause a "serious breach in the Democratic Party," nor did party officials in Washington, who warned the two to keep the campaign on a "high level." Stern also asked for recent congressional material; Lybeck answered that this was difficult as Douglas had nothing interesting coming out. "This whole matter of Helen's long-distance Congressional activities" was a real problem. Unless releases were "sensationally good," they only accentuated that "Helen is not in Washington herself to fight on these causes." From San Jose, Blank wrote Lybeck that she was delighted with the activity out of her office. "Helen says there is a point in the campaign when it becomes the people's campaign. Well it happened to the Fresno County campaign last night—and it was wonderful." [39]

Douglas had been looking forward to a campaign visit from Ickes, who had always delighted in goading Downey. But Boddy was another story. He told Douglas that he no longer saw a visit as appropriate or necessary. Boddy was no challenge; Douglas would do best simply to ignore him. While Boddy had money, he did not have much organization behind him. Douglas apologized— "I guess you are right about not coming out at this time. I hope we haven't pestered you too much." But she did not let this disappointment dampen her spirits. [40]

Douglas viewed labor as her most important voting bloc. CIO's Jack Kroll worked closely with UAW-PAC's head, Roy Reuther. In January the two had dispatched a full-time person, George Douglass, to organize in California, serving as a liaison to all CIO-affiliated unions and district officers. Kroll wrote Douglass that the key to victory was voter registration and a solid turnout in the election; "I am increasingly convinced that a heavy vote is a liberal vote." Douglass wrote Reuther immediately that he had set up appointments for Douglas with various Los Angeles labor leaders. He reported that although only two members of the Los Angeles Council CIO-PAC Committee favored Downey, he anticipated unanimous endorsement of Douglas shortly. "She is gaining force rapidly and of all the meetings I have attended lately, civic, union, and otherwise, Downey isn't even being mentioned." He even felt that AFL might endorse her. In February, the CIO-PAC state convention endorsed her. Although both Downey and Douglas had "acceptable voting records," the resolution read, this only told "part of the story." Douglas had "provided liberals and the labor movement with the kind of courageous and fighting leadership America needs. . . . She is the candidate who can best defeat the reactionary forces behind Nixon. We join her in that fight." Also early in the campaign, she won endorsements from a key labor group, the State Labor League for Political Education, and (as George Douglass had predicted) the Los Angeles CIO Council, the California State CIO-PAC Committee, and affiliated PACS.

These groups pledged to work with Douglass coordinating registration drives. In March, Douglass was detailed just to Douglas's campaign, freeing him from all other races. Tipton and Douglas were pleased with Douglass's work. Tipton commented that the "CIO was doing the best job he had ever seen" in any campaign.[41]

Paul Sifton, the UAW lobbyist who had worked closely with Douglas on labor legislation, wrote her in March that Roy Reuther was "keenly aware" of the need for funds but too many other things had prevented him from helping. At that point, the UAW saw her strength as greater in the north, where she had some AFL support and the railway locals. Reuther felt the state AFL leadership was hesitant to support Downey because it realized the rank-and-file strength behind Douglas and Downey's vacillation about his candidacy hurt him. Once Downey pulled out, however, Douglas received full labor support, including money. California CIO-PAC began distributing Douglas literature to every local. The railroad brotherhood's Railway Labor Political League and the machinists' Non-Partisan Political League joined her campaign. And to Douglas's delight, the state AFL convention voted her their support, although a few local councils refused to go along with the state. George Douglass wrote Roy Reuther near the end of April that Douglas's campaign was "going full blast—she's a cinch to capture the Democratic nomination and in my opinion will run close or take the Republican. I'm working night and day over the whole state."[42]

Women also played a critical role in Douglas's campaign. Most of the grass-roots organizers and many county heads were women. Prominent individual women and women's organizations came out strongly for Douglas. Ellie Heller supported Douglas in part because she was a woman. "I would have been a traitor to the first woman who was running statewide" had she not supported her, Heller later recalled. Many of Heller's political friends also supported Douglas because they did not care for Downey, "who was his own worst enemy, in a way. He was sort of a loner." One statewide "Women for Douglas" group included some of those who had worked closely with the candidate when she was Democratic national committeewoman. Fay Allen, an active black in Douglas's district, wrote Mary McLeod Bethune to see if she could speak at a major meeting for Douglas. Bethune responded that due to ill health she could not come, but asked for specifics on what Douglas had done for her district so that she could do a recording. In mid-May, a half-hour publicity program combining statements from local, state, and nationally prominent women (such as Myrna Loy, Anna Roosevelt Boettinger, and Eleanor Wilson McAdoo) was broadcast over several dozen stations.[43]

Not all women's groups favored Douglas, however. Republican and conservative Democratic women disliked Douglas's liberal views. Some objected to her flamboyant style and acting background, which to them translated into a lack of qualifications. Others would have supported her had she not opposed the ERA. Douglas mailed out 10,000 statements on the ERA in the hope that she could deflect this criticism, but with little success. India Edwards urged the nominally bipartisan National Business and Professional Women's Clubs to endorse Douglas as they had Maine's Margaret Chase Smith in her race for the Senate in 1948. But both the national and the state level refused to support Douglas because of her opposition to the ERA. Despite this official stand, however, various local clubs did invite her to speak. Sometimes Douglas let opportunities slip by. Shortly after declaring her candidacy in October 1949, for example, a ground swell of enthusiasm led to the organizing of a group of influential Democratic women in San Diego to serve as a steering committee. In January, however, the group dissipated because Douglas had failed to give the women any direction.[44]

Blacks, including black women's clubs, ethnic groups, farmers, young Democrats, various liberal intellectual groups, and all sorts of individuals added to the increased campaign momentum at the end of April and early May. Supporters in San Francisco's Chinatown paid for 15,000 leaflets in Chinese and special mailings to every registered Chinese voter. Jews in San Fernando Valley asked her for a Passover message to publish in the *Valley Jewish Press*. The San Joaquin Valley Japanese-American Citizens' League plugged her candidacy on their weekly radio show. Ernesto Galarza, president of the National Farm Labor Union, included statements on farm workers from Roosevelt and Douglas for his Spanish Bulletin, which he mailed to 30,000 Spanish-speaking people. The Teachers' League for Democratic Action endorsed Roosevelt and Douglas, and on many campuses, among them, the University of California, Berkeley, "Students for Douglas" groups formed. Even some patriotic groups invited her to speak, such as the Sacramento Elks Temple and local Veterans of Foreign Wars lodges. Encouraging letters came in from many of the party's county heads. Blank wrote Lybeck that Douglas was making "simply terrific speeches" wherever she went. Staff at headquarters were concerned, however, about the general lethargy of blacks statewide; apparently many felt their vote was being taken for granted. To combat these feelings, black supporters from Douglas's Fourteenth District set up telephone crews in southern California's black districts, and a mass mailing went out to 8,500 members of the California State Association of Colored Women.[45]

While letters between Douglas and her friends were rare during the campaign, those that exist offer revealing glimpses. Lorena Hickok wrote in April to thank Douglas for some birthday presents—a cigarette case, and "exquisite handkerchiefs." Hickok had recently visited Douglas's office on the Hill and "found the girls pretty much upset over Manchester Boddy, the louse. That afternoon I telephoned Daisy Harriman, who was calmer. I gathered that the money situation was still tight." Hickok suggested going to Barney [Bernard]

Baruch. "You know he's a fall-guy for any attractive woman. Nasty old man. Only, so far as I know, he really isn't nasty about it. He just likes 'em. . . . Oh darling, I hate to think of you beating your brains out there. If you don't make it, I shall want to die. And not only for your sake, my pet. You're so badly needed." Douglas hastened to write back to her good friend. Campaigning was like "a Ringling Brothers circus." She got up early every day, made five to ten speeches, and went to bed late. But the campaign was gaining strength. "We still need money, money, money. . . . A tour de force, believe me—just plain elbow grease and a lot of good will." She reported that she had a united labor front behind her. Getting the AFL was hard; George Douglass and others "pushed a lot of rocks out of the road." She needed $30,000 between then and election day. She had no funds for billboards or outside advertising except snipe sheets for Los Angeles. She was hurt by a news blackout in Los Angeles. As far as money from Baruch, she would not accept it if she had to get it in person. Douglas wrote another friend that campaigning the state was "rugged business. . . . Evie is forever after me to either hurry up and get dressed to make an appointment or 'Helen do this' or 'Helen do that.' " She never had a peaceful moment. "The routine in Washington is mild by comparison, believe me."[46]

Douglas rarely saw her family during the campaign. She tried to get home every second weekend, but those times were filled with meetings, phone calls, and speeches. She did occasionally take Mary Helen with her to speaking engagements. Melvyn came home even less; he was performing with a traveling road show, *Two Blind Mice*. But the two did continue their practice of communicating by phone. Melvyn, unhappy with their separation, provided her support and advice. Yet rumors continued to circulate, not only in the press, but among close friends, that success in the election could very likely end their marriage. Two letters from him in the spring of 1950 suggest the distance between the couple. At the end of March, he sent her some newspaper clippings on the "inherent dangers" of HUAC feeding into the "dangerous hysteria" that Senator Joseph McCarthy was rapidly creating with his accusations of Communist infiltration into the government. As for Melvyn, "things are the same," he told her. *Two Blind Mice* would open in Washington on April 24. "I miss you and hope you are not beating yourself to a pulp. Call me when you can." In May he sent her two campaign contributions from friends and one from himself. "Don't bother to thank me for my check," he commented. "I'll keep plugging. Don't kill yourself. Love to yourself and the kids."[47]

Douglas's fast campaign pace exhausted her staff and amazed supporters. Lybeck wrote a publicity release on why Douglas seemed physically able to maintain her intense schedule. He explained that Douglas truly enjoyed meeting people and she "genuinely wants people to like her as a person as well as a candidate"; she also could relax between speeches, often taking catnaps. Lybeck included a story of a woman who asked Douglas how she managed to look so young. Douglas answered: " 'I have a clear conscience, so I sleep well at nights.' " Yet friends knew that her political years had "deepened the lines of character in her face," and she "no longer had the appearance of a movie star." She dressed handsomely, generally in custom-made tailored suits and "health shoes," which apparently Eleanor Roosevelt suggested. Her lack of concern about nails, hair, and makeup gave her a natural windblown look, but did not add glamor.[48]

Early in May, as the pace intensified, Douglas decided to economize on time by campaigning by helicopter in the northern part of the state, an idea she picked up from her friend Lyndon Johnson. On her first day out, she made nine stops and gave nine different speeches, eating candy bars to sustain her energy. She talked about industry in Daly City, farming in San Bruno, civil rights in San Mateo, housing in Belmont, anti-Communism in Redwood City, and labor at the American Legion Hall in South San Francisco at a steelworkers dinner. This mode of transportation, a first for a California political candidate, fit her personal style. While she explained to the press that the helicopter would make her visits to small towns more efficient—she could land in fields, ballparks, empty lots, and on building tops—she also enjoyed the drama of takeoffs and landings. Once she began using her helicopter, the ever-accommodating Chavoor would leave in the car in the middle of a speech and race to the next spot if time permitted. Chavoor was not, however, enchanted with the helicopter idea. "Evie is petrified at the thought of my going up in a helicopter," Douglas wrote Hickok. While many Democratic groups thought the idea novel, some were caustic in their reaction. One Republican lady commented that she found it "unladylike" and disgusting. Some city councils even passed ordinances prohibiting her from landing.[49]

Despite Douglas's success at turning out crowds and attracting campaign workers, the need for money continued to seem overwhelming. Chavoor detailed bills to one supporter: $4,000 for three days of radio spots; $1,600 for her weekly newspaper column; $1,000 for the Los Angeles snipe sheets; $4,000 for ads in daily papers, and $3,000 for ads targeting specialized groups. Douglas spent no money at all on billboards. She cut some one-minute recordings on social security, civil rights, and various other topics with the hope that local groups could raise the money to air the records. Douglas wrote the Siftons that the campaign was going well, "and considering the fact that we have spent hardly any money, we have done a tremendous job. We are still scratching around for money in order to do the minimum things that are necessary in a campaign."[50]

Although Douglas's immediate goal was to beat Boddy, she obviously was conscious of her Republican opponent and Los Angeles neighbor, Congressman

Richard M. Nixon.[51] Nixon lived in Whittier, a small suburb in northeast Los Angeles County, and represented the Twelfth District, an area of small towns and farms. Born in Yorba Linda, he had moved to Whittier as a child, growing up in a devout Quaker family of modest means. Richard often worked after school in his father's grocery store to contribute to the family income. After graduating from Whittier College, he attended Duke University Law School, where he not only excelled academically but also demonstrated leadership skills. Following law school, he returned to the Whittier area, practiced law, and became involved in civic activities. He fell in love with a bright, energetic, and attractive schoolteacher, Pat Ryan, whom he eventually married. In 1941, the couple moved to Washington. Nixon first worked at the Office of Price Administration. Although he had registered as a Republican, he considered himself a liberal and initially felt comfortable in the New Deal agency. But he developed a distaste for government bureaucracy and gradually became more politically conservative. He demonstrated his ability to work extremely hard and intensely, with an eye to moving up the ladder, characteristics that remained Nixon trademarks as a politician. In 1942, despite his Quaker background, he felt an obligation to join the armed forces, and he entered the Navy as an officer.

Nixon returned to the United States in 1945. Before he even returned to Whittier, a hometown conservative, one of a group of mainly small-business Republicans who called themselves the "Committee of 100," asked him if he would be willing to be interviewed as a possible candidate for them to support for Congress against Jerry Voorhis. The Committee hated Franklin Roosevelt, and Voorhis, though popular in the district, had recently antagonized new groups; the committee thought him vulnerable. The Committee of 100 was impressed with Nixon and promised financial backing. Despite his total lack of political experience, Nixon edged out the noted Republican judge, Frederick F. Houser, at the California Republican Assembly, which selected the candidates. Nixon, with the help of campaign manager Murray Chotiner, embarked on what they called "a rocking-socking" campaign designed to associate Voorhis with Communists and fellow-travelers, particularly CIO-PAC. They implied that left-wingers had taken over California's Democratic Party; techniques very typical of many Republican races in 1946. Nixon challenged Voorhis to a series of debates. Voorhis later acknowledged that he let Nixon put him on the defensive. Nixon supporters made anonymous phone calls saying that Voorhis was a Communist. Historian Stephen E. Ambrose summed up the campaign as "characterized by a vicious, snarling approach that was full of half-truths, full lies, and innuendoes, hurled at such a pace that Voorhis could never catch up with them." This ruthlessness shocked Nixon's friends; many felt resentful. But it was a ruthlessness that characterized Nixon throughout his political career. Nixon won by a large margin. Two years later, he beat a little-known attorney, Stephen Zetterberg, in both the Republican and Democratic primaries. Chotiner, again Nixon's manager, added a new technique—the mailing of a Nixon brochure to "Fellow Democrats," taking advantage of the cross-filing system that allowed candidates to file on both tickets and did not identify candidates on the ballot by party. Early on in the Eighty-first Congress, anxious to move to higher office, Nixon made the decision to run for the Senate. Douglas's decision to run in the fall of 1949 "clinched" his decision; he knew that her candidacy would divide the Democratic Party and help his position.[52]

Nixon and Douglas, both members of the southern California delegation, had had a certain amount of interaction on issues pertaining to their common geographical area, but nothing more than minimal contact. On opposite sides in domestic issues, they both supported, in varying degrees, Truman's Marshall Plan. As Douglas carved out her national reputation as a leading Fair Deal liberal, particularly respected on housing, labor, civil rights, and foreign policy issues, Nixon created his own national reputation. He gained some notice with his opposition to Taft-Hartley repeal. As a member of the prestigious House Select Committee on Foreign Aid, informally dubbed the Herter Committee, appointed in 1947 to gather information in Europe in preparation for the Marshall Plan, he gained valuable recognition in the area of foreign affairs. The committee's reports played an important role in developing the Marshall Plan and, as Roger Morris commented, "ran into the acrid jealousy of the House Foreign Affairs Committee" as it "saw its own ambitious legislative proposals languish." But his work as a member of the House Un-American Activities Committee, particularly as the leading investigator in the Alger Hiss case that led to Hiss's conviction for perjury in January 1950, gained headlines for Nixon rarely achieved by a new member of Congress. He had no more success than Douglas in getting legislation passed, although he did co-sponsor the Mundt-Nixon bill requiring the registration of Communist Party members. The bill passed the House in 1948 but died in the Senate.[53]

The two candidates differed in more than political philosophy. Douglas grew up the wealthy daughter of an engineer in Brooklyn, New York; Nixon's father had an unsuccessful citrus farm in Yorba Linda and moved to Whittier where he opened a corner grocery store that eventually became a stable source of income. Both men were respected in their own way in their communities. Nixon's mother Hannah worked hard to help raise the children and to bring extra money into the house. Douglas's mother Lillian did not need to work; indeed, she enjoyed the luxury of household servants. Nixon had two brothers but no sisters, which may explain his adult awkwardness around women; Douglas had both a sister and three brothers with whom she was constantly competing. Organized religion and a religious atmosphere at home dominated Nixon's childhood; while Douglas's mother was a devout Presbyterian, her involvement with the church was not shared by her husband, and the Gahagan home had a generally secular atmosphere. But both grew up as part of large, extended families that were very close. Nixon worked both in the lemon groves and the family store to help the family survive; Douglas did not earn any money until she went on Broadway and brought home a star's salary. Both Nixon and Douglas recall that their fathers had the most influence on them while growing up, encouraging them to believe in themselves, to believe that they could succeed. Both enjoyed reading. Both had had experience as children and young adults in front of groups—Douglas through her acting experience and Nixon in Quaker meetings. As Ambrose described it, when Nixon spoke out in Quaker meeting, "it was more a public speech than it was a personal disclosure."[54] Later on in Whittier, Nixon had some exposure to acting with the Whittier community theater; in fact, it was there that he met Pat. Douglas had had two years of college and a generally poor academic record throughout her education; Nixon had demonstrated high scholarly achievement both in college and at Duke Law School. Both had leadership experience in school.

Despite Nixon's powerful presence, Douglas did not anticipate any difficulties running against him in the fall. She sent Nixon's record to Ickes in early April asking him to write about both Boddy and Nixon. "Just take it for granted that I am going to win the Democratic nomination and that the Republicans are out to vote for me too. There is just a very long chance that I can win the Republican nomination." Later in the month she felt so confident that she called Ickes to tell him that she thought she should concentrate on Nixon to guarantee herself the Republican nomination, and she wanted Ickes to come to California to take on Nixon. Ickes wrote back immediately that he had talked with Washington people including Secretary of the Interior Oscar Chapman and they agreed that her plans were entirely unrealistic. "After all, Nixon will be running on a ticket with Warren, and it is to be expected that Republicans will make every effort to put across a big vote for both." Others warned her as well. A Berkeley student wrote that when Nixon spoke at the university's Sather Gate many realized, much to their dismay, that Nixon was "one of the cleverest speakers" they had heard. "Indeed, he was so skillful—and I might add cagey—that those who came indifferent were sold, and even many of those who came to heckle went away with doubts. I understand that he is carrying his 'grass roots' campaign through the entire state. If he is only a fraction as effective as he was here you have a formidable opponent on your hands." Bert Falconer told Douglas that while Boddy posed no threat, Nixon was a different story. "Anti-Commie sentiment is increasing in volume and intensity and for that reason any Commie or Commie-sympathizer identified with your organization or campaign will do you a very great deal of harm."[55]

Nixon, meanwhile, confident of a primary victory, was carefully laying the groundwork for his fall campaign. He viewed Douglas as a more serious contender than Boddy, and he began to go after the Democratic vote in the primary. He insisted that "socialistic planners" and "political demagogues" favoring the 160-acre limitation in Central Valley were responsible for delaying the project's completion. He charged Truman with causing increasing unemployment; new jobs would come with a fiscally conservative budget and the removal of wartime excise taxes that hurt businesses. His headquarters printed up a pamphlet entitled "As One Democrat to Another," similar to one he used in 1948, which infuriated Democrats. To make himself look like an ordinary American, he generally traveled with Pat in an old station wagon, making dozens of speeches each week. At one point he rented a house trailer that pulled a sound-equipped platform to emphasize carrying his campaign to the "man on the street." [56]

But while Nixon's language did not concern Douglas because he did not attack her personally, she did become concerned in early May with a shift of tactics from the Boddy campaign. Up to that point, Douglas really believed that if she got her message out to the people she would win, regardless of money problems. Despite Boddy's distinguished demeanor—he was a slender gentleman with graying hair and a carefully trimmed mustache—the man exuded vagueness about his political concepts and had little charisma. The first signs that the campaign might become unpleasant appeared in early May. Helen Lustig, the head of Douglas's San Diego County office, wrote Douglas that the Reverend Clayton Russell, a Fourteenth District black and long-time Douglas supporter, made "vague accusations" that Douglas had not kept promises to her district and that she voted for legislation harming blacks while pretending to be their friend; he praised Boddy for his part in founding an interracial hospital. This "seemed to many to be the opening of a 'dirty' campaign," Lustig concluded. [57]

Shortly afterwards, Boddy dramatically shifted ground when he gleefully dubbed Douglas the "Pink Lady" in the *Daily News*. He elaborated in a speech on May 10, claiming that a "subversive clique of 'red hots' " was seeking to control the Democratic county committees. A few days later, he stated that he had on his team "the sound liberals who are genuinely alarmed because a relatively small minority of 'red hots' " were working to win this election "in order to use the sound gains achieved by the Democratic Party as a beachhead from which to launch an un-American attack against the United States on behalf of Communist Russia." In Riverside County speeches, the Boddy people began to deal out the "pink smears strong and heavy." A Fresno Douglas fan trying to be helpful sent headquarters some slogans: "No Boddy wants Boddy" or "No Boddy but Douglas," but the situation demanded more than limp slogans. Nettie Jones delighted in Boddy's attacks and followed suit. Her committee, the Women's Committee for Good Government, took out a newspaper ad that stated, among various charges, that Douglas had voted with the left-wing congressman Vito Marcantonio in March 1950 against HUAC appropriations. Actually, Boddy's charge brought no surprises; anti-Douglas forces had been Red-baiting Douglas since the beginning of the campaign; indeed, throughout her political career. In January 1949, newspapers had brought up the Marcantonio parallel. In January 1950, a leading female Republican state official from Sacramento mentioned that Douglas "had been seen with Communist Party Leaders." "She did not," reported one Douglas supporter, "come right out to call you a Communist; she didn't dare, nor did she say that she saw you personally." But when Boddy made the accusation a central issue, he shifted the tone of his campaign and put Douglas on the defensive. And the term "Pink Lady" proved to have more than passing impact; the label had a ringing appeal that stuck to her throughout the campaign.[58]

While the Douglas campaign did not lose momentum, there was obvious concern at headquarters. Anti-Communist sentiment was increasing rapidly throughout the country as Nationalist China fell to the Communists in 1949, political tensions increased in Korea, and McCarthy pressed forward with his charges. Boddy simply decided to take advantage of this shifting public opinion and "cut loose a terrific last-minute barrage of both radio and newspaper advertising." Press friendly to Boddy gave him free publicity. Douglas made yet another desperate plea for money. She quickly put together statements from Representative John Kee, the chairman of the House Foreign Affairs Committee, McCormack, and Eleanor Roosevelt, stressing her record and loyalty. Tipton tried not to fall apart. He wrote Ruth Lybeck that "we are determined to remain calm in the face of this attack . . . the most despicable yet launched in American politics. . . . Senator McCarthy has been restrained and reserved by comparison. . . . To lose our heads, to become panicky, to be diverted by these unscrupulous tactics would be to fall into a carefully prepared political trap." While the answer was to keep publicizing Douglas's record, "in these hysterical times unlimited funds thrown into false attacks could have the disastrous effect of confusing the voters." The plan for the last two weeks was to concentrate on the local communities with newspaper ads and radio spot announcements made by Washington supporters. One journalist wrote Boddy that his Red-smear campaign "is something that might be expected of Congressman Nixon." Many thought Boddy was "above demagoguery, an illusion that imposed a large measure of public faith in your newspaper." The May primary defeat of the noted liberal Senator Claude Pepper in a messy Red-smear campaign also dampened Douglas's spirits. She wrote Paul Sifton and his wife Claire that "we are sick about it. There is all the more reason now that a real job has to be done here in California and in other states."[59]

Douglas wrote a supporter that she would not retaliate unless the Boddy campaign sank to a "real low," although she did notify various national columnists about Boddy's campaign tactics. Intimations that Truman was not planning to back her made her uneasy. One early May article suggested, for example, that the Democratic National Committee considered both Douglas and Jimmy Roosevelt political liabilities and therefore Truman planned not to campaign for either one of them in the fall. Later in the month, a federal employee in Alameda County spoke on Boddy's behalf, and two San Francisco papers implied that this indicated that Truman had indirectly taken sides in the primary. When this happened, Douglas angrily protested to Chapman, Boyle, and presidential assistant Donald Dawson. "Frankly I am sick and tired of all these shenanigans, and undoubtedly all of you are too." With the onset of the Red-smear charges, Douglas began accusing major newspapers like the *Daily News* of blacking her out of any news coverage. In actuality, they did not completely ignore her. They editorialized unfavorably and did not detail her speeches or her schedule. To compensate, Douglas published weekly advertisements reminiscent of Eleanor Roosevelt's chatty "My Day" column. Entitled "My Senate Campaign," they highlighted her week, listed endorsements, detailed her coming speaking schedule and statewide radio broadcasts, and criticized Boddy. She declared that the papers would at least have to "print news . . . after the primary" when she won the nomination.[60]

While Douglas felt irritated but not surprised by the lack of support from conservative papers such as the *San Francisco Chronicle* or the *Los Angeles Times*, she did become upset when the important liberal McClatchy papers suddenly turned against her, along with the *Santa Barbara News-Press*. Stern commiserated with Douglas over this apparent "sell out" by the *"Bee* endorsement of Boddy." From what Stern could gather, it was a "feminine affair. Orders came from on highest, from editor Eleanor McClatchy," overriding her earlier promise to cover both Douglas and Boddy. Even Mary Ellen Leary, the liberal political editor for the *San Francisco News*, had complimentary things to say about Boddy.[61]

The shift in the tone of the campaign did improve Douglas's campaign funds. Former congresswoman Emily Taft Douglas, former housing administrator Wilson W. Wyatt, the *New Republic* editor Michael Straight, and others sent a letter to 350 people, informing them that Douglas was fighting for her political life in California. Ruth Lybeck wrote every county chairman to "exhaust every possible source of funds." This push brought in enough money to pay for newspaper ads. The smear campaign also brought new support from numerous local and state Democratic leaders. Donald Younger, chairman of the Democratic Central Committee in Santa Cruz County, spearheaded the protest movement; dozens of county, congressional district, and state officers signed a petition at the end of May, only days before the primary, dismissing the "charges and innuendoes" as "false and ridiculous." Eleanor Roosevelt, former governor Culbert Olson, University of California vice-president Monroe Deutsch, and Loren Miller spoke strongly for Douglas on a radio program in early June. Labor increased its activities, and dozens of chapters of the Young Democrats and Students for Democratic Action, the youth division of ADA, added their energies.[62]

To the outside world, Douglas seemed undaunted by Boddy's vicious attacks. She wrote a supporter that "the campaign being waged at the moment by the opposition is one of desperation, but I am convinced that no amount of smearing and no amount of propaganda, no matter how libelous, can change the final vote." Even to Ickes she appeared confident. He had sent Douglas an encouraging word at the end of May. "Confidentially," he wrote, he learned from "an authoritative source" that "the Republicans had taken a test ballot in your state which showed you to be substantially ahead of both of your competitors." Douglas answered, "I think there will be a big vote and I now feel confident that we will win." A memo from a political analyst to Chapman comparing the various California races pointed to generally poor organization and low funding among the Democrats. Warren and Nixon and, to a lesser degree, Roosevelt were well financed. While the Boddy campaign was picking up because of the prestige of the *Daily News*, he wrote, Douglas, running a very personal campaign, still appeared to be the leading candidate and was "much more effective from the standpoint of actual personal campaigning." Boddy's Red-smear campaign did not shift Douglas's grassroots support from labor and agriculture; major county Democratic central committees and dozens of smaller Democratic clubs; plus Hollywood, intellectual, and ethnic groups, including the Chinese and the Latin Americans; some women's organizations; and a variety of enthusiastic small weekly newspapers. Douglas went into the last week of the campaign with buoyant optimism. Her headquarters blitzed newspapers with ads. A *San Francisco Call-Bulletin* staff member commented: "I haven't felt the close, personal interest that I feel in her campaign since 1944 when I worked like mad for FDR." A Mills College professsor reflected: "If I had my choice of being given a permanent teaching job in political science or of having you in the U.S. Senate I would choose the latter without hesitation."[63]

The elated Douglas took the June 6 primary, winning by a wide margin over Boddy, which surprised even some of her close supporters. She garnered close to 735,000 Democratic votes and 154,000 Republican votes; Boddy received 379,000 Democratic votes and 157,000 Republican; and Nixon over 740,000 Republican votes and almost 319,000 Democratic. Douglas's total count was close to 889,000; Boddy's, 532,000; and Nixon's, nearly 1,060,000. Douglas beat Boddy in every county, often by a 2–1 margin or more. She tallied more Republican votes than Boddy in the north-coast urban counties. Her strong county headquarters paid off in several areas; she won more total votes than Nixon in four large counties—Sacramento, Contra Costa, Fresno, and San Francisco—and she came close in Kern. While Roosevelt received more

Democratic votes than Douglas because two Democratic candidates ran for senator, she received considerably more Republican votes than Roosevelt in almost all counties. Warren's vote totaled over 1,800,000, and Roosevelt's almost 1,090,000, with Warren capturing only 200,000 fewer Democratic votes than Roosevelt.[64]

12

Douglas Versus Nixon

FOR A FEW fleeting days, the Douglas forces relaxed and enjoyed the vast number of congratulatory letters and telegrams that flowed into the office. These notes documented the love and respect people felt for Douglas and the appreciation local organizers had for the thousands of hours people had willingly given to her campaign. Douglas returned the affection in many ways. Paul Ziffren, a lawyer who played a key fund-raising role, recalled how he drove the exhausted Douglas home after she had visited all Los Angeles headquarters the night of the election. "The last thing she said to me that night [was to send wires] to thank Mrs. Roosevelt and some of the other people who had helped her." Henry Hill, the executive assigned to Douglas's campaign from the advertising agency she hired, wrote Helen that he had received the expected "businesslike cooperation" from her staff, but he was "totally unprepared" for their "kindness and generosity. . . . Never have I witnessed such devotion to a common aim. It is a source of constant amazement to me that I who am paid for my services should be praised" by volunteers who give services "at great personal sacrifice. . . . It was impossible for me to think and act routinely in behalf of your campaign." The key people were "never too busy or too tired or sick" to provide material, editing, ideas. "If everything went wrong they took the blame. If things went right, they gave me the credit."[1]

From Iva Blank, the talented head of the Fresno office, came an ebullient and chatty letter a week after the election. "I am rambling along" in this letter, she wrote, because she had not had time for months to "ramble." "Why I actually mended some petticoats today that had been held together with safety pins for 2 months. And felt so calm and virtuous doing it. I hate to sew, and so when I do there is the added pleasure of feeling that I am 'keeping myself up' as a woman should. . . . Right now I just love everybody. . . . No I am going to make one exception to my all inclusive feeling of love." A Greyhound bus-driver who had volunteered at her headquarters and kept insisting on seeing her alone. She finally invited him to the election party. "If I didn't feel like a complete jackass when I discovered it was my better acquaintance he sought. I suppose the passion one pours into a campaign does seem transferable to the uninitiated." She felt annoyed with herself for not picking up on the sexual cues; but she sighed, "one gets so used to the sexless world of political work."[2]

Time for the expression of warm feelings proved short. While Douglas, her staff, and the statewide network of volunteers had every right to celebrate her victory, not everyone shared her optimism about her fall battle against Richard Nixon. Most Democrats, including many of Douglas's supporters, believed she faced a campaign that would eclipse the experience of the primary. Anxiety had continued to rise during the spring over Senator McCarthy's periodic revelations of alleged Communist infiltration in the federal government. These fears shifted from hypothetical to real on June 25, 1950, when North Korean Communists attacked South Korea. The President immediately dispatched General Douglas MacArthur and American troops to assist in the south; they, and U.N. troops of fifteen other nations, managed to push the North Koreans above the thirty-eighth parallel, the line of latitude dividing North and South Korea. But as U.N. armed forces edged close to the China border, the Chinese, now under Communist rule, responded with massive numbers of troops that pushed the U.N. forces back into the south. Thus began the undeclared Korean War.[3]

Republicans blamed these frightening events on Truman's China policy, which they contended had caused the fall of the corrupt but pro-Western government of Chiang Kai-shek and the rise of Communism under Party chairman Mao Tse-tung. Democrats blamed Republicans for blocking adequate aid to Korea to build up the country economically and militarily, which they claimed would have prevented the war. For Republicans and Democrats alike, the outbreak of the war confirmed the worst fears about the spread of Communism, increased scrutiny of Truman's foreign policy, heightened concerns about internal security, and certainly compounded the election worries of the Democrats that the war would play well into the Republicans' hands, particularly in the California Senate race. As one analyst bluntly put it, "The Korean war-cloud has blotted out most of the issues that might have made headlines in a politics-as-usual election." India Edwards manifested a brave optimism when she wrote Molly Dewson: "Korea changes the political picture, of course, but we should keep our majority" in both Houses unless the situation became worse or "some of our Democratic boys get more frightened than they are. . . . If only they all had HST's courage and integrity."[4]

It is also important to recognize, as one examines Douglas's fall campaign against Nixon, that since the mid-1930s, Californians had been exposed to charges that not only Communism but Nazism and fascism permeated California society. In fact, the search for Communists in the Los Angeles area dated back to the 1920s. In the late 1930s, Congressman Martin Dies held well-publicized hearings, particularly in Hollywood. But in the 1940s, the California legislature generously financed an Un-American Activities Committee, headed first by Assemblyman Samuel W. Yorty and then by Jack B. Tenney, initially a member of the Assembly and after 1942 a state senator. This committee held hundreds of public and closed hearings and conducted continuous undercover investigations throughout the state looking for evidence of Communists, fascists, Nazis, and their fellow travelers. No major group escaped unscathed— Mexicans, Japanese, blacks, Jews; workers in federal, state, and local offices, including the public school system; unions; and a host of prominent civic organizations. Tenney skillfully publicized these investigations in press releases, lengthy and widely distributed reports (with bright red covers), and interviews that led to the loss of jobs, nervous school personnel and parents, and, ultimately, the passage of numerous laws aimed at "cleansing" California society.[5]

In the summer of 1950, this legislative activity at the state level; investigations by powerful conservative groups, such as the National Association of Manufacturers and the Associated Farmers; uneasiness about the long, exposed coastline, dating back to the war period; and a hotly debated loyalty oath controversy at the University of California beginning in 1949 all fed festering concerns about Truman's response to the Cold War. Social and economic tensions caused by a massive population growth from seven to eleven million people in ten years only added to the "notorious lack of . . . political equilibrium." Douglas supporters were not exempt from these fears. One of Douglas's key people from Tulare County, an agricultural area nestled in the San Joaquin Valley, pointed out to Ruth Lybeck that while the key political issue in the area was water, "many strong [Douglas] supporters never met H.G.D. and have some fear caused by press 'pink' references." This atmosphere, which might well have brought about a Douglas defeat in the primary had Boddy run an effective campaign, had serious implications for the fall. Nixon and his campaign manager Murray Chotiner, among the most skilled politicians in the country, fully intended to utilize every possible tactic to turn these deep-seated anxieties into votes. The beginning of the Korean War merely simplified their job.[6]

Douglas moved into more spacious campaign headquarters at the Alexandria Hotel in Los Angeles as she began revitalizing her campaign organization for fall. Tipton continued to carry the title of statewide director and work in the north; Ruth Lybeck remained assistant director and the pivotal person in the south. Ed Lybeck kept an even lower profile in the fall; he thought Douglas wanted to either be in the Senate or out of politics and he "didn't work in campaigns like that." The fact that the Los Angeles office was referred to as the "State Headquarters" suggests continued confusion of authority between Tipton and Lybeck. Evie Chavoor had moved out to California in March to work constantly by Douglas's side, serving as the liaison between Douglas and her Washington office and the campaign principals. Douglas flew back and forth to Washington as the Foreign Affairs Committee began meeting almost daily to discuss war policy. She wrote Walter Pick in mid-July that "between the office and Korea, life has not been slow." But aside from organizational matters, she indicated no concern about the campaign at this point. As she wrote one supporter, "It is sure to be a good and rough one and that is the kind I like. We will win if everyone does his part." Her campaign would be based on her record and the Democratic program; "the Republicans have nothing more to offer now than they had twenty years ago."[7]

In the two months prior to the formal opening of the campaign, the staff held strategy sessions with numerous groups about fund-raising, registration drives, publicity, and Douglas's fall itinerary; labor, lawyers, Jewish organizations, and Hollywood people figured prominently in this planning. The staff developed strategies to tap new sources of money, including individuals outside of California; began early contact with Douglas-for-Senator offices at the county level; and began to gather more information on Nixon's voting record. They had to work within the ineffectual and expensive pattern of campaigning long typical of the Democratic Party. Each of the three top candidates on the state Democratic ticket—Jimmy Roosevelt, Pat Brown, and Helen Douglas—essentially ran an individual campaign, competing for funds, preparing and distributing campaign literature and other advertising, and carving out space in county party headquarters. While separate campaigns resulted in the duplication of expenses and disorganization, Douglas, although she liked Roosevelt, still considered him more a liability than an asset, and she had no interest in working with Pat Brown. Many of the Douglas loyals from the spring campaign remained in place like Bea Stern in Sacramento, but some chose to work in other campaigns because they believed Douglas had little chance of winning. As one member of the Los Angeles County Democratic Central Committee remembered, Douglas "certainly was a whole lot better than Richard Nixon," but many liberals "did not commit themselves to any all-out effort because they were afraid the cards were stacked in favor of Nixon."[8]

The state party organization, meanwhile, focused on forming policy statements and raising funds to be later divided, urged voter registration, and served as a loose liaison between Democratic groups of various sorts that communicated generally at the county level. The party's newsletter in August brought

Democrats up to date on party activities in various counties. In San Francisco, for example, thirty-five people had gathered from the statewide campaign office, unions, and minority and women's groups; officers were elected. In Sacramento, minority groups for Douglas had begun organizing, while trade unions began activity in Solano County. Groups were urged to concentrate on registering low-income people who were most likely to vote Democratic. In Los Angeles, the Douglas, Roosevelt, and Brown forces, "with other interested groups co-operating," were organizing registration drives by assembly district. County Democrats had capitalized on a very brief and seemingly perfunctory July visit from President Truman, part of a Western campaign swing, to get their organization underway. He arrived late one afternoon and was met by a carefully selected group of active city Democrats, including Douglas. A "little Mexican girl" handed him flowers, with background music supplied by a Mexican band. After a brief press reception, he met for five-minute segments with small numbers representing various groups: the AFL, then the CIO, other labor groups, blacks, Jews, veterans, and the Women's Division (a group of ten that included Douglas). The organizers did not invite either Brown or Roosevelt to a small meeting. Truman addressed general concerns rather than emphasizing endorsement of individuals. A dinner followed, and the President left the city by 10:00 P.M.[9]

Douglas's summer mail suggested the intense personal feelings aroused by the Senate race, feelings that divided generally like-minded groups and even close friendships. For example, the director of the western division of the AFL wrote Douglas a distressed letter saying that he had heard from reliable nonlabor friends that Helen and Melvyn were Communist sympathizers. While he did not necessarily believe the rumors, they worried him. Ethel Richardson Allen, a prominent Los Angeles woman married to a wealthy businessman, told Remsen Bird that she and her husband had recently entertained a very close friend who was from one of San Francisco's oldest families. "We were having a wonderful reunion," she recounted, when the guest asked Allen's husband to fill him in on Nixon. When Clifford Allen indicated he had voted for Douglas, "a solid block of ice was dropped into our cozy weekend." While eventually conversation became comfortable, "it was the supreme test" of their friendship.[10]

Early on, Douglas attempted to join forces with some of Manchester Boddy's workers. One campaign worker wrote that Douglas needed to "smooth the fur" on Boddy, Malone, Rogers, and others for their money and support. A Butte County Democrat attended a summer meeting of the State Executive Committee and learned from "very reliable sources that Will Rogers, Jr., and the rest of the former opposition were waiting to be asked to join the bandwagon." The supporter clearly overestimated the enthusiasm of the Malone forces; Douglas had no reason to expect that oil men like Pauley or anti-feminists like Malone would vote for her, let alone work hard for her. Some continued to resent her vindictive comments about Downey. One Douglas campaign worker had commented that Downey "cannot stand to be ridiculed or belittled. You know [it's] too bad the Old Man is physically unable to campaign. Very unpleasant to criticize an old man with one foot in the grave." The Washington bureau chief of Boddy's *Daily News* told Downey in mid-June that "despite the tactics of Mrs. Douglas, you still hold the highest rank with your friends and supporters." In spite of such lingering feelings, many Boddy Democrats, including Will Rogers, did move over to the Douglas camp, at least publicly. Rogers wrote Douglas, "The best man won, and now is the time for all Democrats to get behind the ticket." At the end of August he joined with two other prominent Boddy Democrats in Los Angeles, Rollin McNitt and Marguerite Scully, to form what they called the California Committee for Douglas. Eventually, Malone and others lent their name to campaign publicity.[11]

Organized labor, however, was Douglas's chief source of campaign help. Walter Reuther told the UAW Executive Board that they would have to "fight like Hell" to prevent the Eighty-second Congress from being another Eightieth. An intensive push for registration and fund-raising began in July with both the Democrats and the labor PACs. In Los Angeles, labor groups sponsored a very successful program of nightly classes for six weeks at Jimmy Roosevelt's headquarters for the thirty-two Los Angeles assembly districts to teach volunteers how to become registrars; efforts resulting in blitzkrieg registration. According to the CIO-PAC director for the area, the CIO responded better than the AFL, and among the various CIO affiliates the hardest-working unions were the Oil Workers, Auto Workers, Shipyard, and Amalgamated Clothing Workers. Steel was "lousy." Kroll urged registration efforts to take place at the shop, at the gate, and in homes.[12]

George Douglass, reappointed from UAW headquarters in Detroit to work on Douglas's fall campaign full-time as well as help raise money and push local registration drives for the entire Democratic ticket, worried about petty squabbles between the UAW and the CIO, but he tried to set himself apart from these problems and work broadly with all CIO affiliates. He reported that Roosevelt thought he ought to have a special labor person assigned to him. But Douglass was pleased with the progress in the Douglas campaign, as he reported to Roy Reuther throughout August, and felt the general organization in the Douglas camp was far superior to the Roosevelt efforts. He met regularly with Chavoor, Tipton, and Lybeck to plan strategy. He helped the campaign managers for Douglas, Roosevelt, and Brown prepare a joint brochure. Douglass also assisted in organizing a major Los Angeles campaign kickoff picnic at Sunland Swimpark to urge registration drives and campaign donations, with Douglas, Roosevelt, and Brown all present to talk. When he wrote Roy Reuther on July 4, he expressed his conviction that Douglas would win; he reiterated this assessment at the end of August.[13]

The Douglas camp continued to cultivate women's groups, but while their effectiveness varied from county to county, these organizations did not figure significantly in Douglas's campaign structure. In June, Los Angeles women party organizers brought together several organizations to urge women to forget their inter-organization hostilities and back the ticket, but with little effect. The lack of a strong Women's Division structure, characteristic of the Truman years, had not presented problems for Douglas's congressional campaigns, but it did affect her Senate race. India Edwards, who spent half of her time in California during the fall campaign, sent Truman an analytical yet poignant memo after the November results had come in. She argued persuasively that, had the National Committee "pursued the course of getting facts to the voters more vigorously," a role the Women's Division had played most effectively during Roosevelt's administration, election results would have been different. "Party stalwarts do not win elections by themselves," she pointed out. As head of the Women's Division and vice-chair of the DNC, she had had no "voice in making policy or planning strategy. . . . I am nothing but an empty title." Edwards later recalled that Douglas certainly could have used the Division's help, had it been well organized, particularly in the north, where she was not well known. Leisa Bronson, director of the Division in California, was so disenchanted with the organization that she resigned to work for Jimmy Roosevelt.[14]

Immediately following the June primary, analysts predicted that Nixon would gain a portion of Boddy's vote and undoubtedly some of Douglas's vote, including rank-and-file union members. Many believed the high Democratic turnout in the spring would diminish in the fall. Al Cohn wrote his friend Matthew J. Connelly, Truman's appointments secretary: "Warren and Nixon are more or less a cinch," because both Roosevelt and Douglas "polled their full strength" in the primary. Nixon would receive "a world of oil money" and his people "knew how to spend it." So "it doesn't look too good for the Democratic Party of the good ole state of Californiay." Cohn enclosed a Kyle Palmer column from the *Los Angeles Times* that Cohn considered a sound analysis of Nixon's advantageous position. Palmer raised the question of Truman's position on the campaign. The journalist pointed out that many Trumanites hoped Douglas would lose, and that the President, while he may not have wished Douglas's defeat, certainly lacked enthusiasm for her, as he did for most women politicians. Furthermore, Truman's long-time antipathy towards Jimmy Roosevelt also diminished his desire to work hard for the party ticket in California. Roosevelt, as head of the Democratic Party in California in 1948 and a Truman delegate to the national convention, had led the efforts to recruit Eisenhower as the party's presidential candidate. Truman's brief, perfunctory visit to Los Angeles in July underscores Palmer's point.[15]

Nixon and his staff wasted no time after the primary in laying out their fall strategy. Unlike Douglas, who had to go day by day in her planning to get her message out as she waited for the funds to dribble in, Nixon had no financial constraints. In fact, his fund-raising became "the most wide-ranging and lavish funding in the history of California politics." The committee searched for money all over the country. One member of Nixon's team wrote a wealthy Houstonian, asking for a contribution to support a "public servant with the fire, honesty, good judgment, and Americanism which has made our country great." His opponent Douglas was backed by left-wing crowds and the Hollywood types. While Douglas had all the money her campaign needed, he went on, Nixon needed funds badly.[16]

The estimated $1,000,000 to $1,500,000 that Nixon raised, much of which began to come in early, permitted him to make decisions early about media publicity—how to blanket newspapers, radio, and even television with ads throughout the campaign. He planned to inundate the state with billboards, stretching even down into Mexico; by August, Nixon supporters had erected more than 1,400 billboards, which constantly greeted the traveler's eye on highways and downtown city streets. A second carefully laid strategy was to organize groups of hecklers to " 'embarrass Douglas' "; to put her on the spot in meetings as well as " 'penetrate Douglas's Democratic strongholds, including Hollywood labor unions' "; and to form " 'groups that knifed into the heart of her support.' " The strategy team also set up advance teams to precede Douglas by several days prior to each of her speeches and distribute literature so that when she arrived she would be forced to respond to Nixon's accusations rather than stay with her own agenda. Nixon also decided to establish the "soft on Communism" issue immediately rather than wait until fall. For example, he suggested in one speech that Douglas's foreign policy record clearly undermined the efforts of American soldiers in Korea.[17]

As the war intensified in July and August and Nixon's strategy gradually became evident, Douglas reluctantly confronted the reality that Communism would become the principal focus of Nixon's campaign. With his accusations that she was "soft on Communism," he could force her into a defensive posture. While this awareness did not daunt the energetic Douglas and her core staff, Douglas had to decide how she would respond. At first she seemed determined to ignore Nixon's tactic. In mid-July she wrote Remsen Bird that she would send a comparison of the Douglas and Nixon voting records to clarify "what's at stake. . . . He really isn't a very good fellow—he's very dangerous." She vowed, however, that she would not let Nixon choose the issues. In responding to a note from a supporter who urged her to take an aggressive position on loyalty questions, she answered that she would "refuse to permit the opposition to make that THE issue in the campaign. Mr. Nixon's record in Congress will not stand up under the enlightened scrutiny of the voters of California and it is my purpose to enlighten them on every facet of it." She also had absolutely no intention of shifting her own position on issues, no matter the consequences. This attitude did not mean, however, that she did not continue to take extreme care to stay away from Communist Party members. When she spoke at a party gathering in Madera County in early August, for example, the woman who introduced Douglas apparently had revealed to neighbors and friends her membership in the Communist Party. A lawyer from Sacramento felt the information was valid and asked Douglas for comment. She immediately answered that she had had nothing to do with selecting the woman; she was "surprised to see her there" and had already reported this to Tipton's office.[18]

Prominent Los Angeles lawyer Irving Hill agreed with Douglas's initial position. He wrote Ruth Lybeck that "the most dangerous issue which we will have to meet in the campaign will be the so-called 'Red' issue. We unfortunately cannot meet the issue head on. It is ridiculous to have a candidate of Helen's stature get up on a platform and deny that she is a 'Red' or a radical." He recommended recording radio and television endorsements from the top Democrats in Washington.[19]

Douglas had actually begun in June to establish an offensive stance. On the thirtieth, she delivered a lengthy speech in the House about the Korean situation. She praised Truman's response to the Communist aggression, action that reinforced the United Nations' establishment of South Korea as an independent nation. She reviewed the efforts of the House to provide an aid package to Korea in January of 1950. The bill, she pointed out, one on which she had worked diligently in the Foreign Affairs Committee, had been defeated by one vote; fortunately the House reconsidered and passed the bill three weeks later. On June 21, she included in the *Congressional Record* a popular speech entitled "This I Believe," which she had delivered in mid-May to respond to Boddy's Red-baiting tactics. She had emphasized that she stood "squarely on the platform of the Democratic Party—and I am proud of it. I not only believe in that platform, I helped build it." She discussed the freedoms Americans cherished, such as the right to own a home and a business, the right to an education, health protection, and a job. She repeated her now-familiar theme that "the way to keep communism out of America is to keep democracy in it." Lawmakers should never have the power to "suppress opposition to those laws or to judge citizens in trials by headlines," power she accused HUAC members of exercising. Foreign policy should "give aid and confidence to free governments and hope and leadership to people ground down by the heel of totalitarianism." Douglas's office released both speeches for circulation to the press and campaign workers a few days later.[20]

Despite Douglas's initially positive stand, one that did not even mention Nixon, it became increasingly evident that she could not ignore the Communist innuendoes as she had with Boddy. Thus, towards the end of July, Douglas began to shift ground to a more aggressive position. On July 22, Douglas addressed the California Federation of Young Democrats with a wide-ranging, strident campaign talk on both Korean and various critical domestic issues. In discussing the January Korean Aid bill, she pointed out that "Mr. Richard Nixon voted against that first Korean Aid Bill along with Mr. Marcantonio," a vote that demonstrated "the failure of so many to understand the communist threat in the far East." In fact, it was hard to predict to what degree the failure of the first bill "influenced the communist decision to strike now in Korea." Certainly if the second bill had not passed, the United States would have given up South Korea "by default." In an attempt to associate Marcantonio with a pro-Soviet stance, she pointed out that in June he had cast the sole vote against funds to send American troops to Korea. She then discussed a 1949 bill providing military aid for Western Europe: Marcantonio, Nixon, and 207 other House members voted to cut the amount of aid. "For one reason or another [they] thought the defense of western Europe was unimportant." She shifted to domestic issues, including federal support for hydroelectric power development. "Those persons who opposed public development in the last five years," she charged, "have been among the most effective saboteurs of our national strength that the Communists could hope to enlist. I nominate for the Order of Stalin those Republicans and private power executives who . . . have obstructed the development of this vital source of energy."[21]

Three weeks after this speech, on August 18, she made a major address at the national convention of the CIO oil workers' union. She referred to her Young Democrats speech and her comments about Nixon. "The mental gyrations of the Republican National Committee in attempting to explain why Mr. Nixon voted against aid to Korea are painful indeed to watch." Despite the support for this bill by Republicans on the Foreign Affairs Committee and "pleas by responsible, alert, and informed members of his own party," Nixon voted against the bill. "This is the record, and these are the facts. No amount of whining, alibiing, or distortion can change them. However, my Republican opponent is busily trying to cover up this fact, trying to confuse the issue, trying to change the subject." She wondered what would happen when campaign issues turned to the minimum wage, tenant farmers, school lunches and other issues for the common American. "I tremble to think of the gyrations and the goings-on we will be forced to witness." While she admitted that "distortion of fact" may exist in any campaign, she believed that voters were always "entitled to the truth." The Democratic Party had no reason to "resort to bogus issues, to trumped-up false charges" because of the validity of its program. As for the California press, which was defending Nixon's explanation that he changed his vote on military aid to Korea in January because the second bill included aid for Formosa while the first did not, she suggested journalists read the *Congressional Record*. She even provided the pertinent page numbers for their convenience.[22]

Shortly after this speech, Bernard Brennan, Nixon's campaign chairman for southern California, released a statement to the press that questioned whether or not Douglas was a true "foe of Communism." Brennan reiterated the principal argument from the Boddy campaign: that Douglas had voted 353 times with Marcantonio, the "notorious Communist party-line" congressman, including votes against HUAC funding, aid to Greece and Turkey, military aid to Korea, and contempt proceedings against people who refused to declare whether or not they were Communists. He quoted the line from "My Democratic Credo," in which she said that "Communism is no real threat to the institutions of this country." Brennan continued, undoubtedly responding to Douglas's comments about Nixon, that Douglas, the heroine of the *Communist Daily Worker* and the *People's World*, had suddenly decided she opposed Communism. "How can Helen Douglas, capable actress that she is, take up so strange a role as a foe of Communism? And why does she, when she has so deservedly earned the title of 'the pink lady'? Perhaps she had just heard of the chameleon that changes color to suit conditions, or perhaps [she] had decided pink isn't becoming any more, or at least while we are in a bloody war with Communism." Brennan's comments clearly pointed out the uselessness of Douglas's weak attempt to counter the ongoing Red-baiting. The *Long Beach Independent*, in the article "Helen's Quandary," pushed Brennan's points a bit further. Douglas wanted federal control of tidelands oil, which included Long Beach's shores; "no one but a crook or a confirmed Socialist would advocate that for a state they called home." Since she was not a crook, then she believed the "federal government should control all wealth . . . the Communist Propaganda line."[23]

On September 6, Douglas opened her campaign. She told her radio audience that her campaign would be one of limited funds; only a handful of papers would support her, and the opposition would distort her record. But California needed a liberal voice. She cited her votes for military and economic aid to Europe because Russia had violated its pledges of cooperation with the free world. She also had supported the Reciprocal Trade Program, the stockpiling of strategic defense materials, the Military Assistance Program, and aid to Korea. She had introduced, along with others, the economic expansion bill that became Title III of the Defense Production Act of 1950. The idea behind this bill was one she had repeated very often—America had to build a strong economy to prevent Communism. American institutions were strong enough, she argued, without destroying basic freedoms.[24]

Nixon, on the other hand, she argued, had "no real comprehension of the challenge of communist imperialism." Nor did he have any concern for the welfare of Americans, or concern for a strong economic base, which was, of course, the key to preventing the spread of Communism. Democrats favored housing for the middle and lower classes, support for small businesses, a strong farming economy, expanded social security, public control over power development, and equal opportunity for all. Nixon had voted against all these Fair Deal programs and against the excess profits tax, designed to take money from the rich and divert it into social programs. Nixon believed the government should handle Communism by repressive measures that had been unclearly drawn. His only legislative effort had been the Mundt-Nixon bill, a bill that both Attorney General J. Howard McGrath and FBI Director J. Edgar Hoover thought ineffective. This bill, an "altar of hysteria," had been created by "those without vision, without faith, without courage, who cringe in fear before a handful of crackpot or traitorous Communists." Citing the *New York Times'* opposition to the bill, Douglas agreed that the country must protect itself against "spies and saboteurs and traitors" but could not "sell American liberties down the river of fear conjured up by the Mundts and the Nixons, [and] the McCarthys."[25]

Ten days after Douglas's opening speech, Nixon gave his kickoff address. He found himself, he announced, "confronted with an unusual situation." His opponent was a woman, and some had advised him that he should not question her qualifications because this might cost him the election. Therefore, he wanted to make his position "crystal clear." There would be "no name-calling, no smears, no misrepresentations in this campaign. We do not need to indulge in such tactics." But on the other hand, he did have the "obligation" to expose Douglas's record to California voters because it "disqualifies her from representing the people in the United States Senate." The next California senator, Nixon argued, needed to understand the international Communist conspiracy at home and abroad, be able to develop a strong foreign policy, and comprehend national defense problems. Douglas did not understand these issues, he claimed. He cited the famous line from her "My Democratic Credo" that Communism was no real threat to the democratic institutions of the United States. He reiterated her votes against funds for HUAC, contempt citations for those who would not testify before Congress, loyalty checks for federal employees, the Selective Service Act, a bill to investigate the whitewash of the Amerasia case, the subversive control bill, and aid to Greece and Turkey and to the anti-Communist forces in China. She believed, he argued, in appeasing the Communists in Asia, which resulted in the outbreak of the Korean War. In these votes she had not voted a party line; she joined Vito Marcantonio and a "small clique of leftwingers and isolationists" who opposed basic security measures.[26]

Both candidates obviously were determined to prove the other "un-American" and themselves the champion of a free country. Both had talent for name-calling. Douglas amused people with "pee-wee" and "Tricky Dick." The latter stayed with Nixon throughout his career. Nixon accused Douglas of being "pink down to her underwear," a term that made audiences snicker. The difference lay in the tone and approach of each candidate. Douglas, with righteous indignation, defended her record, tried to correct Nixon's interpretation of her votes, and criticized Nixon with lengthy, often laborious speeches. Nixon, always on the offense, limited himself to talking only about Douglas; he had little to say about himself. Nixon's manipulation of Douglas's record into a "Red" agenda came across well to the 1950 voter.

Douglas knowingly added ammunition to Nixon's attacks. For example, in September she voted against the McCarran-Wood bill, which was similar to the Mundt-Nixon bill. Chavoor remembers clearly the day before the vote. The staff was conferring at Douglas's Los Angeles headquarters. They knew the vote would be sensitive, that Nixon "would attack her for the wrong reasons." Douglas called to alert them: " 'I just wanted to be sure you all knew because you know what it can mean.' " They reassured her that they were prepared and not to worry; that was why they and others were working for her. Yet while Douglas had no qualms about her record, she took care in selecting speechwriters. For example, when one Hollywood writer offered his services, she sent the letter to Tipton with a note that while he was a good writer, she was not "sure whether he is too far over to the left—you might check and find out from Allen Rivkin," another Hollywood writer and Douglas friend and campaign worker. She could not check too closely. During the primary, at least one Communist Party member, Paul Jerrico, had written a speech for her for a labor rally on May Day.[27]

Nixon did not confine his attacks on Douglas to his speeches; he followed the full strategy planned in June. He used a variety of pamphlets to drive home his message. His most famous handout, comparing his votes with Douglas's, printed on pink paper, became known as the infamous "Pink Sheet." The first widespread use of the document occurred during Eleanor Roosevelt's major campaign address supporting Douglas and her own son Jimmy. Ten thousand people were present. George Douglass wrote Jack Kroll that while the First Lady gave a wonderful speech, "Nixon flooded the meeting with pink leaflets castigating Helen's record of voting 354 times with Marcantonio." Immediately afterwards, Douglas headquarters responded with a very thorough presentation of her record, complete with *Congressional Record* quotes, in the form of a cumbersome twelve-page legal-size brief with a blue cover, entitled "Helen Gahagan Douglas versus Richard Nixon." Douglas had her staff circulate it to key county headquarters and labor groups to use in combating Nixon in hopes of educating all who took the time to read the thick—and ineffective—packet.[28]

Nixon also masterminded a "whispering campaign," perhaps his most devastating and demoralizing tactic. Instead of the public innuendo that Douglas was "soft on Communism," people involved in this activity directly called Douglas a Communist. For example, Douglas's supporters wrote her that Republicans organized postmasters into little groups. Catholic priests worked closely together throughout the state to turn their congregations against Douglas by accusing her of being a Communist. Angry pro-Douglas Catholics responded with "A Message to Catholics from Catholics" defending their candidate's record. Big landowners strove to control the voting of their unorganized farm workers. H. L. Mitchell, head of the National Farm Labor Union, tirelessly fought this approach by organizing and informing these workers and publicizing information about Douglas through his *Farm Labor News*. Eleanor Roosevelt wrote Douglas that a close friend of her grandmother's had been approached on the street by a woman asking whom the friend intended to vote for. When she answered "Douglas," the woman told her that both Douglas and her husband were Communists and furthermore Roosevelt was working for Douglas. "I thought you might like to know of this type of electioneering," Roosevelt wrote Douglas. From Riverside County came a pamphlet entitled "Is Douglas a Democrat? No—But Nixon Is." An Arcadia citizen reported that some Nixon person had put the November first edition of *Legionnaire*, with a very pro-Nixon/Warren and nasty anti-Douglas message, no return address or stamp, in all Arcadia mailboxes. This was against postal regulations, and the writer was furious about this "illegal political work." Other whispering went on in bars. Democrats attributed some of this effort to the fascist Gerald L. K. Smith, who harped on Melvyn's Jewishness rather than the Communist issue.[29]

Democrats made some efforts to combat the whispering campaign, a tactic not confined to California. The Women's Division, for example, assigned a legislative assistant to tour the country to work with women on the techniques of combating the Red-smear tactics that Republicans were using in dozens of campaigns. The approach suggested was to fight the attacks through an intensive grassroots approach, not in large groups. Some Democrats believed that when Douglas made public appearances she could defuse these attacks. In Riverside, for example, she had taken the "town by her charm," and they hoped that would turn the tide. But in reality, most of these efforts were in vain. People did not hesitate to write nasty letters to Douglas or to their friends who found themselves on opposite sides of the campaign. As one Morro Bay lady said, "me and my family we would rather die than vote for you." A statewide broadcasting system permitted a speech so slanderous that Douglas was able to get equal air time to try to combat the charges.[30]

Douglas and campaign workers constantly experienced personal harassment. When Chavoor would work a neighborhood, people would slam doors in her face, "abruptly and with a kind of mean snarl about communists. And you just shake it off and go to the next door." Douglas recalled that "*children* threw rocks at the car. . . . You wondered is this a democratic election, or are we in a *war*, an undeclared war." For Helen Lustig, the personal confrontations were continuous, and some were "pretty ugly." "I was a traveling billboard" because she had had a large billboard mounted on her car. Several times she was forced to the side of the road; once, two cars closed in on her, a "very frightening" occasion. Nixon's campaign paid some people to harass; others joined the crowds.[31]

Long-time prominent Democrat George Creel, a friend of Douglas's until she challenged Downey, worked tirelessly alongside the Republicans and on the Republican payroll to organize "Democrats for Nixon," and he took considerable credit for Nixon's victory. He wrote Republican Jesse Jones in 1951 that he had led the Democratic revolt against Roosevelt and Douglas; the result was "a Republican landslide." Creel and Irene Dockweiler, head of the Women's Division of "California Democrats for Nixon," published Red-baiting literature less subtle than that of Nixon. One pamphlet pointed out that the Communist Party backed her, quoting Downey's charge that Douglas's record gave " 'comfort to Soviet tyranny.' " It also included a list of organizations Douglas had had some contact with that the Attorney General's office had declared "Communist and subversive."[32]

A news blackout of Douglas's activity further bolstered the Nixon campaign. Just as in the primary, Douglas suffered both from a lack of coverage by most California daily papers and news broadcasters and from a barrage of out-of-state journalistic criticism. A *Chicago Tribune* editorial jumped on her for canceling a debate with Nixon scheduled by the Business and Professional Women's Clubs, claiming her explanation that she needed to stay in Washington for some critical votes was merely an excuse. Douglas, a "consistent follower of the Communist party line," probably did not feel she could answer Nixon's questions, it said. Douglas answered the friend who sent her the article that she would have been there if Congress had adjourned, and "one would *not* expect the *Chicago Tribune* to print the truth." Since Douglas also turned down a chance to make a major address to the Amalgamated Clothing Workers for the same reason, her excuse seemed valid despite the fact that she had no interest in debating Nixon.[33]

There were some important exceptions to the news blackout, including the three *Bee* papers, the *Santa Barbara News Press*, the *California Eagle*, and the *San Francisco Daily News*. Although the *News* came out editorially for Nixon, the paper printed a full-page favorable comparison of Douglas's record to Nixon's, which so delighted her managers that they reprinted the page as campaign literature. Douglas congratulated the editor the next day on "high level" reporting. Boddy, "sulking over his defeat," covered both sides in the *Los Angeles Daily News* and sent a questionnaire to Nixon and Douglas and published their responses. Numerous weekly papers came out for her, and at the end of September, Douglas hosted editors of the weekly newspapers (whom she courted vigorously) at the Alexandria Hotel. And the publications of specific groups got out publicity, such as Mitchell's *Farm Labor News* and the *Welfare Advocate*. Not all readers of the *Advocate* liked this support—dozens of irate readers wrote letters protesting an article on Douglas, all of them citing her "un-American" record. Labor publications, mainly the CIO's, gave Douglas heavy coverage. The California edition of the national paper, *Labor*, prepared a special issue October 7 just on Douglas, and all trade union papers supported her, almost always giving her more coverage than the less popular Jimmy Roosevelt.[34]

In September, the Douglas headquarters in Los Angeles had so little money that the staff could not print brochures or pay for newspaper advertising. The only hope at that point was labor, and at first, little money was forthcoming. George Douglass wrote Kroll at the end of September that the Douglas camp still had no money to print literature or buy radio and television time. He worried that if she could not get funds she would lose, simply because she could not get her story across. John Despol from the Los Angeles CIO Central Council told Kroll he had only $1,600 from the "dollar contribution" drive from members, but he planned to give most of it to Douglas. He was quite concerned that Nixon's Red smear was beginning to hurt—even "secondary CIO leadership is asking questions."[35]

Douglas appeared confident despite the grim financial picture, but feelings of insecurity and fear surfaced in her letters to Harold Ickes. She regarded him as the person to rescue her if necessary. Ickes wrote her in July that he had already told Oscar Chapman and Truman that he wanted to stay out of the campaign because he hoped to complete a manuscript. If he made any exception it would be for her, he said, commenting that he hoped her "path will be so rosy that you will decide that you don't need any help." He did promise to do some radio spots, especially if one of Douglas's people sent him draft scripts of what Douglas wanted him to say. He was less certain about being on television—he did not know how he would look. Douglas wrote him she was pleased he would do the spots, but that "doesn't mean I will let you out of coming to California. However I promise not to yell unless I am really in trouble."[36]

In mid-September she begged him to come. If the "red hysteria" became so great that she might be in danger of losing the election, she simply needed him. He refused; this time explaining that the problem was "two horns of my dilemma." He did not want to help Roosevelt but did not want to hurt him, either. She responded with three letters in a row. "Couldn't you talk generally about the Democratic ticket?" she pleaded. Ickes responded that her letters of September 21, 22, and 23 had "caught him in one hell of a jam." The whole family was sick, one child was in the hospital, and for the first time, he was a day late for a column and had the editor "screaming" at him. He refused her pleas once again; he would not even speak for the party. "I am not a party Democrat and never have been." He was a registered independent. And furthermore, he did not care who became governor of California. Douglas was different; she was his representative, as she was to any American. He finally agreed to write and sign a letter with Mrs. Bordon Harriman asking people outside of California for money, an effort that brought in almost $3,100.[37]

He also published a strong statement in the *New Republic* in mid-October supporting both Douglas and New Hampshire senator Charles W. Tobey, who also was struggling through a vicious campaign. "Mrs. Douglas, like Senator Tobey," he wrote, "is outstanding for her courage—if she were a man I would say 'guts.' " If even half of Congress had Douglas's qualities, "we would have the most outstanding parliament in the world." Douglas opposed the police state that Nixon advocated, land monopolists who wanted to destroy the family farm, and the oil powers who did not have the interest of California at heart. "Mrs. Douglas needs money," he concluded, to cover the state. And she needed it quickly to combat Nixon's treasury, which was "bulging" from contributions of "the rich and of the selfish interests." And money came in. Douglas wrote him on October 23: "Thank you a thousand times. I am most appreciative of all that you are doing."[38]

The general financial picture brightened in October. Roy Reuther wrote Douglas to assure her that he would get the most money possible from the national CIO-PAC and would "fully mobilize our efforts to the west coast to insure victory in your campaign." Kroll sent $2,000 to Douglas shortly after that, which quickly was used to print flyers. He apologized that he could not send any more because CIO-PAC was "broke." Numerous local labor organizations, even some from out of state, sent sizable contributions. For example, the Railroad Labor's Political League, the New York City Textile Workers of America, and the Machinists' Non-Partisan League from Washington, D.C., each contributed $1,000, and the Hotel and Restaurant Workers in Cincinnati, $2,000.[39]

Money also began flowing in (relatively speaking) from private contributors in October. Paul Ziffren, with Allan Rivkin working the Hollywood possibilities, contacted hundreds of individuals, with considerable success. Ziffren even pressured his clients to contribute. Donations averaged several thousand dollars per week during October. One peak four-day period in mid-October brought in $15,000. Sometimes money from a particular community came in: thirty-three Chinese supporters sent a total of $500. Several organizations also helped, such as the 1950 Civil Liberties Appeal based in Massachusetts and the National Committee for an Effective Congress. The State Central Committee and the Democratic Senatorial Campaign Committee contributed $6,000 each, the latter including $3,000 from Congressman Clinton P. Anderson.[40]

As donations began to come into the office, Tipton and Lybeck looked for different ways to expose their candidate. Lybeck contracted for billboards and street car and bus advertising, assuming the money would "come from somewhere to pay for it." Douglas gave the first of six statewide radio addresses and planned some television appearances. They scheduled dozens of advertisements in newspapers. Also, as the campaign picked up, people wrote headquarters with various suggestions. Some felt Douglas overdid her involvement with labor. A San Francisco lawyer wrote Tipton that Douglas "should lay off labor organizations," cut the detail in her speeches, and use the words "America" and "Americanism" more often. She needed to speak to service and sectarian groups such as Rotary and the Knights of Labor, and more veterans' organizations and women's groups. She certainly had support to cultivate; for example, not only did the liberal veterans' organizations favor her, even many within the American Legion passed out her literature. She should talk about her roots; simply "exposing Nixon's voting record will not do the trick." Tipton needed to decorate all headquarters with American flags. One suggested that Admiral Chester Nimitz, commander in the central Pacific, wanted to work for her. Tipton should get him to head up a state committee if possible. "We have got to wrap the flag around her and one way of doing it is to get military and naval heroes to become associated with her." While the advice seemed sound, no one took it.[41]

Another important infusion of support came from well-known members of the Truman administration. Vice-President Alben Barkley came first, arriving in California in mid-October, a visit that stimulated Democratic enthusiasm. While he came to back the entire ticket, Douglas spent considerable time at his side. Barkley praised Douglas as "invaluable" to the administration and made the somewhat exaggerated claim that she had played a "prominent and important part" in enacting both New Deal and Fair Deal legislation. And the "dignified body" of the Senate could "stand the shock of the combination of brains and beauty." Iva Blank told Lybeck that Barkley's visit turned the tide in Fresno County. Attorney General McGrath, Secretary of Agriculture Charles Brannan, Secretary of Labor Maurice Tobin, Representative Wright Patman, Mary McLeod Bethune, and India Edwards came to campaign. Oscar Chapman was scheduled to come but at the last minute had a conflict. The Attorneys' Committee for Douglas entertained McGrath at an elegant lunch when he came to campaign. He spoke about civil liberties and national security. Bethune flew out to campaign only for Douglas. Her moving speech emphasized civil rights. "Helen Gahagan Douglas is the voice of American democracy." She cared about the "little people who cannot speak for themselves" and had "stood by the Negro people when they needed a sentinel on the wall."[42]

Tremendous excitement surrounded one particularly distinguished visitor, W. Averell Harriman, Truman's special assistant for foreign affairs. Harriman, who had held many key posts, among them United States Ambassador to Russia, reputedly refused to give campaign speeches. But his anger at the Nixon campaign strategy brought him to Douglas's defense. One Democrat took offense at the invitation to buy a ticket to the Harriman talk at the Biltmore Hotel. It appeared to him that neither Harriman nor the Democratic National Committee favored Roosevelt, and "if the top candidates cannot get together on this kind of function, they cannot expect unified support from the rank and file of the party." Douglas and Roosevelt would "sink or swim together." But most scrambled for one of the 2,000 tickets. Harriman spoke to the overflow crowd about Douglas's intellectual ability as much as her contributions to the Truman administration. He had met her, he recounted, at a hearing of the Foreign Affairs Committee where he was "struck by the penetrating character of her questions, and the understanding nature of her comments. . . . She was determined to know the facts and to see that intelligent action was taken." He called the Mundt-Nixon bill the worse since the 1798 Alien and Sedition Acts.[43]

While not all of Douglas's Washington support group could make it to California, many of them made "spot" endorsements for radio and television. The radio "platters" were sent to Douglas headquarters, where copies were made and mailed to county offices. Those who helped included senators Lyndon Johnson, Warren Magnuson, Robert Murray, John Sparkman, and ex-senator Brien McMahon; House Speaker John McCormack, congressmen Sam Rayburn, Mike Mansfield, Franklin D. Roosevelt, Jr., Wright Patman, Emanuel Celler, John Sabath, and John Kee, chairman of the Foreign Affairs Committee. A. Philip Randolph, president of the sleeping car porters' union, sent her a telegram October 27 that she used for publicity. He praised her record, recalled that she had made the "most telling tribute to the colored soldiers of any representative in the Congress since the days of Charles Sumner" and called her a "great champion of human rights and liberalism." During this period, Senator McCarthy came in to campaign for Nixon, who was not altogether delighted. Fortunately for the rest of the Republicans, McCarthy only mentioned Nixon and his good work on HUAC. To help Nixon avoid embarrassment, the big city newspapers made no mention at all of McCarthy's visit.[44]

Truman could not be persuaded to visit California. Jimmy Roosevelt wrote Truman an effusive four-page letter at the end of September, begging him to come. Presumably because of his past rocky relationship with Truman, Roosevelt brought Douglas into the picture in his plea for Truman to pay a visit. Their financial resources prevented both of them from getting adequate publicity, he argued. Both the press and "whispered statements" indicated Truman was not going to California because he did not support them. It seemed obvious to Roosevelt that the senatorial vote would be less than for governor, and therefore if Roosevelt did poorly, Douglas would lose, and clearly Nixon would not help the Democrats. If Roosevelt became governor, he would help Truman considerably in 1952. In sum, if Truman would fly out on November 3, it would give the campaign the needed "knockout blow." Truman politely but bluntly turned down the invitation. Because of recent developments in Korea, he wrote, he had to meet MacArthur "somewhere in the Pacific." Douglas was encouraged when Truman at least commented about her at a press conference at the end of October. "There has been a lot of misrepresentation of Mrs. Douglas in the press in California," Truman said. If they mentioned her, although they generally boycotted her, she was presented unfavorably, he said. As a member of the House Foreign Affairs Committee, "she is one on whom we depend very much for the legislation which has to be put through the House of Representatives." Despite rumors to the contrary, she was "wholeheartedly in accord with the President's foreign policy, which is more than can be said for most California papers." Not surprisingly, few newspapers mentioned Douglas in their report on the press conference the following day.[45]

As October progressed and the Korean War picture became more discouraging, Douglas felt pulled even more into Nixon's game. She had tried a new approach at the end of September that, like all her ploys, gained her no ground. She argued that Communism was not the issue between her and Nixon. They both opposed it. They differed on methods: how to combat Communism at home and abroad. She then reviewed each of Nixon's charges and offered what seemed to her a logical counter-argument. Yet shortly after that, a special press release to *The Advance* from her office pointed out that Douglas had decided not to answer "each successive slander"; that would only "help them play their game." Instead Douglas planned an "aggressive" campaign.[46]

On October 4, she delivered a lengthy positive talk on American foreign policy since 1945 to the California Committee for Douglas for Senator Dinner. She made little reference to Nixon. But on the stump and over the radio, she lapsed again into her Nixon–Marcantonio comparisons. On October 9, on statewide radio, she contended that the Republican Party was "desperate." The war-weary and "confused" American electorate had "let down their guard" and permitted the Republican Party to take over the Eightieth Congress, allowing "a new group of political opportunists to ride into power. . . . The MacCarthys . . . and the Nixons are the results." These men had interest only in public office, not public service. "I charge them with the high crime of destroying . . . the Republican party" and thus the two-party system. They also had "sabotaged" the American plan of resisting Communist aggression. She compared her votes with Nixon's on social security, housing, and the rights of labor, which no "smokescreen" could hide. "America must go forward [to] lasting peace in the world and security, prosperity and freedom at home." In another speech, she added the point that Nixon's record did not make him a Communist. "It just proves that he and Marcantonio and the Republican majority voted against measures of vital importance." Since Nixon knew he would be "repudiated on his record," he was "throwing up a smokescreen of smears, innuendoes, and half-truths to try to confuse and mislead you."[47]

In mid-October, Lucy Kramer, a staff member, completed a detailed list of Nixon's votes with Marcantonio, information that Douglas and her people began using immediately. Kramer had sent the material to Chavoor with the comment that the White House and a syndicated columnist planned to "make good use" of this material. "You'll note my little whimsy—I used red checks for Nixon and Marc joint votes and true blue for Helen's."[48]

Melvyn played an almost invisible role in the campaign, and Helen saw him and the children only fleetingly. Melvyn, still on tour in Canada and the northeast United States with *Two Blind Mice*, did not make speeches for Helen, in part because he felt his own politics made him a political liability. He mainly served as Helen's confidant by phone, and he sent her money to supplement her living expenses and contributed to her campaign. He wrote her that while reviews of his play ranged from good to excellent, business remained only moderate. He and the cast enjoyed driving between locations. Shortly he would be driving through Vermont, and he expected to be "very homesick." He felt guilty, as if he was on vacation and she knocking herself out but he doubted that he could do much for her. "After all, it's your job and you do it very well." Helen also kept in touch with her family. Her mother contributed $1,000 and her brother Walter and his wife Gay $1,000 each. In a letter to Walter and Gay, who at this point lived in Venezuela, Helen reviewed her schedule and mentioned the Los Angeles press hostility, which did not worry her in terms of final vote. "The people I met . . . are heart-warmingly responsive." She felt very encouraged by the "thrilling" reception at the AFL convention in Santa Barbara and their generous contribution. Peter and Mary Helen had been coming home every other weekend, she reported; "they're both so big I find it hard to believe they're mine." School was progressing well for them; she was particularly pleased that Peter seemed interested in civics.[49]

Melvyn broke his vow not to speak, however, near the end of the campaign because he felt personally maligned. In a radio address, he made it clear that he knew his wife was "eminently qualified" to present her own record and platform, but he was very disturbed that "certain devious persons" were "attempting to defeat her by taking advantage of my absence from the state to spread malicious rumors" suggesting he was a Communist or "fellow-traveler." These rumors were "unmitigated" lies; he reviewed his work and appointments with both Olson's and FDR's administrations and his anti-Communist record. As voting was a "serious responsibility," he assumed that California voters would not be "deluded by a troop of delinquents whose campaign tactics consisted of dirty words and stink bombs."[50]

On election eve, Melvyn spoke again, this time for Helen. The touching speech reflected loyalty and caring. He was angry; there was nothing uglier than a "whispering campaign, a smear campaign, a campaign of rumor and innuendo and vilification," which was being waged against Helen and all across the country. The Republicans, Melvyn charged, took the easy route by doing nothing. They "let want flourish" because they and the people they supported were "comfortable and well-fed and protected." Nixon was not the only guilty party; this was a Republican pattern since the days of Calvin Coolidge in the mid-1920s. "People with sound policies are always attacked," he continued. "The most un-American of all un-American activities" was "false witness against thy neighbor." Republicans attacked Helen as radical and subversive and accused her of being "unstatesmanlike" because she was "just an actress." She was, Melvyn noted, an excellent actress, and had made a good living in that profession. "It's pretty funny, ladies and gentlemen. Anybody who's ever been in show business will tell you what courage and fortitude, what disappointment and perseverance go into the life of an actor." But Helen had also made an outstanding record as a politician. He closed by saying that while the way ahead was difficult, the "principles of freedom and liberty, on which this nation is based alone, offer salvation to the world. . . . We must not let the McCarthys and the Nixons shake that keystone loose." "With no modesty whatever, I ask you to vote for my wife, Helen Gahagan Douglas, for the United States Senate. . . . What is strongest and best in Helen is strongest and best in America . . . love for her fellow man . . . I know of no better quality in a senator." [51]

Predictions on the campaign results varied the week before the election. Douglas felt confident. She took comfort in the fact that registered Democrats outnumbered Republicans by more than one million. The Democratic tabloid *Independent Review* predicted that all three statewide Democratic candidates had a good chance despite assurances that Republicans would "come into the home stretch with a new avalanche of poison-propaganda." "Mrs. Douglas, with dignity, with poise and with confidence, has kept to the record. She has placed Little Nixon in the public pillory and whipped him with his record of obstruction and reaction," and as a result gained "new impetus." The paper's poll showed Douglas with 57 percent of the vote and Nixon with 43 percent. Furthermore, Douglas spoke to enthusiastic and well-attended audiences wherever she went, regularly filling auditoriums seating several thousand and attracting thousands to rallies. Douglas told Drew Pearson, who had written a column strongly supporting her campaign, that "despite the ever-present lack of sufficient money we are in good shape." She sent a note to lawyer Gardner Bullis on November 1 that in spite of the Republican "desperate campaign of vicious lies and innuendoes," she had "confidence in the intelligence of the American people," and she was certain they would vote for her November 7. [52]

The Republicans, for their part, did not assume victory. In the last few days before the campaign, Chotiner orchestrated a finale of fireworks, with new ads in newspapers, a huge rally sprinkled with Hollywood luminaries, and household prizes, including coffeemakers, clocks, and salt and pepper shakers for those who answered their phone with "Vote for Nixon." The Douglas campaign also suspected that the Nixon camp called the Douglas headquarters with questions to keep the lines tied up. But the most devastating tactic of all was the organization of a different phone bank. In this case, the anonymous caller would say, "I think you should know Helen Douglas is a Communist," and then hang up. One study estimated that volunteers made approximately 500,000 such calls.[53]

Newsweek reviewed candidates' positions and accused Douglas of exaggerating what she called Nixon's "big lie" that linked her to Marcantonio; furthermore, "many voters also resent Mrs. Douglas's Hollywood dramatics." Yet, no one could predict the outcome in a state known for its unpredictable politics. The campaign might well turn on personalities, not issues. According to some polls, *Newsweek* continued, many voters still remained undecided at the end of October. The Boddy vote and labor's ability to "deliver at the polls" remained critical. While Nixon seemed to be stronger in the North, the Hollywood community had "reached the screaming stage" in Los Angeles County, which represented 42 percent of the vote.[54]

Liberal Carey McWilliams, writing in *The Nation*, commented that from the beginning, the "California political campaign has been of monumental irrelevance. No significant issues have been raised," and rank-and-file enthusiasm remained low. "Judging even by Democratic standards, this has been a fantastically inept campaign." The candidates had bypassed hundreds of people who normally contributed money and time. He thought labor was poorly organized; furthermore, while labor endorsed candidates, it did not necessarily influence votes. Douglas had tried hard, but the central issue had become whether or not voters approved of Marcantonio's voting record. The administration's "oblique strategy" of sending out a stream of Truman's "big names" probably would not work for Douglas as these top administrators skittishly had avoided mentioning Roosevelt, thus confirming the "weakness of the center." The situation might be different, McWilliams argued, if Douglas had been able to persuade Ickes to come out and "devote his splendid powers of denunciation to a subject worthy of them—namely the brazen demagoguery of Richard Nixon." Douglas had attempted a "sensible and dignified rebuttal" but had had no success in stopping the Nixon theme, " 'Helen Douglas is a red.' " Yet despite these shortcomings, he predicted a victory for Douglas.[55]

On election day, Nixon felt depressed and concerned; but Douglas appeared supremely confident. Susie Clifton, who had worked in Douglas's congressional campaigns but in 1950 headed Jimmy Roosevelt's efforts in southern California, recalled that Jimmy took Helen to a final rally the AFL and CIO had organized for him. "I don't know if she believed it in her heart," Clifton remembered, "but she was playing the role of a successful candidate." She also was convinced that Roosevelt would lose. So she "propositioned" one of Roosevelt's staff members, a talented black woman, to go to Washington with her. This move infuriated Roosevelt's key supporters. But that evening when the numbers came in, Douglas had to face Nixon's victory, by a 3–2 margin. He won in every urban county and most rural ones. As during the primary election night, Paul Ziffren drove her home. She told him she planned to get up at six o'clock to fly to San Francisco to thank her volunteers. As she went to bed, she wondered how she would feel in the morning. She had seen too many other people destroyed by vicious campaigns. But when she woke up, she recalled, she felt *"free, uninjured, whole*; I was prayerfully thankful, because it could have been otherwise." [56]

Nixon garnered 2,183,454 votes to Douglas's 1,502,507, paralleling the Republican sweep in the state. Warren won an even larger percentage of the Republican vote, but Douglas ran ahead of Roosevelt. Nixon took all but four counties, Contra Costa and Solano near the Bay Area, Lassen in the mountain region, and Shasta in the Sacramento Valley. Douglas came close in Sacramento County. In southern California, Nixon ran up enormous margins. For example, in Orange County, he received over 55,000 votes to Douglas's approximately 19,000. In Los Angeles County he garnered close to 932,000 votes to her 612,510; she won only six assembly districts, all of them black, Mexican, or Jewish, a pattern that repeated itself in other urban areas. While she retained strong labor support, she did lose some of these voters to Nixon as well. She even lost her old congressional district to the conservative Republican Sam Yorty. [57]

Nationally, the Republicans gained five seats in the Senate, bringing them within two seats of the Democrats, and twenty-eight seats in the House. Although Republicans hailed these gains as a victory, their wins did not match the 1946 off-year election when the party gained control of both houses. The Democrats were most upset about the loss of key leaders such as Senate Majority Leader Scott Lucas from Illinois; Senator Millard Tydings from Maryland, chairman of the Armed Services Committee; and Utah's Senator Elbert Thomas, Labor Committee chairman. Most contemporary analyses of the national pattern emphasized the impact of the Communist issue. As *U.S. News and World Report* put it, the election demonstrated the degree to which McCarthy's charges "had taken root and grown into votes." In Utah, the prominent Thomas suffered the "hottest off-year contest" in the state's history; the Mormons, like the Catholics in California, had worked closely together to defeat the Democratic senatorial candidate. In Maryland, Tydings' investigation of McCarthy's charges of Communist infiltration in the State Department hurt him. And in California, Nixon's accusations that Douglas was "soft on

Communism" gave him the victory. Political writers also pointed out the resistance of rank-and-file laborers to union leadership pressure to vote Democratic.[58]

Harry Flannery, a California Catholic journalist writing for *Commonweal*, analyzed the results with more care. Newspapers and Nixon clearly helped bring about Douglas's defeat; "they did the smearing, and did it in such a lurid fashion that the people were roundly frightened about voting for Mrs. Douglas." Angry Catholics, many of whom had called his home or written nasty letters about his pro-Douglas stance, really believed Douglas "had at least played footsie with the Communists." But Flannery thought that the Truman administration deserved the principal blame by letting the public think the Democrats and Communists appeared "in the same line-up." It was bad enough to have all the media against you, but "it's worse when you are put in the position of having to spend what time and money you have in trying to explain." Douglas could "pound the rostrum, clench her fist, and cry out her message." But she was "too often talking to those who were already for her and she could not reach enough of the other kind." Douglas further complicated her own position because she "had decided opinions, and was not politically expedient. Once she arrived at a decision, she clung to it tenaciously, and defended it with a burst of flaming words." In sum, she "had a broom trying to sweep back the sea."[59]

Douglas wrote Jack Kroll that she had little to say about the campaign. Voters had repudiated Truman's foreign policy, they were tired, and prices were high. "We lost in California because the opposition was able to split the labor vote and the women's vote." She was not ashamed of her campaign. "Actually there was nothing that we did or did not do that would have made any difference in the result." In an interview with *U.S. News and World Report*, Nixon indicated that he had won because of Truman's Far East policy, which had caused the Korean War; he opposed the policy, Douglas favored it. He claimed she had also had more radio and television coverage at the end of the campaign because she used labor programs. But he had gained from the fact that the "labor boys were a little bit too rough" on their members by pressuring them to vote, even threatening to impose a fine for failure to show up at the polls.[60]

Douglas received hundreds of telegrams and letters in the weeks following the campaign as she and her staff went about the task of taking care of pending financial responsibilities, writing thank-you notes, and terminating business in the Washington office. A letter written to Mary Helen and Peter from Natalye Hall, a university professor of political science, captured the spirit of the dispirited. She had had the "privilege of working actively in your mother's campaign," she wrote, and she felt bad about the loss. It might be difficult for children to understand why "victory does not always go to the man or woman who . . . stands for those principles that are right." But this often happens.

"To stand for the right whatever comes is to win a victory." In fact, "some defeats are better than victories," she pointed out. "We would not have *wanted her to be Senator* if she had used the methods of winning that Mr. Nixon and his followers used," any more than Peter would want a school team to win by "dirty playing." She reminded Mary Helen that "many great women of the past had people laughing at them, even throwing things at them," including those fighting for women's right to vote. Hall knew only a few leaders she considered "as great as your mother and an even fewer number in my own time. For she has a brilliant mind, with a keen grasp of problems of government, and, in addition, she is *good* all the way through . . . a positive, forceful goodness that does not crack under strains and that can be depended on never to let others down." She and her co-workers were proud of Douglas, and "I hope that you are even more proud because she *is* your mother."[61]

More than forty years later, the 1950 Senate campaign in California remains in the collective memory of people who care about American politics. Or, as one biographer said, the race "became a spectral presence in Richard Nixon's subsequent political career, a hoary ghost . . . that would not recede." Yet why is this particular Nixon campaign the one that people remember? Why do people today, who recollect the name Helen Gahagan Douglas, say, "Isn't she the person that Nixon smeared in 1950?" Helen and Melvyn Douglas had both experienced nasty Red-baiting since they entered politics at the end of the 1930s. Chotiner and Nixon had utilized very similar campaign methods in Nixon's congressional defeat of another idealistic liberal, Jerry Voorhis, in 1946. In 1950, equally devastating Red-smear tactics brought down prominent liberals in campaigns using similar techniques to those used in California. During the decade, Chotiner and Nixon devised a Republican campaign strategy modeled on the California experience that then was taught to tens of thousands of Republican volunteers all over the country. But the Douglases' earlier experiences and the Voorhis campaign blended into the general fabric of California politics and did not touch the national conscience.[62]

This particular campaign of excess served as Richard Nixon's steppingstone to another twenty-five years of prominence on the American political scene, prominence marked by his continued pattern of managing political campaigns outside accepted boundaries. Nixon moved up rapidly—to the vice-presidency in 1952 and then to his famous race against John F. Kennedy for President in 1960. After eight years in political exile, marked by a humiliating defeat in the California governor's race in 1962, he rebounded to win two terms as President of the United States in 1968 and 1972. Two years after his re-election, he resigned in deep humiliation after the Watergate scandal. Despite profound national anger, the enigmatic, dark Nixon came out of exile once again in the 1980s, regaining a presence on America's political stage as an international statesman. This continued presence has kept the American public constantly aware of Nixon as a political figure but also as the subject of ongoing analysis. Publishers have sold hundreds of thousands of books about Nixon since the 1950s. In the last few years, massive studies have appeared, and more are expected. Furthermore, Nixon continues to publish variations on his original memoirs, *RN*, brought out in 1978. The television journalists who occasionally gain access to Nixon for an interview enjoy a large audience. Regardless of whether authors support or condemn Nixon, the 1950 campaign always plays a pivotal position in their analysis.

The acuity of the nation's memory of this campaign is intensified because Douglas, Nixon's foe, represented to many the epitome of American liberal idealism. She steadfastly refused to violate the political boundaries like Nixon did with impunity or to let money or votes affect her stand. Nor would she compromise on legislation; half a loaf was worse than nothing if she could not have what she wanted. And she articulated that viewpoint eloquently. As Douglas said, the American political system needed people who could be "used as a yardstick," and, "in a small way," she believed she had played that role. Nixon's excesses, therefore, seemed all the more reprehensible to those with a political conscience. Within this group of people are those who worked on her campaign and believed in her in a very intense, personal fashion. In India Edwards' words, there was an "aura around Helen," "*worship*, it amounted to that." These thousands of people who experienced Nixon's feverish effort to tear "their Helen" apart, many of them young people who had never campaigned before, felt deep anger at the injustice of Nixon's behavior and have never forgotten that fall of 1950. Nixon's continued presence and questionable political behavior—always masterminded by Murray Chotiner—were a constant thorn in the side of those who respected and cared about Douglas. As Sharon Lybeck Hartmann, the Lybecks' daughter, commented about Chotiner, "The man is a rotten son of a bitch." And he kept turning up "over and over." In 1974, many who remembered or worked in the Douglas campaign delighted in reminding the public of the lurid details of the 1950 campaign to demonstrate that Nixon's behavior in Watergate had its own history. Oral history programs have interviewed hundreds of people about California politics, Douglas's and Nixon's careers, and the 1950 race as if there were a campaign on to preserve these memories.[63]

One of the most poignant and dramatic stories emerges from the Lybeck family. Ruth spent a year in bed after the campaign, Hartmann recalled. Her mother was not only physically exhausted and devastated by the Red-smear campaign, but "there was no money, because the people you counted on were falling away in every direction around you, which meant you doubled and redoubled and re-redoubled your own efforts." Furthermore, the Red-baiting became personal. Her father had been Red-baited since the early 1940s, and the Nixon camp intensified the harassment during the 1950 campaign. "It spilled over onto me as a little kid," she continued. School children accused her of being a Communist. "You know, when that kind of terror comes into your home, when people warn you that detectives may be following you, and they are searching through your family's life . . . you get real frightened. . . . It was years after that campaign before I told people that we were associated with [Douglas because] you were taking a substantial chance that some people . . . would think you were a traitor."[64]

Some historians, like Stephen Ambrose, have sought to counter these memories by suggesting that Douglas, not Nixon, started the Red-baiting, an interpretation eagerly picked up by the press and documentary movie producers. What these historians do not point out, however, is that early in the primary campaign the press and conservative groups accused Douglas of being soft on Communism. Manchester Boddy eventually made the accusations part of his campaign, using language that Nixon readily adopted. She had known for months that Nixon planned to accuse her of being a Communist sympathizer. When Douglas compared Nixon's vote with Marcantonio's, she did not suggest Nixon was a Communist or fellow traveler. She accused him of failing to understand how to stop the advance of Communism. Occasionally Douglas did use phrases that approached Red-baiting. But this language resulted from her tendency to become excited, even shrill, particularly when attacked, and to pick up phrases that were being used against her. Nixon made his comments out of calculation—Douglas, out of emotion.[65]

Is there more to say about the nature of Douglas's loss? One can hardly question that the Communist issue, enhanced by the Korean War, dominated the final vote. This, added to the fact that California Republicans had won statewide offices since 1942, suggested a Republican sweep would have happened even without the war as an issue. Other factors include the defection of labor and the disorganization of the Democratic Party. This lack of organization extended to the Douglas campaign, a point very clearly made by her organizers. The popularity of Earl Warren and the lack of enthusiasm for Jimmy Roosevelt also pulled Douglas down. Another issue that has rarely been raised, however, is the question of gender. To what degree did gender issues affect the campaign and ultimately male and female voters? Nixon acknowledged that since he opposed a woman, he would behave accordingly. But that promise of gentlemanliness proved short-lived. In the 1990 gubernatorial race in Texas, the feminist Democratic candidate, Ann Richards, took full advantage of her Republican opponent's failure to "treat her like a woman," ultimately the factor on which the final vote hinged. Why did Helen not take advantage of Nixon's "discourteous" behavior? This idea may never have occurred to Douglas, loath to acknowledge gender differences in politics. This did not mean, of course, that she failed to recognize that voters responded to her flair, her natural beauty, her warmth and exuberance, atypical of the image of women in politics of the period. Lybeck worried more about how her looks would affect female votes than he did the male. He always favored photographs for brochures that did not portray her full beauty.

The larger California picture underscores the reality that a woman did not have a shot at the Senate race. The electorate simply was not ready to trust a woman in this role. The fact that Douglas had a husband and two small children certainly reinforced the gut feeling that women belonged at home. San Diego County reflects a pattern that typified the state. Helen Lustig recalled that some men had the "same idealism" as Douglas. "They respected her and discussions between them were very, very satisfactory." But when the political bosses would meet with her, "I think they were just playing it safe, just in case she was elected." They did little to get out the vote, raise money, or publicize her. The "fierce loyalty" some women felt only intensified male hostility. These gender considerations, added to her idealism and left-of-center political position, further cut into her vote.[66]

The nature of Douglas's personality also played into her defeat. She had refused to play by the rules since the beginning of her life. As an actress, she entered Broadway as a star on sheer talent and little training. After several years she became bored and moved on to become an opera singer. After only two years of intensive lessons, she sang abroad for two summers, fully expecting that the next step would be the Metropolitan Opera. In politics, after five months of working with the Women's Division, it seemed only natural that she head the state's organization and serve as Democratic National Committeewoman. Restless after three years in these positions, she saw the possibility of becoming a member of Congress as a logical next step. Only four years later, she felt ready to run for the Senate. But her lack of political experience and her inflexible stands on political issues, along with gender questions, eroded the support of the Democratic Party in 1950. What in fact may have hurt her the most is that for which she is most remembered—her idealism.

13

Shifting Priorities

THE DOUGLASES' LIFE began to assume some semblance of order after the campaign as Helen and Melvyn redirected their lives. They could not pretend that they had maintained much of a family life during the period after the war, with Helen in Washington, Melvyn doing road shows and movies, and Mary Helen and Peter in boarding school in Los Angeles. For eight years, Mary Helen and Peter had rarely enjoyed life with both parents at home, and even then for no more than a week or two. Yet, despite the fragile condition of the family in the 1940s, Helen had made the decision to run for the Senate in 1950, knowing that her marriage most likely would end.

After her defeat, she received bids to run for Congress from various districts, was proposed for lieutenant-governor of California (the group even printed up brochures without her consent), and an offer came from Truman to become national housing coordinator. Leo Goodman, CIO congressional lobbyist, recalled that the day following Douglas's loss to Nixon, he and Walter Reuther held a post-mortem to discuss how to keep Douglas in politics. They visited at length with Truman, talking about Douglas's qualifications for the then-vacant position of head of the Housing and Home Finance Agency (now the Department of Housing and Urban Development). The President "authorized us to offer her the position." Goodman went to Vermont to talk to Douglas, but she refused. "I begged her. Day after day after day." [1]

But she turned down this and all these other offers; she finally decided the family had "suffered enough," and that her marriage was worth saving. Peter and Mary Helen, seventeen and twelve, respectively, needed her to "be available at all times and not by appointment." As she told Goodman, she and

Melvyn had "decided that she should give up public life. It was very bad psychologically, the defeat. . . . Melvyn wanted her to concentrate on the family." The two had lots of work to do if they hoped to reinforce their marriage and cement relationships with their children. Thus, in 1951, the family sold the California house and moved back to New York so that Melvyn could return to the stage. They rented a lovely, spacious apartment at 983 Park Avenue in Manhattan's fashionable Upper East Side. Peter and Mary Helen entered the Dalton School, and Melvyn opened a play in New York which he had co-authored and directed, *Glad Tidings*.[2]

Helen's round-robin letter to the extended Gahagan family after the first Christmas in New York offers a glimpse into the Douglases's family style and relationships. Melvyn could not be with the family, she reported, as he was in California on business. Celebrations began with a Christmas Eve dinner Peter cooked at his apartment for his mother, sister, and grandmother Lillian, now in her mid-eighties. At the last minute, Mary Helen opted out when George Cehanovsky offered to take her to the Metropolitan Opera. After dinner, Helen accompanied her mother to her apartment and stayed while she opened a few of her presents. Helen then visited her nephew, Lilli's son Herbie Walker, his wife Joan, and their baby, returning home at 2:00 A.M. The household finally settled down around 4:00 A.M., as Mary Helen decided to wash her hair at 2:30 after returning late from the midnight service she attended after the opera. In the morning, after breakfast and the opening of a few presents, Helen went to her mother's apartment to help her dress. Around two, the Douglases, some of Peter's friends, and the Walkers gathered. A Met broadcast supplied background music. Meanwhile, as kitchen help arrived to begin dinner preparations, the family opened gifts.

Helen gave everyone robes from Macy's; Helen had bought herself a "beautiful coral quilted robe" as her gift from Melvyn. "Mary's comment about her presents was very satisfying to me," Helen wrote. "She said this was the first time she felt like a girl instead of a tomboy." Her gifts included petticoats, a bed jacket, and three "beautiful ribbon scarves." And "then came the best present of all—your phone call from California." More guests began arriving around four, and "as usual" no one in the family was ready. Twenty-eight people eventually showed up—various New York friends, some of Mary's teachers, a Venezuelan family, and relatives, each bringing a poem, song, or story as per Helen's instructions. Helen had prepared an eighteen-pound roast beef, but because dinner was served two hours later than planned, the meat was badly overcooked. "I literally almost sat down in the kitchen and wept when I got a look at it just before it was served." She wrote Melvyn that though they missed him tremendously he made them "all very happy at Christmas. What beautiful gifts, mostly the phone call—we all love you darling very deeply and Mary was right, you were with us." Later that week, Helen took the children to see the Lunts in a play, and then she and Mary Helen went to Washington to spend a week over New Year's with Helen Fuller, one of Helen's closest friends. The two had become close during the 1940s; Fuller wrote for *The New Republic*.[3]

Early in 1952, Melvyn embarked on a project that eventually took him away from home for several years. He collaborated on a light, entertaining show, *Time Out for Ginger*. The play opened first in summer playhouses and then went on Broadway in November 1952, where it ran for eight months. Melvyn took the show to Chicago in the early fall of 1953 as the director and leading man. The show played in Chicago and toured the West Coast until mid-1954. Six months later he was off for a four-month run of *Ginger* in Melbourne, Australia. He returned to New York in the fall of 1955 after a lengthy vacation on his trip home. Helen coped with Melvyn's long absences as she had before, by keeping herself busy. But, like in the 1930s, she did not have a driving goal before her, which probably made her realize that she had to take responsibility in a new way for figuring out a satisfying lifestyle.

Helen experimented with getting back into the theater by playing the lead in a short run of a shallow, dated, but amusing 1930s play, *First Lady*. The story revolved around a woman, the granddaughter of a United States president and wife of the secretary of state, who wanted her husband in the White House. When actress Ina Claire backed out of the 1952 production, Douglas agreed to replace her as the lead as long as she could work the two weeks of rehearsals around lecture engagements in Ohio and Minneapolis. Douglas accepted the part, she said, because the repertory company seemed to be "such gay, nice people" and she liked supporting community theater. The play opened in Washington, and political friends, including Truman, came to see her. Reviewers commented more about her political experience for this role than her acting talent. When one theater reporter asked Douglas about her life since Congress, she responded vaguely, revealing perhaps that while she kept herself occupied, she did not have goals. "In Washington my life was study, study, study, and talk, talk, talk." Since then, she had been "walking around looking at people, gazing at the sky and generally getting the most out of life." Comparing dramatic to political acting, she noted that "in politics, the abilities to meet all kinds of people, to use self-discipline and to stay awake for 24 hours at a stretch are absolutely necessary. You need the same stuff on the stage. But the world is your audience in politics and it needs your sense of responsibility as a citizen." She added, in a comment that suggested she still felt a lingering tug to political life, "I'm not through with politics; I may yet turn up at the convention as a delegate from California."[4]

Of more interest to Douglas than a return to the theater was the prospect of singing again. She hired a noted accompanist, Arpad Sandor, and began voice lessons with her old teacher, Madame Cehanovska. She worried about bookings. "People will want me to talk. They won't know I can sing," she wrote Melvyn. But with the help of an agent, she did secure some concert engagements, among them, at long last, her New York concert debut. She performed in Carnegie Hall with a program combining German lieder, French songs, and Hebridean folk songs with poetry reading, primarily her favorite, Emily Dickinson, and Amy Lowell. Reviewers all agreed, undoubtedly to Helen's disappointment, that she could not fine-tune her voice after so much time. The *New York Herald Tribune* reviewer observed that despite her "sturdy and hale" quality, Douglas's songs were beyond her capability as her voice was "technically insecure" and her performance "undisciplined and ragged," problems resulting from so many years without practice. "Thus for all her infinite charm, elegance and grace her recital was musically of only passing interest." Other reviewers praised the dramatic quality and excellent audience communication during her poetry reading but agreed that she had lost her singing voice. Despite the reviews, Douglas continued singing in public for a short while, but finally accepted that her singing career had ended. But she continued to sing at home, which gave her a feeling of inner peace. Even after Madame died, Douglas did not stop practicing regularly until the early 1970s when Sandor was no longer able to play.[5]

When Douglas realized that concertizing would not be a successful pursuit, she stepped up her speaking engagements and accepted more appointments to boards of liberal groups, like Freda Kirchwey's invitation to become a member of the Committee for World Development after she read an article Douglas had written for the group's bulletin. Douglas's speeches focused increasingly on the issue of disarmament. Engagements ranged from speeches for the Students for Democratic Action at Brooklyn College and the CIO National Convention of Women, to the Los Angeles United Jewish Appeal, the American Christian Palestine Committee Conference in Washington, and a major address at the League for Industrial Democracy's conference on the moral decline of America. Douglas also willingly campaigned. The Democratic National Committee and state and local party organizations solicited her help. Her first foray back into campaigning was motivated by her deep affection for Adlai Stevenson. They had become close friends as delegates to the 1946 United Nations General Assembly. In 1956, the California Democrats drew up a frantic two-week schedule for Douglas with six to eight appearances daily, a pace reminiscent of her grueling 1950 campaign. She also signed a letter for mailing to black ministers and other black leaders praising Stevenson's civil rights views. Stevenson's secretary wrote the Democratic National Committee that "the Governor was ever so grateful—and every time I look at that schedule I am breathless!" Later in the decade she spoke at congressional hearings on farm labor in Washington, representing the National Advisory Committee on Farm Labor. She also began speaking on numerous college campuses. She felt it was urgent to shape the minds of college students who were growing up during Eisenhower's administration, which, she argued, had forced the world into the frightening nuclear arms race.[6]

Douglas's popularity as a speaker never dwindled. Fan mail filled files. The Israeli consul general in New York attended a luncheon where Douglas spoke. He had heard hundreds of speeches about Zionism, he wrote. "I thought I was hardened. Your speech has shown me that something can still be said that is worth listening to." After speaking to the Women's National Democratic Club in the late 1950s, the noted political cartoonist Herbert Block wrote that "everyone was still all agog about it" several weeks after. "I can't think of anything nicer to say . . . than to express the simple truth that it was in your own great and courageous tradition—which is the highest compliment there is." A club member wrote to thank Douglas for giving the women a "magnificent piece" of her mind. "That you deeply stirred each one of us was obvious. Your masterly grasp of the facts involved in this life or death issue of disarmament and the clarity and directness with which you expounded these facts is something I can never forget. Your address was one of the finest and most moving I have ever had the privilege of listening to." As one reporter put it, Douglas "is one actress who needs neither a script . . . nor a director's aid . . . to express such time-honored emotions as outrage and moral indignation."[7]

Despite Douglas's keen interest in political questions, she was determined to put the 1950 campaign behind her. But information about Nixon's campaign tactics against her continued to dribble in. Reporters, Nixon biographers, and other curious people periodically dogged her. She wrote Melvyn that Lilli had met a man who said he had worked in Nixon's 1950 campaign and that Republicans "had proof that you and I were 'Simon pure' [i.e., not Communists]. They heard on telephone conversations of how Commies hated both of us but they [the Republicans] had to defeat me and therefore they called both you and I Communists—nice!!" The Nixon issue primarily arose when Nixon ran for office. Despite Douglas's determination to elude questioning, she occasionally made exceptions. She could hardly refuse Eleanor Roosevelt's request for information in 1952 on Nixon, who was running as Eisenhower's vice-presidential candidate, yet Douglas felt reluctant to talk about her campaign even to her closest political friend so soon after the defeat. Four years later, however, she opened up more. In the fall of 1956, during Stevenson's second attempt to beat Eisenhower, a Scripps-Howard newspaper reporter inquired whether Nixon, again the vice-presidential candidate, had called her a Communist. Douglas replied that "he was much too wise to have called me a Communist"; rather, he had "deliberately designed" his campaign to "create the impression that I was a Communist or at least 'communistic.' " She referred the journalist to the pink sheet that compared her to Marcantonio, as well as Nixon's pamphlet "Is Helen Douglas a Democrat? The Record says NO." "What was I supposed to be," she said, "a Republican?" Eleanor Roosevelt boldly stated on television's widely viewed "Meet the Press" that Nixon *had* called Douglas a Communist; Nixon immediately denied this charge, indicating he had merely questioned Douglas's judgement. Closer to election time, Douglas let down her guard even more in an interview with the *New York Post*, stating that Nixon had "dodged the real issues" and "campaigned on character assassination. . . . The 1950 campaign was waged in great part by whispering campaigns, intangible, yet like a spider's web." She recalled the hatred she encountered when, for example, opponents stoned her car. She also remembered the farm woman who looked at her and said, " 'They haven't made you afraid.' . . . That's what I remember—the fear in one's own people."[8]

The 1956 campaign proved to be an overdose of Nixon for Douglas, and for the next several years she refused interviews on the subject, turning inquiries from "right-thinking" people over to Evie Chavoor, who at that point worked for the Gahagan Dredging Company in New York. In 1958, Chavoor helped Selig S. Harrison, associate editor of *The New Republic*, establish a research file on Nixon in preparation for his run for President in 1960. Chavoor wrote Bea Stern in Sacramento for help in finding what she felt was a particularly deceitful Nixon ad portraying Korean War casualties with the comment, "What are we fighting for in Korea when we have [Douglas] representing us in the United States Congress?" She had to find that ad, she wrote Stern, spilling out eight years of bitter, pent-up anger. "I know at the time it nauseated us so, I may well have destroyed it in my rage. But I am even more nauseated today with the kind of drooling palaver that is surrounding our erstwhile Vice-President." Maybe he was different, she continued, as so many were saying. "But I am not ready to believe this. . . . Now after the passage of almost eight years, there appears to be doubt that Nixon did conduct the kind of campaign he did and he now (after a lapse of consciousness when he appeared contrite over it) has cloaked himself in the robe of righteousness and hurt and claims he never did. Statesman or not, able or no, he is a damn liar." While Douglas needed "no defense," the question of "whether or not he is a liar is of importance and that decision the voters will have to arrive at themselves." Chavoor also helped Nixon biographer Earl Mazo, although Douglas warned her to be careful because of his association with the conservative *New York Herald Tribune*. Douglas herself refused to talk to Mazo: "I do not think that anything I would have to say about Mr. Nixon would be considered objective by your readers," she wrote him.[9]

As much as Douglas enjoyed her public engagements, she balanced her time with the family much differently than she had been able to do in the 1940s. Melvyn's continued long absences after 1950 reinforced the pressure on Helen to pick up the pieces, although he did not divorce himself completely from concerns about the family. During the long run of *Ginger*, for example, Mary

Helen spent a spring vacation with him, and Helen visited various times. He corresponded with the children and sent messages to Peter and Mary in his letters to Helen. Helen's letters to Melvyn in the 1950s were principally reports about the children, sketchy outlines of her activities, and often poignant expressions of loneliness. Early in 1953 she told Melvyn about meeting Peter's girlfriend Jane Haber, whom he eventually married. She gave her approval. Jane was a "sober, pretty young woman," studying to be a nurse, and would graduate in June. She had "real character" and furthermore was an "excellent speller and has a large vocabulary so that's good." Helen and Mary listened to the opera on the radio quite frequently; one afternoon, they were listening to the opera *Die Fledermaus*, which was "very amusing, Mary is roaring." Helen recounted a visit to the Metropolitan Museum of Art with Mary. They had discovered the museum's new cafeteria, and Helen described its beauty—fountains, pool, comfortable chairs, plants. She drew several sketches. In the same letter, she commented that she found the Army–McCarthy hearings "most interesting and depressing." She could not resist adding, "Dearest do stop smoking. I am convinced you are poisoning yourself. We love you and miss you so much."[10]

In the summer of 1954, Helen wrote from Vermont that "Peter is improving every day in so many little ways. Furthermore, I believe Peter has real strength if we can help him release it and direct it. . . . Both children hate to be bossed. Both perform best when looked up to and required to be responsible. But they must feel they are loved and *admired* and *trusted*." Melvyn's phone call had made her "feel very lonesome and I felt so badly to have you all alone in Chicago I could not shake off a real depression." She was, however, enjoying a relaxing schedule in Vermont, doing things with the children, planting flowers and vegetables, and playing cards. She wrote how angry she felt at the local power company, which had cut down her dead white birches. "Dead or not they would have stood for another 5 to 10 years," she fumed. Back in New York later that fall, she confessed she missed Melvyn terribly. "Whenever there is a moment of uncertainty I fly to you as an arrow to its target. Your voice is indescribably reassuring, comforting." She had taken a walk with Peter, who had talked at length about his relationship with his father. "It would have made you very proud. It seems life is just one long lesson and the lesson does not get easier."[11]

Visits with Walter and his wife Gay, Lilli, and their children, in addition to a close circle of friends, helped assuage her loneliness. She saw Eleanor Roosevelt and Lorena Hickok frequently, and always enjoyed ER's annual birthday lunch for Hickok. Generally Roosevelt invited the same small group, among them, Douglas, Mary Norton, and Marion Herron. Helen kept in close touch with other New Deal friends, in particular Helen Fuller, the Arthur Goldschmidts and the Myer Cohens, India Edwards, and Jane Ickes. Nan Stevens, who became the Douglases' secretary in the early 1950s, also became a close friend. Stevens handled the Douglases' mail and kept the checkbook. Eventually Nan became a part of the extended Douglas family.

During Melvyn's months in Australia, letters were longer and more frequent. Melvyn had mixed feelings about accepting the offer to do *Ginger* in Melbourne; although it was financially attractive, he did not know if it would help him in the United States. He was pleased because the Australians had recognized him as a first-rate actor and director. After the play closed at the end of April, he took a circuitous route home—Singapore, Bangkok, India, and Rome. Helen's chatty letters reassured Melvyn that she was spending lots of time with Peter, Mary Helen, her mother, Madame and Sandor at intervals, and Nan Stevens every week. A speech at Worcester "went very well—one of my better ones. I did a lot of thinking in preparation." She detailed other engagements and concluded, "Well, that is my life. Unbelievably full [but] nothing special." After Easter she wrote an especially upbeat letter. She and Mary Helen had started off the holiday with "high breakfast," which included some wonderful bran muffins Mary made ("the kind I am sure you would' love"), hardboiled eggs, and tea. Helen painted for three hours (a hobby her nephew Herbie Walker, an artist, had encouraged her to explore), while Mary read. When Peter came by, the three called on Madame. Then Helen's mother Lillian and Lilli picked them all up for a lovely drive down the West Side Highway, across Wall Street, and up the East Side Drive where the ships reflected the sunlight, ending the day with a good dinner at Lillian's. Esther Murray called to wish them a happy Easter. "Is that what one does on Easter?" Douglas wondered. An animated discussion about their idea to prepare a joint program of short story readings permeated every letter to and from Australia, helping to sustain Helen and Melvyn's emotional and intellectual needs. This project would thrust them into a collaboration they had not enjoyed since the mid-1930s. Both began reading—Melvyn sending Helen to the library to look up possibilities and Helen shipping copies of stories to Australia. Mary Helen and Peter even got involved, making their suggestions. Melvyn envisioned a combination of narrative and dialogue, including authors like Chekhov, De Maupassant, O. Henry, and F. Scott Fitzgerald, and maybe a Bible story. They must definitely include a Stephen Vincent Benét story, Helen wrote in June, and she had found two of Benét's for Mel to do alone.[12]

Helen's letters also expressed typical parental worries about Peter, which elicited a deeply caring and emotional response from Melvyn. She apologized for "spilling over," to which Melvyn answered that she should never hold back from "unburdening" herself if it would help her. Sometimes he felt that she kept things from him for fear of making his ulcer worse. But the things that upset him were his problems, the "tensions, indecisions, anxieties," resulting from his own inner conflicts. For example, he became upset when he had to do something he resented doing. She needed to know that despite his erratic behavior, "you, your efforts, your problems, your welfare" were all things he wanted to respond to the best he could.[13]

While Melvyn could understand Helen's concerns about Peter, he continued, he wondered if part of her "torment" was that she felt guilty, felt that she might be to blame for his problems. If so, "you must get rid of it." The best we can do, he reassured her, is to learn as we go along and "apply our accumulated wisdom" to daily problems. Second, he queried if she was upset because Peter had not turned out to be "what you would like him to be," or feeling a fervent hope that he would not be hurt. But the two of them needed to realize that Peter was his own person, and he was on his own. They could best help him, not by protecting him, but by being responsive when he asked for help.[14]

Although Helen tolerated Melvyn's lengthy absences, she felt pushed to the limit at certain times, and the 1950s became increasingly painful. Melvyn had reputedly cultivated several extramarital relationships over the course of their marriage, and at least one during the Chicago run of Ginger. Her answer was to give him the freedom she felt he needed. Despite his absence of over two years, for example, she urged him not to feel guilty about vacationing alone in Europe after leaving Melbourne. She had only recently been there and felt she needed to be home for Peter. "We miss you but are so happy that you are enjoying your trip that it makes up for that. And darling your letters are simply beautiful." Peter seemed happier than he had ever been, she reported cheerfully. His life at Columbia University seemed to be helping him find himself. Thoughts of their short story program helped sustain her. But shortly after Melvyn returned home from Australia, Paul Muni, starring on Broadway as Clarence Darrow in Inherit the Wind, became seriously ill; Melvyn was asked to replace him. He could not bring himself to pass up this opportunity. Although Melvyn only replaced Muni for two months, he subsequently was cast as Darrow for the national tour. The Douglases persuaded their friend Basil Rathbone to replace Melvyn in the short story program, but despite the good reviews, it obviously was not the same. "It was kind of dreary," Helen recalled. Then, in a despondent letter to Nan in August of 1956, Helen wrote that she thought they should rent out the Park Avenue apartment and move into something smaller, because it "looks like Mel is going to England" for a long run of Inherit the Wind after a year-long American tour.[15]

Although the English trip did not materialize, Melvyn accepted work touring in several other plays. The family finally moved to 50 Riverside Drive on the West Side, a sunny, moderate-sized apartment on the corner of Seventy-seventh Street. Melvyn did end up in New York in 1960 with the lead role in The Best Man, which enjoyed a run of over eighteen months before it went on tour. But with Melvyn finally based in New York, Helen often made plans to leave when Melvyn was in town because he seemed so depressed and unhappy at home. She took Mary Helen to Europe for a vacation and participation in a weight-loss program. Although she felt guilty about not making it back for the opening of a show and even more concerned when he collapsed onstage from heat and exhaustion, she did not return, as Mel urged her not to worry. He was fine, he said, and while he wanted her there it would be playing when she returned. If the play was lousy, he reassured her, it would not be worth her coming home early. He took a turn at parenting, calling Peter daily and reporting family doings to Helen and Mary. Helen also continued to go to Vermont, even when Melvyn had work in New York. She missed him, she wrote in the summer of 1960. There were "children under every bush," Peter's, Greg's, and various grandnieces and nephews. The fields were filled with goldenrod, and the only real problem she faced was enduring hip and back pain. She was spending lots of time reading newspapers, particularly about the presidential race between Nixon and John F. Kennedy.[16]

One of Helen's acquaintances who became particularly close during these difficult years with Melvyn was Philip J. Noel-Baker, a long-time distinguished member of the British House of Commons and a leader since World War I in disarmament issues. Douglas had met Noel-Baker in the fall of 1946 at the United Nations when they both sat on the Social and Economic Committee. The two exchanged a few letters during the 1956 election, but in 1958, Noel-Baker began writing more frequently to get her advice about various political issues. He wrote her in detail about a manuscript in progress calling for total abolition of nuclear and conventional weapons. "It is a smashing case against that Son of Belial, John Foster Dulles," President Eisenhower's secretary of state, who had implemented the arms buildup. A year later, Noel-Baker received the Nobel Peace Prize for the published version, *The Arms Race—A Programme for World Disarmament.*

The side benefits of this award, he wrote, were frequent trips to the United States. He looked to Douglas to brief him about American politics and help him make connections in Washington. Douglas did all this as well as serve as a sounding board for Noel-Baker's concerns about disarmament. She sent him copies of speeches and kept him abreast of congressional politics, which she followed through daily home delivery of the *Congressional Record*. They also enjoyed a warm friendship. After their reunion in 1959 he wrote, "I left New York feeling that I wanted to take you out to dinner every night for a year, instead of two nights in ten years." A year later, after dinner together, he wrote how much he missed her and how he did not want to stop talking. After a party Douglas gave for Noel-Baker in 1961, he thanked her profusely for bringing together people who helped him in his talks with Adlai Stevenson, Kennedy's appointment as United States Ambassador to the United Nations. But the most important part of the evening was "listening to you and thinking that your lovely dress showed that you were still as clever as you are beautiful!" He urged her repeatedly to do disarmament talks as a team with him, but she never agreed.[17]

Despite Helen's efforts to stave off frustration and tension in her marriage, the relationship reached a crisis at the end of 1960. Melvyn left the cast of *The Best Man*, physically and emotionally exhausted and depressed, and departed for Malaga, Spain, a place where he felt he could begin to heal. He had no idea of how long he would be gone. He felt guilty and ambivalent about leaving. But he realized his "consciousness, as well as my conscience will continue to be divided. This is the fate of man; the struggle between fireside and adventure—as old as Odysseus." Once he reached Malaga, he settled into a comfortable seaside apartment with a sunny balcony and a swimming pool in the garden. His days were simple. After breakfast in the hotel, beginning Spanish lessons, lunch, and a nap, he then did whatever came along. He had no interest in sightseeing.[18]

Most of Helen's letters to him during this stay in Spain were similar to those of the past. One in particular, however, written a day after the couple's thirtieth wedding anniversary, revealed deep-seated worries. "This business of you not being happy unless you are pursuing your own desires . . . but torn with guilt in the process should be faced and cured if possible." Maybe his guilt would be enough to spur him to action. She urged him to see a doctor she had seen in Rome. "You say when questioned by me on our marriage that you want it to continue. I wonder do you really. The reason I raise the question again and at this time is so that you may be freer to examine your own inner needs and desires . . . in the hope that this trip be more than a pleasant interlude in an otherwise dull and burdensome life." She admitted that she found herself unwilling to accept speaking engagements or even attend any meetings. "I just think I can't go." While she blamed it on people so uninformed or violent "that sane reasoning is drowned in a sea of meaningless words," it seems likely that her personal fears about her relationship with Melvyn also contributed to this withdrawal. She confessed that she felt some "inner distress" herself. "It is not pleasant to be thought of as a charge, and I very often feel that's all I can be for you." She worried that she crowded him in wanting to do things together when he was home. "It is too ridiculous to continue a life that makes you ill, or have you a disposition that needs to be depressed? . . . I keep asking myself if I have been unkind to you in not getting a divorce. . . . Find out how you would like to spend the hours of this last glorious stretch of life—are periodic hunting trips enough? Is there enough for you to come back to?"[19]

She then enumerated the reasons she had not divorced him after his affair twenty years before. She loved him and she did not believe in divorce. She also could not believe what had happened, so she "suffered dumbly." "Now 20 years have passed . . . I do not suffer as I did. I love you differently and deeper, less of myself in it. But you are tormented with ulcers. You are not gay and relaxed about our relationship. Is this your character or do you really want out and do you resent me for not having long ago broken the bonds which you would feel too much guilt to break. Surely Melvyn dear we are friends after 30 years. . . . This letter is not written to make you miserable (and I am not miserable) but to leave you free to do what you want to do if you find out what it is." Her distress was confused by mutual expressions of tender love. Melvyn had written Mary Helen specific instructions for buying flowers to celebrate the Douglases' thirtieth anniversary. He hoped Helen had received the flowers "to remind you that I love you very deeply." She answered, "The flowers are utterly beautiful. . . . Mary has made two sketches of them. Thank you dear. I kiss and embrace you."[20]

Although Melvyn's answer to Helen's letter about divorce is missing, it is clear that he wanted to remain married. Helen responded to one letter that "it was very well reasoned and also leads me to believe you are taking stock of just how you do feel, emotionally as well as physically." She urged him not to hurry home, to return only when he felt ready. "It has nothing to do with us not loving each other, as I see it, just that you need to have the time and trip you have been promising yourself for so long." Money should not be an issue at this point, she emphasized. If necessary she could sell some of her oil stock. He was not in a "frame of mind or spirit or ambition or body to work this summer." She understood this "perfectly" and she was the only one who needed to understand. She was fine, rested from a trip to visit family in Florida, and she looked forward to summer in Vermont. "I will have Mary, my constant delight, and many other pleasures." And Mary Helen felt no resentment. "We love you dearly and want you to have cake and eat it. And what is more I am made very happy to know you want to hear from us. You are not deserting us. . . . In fact I often am walking with you—sitting in a cafe and looking at the passersby." Melvyn worried about Helen. He asked Nan Stevens to let him know if problems occurred at home, like "something worrisome that Helen would rather not burden me with."[21]

In June, Melvyn began to feel emotionally and physically stronger and surprised everyone, even himself, by accepting a small but challenging part in *Billy Budd*, a film in which Peter Ustinov was the star and director. "It is decidedly interesting, a definite cut above the ordinary," and would be filmed on an eighteenth-century warship. The talented and congenial Ustinov wanted Mel to play the part of an "old man of the sea," mystic and rather "mysterious," the "voice" of the play's theme. Melvyn hoped that since part of the filming would take place in London, the opportunity might open up other possibilities. He planned to return home in mid-August and join *The Best Man* cast in Chicago. He felt happy because he was making some money, gaining good experience, yet still feeling free to "move as the spirit suggests." He was pleased that Vermont was providing a real "tonic" for Helen and Mary. "I can visualize the two of you . . . which makes my heart pick up a pleasurable beat."[22]

Helen urged Melvyn not to come home until just before beginning *The Best Man* unless he tired of Europe. She was livid, however, at the Hollywood gossip columnist Louella Parsons for writing that the Douglases had separated. "How can anyone not believe," Helen wrote, "that a couple intend to stay married with one member off in Europe for a vacation. . . . What idiots people are, really. I must say it upsets me even though I know better. . . . The need to *hate* is the strongest of our compulsions." Several days later Helen was even more distraught. People were calling. She begged Melvyn to contact his agent to set the record straight. She felt the way she did when Parsons wrote a similar story about them after only one year of marriage. "What vultures they all are. . . . Incapable of understanding behavior that is the least bit out of the ordinary. That's why they are so dull *and malicious*." Fortunately the issue died down quickly. When Melvyn returned, Helen accompanied him to Chicago. She enrolled in drawing classes at a nearby art school. "I adore drawing," she wrote Nan Stevens; "silly, isn't it." But their happy new routine was suddenly broken when Melvyn developed a perforated ulcer in his stomach and underwent surgery. "Oh, dear me, he has been sick, narrowly escaped death," Helen wrote Stevens.[23]

The long hospital stay, during which Helen remained close by Melvyn's side, culminated a year of turmoil that in retrospect was a turning point in their relationship. After 1961, they began to spend much more time together. Although Melvyn continued to take jobs away from New York, Helen began joining him for long blocks of time, even occasionally during the summer, which took her away from Vermont. In Los Angeles they stayed regularly at the elegant and fashionable Château Marmont. They established a regular pattern of wintering in Mexico. Both Melvyn's and Helen's letters indicate that they had become less restless. They also had entered a stage of life when various health problems often shaped the course of their daily routines, and the tender nurturing of each other, particularly Helen's of Melvyn, became very important to both.

As the couple grew older, their children matured into adulthood and increased independence. They often visited each other and remained in touch with their parents. Helen and Melvyn continued to offer financial support and encouragement. Mary Helen had shown talent early in the arts, and her parents encouraged her in exploring a variety of directions. She painted "with great concentration and pleasure—really lovely patterns and her pictures are simply jumping with colors," Helen wrote Melvyn at one point. Mary Helen also explored life in an Israeli kibbutz and did a stint at the Barter Theatre in

Virginia. In her mid-twenties, her interests broadened to include weaving. Her parents sent her to Europe in the mid-1960s, where she had the opportunity to work with weavers in Israel, Sweden, and other countries. In 1966, Mary entered the Peace Corps. She ended up in Medellín, Columbia, working with children, using theater as a technique to encourage creative writing. Helen visited her and wrote Melvyn that she found Mary "more mature, more positive, independent, very resourceful, very able." Typical parents, the Douglases sometimes worried about her casting about in different directions. But "I don't think we can push Mary," Helen felt. "She will find her way and we must be patient and let her do so. She enchants all whom she meets and the more I see of her, the more I admire and deeply love her. She is a rare human being, unbelievably sweet and good." Melvyn told Helen when their daughter visited him in Texas on the set of *Hud* that she looked "more than ever like a goddess. . . . And she talks—to me, to everyone, questioning, searching, and pouring out her beautiful soul." She shed "a warm and nurturing light on adults, children, animals, flowers—whatever she comes in contact with. She is really remarkable."[24]

Peter graduated from Columbia University, married Jane, and started a family. He completed a master's degree at Columbia in social work. Melvyn commented that Peter had met "all kinds of obstacles . . . frustrations and resentments. . . . He was knocked down and almost out several times but something kept pushing him on. . . . And once he found it, he tended it with such care and consistency that it now throws a clear and steady beam." After graduation, he became certified as a therapist and worked with disturbed children and adults. Letters between the Douglases also reveal concern for Greg. Although he had been a part of the Douglas household for only a brief period during the early years of the war and had moved to Europe and married in the mid-1940s, Helen worried about him. She urged Melvyn to be in touch with his son. "He really never had a home life, *ever*—just when he thought he was going to have you and desperately wanted your love, your advice, the war took you away." After several years in Europe in the 1950s, Greg eventually settled in Connecticut, raising his three children with his third wife. He, too, had artistic talent and held various arts management and teaching positions.[25]

Slowly but noticeably Helen's public life took on a new energy and direction. In 1960 Helen had begun working for her brother Walter as secretary to the board of the Gahagan Dredging Company. She frequented the New York office, advising her brother on overseas projects, undertaking a history of the company, and participating actively in board decisions. The company had prospered; Gahagan had taken on various projects in South America, particularly Venezuela. Helen's sister Lilli also worked for the company during this period, as did Evie Chavoor. This job provided Helen some additional income and an opportunity to be around her brother, sister, and close friend. In May 1962, Helen took a major trip to Central and South America to check out possible new dredging jobs and to investigate the Alliance for Progress that President Kennedy had established in 1961. She planned to visit Peace Corps, CARE, AID, and Food for Peace projects with the hope of using this material for lectures. Although Helen had already made trips to Venezuela and Panama, this trip proved an enormous undertaking emotionally and logistically. Lyndon Johnson, then Kennedy's vice-president, the Rockefeller Foundation, government agency heads, United Nations friends, and her brother helped her set up an impressive itinerary to ten countries in Central and South America. She structured her trip carefully, much as she had previous study trips, such as one to the Middle East in 1952. She had learned her approach from Paul Taylor and Dorothea Lange when she began studying California migrants. Taylor would "feed me statistics" all day long, and Lange taught her what to look at— particularly facial expressions. To help her note-taking, she took a tape recorder and a camera. "For one who can't work the TV or anything else mechanical," she wrote in her round-robin letters to family and friends, "this is very optimistic."[26]

She generally stayed as the guest of the American ambassador in each country, who provided her contacts and set up briefings and transportation, often jeeps into the backcountry. In Guatemala, in addition to visiting village programs, she hoped to find the Indian group who had made her favorite scarf, a "scarf that makes friends for me. . . . All want to touch it. . . . It is gay and comforting." She discovered that the pattern was common throughout the northern part of the country. "We had the same love of the same colors. . . . It related me to their ancient culture in a very personal way." The apparent success of lively programs in Colombia impressed her the most. The massive land ownership of the Catholic Church and resultant Indian poverty in Peru shocked her. She did not particularly like Argentina; the political unrest and Perónist activists disturbed her, as did the economic dislocation brought on by Perón's attempt in the 1950s to industrialize the country. She found Brazil's size impressive and the scenery "awesome." The country seemed "short on everything," but "the richness and potential power is as great as the U.S." Her "stomach was *full of sick babies* and my eyes full of nature's wonders." When she returned, she reported her findings to appropriate Washington agency heads and others who had helped her. Overall, she found the Alliance for Progress a very "sensible" plan. The projects were impressive and stimulated private action. The Latin American countries were "learning how to go about developing—asking for help is understandable when you *see* conditions." She returned "enthusiastic" about the Peace Corps (she had visited every project), CARE, AID, and religious groups. She had not expected to find priests involved in development projects. She emphasized the importance of assessing each country individually; the Latin Americans resented being treated by the United States government as if they were all one nation.[27]

In addition to Douglas's busy schedule away from New York, she worked on projects while at home and resumed an active speaking schedule. When Eleanor Roosevelt died in 1962, the publishing house Hill and Wang contacted her to write a text to accompany a group of photographs spanning Roosevelt's life, collected by Aaron J. Ezickson. Douglas's essay recaptured some of Roosevelt's unique contributions both as First Lady and in the years after FDR died. Douglas based the essay on her personal relationship with ER, and it gave Douglas a chance to put into print what the First Lady had meant to her. The Douglases' first visit to the White House in November 1939, Helen recalled, was "the beginning of a warm and cherished friendship that took me out of the theatre . . . and into politics. The First Lady collected people . . . to cross-fertilize creative minds." Douglas made clear that she had modeled herself after Roosevelt. "Politics for Mrs. Roosevelt . . . meant getting things done. . . . Her way of self-education, study and seeing for yourself, became the ideal for the new political woman. Her example made women believe that individual effort could mean something."[28]

The book, with a handsome cover photo by the noted portrait photographer Philippe Halsman, came out before any other biographies. It was well reviewed and sold nicely. Journalists praised the photographs, anecdotes, the "perceptive" insights, and the "affectionate, warmly personal sketch." Douglas sent the book to dozens of friends and numerous politicians, among them the ambassadors of the Latin American countries she visited in 1962; to LBJ, Frances Bolton, John McCormack, Adlai Stevenson, Philip Noel-Baker, Hubert Humphrey, and Abe Fortas. She also included two dozen organizations on her list, such as the National Consumers League and the Peace Corps. She enjoyed the response. The old New Dealers loved it. Representative Chet Holifield wrote how much it made him miss the old California New Dealers—Douglas, Voorhis, George Outland, and Leisa Bronson. Roosevelt's daughter Anna Roosevelt Halsted wrote that she was really pleased. "You have pointed out, and answered, so many questions about Mother which I do not believe have even occurred to many of the people who felt they knew her and loved her."[29]

In very early January of 1964, Douglas received an urgent request from Lyndon Johnson, now President, to serve as a special ambassador to head the United States delegation to the January 6 inauguration of President William V. S. Tubman of Liberia, an occasion that coincided with the one-hundredth anniversary of formal relations between the two countries. Douglas wrote LBJ January 4, "I am on my way! Believe me, it wasn't easy. Getting the proper attire for the occasion was almost as difficult as trying to get to the moon." As the fourth was a holiday, she had used some connections to get certain department stores opened, particularly Saks Fifth Avenue, so she could shop. President

Kennedy had selected the gift—copies of state papers between President Abraham Lincoln and Liberian leaders. Douglas also took a letter from Kennedy dated November 21, 1963, one of his last official letters before his assassination, and a message from Johnson. The venture was exciting; Tubman was touched by the gifts, and the president of Fisk University, a member of the delegation, wrote LBJ that he could not have selected a "more gracious and articulate person" to head the delegation. Much to some insiders' surprise and disappointment, Johnson did not ask Douglas to consider any other positions, despite his early administrative push to bring more women into high-level appointments. Both Senator Hubert Humphrey and Helen Fuller suggested the President appoint Douglas to the AID Review Committee, and James G. Patton, president of the National Farm Union, urged consideration of Douglas for the Food Investigation Commission. But nothing came of these ideas.[30]

Shortly after she returned from Liberia, the Jane Addams Peace Association invited Douglas to join a delegation of "prominent gals" in March for the second meeting of Russian and American women sponsored by the Women's International League for Peace and Freedom. The fascinating trip, while not a "fact-finding" mission, reinforced her belief that the Russians sought peace and provided her with excellent lecture material. Before accepting, she asked Johnson if he had any objections to her going. When she returned, she wrote him a long summary of the conference. Her letter began "Dear Lyndon, Dear, Dear Lyndon." The Russian women had warmly received the group, she told him. "I think the driving motivation was the desire for peace." Soviet women seemed to want to trust the United States. They asked probing questions about complete disarmament, the role of the United Nations, and possibilities for peaceful coexistence. But the most important information she had to report was a conversation she had at the Moscow Airport as she was leaving. She spoke with the conference hostess, Tamarce Y. Mamedova, secretary of the Institute of Soviet–American Relations and a close friend of the wife of Russian leader Nikita S. Khrushchev. Mamedova asked Douglas if Johnson were really sincere when he spoke of peace and disarmament, and indicated Khrushchev wanted peace. Douglas urged Johnson to reach out to the Russian leader, for he feared "putting his head in a noose." Johnson never acknowledged the letter. Douglas remained convinced he never received it, because "I had word that it would have been helpful to him."[31]

In the fall of 1964, after spending time with Melvyn, who was filming in Spain, she campaigned hard for Johnson both out of loyalty to her old friend and her tremendous fear of the far right, represented by Senator Barry Goldwater, Johnson's opponent. As early as 1961 she began expressing these fears. Speaking in Westport, Connecticut, she had about twenty John Birch Society "enthusiasts" in the large audience. "I thought I handled myself very well. They had come to torment me and break up the meeting," she wrote Melvyn.

After the meeting, Birchers were handing out flyers that were reminiscent of her Red-baited campaigns—"incredible. Nothing to it but fascinating to keep as an exhibit of how these people work." She figured some "intelligent people were behind the movement. Some say Senator Goldwater." Johnson's victory in 1964 reduced her concerns to some degree. After a talk to over 2,000 students at North Georgia College who were "all alert Democrats," she wrote Melvyn that the "strange exhausted feeling, not at all like normal weariness" had subsided. "Perhaps as you say the bad sensation was induced by my great concern over the extreme right wing. Really, Melvyn, they are fascist and too many listen to and believe all that is said. Perhaps my reaction to this campaign *was* physical as well as intellectual. . . . I suddenly remembered my revulsion, my sensations in Europe in 1937 where I felt . . . that I could not return to Vienna and sing in the opera though that had been my heart's desire because those I had respected in the music world had revealed themselves to be Nazis. . . . I am swept by emotions, all that I have done has come out of deep motivations not intellectual analysis. . . . Now I get satisfaction out of these lectures because I resist the evil forces that so repel me. I know in a small way I have helped and this gives me relief." [32]

Despite feeling somewhat less ill-at-ease about the far right, the gradual buildup of American forces in Vietnam intensified her concerns about prospects for world peace and total disarmament. A long-time board member of the National Committee for a Sane Nuclear Policy (SANE), she had co-chaired the 1964 Peace Pledge Campaign to raise funds to pressure the administration for a cease-fire in Vietnam and to support peace candidates. During her campaigning for Johnson, she continuously sounded the alarm about pressures from the military to escalate the war. She desperately wanted Johnson to be the president remembered as the one implementing disarmament. After the 1964 election she sent Johnson a note: "You ask for prayers—you have mine, every day, every hour." Did he still want "reports from informed people in the field?" Johnson answered to send whatever she thought would be helpful. He closed with much love from him and Lady Bird. Initially she thought Johnson might well fulfill her expectations. Six weeks after Johnson took office she praised him for the way he was handling matters and sent him an article by Noel-Baker, "The Way to World Disarmament—Now." Prime Minister Harold Wilson thought Noel-Baker was "the top fellow on the subject of disarmament," she added. [33]

But her relationship with the President deteriorated quickly as Johnson followed the advice of his military advisors and escalated the war, beginning in the spring of 1965. Helen saw him several times at the White House during this period, and he would not listen to her. Johnson's willingness to pursue a foreign policy that Douglas despised and felt was morally wrong ruptured their friendship. A letter to Senator William Fulbright conveyed her feelings. A May 1966 *Washington Post* article, "Fulbright Is Feeling 'Isolated and Discouraged,' " prompted her to write Fulbright: "I almost phoned you in the middle of the night," she told him. She praised his hearings as chairman of the Senate Foreign Relations Committee. They had been so "effective"; it was critical to question America's foreign policy in public. "But I suppose there is no escape from discouragement as long as our foreign policy is so misguided." She agreed with Fulbright that LBJ had "very great capacity. He, more than any president since Roosevelt, could have started us on a sound disarmament program." But the military had pushed him into the role of the "world's police." If he only could admit that American involvement in Vietnam had always been "a tragic miscalculation," he had the political ability and courage to get himself out of the situation. Fulbright wrote back immediately. He felt Johnson was unaware of the dissent "and tends to think I am the only one who is not supporting him." Fulbright found it hard to get in contact with Johnson, given the situation, "to reason with him." Douglas's estrangement extended to Vice-President Hubert Humphrey when he ran for President in 1968. Both Helen and Melvyn refused to campaign for him, despite their long-term support. In fact, Douglas had worked to connect Noel-Baker with Humphrey because of his sympathy with disarmament. But he, like LBJ, could not let go of the Vietnam struggle. At the end of the campaign, Helen finally relented and made some campaign tapes; she felt "so sorry for him" because Nixon was using the same techniques as he had in 1950 against Douglas "to impugn Humphrey's loyalty." [34]

The death of Helen's sister Lilli in the spring of 1968 compounded the melancholy brought on by the war. As children, their differences in personality and interests and Lilli's determination to try to attain Helen's acting success interfered with an intimate relationship. But with time, the two became close friends, seeking out each other's company. Helen later reminisced with tender amusement about their differences. Lilli had no concern for social problems or political matters. While they both liked clothes and "beautiful things," Helen hated to shop and had no interest in the socially élite, while Lilli thrived on keeping up with current fashion and attending fancy society functions. In 1967, Lilli developed cancer, just as her father and brother had. In March 1968, Helen flew to Palm Springs to stay with Lilli as she underwent cobalt treatments. "Nobody took care of her as I did," she recalled. Helen took a break on April 4 to fly to New York and join Melvyn for their anniversary and his birthday the following day. Lilli died alone on the fifth; her son Herbie had left for a walk. Helen accepted her death—"I don't have a bad feeling about death at all"—but it devastated her that Lilli died alone. "I really agonized over this, after Lillian died. Although we were so different, and our values . . . so disparate, I felt so keenly her going that I canceled all engagements. I didn't speak hardly for a year after that . . . and then very slowly came back." [35]

*

Douglas did become active again. Unexpected circumstances, however, added new dimensions to the last eight years of her life. In the spring of 1972, she underwent surgery for breast cancer. Helen's health prior to 1972 had been fairly good, particularly compared to Melvyn's. In addition to the perforated ulcer, he developed heart and back problems and had a bout with skin cancer. Helen had had her share of unpleasant health problems. She, too, suffered increasingly from back pain. In 1962 and 1963 she had serious stomach hemorrhaging resulting in long and difficult recuperative periods without Melvyn because of his work schedule. Melvyn and her friends worried in general about her energy level and frequently admonished her to slow down. But aside from her aching back, she did not experience life-threatening illnesses. When she learned she had cancer, she turned inward for strength. As Nan Stevens said, "She went to Vermont to make peace with her surgery. And then she had it, by herself."[36]

By fall, after a late-spring operation, she began campaigning for the Democratic presidential candidate, Senator George McGovern. She found the campaign impossible to resist—with a peace candidate running against incumbent Richard Nixon. As she told a *New York Post* reporter, when the McGovern people asked her for help during the summer, she did not think she could face it. Then "I looked at what was going on. This administration is the greatest snow job in history." Americans needed a candidate to unify, not divide them, and "I suddenly decided that I just had to get out there and work. Mel looked at me cross-eyed." She did not like Nixon, she stated flatly to students at the State University of New York at Binghamton. His "scandal a day" term had "hurt the American people and the American tradition" by virtually eliminating social programs, and increasing the military budget and the national deficit. Just as in 1950, Nixon did not talk about issues but rather "tricks his opponents into defending their stands." After her swing through upstate New York, she moved to an intense schedule in New Hampshire and Vermont, accompanied at times by Melvyn. She spoke with "undisguised scorn and indignation . . . sounding at times like an orator well-primed for a debate." She accused Nixon of lacking "respect for the processes" of a free society, destroying American prestige abroad, and supporting a conflict "more divisive than the Civil War." In short, a "moral sickness" had resulted. As in 1950, Nixon accused his opponent of being "soft on Communism." A press release on October 30 from the McGovern New York campaign headquarters presented Douglas's detailed comparison of the 1950 and 1972 campaigns, indicating virtually no difference in Nixon's tactics. In her talks, she rarely referred to her surgery except to say, somewhat melodramatically, that she had experienced considerable pain " 'but I welcomed that pain. . . . That was one way I could share what the Vietnamese people are going through.' "[37]

Douglas ignored warnings to slow down; she fought death. As the election drew to a close, she began working on her autobiography and also embarked on a substantial project with the Regional Oral History Office (ROHO) located at The Bancroft Library at the University of California, Berkeley. Amelia Fry conceived of and directed the project. Her preparation for Fry's interviews, which took place over a period of several years, and the transcripts from the interviews became the basis for writing her own book. She consistently turned away potential biographers.

In 1973, as Douglas began to get involved in the autobiography projects, the Watergate hearings began. The intense focus on Nixon's presidency expanded to scrutiny of his entire political career. Political women of the decade not only learned about Douglas but made her, once again, center stage. She had never lost her ability to draw a crowd—during the 1960s she had frequently spoken to groups of one to two thousand. She maintained her access to Washington's liberal circles, and she received recognition and numerous awards. But Douglas's popularity spread from college students and liberal organizations to the large activist women's political organizations responsible for a major push to elect female candidates. In October 1973, the new and popular feminist magazine *Ms* chose her for their cover story. Lee Israel's long and sympathetic article heightened awareness about Douglas among young feminists and brought dozens of speaking invitations to Douglas's door, some addressed to her simply as "Helen Gahagan Douglas, Vermont." [38]

In November 1973, she gave the keynote address at a large New England conference, "The Changing Role of Women in Politics," sponsored by the Democratic National Committee. That same month, the Women's Lobby, Inc., a Washington-based lobby group for women's issues, selected Douglas to sign their major fund-raising letter. In the next two months, she made so many speeches that she had become "thoroughly sick" of the sound of her voice. When she spoke at the Women's National Democratic Club in Washington, her old friend Supreme Court Justice William O. Douglas introduced her. In her speech, entitled "How Did We Get Where We Are, and Where Do We Go from Here?" she assessed the Nixon presidency. The event was so oversubscribed that the organizers eliminated luncheon tables, set up over 500 chairs, and the women juggled their sparse lunches on thin paper plates. [39]

Douglas also spoke to another gathering of Democratic women on the place of women in politics, offering a more pessimistic and realistic view than she had held while in Congress. "Women do not, as yet, participate in any meaningful way in the formulation of national policies." Women "have been brainwashed, made to think we can't think, just as certainly as the minorities." Women need first to be well informed about the facts and then collectively work together to develop "female clout," which meant "becoming aware of issues . . . study, study, study . . . getting at the meat of a matter, developing the capacity to explain and discuss it with those less informed." Two months later, at a big luncheon in Los Angeles sponsored by the Democratic Women's Forum, she called for Nixon's impeachment. The *Los Angeles Times* headlines read "Helen Douglas? They're Paying Attention Now." Yet despite her willingness to speak to these groups, the renaissance of interest rankled Douglas: "Is it only now that [people] are beginning to use their heads again? I don't like being called a cult."[40]

But she kept going, and her prestige continued to climb. Several weeks later she was back in Washington participating in "The 1974 Campaign Conference for Democratic Women," which assembled congresswomen, state legislators, candidates—both men and women—and political activists from all over the country. A month later she was at Dartmouth College for four days as Woman in Residence and then commencement-time alumnae reunion speaker at Barnard College. Later that fall, she joined Margaret Chase Smith and Jeanne Kirkpatrick as the three key speakers for a "Women in Politics" program at Indiana State University. On that occasion she received her first honorary degree. The American Civil Liberties Union of Southern California honored both Helen and Melvyn in December of 1974 as "people who have stood fast for civil liberties and humanitarian principles." In May 1975, Vermont's Marlboro College also awarded her an honorary degree when she came to give the commencement address. In between these major occasions, she made numerous talks for local groups, endorsed candidates, and agreed to dozens of interviews following Nixon's resignation in August 1974.[41]

During this period of the mid-1970s when Helen experienced both personal trauma and the national limelight, Melvyn played some of his best roles and received many awards for his acting. In 1970, he starred in the television movie *I Never Sang for My Father*, and in 1972 he did *The Candidate* with Robert Redford. *I Never Sang for My Father* was a poignant story of a father and grown son who wanted very much to love each other. The father, whose own father had abandoned the family when he was young, lacked the emotional skills to reach out to his son, even as he was dying. The relationship remained unresolved. Both Melvyn and Gene Hackman, who played the son, won Emmy awards. One can only speculate that Melvyn had accepted that role because it fit his own emotional makeup. Melvyn commented that out of his more than eighty films, he felt "most comfortable" with this film and the 1939 *Ninotchka*. Despite the busy film schedule, however, he and Helen continued to spend time with each other and continued their habit of vacationing winters in Mexico and spending much of each summer in Vermont.[42]

In 1976, however, the patterns began to shift again. Helen's cancer recurred in the left lung. She underwent chemotherapy. Doctors suggested that her schedule in the past four years had perhaps been too intense. She agreed to cut her speaking schedule, mainly because her energy level had dropped, and began to work with renewed intensity on her autobiography. But she continued to support organizations such as the Women's International League for Peace and Freedom, the Women's Lobby, and the Women's Campaign Fund by signing solicitation letters. "At these last days of my life," she told Amelia Fry, "it seems important that I endorse. . . . The phone is busy ringing from all parts of the country." She went up to Vermont as early as possible in the spring and returned only after weather became impossibly cold in the fall. Friends visited her frequently in Vermont to "see if I am still standing on my feet—out of love," she wrote Stevens. Fortunately, most of her close friends were still living, and she kept up a lively correspondence, although she deeply missed Helen Fuller, who had died in 1972, and Dan Totheroh, who died in 1976. Occasionally Douglas still made front-page news. In 1977, she could not resist a New Deal reunion, nor could she turn down an opportunity to participate in a reading of the United States Constitution at New York's Broadway Theatre, a program sponsored by the William O. Douglas Inquiry into the State of Individual Freedom. Dartmouth College awarded honorary degrees to both Douglases in 1977.[43]

In March 1979, when the cancer spread to her hip bone, Douglas began another round of chemotherapy and radium treatments. But she managed to attend the ceremony when Barnard College selected her for its Medal of Distinction. She "painfully limped to center stage with the help of a cane and the support of an escort." Nan Stevens, whose sense of humor did much to bolster morale, quipped on the way to the ceremony, "Would you believe you are probably the only college dropout to get an honorary degree?" In August 1979, shortly before painful hip-replacement surgery, she received national coverage when she testified on cancer by phone to the Subcommittee on Aging at the request of the committee chairman, Congressman Claude Pepper. Groups continued to honor her. The Academy of Science Fiction, Fantasy and Horror Films awarded her a Golden Scroll Award for her lead role in *She*, forty-five years after the film had been released. This recognition greatly amused Helen. Walter Hofstötter, her European opera agent, proposed a fifty-year celebration of her performance of *Tosca* with Herbert von Karajan at the Salzburg Festival. But the letter from Austria disturbed her. Even if she were well, she answered, "it would make me very sad to return to Salzburg," where she had realized the political direction of Austria. She also regretted that "the war interrupted my singing career in Europe." In October 1979, she, along with a group of other musicians, including Luciano Pavarotti and Leonard Bernstein, was invited to include one of her numerous paintings in a gallery exhibit, "Musicians as Artists." Also in the fall, PBS did a one-hour interview with her.[44]

Although Melvyn continued to suffer from health problems, he stepped up his pace of filming. Family life at home had become increasingly stressful. Mary Helen spent considerable time at home caring for Helen as she became sicker. But the relationship between Melvyn and his children, particularly Mary Helen, became very tense. Melvyn's solution apparently was to stay away from New York as much as possible, a painful choice for both Helen and Melvyn. But he felt determined to get through his final years "with some dignity, without completely collapsing morally, physically, or mentally," as he put it. Between 1976 and 1980, he made seven feature films and one television movie. He played an old, senile politician in *The Seduction of Joe Tynan*, and a dying industrialist in *Being There* with Peter Sellers and Shirley MacLaine, for which he received his second Academy Award. In 1979, he co-starred in *Tell Me a Riddle*, a touching movie about an aging immigrant couple. With this sort of schedule, Helen and Melvyn spent little time together in New York, although they constantly communicated by phone. Melvyn also did go to Vermont as much as he could.[45]

Despite Helen's determination to keep going, her energy dwindled. Yet she continued to work several hours each day on her autobiography, racing against time to finish; edited ROHO transcripts; and kept up her correspondence. In June 1980, she became too ill to stay at home and entered Sloan-Kettering Cancer Institute; she died on June 28 with her family and Nan Stevens by her side, at the age of seventy-nine. The family gathered for a memorial at Cliff Mull where her ashes were buried. Melvyn planned a public memorial service, held on December 2, 1980, at the simple but elegant First Unitarian Church on the Upper East Side of Manhattan. On April 5, 1981, Melvyn's eightieth birthday and what would have been the couple's fiftieth wedding anniversary, Melvyn had a small dinner party; following an old Chinese tradition, he set an extra place for Helen. Melvyn died four months later.

Helen had come close to completing her autobiography. Melvyn hired a writer to finish the manuscript, and Doubleday published *A Full Life* in 1982. While the book received wide critical attention, it did not sell well. As Abigail McCarthy wrote for *New York Magazine*, the "power and passion" of Douglas's personality did not come through. The book was a "stringing together of reminiscences" and "flatly told anecdotes interspersed with artless quotations from press clippings." It did, however, chronicle important events in which Douglas played a role, with "revealing glimpses" of famous people and a "free and loving marriage." Most of all, it told the story of a person "true to herself in her own place and in her own time"; a very appropriate comment.[46]

Douglas worked so diligently and for so long on this work that perhaps she would have been disappointed with the poor reception. But her legacy goes far beyond the memoirs she left behind, beyond her image as a glamorous Hollywood figure, beyond the myths of the 1950 campaign. She used dynamic scripts—theatrical, operatic, and political—and her powerful presence to bring an audience alive and make them sensitive to the issues she presented. In this fashion, she touched thousands of lives and minds throughout her lifetime. Perhaps the secret to her power was, in her own words, "I never felt I left the stage."[47]

Abbreviations Used in the Notes

AFL	American Federation of Labor Papers, The Wisconsin State Historical Society
B	Box number
BL	Bancroft Library, University of California, Berkeley
CIO-PAC	Congress of Industrial Organizations, Political Action Committee Papers, The Archives of Labor History and Urban Affairs, Wayne State University
CO	Culbert Olson Papers, The Bancroft Library
Dewson	Mary M. (Molly) Dewson Papers, Franklin D. Roosevelt Library
DM	Dorothy McAllister Papers, Grand Rapids, Michigan, private collection
DNC	National Committee of the Democratic Party, Franklin D. Roosevelt Library
ERP	Anna Eleanor Roosevelt Papers, Franklin D. Roosevelt Library
F	Folder number
FDRL	Franklin D. Roosevelt Library
FDRP	Franklin D. Roosevelt Papers, Franklin D. Roosevelt Library
GC	George Creel Collection, Manuscript Division, Library of Congress
GT	George Tyler Papers, Theatre Archives, Princeton University Library
HGD	Helen Gahagan Douglas Papers, Carl Albert Congressional Research and Studies Center, University of Oklahoma
HGD-TMS	Helen Gahagan Douglas Papers, Theater Manuscript Collection, Carl Albert Congressional Research and Studies Center, University of Oklahoma

HI	Harold Ickes Papers, Manuscript Division, Library of Congress
HICCASP	Hollywood Independent Citizens' Committee of the Arts, Sciences, and Professions Papers, Special Collections, University of California, Los Angeles
HM	Hugh B. Mitchell Papers, Manuscripts Division, University of Washington
HMDP	Helen and Melvyn Douglas Papers, New York City, private collection
HSTL	Harry S Truman Library
HSTP	Harry S Truman Papers, Harry S Truman Library
JK	Jack Kroll Papers, Manuscript Division, Library of Congress
LBJL	Lyndon Baines Johnson Library
LBJP	Lyndon B. Johnson Papers, Lyndon B. Johnson Library
LC	Theatre Collection, The New York Public Library at Lincoln Center
LH	Lorena Hickok Papers, Franklin D. Roosevelt Library
MEL	Mary Ellen Leary Papers, The Bancroft Library
MD	Melvyn Douglas Papers, The State Historical Society of Wisconsin
NS	Nan Stevens Papers, New York City, private collection
OC	Oscar Chapman Papers, Harry S Truman Library
OK	Otto Kahn Papers, Theatre Archives, Princeton University Library
REL	Ruth and Ed Lybeck Papers, Special Collections, University of California, Los Angeles
RK	Robert Kenny Papers, The Bancroft Library
RKO	RKO Picture Archives, Los Angeles
ROHO	Regional Oral History Office, The Bancroft Library
SA	Shubert Theatre Archives, New York City
SC	Florence (Susie) Clifton Papers, The Bancroft Library
SD	Sheridan Downey Papers, The Bancroft Library
TWUA	Textile Workers Union of America Papers, The State Historical Society of Wisconsin
UAWPAC RR	United Auto Workers Political Action Committee, Roy Reuther Papers, The Archives of Labor History and Urban Affairs, Wayne State University
WD	Women's Division, National Committee of the Democratic Party Papers, Franklin D. Roosevelt Library
WP	Walter Pick Papers, Los Angeles, private collection
WS	Wayne State University
WSHS	The State Historical Society of Wisconsin

Introduction

1. My article "Helen Gahagan Douglas: Broadway Star as California Politician," *California History* 66 (December 1987): 242–61, 310–14, examines Douglas's public

life. I overview Douglas's Broadway career in "Helen Gahagan Douglas," *Notable Women in the American Theatre: A Biographical Dictionary*, ed. by Alice M. Robinson (New York: Greenwood Press, 1989), 218–22. I have chronicled my intellectual and personal experience in writing this biography in "Writing the Life of a Star: Helen Gahagan Douglas" in the forthcoming book I have co-edited with Sara Alpern, Joyce Antler, and Elizabeth Israels Perry, entitled *The Challenge of Feminist Biography*, which will be published by the University of Illinois Press in 1992.

2. These initial findings were published as "Helen Gahagan Douglas and Her 1950 Senate Race with Richard M. Nixon," *Southern California Historical Quarterly* 63 (Spring 1976): 113–26.

3. See my "Helen and Melvyn Douglas: Two Lives in Vermont," *Vermont Life* 36 (Summer 1982): 35–37, for the importance of Vermont to the Douglases.

4. See my "Helen Gahagan Douglas and the Roosevelt Connection," in Marjorie Lightman and Joan Hoff Wilson, eds., *Without Precedent: The Life and Career of Eleanor Roosevelt* (Bloomington: Indiana University Press, 1984), 153–75.

5. Richard F. Fenno, Jr., *Home Style: House Members in Their Districts* (Boston: Little, Brown, 1978) proved particularly useful in understanding Douglas's style; for quote see Ralph K. Huitt and Robert L. Peabody, *Congress: Two Decades of Analysis* (New York: Harper and Row, Publishers, 1969), 170.

6. I got various ideas from essays on writing biography as this book took shape from James F. Veninga, ed., *The Biographer's Gift: Life Histories and Humanism* (College Station: Texas A & M Press, 1983); Marc Pachter, ed., *Telling Lives: The Biographer's Art* (Philadelphia: University of Pennsylvania Press, 1981); William Zinsser, ed., *Extraordinary Lives: The Art and Craft of American Biography* (Boston: Houghton Mifflin Company, 1986); Leon Edel, *Writing Lives: Principia Biographica* (New York: W.W. Norton and Company, 1984); and Carol Ascher, Louise DeSalvo, and Sara Ruddick, *Between Women* (Boston: Beacon Press, 1984). I learned the most, however, from working with my co-editors on *The Challenge of Feminist Biography* (see note #1 above). The contributors are women historians who have published or are about to publish biographies of twentieth-century public women.

I have read numerous biographies of both men and women during the writing of *Center Stage*. I found several particularly helpful: Joyce Antler, *Lucy Sprague Mitchell: The Making of a Modern Woman* (New Haven: Yale University Press, 1987); Elizabeth Israels Perry, *Belle Moskowitz: Feminine Politics and the Exercise of Power in the Age of Alfred E. Smith* (New York: Oxford University Press, 1987); Kathryn Kish Sklar, *Catharine Beecher: A Study in American Domesticity* (New Haven: Yale University Press, 1973); Nancy J. Weiss, *Whitney M. Young, Jr., and the Struggle for Civil Rights* (Princeton: Princeton University Press, 1989); James T. Patterson, *Mr. Republican: A Biography of Robert A. Taft* (Boston: Houghton Mifflin, 1972); Susan Ware, *Partner and I: Molly Dewson, Feminism, and New Deal Politics* (New Haven: Yale University Press, 1987); and Sara Alpern, *Freda Kirchwey, A Woman of The Nation* (Cambridge: Harvard University Press, 1987).

Chapter 1

1. Helen Gahagan Douglas, *A Full Life* (Garden City, N.Y.: Doubleday, 1982), 20–21.

2. Walter Havighurst, *Ohio: A Bicentennial History* (New York: W. W. Norton, 1976), especially chaps. 3–7, and Harry N. Scheiber, *Ohio Canal Era: A Case Study*

of Government and the Economy, 1820–1861 (Athens, Ohio: Ohio University Press, 1969); Helen Gahagan Douglas, "Congresswoman, Actress, and Opera Singer," an oral history conducted 1973, 1974, and 1976 by Amelia Fry, in Helen Gahagan Douglas Oral History Project, Vol. IV, Regional Oral History Office, The Bancroft Library, University of California, Berkeley, 1982 (hereafter Douglas, ROHO), 1–2; *Historic Troy, Ohio* (Troy, Ohio: Troy Historical Society, 1976), 1–10; Gahagan family tree, Helen Gahagan Douglas and Melvyn Douglas Papers New York City, private collection (hereafter, HMDP). HMDP includes a variety of materials that the Douglases accumulated in their home. Some they used to write their autobiographies. After their deaths in 1980 and 1981, these papers were divided; a portion was sent to the archival collections of their papers at the University of Oklahoma and the State Historical Society of Wisconsin, others were distributed among family members, and others destroyed.

Family records differ as to whether William had a gunshot wound or a serious abdominal disease acquired in the early days of the war. Hannah Gahagan wrote a lengthy family history entitled "Four Families" (unpublished).

3. Martha Allen, interview with author, March 28, 1981; "Reminiscence by Mary Clyde," 1943 (HMDP), Douglas, ROHO, p. 24; and *The National Cyclopedia of American Biography* 22:12; Thomas Bemis Wheeler, *Troy: The Nineteenth Century* (Troy, Ohio: Troy Historical Society, 1970), 182; idem, *Troy Yesterday, Today, and Tomorrow* (Troy, Ohio: Hobart Brothers Co., 1948); Estella Baird Broomhall, *The Story of The Troy Altrurian Club, 1894–1934* (Troy, 1936); *The History of Miami County, Ohio* (Chicago: W. H. Beers and Co., 1880); *Historic Troy, Ohio*; biographical data on Altrurian Club presidents compiled by Virginia Booze; Gahagan, "Four Families"; Allen interview with author; and miscellaneous notes in HMDP.

4. Biographical accounts give both 1873 and 1874 as dates for Tamer's death. See also Douglas, *A Full Life*, 18–20.

5. Douglas, *A Full Life*, 20–21; *Lodi* [Wis.] *Enterprise*, July 26, 1907; and *History of Dane County* (Chicago: Western Historical Company, 1880).

6. Douglas, *A Full Life*, 21.

7. *Trow Business Directory of Brooklyn and Queens* for 1908 lists six contracting, three consulting, twelve electrical, and several dozen mechanical and civil engineers.

8. David Ment, *The Shaping of a City: A Brief History of Brooklyn* (Brooklyn: Brooklyn Rediscovery and Brooklyn Educational and Cultural Alliance, 1979), 56.

9. Ralph Foster Weld, *Brooklyn Is America* (New York: Columbia University Press, 1950), 85. See also Ment, *Shaping of a City*; and Rita Seiden Miller, ed., *Brooklyn, U.S.A.: The Fourth Largest City in America*, vol. 7 of *Brooklyn College Studies on Social Change* (Brooklyn: Brooklyn College Press, 1979).

10. Douglas, ROHO, 23–24; idem, *A Full Life*, 22.

11. For sections on Park Slope, see Brooklyn Rediscovery and Brooklyn Educational and Cultural Alliance, *Building Blocks of Brooklyn: A Study of Urban Growth* (Brooklyn: Brooklyn Educational and Cultural Alliance, 1979), 63–79. See also *Brooklyn Atlas* (1896); "Park Slope Historic District Designation Report," mimeographed, (New York, 1973), iii–vii; *Berkeley Institute* (1986) in Vertical File on Berkeley Institute, and pamphlet on Berkeley Institute [n.d.] in Brooklyn Historical Society; Douglas, ROHO, 27–28; Allen interview; Douglas, A Full Life, 23. A classic history of Brooklyn—Henry W. B. Howard, ed., *The Eagle and Brooklyn: History of the City of Brooklyn* (*Brooklyn Daily Eagle*, 1893)—has a full section on educational institutions. Howard discusses each school for boys at some length. He then lists a school for deaf mutes and concludes the section with brief discussions of the girls' schools (754).

12. Allen interview with author; Douglas, *A Full Life*, 23; idem, ROHO, 31–32;

Percy Waxman, "The Rise of Helen Gahagan," [n.p., n.d.], in Helen Gahagan Douglas Papers, Carl Albert Congressional Research and Studies Center, University of Oklahoma (hereafter, HGD).

13. Douglas, *A Full Life*, 28, 34–35.

14. Douglas, ROHO, 12, 18–19. Gay Gahagan interview with author, October 25, 1980.

15. Douglas, *A Full Life*, 25; idem, ROHO, 3–4.

16. Douglas, ROHO, 6, 18; Walter Gahagan, Jr., interview with author, October 26, 1980.

17. Douglas, ROHO, 19. Over the years, Walter's more than sixty projects for private enterprise and local and United States government, all in the millions of dollars, included constructing the Wanaque Dam for the East Jersey Water Supply Commission; dredging the Chesapeake and Delaware Canal and Hudson River between Coxsackie and Hudson, New York; constructing numerous cutoffs for railroads; and dredging and developing Jamaica Bay. (*New York Times*, December 20, 1930.)

Gahagan was active in the Associated General Contractors of America, the General Contractors Association of America (he was president of the New York chapter in 1925), the American Society of Civil Engineers, the fraternal organization of the Masons, and other organizations. As Walter expanded his business, one business became four: the Gahagan Dredging Company, the W. H. Gahagan Realty Company, Inc., the Gahagan Construction Corporation, and W. H. Gahagan, Inc. Biographical information on Gahagan appeared in the *New York Times*, December 20, 1930; *The National Cyclopedia*, 22:12; and in an obituary for *Transactions*, American Society of Civil Engineers, 1931.

18. Douglas, *A Full Life*, 24; idem, ROHO, 33; Walter Gahagan interview with author.

19. Howard, *The* Eagle *and Brooklyn*, 917; *Montauk Club Directory* for the years 1895 through 1930; Douglas, ROHO, 18.

20. Allen interview with author; Douglas, ROHO, 3, 25.

21. Douglas, *A Full Life*, 31–34; idem, ROHO, 4–5, 11; Scobie, "Helen and Melvyn Douglas: Two Lives in Vermont."

22. For example, see Douglas, *A Full Life*, 3, 24, 27; idem, ROHO draft, 50–51.

23. Douglas, *A Full Life*, 26, 32–33.

24. Ibid., 4; idem, ROHO, 15, 33–37; and *Brooklyn Daily Eagle*, September 22, 1922. Walter Jr. attended Princeton as an undergraduate and then followed his brothers to Columbia, but in law, not engineering. But he experienced his own period of rebellion and vividly remembers his father's reaction. After a series of warnings from the school about his academic performance, he came home one day with a report card of failing grades. His father did not scold him; he "just looked at me in the eye. And he said, 'Well son, if that's the best you can do, I'm satisfied.' " Realizing his problem was "just a matter of application," Walter Jr. made the honor roll from that point on. (Walter Gahagan interview with author.)

25. *Yearbook of the Berkeley Institute*, 1905–1906; *The Berkelydian*, 1905; and *Notes for Girls in School* (Brooklyn: Berkeley Institute, 1911); Douglas, ROHO, 27–29.

26. Transcripts of Helen Gahagan, Berkeley Institute, 1908–1918; Douglas, ROHO, 29, 34. Her contemporary, Katharine Cornell, wrote about herself in a way that also described Helen: "Acting is in my blood. The feeling for it was absolutely born in me." Katharine Cornell, *I Wanted to Be an Actress* (New York: Random House, 1939), 3.

27. Gahagan transcript, 1916–17; *The Berkelydian*, 1916 and 1917; Douglas, *A Full Life*, 6–7; idem, ROHO draft, 44. Despite Gahagan's less than stellar academic

achievements, her fame as an actress elevated her status in the eyes of students who did not remember her. For example, Dr. Maxine Meyer Greene, Class of 1934, said in a 1984 commencement address about legends at Berkeley: "One of our legends had to do with a former student called Helen Twelvetrees, who became a Hollywood actress, but who had indeed been expelled for smoking. She was our bad kid legend; our inspiring one, our really ennobling one was Helen Gahagan . . . later a great liberal states-woman . . . because she was one of our truly radiant symbols of struggle and quest and self-identification and social concern." See Greene, Commencement Address, Berkeley-Carroll Street School, 1984.

28. Numerous books and articles deal with behaviorism. I have found, however, the most useful study of the woman of the 1920s, which includes a discussion of behaviorism, to be Elaine Showalter, ed., *These Modern Women: Autobiographical Essays from the Twenties* (Old Westbury, N.Y.: The Feminist Press, 1978). While Helen recalled in her autobiography that she was the first girl to be admitted, quite a number of girls attended in 1917. Although the Dartmouth College Registrar did not list Helen as attending the regular summer session in 1918, she may have enrolled in a special tutoring class. See *Dartmouth College Bulletin, Summer Session, 1917* (February 1917); *Dartmouth College Bulletin, Directory of Officers and Students, The Summer Session, 1918*; Douglas, *A Full Life*, 4, 6–8; idem, ROHO, 34–35.

29. On the Capen School, see, for example, *Daily Hampshire Gazette*, February 11, 1921; and Bessie T. Capen, "Address of Miss Capen at the 35th Reunion of the Capen School," June 1912, Archives of the Stoneleigh-Burnham School. The school closed in 1921, a year after the death of headmistress Capen, and was taken over by Smith College. Ultimately that institution merged with the Stoneleigh-Burnham School. See also Douglas, ROHO, 37; idem, ROHO draft.

30. Douglas, ROHO, 37.

31. Helen Lefkowitz Horowitz, *Alma Mater: Design and Experience in the Women's Colleges from Their Nineteenth-Century Beginnings to the 1930s* (New York: Alfred A. Knopf, 1984), xviii. The book offers a fine overview of the "Seven Sister Colleges," as they became known in the 1920s. Chaps. 10 and 15 focus on Barnard; other chapters are useful as well.

32. Ibid., 259.

33. In the 1920s, women represented over 47% of all college students; over 80% attended coeducational schools. Of the almost 20% that attended women's schools, only 8% enrolled in private schools. See Mabel Newcomer, *A Century of Higher Education for American Women* (New York, Harper and Row, 1959), 46, 49; Marian Churchill White, *A History of Barnard College* (New York: Columbia University Press, 1954), 42; *The Bulletin of the Associated Alumnae of Barnard College* 14 (December 1924): 27–28. Wealthy families expected their daughters to attend college, particularly the prestigious Eastern women's schools. (Horowitz, *Alma Mater*, 283). Alumnae came to the campus to acquaint students with careers other than teaching. In 1900, almost 90% of Barnard students became teachers; by 1920 the percentage had dropped to below 50%, and graduates worked in a wide variety of positions.

34. Paula S. Fass, *The Damned and the Beautiful: American Youth in the 1920's* (New York: Oxford University Press, 1977), 17–25; and Alice Duer Miller and Susan Myers, *Barnard College: The First Fifty Years* (New York: Columbia University Press, 1939), 109–10, and chaps. 6 and 7, passim; *The Barnard Bulletin*, April 8, April 22, November 18, and December 9, 1921, and February 10, 1922; *Mortarboard 1922*, p. 124; and *The Bulletin of the Associated Alumnae of Barnard College* 10 (April 1921): 24–25. Lefkowitz suggested in *Alma Mater* that curricula of the women's colleges in

the 1920s reflected a "retreat from the public world." This pattern does not appear as prevalent at Barnard as at other institutions.

35. On De Sola, see Alis De Sola, "Helen Gahagan Douglas: College and the Theatre," an oral history conducted 1976 by Amelia Fry, in Helen Gahagan Douglas Oral History Project, Vol. III, ROHO, 1981 (hereafter, De Sola, ROHO); De Sola, interview with Tom Arthur, May 28, 1974; De Sola, interview with author, May 26, 1980; and Douglas, ROHO, 39.

36. De Sola interview with author.

37. Ibid.

38. *The Barnard Bulletin,* April 15, 1921; *Mortarboard 1924,* pp. 107–15; and White, A *History of Barnard College,* 135–36. See also Miller and Myers, *Barnard College,* 127–30; White, *History of Barnard College,* 59; *Mortarboard 1924,* p. 106; and *The Bulletin of the Associated Alumnae of Barnard College* 10 (April 1921): 24–28.

39. *Barnard Bulletin,* December 2, December 16, 1921, and January 13, 1922; and Horowitz, *Alma Mater,* 252.

40. Barnard College transcript, Registrar's Office, 1922. See also De Sola interview with author.

41. *Barnard Bulletin,* May 22, 1922; and De Sola interview with author. On Grimball, see, for example, the essay on her school, "A School That Makes You Think" (1924) in HGD, B1; and the Grimball obituary in the *New York Times,* August 31, 1953.

42. De Sola interview with author.

43. Douglas, A *Full Life,* 13. On George and Brady's reputation for discovering new talent, see *New York Morning Telegram,* October 9, 1923.

Chapter 2

1. On Brady and Davis, see Tyler to Harry Leon Wilson, October 20, 1924, George Tyler Papers, Theatre Archives, Princeton University Library (hereafter, GT); Douglas, A *Full Life,* 13; Burns Mantle, ed., *Best Plays, 1921–22* (Boston: Small, Maynard and Co., 1922), 427–28; H. I. Brock, "Maker of Three Hundred Plays: Thirty Busy Years of George C. Tyler on the Theatre World's 'Main Stem,' " *Personality: A Magazine of Biography* 2 (August 1928): 26–29; and William A. Brady, *Showman* (New York: E. P. Dutton, 1937). Brady obituaries appeared in the *New York Times,* January 8 and 10, 1950.

2. Albert Auster, "Chamber of Diamonds and Delight: Actresses, Suffragists and Feminists in the American Theatre, 1890–1920" (Ph.D. diss., State University of New York at Stonybrook, 1981), 88–89.

3. Douglas, A *Full Life,* 3, 15–16; De Sola interview with author.

4. *Brooklyn Daily Eagle, New York Tribune, Dial,* and *The American*—September 14, 1922; Baker, "Helen Gahagan: A New Acting Sensation," *New York Review,* September 23, 1922; *Theatre Magazine,* September 1922; and *Zit's Weekly Newspaper,* September 1922. I found the majority of clippings cited in the Douglas papers and the extensive theater archives in the Theatre Collection, The New York Public Library at Lincoln Center.

5. *New York Mail* and *Brooklyn Daily Eagle,* September 14, 1922; *Zit's Weekly Newspaper,* September 1922.

6. De Sola interview with author; *Zit's Weekly Newspaper,* September 1922; and Baker, *New York Review,* September 23, 1922.

7. Olive Logan, *Apropos of Women and Theatres with a Paper or Two on Parisian Topics* (New York: Carlton, 1869), 15–16. See also Logan, *Before the Footlights and Behind the Scenes, A Book about the "Show Business" in all its Branches* (Philadelphia: Parmalee and Co., 1870); and Auster, "Chamber of Diamonds and Delight," 41. For a less optimistic view of women in theater, see "Drama: Women and the American Theatre," *The Nation* 106 (June 1, 1918): 665. Douglas commented to Colgate Baker on some of the actresses who inspired her (*New York Review*, September 23, 1922).

8. Howard Taubman, *The Making of the American Theatre* (New York: Coward McCann, 1965), 131.

9. Walter Prichard Eaton, "American Playwrights Not Welcome Here?" *Theatre Magazine* 38 (October 1923): 9ff. A good article on the early goals of the Theatre Guild is Theresa Helburn, "Art and Business: A Record of the Theatre Guild, Inc.," *Theatre Arts Magazine* 5 (October 1921): 268–74. On O'Neill and Broadway, see, for example, Robert Garland, "Eugene O'Neill and This Big Business of Broadway," *Theatre Arts Monthly* 9 (January 1925): 3–16.

10. Barnard Hewitt, *Theatre U.S.A., 1665 to 1957* (New York: McGraw-Hill, 1959), argued that the 1920s saw as many talented writers as in the preceding 170 years altogether. Eleanor Flexner, *American Playwrights: 1918–1938; The Theatre Retreats from Reality* (New York: Simon and Schuster, 1938), was less enthusiastic. Glenn Hughes, *A History of the American Theatre, 1700–1950* (New York: Samuel French, 1951), 406–9. An article in *The Nation* in 1918 noted that few women outside of Rachael Crothers had achieved note as playwrights, and even fewer as producers. See "Drama: Women and the American Theatre," 665.

Only 30% of the plays turned a profit. An excellent study of the economic side of commercial theater is a work commissioned by the Actors' Equity Association, by Alfred L. Bernheim, *The Business of the Theatre: An Economic History of the American Theatre, 1730–1932* (New York: Benjamin Blom, 1932). See also "Why It Costs So Much to Amuse You," *Theatre Magazine* 38 (November 1923): 12ff; Stephen Langsley, *Theatre Management in America: Principle and Practice* (New York: Drama Book Specialists, 1974), chap. 5. Tyler's correspondence during the 1920s is very revealing about the ups and downs of the financial side of Broadway theater (GT).

11. One study suggests that the ratio of women to men seeking roles in New York was 25 to 1 (Percy Hammond, *But—Is It Art* [Garden City: Doubleday, Page, and Co., 1927], 73).

12. *Dreams for Sale* was such a disaster in the playwright's opinion that Davis did not even mention it in his autobiographical *My First Fifty Years in the Theatre* (Boston: Walter H. Bakker Company, 1950). See Kenneth MacGowan and William Melnitz, *Golden Ages of the Theater* (Englewood Cliffs, N.J.: Prentice Hall, 1959), 145; and Emro Joseph Gergely, *Hungarian Drama in New York: American Adaptations, 1908–1940* (Philadelphia: University of Pennsylvania Press, 1947). For reviews, see, for example, *New York World*, December 5, 1922.

13. *The American*, November 11, 1923; Douglas, *A Full Life*, 40; and *Chicago Tribune*, May 22, 1923.

14. *New York News*, December 8, 1923; Baker, "Helen Gahagan: An Acting Prodigy and 'Chains,'" *New York Review*, December 8, 1923; and Thomas to Gahagan (hereafter HGD), November 6, 1923, HGD, B11.

15. *The American*, May 4, 1924. Correspondence between Brady and Lee Shubert and their cooperation on the revival is located in the Shubert Theatre Archives, New York City, (hereafter, SA), Brady Correspondence, Collection 28.

16. Fiske to HGD, April 21, 1924, HGD, Theatre Manuscript Collection (hereafter, HGD-TMS); for New York, see, for example, *New York Sun*, April 22, 1924; *New York Daily News* and *New York Commercial*, April 24, 1924; *New York Herald Tribune*, May 3, 1924. Unidentified article on Sunday night performances, HGD-TMS.

17. *Philadelphia Record*, March 23, 1924; *New York Morning Telegraph*, November 11, 1923; and Gahagan, speech notes, HGD-TMS.

18. *Ma Este* (July 31, 1924). In her autobiography, Douglas indicated that she went to Europe to meet Molnar during the summer of 1923 after *Chains* closed in Chicago, rather than in the summer of 1924. See also Douglas, A *Full Life*, 41–46.

19. *The Nation* 120 (February 15, 1925): 168; *American Mercury* 4 (March 1925): 377; *New York Sun*, January 29, 1925; *New York Morning Tribune*, January 26, 1925; and *New York Evening Post*, January 25, 1925.

20. Brady to HGD, January 25, 1925, HGD-TMS.

21. De Sola interview with author.

22. Douglas, A *Full Life*, 51; Mary Clyde to HGD, July 1, 1940; HMDP; and Douglas, ROHO, 3.

23. De Sola interview with author; De Sola interview with Arthur; and Douglas, A *Full Life*, 46–47.

24. Gahagan, "Away from the Stage," Helen Gahagan Icon File, The State Historical Society of Wisconsin (hereafter, WSHS); De Sola interview with author.

25. De Sola interview with author; Douglas, A *Full Life*, 46. De Sola mentioned that Melvyn told her on several occasions that Helen simply did not want to look inside.

26. Ibid.

27. Mary McGentry to HGD, March 24 and April 7, 1924, HGD, 11; Douglas, ROHO, 42–43; Douglas, A *Full Life*, 37–38; De Sola, ROHO, 15–19; De Sola interviews with author and with Arthur.

28. Martha Banta, *Imaging American Women: Idea and Ideals in Cultural History* (New York: Columbia University Press, 1987), 634, 641.

29. Stengel sketch in *New York Morning Telegraph*, January 26, 1925.

30. Unidentified article in HGD-TMS.

31. In her autobiography, Douglas said that she did this play "despite Brady's objections," implying that she was still under contract to Brady. But by this time she was under contract to Tyler. Since her three-year contract was up, it was logical that she did not exercise the option to renew for two years. (Douglas, A *Full Life*, 52; and HGD to Tyler, November 13, 1925, GT).

32. Brock, "Maker of Three Hundred Plays," 26–29.

33. Hammond, *But—Is It Art*. George Jean Nathan suggested that few critics really wrote true dramatic criticism. He argued that he could predict the sort of positive review that the handful of actresses favored by the critics would get, including Laurette Taylor, Helen Gahagan, Peggy Wood, or Lynn Fontanne. Those out of favor included Irene Fenwick, Doris Keane, and even Margaret Anglin. Nathan, "The Theatre," *American Mercury* 5 (August 1925): 499–501. Also George Abbott, interview with author, July 7, 1983.

34. Van Druten scrapbook on *Young Woodley*, particularly *New York Morning Telegram*, September 19, 1926, Theatre Collection, The New York Public Library at Lincoln Center (hereafter, LC). See also *Brooklyn Times*, January 31, 1926.

35. *Boston Traveller*, October 6, 1925; and *Boston Evening Transcript*, October 6, 1925, HGD, misc. scrapbook; and Tyler to HGD, November 13, 1925; HGD to Tyler, November 17, 1926; and undated letter; all GT.

36. Mantle, *Best Plays*, 1925–26. See also *Peekskill* [N.Y.] *Daily Union*, April 17, 1926; *New York Daily Telegraph* [n.d.] in HGD-TMS; and Van Druten scrapbook on *Young Woodley*, LC.

37. *Cincinnati Daily Times Star*, December 30, 1926.

38. Ibid.; Douglas phone conversation with author, May 19, 1980; *Young Woodley* scrapbook, LC; Fox to HGD, December 31, 1926, HGD, *Moor Born* scrapbook.

39. Tyler to HGD, November 15, 1926; and HGD to Tyler, [n.d.], and November 17, 1926, GT.

40. HGD to Tyler, [n.d.], GT.

41. *Cincinnati Commercial Tribune*, April 17, 1927; and *New York Times*, February 1, 1927. Tyler had actually hoped to do *Trelawney* as early as the spring of 1926, but could not get the right cast together until a year later. (Tyler to Bright, November 4, 1925, GT.)

42. Peggy Wood, "A Splendid Gypsy," *Saturday Evening Post* (September 3, 1927), 12–13, 67–68, and 73.

43. Ibid.; and HGD to Tyler, [n.d.], GT.

44. Dorothy Bromley, "Feminist—New Style," *Harper's* 155 (October 1927): 552–60; Susan Ware, *Modern American Women: A Documentary History* (Chicago: Dorsey Press, 1989), 167. Numerous other works are also helpful in describing the woman of the 1920s, such as Showalter, ed., *These Modern Women*; Estelle Freedman, "The New Woman: Changing Views of Women in the 1920s," *Journal of American History* 61 (September 1974): 372–93; and Nancy F. Cott, *The Grounding of Modern Feminism* (New Haven: Yale University Press, 1987).

Chapter 3

1. HGD to Tyler, [n.d.], GT.

2. Douglas, *A Full Life*, 54, 70–71; and George Cehanovsky, interview with Elizabeth Evans, January 24, 1975.

3. R. Dana Skinner, "The Play," *Commonweal* (February 16, 1927), 412.

4. HGD to Tyler, summer of 1927, GT.

5. Allen interview with author.

6. De Sola, ROHO, 16; *Pittsburgh Post*, September 16, 1927. I have found no evidence to determine how much Gahagan paid Cehanovska.

7. Douglas, *A Full Life*, 54–64; idem, ROHO, 41–42.

8. Tyler to Louis N. Parker, January 17, 1928; and Tyler to Bonstelle, September 4, 1928, GT; *Diplomacy* clips, LC; and *Cincinnati Enquirer*, April 22, 1928.

9. *Pittsburgh Gazette*, March 6, 1928; *St. Paul Pioneer-Press*, April 9 and 10, 1928; *St. Louis Globe Democrat*, April 3, 1928; and *New York American*, June 6, 1928.

10. *New York Morning Telegraph*, May 31, 1928.

11. John Hutchins, "Must Opera Singers Be Fat?" and clipping on art exhibit, Scrapbook, HGD.

12. *New York American*, July 10, 1928.

13. Power to HGD, June 18, 1928, HGD, scrapbook; and Gahagan to Tyler, June 18, 1928, GT.

14. Tyler to HGD, June 24, 1929; and HGD to Tyler, July 2, 1929, GT; HGD to Kahn, [n.d.], and Kahn to HGD, May 15, 1929, Otto Kahn Papers, Theatre Archives, Princeton University Library (hereafter, OK); and *Worcester Telegram*, February 9, 1929.

15. HGD to Tyler, July 2, 1929, GT; and *New York Times*, July 6, 1929.

16. *Moravskoslezský deník*, June 27 and 29, 1930.

17. Tyler to HGD, June 24, 1929; and HGD to Tyler, July 2 and 16, 1929, GT.

18. HGD to Tyler, July 2, 1929; and Tyler to HGD, July 17, 1929, GT.

19. HGD to Lillian Gahagan, July 25, 1929, HMDP.

20. *Der Grenzbote*, July 28, 1929; *Moravskoslezský deník*, September 18, 1929; *Lidove noviny*, September 19, 1929; and *Salzburger Chronik*, October 19, 1929; *Salzburger Volksblatt*, October 19, 1929. (Note on review translations: rather than use the brief and highly complimentary phrases selected from reviews by Helen's American publicists, I hired native translators who specialized in music at Indiana University to translate the entire texts of all reviews.)

21. HGD to Tyler, September 25, 1929, GT.

22. Douglas, *A Full Life*, 75; and *Philadelphia Ledger*, November 7, 1929.

23. *New York Herald Tribune*, May 15, 1931; Jane Dransfield, "Behind the Scenes with Belasco," *Theatre Magazine* 35 (22 April 1922): 228, 230; *New York Sun*, May 4, 1931; and MacGowan and Melnitz, *Golden Ages of the Theater*, 142.

24. Tyler to Parker, February 24, 1930, and Tyler to HGD, September 11, 1930, GT.

25. Tyler to HGD, May 23, 1930; and HGD to Tyler, May 15, August 14, and August 28, 1930, GT. Review quotes from *Salzburger Wacht*, June 30, 1930; *Neue Treie Presse, Wien*, July 22, 1930; and *Wiener Journal*, July 30, 1930. Looking back, Douglas commented that the play was "monumentally silly," yet that was obviously not the primary issue at the time (*A Full Life*, 79).

26. Tyler to HGD, July 28, 1930; and HGD to Tyler, August 14 and 28, 1930, GT.

27. HGD to Tyler, August 28, 1930, GT.

28. Ibid.

29. Ibid.; and Tyler to HGD, September 11, 1930, GT.

30. *New York Herald Tribune*, April 5, 1931; and Melvyn Douglas and Tom Arthur, *See You at the Movies: The Autobiography of Melvyn Douglas* (Lanham, Md.: University Press of America, 1986), 79.

31. Douglas and Arthur, *See You at the Movies*, 79–81; and Douglas, *A Full Life*, 80.

Chapter 4

1. *New York Herald Tribune*, April 5, 1931; and Douglas, *A Full Life*, 80–82.

2. This particular section of biographical information on Melvyn came principally from the Melvyn Douglas interview with Tom Arthur, Indiana University Oral History Office (hereafter, MD interview with Arthur), July 2, 1972. Biographical materials on Melvyn, of varying reliability, abound in various publications. See, for example, Melvyn Douglas Papers, WSHS (hereafter, MD), and HMDP. The full set of Arthur interviews is lengthy and provided the basis for Douglas and Arthur, *See You at the Movies*. For more information on Edouard Hesselberg, see, for example, the *Denver Post*, [n.d.], 1906, and *Sherwood Music School News*, [n.d.], MD, B12–F2.

3. Belasco to HGD, November 18, 1930, HGD, B2–F3; and *New York Morning Telegram*, November 9, 1930.

4. *New York Telegram*, November 19 and 23, 1930; and *New York World*, November 22, 1930.

5. *New York Telegram*, November 19, 1930; and *New York Evening Post*, November 19, 1930. *New York City Variety*, for example, included Lenore Ulric, Helen Ga-

hagan, Jane Cowl, Mary Boland, and Lynn Fontanne, plus Alfred Lunt, as top actors; Ethel Barrymore and Helen Hayes did not count because they had appeared in "flops" that year (January 28, 1931). Another writer commented that this was "woman's year in the theater." His list of four top actresses differed, with the exception of Gahagan— Katharine Cornell in *The Barretts of Wimpole Street*, Helen Gahagan in *Tonight or Never*, Eugenie Leontovich, a Russian actress and dancer in *Grand Hotel*, and Lynn Fontanne in Maxwell Anderson's *Elizabeth the Queen* (*New York Evening World*, February 14, 1931).

6. MD interview with Arthur, May 16, 1974; and De Sola interview with author.

7. *Baltimore News*, November 11, 1930; *Variety*, January 28, 1931; *New York Evening World*, February 14, 1931; *New York Telegram*, November 19 and 23, and December 2 and 3, 1930; *New York Evening Post*, November 19, 1930; *New York Herald Tribune*, November 11, 1930; and *New York Post*, January 19, 1931.

8. Harry Gribble to HGD, December 22, 1930, HMDP; and Douglas, *A Full Life*, 85. Helen inherited a share of her father's estate, valued at $1,315,000 (unidentified clipping, Gahagan File, LC).

9. *New York World Telegram*, March 19, 1931.

10. Bonstelle to Helen and Melvyn Douglas, April 31, 1931, HMDP, B2–F3.

11. Douglas, *A Full Life*, 92; and Douglas and Arthur, *See You at the Movies*, 80.

12. *New York Telegram* and *New York World Telegram*, April 3, 1931; *New York Times*, *Brooklyn Daily Eagle*, and *New York Evening Journal* for April 6, 1931; *New York Sun*, May 4, 1931.

13. Tyler to HGD, April 3, 1931, GT; and Belasco to HGD, April 6, 1931, HMDP, B2–F3.

14. Tino Balio, *United Artists: The Company Built by the Stars* (Madison: University of Wisconsin Press, 1976), 57–58.

15. MD interview with Arthur, May 16, 1974.

16. Murray to Kahn, July 18, 1931; and Kahn to Murray, July 22, 1931, OK; *Cleveland Press*, July 8, 1931.

17. MD to Lena Hesselberg, August 15, 1931, HMDP. On Hollywood, see, for example, Leo C. Rosten, *Hollywood: The Movie Colony, the Movie Makers* (New York: Harcourt, Brace, and Co., 1941), 3–31.

18. Lary May, *Screening Out the Past: The Birth of Mass Culture and the Motion Picture Industry* (New York: Oxford University Press, 1980) details the development of the industry from 1910 to 1929; Arthur Knight, *The Liveliest Art: A Panoramic History of the Movies* (New York: Macmillan, 1957) surveys the industry's development up through the 1950s; and Gerald Mast, *A Short History of the Movies* (Indianapolis: Bobbs-Merrill, 1971) adds the 1960s to his overview, which also includes movie-making outside of the United States. Robert McLaughlin, *Broadway and Hollywood: A History of Economic Interaction* (New York: Arno Press, 1974) details the increasingly complex financial relationship between New York and Hollywood producers from 1910 to 1970; and Rosten's *Hollywood* is a study by a group of social scientists of the politics, economic status, and social life of the film colony. Carey McWilliams discusses Hollywood in various insightful books on California. See for example, *Southern California Country: An Island on the Land* (New York: Duell, Sloan and Pearce, 1946).

19. MD to Lena Hesselberg, August 15, 1931, HMDP.

20. *Los Angeles Daily News*, October 4, 1931; Douglas, ROHO draft; MD interview with Arthur, May 16, 1974.

21. Rosten, *Hollywood*, 189; MD to Lena and Edouard Hesselberg, September 22,

1931, HMDP; MD to HGD, [n.d.], HMDP; *Charleston* [W.Va.] *Gazette,* January 31, 1932; and *New York Times,* December 18, 1931.

22. *Hollywood Citizen News,* November 17, 1931. Tyler tried to arrange an American tour. Helen also had two invitations in early 1932 to go to London but decided against accepting because of the distance from Melvyn. See also HGD to Lena and Edouard Hesselberg, March 26, 1932, HMDP; *Cincinnati Billboard,* January 2, 1932; HGD to Tyler, December 7, 1932, GT.

23. *Worcester Telegram,* January 10, 1932; *New York Journal,* January 11, 1932; *New York Sun,* January 11, 1932.

24. HGD to Tyler, March 26, 1932; and Tyler to HGD, March 29, April 1, and May 19, 1932, GT; Van Druten to HGD, August 23, 1932, HMDP, B11–F4.

25. Louella Parsons noted that RKO was about to sign Gahagan (*Los Angeles Examiner,* January 12, 1932).

26. HGD to Tyler, March 26, 1932, GT; HGD to Lester Cohen, Executive Secretary, Academy of Motion Picture Arts and Sciences, March 7, 1932, RKO Picture Archives, Los Angeles (hereafter, RKO), Helen Gahagan File; RKO Studios attorneys to Cohen, April 11, 1932, RKO, Gahagan File; and *Award of the Conciliation Committee of the Academy of Motion Picture Arts and Sciences in Conciliation Case No. 90,* Helen Gahagan *vs.* RKO Studios, Inc., May 23, 1932, in RKO, Gahagan File. See also Robert H. Stanley, *The Celluloid Empire: A History of the American Movie Industry* (New York, Hastings House Publishers, 1978), 68; Andrew Bergman, *We're in the Money: Depression America and Its Films* (New York: New York University Press, 1971), xix–xxiii; and James Robert Parish, *The RKO Gals* (New Rochelle, N.Y.: Arlington House Publishers, 1974), 854. Helen's comment about "fighting" is interesting, particularly in light of the fact that as a politician she saw every move as a fight.

27. *New York World Telegram,* June 16, 1932.

28. Unidentified clipping, [n.d.], HGD, B10–F3; Melvyn to Lena and Edouard Hesselberg, October 21, 1932, HMDP; Cornelia Palms, "The Carmel and Theater Connections," an oral history conducted in 1977 by Amelia Fry, in Helen Gahagan Douglas Oral History Project, Vol. III, ROHO, 1981 (hereafter, Palms, ROHO), 66.

29. MD to HGD, December 9 and 31, 1931, MDHP; MD interview with Arthur, July 5, 1972; *New York Times* reviews of Melvyn's movies.

30. Carlton Brown, "East, West, Broadway Is Best!," [n.p.], [n.d.], HGD-TMS; MD interview with Arthur, July 5, 1972; *New York Sun,* August 13, 1932; MD to HGD, December 1 and 31, 1931, and January 30, 1932; HGD to Lena and Edouard Hesselberg, March 26, 1932; and MD to Lena and Edouard Hesselberg, August 29, 1932, HMDP.

31. HGD to Lena and Edouard Hesselberg, May 18, 1932, HMDP; Brown, "East, West, Broadway Is Best!"; MD interview with Arthur, July 5, 1972.

32. Douglas, ROHO draft.

33. MD interview with Arthur, July 5, 1972; Brown, "East, West, Broadway Is Best!"

34. MD interview with Arthur, July 7, 1972; *New York Telegram,* April 7, 1934; *San Francisco News,* April 17, 1934.

Chapter 5

1. HGD to Tyler, October 3 and 5, 1933, GT.
2. HGD to Tyler, November 18, 1933, GT.

3. McLaughlin, *Broadway and Hollywood*, 122; *New York Post*, January 22 and April 4, 1934; *New York Herald Tribune*, April 4, 1934; *Stage* 11 (May 1934): 10; and Douglas, *A Full Life*.

4. *Brooklyn Daily Eagle* and *New York Herald Tribune* for April 29, 1934; *New York World Telegram*, July 20, 1935; *New York American*, April 22, 1934; *San Francisco News*, April 17, 1934.

5. *Los Angeles Daily News*, September 11, 1934; *Los Angeles Examiner* and *San Francisco Call-Bulletin*, September 18, 1934.

6. *San Francisco News*, [n.d.] in HGD-TMS.

7. "Mother Lode Players, Inc.," MD, May 7, 1936, B1-1; HGD to MD, [n.d.], HMDP; *New York Times*, April 5, 1934.

8. *Chicago American*, [n.d.], HGD-TMS.

9. B. B. Jahane to R. A. Rowland, February 13, 1935, Helen Gahagan File, RKO. For more complete details of the negotiation on this film, see Gahagan and *She* files, RKO. See also HGD to MD, March 5, 1935, HMDP.

10. HGD to MD, March 18, 1935, HMDP.

11. Ibid.; *Chicago American*, [n.d.], HGD-TMS; De Sola, ROHO, 22.

12. MD to HGD, March 24, 1935; and HGD to MD, March 18, 1935, HMDP.

13. De Sola, ROHO, pp. 21–23.

14. *Miami Herald*, July 21, 1935; *St. Paul Dispatch*, July 25, 1935.

15. MD to HGD, March 7, 12, 18, 24, and 27, 1935; HGD to MD, March 18 and [n.d.], 1935, HMDP; MD interview with Arthur, July 8, 1972; and Douglas and Arthur, *See You at the Movies*, 97.

16. MD to HGD, March 7, 12, 18, 24, and 27, 1935; and HGD to MD, March 18, 1935, HMDP.

17. MD interview with Arthur, May 17 and 30, 1974.

18. *New York Times*, February 4, 1936. For information on the income of Hollywood's executives, actors, and screenwriters, see, for example, *Motion Picture Herald*, January 16 and February 6, 1937; ibid., January 29, 1938; ibid., September 19, 1942. *Managers' Roundtable*, April 8, 1939, documents Melvyn's status as a leading man, not a star.

19. *Los Angeles Examiner*, April 9, 1936; MD interview with Arthur, May 15, 1974.

20. *Los Angeles Times*, March 18, 1936; *New York World Telegram*, July 20, 1935; and De Sola interview with author.

21. *Los Angeles Examiner*, April 9, May 12, and June 16, 1936.

22. *Illustrated Daily News*, March 13, 1936.

23. *Los Angeles Examiner*, May 5, 1936; *Family Circle* 92 (May 6, 1938): 14–15; HGD to MD, September 2, 9, and 21, 1936, and [n.d.], HMDP; and Roy S. Waldau, *Vintage Years of the Theatre Guild, 1928–1939* (Cleveland: Case Western Reserve University Press, 1972), 237–38.

24. HGD to MD, November 4 and 9, 1936, HMDP.

25. Ibid.

26. HGD to MD, September 6, 9, and 15, 1936; October 28 and [n.d.], 1936; November 6, 19, and 28, 1936; and February 1, 4, and 5, 1937; MD to HGD, November 2, 12, and 13, 1936; and December 1, 1936, HMDP.

27. For example, see MD to HGD, November 12, 1936, HMDP.

28. HGD to MD, October 28, 1936; and MD to HGD, November 2, 1936, HMDP.

29. HGD to MD, November 3, 1936, HMDP.

30. Pick to De Sola, April 14, 1937, Walter Pick Papers, Los Angeles, private collection, Los Angeles (hereafter, WP).

31. *Dallas Times Herald*, March 3, 1937; *San Francisco Examiner*, April 3, 1937; Pick to De Sola, April 23, 1937, WP.

32. Douglas, *A Full Life*, 128; and HGD to MD, June 26, 1937, HMDP.

33. *Prager Abendblatt* and *Prager Morgenblatt* for June 25, 1937; *Narodní listy*, June 30, 1937; *Narodní politika*, June 27, 1937; *Pesti Hírlap*, July 3, 1937; *Újság*, July 3, 1937; *Népszava*, July 3, 1937; *Pesti Napló*, July 3, 1937; HGD to MD, June 26, 1937, HMDP.

34. See, for example, *Nieuwe Rotterdam*, July 21, 1937; *Het Aderland*, July 21, 1937; and *Donnerstag*, August 12, 1937.

35. Hollywood Bowl program, August 17–20, 1937; HGD to MD, July 15, 1937, HMDP.

36. Douglas, ROHO, 51–52; Pick to De Sola, August 27, 1937, HMDP; HGD to Kuba, September 5, 1937; and Kuba to HGD, January 19, 1938, HMDP.

37. HGD to Kuba, September 5, 1937, HMDP; Pick to De Sola, July 30, 1937, WP; *Los Angeles Evening News* and *Los Angeles Times* for August 21, 1937; Douglas, *A Full Life*, 133–34.

38. Walter R. Pick, "A Closer Look at the Family and Professional Life of Helen Gahagan Douglas and Melvyn Douglas," an oral history conducted in 1978 by Scobie in *Helen Gahagan Douglas Oral History Project*, Vol. III, ROHO, 1981, (hereafter Pick, ROHO), 123–28; Douglas, *A Full Life*, 138–39; author's tour of the house, April 1984.

39. Pick, ROHO, 128.

40. MD interview with Arthur, July 8, 1972.

41. Pick, ROHO, 158.

42. *Cleveland Plain Dealer*, October 21, 1937; *Dayton Journal*, December 9, 1937; *Los Angeles Herald and Express*, April 7, 1937; and *Toronto Globe and Mail*, April 22, 1938.

43. Pick to De Sola, February 3, 1938; and Cehanovska to HGD, February 3 and 24, 1938, HMDP.

44. Pick, ROHO, 123.

45. Paramount Studios Press Release, 1936, The Margaret Herrick Library, Academy of Motion Pictures Arts and Sciences; Pick, ROHO, 145.

Chapter 6

1. *Motion Picture Herald*, January 15 and February 5, 1937; ibid., January 28, 1938; and ibid., September 19, 1942.

2. MD interview with Arthur, July 8, 1972.

3. John Russell Taylor, *Strangers in Paradise: The Hollywood Émigrés, 1933–1950* (New York: Holt, Rinehart, and Winston, 1983).

4. "My Name Isn't Costello," *Screen Guild's Magazine* (February 1937), 7.

5. Larry Ceplair and Stephen Englund, *The Inquisition in Hollywood: Politics in the Film Community, 1930–1960* (Garden City, N.J.: Anchor Press/Doubleday, 1980), chap. 4. Ceplair and Englund provide a very detailed study of Hollywood's radical life in *The Inquisition in Hollywood*, although screenwriter Philip Dunne, who helped the authors, did not feel they gave enough credit to the less radical anti-Communist liberals in Hollywood. (Dunne interview with author, April 11, 1984.)

6. Paul Jerrico, interview with author, April 10, 1984; and Dunne interview with

author. Dunne discusses the difficulty of knowing who was Communist in *Take Two: A Life in Movies and Politics* (New York: McGraw Hill, 1980).

7. MD to HGD, December 1, 1936; HGD to MD, November 4, 1936; and Pick to De Sola, August 25, 1938, HMDP. Ceplair and Englund comment that "due in large part to the strong support Olson received from the Hollywood film community, Olson was elected" (119). Rosten wrote that this group "helped score a signal victory in California politics" (138–39). But Olson's political biographer, Robert E. Burke, gives the Motion Picture Democratic Committee (MPDC) little credit except to mention that the Hollywood celebrity members organized rallies and dinners for Olson, often in conjunction with other front organizations. See Burke, *Olson's New Deal for California* (Berkeley: University of California Press, 1953), 27. Both Douglases said at different times that Melvyn was asked to head the fall campaign in southern California. After the election, Melvyn ran unsuccessfully for president of the Screen Actors Guild as an independent candidate.

8. Pick, ROHO, 142.

9. For a detailed account of Douglas's involvement in politics from 1938 to 1940, see my "Helen Gahagan Douglas and the Roosevelt Connection," in Hoff-Wilson and Lightman, eds., *Without Precedent*, 153–75.

10. Arthur Goldschmidt, speech, Helen Douglas's memorial service, December 2, 1980, New York City, HMDP; David E. Lilienthal, *The Journals of David E. Lilienthal*, vol. 1, *The TVA Years* (New York: Harper and Row, 1964), 162.

11. Palms, ROHO, 54–55, 69–74; MD interview with Arthur, May 16, 1974.

12. Kevin Lewis, "The Two Careers of Melvyn Douglas," *Films in Review* 32 (October 1981): 453–67; *New York Times*, November 10, 1939; and MD interview with Arthur, July 8, 10, and 12, 1972.

13. Lilienthal, *The War Years*, 162; Williams to FDR, July 18, 1939, Franklin D. Roosevelt Papers (hereafter, FDRP), Official File 444d, Franklin D. Roosevelt Library (hereafter, FDRL); ER to HGD, November 20 and 27, 1940, HGD, B216–F1; Pick, ROHO, 140.

14. Harold L. Ickes, *The Secret Diary of Harold L. Ickes*, vol. 3, *The Lowering Clouds* (New York: Simon and Schuster, 1954), 73. Others they met included Assistant Attorney General Norman Littell, Colonel Francis Harrington (head of the Works Progress Administration), United States Court of Appeals Justice Justin Miller, and others who clustered around the President, such as Ben Cohen, Isador Lubin, and Tom Corcoran.

15. HGD to Thompson, January 6, 1940, HGD, B217–F6; HGD to Voorhis, December 27, 1939; and March 12, 1940, HGD, B212–F9; Arline Coman to HGD, January 18, 1940, HGD, B165–F17; HGD to Executive Board, Committee to Aid Agricultural Workers, March 29, 1940; and the committee's March bulletin, HGD, B165–F17.

16. MD, Report to the Executive Board of the Motion Picture Democratic Committee, December 18, 1939; and MPDC Bulletin, February 22, 1940, MD, B1. For more details on Melvyn's struggle with the MPDC, see MD, B1.

17. Jones to HGD, February 5, 1940; MD, B1; and Pick to Jones, February 6, 1940, HGD, B11–F1. On the early meetings and membership of the California Citizen's Council, see MD, B1. The Democratic Study Clubs as well as the Women's Division of the Democratic Party served as a training ground for women who later moved into elected or appointed political positions. Correspondence in the files suggests the study clubs in California did not date back to the turn of the century nor did they play a significant or active role in California.

18. Guest lists for dinner and reception, HGD, B165–F4; Perkins to HGD, March 1, 1940; and HGD to Perkins, March 29, 1940, HGD, B165–F4; and Pick, ROHO, 138.

19. Gahagan, "FSA Aids Migratory Worker," *The Democratic Digest* 17 (February 1940): 11–13, 37; McAllister to HGD, February 19, 1940, HGD, B165–F14; and W. O. Douglas to HGD, February 17, 1940, HGD, B164–F8.

20. HGD to ER, [n.d.], HGD, B216–F1; Taylor to HGD, March 14 and 29, 1940; and HGD to Taylor, April 8, 1940, HGD, B165–F8; Eleanor Roosevelt, "My Day," April 3, 4, 5, and 6, 1940; and ER to HGD, April 12 and 23, 1940, HGD, B216–F1; and HGD to ER, April 19, 1940, ER Personal Correspondence, B1547, Anna Eleanor Roosevelt Papers (hereafter, ERP), FDRL.

21. Albert Rappaport to MD, November 21, 1941, MD, B2.

22. On Gahagan's Washington trip, see, for example, May entries in the 1940 White House Usher's Book, FDRL; numerous speeches and newspaper clippings, Women's Division, B310, National Committee of the Democratic Party Papers (hereafter, WD), FDRL; Tolan to HGD, May 3, 1940, HGD, B165–F17. The Women's Division papers have extensive correspondence from California members to McAllister revealing the internecine quarrels. The Mary M. Dewson Papers (hereafter, Dewson) and the Lorena Hickok Papers (hereafter, LH), FDRL, are also very helpful.

23. HGD to ER, June 6, 1940; and ER to HGD, June 14, 1940, HGD, B216–F1.

24. Jackson to MD, June 6, 1940; and MD to Olson, May 28, 1940, MD, B1; *Time Magazine* (June 10, 1940): 99–100; MD to Dies, August 18, 1940; and Dies to MD, August 19, 1940, MD, B1.

25. HGD to ER, June 6, 1940; and ER to HGD, June 14, 1940, HGD, B216–F1; Margaret Workman to McAllister, June 23, 1940, WD, B181. On the extensive Red-baiting in California during the late 1930s and 1940s, see my "Jack B. Tenney and Anti-Communist Legislation in California, 1940–1949" (Ph.D. diss., University of Wisconsin, Madison, 1970).

26. McAllister to HGD, June 8 and 12, 1940, HGD, B165–F14; McAllister to Mary W. (Molly) Dewson, June 5, 1940, Dewson, B19; News Briefs, Democratic National Committee Women's Division, July 14, 1940; and McAllister statement, July 15, 1940, WD, B290; *Charlotte Observer*, July 14, 1940; McAllister to ER, July 30, 1940, ERP, B1563.

27. HGD to Perkins, June 6, 1940, HGD, B165–F4.

28. *Los Angeles Times*, March 14, 1940. On the party battles, see, for example, J. R. Files to Olson, January 23, 1940; MD to Olson, February 28, 1940; Ellis Patterson to Olson, March 7, 1940; Florence (Susie) Clifton Papers (hereafter, SC), The Bancroft Library (hereafter, BL); and Carey McWilliams to Olson, March 25, 1940, Culbert L. Olson Papers (hereafter, CO), BL, B1. This period was complicated by grave difficulties in the Olson administrations. See Burke, *Olson's New Deal for California*, esp. chaps. 10 and 11.

29. See for example, Adelaide Metcalf to McAllister, July 6, 1940, WD, B185; Willoughby Rodman to "friend," June 15, 1940, WD, B189; Douglas, *A Full Life*, 157–58; idem, ROHO, 70.

30. Nettie Jones to McAllister, March 16 and April 17, 1940, WD, B189; Nettie Jones to Grace B. Caukins, April 18, 1940, WD, B188; Nettie Jones to Paul Peek, March 16, 1940; and Mattison Boyd Jones to Olson, March 12, 1940, CO, B1, BL; Lucy McWilliams to McAllister, March 29, 1940, WD, B190.

31. Douglas, ROHO, 70; Susie Clifton interview with author, April 12, 1984. On

the whole Jones–Gahagan fight, see my "Helen Douglas and the Roosevelt Connection," 169–73.

32. McAllister to HGD, August 1, 1940, HGD, B165–F14. On Douglas's activities, see press release, Women's Division, Democratic National Committee, WD, B290. Review of *Tonight or Never* in *New York World Telegram*, August 8, 1940.

33. *Los Angeles Examiner*, August 12, 1940; *Covina Citizen*, August 15, 1940; Clifton interview with author; Mrs. Willoughby Rodman to ER, September 13, 1940, WD, B181; McAllister to HGD, September 23, 1940, HGD, B165–F14.

34. Aldrich Blake to McAllister, August 29, 1940, WD, B183. Packard admitted that the Democrats in southern California were split but believed they were all pro-Roosevelt. See *Los Angeles Herald Express*, October 11, 1940.

35. H. William Ihrig to HGD, November 5, 1940, HGD, B164–F20.

36. Melvyn Douglas speech before the Wallace meeting, September 28, 1940, MD, B10–F1; HGD to Ickes, November 17, 1940, HGD, B212–F23.

37. Pick to De Sola, October 17, 1940, HMDP.

38. Ickes to HGD and MD, November 7, 1940, HGD, B212–F23; HGD to Lorena Hickok, January 9, 1941, HGD, B165–F12.

39. *Times-Herald*, January 29, 1941.

40. HGD to ER, February 12, 1941, HGD, B216–F1; HGD to Jane Ickes, February 12, 1941, HGD, B212–F24.

41. HGD to Jane Ickes, February 12, 1941, HGD, B212–F24.

42. Bird to ER, December 14, 1940; and ER to Bird, December 20, 1940, ERP, B1537.

43. Douglas, ROHO, 59. Melvyn did not recall being resentful, although Alis De Sola emphasized that he was.

44. HGD to MD, April 6, 1961, HMDP; Malone interview with author, September 28, 1978.

Chapter 7

1. Irwin N. Gertzog, *Congressional Women: Their Recruitment, Treatment, and Behavior* (New York: Praeger Publishers, 1984); and Hope Chamberlin, *A Minority of Members: Women in the U.S. Congress* (New York: New American Library, 1973). The literature on women in politics grew rapidly in the 1970s, increasing in the 1980s. Mae Ella Nolan entered Congress on January 23, 1923, and completed her husband's term; Florence Kahn served in Congress from February 17, 1925, until the end of 1936.

2. Gahagan to Hickok, January 9, 1941, HGD, B165–F12; Report of the Activities of the Women's Division, DNC, in the 1940 campaign, Dorothy McAllister Papers, Grand Rapids, Michigan, private collection (hereafter, DM).

3. FDR to McAllister, April 26, 1939, DM; Elizabeth Israels Perry, "Training for Public Life: ER and Women's Political Networks in the 1920s," in Hoff-Wilson and Lightman, eds., *Without Precedent*, 28–45. For a discussion of the importance of Molly Dewson and her work with the Women's Division, see Susan Ware, *Partner and I: Molly Dewson, Feminism, and New Deal Politics* (New Haven: Yale University Press, 1987); idem, *Holding Their Own: American Women in the 1930s* (Boston: Twayne Publishers, 1982); and idem, *Beyond Suffrage: Women in the New Deal* (Cambridge, Mass.: Harvard University Press, 1981). See also Eleanor Roosevelt and Lorena A. Hickok,

Ladies of Courage (New York: Putnam and Sons, 1954); and Eleanor Roosevelt, *It's Up to the Women* (New York: Frederick A. Stokes Company, 1933).

4. The friendship of Roosevelt and Hickok is the central focus of Doris Faber, *The Life of Lorena Hickok: ER's Friend* (New York: William Morrow, 1980), in which she suggests that the two women had a long-time lesbian relationship. William H. Chafe, in "Biographical Sketch" in Hoff-Wilson and Lightman, eds., *Without Precedent*, 3–27, agrees that the two had a lesbian relationship but disagrees about the degree to which it dominated Roosevelt's life. Blanche Weisen Cook in her forthcoming biography of Eleanor Roosevelt also treats this relationship in detail.

The disorganization of the Democratic Party in California is well documented; see, for example, Chet Holifield to Frank C. Walker, February 23, 1943, National Committee of the Democratic Party Papers, FDRL (hereafter, DNC), B1122. Jackson K. Putnam, in *Modern California Politics*, 2nd ed. (San Francisco: Boyd and Fraser Publishing Co., 1984) argues that the California Republican Assembly, the party's club system initiated in 1934, deserves considerable credit for the Republican victories in state offices. See also Michael P. Rogin and John L. Shover, *Political Change in California: Critical Elections and Social Movements, 1890–1966* (Westport, Conn.: Greenwood Publishing Co., 1970). See also the considerable Dewson and McAllister correspondence on political disorganization in California in DNC, WD, and Dewson. Dewson also comments in "An Aid to the End," unpublished MS, Dewson.

5. HGD, ROHO, 62; and HGD to Porter, May 3, 1941, HGD, B165–F3.

6. HGD to Hickok, March 17, 1941, HGD, B212–F17; Tillett to Dewson, July 9, 1941, WD Papers, B292; HGD to Ickes, April 9, 1941, and Ickes to HGD, May 12, 1941, Harold Ickes Papers, Manuscript Division, Library of Congress (hereafter, HI), B97.

7. Malone interview with author, September 28, 1978.

8. HGD to ER, March 31 and April 23, 1941, ER to HGD, April 17, 1941; Disney to ER, May 2, 1941, and various guest lists, all HGD, B216–F1; Aubrey Williams to HGD, March 27, 1941, HGD, B165–F10; *Los Angeles Examiner*, April 29, 1941.

9. *New York Times*, May 17 and 21, and July 20, 1941. ER was continually urging women to join the civilian defense efforts. See FDR to HGD, July 18, 1941, HGD, B216–F3; Civilian Defense Order, May 20, 1941, Dewson, B4; and verbatim transcript of Voluntary Participation Committee Meeting, July 24, 1941, DM.

10. Douglas, ROHO, 71–75.

11. Douglas wrote ER of the tremendous success of the luncheon meeting (HGD to ER, July 18, 1941, HGD, B216–F1). See also Roosevelt, *Ladies of Courage*, 22.

12. Tillett to HGD, June 27, 1941, HGD, B164–F20. Considerable correspondence exists on the details of organizing this conference, particularly in HGD, B164.

13. Malone to HGD, July 28, 1941; HGD to Malone, August 2, 1941; Hickok to HGD, August 20, 1941; HGD to Hickok, August 21, 1941, all HGD, B164–F23. The Fight for Freedom group also contributed $300.

14. *The Democratic Digest* (September 1941), 18–19; and ibid. (October 1941), 16–21; Burke, *Olson's New Deal for California*; HGD to Norman Littell, September 27, 1941, HGD, B164–F16; *Los Angeles Times*, September 14, 1941.

15. Roosevelt, *Ladies of Courage*, 50; HGD to Littell, September 27, 1941, HGD, B164–F16.

16. *Oregon Democratic News*, October 1, 1941; Tillett and Hickok to HGD, September 26, 1941; and Tillett to HGD, September 24, 1941, WD, B335; Norton to HGD, September 26, 1941, HGD, B165–F1; Joseph P. Lash, *Eleanor and Franklin: The Story of Their Relationship* (New York: W. W. Norton and Co., 1971), 634–53.

17. MD interview with Arthur, July 13–16, 1972; Anthony A. Bliss to MD, November 19, 1941, and other correspondence on Fight for Freedom, in MD, B2; Donald B. Robinson to MD, December 3, 1941; and Landis to MD, January 25, 1942, MD, B2; ER to MD, January 19, 1942, HGD, B216–F1; MD memo to Landis, February 8, 1942, MD, B2.

18. *Los Angeles Examiner*, February 5 and 13, 1942; *Los Angeles Times*, February 4, 1942; Landis press conference, February 11, 1942, MD, B11–F5.

19. *Congressional Record*, House of Rep., 77th Cong. 2nd sess. (February 3, 1942), Vol. 88. pt. 1, pp. 975–76; ibid. (February 4, 1942), 1,028–29; ibid. (February 6, 1942), 1,129–34, 1,145–51; ibid. (February 9, 1942), 1,144–56, 1,189–90; and ibid., pt. 8, *Appendix*, pp. A451–52. Senate, 77th Cong., 2nd sess., (February 3, 1942), vol. 88, pt. 1, p. 1,000; ibid. (February 11, 1942), 1,189. Duncan Underhill, "The Truth About Melvyn Douglas's Defense Job," [n.d., n.p.], Melvyn Douglas Icon File, WSHS. Melvyn received numerous letters of support; see MD, B2.

20. *Los Angeles Examiner*, February 23, 1942; ER to MD, February 23, 1942, MD, B2; Littell to HGD, February 16, 1942, HGD, B164–F16; MD statement, Office of Civilian Defense, February 9, 1942; and Screen Actors Guild statement, February 8, 1942, MD, B2; Mary Norton to HGD, February 11, 1942, HGD, B165–F1.

21. HGD to Littell, March 6, 1942, HGD, B164–F16.

22. Dewson notes, March 12, 1942, Dewson, B19; Nelda Salinger (for HGD) to Hickok, March 17, 1942, HGD, B212–F17; Porter to HGD, March 30, 1942, HGD, B165–F13; HGD to Dewson, April 2, 1942, Dewson, B19.

23. HGD to Tillett and Hickok, April 2, 1942, HGD, B165–F12; HGD to Dewson, April 15, 1942, Dewson, B19; HGD to MD, April 15, 1942; and MD to HGD, April 28, 1942, HMDP.

24. HGD to Stephen Early, June 1, 1942, HGD, B216–F4; Thomas F. Ford to HGD, October 8, 1942, HGD, B164–F10; HGD to Tillett, October 9, 1942, HGD, B165–F12; HGD radio address, August 24, 1942, HGD, B167–F5; *Los Angeles Daily News*, August 27, 1942.

25. Porter to HGD, August 2, 1942; and Porter to Tillett, September 22, 1942, HGD, B165–F13.

26. Pauley to HGD, November 19, 1942, DNC, B1144; Hickok to HGD, November 10 and 11, 1942, HGD, B212–F17. See also "Vote for Victory: A Voters' Handbook," *The New Republic* 107 (October 5, 1942): 42.

27. MD to ER, September 7, 1942, MD, B2–F5.

28. Voorhis to HGD, December 9, 1942; and Voorhis to MD, December 23, 1942, MD, B2; *New York Times*, August 25 and December 7, 1942; HGD to MD, December 10, 1942, HMDP.

29. ER to Walter Pick, June 9 and July 30, 1943, Pick; FDR memo to ER, and memo to Grace Tully, FDRP, President's Secretary's File, 144, Melvyn Douglas; Adjutant General to MD, July 8, 1943, MD, B2; unidentified newspaper article, July 14, 1943, DNC, B1144; ER to Pick, July 30, 1943, WP; ER to MD, September 27, 1943, Dewson, B2–F6.

30. HGD to MD, December, 1943, HMDP; HGD to ER, December 23, 1943, ER, 1943 pers corresp., B1682.

31. HGD to MD, August 19, December 10, [December], 1942, and June 23, 1943, HMDP; Douglas, *A Full Life*, 185. On women managing at home during the war, see, for example, D'Ann Campbell, *Women at War with America: Private Lives in a Patriotic Era* (Cambridge: Harvard University Press, 1984); and Susan M. Hartmann, *The

Home Front and Beyond: American Women in the 1940s (Boston: Twayne Publishers, 1982).

32. HGD to MD, August 19, 1943, HMDP; HGD to ER, HGD, B216–F1; Douglas, *A Full Life*, 185–86.

33. HGD to MD, August 16, 1943; and HGD to De Sola, April 21, 1942, HMDP.

34. HGD to MD, August 16, 1943, HMDP.

35. HGD to MD, May 19 and June 23, 1943; MD to HGD, May 18, June 1, August 8, 1943, HMDP.

36. HGD to MD, June 23, 1943, HMDP.

37. MD to HGD, May 4 and 18, October 31, 1943, HMDP.

38. HGD to MD, June 23, 1943; MD to HGD, December 20, 1942, May 4 and May 18, 1943, and October 31, 1943, HMDP. On separation, see Hartmann, *Home Front and Beyond*, especially chap. 9.

39. Holifield to HGD, November 9, 1943, HGD, B164–F13; White House Usher's Book for 1943, January 20–30 and February 14–24 entries; HGD to De Sola, January 13, 1943; and HGD to MD, January 25, 1943, HMDP.

40. HGD to MD, January 25, 1943, and June 1943, HMDP.

41. HGD to ER, August 19, 1943, HGD, B216–F1; HGD to MD, [n.d.], HMDP.

42. Douglas to Ickes, March 12, November 18, and December 13, 1941; and Ickes to Douglas, April 19, November 21, and December 17, 1941, HI, B97; HGD to ER, November 18, 1941, HGD, B216–F1; George Creel to Douglas, November 17, 1941, HGD, B164–F2; Douglas to Francis Biddle, November 18, 1941; and Biddle to Douglas, February 13, 1942, HGD, B164–F2; Hickok to HGD, May 26, 1943, HGD, B212–F17; Ickes to Creel, November 21, 1941, HI; HGD to MD, June 23, 1943, and August 19, 1943, HMDP.

43. HGD to MD, June 23, 1943, HMDP.

44. Lillian and Tom Ford to HGD, May 27 and June 1, 1943, HGD, B212–F9; Lillian Ford to HGD, October 20, 1943, HGD, B163–F11; HGD to Aubrey Williams, October 11, 1943, Aubrey Williams Papers, FDRL, B12–G; Douglas, *A Full Life*, 186–87.

45. Lillian Ford to HGD, May 27, 1943, HGD, B212–F9.

46. Lillian Ford to HGD, October 11, 1943, HGD, B163–F1; HGD to Harold Young, September 29, 1943; and Young to HGD, December 20, 1943, Henry A. Wallace Papers, FDRL, B40; HGD to McAllister, October 11, 1942, DM; HGD to Frank Walker, November 29, 1943, DNC; Douglas, *A Full Life*, 185.

47. Douglas, *A Full Life*, 189. See Gertzog, *Congressional Women*, for background of congresswomen, especially chaps. 2 and 3.

48. The statistical material in the following paragraphs is from the U.S. Dept. of Commerce, Bureau of the Census, Sixteenth Census of the U.S.: 1940, Pop., Vol. 2, *Characteristics of the Population*, Pt. 1, Alabama–District of Columbia (Washington, D.C.: U.S. Gov't. Printing Office, 1943), 541, 630; and U.S. Dept. of Commerce, Bureau of the Census, Special Census of Los Angeles, California, Population by Age, Race, and Sex by Census Tracts: January 29, 1946, Series P-SC, No. 188 (Washington, D.C.: U.S. Gov't. Printing Office, October 29, 1945), 1–9.

49. HGD, "The House That Jack Can't Build," speech before the Regional Conference of the National Association of Housing Officials, September 25, 1947, HI, B55.

50. Census data show a total of 13,000 in the category of "Other" in 1940, and 8,400 in 1946. If one assumes that few Japanese-Americans moved back into their 1940 homes when released from the detention camps, then the district had only about 4,600

Japanese in 1940, or approximately 12% of the county's 37,000 Japanese, a small number compared to the 47,000 blacks. See also Douglas to De Sola, June 20, 1944, HMDP. In 1940, the district included approximately 47,000 blacks, more than three-fourths of the city's total black population. In that year, blacks made up 15% of the district's 312,000 people.

During the war, blacks spilled over into the other assembly districts, particularly the 44th, when they moved north across Olympic Avenue up to Sixth Street and east to the river. The number of blacks in the 44th increased from 1,000 to 10,000. In the 64th, the 1940 black population of about 1,300—living in an area bounded by Third Avenue, Beverly, Hoover, and Main—increased only by about 400. The 55th, which had 93 blacks in 1940, increased to 400 in the small area between Maple and Main. In the 62nd Assembly District, the black population increased from 45,000 to over 73,000 during the war. Although some census tracts in the 62nd showed an increase of only 17–25% in the number of blacks, numbers in other tracts increased by several hundred percent.

For descriptive material on the district, see Clifton interview with author, material throughout the Ruth and Ed Lybeck Collection, Special Collections, University of California, Los Angeles (hereafter, REL); *Redbook* (February 1945), 60.

51. Lillian Ford to HGD, October 20, 1943, HGD, B183–F11; and Ford to Esther Murray, December 21, 1943, HGD, B163–F1.

52. Ford to Philip M. Connelly, February 3, 1944; J. R. Files to Ford, February 7, 1944; Ford to Files, February 10, 1944; and Ford to Neal Haggerty, February 12, 1944, HGD, all B163–F1. Ford to Sam Lindauer, February 3, 1944; and Ford to Dan Green, February 14, 1944, HGD, B163–F3.

53. Ford to "Friends," February 3, 1944; and Ford to Lindauer, February 10, 1944, HGD, B163–F3.

54. Ford to Neal Haggerty, February 12, 1944; C. J. Haggerty to Ford, February 17, 1944; Ford to HGD, October 20, 1943; C. B. Baldwin to Ford, February 28, 1944; and Boddy to Ford, February 15, 1944; all HGD, B163–F1. On labor's indecision, see HGD to the Fords, March 16, 1944, HGD, B193–F3.

55. Amerigo Bozzani to Ford, February 13, 1944, HGD, B163–F1.

56. Juanita Terry Barbee, "Helen Gahagan Douglas's Office Staff—Work and Relaxation," an oral history conducted 1976 by Fern Ingersoll, in Helen Gahagan Douglas Oral History Project, Vol. II, ROHO, 1981 (hereafter, Barbee, ROHO), 11–12.

57. HGD to MD, August 19, 1943, HMDP.

58. Thomas Ford to HGD, February 1, 1944; Lillian Ford to HGD, February 2, 1944, HGD, B163–F1; HGD to ER, February 21, 1944; and ER to HGD, February 28, 1944, ERP, Personal Correspondence, 1944, B1723; FDR to HGD, March 2, 1944, HGD, B193–F3; Douglas, *A Full Life*, 187–88.

Chapter 8

1. Clifton interview with author.

2. For example, see "Spot News," Charles E. Taintor campaign brochure, Spring 1944; HGD to ER, March 16, 1944; Ford to Lindauer, March 9, 1944, all HGD, B163–F3.

3. See, for example, Samuel Selden, *The Stage in Action* (New York: Appleton-Century Crofts, 1941); and idem, *First Steps in Acting* (New York: Appleton-Century Crofts, 1947); Francis Cowles Strickland, *The Technique of Acting* (New York: McGraw-

Hill, 1956); Louis Calvert, *Problems of the Actor* (New York: Henry Holt and Co., 1918); and Shirley McLaine interview with Larry King, *Larry King Live*, CNN, September 10, 1985. Also *Highlights*, WD, B26; Clifton interview with author; Sharon Lybeck Hartmann, interview with author, April 11, 1984; HGD to Dewson, March 31, 1944, Dewson, B20.

4. HGD to De Sola, June 20, 1944, HMDP; Thomas Ford to HGD, May 30, 1944, HGD, B163–F1; Clifton interview with author; State of California, Statement of Vote, Primary, 8th Senate Dist, May 16, 1944, p. 10.

5. MD to HGD, May 29, 1944, HMDP. Melvyn recalled in his autobiography that he did not learn she had run for Congress until she had won the fall campaign and she had moved to Washington. "My God, how out of touch I had become with my own life!" Although he in fact did learn in the spring that she was a candidate, his recollections thirty years later are poignant and telling. (Douglas and Arthur, *See You at the Movies*, 143.)

6. *New York Daily News*, July 10, 1944; *New York Post*, July 19, 1944; *Boston Daily Globe*, July 14, 1944; *Christian Science Monitor*, July 16, 1944; Walter Gahagan to HGD, July 6, 1944, HMDP.

7. HGD to MD, July 13, 1944, HMDP; ER to Pick, July 8, 1944, WP; HGD to Ann Oliphant, July 15, 1944, HGD, B163–F3.

8. *New York Times*, July 13, 14, 15, 19, and 21, 1944; *Los Angeles Examiner*, July 21 and 22, 1944; MD to HGD, August 4, 1944, HMDP.

9. Unofficial minutes of Western Democrats Meeting, July 20, 1944, HGD, B153–F5; *Los Angeles Examiner*, July 22, 1944; ER to Pick, July 23, 1944, WP. For ER on Wallace, see, for example, Richard S. Kirkendall, "ER and the Issue of FDR's Successor," Hoff-Wilson and Lightman, eds., *Without Precedent*, 176–97.

10. *Democratic Digest* (August 1944), 9–12; Tillett to Dewson, July 20, 1944, Dewson, B20–Scrapbook.

11. ER to Pick, September 14, 1944, WP. On labor, see, for example, Philip Murray and Sidney Hillman to "Sir and Brother," April 3, 1944, Textile Workers Union of America Papers (hereafter, TWUA), Series 1A, B3, WSHS.

12. Lybeck interview with author and various HICCASP publications in HICCASP Papers, Special Collections, UCLA, and HICCASP Papers, Special Collections, WSHS; see, for example, *The Free Press* for the fall of 1944. See *PM*, October 6, 1944, on HICCASP. AFL's president William Green refused to let any of his locals work with the CIO. For example, see Marshall Shafer to William Green, September 5, 1944; Thomas M. Brett and Thomas H. Deane to Green, April 4, 1944; Stanley L. Sapp to Green, April 17, 1944; Green to Sapp, April 25, 1944; and Green to Barrow, March 25, 1944; all in American Federation of Labor Papers, WSHS (hereafter, AFL); MD, B26. See also Fenno, *Home Style*, chap. 4, on the nature of constituencies.

13. Campbell and Douglas campaign literature, HMDP.

14. Clifton interview with author.

15. *New York Herald Tribune*, October 22, 1944.

16. HGD to MD and Pick, October 20, 1944, WP; Hannigan to HGD, October 19, 1944, DNC, B1144; Hickok to HGD, October 24, 1944, HGD, B171–F5.

17. Stuart P. Dobbs to HGD, November 10, 1944, HGD, B171–F2; FDR to HGD, November 27, 1944, HGD, B216–F3; Hickok to Douglas, November 15, 1944, HGD, B171–F2; ER to HGD, November 16, 1944, HGD, B216–F1.

18. State of California, Statement of Vote, General Election, November 7, 1944, p. 9; Clifton interview with author; HGD to FDR, November 27, 1944, FDRP, President's Secretary's Files, Gahagan, 3–44.

19. Robert Kenny to Clair Engle, November 9, 1944, Robert Kenny Papers (hereafter, RK), B7, BL; Fred Houser to "Friend," December 23, 1944, Sheridan Downey Papers (hereafter, SD), B4, BL; and New York Times, November 10, 1944, on the importance of the women's vote.

There is extensive literature on women as candidates, although the literature on political women in general and specifically women in elected office, particularly Congress, was quite sparse prior to the late 1960s. But in the last twenty years, the topic has become a major focus of scholarly examination by both historians and social scientists. Much of the political-science interest has been spearheaded by Ruth Mandel, director of the Center for the American Woman and Politics, Eagleton Institute of Politics, Rutgers University. The center sponsors conferences, publishes scholarly materials, collects materials, particularly newsclips, and conducts oral interviews. Examples of publications include Kathy A. Stanwick, Political Women Tell What It Takes (1983), and Susan J. Carroll and Wendy S. Strimling, Women's Routes to Elective Office: A Comparison with Men's (1983), both part of a major study concerned with recruiting more women to run for political office.

Prior to the late 1960s, periodicals, including Independent Women, the journal of the Federation of Business and Professional Women, and the Democratic Digest, the publication of the Women's Division of the Democratic Party, provided the richest sources on women in politics. The American Association of Political and Social Science devoted a complete issue of its journal, Annals of the American Association of Political and Social Science, to an overview of women in politics in 1947. Works on congresswomen, such as Annabel Paxton, Women in Congress (Richmond, Va.: Dietz Press, 1945), are sketchy, but Roosevelt and Hickok, Ladies of Courage, offers insights into women's political activities in the 1940s, as do Louis M. Young's Understanding Politics: A Practical Guide for Women (New York: Pellegrini and Cudahy, 1950), India Edwards' autobiography, Pulling No Punches: Memoirs of a Woman in Politics (New York: G. P. Putnam's Sons, 1977), Eleanor Roosevelt's "My Day" column, It's Up to the Women, and her several books on her life. Some rather superficial biographies on congresswomen include Alden Hatch's Ambassador Extraordinary, Clare Boothe Luce (New York: Henry Holt and Company, 1955), and David G. Loth's A Long Way Forward: The Biography of Congresswoman Frances P. Bolton (New York: Longmans, Green, 1957).

Books by historians on women in politics since suffrage include William H. Chafe's The American Woman: Her Changing Social, Economic, and Political Roles, 1920–1970 (New York: Oxford University Press, 1972), esp. pp. 25–67, and his revised edition, The Paradox of Change: American Women in the Twentieth Century (New York: Oxford University Press, 1991); Ware's Beyond Suffrage and her Holding Their Own; Hartmann's The Home Front and Beyond. Nancy J. Weiss's Farewell to the Party of Lincoln: Black Politics in the Age of FDR (Princeton, N.J.: Princeton University Press, 1983) has an excellent chapter on Eleanor Roosevelt, as well as important material on Mary McLeod Bethune. Without Precedent, edited by Joan Hoff-Wilson and Marjorie Lightman, offers a variety of new ways to examine political women. Much of the scholarship on political women prior to the suffrage amendment is useful, including Griffith's In Her Own Right: The Life of Elizabeth Cady Stanton (New York: Oxford University Press, 1984), and the work of Kathryn Kish Sklar on Florence Kelley.

Political science literature is also very helpful. A quite lengthy bibliography by Kathy A. Stanwick and Christine Li, The Political Participation of Women in the United States: A Selected Bibliography, 1950–1976 (New Brunswick: Center for the American Woman and Politics, 1977), is useful, although outdated. See also Martin Gruberg,

Women in American Politics: An Assessment and Sourcebook (Oshkosh, Wisc.: Academia Press, 1968); Susan and Martin Tolchin, *Clout: Womanpower and Politics* (New York: Coward, McCann, and Geoghegan, 1974); Jeane J. Kirkpatrick, *Political Woman* (New York: Basic Books, 1974); Rita Mae Kelly and Mary Boutilier, *The Making of Political Women: A Study of Socialization and Role Conflict* (Chicago: Nelson-Hall, 1978); Sandra Baxter and Marjorie Lansing, *Women and Politics: The Visible Majority*, rev. ed. (Ann Arbor: University of Michigan Press, 1983); Ruth Mandel, *In the Running: The New Woman Candidate* (New Haven, Conn.: Ticknor and Fields, 1981); and the very helpful Gertzog, *Congressional Women*. Autobiographies by political women, particularly Geraldine A. Ferraro, *Ferraro: My Story* (New York: Bantam Books, 1985), offer insights into the difficulties women face when they enter high-level politics. Periodical literature abounds.

For a discussion of different ways congressional candidates and members of Congress gain support and legitimacy, see chap. 3 in Richard F. Fenno, Jr., *Home Style*. Ervin Goffman, in *The Presentation of Self in Everyday Life* (Woodstock, N.Y.: The Overlook Press, 1973), discusses the impact of an individual's use of theatrical vocabulary on a group. See also Lewis A. Dexter, "The Representative and His District," in Theodore J. Lowi, ed., *Legislative Politics, U.S.A.: Congress and the Forces That Shape It*, 2nd ed. (Boston: Little, Brown, 1962), chap. 8.

20. ER to HGD, November 12, 1944, FDRP, President's Personal File, 7371, Helen Gahagan.

21. HGD to MD, December 15, 1944, HMDP.

22. Ibid.

23. HGD and Jamila Marton to Walter Pick, December 31, 1944, WP; Lilienthal, *The TVA Years*, 674, 678.

24. *Washington Post*, December 31, 1944. See *St. Louis Post-Dispatch*, March 4, 1945, for interesting profiles of selected members. For a good discussion of the "extraordinary looseness in party performance" and yet a "passionate attachment to party labels," see Clarence Berdhahl, "American Government and Politics: Some Notes on Party Membership in Congress, III," *American Political Science Review* 45 (August 1949): 721–34. Colleen O'Connor has treated Douglas's congressional years in "Through the Valley of Darkness: Helen G. Douglas' Congressional Years" (Ph.D. diss., University of California, San Diego, 1982).

25. *Democratic Digest* (December 1944–January 1945). The *New York Times*, November 12, 1944, discussed committee appointments of women in Congress. Gertzog lists the committees on which women have most commonly served. From 1947–1964, for example, these committees included District of Columbia, Education and Labor, Foreign Affairs, Government Operations, and Veterans' Affairs (Gertzog, *Congressional Women*, 263–69).

26. *San Diego Journal*, January 17, 1945. Richard Fenno, *Congressmen in Committees* (Boston: Little, Brown, 1973), amply describes examples of each type. See also Nicholas A. Masters, "Committee Assignments in the House of Representatives," *American Political Science Review* 55 (June 1961): 345–57. The importance of committee assignments is discussed in other works, including Masters, op. cit.; Randall B. Ripley, *Congress: Process and Policy* (New York: W. W. Norton, 1975), esp. 102ff.; Ralph K. Huitt and Robert L. Peabody, *Congress: Two Decades of Analysis* (New York: Harper and Row, 1969); Ralph K. Huitt, "The Congressional Committee: A Case Study," *American Political Science Review* 48 (June 1954): 340–65; and Steven S. Smith and Christopher Dering, *Committees in Congress* (Washington, D.C.: Congressional Quarterly Press, 1984).

On the powers of the Foreign Affairs Committee, see, for example, Fenno, *Congress in Committees*; Holbert N. Carroll, *The House of Representatives and Foreign Affairs*, rev. ed. (Boston: Little, Brown, 1966); Raymond M. Lahr and J. William Theis, *Congress: Power and Purpose on Capitol Hill* (Boston: Allyn and Bacon, 1974), chap. 7; George P. Galloway, *History of the House of Representatives*, ed. Sidney Wise (New York: Thomas Y. Crowell, 1976; 2nd rev. ed.), chap. 12; Rochelle Jones and Peter Woll, *The Private World of Congress* (New York: Free Press, 1979); and Donald G. Tacheron and Morris K. Udall, *The Job of the Congressman: An Introduction to Service in the U.S. House of Representatives* (Indianapolis: Bobbs-Merrill, 1966), esp. pp. 13ff. For women's progress in the informal and formal power structure, see Gertzog, *Congressional Women*, chaps. 4–8.

From the very beginning, Douglas cultivated her relationship with Sam Rayburn. Although she had no place in his power structure, the Speaker of the House listened to her and valued her articulate and outspoken backing of the President's program.

27. *Baltimore Sun*, January 28, 1945; Douglas, *A Full Life*, 201–2.

Congress Off the Record (Washington, D.C.: American Enterprise Institute, 1983) mentions that a "quiet period of apprenticeship" was typical of new members of Congress prior to the 1970s. Charles L. Clapp, *The Congressman: His Work As He Sees It* (Garden City, N.Y.: Doubleday, 1963) discusses the importance of "learning the ropes" quickly, including the subtleties of the legislative process. He also points out that the prior experience of a new member of Congress has little or no relevance to his or her stature in the House. Everyone begins at the bottom (e.g., 10, 23, 49). See also Fenno, "The Freshman Congressman: His View of the House," in Nelson W. Polsby, ed., *Congressional Behavior* (New York: Random House, 1971), 129–35; Tacheron and Udall, *Job of the Congressman*, 152–53; and Gertzog, *Congressional Women*, 52–53. Emanuel Celler wrote that freshmen "chafe at the tardiness with which their talents are recognized and rewarded by assignments to coveted posts"; Douglas was much too impatient to wait out the system. (Celler, "The Seniority Rule in Congress," *Western Political Quarterly* 14 (March 1961): Part. 1, pp. 160–67; and Gerald D. Sturges, "The Freshman Faces Congress," and Ernest A. Chaples, Jr., "Congress Gets New Ideas from Outside Experts," in Swen Groennings and Jonathan P. Hawley, eds., *To Be a Congressman: The Promise and the Power* (Washington, D.C.: Acropolis Books, 1983).

The first half of Huitt and Peabody, *Congress: Two Decades of Analysis*, includes an excellent historiographical essay on changing views of the House. Good general works on the House of Representatives include Richard Bolling, *Power in the House: A History of the Leadership of the House of Representatives* (New York: E. P. Dutton, 1968); Joseph Cooper and G. Calvin MacKenzie, *The House at Work* (Austin: University of Texas Press, 1981); Galloway, *History of the House of Representatives*; Neil McNeil, *Forge of Democracy: The House of Representatives* (New York: D. McKay, 1963). See also Barbara Sinclair, *Congressional Realignment, 1925–1978* (Austin: University of Texas Press, 1982); V. O. Key, Jr., *Politics, Parties, and Pressure Groups* (New York: Thomas Y. Crowell, 1946—and numerous subsequent editions); and Norman J. Ornstein, ed., *Congress in Change: Evolution and Reform* (New York: Praeger Publishers, 1975).

Useful works for this book that specifically look at the behavior of individual members of Congress include Roger H. Davidson, *The Role of the Congressman* (New York: Pegasus, 1969); Clem Miller, *Member of the House: Letters of a Congressman*, ed. John W. Baker (New York: Charles Scribner, 1962); and Clapp, *The Congressman*. Helpful scholarly books on individual congressmen include in particular James T. Patterson,

Mr. Republican: A Biography of Robert A. Taft (Boston: Houghton Mifflin, 1972), as well as Anthony Champagne, *Congressman Sam Rayburn* (New Brunswick: Rutgers University Press, 1985), and Edward L. and Frederick H. Schapsmeier, *Dirksen of Illinois: Senatorial Statesman* (Urbana: University of Illinois Press, 1985).

28. Douglas, *A Full Life*, 203–4.

29. Clapp, *The Congressman*, esp. chap. 9 on wives and children. See also Evelyn Chavoor, "Twenty-Four-Hour-a-Day Support Person," an oral history conducted in 1976 by Fern S. Ingersoll, in Helen Gahagan Douglas Oral History Project, Vol. II, ROHO, 1981 (hereafter, Chavoor, ROHO), particularly 263–72 and 289–98; Douglas, ROHO, 87–100.

30. Chavoor to Ruth and Ed Lybeck, February 7, 1945, REL, B1-F2.

31. *Redbook* (February 1945), 60.

32. Ibid.

33. Ibid. See also Chavoor to the Lybecks, February 7, 1945, REL, B1-F2.

34. Benjamin I. Page, *Choice and Echoes in Presidential Elections: Rational Man and Electoral Democracy* (Chicago: University of Chicago Press, 1978), 267. See also V. O. Key, *Politics, Parties, and Pressure Groups*, 5–12. Douglas refused to see that "politics is not a branch of moral philosophy," as Key put it (11).

35. *Congressional Record*, House of Rep., 79th Cong. 1st sess. (March 26, 1945), Vol. 91, pt. 11, Appendix, p. A1491.

36. Ibid., A1491–92, and March 14, 1945, Vol. 91, pt. 10 Appendix, pp. A1186–87.

37. HGD to ER, November 12, 1944, FDRP, President's Personal File, 7371, Helen Gahagan. Celler, "The Seniority Rule in Congress," 160–67. See Davidson, *The Role of the Congressman*; Donald R. Matthews, *U.S. Senators and Their World* (Chapel Hill: University of North Carolina Press, 1960); and William S. White, *Citadel: The Story of the U.S. Senate* (New York: Harper and Row, 1957). Harold Lasswell in *Power and Personality* (New York: W. W. Norton, 1948) makes a number of points concerning motivation and skill that suggest Douglas's peculiar quest for power and influence. Various essays in Theodore J. Lowi, ed., *Legislative Politics, U.S.A.*, suggest profiles of the typical member of Congress that underscore the fact that Douglas was atypical in almost every way.

38. See note #27, this chapter, for citations on rules for gaining power for newcomers, and Hartmann interview with author. Also useful is Richard Fenno, "U.S. House Members in Their Constituencies: An Exploration," *American Political Science Review* 71, pt. 2 (September 1977), 898. In this article, Fenno introduced some of the ideas that he eventually developed in *Home Style*.

39. Political scientists have attempted to arrive at various schemes for typing congressmen. Most scholars examine the members' Washington style, although Fenno in *Home Style* and Lewis Anthony Dexter in *The Sociology and Politics of Congress* (Chicago: Rand McNally, 1969) analyzed a member's relationship to his constituency. See also Tacheron and Udall, *The Job of the Congressman*, Chapter 9. Some experts use a member's background—age, socioeconomic status, education, occupation, and geographic mobility (although never gender) to distinguish congressional types. Davidson, however, in *The Role of the Congressman*, contended that only occupation influences the "perceptual role." He divided congressional behavior into five categories (a member might combine more than one category). The first type is tribunal, or constituent-based. This type of member focuses on popular needs or wants. The ritualistic member masters legislative procedures so he can write the laws. This member does his legislative homework; floor and committee work are of utmost importance. Davidson contends that most

legislators become more ritualistic after the first term. Ninety percent of members fall in either or both of these categories. A third type is the inventor, a crusader who "emphasizes problem solving or policy innovation." This person sees himself as representing a whole state, the country, or even the world. Some contend, Davidson argues, that the inventor role results from a member's committee assignment; others argue that it complements the tribunal role. The fourth category is the brokerage role, a designation applicable to the member who wants to balance diverse geographical, occupational, ideological interests. The brokerage type differs from the tribunal type, who concentrates solely on constituents' needs. Finally, there is the opportunist, who stresses campaigning and re-election exclusively.

Matthews, in *U.S. Senators and Their World*, has another set of categories: the patrician who has an inherited political position; the amateur who has significant business and professional accomplishments; the professional politician who has enjoyed considerable political accomplishments; and the agitator who is generally of lower social origins and from the West, where society is less stratified and party leadership has less control over the nominating process than in other parts of the country. Also, the agitator has no inherited position or important accomplishments. From 1947–1957, says Matthews, only 4% of the members fell into this category.

It is difficult to "type" Douglas. Her acting background does not parallel that of any other member of Congress, except perhaps Glenn Taylor or, to a degree, Everett Dirksen. Although she did have an apprenticeship in party politics, it was at the top level in California. She believed the voter should be educated to vote good members in and bad ones out. She also believed in the power of letter-writing to members of Congress. For an article providing stimulating material for understanding Douglas, see Jean E. Torcom, "Leadership: The Role and Style of Senator Everett Dirksen," in Groennings and Hawley, eds., *To Be a Congressman*.

40. Huitt and Peabody, *Congress*, 170. Political scientists do not agree on the definition of "outsider." See, for example, the work of Matthews, Huitt, and Dexter, *Sociology and Politics of Congress*.

41. Huitt makes his argument for outsiders and includes senators George Norris, Paul Douglas, Wayne Morse, Herbert Lehman, and William Proxmire, all of whom, he contends, made a significant contribution to legislative politics. Although he does not mention women, his position is critical in forcing a re-evaluation of women in Congress.

42. Chavoor to Ed Lybeck, March 19, 1945, REL, B1-F2; and Samuel A. Weiss to Hannegan, May 15, 1945, DNC, B1144.

43. F. Cowles Strickland, *The Techniques of Acting*; and Josephine Dillon [Gable], *Modern Acting: A Guide for Stage, Screen, and Radio* (New York: Prentice-Hall, 1940). In *The Job of the Congressman*, Tacheron and Udall make the point (as do others) that speaking ability is not a necessary tool for power within the House. Rayburn, for example, was not noted for his oratorical skills (Champagne, *Congressman Sam Rayburn*). Halliam Boswell, *Techniques in Dramatic Art* (New York: Macmillan, 1928) has an interesting discussion comparing acting and public speaking (399–416).

44. *Dallas Morning News*, January 11, 1945; and *Louisville Courier-Journal*, June 6, 1945.

45. *Dallas Morning News*, January 11, 1945.

46. *Baltimore Sun*, January 28, 1945; and *Louisville Courier-Journal*, June 3, 1945.

47. Chavoor to Ed and Ruth Lybeck, February 7, 1945, REL; HGD to Bennet,

March 7, 1945, HGD, B207-F9. On October 17, 1945, John Coffee was selected chairman of the liberal bloc (Coffee to HGD, October 10, 1945, HGD, B207-F9).

48. Pick, ROHO, 165; Chavoor, ROHO, passim; Creekmore Fath, interview with author, March 4, 1983. The relationship of Douglas and Johnson has never been discussed to any extent. Robert Caro, in *The Years of Lyndon Johnson: The Path to Power* (New York: Alfred A. Knopf, 1982), says only that Douglas "spent a lot of time" with Johnson (550).

49. ER to Pick, January, 1945, WP; and Douglas, *A Full Life*, 210.

50. Douglas, *A Full Life*, 210; *Milwaukee Journal*, April 13, 1945; Outland et al., "To the Democrats of Southern California," April 16, 1945, HGD, B27-F2; Chavoor to Ed Lybeck, April 23, 1945, REL, B1-F2.

51. Chavoor to Ed Lybeck, April 23, 1945, REL, Bl-F2.

Chapter 9

1. Numerous books deal with women and the war, among them, Susan Hartmann, *Home Front and Beyond*; Karen Anderson, *Wartime Women: Sex Roles, Family Relations, and the Status of Women During World War II* (Westport, Conn.: Greenwood Press, 1941); D'Ann Campbell, *Women at War with America: Private Lives in a Patriotic Era* (Cambridge, Mass.: Harvard University Press, 1984).

2. See, for example, Weiss, *Farewell to the Party of Lincoln*, 120–22; and Joanna Schneider Zangrando and Robert L. Zangrando, "ER and Black Civil Rights," in Hoff-Wilson and Lightman, *Without Precedent*, 88–92. Douglas, *A Full Life*, 58–59.

3. Ibid., 165–66.

4. Barbee, ROHO, 10.

5. *Chicago Defender*, January 13, 1945.

6. See Zangrando and Zangrando, "ER and Black Civil Rights," 91; ER article in *The New Republic* 106 (May 11, 1942): 630; and Douglas, "If I Were a Negro," *Negro Digest* (October 1943), 49–50.

7. Bethune to HGD, March 14, 1945; and HGD to Walter Wanger, April 25, 1945, HGD, B23-F4. ER was attempting to reduce publicity about her civil rights activity. As she wrote her good friend Bess Furman, who covered women's issues for the *New York Times*, "I think it would be wonderful to write about the Negroes and their accomplishments, mentioning their presence at the Inauguration, and their quiet dignity and acceptance of their rights. If you mention me [however], it will do them harm and hurt my ability to help them (ER to Furman, January 23, 1945, ERP, Series 100, B1757).

8. Helen G. Douglas, Howard M. LeSourd, and Carl Hermann Voss to Members of Congress, [n.d.], HGD, B15-F4; for an example of the dialogue the letter elicited, see John H. Folger to HGD, May 28, 1945; and HGD to Folger, June 5, 1945, HGD, B15-F4.

9. Examples of her writings include Douglas, "Back from Babylon," *The Christian Register* 124 (October 1945): 364–65; *To Christian Youth* and *Questions and Answers on Palestine* (New York: American Christian Palestine Committee, 1945); "Back from Babylon," *Zion's Herald* (October 17, 1945), 661, 665; positive responses include Nussbaum to HGD, October 10, 1945, HGD B15-F4; HGD to Mrs. Arthur J. Rubel, October 12, 1945; Theodore Strimling to HGD, November 15, and December 20, 1945; and Arthur O. Turbow to HGD, December 21, 1945, all HGD, B26-F5;

Congressional Record, House of Rep., 79th Cong., 1st sess. (October 16, 1945), Vol. 91, pt. 7, pp. 9,692–93; and ibid., *Appendix* (October 4, 1945), Vol. 91, pt. 12, pp. A4,183–85; *New York Times*, October 15, 1945. For HGD on Arab rights, see HGD to Arthur B. Dewberry, November 26, 1945, HGD, B26-F5.

10. Chavoor to Ed Lybeck, February 26 and May 26, 1945; and HGD to Ruth and Ed Lybeck, February 22, 1945, REL, B1-F2. B207, includes some of her invitations to speak for 1945.

11. HGD to Posner, May 26, 1945, HGD, B26-F4.

12. MD to HGD, January 30 and April 15, 1945, HMDP.

13. Chavoor to Ed Lybeck, July 3, 1945, REL, B1-F2.

14. MD interview with Arthur, July 19–22, 1972; Chavoor to Ed Lybeck, April 17 and 27, 1946, REL, B1-F3.

15. *Congressional Record*, House of Rep., 79th Cong., 1st sess. (October 4, 1945), Vol. 91, pt. 7, pp. 9,460–61.

16. Richard G. Hewlett and Oscar E. Anderson, Jr., *A History of the United States Atomic Energy Commission*, Vol. 1, *The New World, 1939–1946* (University Park: Pennsylvania State University Press, 1962), particularly chaps. 10, 13, and 14, provides a very detailed legislative history of the Atomic Energy Act. Other useful books include James R. Newman and Byron S. Miller, *The Control of Atomic Energy: A Study of Its Social, Economic, and Political Implications* (New York: Whittlesey House, 1948); Harold P. Green and Alan Rosenthal, *Government of the Atom: The Integration of Powers* (New York: Atherton Press, 1963); and Corbin Allardice and Edward R. Trapnell, *The Atomic Energy Commission* (New York: Praeger Publishers, 1974). Douglas is not given much credit for her role, however, in the general histories of the Atomic Energy Act or the Atomic Energy Commission. Hewlett and Anderson, for example, note the importance of public protest but do not identify the key organizers. This type of omission has tended to prevent recognition of women's lobbying roles in the legislative process.

See Douglas, statement to the press, October 12, 1945, HGD, B16-F1; idem, *A Full Life*, 215; and idem, ROHO, 141–42.

17. Newman and Miller, *Control of Atomic Energy*, 9; Freda Kirchwey to Robert Kenny, October 22, 1945, RK, B1, BL. Joyce and Zlatko Balokovic to HGD, October 15, 1945; HGD to Tris Coffin, October 29, 1945; and the Executive Committee of the Association of Manhattan District Scientists, New York City Area, to HGD, October 16, 1945, all HGD, B16-F4.

18. Chavoor to Hickok, October 17, 1945, LH, B13.

19. November 13, 1945, press list and draft of resolution in HGD, B48-F6, 7; HGD to J. H. Oppenheimer, Albert Einstein, James Franck, and ten other atomic scientists, November 20, 1935, HGD, B16-F1; Oppenheimer to HGD, November 21, 1945, HGD, B16-F1.

20. *Congressional Record*, House of Rep., 79th Cong., 1st sess. (November 23, 1945), Vol. 91, pt. 8, pp. 10,940–46; and ibid., *Appendix* (December 5, 1945), Vol. 91, pt. 3, pp. A5,306–307; Charles D. Coryell to HGD, November 26, 1945, in HGD, B16-F1; HGD to Griselda Kuhlman, November 12, 1945, HGD, B13-F15; James F. Byrnes, *All in One Lifetime* (New York: Harper and Row, 1958), 326, 331–33; Hewlett and Anderson, *The New World*, 470–77.

21. *San Francisco Chronicle*, November 27, 1945; Frieda F. Halpern to National Working Committee, ICCASP, November 21, 1945; and Halpern to HGD, November 28, 1945, HGD, B16-F1; George Pepper to Members of HICCASP, November 30, 1945; minutes of ICCASP Conference, December 3, 1945; and other materials relating

to the two conferences, HICCASP Papers, Special Collections, University of California, Los Angeles (hereafter, HICCASP); ad for mass meeting with Douglas, Reagan, and Pauling, HICCASP.

22. *NAACP Bulletin* (August–September 1945), 1–2; *San Francisco Chronicle*, October 30 and December 12, 1945; *New York Post*, January 22, 1946; Mrs. J. E. Guinn to HGD, October 22, 1945, HGD, B12-F6; Sylvia Herron to HGD, December 13, 1945, HGD, B32-F5; "List of House Members Who Have Not Signed Discharge Petition No. 4 for a Permanent FEPC Bill," December 1945, HGD, B44-F1; Alfred E. Smith to HGD, October 30, 1945, HGD, B12-F6; publicity on FEPC debate, November 2, 1945, HGD, B12-F8; HGD, "The Negro Soldier," January 22, 1946, HMDP; and Douglas, *A Full Life*, 226–29. Books on black soldiers do not acknowledge Douglas's project. See, for example, A. Russell Buchanan, *Black Americans in World War II* (Santa Barbara, Calif.: Clio Books, 1977); Gunnar Myrdal, *An American Dilemma: The Negro Problem and Modern Democracy* (New York: Harper and Row, 1962); and Richard M. Dalfiume, *Desegregation of the Armed Forces: Fighting on Two Fronts, 1939–1953* (Columbia: University of Missouri Press, 1969).

23. According to Hewlett and Anderson, McMahon had met Newman at Douglas's house during the summer of 1945 (*The New World*, 439); press release on atomic energy, Douglas and McMahon bills, [n.d.], HGD, B48-F6; Douglas, *A Full Life*, 216.

24. Douglas, "What You Can Do About Civilian Control of Atomic Energy," [March 1946], HGD, B48-F7; F. R. Von Wendegger, President, Plaza Bank of St. Louis, March 6, 1945, to Truman, Congressman May, and other members of Congress, HGD, B16-F10. HGD to "Dear Friend," March 5, 1946; and John B. Hawkes, Stevens Institute of Technology, to HGD, March 12, 1946, both in HGD, B48-F6. Lee Norgans to McMahon, March 22, 1946; and Cora H. Baehr to HGD, March 20, 1946, HGD, B16-F6; Douglas, "Women and Atomic Energy," [March 1946], HGD, B13-F8; HICCASP Papers, UCLA; Hewlett and Anderson, *The New World*, 501. Holifield, Douglas, Walter H. Judd, and Charles M. La Follette were the most active members of Congress during March. See Holifield, Douglas, Charles M. La Follette, and Walter Judd to "Colleagues," March 19, 1946, HGD, B16-F6; *Christian Science Monitor*, March 19, 1946; *New York Times*, March 22, 1946; *PM*, March 22, 1946; and *New York Herald Tribune*, March 24, 1946.

25. "Summary of Action by Emergency Conference on Civilian Control of Atomic Energy," April 1946, HGD, B48-F6; Hewlett and Anderson, *The New World*, 514–15; *Congressional Record*, House of Rep., 79th Cong., 2nd sess. (July 18, 1946), Vol. 92, pt. 7, pp. 9,350–53.

26. HGD to Roy K. Marshall, July 23, 1946, HGD, B16-F3; *PM*, July 22, 1946; *New York Herald-Tribune*, July 3, 1946; *Washington Post*, July 18, 1946; *New York Evening Post* and *PM*, July 22, 1946; *Baltimore Sun*, July 26, 1946.

27. David E. Lilienthal to HGD, April 2, 1946, HGD, B21-F9; Irving Richter, "Behind Washington Headlines," March 8, 1946, REL, B1-F3, UCLA; W. A. Higinbotham and J. A. Rush to HGD, August 5, 1946, HGD, B212-F11; Newman and Miller, *The Control of Atomic Energy*, dedication. Copy in HGD's private library includes the personal inscription from Newman.

28. Albert Cahn, "Helen Gahagan Douglas—The Lobby for Civilian Control of Atomic Energy," an oral history conducted 1978 by Scobie, in Helen Gahagan Douglas Oral History Project, Vol. III, ROHO, 1981, pp. 196–99; and Chester E. Holifield, "Helen Gahagan Douglas—Perspectives of a Southern California Colleague," an oral history conducted 1978 by Scobie, op. cit., 176.

29. *Congressional Record*, House of Rep., 79th Cong., 2nd sess. (March 29, 1946), Vol. 92, pt. 3, pp. 2,856–59.

30. Ibid., and draft of Douglas biography. HMDP.

31. HGD to Ed Lybeck, June 24, 1946, REL, B1-F3; and Lybeck to HGD, [n.d., June 1946], REL, B1-F9.

32. Clifton interview with author.

33. L.A. Freeway Evictions, Factual Summary, December 11, 1945, HGD, B20-F14. Douglas and Holifield wired Warren on November 28, 1945: "Condemnation of houses in path of proposed Los Angeles Freeway must be stopped at once and whole project postponed until housing crisis in Los Angeles has passed. . . . Situation so serious that breakdown of sanitation threatened, with danger of plague [which] could mean wiping out half million people. . . . We have to have a freeway sometime, but first things come first. People must have a place to live before they are given a freeway to drive automobiles on" (HGD, B20-F14). See also Citizens Evictee Committee to HGD, November 28, 1946, HGD, B27-F1; HGD to Ed Lybeck, REL, B1-F2; HGD to Birdie and Ellan Juda, December 20, 1945, HGD, B20-F14; Temple to HGD, May 4 and July 2, 1945; and HGD to Temple, September 21, 1945, HGD, B29-F1; HGD to Allen Rivkin, September 21, 1945, HGD B29-F1; HGD to Robert E. Hannigan, November 26, 1945, HGD, B27-F1; C. G. Woodson to HGD, January 31, 1945, HGD, B207-F1; *Los Angeles Sentinel* to HGD, February 5, 1945; George Gleason to HGD, April 6, 1945, HGD, B20-F11; HGD to John H. Fahey, June 25, 1946, REL, B1-F4.

34. Chavoor to Ed Lybeck, July 3, 1945, REL, B1-F2; Ed Lybeck to Chavoor, June 1946, and Lybeck to HGD, [n.d. November 1946], REL, B1-F9.

35. Lybeck, "Fear of Douglas Speech Blocks Plans for Distributing Nazi Films," [July 1945], and Chavoor to Ed Lybeck, July 3, 1945, REL, B1-F2; *California Democrat*, October 15, 1946.

36. Rollin L. McNitt to HGD, April 22, 1946; HGD to McNitt, April 27, 1946; McAllister to Esther Murray, May 7, 1946; McAllister to HGD, May 7, 1946, all HGD, B12-F7. *Los Angeles Daily News*, May 8, 1946; *New York Tribune*, March 9, 1946; and *Congressional Record*, House of Rep., 79th Cong., 2nd sess. (February 27, 1946), Vol. 92, pt. 2, pp. 1,724–32; HGD to Ed Lybeck, August 7, 1945, HGD to Truman, August 7, 1945, and Chavoor to Ed Lybeck, May 9, 1946, REL, B1-F3.

37. California, *Statement of Vote*, General Election, November 5, 1946, p. 15; HGD to Hickok, June 18, 1946, LH, B13; Ed Lybeck to Chavoor, June 1946; Ed Lybeck to Chavoor, June 16, 1946; and Ed Lybeck to Douglas, n.d. [prob. June 1946], REL, B1-F9.

38. Douglas interview with Arthur, July 18–21, 1972; Chavoor, ROHO, 292–293; Chavoor to Ed Lybeck, March 11 and April 16, 1946, REL, B1-F3.

39. Chavoor to Ed Lybeck, May 18 and 23, 1946, REL, B1-F3; and Chavoor to Ruth and Ed Lybeck, January 17, 1947, REL, B1-F5.

40. HGD to MD, June 17, 1946; and MD to HGD, June 20, 1946, HMDP.

Chapter 10

1. HGD to MD, October 18, 1946; and MD to HGD, October 22, 1946, HMDP.

2. *Brooklyn Eagle*, November 20, 1946.

3. HGD to MD, October 18 and 22, 1946, HMDP. Douglas's name does not appear in the daily meeting summaries. See United Nations, Official Records of the Second Part of the First Session of the General Assembly, *Second Committee, Economic and Financial Questions, Summary Record of Meetings,* November 1 to December 9, 1946 (Lake Success, New York: 1947); and *Joint Committee of the Second and Third Committees, Summary Record of Meetings,* November 18 to December 10, 1946 (Lake Success, New York: 1947). On her talk, see United Nations, Official Records of the Second Part of the First Session of the General Assembly, *Plenary Meetings of the General Assembly,* verbatim record, October 23 to December 16, 1946 (Flushing, New York: 1947), 66th Plenary Meeting, December 15, 1946, pp. 1,399–1,404; *New York Times,* December 16, 1946. See also draft of letter to Truman, November 26, 1946; Truman to HGD, November 26, 1946; and Douglas's opening remarks, November 27, 1946, all HGD, B90-F8; *New York Times,* November 28, 1946.

4. HGD and Hickok to MD, October 30, 1946, HMDP.

5. HGD to Ed Lybeck, June 24, 1946, REL, B1-F3.

6. Lybeck to HGD, [June 1946]; and Douglas statement, [November 1946], REL, B1-F9; Connelly to HGD, July 9, 1946, REL, B1-F4; HGD to Ed Lybeck, June 24, 1946, REL, B1-F3; *Los Angeles Sentinel,* June 13, September 26, October 14, 17, and 31, 1946; *California Eagle,* September 12 and 26, October 10 and 24, 1946.

7. Miscellaneous campaign literature in Jake Zeitlin Papers, Los Angeles; *Los Angeles Sentinel,* June 20, 1946; Douglas campaign literature, SC; Adam Clayton Powell to HGD, November 1, 1946, REL, B1-F5. On national black support, see, for example, Adam Clayton Powell, Jr., to HGD, November 1, 1946, REL, B1-F5.

8. Campaign flyers, SC; survey prepared by Ralph H. Gundlach, University of Washington, [prob. October 1946], HGD, B90-F8; *Washington Star,* October 9, 1946; Ickes' column ran in the *Los Angeles Daily News,* as well as numerous other papers; HGD to Ickes, September 11 and October 2, 1946, HI, B55.

9. Clifton to Frank Jordan, November 26, 1946; and treasurer's report for the Douglas campaign, SC; Roosevelt joined with CIO-PAC, HICCASP, the Progressive AFL, and the Railroad Brothers' Union to bring Wallace to California. In Los Angeles, 10,000 packed the hall, with over 5,000 outside. See George B. Roberts to Jack Kroll, October 7 and 31, 1946, CIO-PAC Papers (hereafter, CIO-PAC), The Archives of Labor History and Urban Affairs, Wayne State University (hereafter, WS), B1-F1946; Jimmy Roosevelt to Truman, August 29, 1946, SC; *Christian Science Monitor,* October 25, 1946; *Labor Herald,* October 18, 1946. In August, the CIO released to the press a tally on how Congress voted on twelve issues critical to labor. Within the notedly liberal southern California delegation, seven, including Douglas, received perfect scores. See *Washington Post,* August 18, 1946; *Los Angeles Daily News,* September 30, 1946; Mervyn Rathborne to Sidney Hillman, March 14, 1946, CIO-PAC, B1-F1946; HGD to Charlotta Bass, November 9, 1946, HGD, B17-F1.

10. 14th District League flyer, SC; *Los Angeles Daily News,* October 26 and 31, 1946; *Chicago Times,* October 12, 1946; HGD to Noel Sullivan, November 19, 1946, Noel Sullivan Papers, The Bancroft Library, B19. Jane Ickes to HGD, October 31, 1946; and Harold Ickes to HGD, November 9, 1946, HI, B55.

11. Ed Lybeck to HGD, [November 1946], REL, B1-F9.

12. Ibid.; *Los Angeles Sentinel,* November 7 and 14, 1946; HGD to Ed and Ruth Lybeck, November 6, 1946, REL, B1-F4.

13. *Washington News,* November 12, 1946; Jimmy Roosevelt to the Executive Com-

mittee Meeting, December 13, 1946, SC; Eleanor Roosevelt, "My Day," November 8, 1946; Ed Lybeck to HGD, [November 1946], REL, B1-F9; HGD to Ed and Ruth Lybeck, November 6, 1946, REL, B1-F4.

14. Chavoor to Ed Lybeck, March 7, 1947; and Chavoor to Ruth and Ed Lybeck, May 15, 1947, REL, B1-F5.

15. Bella Abzug, *Gender Gap: Bella Abzug's Guide to Political Power for American Women* (Boston: Houghton Mifflin, 1984).

16. HGD to Stella Jakobitz, March 4, 1947; HGD to Ed Lybeck, May 14, 1947; Clyde Doyle to HGD, April 28, 1947; Chavoor to Ed Lybeck, March 26, 1947; Chavoor to Ed Lybeck, April 28, 1947; all REL, B1-F5.

17. Ed Lybeck to HGD, [November 1946], REL, B1-F9.

18. *Los Angeles Sentinel*, January 16, 1947. On housing during the Truman period, see Richard O. Davies, *Housing Reform During the Truman Administration* (Columbia: University of Missouri Press, 1966). Patterson, in *Mr. Republican*, discusses Taft's involvement in housing legislation. *Congressional Record*, House of Rep., 80th Cong., 1st sess. (February 20, 1947), Vol. 93, pt. 10, *Appendix*, pp. A627, A684, and A790.

19. Ed Lybeck to HGD, [November 1946], REL, B1-F9; Douglas quote in Barbee, ROHO, 5.

20. Chavoor to Ed Lybeck, July 1 and 7, 1947, REL, B1-F5; Barbee, ROHO, 5–9. Senator Paul Douglas from Illinois, the first senator to hire a black secretary, forced the segregation issue in the senatorial dining area. Barbee learned enough in Douglas's office to move to Senator Hubert H. Humphrey's office as a caseworker when Douglas lost the Senate race in 1950. And when Jimmy Roosevelt was elected to Congress in 1954, Terry became his office manager. Her final move was to Gus Hawkins when he replaced Roosevelt in 1962. Douglas's decision to hire her also had an impact on the House by encouraging other white representatives with large blocs of black voters to employ blacks in the office.

21. Hartmann, *Home Front and Beyond*, chap. 8.

22. *Congressional Record*, House of Rep., 80th Cong., 1st sess. (February 6, 1947), Vol. 93, pt. 10, *Appendix*, p. A127; ibid., 2nd sess. (May 19, 1948), Vol. 94, pt. 11, *Appendix*, p. A5256.

23. Douglas Statement to Japanese Women, [n.d.], HGD, B212-F5; *Congressional Record*, House of Rep., 80th Cong., 2nd sess. (May 19, 1948), Vol. 94, pt. 11, p. A3156.

24. *New York Herald Tribune*, July 1, 1945; McAllister to HGD, May 21, 1945, HGD, B12-F7; Report of the Secretary, National Committee to Defeat the Un-Equal Rights Amendment, June 1945, HGD, B12-F7; Florence L. C. Kitchelt to HGD, July 31, 1945, HGD, B12-F7; HGD to Mary Reed, April 14, 1948, HGD, B43-F4; Hearings before Subcommittee No. 1 of the Committee on the Judiciary, House of Representatives, on Equal Rights Amendment, and Commission on the Legal Status of Women, 80th Cong., 2nd sess. (March 10 and 12, 1948), 196–98; Douglas, "Women of the World Unite!" *Magazine Digest* (May 1945): 14–16; program, Foreign Policy Association luncheon, March 10, 1945, HGD, B207-F3. She also responded to various calls for messages or bills to assist foreign women.

25. *Congressional Record*, House of Rep., 80th Cong., 1st sess. (February 20, 1947), Vol. 93, pt. 10, Appendix, p. A635; *Second Report*, January 1946–April 1947, National Committee on the Status of Women in the United States, with memo from national chairman, Mary Anderson, October 15, 1947, HGD, B36-F2; memo on Status of Women bill, National Committee on the Status of Women in the United States, February 19, 1947, with letter from national chairman, Dorothy McAllister, February 21, 1947,

AFL, Series 8A, B44; letter from lawyers favoring the Women's Status Bill, February 1947, HGD, B43-F4.

26. *Congressional Record*, House of Rep., 80th Cong., 1st sess. (March 13, 1947), Vol. 93, pt. 2, pp. 2038–42.

27. Ibid.

28. *Los Angeles Daily News*, March 4, 1946; *Los Angeles Tribune*, November 8, 1947; *New York Post*, March 8, 1948; list of "friends of Housing" who had signed Discharge Petition #6 to bring the TEW (Taft-Ellender-Wagner) bill onto the House floor, CIO-UAW Papers, [n.d.] B37-F5; Douglas, "The House That Jack Can't Build," speech before the Regional Conferences of the National Association of Housing Officials, September 18, 1947; and Ickes to HGD, September 27, 1947, HI, B55.

29. *Chicago Tribune*, May 2, 1947.

30. Douglas, press release on Taft-Hartley, April 17, 1947; HGD to Philip Connelly, April 25, 1947; HGD to labor friends, May 1, 1947, HGD, B37-F1; HGD to Ed Lybeck, April 15, 1947, REL, B1-F5.

31. *AVC News*, January 27, 1947; Ickes to HGD, September 17 and October 8, 1947, HI, B55.

32. See, for example, Douglas, "Greek-Turkish Loan" (1947), HGD, B181-F/ "Speeches 1950."

33. *Congressional Record*, House of Rep., 80th Cong., 1st sess. (May 7, 8, 1947), Vol. 93, pt. 11, Appendix, pp. A2158, A2198–99; *St. Louis Star-Times*, May 9, 1947. Congress debated at length over the Greek-Turkish loan. See, for example, *Congressional Record* (May 8, 9, 1947), Vol. 93, pt. 4, pp. 4,791–4,823; ibid., (May 8, 1947), Vol. 93, pt. 11, *Appendix*, p. A2177.

34. *Congressional Record*, House of Rep., 80th Cong., 1st sess. (July 15, 1947), Vol. 93, pt. 7, pp. 8,948–49; and ibid., pt. 12, Appendix, pp. A3555–36.

35. Chavoor, ROHO, 287–89; Chavoor to Ruth Lybeck, April 22, 1947, REL, B1-F5; Chavoor to Hickok, July 9, 1947, LH, B13, FDRL.

36. MD to HGD, [n.d.], HMDP; Paul Sifton, Jr., interview with author, June 15, 1982.

37. MD to HGD, [n.d.]; Chavoor to Hickok, REL, B1-F5; Chavoor, ROHO, 292–93; Chavoor to Ruth and Ed Lybeck, January 17, 1947, REL, B1-F5.

38. HGD to Ed and Ruth Lybeck, March 3, 1948, REL, B1-F5; Lybeck to HGD, March 15, 1948, REL, B1-F9; *New Republic* (April 12, 1948), 12.

39. Ed Lybeck to HGD, March 15, 1948, REL, B1-F9; *New Republic* (April 12, 1948), 12.

40. Resolution, Executive Board of UAW, Minutes of the International Executive Board (March 1–5, 1948), 12, UAW Papers, WSHS, B10; Jerome Posner to Kroll, March 9, 1948; Morris Zusman to Kroll, March 24, 1948; Irwin Deshelter to Kroll, March 27, 1948; all CIO-PAC, B1-F/CIO-PAC, Political.

41. Ed Lybeck, Post-Campaign Report, 1948, REL, B4-F2.

42. Ralph Brown to HGD, July 21, 1948, HGD, B49-F4; Ed Lybeck, Post-Campaign Report, 1948, REL, B4-F2; "A Day to Day Account of the Activities of CIO-PAC at the Democratic National Convention," Jack Kroll Papers, Manuscript Division, Library of Congress (hereafter, JK), B7.

43. Kroll to Zusman, June 19, 1948, CIO-PAC Papers, B1-F/CIO-PAC, Political. The CIO's assessment of the fall campaign: 13th, marginal; 14th, difficult; 16th, probable; 17th, either way; 18th, close; 20th—Democrats think they might beat Hinshaw with a strong candidate; 21st, close; 23rd, close. See CIO-PAC Contributions by State and Federal Campaigns, December 31, 1948, United Auto Workers Political Action

Committee, Roy Reuther Papers, WS (hereafter, UAWPAC RR), B48-F17. In June the California CIO split into two groups in a fight over Wallace, but this did not affect the existing PAC structure.

Other examples of donations are Connecticut: Chester Bowles, $16,000; Woodhouse, $1,850; Abraham Ribicoff, $500; Illinois: Paul Douglas, $13,000; various congressmen, $1,000; Adlai Stevenson, $6,500. In no other state did any congressional candidate receive more than $1,000, although various senatorial and gubernatorial candidates enjoyed larger contributions, such as Humphrey in Minnesota and Murray in Montana. See long, handwritten list and typed list of just CIO-PAC contributions, UAWPAC RR, B48-F17. See also *Los Angeles Daily News*, June 21, 1948.

44. They also used Holifield's comments as written by Douglas's office. Text for flyers, REL, B4-F2; Douglas press release draft, [n.d.], HMDP.

45. HGD Post-Campaign Statement and Post-Campaign Report, REL, November 1948, B4-F2; post-election memorandum for Mr. Kroll, JK, B7; State of California, *Statement of Vote*, General Election, November 2, 1948, p. 8.

Chapter 11

1. See report by CIO-PAC director Jack Kroll, March 3, 1949, evaluating labor's electoral success. Labor's agenda for 1949 paralleled Truman's Fair Deal; see, for example, "PAC: America's Middle Way," [1949]; JK, B48-F18. Most Truman scholars have overlooked Douglas in their treatment of postwar politics, in part, perhaps, because of her non-traditional political role and her sex. One exception is Alonzo L. Hamby, *Beyond the New Deal: Harry S. Truman and American Liberalism* (New York: Columbia University Press, 1973).

2. Weekly broadcast transcripts, HGD, 1991–2; Ed Lybeck to Chavoor, March 30, 1949, REL, B1-F9; Chavoor to Ed Lybeck, April 1, 1949, REL, B1–F7.

3. *Baltimore Afro-American*, January 29, 1949; *California Eagle*, February 10, 1949; HGD to Ed Lybeck, February 10, 1949, REL, B1-F7; Murray to HGD, June 21, 1949, HGD, B92-F11. For a full list of legislation Douglas introduced, see HGD, B108-F1; see also Douglas press release on Migrant Commission, June 1, 1950, HGD, B69-F5. Douglas commented in a letter to Representative Andrew Jacobs that her Women's Status bill received a good presentation in March 1948 before a subcommittee of the House Judiciary Committee (HGD to Jacobs, March 17, 1949, HGD, B102-F/81st Congress—Status of Women). For a sampling of correspondence on women's issues, see HGD to Josephine Terrill, June 8, 1949; Terrill to HGD, May 17, 1949; HGD to Lucy Rice Winkler, March 26, 1949; HGD to Helen Sourds, August 22, 1949; HGD to Maurice Tobin, March 30, 1949, all HGD, B101-F/81st Congress—Status of Women.

4. Despite her support for assistance to migrants, she raised questions with Truman's office about allowing any foreign labor into the country, given current employment problems. See Harry S Truman Papers (hereafter, HST), General File, B653-F/HGD, Harry S Truman Library (hereafter, HSTL). Quote from *Congressional Record*, House of Rep., 81st Cong., 1st sess. (August 18, 1949), Vol. 95, pt. 1, p. 11,755; *Washington Post*, January 26, 1949; on Station K, see Chavoor to Ed Lybeck, October 15, 1949, REL B1-F7. Examples of various statements on bills include Statement for FEPC, May 11, 1949, HGD, B58-F4; Testimony on Children's Day, May 4, 1950, B91-F16; Administrator to HGD, April 15, 1949, HGD, B59-F10.

5. *Congressional Record*, House of Rep., 81st Cong., 1st sess. (March 8, 1949), Vol. 95, pt. 2, p. 2,027.

6. Ed Lybeck to Chavoor, March 30, 1949, REL, B1-F9; Chavoor to Lybeck, April 1, 1949, REL, B1-F7; *Fortnight* 6 (January 21, 1949): 8.

7. Pick to Ed Lybeck, February 10, 1949, REL, B1-F7; Wilhelmina G. Benes to HGD, January 10, 1949, HGD, B204-F/Endorsements; *Los Angeles Daily News*, January 31, 1949; Ickes column, Jan. 28, 1950; Alvin Meyers, "Helen Gahagan Douglas and the Campaigns for Congress," an oral history conducted in 1978 by Scobie, Helen Gahagan Douglas Oral History Project, Vol. 1, ROHO (hereafter, Meyers, ROHO), 225–26.

8. Mille Logan to HGD, June 8, 1949, HGD, B199-F/L—San Francisco; and Falconer to HGD, June 27, 1949, HMDP.

9. Chavoor to Ed Lybeck, April 6, 1949, REL, B1-F7; Al Barkan to Harry Stillman, August 12, 1949, TWUA, Series 3, WSHS, B477-F/California; HGD to Ed Lybeck, July 18, 1949, REL, B1-F7; Ed Lybeck to HGD, July 22, 1949, and to Chavoor, September 9, 1949, REL, B1-F9.

10. HGD to Jack Abel, May 24, 1949, HGD, B198-F/A-San Francisco; Wallace N. Atherton to HGD, August 13, 1949, HGD, B145-F/A-Alameda. Shelley favored Douglas's candidacy but wanted to be assured she could win.

11. Chavoor to Ed Lybeck, May 12 and June 16, 1949, REL, B1-F7; Ed Lybeck to Chavoor, June 28 and July 19, 1949, REL, B1-F9; Ed Lybeck to HGD, July 22, 1949, REL, B1-F9.

12. Chavoor to Ed Lybeck, August 29, 1949, REL, B1-F7; and Lybeck to Chavoor, August 19, 1949, REL, B1-F9.

13. HGD, "Opening Campaign Speech," October 5, 1949, HGD, B203-F/1950 Campaign Speeches; press release, October 5, 1949, HGD, B177-F/Press Releases.

14. HGD to Ickes, December 27, 1949, HGD, B212-F22.

15. HGD to Amerigo Bozzani, October 14, 1949, HGD, B195-F/Los Angeles-B; HGD to Allen Rivkin, October 20, 1949, HGD, B178-F/Personal Corres., 1951.

16. Kroll to Mazey, October 4, 1949, UAWPAC RR, B47-F25.

17. Myers to HGD, June 8, 1949; and HGD to Myers, October 25 and November 16, 1949, HMDP; Elizabeth R. Smith to HGD, February 3, 1950, HGD, B197-F/S-Marin.

18. Patrick Cooney to Matthew Connelly, February 4, 1950; Cooney to William M. Boyle, Jr., February 4, 1950, HSTP, Official File, B976, FCA-C. These letters include information about anti-Roosevelt factions, comments that Douglas would clearly beat Downey, and mention that those controlling the *Los Angeles Daily News* saw Roosevelt and Douglas as threats to their political power and wanted them out.

19. Notes on Downey Speech, December 6, 1949; and Downey to HGD, December 12, 1949, HGD, B179-F/Downey Speech; HGD to Downey, December 16, 1949, January 31 and February 1, 1950; and Downey to HGD, February 1, 1950, SD, B1; *Independent Review*, February 3, 1950.

20. Marquis Childs column, [n.d.], SC.

21. Douglas's official opening campaign speech, February 28, 1950, HGD, B203. See Statement of Policy, Western States Conference, Fall 1949—reinforcing Douglas's campaign platform, Hugh B. Mitchell Papers, Accession #281, Manuscripts Division, University of Washington (hereafter, HM), B70-F3.

22. Tipton to Mitchell, [early February 1950], HM, B70-F3. Various letters indicate the tensions between the Douglas and Roosevelt camps. See, for example, Chavoor to Monte Montrezza, May 3, 1950, HGD, B199-F/M-Santa Clara; Chavoor phone interview with author, May 24, 1991; Hartmann interview with author.

23. Ruth Lybeck to Glad Hall Jones, March 17, 1950, HGD, B196-F/J-Los Angeles;

memo, "Douglas for Senator" Club, San Jose, February 26, 1950, HGD, B199-F/M-Santa Clara; Tipton to Ruth Lybeck, May 22, 1950, HGD, B199-F/T-San Francisco. On the north relying on Lybeck, see, for example, May C. Montrezza to Ruth Lybeck, February 26, 1950, HGD, B199-F/M-Santa Clara.

24. On Downey support regarding Roosevelt, see Cliff Waters to Earl Irwin, HGD, B199-F/I-Sacramento.

25. Stern to Ruth Lybeck, March 6 and 17, 1950; and Ruth Lybeck to Stern, March 27, 1950, HGD, B199-F/S-Sacramento.

26. See, for example, Alice Hoien to HGD, January 11, 1950, HGD, B195-F/H-Fresno; Cliff Brock to HGD, January 19, 1950; Blank to Ruth Lybeck, March 23 and April 19, 1950, both HGD, B195-F/B-Fresno; *Mountain View Register*, April 7, 1950.

27. "Tour Schedules," HGD, B180, and REL, B2-F1, 2.

28. Meyers, ROHO, 226ff; Douglas speech to the Business and Professional Women's Club of Fresno, February 20, 1950, Mary Norton Papers, Special Collections, Rutgers University Library, General File, B7. On the Hollywood Ten, see, for example, HGD to Clyde Giles, May 5, 1950, HGD, B194-F/"Melvyn Douglas."

29. Bill Field to HGD, [n.d.]; and HGD to Field, May 20, 1950, HGD B196-F24.

30. HGD to Ickes, December 27, 1949, HI, B55; Roosevelt Fund-raiser Invitation List, HMDP; HGD to ER, March 10, 1950, HGD, B200-F/"Out of State"; "My Day," February 28, 1950; HGD to ER, March 10, 1950, ERP, B3839.

31. Mrs. J. Borden Harriman to _____, April 4, 1950, HMDP; Douglas press release, March 21, 1950, HGD, B177-F/"Primary Campaign, 1950"; Guffey to Harriman, April, 1950, HMDP.

32. James Walter to HGD, March 1, 1950, HGD, B198-F/W-Orange; Gaye Bjornsen to W. H. Sullivan, SD, B1; *Los Angeles Times*, March 5 and 29, 1950.

33. Ickes to HGD, March 31 and April 13, 1950, HGD, B179-F/"Boddy Material"; Edwin Pauley to Downey, April 12, 1950, SD, B4.

34. *Frontier* (May 15, 1950), 7–8; Stern–Amelia Fry phone conversation, April 20, 1973, ROHO, Fry research materials.

35. Eleanor Heller, ROHO, Fry interview notes, and Heller to Fry, phone conversation, March 28, 1973, ROHO, Fry research materials.

36. Clarvoe to HGD, March 29, 1950; and HGD to Clarvoe, April 4, 1950, HGD, B198-F/C-San Francisco; HGD to Jones, April 8, 1950, HGD, B199-F/J-Sacramento.

37. *New York Post*, March 31, 1950; Ickes to HGD, March 31 and April 13, 1950, HGD, B212-F22; Fanning to Downey, March 29, 1950, SD, B3; Rogers to Downey, March 30, 1950, SD, B5; Harry Crowe to Downey, March 29, 1950; and Workman to Downey, May 5, 1950, SD, B1.

38. HGD to Ickes, April 9, 1950, HI, B55; Fay Allen to Mary McLeod Bethune, April 12, 1950, HGD, B204-F/"Statements of Endorsements—1950"; HGD to Clarvoe, May 5, 1950, HGD, B198-F/C-San Francisco; HGD to Edwards, April 11, 1950, HGD, B194-F/"Personal Correspondence"; *Independent Review*, April 21, 1950; *Los Angeles Times*, April 23, 1950; HGD to Tipton, April 9, 1950, HI, B55; Tipton to Mitchell, April 20, 1950; and Mitchell to Tipton, April 24, 1950, HM, B70-F3.

39. Stern to Ruth Lybeck, April 14, 1950; and Ruth Lybeck to Stern, April 21, 1950, HGD, B199-F/S-Sacramento; Ruth Lybeck to Virginia Jennings, HGD, B199-F/J-Santa Barbara; *Los Angeles Times*, April 13, 1950; Blank to Ruth Lybeck, April 22, 1950, HGD, B194-F/"Melvyn Douglas."

40. Ickes to HGD, April 13, 1950; and HGD to Ickes, April 9, 1950, HI, B55; HGD to Ickes, April 26, 1950, HGD, B212-F22.

41. For details on labor's role and position on Senate races and California House

races, see "Elections 1950: Confidential," CIO-PAC Research Department, January 19, 1950, JK, B7; Roy Reuther to Douglass, January 4, 1950; Kroll to Douglass, January 11, 1950; Douglass to Reuther, January 14, 1950; Roy Reuther to Douglass, January 23, 1950; all UAWPAC RR, B48-F27. Minutes, Executive Board Meeting, California National CIO-PAC State Central Committee, February 4, 1950; and Minutes of the State Central Committee, February 5, 1950, Irwin L. DeShelter Collection, The Archives of Labor History and Urban Affairs, WS, B26-F/Board Minutes, 1949–50, and Minutes Collection; Roberts to Kroll, [n.d.], CIO-PAC, B1-F/1949–50; Jack Goldberger to HGD, April 3, 1950, HGD, B199-F/U-San Francisco; HGD press release, [n.d.], HGD, B177-F/"Primary Campaign 1950."

42. Sifton to HGD, March 7, 1950, HGD, B200-F/Out of State; *Independent Review*, April 21, 1950; weekly newsletter from the California State Federation of Labor, April 19, 1950, Mary Ellen Leary Papers, BL, B7; Jack A. Despol to California CIO Local Unions, WS, CIO-PAC, B1-F/1949–50; *Long Beach Press Telegram*, May 10, 1950; Douglass to Reuther, and Douglass to Kroll, both April 20, 1950, UAWPAC RR, B48-F27.

43. Bethune to John Somerville, April 21, 1950, HGD, B204-F/"Statements of Endorsements—1950"; HGD Headquarters press release, May 6, 1950, B177-F/Primary; Heller, ROHO draft; Allen to Bethune, April 12, 1950; and Bethune to John Somerville, April 21, 1950, HGD, B204-F/"Statements of Endorsements." But the Democratic Party Women's Division lacked the mass support it enjoyed earlier in the 1940s.

44. Edwards to K. Frances Scott, November 2, 1949, HGD, B178-F/"Endorsements"; memo, Report on ERA, HGD, B92-F13; Louise Darby to HGD, October 17 and October 30, 1949, and January 7, 1950, HGD, B198-F/D-San Diego; Dorothy M. Donohoe to Blank, March 23, 1950, HGD, B92-F13.

45. Blank to Chavoor, April 19, 1950; Blank to Ruth Lybeck, April 22, 1950; and Blank to Frank Wigham, April 22, 1950, all HGD, B195-F/B-Fresno; Rose Baupaugh to Ruth Lybeck, April 5, 17, and 20, 1950; and Baupaugh to HGD, January 28, 1950, HGD, B195-F/B-Los Angeles. On USC incident, see, for example, HGD, B201-F2, and B180-F/"USC Incident." On Galarza, see Alexander Schullman to Chavoor, April 27, 1950; and HGD to Galarza, April 27, 1950, HGD, B179-F/"Farm Legislation."

46. Hickok to HGD, April 18, 1950; HGD to Hickok, May 3, 1950; Sidney Wilkerson to HGD, April 26, 1950; HGD to Wilkerson, May 5, 1950, all HGD, B200-F/"Out of State Correspondence."

47. MD to HGD, March 29 and May 13, 1950, HMDP; Meyers, ROHO, 238–39.

48. HGD Headquarters press release, May 1950, HGD, B177-F/Primary Campaign 1950.

49. Helicopter schedule, May 9, 1950, HGD, B180-F/"Tour Schedules"; Mercedes Davidson to Flora Rothenberg, May 9, 1950; and HGD to Hickok, May 3, 1950, HMDP; *Porterville Recorder*, May 25, 1950.

50. Chavoor to V. K. Auxier, May 5, 1950, HGD, B194-F/1950 Correspondence; HGD to Claire and Paul Sifton, May 5, 1950, HGD, B197-F/S-Los Angeles; HGD to Hickok, April 18, 1950, HMDP.

51. For recent major studies of Nixon's background, see in particular Fawn M. Brodie, *Richard Nixon: The Shaping of His Character* (New York: W. W. Norton, 1981); Roger Morris, *Richard Milhous Nixon: The Rise of an American Politician* (New York: Henry Holt and Co., 1990); Stephen E. Ambrose, *Nixon: The Education of a Politician, 1913–1962* (New York: Simon and Schuster, 1987); and Herbert S. Parmet, *Richard Nixon and His America* (Boston: Little, Brown and Company, 1990). Numerous other books track Nixon's path to the presidency, such as Frank Mankiewicz, *Perfectly*

Clear: Nixon from Whittier to Watergate (New York: Quadrangle Books, 1973); William Costello, *The Facts About Nixon: An Unauthorized Biography* (New York: Viking Press, 1960); Bela Kornitzer, *The Real Nixon: An Intimate Biography* (New York: Rand McNally, 1960); Bruce Mazlish, *In Search of Nixon: A Psychohistorical Inquiry* (New York: Basic Books, 1972); Earl Mazo, *Richard Nixon: A Political and Personal Portrait* (New York: Harper and Brothers, 1959); Earl Mazo and Stephen Hess, *Nixon: A Political Portrait* (New York: Harper and Row, 1968); and Nixon's *The Memoirs of Richard Nixon* (New York: Grosset and Dunlap, 1978). On Nixon as a "formidable candidate," see, for example, *Los Angeles Times*, April 11, 1950. I very much appreciate Robert Sklar's sending me a copy of his senior thesis on Nixon, which is missing from the Princeton University Library ("The 'Old' Nixon: The Political Career of Vice President Richard M. Nixon from 1945 to 1952," senior thesis, Princeton University, 1958).

52. Paul Bullock, *Jerry Voorhis: The Idealist as Politician* (New York: Vantage Press, 1978), 138; Voorhis, *The Confessions of a Congressman* (Garden City, N.Y.: Doubleday, 1947), and idem, *The Strange Case of Richard Milhous Nixon* (New York: P. S. Ericksson, 1972); Ambrose, *Nixon*, 138. Brodie in *Richard Nixon*, chap. 13, agreed with this assessment. See also *Independent Review*, February 3, 1950; Wicker, *One of Us*, 71.

53. Morris, *Richard Milhous Nixon*, 365.

54. Ambrose, *Nixon*, 31.

55. HGD to Ickes, April 9, 1950; Ickes to HGD, April 26, 1950, HGD, B212-F22; Falconer to HGD, May 10, 1950; and Dick Miller to HGD, April 20, 1950, HMDP.

56. *Los Angeles Daily News*, June 5, 1950; *Fresno Labor Citizen*, April 14, 1950; *Alhambra Post Advocate*, April 7, 1950; *Oakland Tribune*, April 13, 1950; *Merced Sun*, May 12, 1950.

57. Lustig to HGD, May 2, 1950, HGD, B198-F/L-San Diego; Stern to HGD, May 5, 1950, HGD, B199-F/W-Sacramento.

58. *Los Angeles Daily News*, May 18, 1950; Woodrow May to Cliff Waters, June 4, 1950, HGD, B199-F/M-Riverside; *Redding Record-Searchlight*, May 25, 1950; Aurora Dufour to HGD, January 27, 1950, HGD, B204-F/"Letters of Endorsement"; *Sun*, January 1, 1949; *Los Angeles Times*, March 28, 1950.

59. Tobriner to friend, May 22, 1950; and Tipton to Ruth Lybeck, May 23, 1950, HGD, B199-F/T-San Francisco; Sutton Christian to Boddy, May 24, 1950, HGD, B199-F/C-Santa Clara; HGD to Paul and Claire Sifton, HGD, B197-F/S-Los Angeles.

60. HGD to Ricks, May 5, 1950, HMDP; HGD to Doris Fleeson, May 29, 1950, HGD, B179-F/"Boddy Material"; see May 4, 1950, HSTP, Official File, Box 976, FCa–D; HGD to Chapman, OC, B86-F/Pol 1950 CA, HSTL; *Independent Review*, June 2, 1950; Ruth Lybeck to Leonard Dieden, May 20, 1950, HGD, B195-F/D-Alameda; HGD press release, June 2, 1950, HGD, B177-F/"Primary Campaign 1950"; see also B203-F/"1950 Campaign Materials; Douglas, et al. to _____, May 26, 1950, HGD, B180-F/"Fund Raising"; *New York Post*, May 21, 1950.

61. Stern to HGD, May 27, 1950, HGD, B194-F/"Bea Stern"; *San Francisco News*, May 4, 1950; *San Diego Voter*, June 1, 1950, HGD, B194-F/"1950 Campaign."

62. Tobriner to friend, May 22, 1950, HGD, B199-F/T-San Francisco; Emily Taft Douglas et al., to _____, May 26, 1950, HGD, B180-F/"Fund-raising."

63. HGD to James Wilson, May 20, 1950, HGD, B199-F/W-Sacramento; Ickes to HGD, May 26, 1950; and HGD to Ickes, May 31, 1950, HI, B55; Robert W. Gilbert to Chapman, May 6, 1950, OC Papers, HSTL (hereafter, OC) B86-F/Political 1950-CA; Julius Castelan to HGD, June 2, 1950, HGD, B177-F/"Primary Congratulations"; List, B179-F/"Los Angeles County"; Torrey Smith to Gloria Best, June 10, 1950, HGD,

B179-F/"Santa Clara County"; telegrams from labor groups, HGD, B177-F/"Telegrams"; ZF to Eloise Dungan, June 2, 1950, HGD, B198-F/D-San Francisco; Natalye Hall to HGD, June 4, 1950, HGD, B199-F/W-San Mateo.

64. State of California, *Statement of Vote,* Direct Primary Election and Special State-Wide Election, June 6, 1950; *Los Angeles Times,* June 30, 1950; Boyle to HGD, June 8, 1950, HGD, B177-F/"Telegrams"; Truman to HGD, HGD, B217-F8; Johnson to HGD, June 16, 1950, Lyndon B. Johnson Papers (hereafter, LBJP), Congressional File, B42, Lyndon B. Johnson Library (hereafter, LBJL).

Chapter 12

1. Rich to HGD, June 8, 1950, HGD, B194-F/Radio; Paul Ziffren, interview with author, April 2, 1980.

2. Blank to Chavoor, June 13, 1950, HGD, B195-F/B-Fresno.

3. The bibliography on McCarthyism and Communist hysteria is extensive; see, for example, Earl Latham, *The Communist Controversy in Washington: From the New Deal to McCarthy* (Cambridge: Harvard University Press, 1966); Robert Griffith, *The Politics of Fear: Joseph R. McCarthy and the Senate* (Lexington: University Press of Kentucky, 1970); Richard M. Fried, *Men Against McCarthy* (New York: Columbia University Press, 1976); Richard H. Rovere, *Senator Joe McCarthy* (New York: Harcourt, Brace, Jovanovich, 1959); and Stanley I. Kutler, *The American Inquisition: Justice and Injustice in the Cold War* (New York: Hill and Wang, 1982).

4. Eric Boden, "A Preliminary Report on Media and Readability in California Political Campaigns and the Primary Election, June 6, 1950" (Eric Boden Research Consultant, San Francisco, [n.d.]), 32, MEL, B1; Edwards to Dewson, August 7, 1950, Dewson, B21, FDRL.

5. Annual *Reports* of the Joint Fact-Finding Committee on Un-American Activities in California that began in 1940; Tenney, *Cry Brotherhood* (Sacramento, Calif.: Standard Publications, 1965); Scobie, "Jack B. Tenney and the 'Parasitic Menace,' " *Pacific Historical Review* 43 (May 1974): 188–211; idem, "Tenney and Anti-Communist Legislation in California"; Jack Tenney interview with author, April 7, 1968; Jack B. Tenney interview, Oral History Program, UCLA; Carey McWilliams, "Look What's Happened to California," *Harper's* magazine (October 1949), 25.

6. George R. Stewart, *The Year of the Oath: The Fight For Academic Freedom at the University of California* (Garden City, N.Y.: Doubleday and Company, 1950); Cliff Waters to Ruth Lybeck, March 1950, HGD, B197-F/W-Los Angeles.

7. HGD to Pick, July 17, 1950, WP; HGD to William E. Kent, July 10, 1950; HGD to Mr. DeLong, June 26, 1950; HGD to Bert W. Thomas, June 29, 1950, all HMDP; Hartmann interview with author.

8. Campaign literature, HMDP; County correspondence, BX-Y; John A. Vieg, interview with author, March 20, 1980. Vieg wrote Will Rogers, Jr., however, that he wanted to do everything he could to help elect Douglas. See Vieg to Rogers, September 27, 1950, HGD, B197-F/V-Los Angeles. Paul Ziffren also made it clear that people left the campaign; see Ziffren interview with author.

9. Democratic State Central Committee of California Newsletter, No. 2, August 4, 1950, RK, B16; HSTP, Official File, B971-F/Ca.

10. Daniel V. Flanagan to HGD, June 8, 1950, HGD, HMDP; and Allen to Bird, July 5, 1950, HGD, B65-F8.

11. Cappy Ricks to HGD, June 7, 1950, HMDP; S. E. Shapiro to HGD, July 20,

1950, HMDP; Rogers to HGD, August 17, 1950, HGD, B197-F/R-Los Angeles; misc. campaign literature, HMDP; Cliff Waters to Ruth Lybeck, March 1950, HGD, B197-F/W-Los Angeles; Frank Rogers to Downey, June 15, 1950, SD, B5; press release to southern California weeklies, August 25, 1950, HGD, B177-F/General Election 1950.

12. "Registration Drive News," Democratic State Central Committee of California, August 4, 1950, RK, B16; Harold Shapiro to Jack Kroll, September 6, 1950, CIO-PAC, B1-F/1949–50; Kroll to Sir and Brother, September 15, 1950, UAWPAC RR, B48-F1; Hank Hasiwar to HGD, August 29, 1950, HGD, B93-F3; H. L. Mitchell to HGD, September 7, 1950, HMDP. Reuther made a revealing comment when he mentioned a Republican woman whom Democrats probably could beat because "as a rule women are not too popular in most Congressional situations." See UAW Executive Board Minutes, CIO-PAC, Series 2/7, September 14, 1950, 179–80.

13. Douglass to Kroll, August 11 and 21, 1950; and Albert T. Lunceford to Tilford Dudley, August 28, 1950, CIO-PAC, B1-F/49-50; Douglass to Kroll, August 29, 1950; Douglass to Roy Reuther, July 4 and August 31, 1950; and Reuther to Douglass, August 30, 1950; all UAWPAC RR, B48-F27. Other groups working for her included the National Farm Labor Union headed by H. L. Mitchell, and veterans who worked to organize statewide in congressional districts. See Mitchell to HGD, September 7, 1950; and Veterans' Douglas-for-Senator Organization proposal, HGD, B180-F/Misc.

14. *Independent Review*, June 16, 1950; Edwards to Truman, draft letter, [n.d.], India Edwards Papers, HSTL, B2-F/General Corresp. 1950; Bronson interview with author.

15. Hill to Ruth Lybeck, June 13, 1950, HGD, B196-F/H-Los Angeles.

16. Bernard Brennan to J. R. Parten, October 3, 1950, B86-F/"Pol. 1950 CA."

17. Morris, *Richard Milhous Nixon*, 566–69.

18. HGD to Bird, July 18, 1950, HGD, B65-F8; Macklin Fleming to HGD, June 22, 1950; and HGD to Fleming, June 7, 1950, HGD, B198-F/San Francisco; Cecil J. Bishop to HGD, August 2, 1950; and HGD to Bishop, August 8, 1950, HGD, B49-F1; Confidential from AFL lobby in Washington, Spring 1950, HGD, B179-F/"Downey Material."

19. Cohn to Connelly, June 12, 1950, HSTP, Official File, B976-F-CA/C.

20. *Congressional Record*, House of Rep., 81st Cong., 2nd sess. (June 21, 1950), Vol. 96, pt. 16, Appendix, p. 4,753; ibid. (June 30, 1950) Vol. pt. 7, pp. 9,625–9,627; Rich to HGD, May 12, 1950, HGD, B194-F/Radio; press release, June 30, 1950, B178-F/statements-1950.

21. "Address of the Hon. Helen Gahagan Douglas Before the California Federation of Young Democrats," Los Angeles, July 22, 1950, HGD, B181-F/1950 Campaign; *San Francisco News*, June 29, 1950; "Drew Pearson's *Merry-Go-Round*," July 11, 1950.

22. "An Address Given by Helen Gahagan Douglas Before the Twentieth National Convention, Oil Workers International Union CIO," August 18, 1950, HMDP.

23. Nixon Headquarters' press release, August 30, 1950, HGD, B204-F6; *Long Beach Independent*, August 28, 1950.

24. Douglas speech, September 6, 1950, HGD, B203-F9.

25. Ibid.

26. Nixon "Kickoff" speech, September 18, 1950, HGD, B204-F6.

27. Chavoor, ROHO, 330; Howard Dimsdale to HGD, July 30, 1950; and HGD to Dimsdale, August 29, 1950, in HGD, B194-F/"1950 Campaign Correspondence"; Paul Jerrico, interview with author, April 7, 1984.

28. Douglass to Kroll, September 11, 1950, CIO-PAC, B1-F/1949–50; "Let's Look at the Record," Nixon campaign literature; and "Douglas *v.* Nixon," Douglas campaign

literature, HGD, B203-F/HGD-Nixon Voting Record; "Douglas Blue Book," HGD, B191; Mitchell to HGD, September 7, 1950, HMDP.

29. Raymond J. Smith to HGD, June 10, 1950; Bryan Rose to HGD, June 22, 1950; J. H. Hoeppel to HGD, October 29, 1950; all in HMDP; ER to HGD, September 16, 1950, HGD, B216-F1; Townsend to HGD, Fall 1950, HGD, B199-F/W-San Bernadino; Thelma Zulch to Ruth Lybeck, October 30, 1950, HGD, B199-F/"XYZ-Riverside"; "A Message to Catholics from Catholics," HGD, B203-F3.

30. Edith S. Noyes to HGD, October 30, 1950, HGD, B199-F/N-San Luis Obispo; *Independent Review*, September 29, 1950; Douglas press release, November 2, 1950, HGD, B177-F/"General Election 1950"; Sue Lilienthal Report, 1952, Chavoor, ROHO, 358–61.

31. Chavoor, ROHO, 319; Douglas, ROHO, 179; Lustig, ROHO, 188–89.

32. California Democrats for Nixon campaign literature; Creel to Jones, December 12, 1951; and Jones to Creel, December 18, 1951, George Creel Collection, Manuscripts Division, Library of Congress (hereafter, GC) B4. Creel continued to organize Democrats for Nixon nationally in 1952.

33. Frank McCallister to HGD, September 25, 1950, and HGD to McCallister, September 29, 1950, HGD, B194-F/"1950 Corres."

34. The *San Francisco News* article appeared October 5, 1950; HGD to Frank A. Clarvoe, *San Francisco News*, October 6, 1950, HGD, B180-F/"Corr. with Press"; W. A. Anderson to Rollin L. McNitt, September 23, 1950, HMDP; Trudy Chern to Ruth Lybeck, September 24; and Ruth Lybeck to Chern, September 29, 1950, HGD, B199-F/C-Santa Barbara; *Labor*, October 7, 1950.

35. Douglass to Roy Reuther, August 11 and 31, 1950, UAWPAC RR, B48-F27. Douglass to Kroll, September 28, 1950; Despol to Kroll, October 6, 1950; Kroll to Tipton, October 10, 1950; all CIO-PAC, B1-F/1949–50; Reuther to HGD, October 12, 1950, UAWPAC RR, B42-F3. See also HGD, B91-2-F/Thank You Letters. At the end of October, Douglas used a support statement from numerous CIO groups for publicity. Those signing included all CIO area officers plus the district directors of the Steelworkers, Auto Workers, Rubber Workers, Oil Workers, Packinghouse Workers, Textile Workers, Shipyard Workers, Telephone Workers, Utility Workers, Woodworkers, Clothing Workers, American Radio Association, Transportation Service Workers, National Maritime Union, and the Newspaper Guild. See HGD Press Release, October 25, 1950, HGD, B177-F/"General election 1950."

36. HGD to Ickes, August 7, September 12, September 21, and September 22, 1950; and Ickes to HGD, July 15, August 16, September 20, October 2, 1950, HI, B55.

37. HGD to Ickes, October 2, 1950, HI, B55; HGD to Ickes, September 22, 1950, HGD, B212-F22; Ickes, "Helen Douglas and Tobey," *New Republic* 123 (October 16, 1950): 18; List of Donors, HMDP.

38. HGD to Ickes, October 23, 1950, HGD, B91-2.

39. HGD, B91-2-F/Thank You Letters.

40. Ibid.

41. David Freidenrich to Tipton, September 15, 1950, HGD, B180-F/"Tipton"; Alfred Janssens to HGD, August 18, 1950, HGD, B194-F/"1950 Campaign Correspondence"; HGD, B177-F/Gen. Elec 1950; *Huntington Park Daily Signal*, September 1, 1950; HGD to Carol Crispin, Laguna Beach, September 29, 1950, HGD, B194-F/"1950 Campaign correspondence"; Douglas speeches, October 23 and 30, 1950, HGD, B203; HGD to LeRoy Francis, October 12, 1950, HMDP.

42. *CIO News*, October 16, 1950; Blank to Lybeck, October 1950, HMDP; Blank to Ruth Edwards, October 13, 1950, B206-F2; Chapman to Maurice Saeta, October

23, 1950, HSTP, Official File, B1515; Bethune speech excerpts, October 23, 1950, HMDP.

43. *Independent Review*, October 27, 1950; Douglas press release, October 25, 1950, HGD, B177-F/"General Election 1950"; Joseph S. Best to Tipton, HGD, B195-F/B-Los Angeles; text of Harriman speech, October 30, 1950, HGD, B204-F/"Speeches of Endorsements, 1950"; Douglas press release, October 31, 1950, HGD, B177-F/"General Election 1950."

44. B203-F/"Spot Endorsements"; Clinton P. Anderson to HGD, [September 1950], HMDP; press release, October 1950, HGD, B177-F/"General Election 1950"; Randolph to HGD, October 27, 1950, B177-F/"June Senate Primary 1950."

45. Truman trip to Los Angeles—see guest list, July 20, 1950, Douglas on list, HSTP, B971-F/Ca; Roosevelt to Truman, September 28, 1950, and Truman to Roosevelt, October 10, 1950, HSTP, Official File, B976-F/Ca-R; memo on Press Conference 244, November 2, 1950, HSTP, President's Personal File, B5-F/"Reports"; and HGD, B217-F8; Sharpless Walker telegram to HST, reported in November 5, 1950, memo, HSTP, General File, B653-F/Helen Gahagan Douglas.

46. Douglas speech, September 1950, HGD, B181-F/Speeches 1950; press release, October 4, 1950, HGD, B177-F/General Election 1950.

47. Speech before the California Committee for Douglas for Senator dinner, October 4, 1950, HGD, B181-F/Speeches 1950; speech excerpts, state-wide broadcast, October 9, 1950, HGD, B177-F/General election 1950.

48. Kramer to Chavoor, October 9, 1950, HGD, B212-F22. See also speeches, October 23 and 30, 1950, HGD, B203.

49. HGD speeches, October 23 and 30, 1950, HGD, B203-F9.

50. MD to HGD, October 11, 1950; Gay and Walter Gahagan to HGD, October 2, 1950; HGD to Gay and Walter Gahagan, October 20, 1950; Herbert F. Atwater to HGD, October 13, 1950, all HMDP.

51. "Statement of Melvyn Douglas," October 18, 1950, HMDP.

52. HGD to Drew Pearson, October 2, 1950, HGD, B200-F/"Out of State Correspondence"; HGD to Bullis, November 1, 1950, HGD, B194-F/"1950 Correspondence"; *Independent Review*, October 20, 1950; "Know Nixon" material, CIO-PAC, unprocessed, B26.

53. Morris, *Richard Milhous Nixon*, 607-10; Ziffren interview with author.

54. *Newsweek* (October 30, 1950), 21–22.

55. McWilliams, "VIII. Bungling in California," *The Nation* (November 4, 1950), 411–12.

56. Clifton interview with author; Ziffren interview with author, Douglas, ROHO, 170; text of speech, Douglas press release, November 6, 1950, HMDP. The *Los Angeles Times* commented about her lack of qualifications because she was an actress. See Maude M. Braden to Juanita Terry, September 11, 1950; and Terry to Braden, September 26, 1950, HGD, B195-F/Kings.

57. State of California, *Statement of Vote*, comp. by Frank M. Jordan, Secretary of State, General Election (November 7, 1950), 11; Ruth Lybeck to HGD, November 1950, HGD, B180-F/Primary Results.

58. *Newsweek* (November 13, 1950), 23–27; *Time* (November 13, 1950), 19–20; *U.S. News and World Report* (November 17, 1950), 15; *New Republic* (November 20, 1950), 8.

59. Flannery, "Red Smear in California," *The Commonweal* (December 8, 1950), 223–25; see for example, letters in JK, Box 7.

60. HGD to Kroll, November 13, 1950, CIO-PAC, B1-F49–50; *U.S. News and World Report* (November 17, 1950), 29–30.

61. Hall to Peter and Mary Helen Douglas, November 10, 1950, HMDP.

62. Morris, *Richard Milhous Nixon*, 615. 1950 Republican National Committee radio spots, for example, played on Hiss and Truman's "appeasement" of Communism. See "Spots for Your Radio," Republican National Congressional Committee, WSHS, Iconography, Disc 3A, Republican National Congressional Committee/Advertising-Radio.

63. Edwards, ROHO, 18; Douglas, ROHO, 168; Hartmann interview with author.

64. Lybeck interview with author.

65. Ambrose, *Nixon*, 215.

66. Lustig, ROHO, 176–79. Brodie addressed the gender issue in her chapter entitled "On Women and Power: Pat and the Pink Lady," in *Richard Nixon*.

Chapter 13

1. Leo Goodman, "Helen Gahagan Douglas and Her Work with Labor on Housing and Atomic Energy," an oral history conducted 1978 by Fern S. Ingersoll, in Helen Gahagan Douglas Oral History Project, Vol. I, ROHO, 1981 (hereafter, Goodman, ROHO), 58; Ed Lybeck to HGD, [n.d.], REL, B1-F9, on running for a congressional seat; *Los Angeles Daily News*, August 26, 1952; and Avery C. Moore to HGD, February 10, 1954, HGD, B212-F6, reporting a boomlet advocating Douglas for lieutenant governor.

2. Goodman, ROHO, 57–59; Douglas, A *Full Life*, 345–50; and idem, ROHO, 217–18.

3. HGD family letter, December 27, 1951; and HGD to MD, [December 1950], HMDP.

4. *New York Post*, May 28, 1952; newspaper quote, [n.d., n.p.], Lester Sweyd Collection, Gahagan Clips, LC.

5. HGD to MD, [n.d.]; and HGD to MD, January 11, 1953, HMDP; *New York Herald Tribune* and *New York Times* for September 28, 1956; *Variety*, October 3, 1956.

6. Roger Kent to HGD, May 24, 1956, Roger Kent Papers, BL; HGD to MD, [n.d.], HMDP; *New York Times*, April 27, 1952; Fay Bennett to HGD, January 22, 1959, National Sharecroppers' Fund Papers, B2-F2-17, The Archives of Labor History and Urban Affairs, WS; Kirchwey to HGD, September 18, 1959, HGD, B212-F11; Carol Evans to Dorothy Wilson, June 15, 1956; Evans to Wilson, [n.d.], and attached Douglas speaking schedule, Adlai Stevenson Papers, B3, Helen Gahagan Douglas File, Manuscript Division, Princeton University Library.

7. S. C. Hyman to HGD, January 26, 1956, HGD, B214-F2; Block to HGD, January 1, 1959, HGD, B212-F10; Agnes Wolf to HGD, April 8, 1959, HGD, B212-F11; *New York Post*, February 2, 1960.

8. HGD to MD, [n.d.], HMDP; HGD to ER, October 1, 1952, ERP, B3980; HGD to Edson, September 20, 1956, ERP, B4220; *New York Times*, *Washington Post*, and *New York Times Herald*, for September 21, 1956; *New York Post*, October 26, 1956; Sam C. Jackson to HGD, October 14, 1956, and HGD to Jackson, October 17, 1956, HGD, B205-F4.

9. Stewart Alsop to HGD, February 28, 1958; and HGD to Alsop, March 20, 1958, HGD, B205-F2. Selig Harrison to Chavoor, May 27 and June 9, 1958; Chavoor to

Harrison, June 3, 1958; Chavoor to HGD, June 4, 1958; Chavoor to Bea Stern, June 9, 1958, all HGD, B205-F5. "Profiles of Nixon," HMDP; Mazo to HGD, March 12, 1958; HGD to Mazo, March 17, 1958; Mazo to Chavoor, April 27 and October 1, 1959; Chavoor to Mazo, October 9, 1958; all HGD, B205-F4; Kornitzer to HGD, November 16, 1959; and Chavoor to Kornitzer, January 13, 1960, HMDP.

10. HGD to MD, [n.d.] and January 11, 1953, HMDP.

11. HGD to MD, July 28 and November 11, 1954, HMDP.

12. The next few paragraphs are from MD to HGD, March 8, 9, 25, April 1, 7, 13, and 22, 1955; HGD to MD, March 31, April 11, June 15 and 24, 1955, HMDP.

13. MD to HGD, March 8, 9, 25, April 1, 7, 13, and 22, 1955; HGD to MD, March 31, April 11, June 15 and 24, 1955, HMDP.

14. MD to HGD, March 8, 9, 25, April 1, 7, 13, and 22, 1955; HGD to MD, March 31, April 11, June 15 and 24, 1955, HMDP.

15. Ibid.; HGD to Stevens, August 10, 1956; and MD to Stevens, February 29, 1956, Nan Stevens Papers, New York City, private collection (hereafter, NS); MD to HGD, September 7, 1959, and HGD to MD, August 11, 1960, HMDP.

16. HGD to MD, August 11, 1960, HMDP.

17. Noel-Baker to Douglas, April 4, May 13, 1960, and April 15, 1961, HMDP. See also Philip J. Noel-Baker, "Disarmament, the United Nations, and Helen Gahagan Douglas," an oral history conducted 1976 by Amelia Fry, in Helen Gahagan Douglas Oral History Project, Vol. II, ROHO, 1981.

18. MD to HGD, [n.d.], HMDP.

19. HGD to MD, April 6, 1961.

20. Ibid.

21. HGD to MD, May 17, 1961, HMDP; MD to Stevens, May 5 and June 20, 1961, NS.

22. MD to HGD, June 9 and 18, 1961, HMDP.

23. HGD to MD, May 17, June 12 and 16, 1961; and MD to HGD, June 26, 1961, HMDP; HGD to Stevens, October 15 and November 9, 1961, NS.

24. MD to HGD, March 29, April 3, 1961, June 9, 1961, June 2 and 13, 1962; HGD to MD, May 27, June 5, 1961; and Peace Corps letters, all HMDP; MD to Stevens, October 7, 1962, and HGD to Stevens, April 13, 1966, NS.

25. MD to HGD, June 24, 1955, and June 9, 1961; HGD to MD, December 27, 1951, and January 11, 1953, May 27 and June 12, 1961, all HMDP. Letters from Greg to Helen in 1973–1974 in HMDP suggest a rupture with Melvyn and resentment both at what he feels are strings attached to money and the impact on him as a child resulting from the Douglases' lives as public figures.

26. HGD to MD, [n.d.], HMDP; and Douglas, ROHO draft.

27. Reports, round-robin letters to family and friends, letters to Melvyn and Mary Helen, and a taped interview with ROHO that was cut from the final transcript (taped August–September 1976); HGD to MD, April 20, 1962; Miami-Guatamala letter, "The Story of My Scarf"; HGD to Melvyn and Mary Helen Douglas, Buenos Aires; all ROHO.

28. Douglas, *The Eleanor Roosevelt We Remember* (New York: Hill and Wang, 1963), 19–20, 29.

29. Halsted to HGD, June 5, 1963, HGD, B215, scrapbook 2; Holifield to HGD, June 5, 1963, HGD, 215, scrapbook 3. The Jewish Theological Seminary of America televised a reading from the book, with Douglas participating (transcript, November 3, 1963, B215, scrapbook 1). Examples of reviews are in the *National Observer* and *Baltimore American*, June 9, 1963.

30. Rusk to Johnson, January 3, 1964, Executive Files, FG1-2/C063; HGD to LBJ,

January 4, 1964, LBJP, Executive Files, PC1, PU 2–6; Stephen J. Wright to LBJ, January 21, 1964, LBJP, Executive Files, FG1-2/CO163; John Macy Files, Folder "Douglas, Helen G."; *New York Post Weekend Magazine,* January 12, 1964. The appointment brought a nasty comment by the conservative *Long Beach Independent* indicating that Communists would welcome the choice of Douglas (January 4, 1964). Johnson appointed Esther Peterson to head the Status of Women study to bring more women in policy-making positions. See, for example, talk for Cabinet meeting, January 19, 1964, LBJP, Executive Files, FG100, PU1, FG 11–1.

31. Stevens to Jack Valenti, enclosures, June 15, 1964, LBJP, Executive Files, FO, CO305, CO303, LBJL; Douglas, ROHO draft.

32. HGD to MD, June 12, 1961, and November 13, 1964, HMDP.

33. She remained active in SANE until in-house fighting led to a forced resignation from the board in 1967. That year, fourteen board members, including Douglas, Norman Cousins, Victor Reuther, and several founding members, threatened to quit because of Dr. Benjamin Spock's extremist position supporting liberation movements " 'no matter what their political character or threat to world peace.' " The group also opposed the board's failure to take a united position. Douglas did not resign at this point, but several months later she was asked to leave the board and become a national sponsor on the grounds that she had not had an opportunity to be an active participant. She declined, deciding to withdraw from the fractured organization (*New York Times,* October 20, 1967; SANE flyer and H. Stuart Hughes to HGD, December 18, 1967, HMDP). HGD to LBJ, January 4, 1964, LBJP, Executive Files, PC1, PU 2–6; and HGD to LBJ, November 16, 1964, LBJP, Executive Files, FO, PP2–2, FG216; HGD to Stevens and family, June 1964, NS.

34. HGD to Fulbright, May 16, 1966; and Fulbright to HGD, May 18, 1966, HGD, B212-F9; Douglas, *A Full Life,* 390; idem, ROHO draft.

35. Douglas, ROHO draft; idem, *A Full Life,* 390.

36. Stevens interview with author, June 10, 1979.

37. *New York Post,* October 30, 1972; *Binghamton* (N.Y.) *Press,* October 4, 1972; *Claremont Daily Eagle,* October 17 and 20, 1972; *Rutland* (Vt.) *Daily Herald,* October 18, 1972; *White River Valley* (Vt.) *Herald,* October 19, 1972; McGovern-Shriver press release, October 30, 1972, HMDP. A *New York Times* editorial on October 18, 1972, backed up Douglas's charge of Nixon's lack of commitment to American values.

38. Israel, "Helen Gahagan Douglas," *Ms.* 11 (October 1973): 55–59, 112–19.

39. Conference brochure, November 3, 1973; HGD to _____ [Woman's Lobby mailing list], November 26, 1973; Women's Lobby brochure; Esther Peterson to HGD, December 11, 1973, all HMDP; HGD to Fry, January 26, 1974, ROHO; *Boston Herald American,* November 2, 1973; *Washington Post* and *Washington Star-News* for January 4, 1974.

40. Speech, January 3, 1974, HMDP; *Los Angeles Times,* March 8, 1974.

41. Washington Conference program, March 29–31, 1974; Dartmouth schedule, April 29–May 2, 1974; Dena Warshaw to HGD, May 7, 1974; "Women in Politics" program, Indiana State University, October 1974; honorary Doctor of Civil Law citation, October 19, 1974; Fath to Douglas, March 20, 1974; HGD to Roberts, May 21, 1974; Douglas statement for Roth, May 23, 1974; "The Way We Were," ACLU Program, December 14, 1974; all HMDP. HGD to NS, February 27, 1975, NS.

Groups had also recognized Douglas in the 1960s. For example, she was one of three to receive the second Eleanor Roosevelt Humanitarian Award sponsored by the Philadelphia Women's Division, State of Israel Bonds. On March 22, 1968, she was awarded the Louise Waterman Wise Award for work in human rights from the Women's Division of the American Jewish Congress (HGD, B222-F11). Congressman Wright Patman invited Douglas in 1966 to join a symposium and dinner to celebrate the twentieth anniversary of the 1946 Full Employment bill. He wanted her to sit at a front table with a small number of people who "contributed outstandingly to the original enactment and early beginnings of the legislation" (Patman to HGD, February 3, 1966; and HGD to Patman, February 21, 1966, HGD, B212-F9).

42. *Los Angeles Times*, May 16, 1976.

43. HGD to Stevens, [n.d.], NS; HGD to Fry, [n.d.], ROHO; Dartmouth College Commencement and Baccalaureate Exercises program, June 12, 1977; Jacquelyn Anderson Mattfeld to HGD, April 24, 1979; Donald A. Reed to HGD, June 26, 1979; Otto Christ to HGD, July 31, 1979; all HMDP. The Constitution reading was sponsored by the Center for the Study of Democratic Institutions in Santa Barbara.

44. Stevens interview with author; WNYC press release, June 27, 1979; and invitation to "Musicians as Artists" benefit, October 10, 1979, HMDP.

45. *Miami Herald*, February 24, 1980; *New York Times*, March 30, 1980; and *Women's Wear Daily*, March 7, 1980.

46. Dozens of obituaries were written; see in particular *New York Times*, June 29, 1980. *New York Magazine*, August 2, 1982.

47. *San Francisco Chronicle*, April 2, 1976.

Index

Hollywood (*continued*)
1940, 109, 110; glamor of, 109, 110, 111, 130; Jewish immigrants in, 103; movie stars at 1941 inauguration, 121; and 1950 campaign, 256, 269; radical politicization of, 102–6, 321n5; stars support Douglas, 156, 178, 219–20. *See also* Actors; Douglas, Helen Gahagan—movie; Douglas, Helen Gahagan and Melvyn, attitude toward Hollywood; Douglas, Melvyn, movies; *specific organizations and individuals.*
Hollywood Anti-Nazi League, 104–5, 106
Hollywood Bowl, 97, 98, 100–101, 118–19
Hollywood for Roosevelt Committee, 128
Hollywood Independent Citizens' Committee on the Arts, Sciences, and Professions (HICCASP), 155, 156, 185
Hollywood Ten, 235
Honeyman, Nan Wood, 116, 130
Hoover, J. Edgar, 264
Hopper, Hedda, 99
Horne, Lena, 236
House Foreign Affairs Committee, 246; Douglas as member of, 162, 164, 214, 223, 224, 226, 261, 271, 272; and foreign aid, 214; issues in and congeniality of, 223; power, 162
House Un-American Activities Committee (HUAC): Douglas opposes, 193, 215, 243, 248, 261; investigates California, 104, 106; Nixon as member of, 246, 271
Houser, Frederick F., 245
Housing: Douglas's concern for, 207, 211, 212–13, 222, 223, 234, 338n33; Truman respects Douglas's work on, 282. *See also* Douglas, Helen Gahagan, issues in Congress.
Howard, H. A., 192
Humphrey, Hubert H., 297, 298, 300, 340n20
Hunter, Glenn, 38, 40
Huston, Walter, 155

Ibsen, Henrik, 25, 26, 28
ICCASP. *See* Independent Citizens' Committee on the Arts, Sciences, and Professions.
Ickes, Harold, 107, 109, 121, 165; as confidante to Douglas, 120; on Downey, 225; and 1946 campaign, 201–2; and 1950 campaign, 237, 240, 247, 251, 268–69, 275
Ickes, Jane, 121, 165, 288; Douglas offers beauty advice to, 122
Independent Citizens' Committee on the Arts, Sciences, and Professions (ICCASP), 155, 156, 185
Independent Progressive Party (IPP), and 1948 election, 217–20

Inflation, 207, 211–12. *See also* Douglas, Helen Gahagan, issues in Congress.
Inter-Theatre-Arts, Inc., 16, 20–21, 27
IPP. *See* Independent Progressive Party.
It's Up to the Women, 125
Izac, Ed, 135, 203

Jackson, Robert H., 115
Jane Addams Peace Association, 298
Japanese, in Fourteenth Congressional District, 144, 145, 327–28n50
Jeffers, Robinson, 108
Jeffers, Una, 108
Jerrico, Paul, 105, 265
John Birch Society, 298
John Steinbeck Committee to Aid Migratory Workers, 106–7, 110. *See also* Migrants; Steinbeck, John.
Johnson, Erwin, 183, 187
Johnson, Hiram, 229
Johnson, Lyndon B., 168, 244; advice to Douglas, 163, 190; close friendship with Douglas, 171–72, 173, 189; Douglas advises, on Khrushchev, 298; Douglas and official appointments of, 297–98; Douglas campaigns for, 298–99; Douglas opposes Vietnam policy of, 299–300; and Douglas's Latin American trip, 296, 297; and 1950 fall campaign, 271
Joint Anti-Fascist Refugee Committee, 104, 105
Jolson, Al, 15, 69
Jones, Nettie (Mrs. Mattison Boyd), 111, 112, 129–30; fight over Democratic National Committeewoman post, 117–19; and 1950 campaign, 230, 248
Judd, Walter H., 337n24

Kahn, Otto, 50, 54, 70
Keane, Doris, 315n33
Kee, John, 249, 271
Keefe, Frank B., 211–12
Keith, Ian, 82
Kemble-Cooper, Violet, 82
Kennedy, John F., 278, 291, 296, 297–98
Kenny, Robert, 146
Kern, Jerome, 74, 75
Khrushchev, Nikita S., 298
Kilpatrick, Vernon, 144
King, Cecil R., 218, 239
Kirchwey, Freda, 183, 285
Kirkpatrick, Jeanne, 303
Knowland, William, 226
Korean War, impact on 1950 campaign, 254, 260, 262, 272, 280, 287
Kramer, Lucy, 273
Kroll, Jack, 218, 229, 240, 277; and 1950 fall campaign, 258, 269
Kuba, Fritz, 95, 96, 100